VOLUME TWO

CONTEMPORARY AMERICAN POETRY

ANTHOLOGY OF MODERN & CONTEMPORARY

American Poetry

VOLUME TWO

CONTEMPORARY AMERICAN POETRY

Second Edition

Edited by Cary Nelson

NEW YORK OXFORD
OXFORD UNIVERSITY PRESS

Oxford University Press is a department of the University of Oxford. It furthers the University's objective of excellence in research, scholarship, and education by publishing worldwide.

Oxford New York
Auckland Cape Town Dar es Salaam Hong Kong Karachi
Kuala Lumpur Madrid Melbourne Mexico City Nairobi
New Delhi Shanghai Taipei Toronto

With offices in
Argentina Austria Brazil Chile Czech Republic France Greece
Guatemala Hungary Italy Japan Poland Portugal Singapore
South Korea Switzerland Thailand Turkey Ukraine Vietnam

For titles covered by Section 112 of the US Higher Education Opportunity Act, please visit www.oup.com/us/he for the latest information about pricing and alternate formats.

Published by Oxford University Press
198 Madison Avenue, New York, NY 10016
http://www.oup.com

Cataloging-in-Publication Data is on file with the Library of Congress.
ISBN: 978-0-19-992073-0

Printing number: 9 8 7 6 5 4 3 2 1

Printed in the United States of America
on acid-free paper

Editorial Advisory Board

Contents

Topical Contents

The list of poets under several of the headings identifies writers whose work broadly fits that category. I also list individual poems when the selection here may not show a comprehensive commitment to that topic. To give people maximum flexibility and room for invention, I have left the categories very broad, but many more specific grouping are possible. One might, for example, compare Walt Whitman's, Allen Tate's, Robert Lowell's, Natasha Trethewey's, and Andrew Hudgins's poems about the Civil War, or Natasha Trethewey's and Patricia Smith's poems about Hurricane Katrina.

AFRICAN AMERICAN HISTORY AND CULTURE, Vol. 1: POETS—W. E. B. Du Bois, James Weldon Johnson, Paul Laurence Dunbar, Alice Dunbar-Nelson, Angelina Weld Grimké, Georgia Douglas Johnson, Anne Spencer, Claude McKay, Jean Toomer, Melvin B. Tolson, Sterling A. Brown, Langston Hughes, Arna Bontemps, Gwendolyn Bennett, Countee Cullen, Aqua Laluah. **Vol. 2: POETS**—Robert Hayden, Dudley Randall, Margaret Walker, Gwendolyn Brooks, Bob Kaufman, Derek Walcott, Etheridge Knight, Henry Dumas, Amiri Baraka, Audre Lorde, Jayne Cortez, Lucille Clifton, Michael S. Harper, Ishmael Reed, Welton Smith, Carolyn M. Rodgers, Yusef Komunyakaa, Ai, Rita Dove, Harryette Mullen, Thylias Moss, Patricia Smith, Janice N. Harrington, Claudia Rankine, Natasha Trethewey. **Vol. 1: POEMS**—Carl Sandburg, "Nigger," "Man, the Man-Hunter," "Elizabeth Umpstead"; Vachel Lindsay, "The Congo"; Elinor Wylie, "August"; Dorothy Parker, "The Dark Girl's Rhyme"; Genevieve Taggard, "To the Negro People"; Charles Reznikoff, "Negroes"; V. J. Jerome, "A Negro Mother to Her Child"; John Wheelwright, "Plantation Drouth"; Lucia Trent, "Black Men"; Hart Crane, "Black Tambourine"; Kay Boyle, "A Communication to Nancy Cunard"; John Beecher, "Beaufort Tides"; Sol Funaroff, "Goin Mah Own Road." **Vol. 2: POEMS**—Charles Henri Ford, "Plaint"; Thomas McGrath, "Deep South"; Robert Lowell, "A Mad Negro Soldier Confined at Munich"; Aaron Kramer, "Denmark Vesey."

NATIVE AMERICAN HISTORY AND CULTURE, Vol. 1: POETS—Too-qua-stee, Alexander Posey, Arsenius Chaleco, Ruth Margaret Muskrat, Lynn Riggs. **Vol. 1: POEMS**—Robert Frost, "The Vanishing Red." **Vol. 2: POETS**—Mary Cornelia Hartshorne, N. Scott Momaday, Adrian Louis, Wendy Rose, Ray A. Young Bear, Anita Endrezze, Louise Erdrich, Heid E. Erdrich, Sherman Alexie. **Vol. 2: POEMS**—James Wright, "A Centenary Ode: Inscribed to Little Crow, Leader of the Sioux Rebellion in Minnesota, 1862"; Lucille Clifton, "the message of crazy horse"; William Heyen, *Crazy Horse in Stillness.*

ASIAN AMERICAN HISTORY AND CULTURE, Vol. 1: POETS—Sadakichi Hartman, Angel Island: Poems by Chinese Immigrants. **Vol. 2: POETS**—Japanese American Concentration Camp Haiku, Lawson Fusao Inada, Jessica Hagedorn, Garrett Kaoru Hongo, Marilyn Chin, Sesshu Foster, Li-Young Lee.

LATINO/LATINA AMERICAN HISTORY AND CULTURE, Vol. 2: POETS—Jimmy Santiago Baca, Alberto Ríos, Ana Castillo, Lorna Dee Cervantes, Sandra Cisneros, Martín Espada.

EXPERIMENTAL TRADITIONS, Vol. 1: POETS—Emily Dickinson, Gertrude Stein, Mina Loy, Ezra Pound, Marianne Moore, T. S. Eliot, E. E. Cummings, Harry Crosby,

Andrew Hudgins, "The Summer of the Drought"; Anita Endrezze, "Birdwatching at Fan Lake," "Return of the Wolves"; Lorna Dee Cervantes, "Starfish"; Thylias Moss, "There Will Be Animals"; Atsuro Riley, "Roses."

POETRY AND RELIGION, Vol. 1: POEMS—Emily Dickinson, "I felt a Funeral, in My Brain," "I'm ceded—I've stopped being Theirs," "Title divine—is mine!"; James Weldon Johnson, "The Creation"; Paul Lawrence Dunbar, "When Malindy Sings"; Wallace Stevens, "A High-Toned Old Christian Woman," "Sunday Morning"; T. S. Eliot, "Journey of the Magi," "Burnt Norton"; Langston Hughes, "Christ in Alabama," "Goodbye Christ"; Countee Cullen, "Christ Recrucified." **Vol. 2: POEMS**—William Everson, "The Making of the Cross," "Canticle of the Waterbirds"; Jack Kerouac, "The Perfect Love of Mind Essence"; Gwendolyn Brooks, "of De Witt Williams on his way to Lincoln Cemetery"; Donald Justice, "The Wall," "An Old Fashioned Devil"; Robert Creeley, "After Lorca"; James Wright, "Saint Judas"; Anne Sexton, "Jesus Asleep," "Jesus Raises Up the Harlot"; Amiri Baraka, "When We'll Worship Jesus"; N. Scott Momaday, "Carriers of the Dream Wheel," "The Shield That Came Back"; Lucille Clifton, "at the cemetery, / walnut grove plantation, south carolina, 1989"; Sharon Olds, "The Pope's Penis"; Louise Glück, "A Village Life"; Carolyn M. Rodgers, "and when the revolution came," "mama's god"; Adrian C. Louis, "Wakinyan," "Looking for Judas," "Jesus Finds His Ghost Shirt"; D. A. Powell, "(came a voice in my gullet)"; Natasha Trethewey, "Believer."

GAY AND LESBIAN POETRY, Vol. 1: POEMS—Walt Whitman, "As Adam Early in the Morning," "For You O Democracy," "A Glimpse"; Hart Crane, "Episode of Hands," "Voyages," "Cape Hatteras"; Amy Lowell, "Venus Transiens," "Madonna of the Evening Flowers," "The Weather-Cock Points South," "Taxi"; Gertrude Stein, "Susie Asado," "Patriarchal Poetry"; Angelina Weld Grimké, "A Mona Lisa"; Countee Cullen, "In Praise of Boys," "Tableau." **Vol. 2: POEMS**—Charles Henri Ford, "Pastoral for Pavlik," "28"; Robert Duncan, "My Mother Would Be a Falconress," "The Torso"; Frank O'Hara, "The Day Lady Died," "A True Account of Talking to the Sun at Fire Island," "Thinking of James Dean"; Allen Ginsberg, "Love Poem on Theme by Whitman," "A Supermarket in California," "Rain-wet asphalt heat, garbage curbed cans overflowing," "Sphincter"; Adrienne Rich, "Trying to Talk with a Man," "Twenty-One Love Poems"; Audre Lorde, "Outlines"; Judy Grahn, "Carol"; Ana Castillo, "Seduced by Natassja Kinski"; Mark Doty, "Homo Will Not Inherit," "The Embrace"; D. A. Powell, "(the cocktail hour finally arrives)," "(dogs and boys can treat you like trash)," "(came a voice in my gullet)"; Richard Siken, "Visible World," "A Primer for the Small Weird Loves."

HOLOCAUST POETRY, Vol. 1: POEMS—Charles Reznikoff, "Massacres"; George Oppen, "Exodus"; Muriel Rukeyser, "(To Be a Jew in the Twentieth Century)." **Vol. 2: POEMS**—Randall Jarrell, "Protocols"; Anthony Hecht, "'More Light! More Light!,'" "The Book of Yolek"; Sylvia Plath, "Daddy"; Robert Pinsky, "The Unseen"; William Heyen, "Riddle"; Jorie Graham, "History," "From the New World."

POETRY AND WAR, Vol. 1: POEMS—Walt Whitman, "Vigil Strange I Kept on the Field One Night"; Stephen Crane, "Do Not Weep, Maiden, for War Is Kind"; Amy Lowell, "September, 1918"; Alice Dunbar-Nelson, "I Sit and Sew"; Carl Sandburg, "Buttons," "Planked Whitefish," "Grass"; Wallace Stevens, "The Death of a Soldier"; Sara Teasdale, "Spring in the Naugatuck Valley," "There Will Come Soft Rains"; Ezra Pound, "Canto IX"; H.D., "The Walls Do Not Fall"; Robinson Jeffers, "Antrim," "(I saw a regiment of soldiers)"; T. S. Eliot, *The Waste Land*; Edna St. Vincent Millay, "Say That We Saw Spain Die"; Archibald MacLeish, "The Silent Slain"; E. E. Cummings, "my sweet old etcetera," "i sing of Olaf glad and big"; Langston Hughes, "Letter from Spain"; Allen Tate, "Ode to the Confederate Dead"; W. H. Auden, "September 1, 1939," "The Shield of Achilles"; George Oppen, "Survival: Infantry," "In Alsace"; Sol Funaroff, "The Bull in the Olive Field"; Muriel Rukeyser, "Poem (I lived in the first century of world

Tree"; Dorothy Parker, "One Perfect Rose"; Genevieve Taggard, "Everyday Alchemy," "With Child"; Jean Toomer, "Her Lips Are Copper Wire"; Lucia Trent, "Breed, Women Breed"; Louise Bogan, "Medusa," "Women," "Cassandra"; Sterling A. Brown, "Scotty Has His Say"; Laura (Riding) Jackson, "Helen's Burning"; Langston Hughes, "To the Dark Mercedes of 'El Palacio de Amor'"; Gwendolyn Bennett, "To a Dark Girl," "(Rapacious women who sit on steps at night)"; Countee Cullen, "For a Lady I Know"; Kenneth Rexroth, "The Love Poems of Marichiko"; Robert Penn Warren, "Mother Makes the Biscuits"; Theodore Roethke, "I Knew a Woman"; Muriel Rukeyser, "Rite," "The Poem as Mask." **Vol. 2: POEMS**—Tillie Lerner Olsen, "I Want You Women Up North to Know"; Robert Hayden, "A Letter from Phillis Wheatley," "Aunt Jemima of the Ocean Waves"; Joy Davidman, "This Woman"; Ruth Stone, "Pokeberries," "I Have Three Daughters"; Robert Lowell, "Man and Wife"; Gwendolyn Brooks, "To Those of My Sisters Who Kept Their Naturals"; Mona Van Duyn, "Toward a Definition of Marriage"; James Dickey, "Falling"; Denise Levertov, "The Ache of Marriage," "Olga Poems"; Maxine Kumin, "Voices from Kansas"; John Ashbery, "Mixed Feelings"; Anne Sexton, "Her Kind," "And One for My Dame," "The Room of My Life"; Adrienne Rich, "Aunt Jennifer's Tigers," "Diving into the Wreck," "Twenty-One Love Poems," "Power," "Behind the Motel"; Gregory Corso, "Marriage"; Sylvia Plath, "The Colossus," "Daddy," "Ariel," "Lady Lazarus"; Audre Lorde, "Sisters in Arms," "Outlines"; Lucille Clifton, "poem to my uterus," "to my last period"; Michael S. Harper, "Blue Ruth: America"; Judy Grahn, "I Have Come to Claim Marilyn Monroe's Body," "Carol," "The Woman Whose Head Is on Fire"; Robert Hass, "A Story About the Body"; Sharon Olds, "Known to Be Left," "Left-Wife Goose"; Louise Glück, "Penelope's Song"; Thomas James, "Mummy of a Lady Named Jemutesonekh"; Ai, "Twenty-Year Marriage"; Anita Endrezze, "La Morena and Her Beehive Hairdo"; Sandra Cisneros, "Little Clown, My Heart"; Thylias Moss, "Crystals"; Patricia Smith, "Blond White Women"; Heid E. Erdrich, "Some Elsie."

EXPLICIT POET-TO-POET DIALOGUES, Vol. 1: POEMS—Too-qua-stee, "The White Man's Burden" (Kipling); Alexander Posey, "The Fall of the Redskin" (Markham); Anne Spencer, "Dunbar"; Ezra Pound, "A Pact" (Whitman), "A River Merchant's Wife" (Rihaku/Li Po), "Canto I" (Homer); Marianne Moore, "Spenser's Ireland"; Dorothy Parker, "Walter Savage Landor"; Hart Crane, "Porphyro in Akron" (Keats), "Cape Hatteras" (Whitman); W. H. Auden, "In Memory of W. B. Yeats." **Vol. 2: POEMS**—Robert Hayden, "A Letter from Phillis Wheatley"; Allen Ginsberg, "Love Poem on Theme by Whitman," "A Supermarket in California" (Whitman); Robert Bly, "Hearing Gary Snyder Read"; Philip Levine, "On the Meeting of García Lorca and Hart Crane"; Adrian C. Louis, "How Verdell and Dr. Zhivago Disassembled the Soviet Union" (Pasternak); Garrett Kaoru Hongo, "Kubota to Miguel Hernandez in Heaven, Leupp, Arizona, 1942"; Thylias Moss, "Interpretation of a Poem by Frost"; Martín Espada, "Hard-Handed Men of Athens" (Shakespeare); Heid E. Erdrich, "The Theft Outright" (Frost), "Some Elsie" (Williams).

MODERN INTERPRETATIONS OF CLASSICAL MYTH, Vol. 1: POEMS—Edwin Markham, "A Look Into the Gulf," William Carlos Williams, "Landscape with the Fall of Icarus"; H.D., "Eurydice," "Helen"; Robinson Jeffers, "Cassandra"; Charles Reznikoff, "Aphrodite Vrania"; Louise Bogan, "Medusa," "Cassandra"; Laura (Riding) Jackson, "Helen's Burning"; Countee Cullen, "Yet I Do Marvel"; W. H. Auden, "The Shield of Achilles"; Muriel Rukeyser, "The Minotaur," "The Poem as Mask." **Vol. 2: POEMS**—Robert Hayden, "O Daedalus, Fly Away Home"; Maxine Kumin, "Pantoum, with Swan"; Derek Walcott, *Omeros*; Louise Glück, *Meadowlands*; Janice N. Harrington, "Falling."

THE POETRY OF LOVE, Vol. 1: POEMS—Walt Whitman, "A Glimpse"; Amy Lowell, "Venus Transiens," "Madonna of the Evening Flowers," "The Weather-Cock Points South," "The Taxi"; Gertrude Stein, "Susie Asado"; Angelina Weld Grimké, "A Mona Lisa"; William

Preface

This anthology has been compiled at the intersection of aesthetics and history. By "history" I refer not only to literary history but also broadly to national and international history and to current events. Whether responding to the long traumatic story of race relations in the United States, to the devastating record of World War I trench warfare in France, to the unassimilable reality of the Holocaust, or to historically emergent forms of cultural and sexual practice and identity, American poets have been compelling witnesses. Their poetry responds with unique linguistic compression and metaphoric density to both national experience and international events.

The forms of historical testimony and intervention possible in poetry are consistently distinctive and sometimes incomparable. Lived time without these poems, this collection aims to prove, is impoverished time. I offer that claim in keeping with William Carlos Williams's observation that people die every day for lack of the knowledge available in poems. But poetic witness, at its best, as readers will find, is not designed to offer ready consolation or to make life easier. Unforgettable witness can make life at once richer and more difficult. Too many other anthologies slight the difference poetry can make in historical understanding. As a result, they deny readers the full epistemological, psychological, and aesthetic resources poetry continues to provide. My goal is thus partly corrective.

Yet, to warrant rereading decade after decade poems must meet high aesthetic standards, though no comprehensive anthology of modern and contemporary poetry can do its job by hewing to only one set of aesthetic criteria. An anthologist's job, I believe, is to combine flexible taste with sound editorial principles. The astonishing and endlessly energetic diversity of American poetry throughout much of its history is one of its strengths, but diversity alone is not a virtue in an anthology. At least for me, all these poems merit our admiration based on their quality, though the terms on which they do so vary. The canon reform movement of the 1970s and 1980s taught us to value and find pleasure in the immensely varied interplay of tradition and innovation that continues to surprise readers of American poetry to the present day. It also made us realize that aesthetic impulses can be local, embedded in particular historical and literary contexts. The challenge is to find the poems from those contexts that manage at once to honor their historical moment and speak to our own.

These are ambitious aims. Underlying them, however, is a conviction that American poetry represents a major contribution to human culture. Proving all this, of course, depends on making hundreds of individual choices about what poems to include. Sometimes I try to represent a poet's whole career. From Emily Dickinson, Amy Lowell, Robert Frost, Wallace Stevens, and William Carlos Williams to Gwendolyn Brooks, John Ashbery, and W. S. Merwin I offer what I hope are sufficiently generous selections to give a fair picture of those poets' accomplishments over time. At other times, I felt a particular period in a career—or even a single long poem or poem sequence—to be so compelling that readers would be best served by concentrating on it. The obvious consensual example is Sylvia Plath's 1963 *Ariel* poems. But there are many more instances here—from Randall Jarrell's World War II poems to the fusion of autobiography and history that Michael Harper achieved in the 1970s. I give maximum space to these major achievements at the expense of other fine poems throughout such poets' careers.

The most extreme choices, however, are the cases in which I devote all or most of a poet's space to a single text—from Gertrude Stein's "Patriarchal Poetry," Edna St. Vincent Millay's "Sonnets from an Ungrafted Tree," Melvin Tolson's "Libretto for the Republic of Liberia," Kenneth Rexroth's "The Love Poems of Marichiko," and Muriel Rukeyser's "The Book of the Dead" to Aaron Kramer's "Denmark Vesey," Kathleen Fraser's "In Commemoration of the Visit of Foreign Commercial Representatives to Japan, 1947," and Natasha Trethewey's "Native Guard." "Denmark Vesey" combines a dramatic narrative of a potential slave revolt with complex musical, metrical, and formal choices that make for a poem that has nothing comparable in American literary history. The integration of African and European history and culture in "Libretto for the Republic of Liberia," combined with Tolson's high rhetorical style has no match I know of save perhaps Derek Walcott's layered account of Caribbean culture and Western imperialism, despite textual affinities with such diverse texts as Eliot's *Waste Land,* Pound's *Cantos,* and Olson's *Maximus Poems.*

When possible, I added a few short poems to one long one, or at least prefaced a longer, more difficult poem with one that might prove more accessible. "Susie Asado" precedes "Patriarchal Poetry." Mina Loy's "(There is no Life or Death)" and "O Hell" come before "Songs to Joannes." Charles Wright's "Spider Crystal Ascension" and "Clear Night" precede his "Homage to Paul Cezanne." Even when I try to represent a whole career, however, I am willing to grant space to longer poems—including William Carlos Williams's "The Descent of Winter," Theodore Roethke's "North American Sequence," Allen Ginsberg's "Howl," Gwendolyn Brook's "Gay Chaps at the Bar," Denise Levertov's "Olga Poems," and Adrienne Rich's "Twenty-One Love Poems." With Marianne Moore I opted for two long poems, "The Octopus" and "Marriage," because their referential divide between nature and culture makes them inescapable companion poems. I believe there are more long poems and poem sequences in this collection than in any other comprehensive anthology.

On the other hand, in a few cases a lone poem is here not to encapsulate a major career but rather to help capture the spirit of a literary movement. Herman Spector's "Wiseguy Type," V. J. Jerome's "A Negro Mother to Her Child," and Joseph Freeman's "Our Age Has Caesars" perfectly embody the cultural commitments of 1930s proletarian poetry and thus help make possible the account of that period mentioned above. Welton Smith's "Malcolm" is one of the most indicative products of the Black Arts Movement. I point this out here lest readers assume I am making larger claims about the contributions these writers have made to our literary history. On the other hand, Arsenius Chaleco's "Requiem" is here because it is one of the more powerful examples of American Indian elegies to appear over several decades. What it says about his career we can only guess, since it is the only poem by him known to have survived. And Tillie Olsen's "I Want You Women Up North to Know," a classic poem about women's work by a writer widely celebrated for her fiction and nonfiction prose, is a compelling poem reprinted here in part to challenge disciplinary notions about the transitory character of topical poetry. It should also encourage readers to think anew about the kinds of cultural and political work a poem can do, for it is unfortunately just as relevant today as it was decades ago. Indeed, given women's working conditions in Asia—and the relationship between their exploitation and those in America who buy the clothing they produce—the poem could also be revised to read "I Want You Women in the West to Know." What kind of difference, we might ask, does poetic language make to a subject like this?

The two volumes, "modern" and "contemporary," volumes; divide roughly at 1910 birth dates, but the differentiation is necessarily imperfect. Some careers—both long ones and curtailed ones—notably straddle the divide between modernity and contemporaneity. Muriel Rukeyser began in part as a 1930s poet devoted to labor issues and captured, like so many progressive writers, by the lure of antifascism and the cause of democratic Spain, but she concluded her career decades later by writing key poems speaking for contemporary feminism. Like Rukeyser, Edwin Rolfe began firmly in 1930s culture and politics, but he composed some of our most telling poems against McCarthyism in the early 1950s. As part of an effort to make the two volumes internally coherent, I made a judgment about where the main weight of a poet's reputation fell, thus assigning some poets born in 1910–1913 to the first volume and some born in 1910 to the second.

In addition to a standard chronological table, we provide a topical table of contents. Some critical topics bridge multiple categories. The long American poetic dialogue about the culturally constructed but powerful subject of race that came to a head in the nineteenth-century Abolitionist movement becomes a major feature of twentieth-century poetry. Poets of white, black, Asian, Native American, Latino, and multiple heritages reflect on that history here, interrogating both whiteness and blackness and producing searing statements to be found perhaps nowhere else in our literature—perhaps nowhere else in our culture.

None of the classifications in the topical table of contents are definitive. And there are many topics not listed. You can also read Marianne Moore, Robert Lowell, Denise Levertov, Mona Van Duyn, Gregory Corso, and Ai about marriage. You can compare poems about Helen of Troy by H.D. and Laura Riding, poems about Cassandra by Robinson Jeffers and Louise Bogan. You can gather together poems by Joseph Freeman, Kenneth Fearing, John Beecher, Joseph Kalar, Edwin Rolfe, Sol Funaroff, Muriel Rukeyser, Genevieve Taggard, and Tillie Olsen to revisit the political 1930s. You can read love poems on the list in the topical table of contents, then unsettle the category by reading Edna St. Vincent Millay's "Sonnets from an Ungrafted Tree" or Richard Siken's "A Primer for the Small Weird Loves." Importantly, poets often appear in more than one category, sometimes even contributing to both experimental and formalist traditions. While polemical claims about what constitutes either an experimental or a formalist poem abound—and certainly play a role in literary history—they did not seem to me to have a place in the groupings here. These classifications are designed to be suggestive, inclusive, and exploratory. They are a starting place for a discussion of these categories. Thus Anthony Hecht's adaptation of traditional poetic forms shares the paragraph with the new forms Langston Hughes invented.

This effort to be receptive to different kinds of open and closed forms matches the realization that both our personal and our institutional evaluations change over time. Ten years ago I thought Joseph Kalar wrote only one important poem. Now I realize he has more than a score of them. For years I missed hearing the special music of "Denmark Vesey." Eventually I coedited Kramer's selected poems. But the material facts of history shift and evolve over time as well. Every literary history and reference work I know dates Native American poetry from the 1960s. Indian texts standing in for poems before then often amounted to transcriptions and adaptations of chants and other oral performances, not infrequently recorded by missionaries or anthropologists. But what every poetry scholar believed, wrote, and taught was not true. Native Americans worked in traditional rhymed and metered forms from the nineteenth century on—but they published them in Indian magazines that never reached the dominant culture. Enough of that stunning history has now been recovered so that I can include the work of six Native American poets who wrote prior to the 1950s. The first three authors in the modern half of the collection are Walt Whitman, Too-qua-stee, and Emily Dickinson. The newly recovered Native American poems in the book also force us to reconceive the role of poetry in Native American life, along with any assumptions we may have about what Indians were reading and thinking about in the nineteenth and early twentieth centuries. Two of the poems partly parody widely read poems by white authors, and the poems include references to events elsewhere in the world.

Some of these recovered poems, like Alexander Posey's "The Fall of the Redskin," include historical references no longer part of most Americans' cultural memory and thus benefit from annotation. The most extreme case of this is Tolson's "Libretto for the Republic of Liberia," where the poem is fundamentally inaccessible without extensive notes. We are proud to publish "Libretto" in its first fully annotated version and hope it can gain wider readership as a result. Despite occasionally worrying that a footnote might seem to narrow an allusion's implications, like most text editors I have opted to annotate. It is worth knowing, for example, that Anthony Hecht served in the army and was there when a concentration camp was liberated. That doesn't diminish the power of his Holocaust poems. Perhaps instead it reminds us both that proximity to horror can increase the necessity of witness and that distance from horror complicates our own commitment. On the other hand, on a few occasions, as with Edwin Rolfe's "June 19, 1953," I chose not to annotate the poem, thereby encouraging readers who do not recognize the reference to pause, look it up on the internet, and perhaps ask themselves why they do not already know the answer, why the knowledge has been erased from general cultural awareness.

The arrangement of each poet's work is most often chronological, but I diverge from chronology when doing so made for a more coherent selection. Thus it would have been pointlessly disruptive to have interrupted a group of rather serious poems by Sharon Olds with her witty "The Pope's Penis," so I open her selection with that irreverent poem instead. One decision about how to represent a poet's work was driven by copyright law. In the case of poems first published in 1922 or earlier, then later revised, we print the earlier version here. That results in recovering earlier and less familiar versions of poems by Amy Lowell, Robert Frost, Marianne Moore, John Crowe Ransom, E. E. Cummings, and Hart Crane. To put matters bluntly, some publishers now charge substantial reprint fees for the post-1922 versions of many poems first published earlier. Staying within budget meant making the strategic choice of opting for the pre-1923 public domain versions of several poems.

On the other hand, some poets responding to the cultural and political climate of the 1960s made public gifts of a few poems either then or in the 1970s by issuing broadsides without copyright notices. That tradition began earlier in the century with poems contributed to the labor movement, but it continued decades later with poems that contributed to the antiwar, feminist, and gay liberation movements. Even poets who copyrighted the majority of their broadsides occasionally selected poems for public domain distribution. In the early part of the century, neither Edwin Markham nor Vachel Lindsay ever copyrighted their broadsides.

The illustrated version of Markham's "The Man with the Hoe" was first published as an insert in the *San Francisco Examiner* in 1899. Lindsay distributed his two-panel "Drink for Sale" broadside at a July 29, 1909, anti-saloon lecture in Springfield, Illinois. Decades later, Allen Ginsberg's "Rain-Wet Asphalt Heat, Garbage Curbed Cans Overflowing" would be issued as "a free poem" from Detroit's Alternative Press, and Robert Bly's Unicorn Broadside version of "Hearing Gary Snyder Read" would be labeled "may be reproduced without permission." Such notices underlined the legal status of poems published without copyright notice from 1923 to 1976. "The Form Falls in on Itself" by David Ignatow (1914–1997) was one of two Ignatow broadsides with lettering by Wang Hui-Ming distributed in 1971. The following year Hui-Ming collected a series of his broadside poems by various authors in his book *The Land on the Tip of a Hair: Poems in Wood*. Hughes's "Christ in Alabama" was illustrated by his longtime companion Zell Ingram; the illustrated version appeared in *Contempo* in 1931. Charles Henri Ford's "Serenade to Leonor" is illustrated with paintings by Leonor Fini. Alan Halsey's illustrated version of Gary Snyder's "O Mother Gaia" was issued by Glenn Storhaug at Five Seasons Press. Ginsberg's "Kraj Majales" was illustrated by Robert LaVigne, his "Moloch" by Lyn Ward. The illustrations to Lindsay's "Drink for Sale" and "The Virginians Are Coming," Ginsberg's "Consulting I Ching Smoking Pot Listening to the Fugs Sing Blake," and Richard Wilbur's "A Difference" are by the poets themselves. Everson's "A Canticle to the Waterbirds" has a woodblock version of a heron by Daniel O. Stolpe. Except for "Christ in Alabama," which is reproduced (in a form restored by the editor) from the copy in the rare books collection at the University of Illinois at Urbana–Champaign, all the illustrated poems come from the editor's personal collection.

A vast amount of critical commentary and historical background for the poets and many of the poems included here can be found on the website we have been constructing since 1999. Hundreds of poems have individual entries with extensive commentary devoted to them. Titled Modern American Poetry Site (MAPS), it was originally constructed at www.english.uiuc.edu/maps. It is now being reconstructed as a database.

The website's first incarnation was designed by Matthew Hurt and edited by Cary Nelson and many other scholars. Bart Brinkman has now joined me as overall editor and designer of MAPS. The site is open to all and widely used by hundreds of thousands of poetry readers across the world. It includes scores of new essays published there for the first time, along with unique photo arrays that supplement the commentary on Angel Island, the Great Depression, the Holocaust, World War II, and the subject matter of many other poems. Detailed individual background essays for many of the individuals mentioned in particular poems can be found there as well.

My first appreciation is due Oxford University Press for offering me the opportunity to revise and update the anthology. Sincere thanks is also due the long list of poets, literary agents, and publishers who worked with us to make this edition possible. Special thanks go out to Philip Levine, without whose timely intervention on behalf of the book's uniquely progressive aims—aims Oxford University Press consistently supported—the project would quite simply have failed.

As part of its review process, Oxford solicited a number of very helpful comments about the first edition. A new set of comments arrived in response to the draft table of contents for this revised edition. My thanks to all those who took the time to offer their suggestions.

CHANGES TO THE SECOND EDITION

As the law requires, we conclude with a brief summary of the changes to the second edition of this anthology. Forty-four named poets are new to the second edition, along with several anonymous poets who carved poems on the walls of Angel Island. We have continued the practice we established over a decade ago of including poets who will be unknown to many readers. If the little-known poets of the first edition are now better known, I expect some of the poets new to this edition will once again represent fresh discoveries for most readers. Perhaps their work will spread to other collections as a result. The first edition was the only anthology to include Edwin Rolfe in over half a century; you can now find his poetry in over twenty collections. On the other hand, we repeated our earlier decision to omit songs. A full and fair representation of American song would have required another hundred pages. Unable to do the tradition justice, I chose not to do it at all. Are there a few poets who would have a more generous selection if their publishers did not demand such exorbitant reprint fees? To be sure. As I will argue in a separate essay, modern poetry anthologies will soon become financially impossible unless escalating reprint fees are moderated. But overall I believe this anthology more than fulfills its aims. Only one poet has been dropped—because we were unable to reach the holder of rights to his work. A remarkable ninety-one poets have had the selection of their work expanded. Over 350 poems are new to the book. The topical table of contents is a new feature as well. And the sheer fact of increased length has led us to divide the book into two volumes, modern and contemporary, though, as the topical list demonstrates, there are many fruitful comparisons and contrasts to be made between poems in the two volumes and several traditions that run through both halves of the anthology. Here, in a convenient bulleted list, are the highlights of the second edition:

- **New poets**: Too-qua-stee/Dewitt Clinton Duncan, W. E. B. Du Bois, Stephen Crane, Alexander Posey, Sara Teasdale, Elinor Wylie, Ruth Margaret Muskrat, Arsenius Chaleco, Lynn Riggs, W.H. Auden, Mary Cornelia Hartshorne, Taro Katay, Kyokusui, Oshio, Barbara Guest, Aaron Kramer, Jack Kerouac. Donald Justice, Derek Walcott, Kathleen Fraser, William Heyen, Lyn Hejinian, Thomas James, Timothy Steele, Albert Goldbarth, David Ignatow, Charles Bernstein, Jorie Graham, Andrew Hudgins, Alberto Ríos, Lorna Dee Cervantes, Janice N. Harrington, Li-Young Lee, Atsuro Riley, Claudia Rankine, D. A. Powell, Heid E. Erdrich, Natasha Trethewey, and Richard Siken.
- **Expanded selections by**: Emily Dickinson, Edwin Markham, Edgar Lee Masters, Edwin Arlington Robinson, James Weldon Johnson, Amy Lowell, Gertrude Stein, Robert Frost, Carl Sandburg, Vachel Lindsay, Wallace Stevens, Georgia Douglas Johnson, Anne Spencer, William Carlos Williams, Ezra Pound, H.D., Robinson Jeffers, Marianne Moore, T. S. Eliot, Archibald MacLeish, Dorothy Parker, Charles Reznikoff, John Wheelwright, Louise Bogan, Hart Crane, Yvor Winters, Sterling A. Brown, Laura (Riding) Jackson, Langston Hughes, Arna Bontemps, Gwendolyn Bennett, Countee Cullen, Lorine Niedecker, John Beecher, Robert Penn Warren, Stanley Kunitz, Joseph Kalar, Theodore Roethke, George Oppen, Edwin Rolfe, Sol Funaroff, Charles Henri Ford, Charles Olson, William Everson, Robert Hayden, Weldon Kees, William Stafford, Dudley Randall, Thomas McGrath, Robert Lowell, Gwendolyn Brooks, William Bronk, Richard Wilbur, Anthony Hecht, Bob Kaufman, Maxine Kumin, Paul Blackburn, Frank O'Hara, James Wright, John Ashbery, Galway Kinnell, W. S. Merwin, Anne Sexton, Philip Levine, Adrienne Rich, Gary Snyder, Etheridge Knight, Henry Dumas, N. Scott Momaday, Mark Strand, Charles Wright, Ishmael Reed, Robert Pinsky, Robert Hass, Sharon Olds, Louise Glück, Paul Violi, Adrian Louis, C. D. Wright, Carolyn Forché, Garrett Kaoru Hongo, Rita Dove, Jimmy Santiago Baca, Anita Endrezze, Ana Castillo, Mark Doty, Louise Erdrich, Thylias Moss, Patricia Smith, Marilyn Chin, Sesshu Foster, and Martín Espada.
- **Topical table of contents.**
- **New (previously unpublished) translations and an expanded selection of Angel Island poems.**
- **Previously unpublished poems by Gwendolyn Bennett.**
- **Expanded sections of illustrated poems**: new illustrated poems by Vachel Lindsay, Charles Henri Ford, Allen Ginsberg, William Everson, David Ignatow, W.S. Merwin, Gary Snyder, and Richard Wilbur.
- **New special section**: wartime poems by William Butler Yeats, Edward Thomas, Siegfried Sassoon, Isaac Rosenberg, and Wilfred Owen to compare with their American counterparts.

We wish to thank the following reviewers who provided feedback for this book:

Dorothy Barresi, California State University–Northridge; **Anthony Cuda**, University of North Carolina–Greensboro; **Joseph Duemer**, Clarkson University; **Cathy E. Fagan**, Nassau Community College; **Louis Gallo**, Radford University; **Siân Griffiths**, Piedmont College; **Christine Hume**, Eastern Michigan University; **Ruth Jennison**, University of Massachusetts; **Linda A. Kinnahan**, Duquesne University; **Elizabeth Majerus**, University of Illinois Laboratory High School; **Brian McHale**, Oho State University; **Peter Nicholls**, New York University; **Rhonda Pettit**, University of Cincinnati; **Paul Robichaud**, Albertus Magnus College; **Catherine A. Rogers**, Savannah State University; **Jennifer Ryan**, Buffalo State College; **Eric Murphy Selinger**, DePaul University; **Heather H. Thomas**, Kutztown University of Pennsylvania.

Thanks as well to Phillip Ernstmeyer and Caroline Nappo for their help in proofreading this large manuscript.

VOLUME TWO

CONTEMPORARY AMERICAN POETRY

MARY CORNELIA HARTSHORNE (BORN C. 1910)

American Indian magazine described Mary Cornelia Hartshorne as "descended from two of the most influential families of the Choctaw tribe." She had been contributing poems to the magazine and joined it as contributing editor of its "Poetry Page." They placed a picture of her on the cover of the July 1928 issue. At the University of Oklahoma, she joined the Indian, Spanish, and poetry clubs. After illness interrupted her education, she resumed her studies at the University of Tulsa. An essay contest won her and twenty-three other students a trip to Hollywood, and *American Indian* featured a photo of her with actress Mary Pickford on another cover. After that, Hartshorne vanishes from the historical record. We know nothing of the rest of her life, but, as Robert Parker has written, her "sophisticated sense of the poetic life, with its flexible length and its flexible array of enjambments and caesuras, anticipates the style of later poetry."

FALLEN LEAVES

(An Indian Grandmother's Parable)

Many times in my life I have heard the white sages,
Who are learned in the knowledge and lore of past ages,
Speak of my people with pity, say, "Gone is their hour
Of dominion. By the strong wind of progress their power,
Like a rose past its brief time of blooming, lies shattered;
Like the leaves of the oak tree its people are scattered."
This is the eighty-first autumn since I can remember.
Again fall the leaves, born in April and dead by December;
Riding the whimsied breeze, zigzagging and whirling,
Coming to earth at last and slowly upcurling,
Withered and sapless and brown, into discarded fragments
Of what once was life; dry, chattering parchments
That crackle and rustle like old women's laughter
When the merciless wind with swift feet coming after
Will drive them before him with unsparing lashes
'Til they are crumbled and crushed into forgotten ashes;
Crumbled and crushed, and piled deep in the gulches and hollows,
Soft bed for the yet softer snow that in winter fast follows
But when in the spring the light falling
Patter of raindrops persuading, insistently calling,
Wakens to life again forces that long months have slumbered,
There will come whispering movement, and green things
unnumbered

Will pierce through the mould with their yellow-green, sun-
searching fingers,
Fingers—or spear-tips, grown tall, will bud at another year's
breaking,
One day when the brooks, manumitted by sunshine, are making
Music like gold in the spring of some far generation.
And up from the long-withered leaves, from the musty stagnation,
Life will climb high to the furthermost leaflets.
The bursting of catkins asunder with greed for the sunlight; the
thirsting
Of twisted brown roots for earth-water; the gradual unfolding
Of brilliance and strength in the future, earth's bosom is holding
Today in those scurrying leaves, soon to be crumpled and broken.
Let those who have ears hear my word and be still. I have spoken.

1927

HILLS OF DOON°

When I beheld the squatted Hills of Doon,
Blistered and bald and bare,
Sketched in a ragged semi-circle on the air
That quivered up from the parched earth at noon;
When I beheld the stately pale-green spears
Of cottonwood arrayed against the sky,
Sternly aloof and high,
My heart grew heavy, but there were no tears.
And when I felt the lonely quietness that crept
Down from the brooding hills at dusk,
On breezes tinctured with faint woodland musk
That lulled my brain, like poppies, 'til I slept,
I pictured the low house near the great bay,
The down-plunging cliffs of rock
Battling the waves' recurrent shock,
The stretch of pebbled beach where, day by day,
I used to stand and watch the sea birds swerve
On sunlit wings swift and alive and free,
And fancied that the unleashed soul of me
Raced with them there above the ocean's curve.

The Hills of Doon were huge and strange and old,
I had seen great liners slowly pass.
There were long blades of lightly stirring grass;

---

poem title: *Doon:* most likely Ireland.

I had played with whitecaps salt and cold.
I had seen mad waters lashed to foam;
I had heard sea-voices' friendly taunt;
These inland hills and trees, indifferent and gaunt,
Filled my sick soul with longing for my home.

But that was years ago. Today the sound
Of leaves, whirled by some hurried breeze,
Dancing a silver dance in the prim trees,
Quenches the scrape of fishing boats coming aground.
And there is golden magic under a golden moon;
Magic of bird-song and small, shrill-mouthed things at play:
The boom of waters fainter grows each day.
I am at home again—here in my Hills of Doon.

1928

WIND IN MEXICO

Purple and white, the water-flowers are resting
On a pool of ink-blackness. So they had rested
When she had come to them. So they had lain quiet, quiet,
While the wind played in the tall bordering grasses.

White sunlight falls through the ebony branches,
The sunlight is old; she once dipped her brown hands in it.
The silence is old; she loved the great stillness
Two thousand years away from this thundering greed.

Her feet were small: they pressed lightly among the rushes;
They did not disturb the turtles asleep in the mud.
Her hands were like moths skimming over the glowing blossoms.
Her eyes were a-dream with the beauty of high-noon in Mexico.

The coolness of sheltering shadows engulfed her;
A breeze, sweet with the breath of the forest, brushed by her;
She heard a lute's voice and a drum's throb afar in the village,
Warp and woof of a skillfully woven old dream-telling pattern.

Her own fingers sought after music and found it
On thin harp-strings when the heat of the day was asleep;
And night was awake and she sat in the house of her father
And the song of frogs floated up from the pool of white flowers.

Harp-strings a-quiver flung silver afar in the starlight,
And her silver singing went surging around and above it;

The wind bore it outward, caressing the land of the Aztecs,
Spilling it into the hearts of the Children of Freedom.

But the wind that wearily ripples the palm-leaves,
That glides through the pool-margining grasses here in the sun's glare,
Bending them low like swords bent low in subjection,
Has been robbed of its treasure. It moans in the ebony branches.

For the ages have muffled the music of her who once walked here,
Have choked out the echoes of laughter, have stifled the flute notes,
And the wind is filled with the weeping of Mexico's daughters.
The Children of Freedom are slaves in the home of their fathers.

1928

CHARLES HENRI FORD (1910–2002)

Born in Brookhaven, Massachusetts, Ford was first known as the editor of *Blues: A Magazine of Verse* (1929–1930), after which he lived in Paris for several years. He edited the beautiful surrealist magazine *View* in New York from 1940 to 1947 and lived in Italy from 1952 to 1957. He began publishing his own surrealist poetry in the 1930s and exhibiting his paintings worldwide in the 1950s. In the 1960s, he collaborated with Andy Warhol on film and multimedia projects and exhibited his collage poems (including "28")—composed of words cut out of newspapers and magazines—in galleries. Ford frequently lived in Greece and spent some time in Tibet.

PLAINT

Before A Mob of 10,000 At Owensboro, Ky.

I, Rainey Bethea,° 22,
from the top-branch of race-hatred look at you.
My limbs are bound, though boundless the bright sun
like my bright blood which had to run
into the orchard that excluded me:
now I climb death's tree.

The pruning hooks of many mouths
cut the black-leaved boughs.
The robins of my eyes hover where
sixteen leaves fall that were a prayer:
sixteen mouths are open wide;
the minutes like black cherries
drop from my shady side.

Oh, who is the forester must tend such a tree, Lord?
Do angels pick the cherry-blood of folk like me, Lord?

1937

1. *Bethea:* Rainey Bethea (c. 1909–August 14, 1936) was the last person to be publicly executed in the United States. Bethea, an indigent black man, confessed to the rape and murder of a seventy-year-old white woman named Liscia Edwards. His lawyers essentially presented no defense. The trial jury returned a verdict of death by hanging in less than five minutes. Thousands traveled to Owensboro, Kentucky, to witness the public execution. The executioner arrived drunk.

PASTORAL FOR PAVLIK°

The tree with the umbilical eyes
voids the dress of sunrise;

the pink wool of the hill rat
curves like the whinny of a caught cat.

The lichen wattle of the senseless rocks
votes the last lizard smallpox,

while the venereal sumac does
nothing until the endless wind blows.

Twigs, bones of the boy you were,
wait for the bird with the kindling fur.

Which bole huts, like a pianola,
the perforated bleat of the sick boa?

Bridges, furniture of roads,
test our superiority to toads.

The back of the fluffy dead bush
may be a relinquished wish.

Feet on the ground, bulbs without beds,
sprout with bodies, bloom with heads,

while the young cow in doddering dews
paradisiacally chews.

1937

FLAG OF ECSTASY

for Marcel Duchamp

Over the towers of autoerotic honey
Over the dungeons of homicidal drives

---

poem title: Pavlik: Ford's longtime partner and companion, the painter and designer Pavel Tchelitchew (1898–1957), who illustrated Ford's magazine *View.* The two men shared an interest in surrealism.

Over the pleasures of invading sleep
Over the sorrows of invading a woman

Over the voix céleste°
Over vomito negro°

Over the unendurable sensation of madness
Over the insatiable sense of sin

Over the spirit of uprisings
Over the bodies of tragediennes

Over tarantism:° "melancholy stupor and an
    uncontrollable desire to dance"
Over all

Over ambivalent virginity
Over unfathomable succubi°

Over the tormentors of Negresses
Over openhearted sans-culottes°

Over a stactometer° for the tears of France
Over unmanageable hermaphrodites

Over the rattlesnake sexlessness of art lovers
Over the shithouse enigmas of art haters

Over the sun's lascivious° serum
Over the sewage of the moon

Over the saints of debauchery
Over criminals made of gold

---

5. *voix céleste*: (French) "heavenly voice," an organ stop producing a sound of stringlike quality.

6. *vomito negro:* (Italian) "black vomit." Cf. "vomitus niger" (Latin), "black vomit."

11. *tarantism:* a dancing mania of late medieval Europe, defined in the quoted phrase.

15. *succubi:* demons who take female form in order to have intercourse with men in their sleep; also, more broadly, prostitutes.

17. *sans-culottes:* (French) "without breeches," a term of reproach used by the aristocrats for the extreme republicans (wearers of pantaloons rather than knee breeches) in the French Revolution; in other words, a violent revolutionist.

18. *stactometer:* a device used to measure the number of drops in a given volume of liquid.

22. *lascivious:* wanton, lewd.

Over the princes of delirium
Over the paupers of peace

Over signs foretelling the end of the world
Over signs foretelling the beginning of a world

Like one of those tender strips of flesh
On either side of the vertebral column

Marcel,° wave!

1944

32. *Marcel:* Duchamp (1887–1968), French painter and theorist, an avant-garde icon who moved to New York in 1915 and became the center of a group of Dada artists. Note in the poem the element of collage, the use of phrases that are almost the equivalent of found objects, and the unstable dichotomies in the couplets.

CHARLES OLSON (1910–1970)

Born and raised in Worcester, Massachusetts, the son of a postal worker, Olson was educated at Wesleyan, Harvard, and Yale Universities. As a child, he spent summers on the Massachusetts coast at Gloucester, the city that would be the setting for his major poem sequence *The Maximus Poems*. Anticipating a scholarly career, he completed doctoral research for a project on Herman Melville. It was interrupted by work for the American Civil Liberties Union in New York and for the Office of War Information in Washington. After resigning the latter job in protest against censorship, he proceeded to write *Call Me Ishmael,* a powerful, visionary study of Melville and the American obsession with space. Then he had the opportunity to fill in at Black Mountain College in North Carolina, which would become his home until 1956. He ended up running the college and wrote many of his key early poems there, along with his widely read manifestos on poetics, "Projective Verse" and "Human Universe." One of the major practitioners of open form poetry, Olson often sought to record the mental process of composition in his poetry. *The Maximus Poems* in particular tracks ongoing perceptions while drawing in both classical allusions and references to modern science and philosophy. Often disjunctive, the poems can be lyrical at some moments, decidedly didactic at others. We have chosen two poems from the sequence, "Maximus, to himself" and "Cole's Island," that work well on their own, along with one of Olson's more appealing independent poems, as introductions to his work.

VARIATIONS DONE FOR GERALD VAN DE WIELE°

I. LE BONHEUR°

dogwood flakes
what is green

the petals
from the apple
blow on the road

mourning doves
mark the sway
of the afternoon, bees
dig the plum blossoms

---

poem title: Van De Wiele was a student at Black Mountain College in the 1950s while Olson was director there.

Part I: *Le Bonheur:* (French) "Happiness," title of a poem by French poet Arthur Rimbaud (1854–1891), the last text of Rimbaud's experimental sequence *A Season in Hell* (1873). A number of echoes of Rimbaud's book are woven into Olson's poem.

the morning
stands up straight, the night
is blue from the full of the April moon

iris and lilac, birds
birds, yellow flowers
white flowers, the Diesel
does not let up dragging
the plow

as the whippoorwill,
the night's tractor, grinds
his song

and no other birds but us
are as busy (O saisons, o chateaux!°

Délires!°

What soul
is without fault?

Nobody studies
happiness

Every time the cock crows
I salute him

I have no longer any excuse
for envy. My life

has been given its orders: the seasons
seize

the soul and the body, and make mock
of any dispersed effort. The hour of death

is the only trespass

II. THE CHARGE

dogwood flakes
the green

---

22. O *saisons, o chateaux!:* "Oh seasons, oh castles!"; the first line of "Le Bonheur."
23. *Délires:* (French) "Frenzies," the title of two sections of *A Season in Hell.*

the petals from the apple-trees
fall for the feet to walk on

the birds are so many they are
loud, in the afternoon

they distract, as so many bees do
suddenly all over the place

With spring one knows today to see
that in the morning each thing

is separate but by noon
they have melted into each other

and by night only crazy things
like the full moon and the whippoorwill

and us, are busy. We are busy
if we can get by that whiskered bird,

that nightjar,° and get across, the moon
is our conversation, she will say

what soul
isn't in default?

can you afford not to make
the magical study

which happiness is? do you hear
the cock when he crows? do you know the charge,

that you shall have no envy, that your life
has its orders, that the seasons

seize you too, that no body and soul are one
if they are not wrought

in this retort? that otherwise efforts
are efforts? And that the hour of your flight

will be the hour of your death?

---

53. *nightjar:* a European bird of the goatsucker family, named for its harsh call.

III. SPRING

The dogwood
lights up the day.

The April moon
flakes the night.

Birds, suddenly,
are a multitude

The flowers are ravined°
by bees, the fruit blossoms

are thrown to the ground, the wind
the rain forces everything. Noise—

even the night is drummed
by whippoorwills, and we get

as busy, we plow, we move,
we break out, we love. The secret

which got lost neither hides
nor reveals itself, it shows forth

tokens. And we rush
to catch up. The body

whips the soul. In its great desire
it demands the elixir

In the roar of spring,
transmutations. Envy

drags herself off. The fault of the body and the soul
—that they are not one—

the matutinal° cock clangs
and singleness: we salute you

season of no bungling

1960

---

74. *ravined:* emptied out.
92. *matutinal:* morning.

MAXIMUS, TO HIMSELF

I have had to learn the simplest things
last; Which made for difficulties.
Even at sea I was slow, to get the hand out, or to cross
a wet deck.
The sea was not, finally, my trade.
But even my trade, at it, I stood estranged
from that which was most familiar.° Was delayed,
and not content with the man's argument
that such postponement
is now the nature of
obedience,
that we are all late
in a slow time,
that we grow up many
And the single
is not easily
known
It could be, though the sharpness (the *achiote*°)
I note in others,
makes more sense
than my own distances. The agilities

they show daily
who do the world's
businesses
And who do nature's
as I have no sense
I have done either

I have made dialogues,
have discussed ancient texts,
have thrown what light I could, offered
what pleasures
doceat° allows

But the known?
This, I have had to be given,
a life, love, and from one man
the world

---

7. *most familiar:* Cf. Heracleitus (c. 540–c. 480 B.C.)—"We are estranged from that with which we are most familiar."

18. *achiote:* seed crushed to produce a dye the color of red pepper (thus, sharp).

32. *doceat:* (Latin) teaching.

Tokens.
But sitting here
I look out as a wind
and water man, testing
And missing
some proof

I know the quarters
of the weather, where it comes from,
where it goes. But the stem of me,
this I took from their welcome,
or their rejection, of me

And my arrogance
was neither diminished
nor increased,
by the communication

It is undone business
I speak of, this morning,
with the sea
stretching out
from my feet

1960

COLE'S ISLAND

I met Death—he was a sportsman—on Cole's
Island.° He was a property-owner. Or maybe
Cole's Island, was his. I don't know. The
point was I was there, walking, and—as it
often is, in the woods—a stranger, suddenly
showing up, makes the very thing you were do-
ing no longer the same. That is suddenly
what you thought, when you were alone, and
doing what you were doing, changes because someone else
shows up. He didn't bother me, or say anything. Which is
not surprising, a person might not, in the circumstances;

2. *Cole's Island:* located in West Gloucester on the Essex River, Cole's Island is not a true island but is attached to the mainland by marshes and a road.

or at most a nod or something. Or they would. But they wouldn't,
or you wouldn't think to either, if it was Death. And
He certainly was, the moment I saw him. There wasn't any
    question
about that even though he may have looked like a sort of country
gentleman, going about his own land. Not quite. Not it being He.

A fowler, maybe—as though he was used to
hunting birds, and was out, this morning, keeping
his hand in, so to speak, moving around, noticing
what game were about. And how they seemed. And how the woods
were. As a matter of fact just before he had shown up,
so naturally, and as another person might walk
up on a scene of your own, I had noticed
a cock and hen pheasant cross easily the
road I was on and had tried, in fact,
to catch my son's attention quick enough for him
to see before they did walk off into the bayberry
or arbor vitae along the road.

                    My impression is we did—
that is, Death and myself, regard each other. And
there wasn't anything more than that, only that he had appeared,
and we did recognize each other—or I did, him, and he seemed
to have no question
about my presence there, even though I was uncomfortable.
    That is,
Cole's Island
is a queer isolated and gated place, and I was only there by will
to know more of the topography of it lying as it does out
over the Essex River. And as it now is, with no tenants that one
    can speak of,
it's more private than almost any place one might imagine.
And down in that part of it where I did meet him (about half way
    between the
two houses over the river and the carriage house
at the entrance) it was as quiet and as much a piece
of the earth as any place can be. But my difficulty,
when he did show up, was immediately at least that I was
an intruder, by being there at all
and yet, even if he seemed altogether
used to Cole's Island, and, like I say, as though he owned it,
even if I was sure he didn't, I noticed him, and he me, and he
went on without anything extraordinary at all.

Maybe he had gaiters on, or almost
a walking stick, in other words much more
habited than I,
who was in chinos actually and
only doing what I had set myself to do here
& in other places on Cape Ann.

It was his eye perhaps which makes me
render him as Death? It isn't true, there wasn't anything
that different about his eye,
it was not one thing more than that he was Death instantly
that he came into sight. Or that I was aware there was a person
here as well as myself. And son.

We did exchange some glance. That is the fullest possible
account I can give, of the encounter.

1964

ELIZABETH BISHOP (1911–1979)

Born in Worcester, Massachusetts, Bishop endured a childhood that was structured around a sequence of tragedies. Her father died when she was less than one year old. Her mother endured a series of emotional breakdowns and was permanently institutionalized when Bishop was five years old; they never saw each other again. At that point, she was living in Nova Scotia, but after a few years her grandparents returned with her to Worcester. Then she lived with an aunt, meanwhile suffering from asthma and other illnesses. After an education at Vassar, she lived in New York and Florida, but on a fellowship to Brazil she decided to stay there with Lota de Macedo Soares, a Brazilian architect, as her partner, which she did for sixteen years, until Soares committed suicide in 1967. In 1970 Bishop began a seven-year teaching career at Harvard.

If other poets of her generation were to exploit their pain, Bishop instead chose restraint in her early work. She practiced exacting description coupled with distinctly unsentimental introspection, but she also discovered a style of frank, but crafted, spontaneity. With her third book, *Questions of Travel* (1965), which focused on her Brazil experience, her technical skills and unsentimental wit supported her in a journey into boldly unconventional social and cultural commentary of a sort no other American poet has attempted. If anything, the Brazil poems have become more surprising with a few decades' distance. It would be hard to imagine anyone writing them now.

THE FISH

I caught a tremendous fish
and held him beside the boat
half out of water, with my hook
fast in a corner of his mouth.
He didn't fight.
He hadn't fought at all.
He hung a grunting weight,
battered and venerable
and homely. Here and there
his brown skin hung in strips
like ancient wallpaper,
and its pattern of darker brown
was like wallpaper:
shapes like full-blown roses
stained and lost through age.
He was speckled with barnacles,

fine rosettes° of lime,
and infested
with tiny white sea-lice,
and underneath two or three
rags of green weed hung down.
While his gills were breathing in
the terrible oxygen
—the frightening gills,
fresh and crisp with blood,
that can cut so badly—
I thought of the coarse white flesh
packed in like feathers,
the big bones and the little bones,
the dramatic reds and blacks
of his shiny entrails,
and the pink swim-bladder
like a big peony.
I looked into his eyes
which were far larger than mine
but shallower, and yellowed,
the irises backed and packed
with tarnished tinfoil
seen through the lenses
of old scratched isinglass.°
They shifted a little, but not
to return my stare.
—It was more like the tipping
of an object toward the light.
I admired his sullen face,
the mechanism of his jaw,
and then I saw
that from his lower lip
—if you could call it a lip—
grim, wet, and weaponlike,
hung five old pieces of fish-line,
or four and a wire leader°
with the swivel still attached,
with all their five big hooks
grown firmly in his mouth.

---

17. *rosettes:* roselike marking, like an ornamental badge.

40. *isinglass:* thin, transparent sheets of mica, a crystallized mineral, used for windows; in context, we are to remember that "isinglass" also refers to a very pure form of gelatin made from the air bladders of sturgeons or other fish.

52. *leader:* connects fish hook and fishline.

A green line, frayed at the end
where he broke it, two heavier lines,
and a fine black thread
still crimped from the strain and snap
when it broke and he got away.
Like medals with their ribbons
frayed and wavering,
a five-haired beard of wisdom
trailing from his aching jaw.
I stared and stared
and victory filled up
the little rented boat,
from the pool of bilge
where oil had spread a rainbow
around the rusted engine
to the bailer rusted orange,
the sun-cracked thwarts,
the oarlocks on their strings,
the gunnels°—until everything
was rainbow, rainbow, rainbow!
And I let the fish go.

1946

THE MAN-MOTH°

Here, above,
cracks in the buildings are filled with battered moonlight.
The whole shadow of Man is only as big as his hat.
It lies at his feet like a circle for a doll to stand on,
and he makes an inverted pin, the point magnetized to the moon.
He does not see the moon; he observes only her vast properties,
feeling the queer light on his hands, neither warm nor cold,
of a temperature impossible to record in thermometers.

But when the Man-Moth
pays his rare, although occasional, visits to the surface,
the moon looks rather different to him. He emerges
from an opening under the edge of one of the sidewalks
and nervously begins to scale the faces of the buildings.
He thinks the moon is a small hole at the top of the sky,

71–74. *bailer . . . gunnels:* "bailer," bucket used to bail water out of the boat; "thwarts," seats or benches across a boat for rowers to sit on; "oarlocks," metal brackets that anchor the oars but allow them to swivel; "gunnels," the upper edges on the sides of a boat.

poem title: Bishop's note—"a newspaper misprint for mammoth."

proving the sky quite useless for protection.
He trembles, but must investigate as high as he can climb.

Up the façades,
his shadow dragging like a photographer's cloth behind him,
he climbs fearfully, thinking that this time he will manage
to push his small head through that round clean opening
and be forced through, as from a tube, in black scrolls on the light.
(Man, standing below him, has no such illusions.)
But what the Man-Moth fears most he must do, although
he fails, of course, and falls back scared but quite unhurt.

Then he returns
to the pale subways of cement he calls his home. He flits,
he flutters, and cannot get aboard the silent trains
fast enough to suit him. The doors close swiftly.
The Man-Moth always seats himself facing the wrong way
and the train starts at once at its full, terrible speed,
without a shift in gears or a gradation of any sort.
He cannot tell the rate at which he travels backwards.

Each night he must
be carried through artificial tunnels and dream recurrent dreams.
Just as the ties recur beneath his train, these underlie
his rushing brain. He does not dare look out the window,
for the third rail, the unbroken draught of poison,
runs there beside him. He regards it as a disease
he has inherited the susceptibility to. He has to keep
his hands in his pockets, as others must wear mufflers.

If you catch him,
hold up a flashlight to his eye. It's all dark pupil,
an entire night itself, whose haired horizon tightens
as he stares back, and closes up the eye. Then from the lids
one tear, his only possession, like the bee's sting, slips.
Slyly he palms it, and if you're not paying attention
he'll swallow it. However, if you watch, he'll hand it over,
cool as from underground springs and pure enough to drink.

1946

AT THE FISHHOUSES

Although it is a cold evening,
down by one of the fishhouses

an old man sits netting,
his net, in the gloaming almost invisible,
a dark purple-brown,
and his shuttle worn and polished.
The air smells so strong of codfish
it makes one's nose run and one's eyes water.
The five fishhouses have steeply peaked roofs
and narrow, cleated gangplanks slant up
to storerooms in the gables
for the wheelbarrows to be pushed up and down on.
All is silver: the heavy surface of the sea,
swelling slowly as if considering spilling over,
is opaque, but the silver of the benches,
the lobster pots, and masts, scattered
among the wild jagged rocks,
is of an apparent translucence
like the small old buildings with an emerald moss
growing on their shoreward walls.
The big fish tubs are completely lined
with layers of beautiful herring scales
and the wheelbarrows are similarly plastered
with creamy iridescent coats of mail,
with small iridescent flies crawling on them.
Up on the little slope behind the houses,
set in the sparse bright sprinkle of grass,
is an ancient wooden capstan,
cracked, with two long bleached handles
and some melancholy stains, like dried blood,
where the ironwork has rusted.
The old man accepts a Lucky Strike.
He was a friend of my grandfather.
We talk of the decline in the population
and of codfish and herring
while he waits for a herring boat to come in.
There are sequins on his vest and on his thumb.
He has scraped the scales, the principal beauty,
from unnumbered fish with that black old knife,
the blade of which is almost worn away.

Down at the water's edge, at the place
where they haul up the boats, up the long ramp
descending into the water, thin silver
tree trunks are laid horizontally
across the gray stones, down and down
at intervals of four or five feet.

Cold dark deep and absolutely clear,
element bearable to no mortal,
to fish and to seals . . . One seal particularly
I have seen here evening after evening.
He was curious about me. He was interested in music;
like me a believer in total immersion,
so I used to sing him Baptist hymns.
I also sang "A Mighty Fortress Is Our God."
He stood up in the water and regarded me
steadily, moving his head a little.
Then he would disappear, then suddenly emerge
almost in the same spot, with a sort of shrug
as if it were against his better judgment.
Cold dark deep and absolutely clear,
the clear gray icy water . . . Back, behind us,
the dignified tall firs begin.
Bluish, associating with their shadows,
a million Christmas trees stand
waiting for Christmas. The water seems suspended
above the rounded gray and blue-gray stones.
I have seen it over and over, the same sea, the same,
slightly, indifferently swinging above the stones,
icily free above the stones,
above the stones and then the world.
If you should dip your hand in,
your wrist would ache immediately,
your bones would begin to ache and your hand would burn
as if the water were a transmutation of fire
that feeds on stones and burns with a dark gray flame.
If you tasted it, it would first taste bitter,
then briny, then surely burn your tongue.
It is like what we imagine knowledge to be:
dark, salt, clear, moving, utterly free,
drawn from the cold hard mouth
of the world, derived from the rocky breasts
forever, flowing and drawn, and since
our knowledge is historical, flowing, and flown.

1955

FILLING STATION

Oh, but it is dirty!
—this little filling station,
oil-soaked, oil-permeated

to a disturbing, over-all
black translucency.
Be careful with that match!

Father wears a dirty,
oil-soaked monkey suit
that cuts him under the arms,
and several quick and saucy
and greasy sons assist him
(it's a family filling station),
all quite thoroughly dirty.

Do they live in the station?
It has a cement porch
behind the pumps, and on it
a set of crushed and grease-
impregnated wickerwork;
on the wicker sofa
a dirty dog, quite comfy.

Some comic books provide
the only note of color—
of certain color. They lie
upon a big dim doily
draping a taboret°
(part of the set), beside
a big hirsute begonia.

Why the extraneous plant?
Why the taboret?
Why, oh why, the doily?
(Embroidered in daisy stitch
with marguerites,° I think,
and heavy with gray crochet.)

Somebody embroidered the doily.
Somebody waters the plant,
or oils it, maybe. Somebody
arranges the rows of cans
so that they softly says:
Esso°—so—so—so

---

25. *taboret:* small, drum-shaped table or stand.

32. *marguerites:* small daisies.

39. *Esso:* a brand of gasoline.

to high-strung automobiles.
Somebody loves us all.

1965

QUESTIONS OF TRAVEL

There are too many waterfalls here; the crowded streams
hurry too rapidly down to the sea,
and the pressure of so many clouds on the mountaintops
makes them spill over the sides in soft slow-motion,
turning to waterfalls under our very eyes.
—For if those streaks, those mile-long, shiny, tearstains,
aren't waterfalls yet,
in a quick age or so, as ages go here,
they probably will be.
But if the streams and clouds keep travelling, travelling,
the mountains look like the hulls of capsized ships,
slime-hung and barnacled.

Think of the long trip home.
Should we have stayed at home and thought of here?
Where should we be today?
Is it right to be watching strangers in a play
in this strangest of theatres?
What childishness is it that while there's a breath of life
in our bodies, we are determined to rush
to see the sun the other way around?
The tiniest green hummingbird in the world?
To stare at some inexplicable old stonework,
inexplicable and impenetrable,
at any view,
instantly seen and always, always delightful?
Oh, must we dream our dreams
and have them, too?
And have we room
for one more folded sunset, still quite warm?

But surely it would have been a pity
not to have seen the trees along this road,
really exaggerated in their beauty,
not to have seen them gesturing
like noble pantomimists, robed in pink.
—Not to have had to stop for gas and heard

the sad, two-noted, wooden tune
of disparate wooden clogs
carelessly clacking over
a grease-stained filling-station floor.
(In another country the clogs would all be tested.
Each pair there would have identical pitch.)
—A pity not to have heard
the other, less primitive music of the fat brown bird
who sings above the broken gasoline pump
in a bamboo church of Jesuit baroque:
three towers, five silver crosses.
—Yes, a pity not to have pondered,
blurr'dly and inconclusively,
on what connection can exist for centuries
between the crudest wooden footwear
and, careful and finicky,
the whittled fantasies of wooden cages.
—Never to have studied history in
the weak calligraphy of songbirds' cages.
—And never to have had to listen to rain
so much like politicians' speeches:
two hours of unrelenting oratory
and then a sudden golden silence
in which the traveller takes a notebook, writes:

"Is it lack of imagination that makes us come
to imagined places, not just stay at home?
Or could Pascal have been not entirely right
about just sitting quietly in one's room?

Continent, city, country, society:
the choice is never wide and never free.
And here, or there . . . No. Should we have stayed at home,
wherever that may be?"

1965

THE ARMADILLO

(For Robert Lowell)

This is the time of year
when almost every night
the frail, illegal fire balloons appear.
Climbing the mountain height,

rising toward a saint
still honored in these parts,
the paper chambers flush and fill with light
that comes and goes, like hearts.

Once up against the sky it's hard
to tell them from the stars—
planets, that is—the tinted ones:
Venus going down, or Mars,

or the pale green one. With a wind,
they flare and falter, wobble and toss;
but if it's still they steer between
the kite sticks of the Southern Cross,°

receding, dwindling, solemnly
and steadily forsaking us,
or, in the downdraft from a peak,
suddenly turning dangerous.

Last night another big one fell.
It splattered like an egg of fire
against the cliff behind the house.
The flame ran down. We saw the pair

of owls who nest there flying up
and up, their whirling black-and-white
stained bright pink underneath, until
they shrieked up out of sight.

The ancient owls' nest must have burned.
Hastily, all alone,
a glistening armadillo left the scene,
rose-flecked, head down, tail down,

and then a baby rabbit jumped out,
short-eared, to our surprise.
So soft!—a handful of intangible ash
with fixed, ignited eyes.

Too pretty, dreamlike mimicry!
O falling fire and piercing cry

16. *Southern Cross:* a constellation.

and panic, and a weak mailed fist
clenched ignorant against the sky!

1965

IN THE WAITING ROOM

In Worcester, Massachusetts,
I went with Aunt Consuelo
to keep her dentist's appointment
and sat and waited for her
in the dentist's waiting room.
It was winter. It got dark
early. The waiting room
was full of grown-up people,
arctics and overcoats,
lamps and magazines.
My aunt was inside
what seemed like a long time
and while I waited I read
the *National Geographic*
(I could read) and carefully
studied the photographs:
the inside of a volcano,
black, and full of ashes;
then it was spilling over
in rivulets of fire.
Osa and Martin Johnson°
dressed in riding breeches,
laced boots, and pith helmets.
A dead man slung on a pole
—"Long Pig,"° the caption said.
Babies with pointed heads
wound round and round with string;
black, naked women with necks
wound round and round with wire
like the necks of light bulbs.
Their breasts were horrifying.
I read it right straight through.
I was too shy to stop.
And then I looked at the cover:
the yellow margins, the date.

---

21. *Johnson:* Osa Johnson (1894–1953) and her husband Martin Johnson (1884–1937) filmed Africa's vanishing wildlife for the American Museum of Natural History.

25. *Long Pig:* the name Polynesian cannibals used for the body of a dead person.

Suddenly, from inside,
came an *oh!* of pain
—Aunt Consuelo's voice—
not very loud or long.
I wasn't at all surprised;
even then I knew she was
a foolish, timid woman.
I might have been embarrassed,
but wasn't. What took me
completely by surprise
was that it was *me:*
my voice, in my mouth.
Without thinking at all
I was my foolish aunt,
I—we—were falling, falling,
our eyes glued to the cover
of the *National Geographic,*
February, 1918.

I said to myself: three days
and you'll be seven years old.
I was saying it to stop
the sensation of falling off
the round, turning world
into cold, blue-black space.
But I felt: you are an *I,*
you are an *Elizabeth,*
you are one of *them.*
Why should you be one, too?
I scarcely dared to look
to see what it was I was.
I gave a sidelong glance
—I couldn't look any higher—
at shadowy gray knees,
trousers and skirts and boots
and different pairs of hands
lying under the lamps.
I knew that nothing stranger
had ever happened, that nothing
stranger could ever happen.
Why should I be my aunt,
or me, or anyone?
What similarities—
boots, hands, the family voice
I felt in my throat, or even

the *National Geographic*
and those awful hanging breasts—
held us all together
or made us all just one?
How—I didn't know any
word for it—how "unlikely"...
How had I come to be here,
like them, and overhear
a cry of pain that could have
got loud and worse but hadn't?

The waiting room was bright
and too hot. It was sliding
beneath a big black wave,
another, and another.

Then I was back in it.
The War° was on. Outside,
in Worcester, Massachusetts,
were night and slush and cold,
and it was still the fifth
of February, 1918.

1976

PINK DOG

[Rio de Janeiro]°

The sun is blazing and the sky is blue.
Umbrellas clothe the beach in every hue.
Naked, you trot across the avenue.

Oh, never have I seen a dog so bare!
Naked and pink, without a single hair...
Startled, the passersby draw back and stare.

Of course they're mortally afraid of rabies.
You are not mad; you have a case of scabies°
but look intelligent. Where are your babies?

---

95. *The War:* World War I.

epigraph: *Rio de Janeiro:* port city in southeast Brazil.

8. *scabies:* an itchy skin condition caused by infestation of parasitic mites; in the tropics, sometimes accompanied by secondary infections.

(A nursing mother, by those hanging teats.)
In what slum have you hidden them, poor bitch,
while you go begging, living by your wits?

Didn't you know? It's been in all the papers,
to solve this problem, how they deal with beggars?
They take and throw them in the tidal rivers.

Yes, idiots, paralytics, parasites
go bobbing in the ebbing sewage, nights
out in the suburbs, where there are no lights.

If they do this to anyone who begs,
drugged, drunk, or sober, with or without legs,
what would they do to sick, four-leggèd dogs?

In the cafés and on the sidewalk corners
the joke is going round that all the beggars
who can afford them now wear life preservers.

In your condition you would not be able
even to float, much less to dog-paddle.
Now look, the practical, the sensible

solution is to wear a *fantasía*.°
Tonight you simply can't afford to be a-
n eyesore. But no one will ever see a

dog in *máscara* this time of year.
Ash Wednesday'll° come but Carnival is here.
What sambas° can you dance? What will you wear?

They say that Carnival's degenerating
—radios, Americans, or something,
have ruined it completely. They're just talking.

Carnival is always wonderful!
A depilated dog would not look well.
Dress up! Dress up and dance at Carnival!

1979

---

28. *fantasía:* Bishop's note—"carnival costume".

32. *Ash Wednesday:* in the Christian calendar, the first day of Lent, the forty days leading up to the date of Christ's crucifixion. Catholics mark the day by placing a cross of ash on their foreheads, a token of penitence and mortality.

33. *sambas:* Brazilian dances.

CRUSOE IN ENGLAND

A new volcano has erupted,
the papers say, and last week I was reading
where some ship saw an island being born:
at first a breath of steam, ten miles away;
and then a black fleck—basalt, probably—
rose in the mate's binoculars
and caught on the horizon like a fly.
They named it. But my poor old island's still
un-rediscovered, un-renamable.
None of the books has ever got it right.

Well, I had fifty-two
miserable, small volcanoes I could climb
with a few slithery strides—
volcanoes dead as ash heaps.
I used to sit on the edge of the highest one
and count the others standing up,
naked and leaden, with their heads blown off.
I'd think that if they were the size
I thought volcanoes should be, then I had
become a giant;
and if I had become a giant,
I couldn't bear to think what size
the goats and turtles were,
or the gulls, or the overlapping rollers
—a glittering hexagon of rollers
closing and closing in, but never quite,
glittering and glittering, though the sky
was mostly overcast.

My island seemed to be
a sort of cloud-dump. All the hemisphere's
left-over clouds arrived and hung
above the craters—their parched throats
were hot to touch.
Was that why it rained so much?
And why sometimes the whole place hissed?
The turtles lumbered by, high-domed,
hissing like teakettles.
(And I'd have given years, or taken a few,
for any sort of kettle, of course.)
The folds of lava, running out to sea,
would hiss. I'd turn. And then they'd prove

to be more turtles.
The beaches were all lava, variegated,
black, red, and white, and gray;
the marbled colors made a fine display.
And I had waterspouts. Oh,
half a dozen at a time, far out,
they'd come and go, advancing and retreating,
their heads in cloud, their feet in moving patches
of scuffed-up white.
Glass chimneys, flexible, attenuated,
sacerdotal beings of glass . . . I watched
the water spiral up in them like smoke.
Beautiful, yes, but not much company.

I often gave way to self-pity.
"Do I deserve this? I suppose I must.
I wouldn't be here otherwise. Was there
a moment when I actually chose this?
I don't remember, but there could have been."
What's wrong about self-pity, anyway?
With my legs dangling down familiarly
over a crater's edge, I told myself
"Pity should begin at home." So the more
pity I felt, the more I felt at home.

The sun set in the sea; the same odd sun
rose from the sea,
and there was one of it and one of me.
The island had one kind of everything:
one tree snail, a bright violet-blue
with a thin shell, crept over everything,
over the one variety of tree,
a sooty, scrub affair.
Snail shells lay under these in drifts
and, at a distance,
you'd swear that they were beds of irises.
There was one kind of berry, a dark red.
I tried it, one by one, and hours apart.
Sub-acid, and not bad, no ill effects;
and so I made home-brew. I'd drink
the awful, fizzy, stinging stuff
that went straight to my head
and play my home-made flute
(I think it had the weirdest scale on earth)
and, dizzy, whoop and dance among the goats.

Home-made, home-made! But aren't we all?
I felt a deep affection for
the smallest of my island industries.
No, not exactly, since the smallest was
a miserable philosophy.

Because I didn't know enough.
Why didn't I know enough of something?
Greek drama or astronomy? The books
I'd read were full of blanks;
the poems—well, I tried
reciting to my iris-beds,
"They flash upon that inward eye,
which is the bliss . . ." The bliss of what?
One of the first things that I did
when I got back was look it up.

The island smelled of goat and guano.
The goats were white, so were the gulls,
and both too tame, or else they thought
I was a goat, too, or a gull.
Baa, baa, baa and *shriek, shriek, shriek,*
baa . . . shriek . . . baa . . . I still can't shake
them from my ears; they're hurting now.
The questioning shrieks, the equivocal replies
over a ground of hissing rain
and hissing, ambulating turtles
got on my nerves.

When all the gulls flew up at once, they sounded
like a big tree in a strong wind, its leaves.
I'd shut my eyes and think about a tree,
an oak, say, with real shade, somewhere.
I'd heard of cattle getting island-sick.
I thought the goats were.
One billy-goat would stand on the volcano
I'd christened *Mont d'Espoir* or *Mount Despair*
(I'd time enough to play with names),
and bleat and bleat, and sniff the air.
I'd grab his beard and look at him.
His pupils, horizontal, narrowed up
and expressed nothing, or a little malice.
I got so tired of the very colors!
One day I dyed a baby goat bright red
with my red berries, just to see

something a little different.
And then his mother wouldn't recognize him.

Dreams were the worst. Of course I dreamed of food
and love, but they were pleasant rather
than otherwise. But then I'd dream of things
like slitting a baby's throat, mistaking it
for a baby goat. I'd have
nightmares of other islands
stretching away from mine, infinities
of islands, islands spawning islands,
like frogs' eggs turning into polliwogs
of islands, knowing that I had to live
on each and every one, eventually,
for ages, registering their flora,
their fauna, their geography.

Just when I thought I couldn't stand it
another minute longer, Friday came.
(Accounts of that have everything all wrong.)
Friday was nice.
Friday was nice, and we were friends.
If only he had been a woman!
I wanted to propagate my kind,
and so did he, I think, poor boy.
He'd pet the baby goats sometimes,
and race with them, or carry one around.
—Pretty to watch; he had a pretty body.

And then one day they came and took us off.

Now I live here, another island,
that doesn't seem like one, but who decides?
My blood was full of them; my brain
bred islands. But that archipelago
has petered out. I'm old.
I'm bored, too, drinking my real tea,
surrounded by uninteresting lumber.
The knife there on the shelf—
it reeked of meaning, like a crucifix.
It lived. How many years did I
beg it, implore it, not to break?
I knew each nick and scratch by heart,
the bluish blade, the broken tip,
the lines of wood-grain on the handle . . .

Now it won't look at me at all.
The living soul has dribbled away.
My eyes rest on it and pass on.

The local museum's asked me to
leave everything to them:
the flute, the knife, the shrivelled shoes,
my shedding goatskin trousers
(moths have got in the fur),
the parasol that took me such a time
remembering the way the ribs should go.
It still will work but, folded up,
looks like a plucked and skinny fowl.
How can anyone want such things?
—And Friday, my dear Friday, died of measles
seventeen years ago come March.

1976

ONE ART

The art of losing isn't hard to master;
so many things seem filled with the intent
to be lost that their loss is no disaster.

Lose something every day. Accept the fluster
of lost door keys, the hour badly spent.
The art of losing isn't hard to master.

Then practice losing farther, losing faster;
places, and names, and where it was you meant
to travel. None of these will bring disaster.

I lost my mother's watch. And look! my last, or
next-to-last, of three loved houses went.
The art of losing isn't hard to master.

I lost two cities, lovely ones. And, vaster,
some realms I owned, two rivers, a continent.
I miss them, but it wasn't a disaster.

—Even losing you (the joking voice, a gesture
I love) I shan't have lied. It's evident
the art of losing's not too hard to master
though it may look like (*Write* it!) like disaster.

1976

WILLIAM EVERSON (1912–1994)

Born in Sacramento, California, Everson was the son of a Norwegian composer. He attended Fresno State College until leaving in 1935 to write poetry. Robinson Jeffers was one of his strongest literary influences at the time. He was a conscientious objector during World War II, working as a forester in Oregon for three years, and soon afterward joined the San Francisco anarcho-pacifist group centered around poet Kenneth Rexroth. In 1949, Everson converted to Roman Catholicism and wrote "The Making of the Cross"; the following year he joined the Catholic Worker Movement. In 1951 he entered the Dominican Order as a lay brother without vows. He took the name Brother Antoninus, but he left the monastery and rejoined the secular world in 1969. Before his conversion Everson had written poems of erotic mysticism and pantheism, as well as poems against war. In the early 1950s, the period when "A Canticle to the Waterbirds" was written, he wrote poems of great religious passion, but the differences with his earlier poetry were not absolute. "Canticle" is essentially a proof of the existence of God based on the evidence of nature's fecundity.

THE MAKING OF THE CROSS

Rough fir, hauled from the hills. And the tree it had been,
Lithe-limbed, wherein the wren had nested,
Whereon the red hawk and the grey
Rested from flight, and the raw-head vulture
Shouldered to his feed—that tree went over
Bladed down with a double-bitted axe; was snaked with winches;
The wedge split it; hewn with the adze
It lay to season toward its use.

So too with the nails: milleniums under the earth,
Pure ore; chunked out with picks; the nail-shape
Struck in the pelt-lunged forge; tonged to a cask,
And the wait against that work.

Even the thorn-bush flourished from afar,
As do the flourishing generations of its kind,
Filling the shallow soil no one wants.
Wind-sown, it cuts the cattle and the wild horse;
It tears the cloth of man, and hurts his hand.

Just as in life the good things of the earth
Are patiently assembled: some from here, some from there;
Wine from the hill and wheat from the valley;
Rain that comes blue-bellied out of the sopping sea;

Snow that keeps its drift on the gooseberry ridge,
Will melt with May, go down, take the egg of the salmon,
Serve the traffic of otters and fishes,
Be ditched to orchards . . .

So too are gathered up the possibles of evil.

And when the Cross was joined, quartered,
As is the earth; spoked, as is the Universal Wheel—
Those radials that led all unregenerate act
Inward to innocence—it met the thorn-wove Crown;
It found the Scourges and the Dice;
The Nail was given and the reed-lifted Sponge;°
The Curse caught forward out of the heart corrupt;
The excoriate Foul, stoned with the thunder and the hail—
All these made up that miscellaneous wrath
And were assumed.

The evil and the wastage and the woe,
As if the earth's old cyst, back down the slough
To Adam's sin-burnt calcinated bones,
Rushed out of time and clotted on the Cross.
Off there the cougar
Coughed in passion when the sun went out; the rattler
Filmed his glinty eye, and found his hole.

1949

A CANTICLE° TO THE WATERBIRDS

Clack your beaks you cormorants° and kittiwakes,
North on those rock-croppings finger-jutted into the rough Pacific
surge;

31–32. *Dice, Sponge:* during the Crucifixion, Roman soldiers threw dice to claim Christ's robes and quenched his thirst by lifting to his lips a vinegar-soaked sponge on a reed.

poem title: *canticle:* a song or chant, often a hymn with words taken from a biblical text. The poem is devoted to the waterbirds on a long stretch of Pacific coast from San Francisco/Oakland, California, north along Oregon and Washington to British Columbia, Canada. In a preface to the poem, Everson explains: "In the long summer dusks we used to walk to the Oakland estuary among the deserted factories and warehouses, and out along the silent piers. Where all day long an inferno of deafening racket enveloped the machines, now lay a most blessed peace. In these moments of solitude we thought of the men back at the hospice, broken, shabby, wine-sotted, hopeless. Out there on the estuary, over the water, the gulls lifted their wings in a gesture of pure felicity. Something hidden and conclusive broke bondage within me, something born of the nights and the weeks and the months. My mind shot north up the long coast of deliverance, encompassing all the areas of my ancient quest, that ineluctable instinct for the divine—the rivermouths and the sand-skirted beaches, sea-granite capes and bastions and basalt-founded cliffs—where despite all man's meanness a presence remains unspoiled, the sacred zone between earth and sea, and pure."

1. *cormorants:* marine diving birds with webbed feet and slender, hooked bills; kittiwakes: cliff-nesting gulls. These are among the many species of sea and fresh waterbirds, large and small, mentioned in the poem; we have identified only a few.

You migratory terns and pipers who leave but the temporal claw-track written on sandbars there of your presence;
Grebes and pelicans; you comber-picking° scoters° and you shorelong gulls;
All you keepers of the coastline north of here to the Mendocino° beaches;
All you beyond upon the cliff-face thwarting the surf at Hecate Head;
Hovering the under-surge where the cold Columbia° grapples at the bar;
North yet to the Sound,° whose islands float like a sown flurry of chips upon the sea;
Break wide your harsh and salt-encrusted beaks unmade for song
And say a praise up to the Lord.

And you freshwater egrets° east in the flooded marshlands skirting the sea-level rivers, white one-legged watchers of shallows;
Broad-headed kingfishers minnow-hunting from willow stems on meandering valley sloughs;
You too, you herons, blue and supple-throated, stately, taking the air majestical in the sunflooded San Joaquin,°
Grading down on your belted wings from the upper lights of sunset,
Mating over the willow clumps or where the flatwater rice fields shimmer;
You killdeer, high night-criers, far in the moon-suffusion sky;
Bitterns, sand-waders, all shore-walkers, all roost-keepers,
Populates of the 'dobe° cliffs of the Sacramento:
Open your water-dartling beaks,
And make a praise up to the Lord.

For you hold the heart of His mighty fastnesses,
And shape the life of His indeterminate realms.

---

4. *comber-picking:* searching for food among long waves that have reached their peak or broken into foam.

4. *scoters:* ducks of northern coastal areas.

5. *Mendocino:* Northern California coastal county and city.

7. *cold Columbia:* the Columbia River rises in southeast British Columbia, Canada, and flows south and west toward the Pacific Ocean along the Washington-Oregon border.

8. *the Sound:* probably Queen Charlotte Sound, running from Vancouver Island north to Hecate Strait and the Queen Charlotte Islands along the Pacific coast in British Columbia, Canada; a sound is a long, wide body of water, larger than a strait or channel, as in an ocean inlet.

11. *egret:* a species of heron, often white, displaying long, dramatic drooping plumes during the mating season.

13. *San Joaquin:* river in central California rising in the Sierra Nevada and flowing northwest to form a large delta with the Sacramento River.

18. *'dobe:* adobe, a form of clay.

You are everywhere on the lonesome shores of His wide creation.
You keep seclusion where no man may go, giving Him praise;
Nor may a woman come to lift like your cleaving flight her clear contralto° song
To honor the spindrift° gifts of His soft abundance.
You sanctify His hermitage° rocks where no holy priest may kneel to adore, nor holy nun assist;
And where His true communion-keepers are not enabled to enter.

And well may you say His praises, birds, for your ways
Are verved with the secret skills of His inclinations,
And your habits plaited and rare with the subdued elaboration of His intricate craft;
Your days intent with the direct astuteness needful for His out-working,
And your nights alive with the dense repose of His infinite sleep.
You are His secretive charges and you serve His secretive ends,
In His clouded, mist-conditioned stations, in His murk,
Obscure in your matted nestings, immured in His limitless ranges.
He makes you penetrate through dark interstitial° joinings of His thicketed kingdoms,
And keep your concourse in the deeps of His shadowed world.

Your ways are wild but earnest, your manners grave,
Your customs carefully schooled to the note of His serious mien.
You hold the prime condition of His clean creating,
And the swift compliance with which you serve His minor means
Speaks of the constancy with which you hold Him.
For what is your high flight forever going home to your first beginnings,
But such a testament to your devotion?
You hold His outstretched world beneath your wings, and mount upon His storms,
And keep your sheer wind-lidded sight upon the vast perspectives of His mazy latitudes.

But mostly it is your way you bear existence wholly within the context of His utter will and are untroubled.
Day upon day you do not reckon, nor scrutinize tomorrow, nor multiply the nightfalls with a rash concern,

---

25. *contralto:* the lowest female voice, intermediate between soprano and tenor.
26. *spindrift:* windblown sea spray.
27. *hermitage:* monastery.
37. *interstitial:* narrow spaces created between multiple connections.

But rather assume each instant as warrant sufficient of His final seal.
Wholly in Providence you spring, and when you die you look on death in clarity unflinched,
Go down, a clutch of feather ragged upon the brush;
Or drop on water where you briefly lived, found food,
And now yourselves made food for His deep current-keeping fish, and then are gone:
Is left but the pinion-feather° spinning a bit on the uproil°
Where lately the dorsal° cut clear air.

You leave a silence. And this for you suffices, who are not of the ceremonials of man,
And hence are not made sad to now forgo them.
Yours is of another order of being, and wholly it compels.
But may you, birds, utterly seized in God's supremacy,
Austerely living under His austere eye—
Yet may you teach a man a necessary thing to know,
Which has to do of the strict conformity that creaturehood entails,
And constitutes the prime commitment all things share.
For God has given you the imponderable grace to *be* His verification,
Outside the mulled incertitude of our forensic° choices;
That you, our lessers in the rich hegemony of Being,
May serve as testament to what a creature is,
And what creation owes.

Curlews, stilts and scissortails, beachcomber gulls,
Wave-haunters, shore-keepers, rockhead-holders, all cape-top vigilantes,
Now give God praise.
Send up the strict articulation of your throats,
And say His name.

1950

---

55. *pinion-feather:* one of a bird's primary wing feathers.
55. *uproil:* small section of turbulent water (or air) moving rapidly upward.
56. *dorsal:* main fin located on the back of fishes and marine mammals.
66. *forensic:* rhetorical, argumentative.

TILLIE LERNER OLSEN (1912–2007)

Born in Nebraska of Russian parents who participated in the 1905 Revolution and fled when it failed, Tillie Lerner had to leave school to work after the eleventh grade. She trimmed meat in a packinghouse, worked as a waitress and a domestic, and meanwhile joined the Young Communist League. Her father had become state secretary of the Nebraska Socialist Party. Lerner herself went to jail for trying to organize packinghouse workers. Meanwhile, she began to write, starting the novel that would become *Yonnondio* years later, when she was only nineteen. She moved to California in the early 1930s, publishing "I Want You Women Up North to Know" in the West Coast John Reed Club magazine *Partisan* in 1934. She was harassed repeatedly by the FBI during the McCarthy period. Her story "Tell Me a Riddle" is her most famous work.

I WANT YOU WOMEN UP NORTH TO KNOW

(Based on a Letter by Felipe Ibarro in New Masses, *Jan. 9th, 1934.)*

I want you women up north to know
how those dainty children's dresses you buy
    at macy's, wanamakers, gimbels, marshall fields,°
are dyed in blood, are stitched in wasting flesh,
down in San Antonio,° "where sunshine spends the winter."°

I want you women up north to see
the obsequious smile, the salesladies trill
    "exquisite work, madame, exquisite pleats"
vanish into a bloated face, ordering more dresses,
    gouging the wages down,
dissolve into maria, ambrosa, catalina,
    stitching these dresses from dawn to night,
    in blood, in wasting flesh.

Catalina Rodriguez, 24,
    body shrivelled to a child's at twelve,
catalina rodriguez, last stages of consumption,
    works for three dollars a week from dawn to midnight.
A fog of pain thickens over her skull, the parching heat
    breaks over her body.

3. *macy's . . . marshall fields:* four U.S. department stores.

5. *San Antonio:* Texas city.

5. *winter:* phrase from a San Antonio Chamber of Commerce brochure.

and the bright red blood embroiders the floor of her room.
White rain stitching the night, the bourgeois poet would say,
white gulls of hands, darting, veering,
white lightning, threading the clouds,
this is the exquisite dance of her hands over the cloth,
and her cough, gay, quick, staccato,°
like skeleton's bones clattering,
is appropriate accompaniment for the esthetic dance
of her fingers,
and the tremolo, tremolo° when the hands tremble with pain.
Three dollars a week,
two fifty-five,
seventy cents a week,
no wonder two thousands eight hundred ladies of joy
are spending the winter with the sun after he goes down—
for five cents (who said this was a rich man's world?) you can
get all the lovin you want
"clap and syph aint much worse than sore fingers, blind eyes, and
t.m."

Maria Vasquez, spinster,
for fifteen cents a dozen stitches garments for children she has
never had,
Catalina Torres, mother of four,
to keep the starved body starving, embroiders from dawn to
night.
Mother of four, what does she think of,
as the needle pocked fingers shift over the silk—
of the stubble-coarse rags that stretch on her own brood,
and jut with the bony ridge that marks hunger's landscape
of fat little prairie-roll bodies that will bulge in the
silk she needles?
(Be not envious, Catalina Torres, look!
on your own children's clothing, embroidery,
more intricate than any a thousand hands could fashion,
there where the cloth is ravelled, or darned,
designs, multitudinous, complex and handmade by Poverty
herself.)

Ambrosa Espinoza trusts in god,
"Todos es de dios, everything is from god,"
through the dwindling night, the waxing day, she bolsters herself
up with it—

25. *staccato:* series of short, abrupt, disjointed sounds or motions.
29. *tremolo:* from music, a rapid reiteration of a tone or rapid variation of pitch; here the music of pain.

but the pennies to keep god incarnate, from ambrosa,
and the pennies to keep the priest in wine, from ambrosa,
ambrosa clothes god and priest with hand-made children's dresses.
Her brother lies on an iron cot, all day and watches,
on a mattress of rags he lies.
For twenty-five years he worked for the railroad, then they laid him off.
(racked days, searching for work; rebuffs; suspicious eyes of policemen.)
goodbye ambrosa, mebbe in dallas I find work; desperate swing for a freight,
surprised hands, clutching air, and the wheel goes over a
leg,
(the railroad cuts it off, as it cut off twenty-five years of his life.)
She says that he prays and dreams of another world, as he lies
there, a heaven (which he does not know was brought to earth
in 1917 in Russia,° by workers like him).

Women up north, I want you to know
when you finger the exquisite hand made dresses
what it means, this working from dawn to midnight,
on what strange feet the feverish dawn must come
to maria, catalina, ambrosa,
how the malignant fingers twitching over the pallid faces jerk them to work,
and the sun and the fever mounts with the day—
long plodding hours, the eyes burn like coals, heat jellies the flying fingers,
down comes the night like blindness.
long hours more with the dim eye of the lamp, the breaking back,
weariness crawls in the flesh like worms, gigantic like earth's in winter.
And for Catalina Rodriguez comes the night sweat and the blood
embroidering the darkness.
for Catalina Torres the pinched faces of four huddled
children,
the naked bodies of four bony children,
the chant of their chorale of hunger.
And for twenty eight hundred ladies of joy the grotesque act gone over—
the wink—the grimace—the "feeling like it baby?"
And for Maria Vasquez, spinster, emptiness, emptiness.
flaming with dresses for children she can never fondle.

74. *Russia:* the 1917 Russian Revolution ushered in the era of communism.

And for Ambrosa Espinoza—the skeleton body of her brother on his mattress
of rags, boring twin holes in the dark with his eyes to the image of christ
remembering a leg, and twenty-five years cut off from his life by the railroad.

Women up north, I want you to know,
I tell you this can't last forever.

I swear it won't.

1934

ROBERT HAYDEN (1913–1980)

Hayden was born Asa Bundy Sheffey to a couple in financial and personal difficulty. When they separated, Hayden was taken in by a foster family and received a new name. The new family, unfortunately, was equally conflicted, and Hayden's childhood—spent in the Detroit ghetto called "Paradise Valley"—was frequently traumatic. Reading was a form of escape, but it also prepared him for a career. He enrolled at Detroit City College, but left in 1936 to research black history and culture, including Michigan's Underground Railroad, for the Federal Writers' Project. Then in the early 1940s, he studied with W. H. Auden at the University of Michigan. The other major development in his life occurred when he committed himself to the Baha'i faith in the 1940s, eventually editing its journal *World Order* in the late 1960s and in the 1970s.

All this experience finds its way into his poetry, for he wrote about his Detroit neighborhood and about black history, as in "Middle Passage" and "Runagate, Runagate." Technically meticulous, Hayden adapted his style and voice to the subject matter, using montage, and mixing narrative and lyric passages in "Middle Passage," adopting imagist and symbolist techniques, varying line length considerably. Some of his poems are meditative, others strongly narrative. He also aimed for a universal audience, believing that African American history had vital lessons for all readers. And he refused to write exclusively about black subject matter, despite crafting a distinctive form of rhetorically intricate protest and deploying it for decades. Hayden taught for many years at Fisk University, returning at the end of his career to the University of Michigan.

MIDDLE PASSAGE°

I

Jesús, Estrella, Esperanza, Mercy:°
Sails flashing to the wind like weapons,
sharks following the moans the fever and the dying;
horror the corposant° and compass rose.°

---

poem title: the "middle passage" was the name of the route slave ships took across the Atlantic Ocean from Africa to North or South America. Robert Hayden's note—"Part III follows in the main the account of the *Amistad* mutiny given by Muriel Rukeyser in her biography of Willard Gibbs."

1. *Jesús, Estrella, (Spanish, "star"), Esperanza (Spanish, "hope"), Mercy:* names of slave ships.

4. *corposant:* Saint Elmo's fire, named after the patron saint of sailors—an eerie light, actually an electrical discharge, appearing on a ship's mast during a storm.

4. *compass rose:* the printed guide to compass directions included on maps.

Middle Passage:
voyage through death
to life upon these shores.

"10 April 1800—
Blacks rebellious. Crew uneasy. Our linguist says
their moaning is a prayer for death,
ours and their own. Some try to starve themselves.
Lost three this morning leaped with crazy laughter
to the waiting sharks, sang as they went under."

Desire, Adventure, Tartar, Ann:

Standing to America, bringing home
black gold, black ivory, black seed.

Deep in the festering hold thy father lies,
of his bones New England pews are made,
those are altar lights that were his eyes.°

Jesus Saviour Pilot Me°
Over Life's Tempestuous Sea

We pray that Thou wilt grant, O Lord,
safe passage to our vessels bringing
heathen souls unto Thy chastening.

Jesus Saviour

"8 bells. I cannot sleep, for I am sick
with fear, but writing eases fear a little
since still my eyes can see these words take shape
upon the page & so I write, as one
would turn to exorcism. 4 days scudding,°
but now the sea is calm again. Misfortune
follows in our wake like sharks (our grinning
tutelary° gods). Which one of us
has killed an albatross?° A plague among

---

19. *eyes:* a devastating adaptation of Ariel's song in Shakespeare's *The Tempest.* In the play, it was to offer a certain consolation to Ferdinand about the father he feared had drowned: "Full fathom five thy father lies, / Of his bones are coral made; / Those are pearls that were his eyes; / Nothing of him that doth fade, / But doth suffer a sea-change / Into something rich and strange."

20. *Jesus Saviour Pilot Me . . . :* from a Protestant hymn.

30. *scudding:* running before a strong wind with little or no sail set.

33. *tutelary:* protector or guardian.

34. *albatross:* a large, web-footed seabird. They are considered to bring luck unless they are killed. In Samuel Taylor Coleridge's (1772–1834) poem "The Rime of the Ancient Mariner," a sailor who kills an albatross must wear it around his neck as a penance.

our blacks—Ophthalmia: blindness—& we
have jettisoned the blind to no avail.
It spreads, the terrifying sickness spreads.
Its claws have scratched sight from the Capt.'s eyes
& there is blindness in the fo'c'sle°
& we must sail 3 weeks before we come
to port."

What port awaits us, Davy Jones'
or home? I've heard of slavers drifting, drifting,
playthings of wind and storm and chance, their crews
gone blind, the jungle hatred
crawling up on deck.

Thou Who Walked On Galilee

"Deponent° further sayeth *The Bella J*
left the Guinea Coast
with cargo of five hundred blacks and odd
for the barracoons° of Florida:

"That there was hardly room 'tween-decks for half
the sweltering cattle stowed spoon-fashion there;
that some went mad of thirst and tore their flesh
and sucked the blood:

"That Crew and Captain lusted with the comeliest
of the savage girls kept naked in the cabins;
that there was one they called The Guinea Rose
and they cast lots and fought to lie with her:

"That when the Bo's'n piped all hands,° the flames
spreading from starboard already were beyond
control, the negroes howling and their chains
entangled with the flames:

"That the burning blacks could not be reached,
that the Crew abandoned ship,

---

39. *fo'c'sle:* forecastle, a superstructure at the bow of a merchant ship where the crew is housed.
48. *Deponent:* person offering evidence.
51. *barracoons:* temporary confinement for slaves or convicts.
60. *Bo's'n piped all hands:* boatswain called the crew.

leaving their shrieking negresses behind,
that the Captain perished drunken with the wenches:

"Further Deponent sayeth not."

Pilot Oh Pilot Me

II

Aye, lad, and I have seen those factories,
Gambia, Rio Pongo, Calabar;°
have watched the artful mongos° baiting traps
of war wherein the victor and the vanquished

Were caught as prizes for our barracoons.
Have seen the nigger kings whose vanity
and greed turned wild black hides of Fellatah,
Mandingo, Ibo, Kru° to gold for us.

And there was one—King Anthracite we named him—
fetish face beneath French parasols
of brass and orange velvet, impudent mouth
whose cups were carven skulls of enemies:

He'd honor us with drum and feast and conjo°
and palm-oil-glistening wenches deft in love,
and for tin crowns that shone with paste,
red calico and German-silver trinkets

Would have the drums talk war and send
his warriors to burn the sleeping villages
and kill the sick and old and lead the young
in coffles° to our factories.

Twenty years a trader, twenty years,
for there was wealth aplenty to be harvested
from those black fields, and I'd be trading still
but for the fevers melting down my bones.

---

71. *Calabar:* a Nigerian city; Gambia: a country in west Africa; Rio Pongo: African river.

72. *mongos:* Bantu-speaking people native to the African country of Democratic Republic of the Congo.

76–77. *Fellatah, Mandingo, Ibo, Kru:* African tribes. The Mandingo are Mande-speaking agricultural people from Mali, Guinea, and Senegal; the Ibo are agricultural tribes from Nigeria; the Kru are fishermen from Liberia and the Ivory Coast.

82. *conjo:* dance.

89. *coffles:* slaves chained together in a line; the term also refers to the same practice applied to criminals or animals.

III

Shuttles in the rocking loom of history,
the dark ships move, the dark ships move,
their bright ironical names
like jests of kindness on a murderer's mouth;
plough through thrashing glister toward
fata morgana's° lucent melting shore,
weave toward New World littorals° that are
mirage and myth and actual shore.

Voyage through death,
voyage whose chartings are unlove.

A charnel stench, effluvium of living death
spreads outward from the hold,
where the living and the dead, the horribly dying,
lie interlocked, lie foul with blood and excrement.

Deep in the festering hold thy father lies,
the corpse of mercy rots with him,
rats eat love's rotten gelid eyes.

But, oh, the living look at you
with human eyes whose suffering accuses you,
whose hatred reaches through the swill of dark
to strike you like a leper's claw.

You cannot stare that hatred down
or chain the fear that stalks the watches
and breathes on you its fetid scorching breath;
cannot kill the deep immortal human wish,
the timeless will.

"But for the storm that flung up barriers
of wind and wave, *The Amistad*° señores,
would have reached the port of Príncipe in two,
three days at most; but for the storm we should

---

99. *fata morgana:* mirage.

100. *littorals:* shores or coastal regions.

121. *Amistad:* (Spanish) "Friendship," a Spanish slave ship out of Havana that was the site of a famous 1839 rebellion. Cinquez led the fifty-three slaves in revolt, in which the captain, the mate, and the captain's slave Celestino were killed. The *Amistad* was held when it arrived at Long Island; the owners, who were spared during the mutiny, tried to have the slaves sent to Cuba to be tried for murder. The case was decided in the U.S. Supreme Court in 1841, with John Quincy Adams, former U.S. president, helping (successfully) to defend the surviving slaves.

have been prepared for what befell.
Swift as the puma's leap it came. There was
that interval of moonless calm filled only
with the water's and the rigging's usual sounds,
then sudden movement, blows and snarling cries
and they had fallen on us with machete
and marlinspike. It was as though the very
air, the night itself were striking us.
Exhausted by the rigors of the storm,
we were no match for them. Our men went down
before the murderous Africans. Our loyal
Celestino ran from below with gun
and lantern and I saw, before the cane-
knife's wounding flash, Cinquez,
that surly brute who calls himself a prince,
directing, urging on the ghastly work.
He hacked the poor mulatto down, and then
he turned on me. The decks were slippery
when daylight finally came. It sickens me
to think of what I saw, of how these apes
threw overboard the butchered bodies of
our men, true Christians all, like so much jetsam.
Enough, enough. The rest is quickly told:
Cinquez was forced to spare the two of us
you see to steer the ship to Africa,
and we like phantoms doomed to rove the sea
voyaged east by day and west by night,
deceiving them, hoping for rescue,
prisoners on our own vessel, till
at length we drifted to the shores of this
your land, America, where we were freed
from our unspeakable misery. Now we
demand, good sirs, the extradition of
Cinquez and his accomplices to La
Havana. And it distresses us to know
there are so many here who seem inclined
to justify the mutiny of these blacks.
We find it paradoxical indeed
that you whose wealth, whose tree of liberty
are rooted in the labor of your slaves
should suffer the august John Quincy Adams
to speak with so much passion of the right
of chattel slaves to kill their lawful masters
and with his Roman rhetoric weave a hero's
garland for Cinquez. I tell you that

we are determined to return to Cuba
with our slaves and there see justice done. Cinquez—
or let us say 'the Prince'—Cinquez shall die."

The deep immortal human wish,
the timeless will:

Cinquez its deathless primaveral image,
life that transfigures many lives.

Voyage through death
to life upon these shores.

1962

RUNAGATE RUNAGATE°

I.

Runs falls rises stumbles on from darkness into darkness
and the darkness thicketed with shapes of terror
and the hunters pursuing and the hounds pursuing
and the night cold and the night long and the river
to cross and the jack-muh-lanterns° beckoning beckoning
and blackness ahead and when shall I reach that somewhere
morning and keep on going and never turn back and keep on going

Runagate
Runagate
Runagate

Many thousands rise and go
many thousands crossing over

O mythic North
O star-shaped yonder Bible city°

Some go weeping and some rejoicing
some in coffins and some in carriages
some in silks and some in shackles

Rise and go or fare you well

---

poem title: *Runagate:* archaic for "runaway," the poem is about America's Underground Railroad, a pre-Civil War system set up by Abolitionists to help slaves escape to the North.

5. *lanterns:* Jack-o'-lanterns, or will-o'-the-wisps, elusive lights seen over marshes at night.

14. *Bible city:* Bethlehem, Pennsylvania, just north of the Mason-Dixon line, the line dividing slave from free states, in pre-Civil War days.

No more auction block for me
no more driver's lash for me

If you see my Pompey, 30 yrs of age,
new breeches, plain stockings, negro shoes;
if you see my Anna, likely young mulatto°
branded E on the right cheek, R on the left,
catch them if you can and notify subscriber.
Catch them if you can, but it won't be easy.
They'll dart underground when you try to catch them,
plunge into quicksand, whirlpools, mazes,
turn into scorpions when you try to catch them.

And before I'll be a slave
I'll be buried in my grave

North star and bonanza gold
I'm bound for the freedom, freedom-bound
and oh Susyanna don't you cry for me°

Runagate

Runagate

II.

Rises from their anguish and their power,
Harriet Tubman,°

woman of earth, whipscarred,
a summoning, a shining

Mean to be free

And this was the way of it, brethren brethren,
way we journeyed from Can't to Can.
Moon so bright and no place to hide,
the cry up and the patterollers° riding,

---

23. *mulatto:* a person of mixed race, child of both black and white parents.

34. *cry for me:* the first line of the song "Oh Susanna" (1848) by the composer of popular music Stephen Collins Foster (1826–1864).

38. *Tubman:* (1820?–1913), an escaped slave who helped others escape to the North through the Underground Railroad.

45. *patterollers:* patrollers.

hound dogs belling in bladed air.
And fear starts a-murbling, Never make it,
We'll never make it. *Hush that now,*
and she's turned upon us, levelled pistol
glinting in the moonlight:
Dead folks can't jaybird-talk, she says;
you keep on going now or die, she says.

Wanted Harriet Tubman alias The General
alias Moses Stealer of Slaves

In league with Garrison Alcott Emerson
Garrett Douglass Thoreau John Brown°

Armed and known to be Dangerous

Wanted Reward Dead or Alive

Tell me, Ezekiel,° oh tell me do you see
mailed Jehovah coming to deliver me?

Hoot-owl calling in the ghosted air,
five times calling to the hants° in the air.
Shadow of a face in the scary leaves,
shadow of a voice in the talking leaves:

Come ride-a my train

Oh that train, ghost-story train
through swamp and savanna movering movering,
over trestles of dew, through caves of the wish,
Midnight Special on a sabre track movering movering,
first stop Mercy and the last Hallelujah.

Come ride-a my train

Mean mean mean to be free.

1962

55–56. *Garrison . . . Brown:* Abolitionists. The editor William Lloyd Garrison (1805–1879); the educator and reformer Amos Bronson Alcott (1799–1888); the essayist and poet Ralph Waldo Emersom (1803–1882); the Quaker leader Thomas Garrett (1789–1871); the African American journalist and statesman Frederick Douglass (1818?–1895); the writer and naturalist Henry David Thoreau (1817–1862); John Brown (1800–1859), the leader of a raid on the arsenal at Harper's Ferry, West Virginia, to start a slave uprising.

59. *Ezekiel:* sixth-century B.C. Hebrew prophet; Jehovah is the Judeo-Christian God.

62. *hants:* haunts, ghosts.

A LETTER FROM PHILLIS WHEATLEY°

London, 1773

Dear Obour°
Our crossing was without
event. I could not help, at times,
reflecting on that first—my Destined—
voyage long ago (I yet
have some remembrance of its Horrors)
and marvelling at God's Ways.
Last evening, her Ladyship° presented me
to her illustrious Friends.
I scarce could tell them anything
of Africa, though much of Boston
and my hope of Heaven. I read
my latest Elegies to them.
"O Sable° Muse!" the Countess cried,
embracing me, when I had done.
I held back tears, as is my wont,
and there were tears in Dear
Nathaniel's° eyes.
At supper—I dined apart
like captive Royalty—
the Countess and her Guests promised
signatures affirming me
True Poetess, albeit once a slave.
Indeed, they were most kind, and spoke,
moreover, of presenting me
at Court (I thought of Pocahontas)°—
an Honor, to be sure, but one,
I should, no doubt, as Patriot decline.
My health is much improved;

---

poem title: Wheatley (c. 1753–1784) was brought to the United States as a slave from Gambia in West Africa. She was put up for auction on the Boston slave block in 1761 and sold to John and Susannah Wheatley. Despite being a slave, she mastered English well enough to begin writing letters and poems. A few were published and she came to the attention of people both in the United States and in England. It was the British attention that persuaded John Wheatley to set her free. By then, her book *Poems on Various Subjects, Religious, and Moral* had already appeared. Only the second woman (and the first African American) to publish a book in the colonies on any subject, Wheatley is considered a founding figure of the black literary tradition.

1. *Obour* (Tanner)*:* a young, free black woman who was Wheatley's most regular correspondent.

8. *Ladyship:* Selina Hastings, philanthropist and Countess of Hastings, who helped Wheatley find a publisher for her book.

14. *Sable:* Cf. Wheatley's line "Some view our sable [black] race with scornful eye" in her delicately sardonic poem "On Being Brought from Africa to America."

18. *Nathaniel:* Wheatley's son, who accompanied Wheatley on her 1773 trip to London.

26. *Pocahontas:* an Indian princess who reportedly saved the life of Captain John Smith, leader of a group of American colonists. She married an Englishman, John Rolfe (1585–1622), who presented her to the British court in 1616.

I feel I may, if God so Wills,
entirely recover here.
Idyllic England! Alas, there is
no Eden without its Serpent. Under
the chiming Complaisance I hear him Hiss;
I see his flickering tongue
when foppish would-be Wits
murmur of the Yankee Pedlar
and his Cannibal Mockingbird.°
        Sister, forgive th'intrusion of
my Sombreness—Nocturnal Mood
I would not share with any save
your trusted Self. Let me disperse,
in closing, such unseemly Gloom
by mention of an Incident
you may, as I, consider Droll:
Today, a little Chimney Sweep,
his face and hands with soot quite Black,
staring hard at me, politely asked:
"Does you, M'lady, sweep chimneys too?"
I was amused, but dear Nathaniel
(ever Solicitous) was not.
        I pray the Blessings of our Lord
and Saviour Jesus Christ be yours
Abundantly. In his Name,
                                        Phillis

1978

THOSE WINTER SUNDAYS

Sundays too my father got up early
and put his clothes on in the blueblack cold,
then with cracked hands that ached
from labor in the weekday weather made
banked fires blaze. No one ever thanked him.

I'd wake and hear the cold splintering, breaking.
When the rooms were warm, he'd call,
and slowly I would rise and dress,
fearing the chronic angers of that house,

37. *Yankee Pedlar and his Cannibal Mockingbird:* derogatory terms for John Wheatley and poet Phillis Wheatley; as a "mockingbird," she is in effect only mimicking other poets.

Speaking indifferently to him,
who had driven out the cold
and polished my good shoes as well.
What did I know, what did I know
of love's austere and lonely offices?

1962

NIGHT, DEATH, MISSISSIPPI

I

A quavering cry. Screech-owl?
Or one of them?
The old man in his reek
and gauntness laughs—

One of them, I bet—
and turns out the kitchen lamp,
limping to the porch to listen
in the windowless night.

Be there with Boy and the rest
if I was well again.
Time was. Time was.
White robes like moonlight

In the sweetgum dark.°
Unbucked that one then
and him squealing bloody Jesus
as we cut it off.

Time was. A cry?
A cry all right.
He hawks and spits,
fevered as by groinfire.

Have us a bottle,
Boy and me—
he's earned him a bottle—
when he gets home.

---

13. *sweetgum dark:* the deep woods of the North American sweet gum tree.

II

Then we beat them, he said,
beat them till our arms was tired
and the big old chains
messy and red.

O Jesus burning on the lily cross

Christ, it was better
than hunting bear
which don't know why
you want him dead.

O night, rawhead and bloodybones night

You kids fetch Paw
some water now so's he
can wash that blood
off him, she said.

O night betrayed by darkness not its own

1966

AUNT JEMIMA OF THE OCEAN WAVES°

I

Enacting someone's notion of themselves
(and me), The One And Only Aunt Jemima
and Kokimo The Dixie Dancing Fool
do a bally for the freak show.

I watch a moment, then move on,
pondering the logic that makes of them
(and me) confederates
of The Spider Girl, The Snake-skinned Man. . . .

---

poem title: adapted from a minstrel show, Aunt Jemima has been the symbol for a popular pancake mix since 1899. As Nagueyalti Warren writes in the *Oxford Companion to African American Literature.* "Jemima, the offshoot of irascible mammy [a still earlier popular stereotype], was sweet, jolly, even-tempered, and polite. Jemima, Hebrew for 'dove,' was Job's youngest daughter, symbolizing innocence, gentleness, and peace. But the name belies its meaning. The caricature connotes not naiveté but stupidity, not peace but docility. Jemima was an obese, darkly pigmented, broad-bosomed, handkerchief-headed, gingham-dressed, elderly servant content in her subjugation. . . . By 1900, more than 200,000 Jemima dolls, 150,000 Jemima cookie jars, and numerous memorabilia in the form of black-faced buttons and toothpick holders had been sold."

Poor devils have to live somehow.

I cross the boardwalk to the beach,
lie in the sand and gaze beyond
the clutter at the sea.

II

Trouble you for a light?
I turn as Aunt Jemima settles down
beside me, her blue-rinsed hair
without the red bandanna now.

I hold the lighter to her cigarette.
Much obliged. Unmindful (perhaps)
of my embarrassment, she looks
at me and smiles: You sure

do favor a friend I used to have.
Guess that's why I bothered you
for a light. So much like him that I—
She pauses, watching white horses rush

to the shore. Way them big old waves
come slamming whopping in,
sometimes it's like they mean to smash
this no-good world to hell.

Well, it could happen. A book I read—
Crossed that very ocean years ago.
London, Paris, Rome,
Constantinople too—I've seen them all.

Back when they billed me everywhere
as the Sepia High Stepper.
Crowned heads applauded me.
Years before your time. Years and years.

I wore me plenty diamonds then,
and counts or dukes or whatever they were
would fill my dressing room
with the costliest flowers. But of course

there was this one you resemble so.
Get me? The sweetest gentleman.

Dead before his time. Killed in the war
to save the world for another war.

High-stepping days for me
were over after that. Still I'm not one
to let grief idle me for long.
I went out with a mental act—

mind-reading—Mysteria From
The Mystic East—veils and beads
and telling suckers how to get
stolen rings and sweethearts back.

One night he was standing by my bed,
seen him plain as I see you,
and warned me without a single word:
Baby, quit playing with spiritual stuff.

So here I am, so here I am,
fake mammy to God's mistakes.
And that's the beauty part,
I mean, ain't that the beauty part.

She laughs, but I do not, knowing what
her laughter shields. And mocks.
I light another cigarette for her.
She smokes, not saying any more.

Scream of children in the surf,
adagios of sun and flashing foam,
the sexual glitter, oppressive fun. . . .
An antique etching comes to mind:

"The Sable Venus" naked on
a baroque Cellini shell—voluptuous
imago floating in the wake
of slave-ships on fantastic seas.

Jemima sighs, Reckon I'd best
be getting back. I help her up.
Don't you take no wooden nickels, hear?
Tin dimes neither. So long, pal.

1978

from ELEGIES FOR PARADISE VALLEY

I

My shared bedroom's window
opened on alley stench.
A junkie died in maggots there.
I saw his body shoved into a van.
I saw the hatred for our kind
glistening like tears
in the policemen's eyes.

1978

THE DOGWOOD TREES

(for Robert Slagle)

Seeing dogwood trees in bloom,
I am reminded, Robin,
of our journey through the mountains
in an evil time.

Among rocks and rock-filled streams
white bracts of dogwood
clustered. Beyond, nearby, shrill slums
were burning,

the crooked crosses flared. We drove
with bitter knowledge
of the odds against comradeship we dared
and were at one.

1978

O DAEDALUS, FLY AWAY HOME°

(For Maia and Julie)

Drifting night in the Georgia pines,
coonskin drum and jubilee banjo.
        Pretty Malinda, dance with me.

Night is juba, night is conjo.°
        Pretty Malinda, dance with me.

---

poem title: in Greek mythology, Daedalus and his son Icarus set out to free themselves from the Minotaur's labyrinth. Daedalus made wings for his son out of wax and feathers, but Icarus flew too near the sun, and the wax melted. Icarus perished when he fell into the sea, but Daedalus escaped.

4. *juba, conjo:* dances.

Night is an African juju man
weaving a wish and a weariness together
        to make two wings.

        O fly away home fly away

Do you remember Africa?

        O cleave the air fly away home

My gran, he flew back to Africa,
just spread his arms and
        flew away home.

Drifting night in the windy pines;
night is a laughing, night is a longing.
        Pretty Malinda, come to me.

Night is a mourning juju man°
weaving a wish and a weariness together
        to make two wings.

        O fly away home fly away

1962

---

18. *juju man:* one adept in the system of conjuring or magic known as "hoodoo," "mojo," "obeah," or "juju" A juju man is a practioner of folk medicine, a visionary, a spiritual guide, a shape changer, and a practicer of black magic.

WELDON KEES (1914–1955)

Born in Beatrice, Nebraska, Kees graduated from the University of Nebraska. After an editorial job with the Federal Writers' Project in Lincoln, he moved to Denver to direct its bibliographic center. A few years later, he left for New York, where he earned a living for a while writing for *Time* magazine, until he moved to San Francisco in 1951. He also became a committed Trotskyite, the Marxist group cast out of the official Communist Party. Kees was not only a poet—one often cynical about American middle-class values—but also a painter, a pianist, and a jazz composer. In California, he also collaborated with psychiatrist Jurgen Ruesch on the book *Non-Verbal Communication,* which is illustrated with Kees's photographs. Little known as a poet during his own life, he disappeared in 1955 and is presumed to have committed suicide; his car was found abandoned on the approach to Golden Gate Bridge, but his body was never found. His fictional satire of scholarly life, *Fall Quarter,* was written in the 1930s but not published until 1990.

JUNE 1940

"Yet these elegies are to this generation in no sense consolatory.
They may be to the next. All a poet can do today is warn."

"The old Lie: Dulce et decorum est
Pro patria mori."

—Wilfred Owen

It is summer, and treachery blurs with the sounds of
    midnight,
The lights blink off at the closing of a door,
And I am alone in a worn-out town in wartime,
Thinking of those who were trapped by hysteria once
    before.

Flaubert and Henry James and Owen,
Bourne with his crooked back, Rilke and Lawrence,
    Joyce—
Gun-shy, annoyers, sick of the kill, the watchers,
Suffered the same attack till it broke them or left its
    scars.

Now the heroes of March are the sorriest fools of April:
The beaters of drums, the flag-kissing men, whose eyes
Once saw the murder, are washing it clean, accusing:

"You are the cowards! All that we told you before was
lies!"

It is summer again, the evening is warm and silent.
The windows are dark and the mountains are miles away.
And the men who were haters of war are mounting the
platforms.
An idiot wind is blowing; the conscience dies.

1940

TRAVELS IN NORTH AMERICA

(To Lorraine and Robert Wilbur)

Here is San Luis Obispo. Here
Is Kansas City, and here is Rovere,
Kentucky. And here, a small black dot,
Unpronounceable but hard to forget,
Is where we stopped at the Seraphim Motel,
And well-fed moths flew out to greet us from the walls
On which a dado of petunias grew.
We threw a nickel in the wishing well,
But the moths remained, and the petunias too.

And here is Santa Barbara where
They had the heated swimming pool.
Warm in our room, we watched the bathers' breaths. My hair
Fell out in Santa Barbara, and the cold
Came blowing off the sea. An ancient gull
Dropped down to shiver gravely in the steady rain.
The sea-food dinner Duncan Hines° had praised
Gave off a classic taste of tin. The weather was unseasonable.
There was a landmark, I remember, that was closed.

Here is the highway in and out of Cincinnati.
An inch or so of line along the river. Driving west
One Sunday in a smoky dawn, burnt orange along the land-
scape's rim,
The radio gave forth five solid and remembered hours
Of gospel singers and New Orleans jazz,
With terse, well-phrased commercials for a funeral home.
They faded out—Cleves, Covington, North Bend

---

16. *Hines:* (1880–1959); he published the notes he accumulated from years of eating at American restaurants as a traveling salesman as *Adventures in Good Eating* (1936). The book launched him on a career as a publisher and sponsor of packaged food products.

Made way for Evansville and Patti Page.[o] The roads end
At motels. The one that night had an Utrillo[o] in a velvet frame.

The stars near Santa Fe are blurred and old, discolored
By a milky haze; a ragged moon
Near Albuquerque shimmers the heat. Autumnal light
Falls softly on a file of candy skulls
And metal masks. Sand drifts at noon, at nine,
And now at midnight on a Navajo in levis reading
Sartre[o] in an Avon Pocket Book, against the window
Of a Rexall store. Here one descends
To shelvings of the pit. The valleys hollow out.

The land is terraced near Los Alamos[o]: scrub cedars,
Piñon pines and ruined pueblos, where a line
Of tall young men in uniform keep watch upon
The University of California's atom bomb.
The sky is soiled and charitable
Behind barbed wire and the peaks of mountains—
Sangre de Christo, Blood of Christ, this "fitting portent
For the Capital of the Atomic Age." We meant
To stop, but one can only see so much. A mist
Came over us outside Tryuonyi: caves, and a shattered cliff.

And possibly the towns one never sees are best,
Preserved, remote, and merely names and distances.
Cadiz, Kentucky, "noted for the quality of hams it ships,
The home of wealthy planters," Dalton, Georgia,
"Center of a thriving bedspread industry, where rainbow lines
Of counterpanes may be observed along the highway. Here
The man whose *Home, Sweet Home* is known to all,
The champion of the Cherokee, John Howard Payne,[o] was tried."
—Wetumka, Oklahoma; Kipling, Michigan;

Glenrock, Wyoming; and Chehalis, Washington
Are momentarily the shifting centers of a dream,
Swept bare of formica and television aerials

---

26. *Page:* (b. 1927), American singer who recorded a number of hit records in the 1950s and was often heard on the radio.

27. *Utrillo:* Maurice Utrillo (1883–1955), French painter.

34. *Sartre:* Jean-Paul Sartre (1905–1980), French existentialist philosopher, novelist, and critic.

37. *Los Alamos:* New Mexico site where the atom bomb was constructed from 1943 to 1945.

54. *Payne:* (1791–1852), American actor, playwright, and composer (and frequent debtor) who wrote the words to the song "Home, Sweet Home" for his operetta *Clari* (1823). He once took on a campaign to help the Cherokee.

And rows of cars that look a little more like fish each year.
—A dream that ends with towns that smell of rubber smouldering;
A brownish film sticks to the windshields
And the lungs; the skies are raining soot
And other specks that failed to fit into the paint
Or the salami. A cloud of grit sweeps over you and down the street.

And sometimes, shivering in St. Paul or baking in Atlanta,
The sudden sense that you have seen it all before:
The man who took your ticket at the Gem in Council Bluffs
Performed a similar function for you at the Shreveport Tivoli.
Joe's Lunch appears again, town after town, next door
To Larry's Shoe Repair, adjoining, inescapably, the Acme
    Doughnut Shop.
Main, First, and Market fuse together.
Bert and Lena run the laundromat. John Foster, D.D.S.,
Has offices above the City Bank.—At three or four,
On winter afternoons, when school is letting out
And rows of children pass you, near the firehouse,
This sense is keenest, piercing as the wind
That sweeps you toward the frosted door of your hotel
And past the portly hatted traveler with moist cigar
Who turns his paper as you brush against the rubber plant.
You have forgotten singularities. You have forgotten
Rooms that overlooked a park in Boston, brown walls hung

With congo masks and Mirós,° rain
Against a skylight, and the screaming girl
Who threw a cocktail shaker at a man in tweeds
Who quoted passages from Marlowe and *'Tis Pity She's a Whore.*°
You have forgotten yellow lights of San Francisco coming on,
The bridges choked with cars, and islands in the fog.
Or have forgotten why you left or why you came to where you are,
Or by what roads and passages,
Or what it was, if anything, that you were hoping for.

Journeys are ways of marking out a distance,
Or dealing with the past, however ineffectually,
Or ways of searching for some new enclosure in this space
Between the oceans.—Now the smaller waves of afternoon retrace
This sand where breakers threw their cargoes up—

---

82. *Mirós:* paintings by Spanish artist Joán Miró (1893–1983).

85. *'Tis: Pity She's a Whore:* 1628 play by British dramatist John Ford (1586–1640); Christopher Marlowe (1564–1593), British dramatist.

Old rafts and spongy two-by-fours and inner tubes,
The spines of sharks and broken codheads,
Tinned stuff with the labels gone, and yellow weeds
Like entrails; mattresses and stones, and, by a grapefruit crate,
A ragged map, imperfectly enclosed by seaworn oilskin.
Two tiny scarlet crabs ran out as I unfold it on the beach.
Here, sodden, fading, green ink blending into blue,
Is Brooklyn Heights, and I am walking toward the subway
In a January snow again, at night, ten years ago. Here is Milpitas,
California, filling stations and a Ford
Assembly plant. Here are the washboard roads
Of Wellfleet, on the Cape, and summer light and dust.
And here, now textured like a blotter, like the going years
And difficult to see, is where you are, and where I am,
And where the oceans cover us.

1952

RANDALL JARRELL (1914–1965)

Born in Nashville, Tennessee, Jarrell was educated at Vanderbilt University, and taught at a number of colleges and universities, meanwhile acquiring a reputation as a devastatingly witty reviewer of other people's poetry. After enlisting in the Army Air Force in 1942, he was assigned to an aviation facility in Tucson, Arizona, where he became a celestial training navigator. It may well have been his very distance from the World War II front that made him an attentive listener to B-29 crews, other returning soldiers, and home front family members, and led him to retell their stories so effectively. Influenced by W. H. Auden early on, the war inspired him to use a less intricate, more conversational idiom. Both then and later in his career, he sometimes adopted a woman's persona to tell a gendered narrative. Overall, it is the body of poetry he wrote about World War II, some of the most successful written by any American, that constitutes his most distinctive and important contribution to his country's literature. A 1954 novel, *Pictures from an Institution,* uses Sarah Lawrence College as a model for its satire.

THE DEATH OF THE BALL TURRET GUNNER°

From my mother's sleep I fell into the State,
And I hunched in its belly till my wet fur froze.
Six miles from earth, loosed from its dream of life,
I woke to black flak° and the nightmare fighters.
When I died they washed me out of the turret with a hose.

1945

A FRONT°

Fog over the base: the beams ranging
From the five towers pull home from the night
The crews cold in fur, the bombers banging
Like lost trucks down the levels of the ice.
A glow drifts in like mist (how many tons of it?),

---

poem title: Jarrell's note—"A ball turret was a plexiglass sphere set into the belly of a B-17 or B-24 [bomber], and inhabited by two .50 caliber machine-guns and one man, a short, small man. When this gunner tracked with his machine-gun a fighter attacking his bomber from below, he revolved with the turret; hunched upside-down in his little sphere, he looked like the foetus in the womb. The fighters that attacked him were armed with cannon firing explosive shells. The hose was a steam hose."

4. *flak:* noise and fire of anti-aircraft guns.

poem title: Jarrell's note—"A front is closing in over a bomber base; the bombers, guided in by signals from the five towers of the radio range, are landing. Only one lands before the base is closed; the rest fly south to fields that are still open. One plane's radio has gone bad—it still transmits, but doesn't receive—and this plane crashes."

Bounces to a roll, turns suddenly to steel
And tires and turrets, huge in the trembling light.
The next is high, and pulls up with a wail,
Comes round again—no use. And no use for the rest
In drifting circles out along the range;
Holding no longer, changed to a kinder course,
The flights drone southward through the steady rain.
The base is closed.... But one voice keeps on calling,
The lowering pattern of the engines grows;
The roar gropes downward in its shaky orbit
For the lives the season quenches. Here below
They beg, order, are not heard; and hear the darker
Voice rising: *Can't you hear me? Over. Over—*
All the air quivers, and the east sky glows.

1945

LOSSES

It was not dying: everybody died.
It was not dying: we had died before
In the routine crashes—and our fields
Called up the papers, wrote home to our folks,
And the rates rose, all because of us.
We died on the wrong page of the almanac,
Scattered on mountains fifty miles away;
Diving on haystacks, fighting with a friend,
We blazed up on the lines we never saw.
We died like aunts or pets or foreigners.
(When we left high school nothing else had died
For us to figure we had died like.)

In our new planes, with our new crews, we bombed
The ranges by the desert or the shore,
Fired at towed targets, waited for our scores—
And turned into replacements and woke up
One morning, over England, operational.
It wasn't different: but if we died
It was not an accident but a mistake
(But an easy one for anyone to make).
We read our mail and counted up our missions—
In bombers named for girls, we burned

The cities we had learned about in school—
Till our lives wore out; our bodies lay among
The people we had killed and never seen.

When we lasted long enough they gave us medals;
When we died they said, "Our casualties were low."
They said, "Here are the maps"; we burned the cities.

It was not dying—no, not ever dying;
But the night I died I dreamed that I was dead,
And the cities said to me: "Why are you dying?
We are satisfied, if you are; but why did I die?"

1948

SECOND AIR FORCE

Far off, above the plain the summer dries,
The great loops of the hangars sway like hills.
Buses and weariness and loss, the nodding soldiers
Are wire, the bare frame buildings and a pass
To what was hers; her head hides his square patch
And she thinks heavily: My son is grown.
She sees a world: sand roads, tar-paper barracks,
The bubbling asphalt of the runways, sage,
The dunes rising to the interminable ranges,
The dim flights moving over clouds like clouds.
The armorers in their patched faded green,
Sweat-stiffened, banded with brass cartridges,
Walk to the line; their Fortresses, all tail,
Stand wrong and flimsy on their skinny legs,
And the crews climb to them clumsily as bears.
The head withdraws into its hatch (a boy's),
The engines rise to their blind laboring roar,
And the green, made beasts run home to air.
Now in each aspect death is pure.
(At twilight they wink over men like stars
And hour by hour, through the night, some see
The great lights floating in—from Mars, from Mars.)
How emptily the watchers see them gone.

They go, there is silence; the woman and her son
Stand in the forest of the shadows, and the light
Washes them like water. In the long-sunken city
Of evening, the sunlight stills like sleep
The faint wonder of the drowned; in the evening,
In the last dreaming light, so fresh, so old,
The soldiers pass like beasts, unquestioning,
And the watcher for an instant understands

What there is then no need to understand;
But she wakes from her knowledge, and her stare,
A shadow now, moves emptily among
The shadows learning in their shadowy fields
The empty missions.
Remembering,
She hears the bomber calling, *Little Friend*!
To the fighter hanging in the hostile sky,
And sees the ragged flame eat, rib by rib,
Along the metal of the wing into her heart:
The lives stream out, blossom, and float steadily
To the flames of the earth, the flames
That burn like stars above the lands of men.

She saves from the twilight that takes everything
A squadron shipping, in its last parade—
Its dogs run by it, barking at the band—
A gunner walking to his barracks, half-asleep,
Starting at something, stumbling (above, invisible,
The crews in the steady winter of the sky
Tremble in their wired fur); and feels for them
The love of life for life. The hopeful cells
Heavy with someone else's death, cold carriers
Of someone else's victory, grope past their lives
Into her own bewilderment: The years meant *this*?

But for them the bombers answer everything.

1945

PROTOCOLS

(Birkenau,° Odessa;° the children speak alternately.)

We went there on the train. *They had big barges that they towed,*
We stood up, there were so many I was squashed.
There was a smoke-stack, then they made me wash.
It was a factory, I think. *My mother held me up*
And I could see the ship that made the smoke.

---

subtitle: *Birkenau:* a village in southern Poland next to the Auschwitz-Birkenau concentration camp, the most notorious World War II Nazi death camp. *Odessa:* a city in the Ukraine in the former Soviet Union, located on Odessa Bay off the Black Sea; a major seaport and industrial center. After experiencing heavy damage and loss of life from bombardment and being largely cut off, the city was evacuated and abandoned by the Russians in 1941. The Nazis occupied Odessa from 1941 to 1944 at the height of World War II. The Germans also brought the "final solution," their plan for the murder of all the Jews of Europe, with them to the Ukraine, where they killed Jews whenever the opportunity arose.

When I was tired my mother carried me.
She said, "Don't be afraid." But I was only tired.
Where we went there is no more Odessa.
They had water in a pipe—like rain, but hot;
The water there is deeper than the world

And I was tired and fell in in my sleep
And the water drank me. That is what I think.
And I said to my mother, "Now I'm washed and dried,"
My mother hugged me, and it smelled like hay
And that is how you die. And that is how you die.

1948

JAPANESE AMERICAN CONCENTRATION CAMP HAIKU, 1942–1944

Shortly after Japan bombed Pearl Harbor and the United States entered World War II, U.S. president Franklin Delano Roosevelt signed the now infamous Executive Order 9066, which authorized the forced roundup, relocation, and detention of Japanese Americans. The executive order would later be declared unconstitutional, but such legal niceties were ignored during the war. Its motivation was racist. No comparable abrogation of citizenship and due process was effected for German Americans. So over 120,000 Japanese Americans, most of them American born, were suddenly taken from their homes and confined in concentration camps set up in the swampland of Arkansas or the deserts of Arizona, California, and New Mexico. Meanwhile, some Japanese Americans fought and died in the U.S. Army, on behalf of the country that was imprisoning their families.

Among the imprisoned Japanese Americans were members of California haiku-writing clubs that had adopted the free-verse haiku. First developed after 1915 and more widely popularized in the 1930s, these modernist haiku were not restricted to seasonal vocabularies or to the strict syllable structure of traditional haiku. When these amateur poets found themselves exiles in their own country, they turned to haiku to express their feelings, and some haiku were issued in camp newspapers. Many of the poems did not survive the war, but Violet Kazue de Cristoforo translated over 300 of them from the Japanese in *May Sky—There Is Always Tomorrow: An Anthology of Japanese American Concentration Camp Kaiko Haiku* (1997), from which the following selection is taken.

Of the twenty-one poets represented here, few biographical details are known. Neiji Ozawa (1886–1967) was born in Nagano Prefecture in Japan. He came to the United States in 1907, studied pharmacology at Berkeley, and opened a drugstore in Fresno, California, where he also organized a haiku club. Kyotaro Komuro (1885–1953) came to the United States on the same boat as Ozawa; before being taken from his home he had become president and publisher of the *Stockton Times* in California. Hekisamei Matsuda (1906–1970) was owner and manager of the Matsuda Book Shop in Fresno when war broke out; he was repatriated to Japan in 1945. Taro Katay was sent first to Tanforan and then interned at Topaz in Utah; he later volunteered for the U.S. Army. Sadayo Taniguchi, born in Japan in 1905, was separated from her family during her five-year internment; she later died in Texas. Hankuro Wada was born in Stockton, California, but was also expatriated to Japan in 1945. Shokoshi Saga, the pen name of Hideo Ito, was born in Mie Prefecture, Japan. Before the war he was a Japanese language school teacher and a correspondent for a Japanese newspaper. He settled in San Francisco after the war and died there in 1988. Shizuku Uyemaruko, the pen name of Sachiko Uyemaruko (1898–1992), was born in Hiroshima and emigrated to the United States in 1917; she declined to share other details of her biography with de Cristoforo. Shiho Okamoto (1888–1967) wrote haiku for many decades. Senbinshi Takaoka was both a poet and an artist; he returned to Japan and died in

Kyoto. Jyosha Yamada (1883–1969) was born in Japan and died in Stockton, California. Hangetsu Tsunekawa returned to Stockton, California, after being released. Ryokuin Matsui died soon after the war. About fifty of Hyakuissei's haiku survive, including some composed as a travel diary between Rohwer concentration camp in Arkansas to the Tule Lake camp in northern California in 1943. Little is known about Shonan Suzuki, Hyakuissei Okamoto, Tokuji Hirai, Suiko Matsushita, or Sei Sagara. In order to emphasize the narrative potential that is revealed when the poems are treated as a collective enterprise, we have removed the poets' names from the poems here, though they are listed in the table of contents and in the index. This sequence begins with arrest in summer and moves through the experience of internment.

Being arrested—
at home peony bud
still firm

Hand-cuffed and taken away
I see my husband
even today

Lingering summer heat—
Japanese proceeding under guard
on dusty white road

Shouldering
a house without a husband
letter from my wife

Passed guard tower
without glancing up
before summer daybreak

In the shade of summer sun
guard tapping rock
with club

Withered grass on ground
army tank creaking
in the wind

Young grass red and shriveled
wide sandy flat
and gritty wind

Dandelion has bloomed
a moment of bitterness—
of what consequence?

On certain days
heart is full of hypocrisy
flowers of *gobo*° are purple

Released seagull
after writing NIPPON° in red on its belly
summer morning in highlands

Sprinkling water outside
barracks occupants
in full force and barefooted

Want to be with children
playing in water
of irrigation ditch

Even the croaking of frogs
comes from outside the barbed wire fence
this is our life

Sentry at main gate
face clearly exposed
in evening sun

Thin shadow of tule reed
blazing sunset
on barbed wire fence

Looking at summer moon
on Castle Rock
we are living in alien (enemy) land

Moon shadows on internment camp
I hear the cries of geese
again this year

Early moon has set
people unable to sleep
whispering

Rain shower from mountain
quietly soaking
barbed wire fence

---

30. *gobo:* burdock.
32. *Nippon:* (Japanese) "Japan,"

Thorns of the iron fence
pointed inward
toward camp

Desert rain falling
spitting blood
then fall asleep

Frosty morning
handed a hatchet
today I became a woodcutter

Stepping through snow
in predawn haste
a kitchen worker

Black clouds instantly shroud
autumn sky
hail storming against us today also

Winter wind
relentlessly blasting shed
goat bleating

Doll without a head
lying on desk top
one evening

Suddenly awakened
listening to bugle from guard house
moonlight

Jeep patrolling slowly
stove is glowing
at night

Grieving within
another victim°
oats on the ground

---

89. *victim:* Soichi James Okamoto, a construction worker, was asking permission to pass through the Tule Lake Camp gate when he was fatally shot, on May 24, 1944. The sentry who fired the fatal bullet was later acquitted after being fined $1.00 for the "unauthorized use of government property."

In the sage brush
two new earth mounds°
torrid wind blows

Oh shells—
the cliff, your bygone world
is slowly crumbling

93. *mounds:* the mounds (graves) were for two critically ill internees who had just arrived from a camp in Bismarck, North Dakota, and were shot dead by sentries who later alleged the two were "trying to escape from the camp."

JOHN BERRYMAN (1914–1972)

Berryman was born John Smith in McAlester, Oklahoma. At age twelve, after his family had moved to Florida, Berryman's father shot himself to death outside his son's window. His surname comes from his mother's second marriage, which occurred after the family moved to New York. Berryman was educated at Columbia and Cambridge Universities and himself became an influential teacher at Harvard, Princeton, and Minnesota. But he struggled with alcoholism and madness throughout his life. In the end, he leapt to his death from a bridge in Minneapolis.

Although he wrote short poems, a long poem and a 385-poem sequence, *Homage to Mistress Bradstreet* (1956) and *The Dream Songs* (1964–1968) are his major achievements. In the later work Berryman performs, exhibits, and burlesques his psychic struggles and his attitudes toward contemporary culture through a series of personae. Stylistically and rhetorically inventive, these poems are quite unlike anything else in modem poetry.

from THE DREAM SONGS°

I

Huffy Henry hid the day,
unappeasable Henry sulked.
I see his point,—a trying to put things over.
It was the thought that they thought
they could *do* it made Henry wicked & away.
But he should have come out and talked.

All the world like a woolen lover
once did seem on Henry's side.
Then came a departure.
Thereafter nothing fell out as it might or ought.
I don't see how Henry, pried
open for all the world to see, survived.

---

volume title: most of these poems were first published in *77 Dream Songs* (1967) or in *His Toy, His Dream, His Rest* (1968) and then collected in *The Dream Songs* (1969). Throughout the "dream songs" appear Berryman's persona, Henry, and Henry's alter ego, Mister Bones (a name given to the character who rattled bones as a sound effect in minstrel shows). Berryman's note—"The poem, then, whatever its wide cast of characters, is essentially about an imaginary character (not the poet, not me) named Henry, a white American in early middle age sometimes in blackface, who has suffered an irreversible loss and talks about himself sometimes in the first person, sometimes in the third, sometimes even in the second; he has a friend, never named, who addresses him as Mr. Bones and variants thereof. Requiescant in pace" [(Latin) "Rest in peace"].

What he has now to say is a long
wonder the world can bear & be.
Once in a sycamore I was glad
all at the top, and I sang.
Hard on the land wears the strong sea
and empty grows every bed.

1964

4

Filling her compact & delicious body
with chicken páprika, she glanced at me
twice.
Fainting with interest, I hungered back
and only the fact of her husband & four other people
kept me from springing on her

or falling at her little feet and crying
'You are the hottest one for years of night
Henry's dazed eyes
have enjoyed, Brilliance.' I advanced upon
(despairing) my spumoni.— Sir Bones: is stuffed,
de world, wif feeding girls.

—Black hair, complexion Latin, jewelled eyes
downcast . . . The slob beside her feasts . . . What wonders is
she sitting on, over there?
The restaurant buzzes. She might as well be on Mars.
Where did it all go wrong? There ought to be a law against Henry.
—Mr. Bones: there is.

1964

5

Henry sats in de bar & was odd,
off in the glass from the glass,
at odds wif de world & its god,
his wife is a complete nothing,
St Stephen
getting even.

Henry sats in de plane & was gay.
Careful Henry nothing said aloud
but where a Virgin out of cloud
to her Mountain dropt in light,

his thought made pockets & the plane buckt.
'Parm me, lady.' 'Orright.'

Henry lay in de netting, wild,
while the brainfever bird did scales;
Mr Heartbreak,° the New Man,
come to farm a crazy land;
an image of the dead on the fingernail°
of a newborn child.

1964

14

Life, friends, is boring. We must not say so.
After all, the sky flashes, the great sea yearns,
we ourselves flash and yearn,
and moreover my mother told me as a boy
(repeatingly) 'Ever to confess you're bored
means you have no

Inner Resources.' I conclude now I have no
inner resources, because I am heavy bored.
Peoples bore me,
literature bores me, especially great literature,
Henry bores me, with his plights & gripes
as bad as achilles,°

who loves people and valiant art, which bores me.
And the tranquil hills, & gin, look like a drag
and somehow a dog
has taken itself & its tail considerably away
into mountains or sea or sky, leaving
behind: me, wag.

1964

---

15. *Heartbreak:* translates the last name of J. Hector St. John Crèvecoeur, whose *Letters from an American Farmer* (1782) introduces the notion of the American as the "New Man" in its third chapter.

17. *fingernail:* from Miguel de Cervantes, whose *The Colloquoy of the Dogs* (1613) notes that the witch of Kamacha could "cause the living or dead to appear in a mirror on the fingernail of a newborn child."

12. *achilles:* hero of *The Iliad,* by the Greek epic poet Homer (eighth century B.C.); because of injured pride after a slight from Agamemnon, Achilles sulked in his tent, refusing to fight the Trojans. Berryman commented that *The Dream Songs* borrows some of its structure from *The Iliad.*

22

Of 1826

I am the little man who smokes & smokes.
I am the girl who does know better but.
I am the king of the pool.
I am so wise I had my mouth sewn shut.
I am government official & a goddamned fool.
I am a lady who takes jokes.

I am the enemy of the mind.
I am the auto salesman and lóve you.
I am a teenage cancer, with a plan.
I am the blackt-out man.
I am the woman powerful as a zoo.
I am two eyes screwed to my set, whose blind—

It is the Fourth of July.
Collect: while the dying man,°
forgone by you creator, who forgives,
is gasping 'Thomas Jefferson still lives'
in vain, in vain, in vain.
I am Henry Pussy-cat! My whiskers fly.

1964

29

There sat down, once, a thing on Henry's heart
só heavy, if he had a hundred years
& more, & weeping, sleepless, in all them time
Henry could not make good.
Starts again always in Henry's ears
the little cough somewhere, an odour, a chime.

And there is another thing he has in mind
like a grave Sienese face° a thousand years
would fail to blur the still profiled reproach of. Ghastly,
with open eyes, he attends, blind.
All the bells say: too late. This is not for tears;
thinking.

---

14. *dying man:* John Adams (1735–1826), second president of the United States, defeated for reelection by Thomas Jefferson (1743–1826). They died on the same day, July 4, 1826, with Jefferson dying first, but Adams did not know that when he gasped his last words.

8. *Sienese face:* like an austere face seen in the religious paintings by thirteenth- and fourteenth-century Italian artists in Siena.

But never did Henry, as he thought he did,
end anyone and hacks her body up
and hide the pieces, where they may be found.
He knows: he went over everyone, & nobody's missing.
Often he reckons, in the dawn, them up.
Nobody is ever missing.

1964

40

I'm scared a lonely. Never see my son,
easy be not to see anyone,
combers° out to sea
know they're goin somewhere but not me.
Got a little poison, got a little gun,
I'm scared a lonely.

I'm scared a only one thing, which is me,
from othering I don't take nothin, see,
for any hound dog's sake.
But this is where I livin, where I rake
my leaves and cop my promise,° this' where we
cry oursel's awake.

Wishin was dyin but I gotta make
it all this way to that bed on these feet
where peoples said to meet.
Maybe but even if I see my son
forever never, get back on the take,
free, black & forty-one.°

1964

45

He stared at ruin. Ruin stared straight back.
He thought they was old friends. He felt on the stair
where her papa found them bare
they became familiar. When the papers were lost
rich with pals' secrets, he thought he had the knack
of ruin. Their paths crossed

---

3. *combers:* long, breaking waves.

11. *cop my promise:* the phrase cuts two ways, suggesting at once *increasing* his promise or capacities and backing down on, or going back on, his word.

18. *free, black: & forty-one:* a play on "free, white, and twenty-one," a colloquialism for "legally independent."

and once they crossed in jail; they crossed in bed;
and over an unsigned letter their eyes met,
and in an Asian city
directionless & lurchy at two & three,
or trembling to a telephone's fresh threat,
and when some wired his head

to reach a wrong opinion, 'Epileptic'.°
But he noted now that: they were not old friends.
He did not know this one.
This one was a stranger, come to make amends
for all the imposters, and to make it stick.
Henry nodded, un-.

1964

46

I am, outside. Incredible panic rules.°
People are blowing and beating each other without mercy.
Drinks are boiling. Iced
drinks are boiling. The worse anyone feels, the worse
treated he is. Fools elect fools.
A harmless man at an intersection said, under his breath: "Christ!"

That word, so spoken, affected the vision
of, when they trod to work next day, shopkeepers
who went & were fitted for glasses.
Enjoyed they then an appearance of love & law.
Millenia whift & waft—one, one—er, er . . .
Their glasses were taken from them, & they saw.

Man has undertaken the top job of all,
son fin.° Good luck.
I myself walked at the funeral of tenderness.
Followed other deaths. Among the last,
Like the memory of a lovely fuck,
was: *Do, ut des.*°

1964

---

13. *Epileptic:* Berryman was incorrectly diagnosed with epilepsy in 1939.

1. *rules:* the first line alludes to a dream recorded by Wilhelm Stekel in *Sadism and Masochism* (1935).

14. *son fin:* (French) "his end."

18. *Do, ut des:* (German) "I give that thou shalt give," Wilhelm Stekel.

55

Peter's not friendly. He gives me sideways looks.
The architecture is far from reassuring.
I feel uneasy.
A pity,—the interview began so well:
I mentioned fiendish things, he waved them away
and sloshed out a martini

strangely needed. We spoke of indifferent matters—
God's health, the vague hell of the Congo,
John's energy,
anti-matter matter. I felt fine.
Then a change came backward. A chill fell.
Talk slackened,

died, and he began to give me sideways looks.
'Christ,' I thought 'what now?' and would have askt for another
but didn't dare.
I feel my application   failing. It's growing dark,
some other sound is overcoming. His last words are:
'We betrayed me.'

1964

76

Henry's Confession

Nothin very bad happen to me lately.
How you explain that?—I explain that, Mr Bones,
terms o' your bafflin odd sobriety.
Sober as man can get, no girls, no telephones,
what could happen bad to Mr Bones?
—*If* life is a handkerchief sandwich,

in a modesty of death I join my father
who dared so long agone leave me.
A bullet on a concrete stoop
close by a smothering southern sea
spreadeagled on an island, by my knee.
—You is from hunger, Mr Bones,

I offers you this handkerchief, now set
your left foot by my right foot,
shoulder to shoulder, all that jazz,

arm in arm, by the beautiful sea,°
hum a little, Mr Bones.
— I saw nobody coming, so I went instead.

1964

382

At Henry's bier let some thing fall out well:
enter there none who somewhat has to sell,
the music ancient & gradual,
the voices solemn but the grief subdued,
no hairy jokes but everybody's mood
subdued, subdued,

until the Dancer comes, in a short short dress
hair black & long & loose, dark dark glasses, uptilted face,
pallor & strangeness, the music changes
to 'Give!' & 'Ow!' and how! the music changes,
she kicks a backward limb

on tiptoe, pirouettes, & she is free
to the knocking music, sails, dips, & suddenly
returns to the terrible gay
occasion hopeless & mad, she weaves, it's hell,
she flings to her head a leg, bobs, all is well,
she dances Henry away.

1968

384

The marker slants, flowerless, day's almost done,
I stand above my father's grave with rage,
often, often before
I've made this awful pilgrimage to one
who cannot visit me, who tore his page
out: I come back for more,

I spit upon this dreadful banker's grave
who shot his heart out in a Florida dawn
O ho alas alas
When will indifference come, I moan & rave

16. *beautiful sea:* from a popular song of 1914.

I'd like to scrabble till I got right down
away down under the grass

and ax the casket open ha to see
just how he's taking it, which lie sought so hard
we'll tear apart
the mouldering grave clothes ha & then Henry
will heft the ax once more, his final card,
and fell it on the start.

1968

WILLIAM STAFFORD (1914–1993)

Born in rural Kansas, Stafford was a conscientious objector during World War II and was active in pacifist organizations. After earning degrees from the University of Kansas, he went on to study at the Writers' Workshop at the University of Iowa, where he also earned a Ph.D. He taught at Lewis and Clark College in Portland, Oregon, from 1956 to 1979, publishing his first book, *West of Your City,* in 1960. Stafford's writing process, as he explained it, was to rise early and work in the quiet before others awoke. One way to describe his poetry is to compare it with the pure quiet of the predawn hours. Everything about his writing, from its careful parceling into stanzas to the clear steps that guide us from passage to passage, suggests there is a virtue to calm, thoughtful, understated observation. Many of his poems depict Midwestern towns and landscapes; others take up personal and family experiences, but he has also frequently addressed public topics.

TRAVELING THROUGH THE DARK

Traveling through the dark I found a deer
dead on the edge of the Wilson River road.
It is usually best to roll them into the canyon:
that road is narrow; to swerve might make more dead.

By glow of the tail-light I stumbled back of the car
and stood by the heap, a doe, a recent killing;
she had stiffened already, almost cold.
I dragged her off; she was large in the belly.

My fingers touching her side brought me the reason—
her side was warm; her fawn lay there waiting,
alive, still, never to be born.
Beside that mountain road I hesitated.

The car aimed ahead its lowered parking lights;
under the hood purred the steady engine.
I stood in the glare of the warm exhaust turning red;
around our group I could hear the wilderness listen.

I thought hard for us all—my only swerving—,
then pushed her over the edge into the river.

1960

AT THE BOMB TESTING SITE

At noon in the desert a panting lizard
waited for history, its elbows tense,

watching the curve of a particular road
as if something might happen.

It was looking for something farther off
than people could see, an important scene
acted in stone for little selves
at the flute end of consequences.

There was just a continent without much on it
under a sky that never cared less.

1966

AT THE UN-NATIONAL MONUMENT ALONG THE CANADIAN BORDER

This is the field where the battle did not happen,
where the unknown soldier did not die.
This is the field where grass joined hands,
where no monument stands,
and the only heroic thing is the sky.

Birds fly here without any sound,
unfolding their wings across the open.
No people killed—or were killed—on this ground
hallowed by neglect and an air so tame
that people celebrate it by forgetting its name.

1960

THE INDIAN CAVE JERRY RAMSEY FOUND°

Brown, brittle, wait-a-bit weeds
block the entrance. I untangle their
whole summer embrace. Inside—soot from
a cold fire, powder of bones,
a piece of ceremonial horn: cool
history comes off on my hands.
Outside, I stand in a canyon so
quiet its pool almost remembers its
old reflections. And then I breathe.

1983

poem title: Jarold Ramsey (b. 1937), American poet and critic who studied Native American literature.

DUDLEY RANDALL (1914–2000)

Randall was born in Washington, D.C., but moved to Detroit in 1920. He worked in a foundry early on, then served in the military during World War II, an experience described in some of his poems. He earned degrees in English and library science and took several library positions during his career, but he is perhaps most famous as the 1965 founder of Detroit's Broadside Press. The press issued the first books of a considerable number of black writers, along with an extensive series of historic poetry broadsides. Randall himself worked both in traditional stanzaic forms and in blues styles, often writing poems of articulate protest. See his *A Litany of Friends: New and Selected Poems* (1983).

BALLAD OF BIRMINGHAM°

(On the bombing of a church in Birmingham, Alabama, 1963)

"Mother dear, may I go downtown
Instead of out to play,
And march the streets of Birmingham
In a Freedom March today?"

"No, baby, no, you may not go,
For the dogs are fierce and wild,
And clubs and hoses, guns and jails
Aren't good for a little child."

"But, mother, I won't be alone.
Other children will go with me,
And march the streets of Birmingham
To make our country free."

"No, baby, no, you may not go,
For I fear those guns will fire.
But you may go to church instead
And sing in the children's choir."

She has combed and brushed her night-dark hair,
And bathed rose petal sweet,

---

poem title: the Rev. Martin Luther King Jr. led nonviolent civil rights demonstrations in Birmingham, Alabama, two weeks after his famous August 23rd March on Washington, D.C.; the Birmingham demonstrators were confronted with attack dogs, tear gas, fire hoses, and cattle prods.

And drawn white gloves on her small brown hands,
And white shoes on her feet.

The mother smiled to know her child
Was in the sacred place,
But that smile was the last smile
To come upon her face.

For when she heard the explosion,
Her eyes grew wet and wild.
She raced through the streets of Birmingham
Calling for her child.

She clawed through bits of glass and brick,
Then lifted out a shoe.
"O, here's the shoe my baby wore,
But, baby, where are you?"

1969

A DIFFERENT IMAGE

The age
requires this task:
create
a different image;
re-animate
the mask.

Shatter the icons of slavery and fear.
Replace
the leer
of the minstrel's burnt-cork face
with a proud, serene
and classic bronze of Benin.°

1968

12. *Benin:* African country.

JOY DAVIDMAN (1915–1960)

Davidman's first publications appeared while she was still an undergraduate at Hunter College. *Poetry* began to publish her poems in 1936. Within a year or two, she had joined the Communist Party. *Letter to a Comrade,* the only collection of her own poems, was published in the Yale Series of Younger Poets in 1938. She spent the latter half of 1939 in Hollywood as an assistant screen writer for MGM, an experience that led her to write a number of film reviews for *New Masses* in the early 1940s. She contributed new poems to her massive anthology *War Poems of the United Nations* (1943) and to *Seven Poets in Search of an Answer* (1944), from which "For the Nazis" is reprinted. She wrote two novels, and converted to Christianity after a religious experience in 1946. She divorced her first husband, the Spanish Civil War veteran William Gresham, and married the British writer C. S. Lewis in 1956; the 1993 feature film *Shadowlands* tells a version of her relationship with Lewis.

THIS WOMAN

Now do not put a ribbon in your hair;
Abjure the spangled insult of design,
The filigree sterility, nor twine
A flower with your strength; go bare, go bare.

The elements foregathered at your birth
Gave your hard throat an armor for despair,
Burned you and bathed you, nourished you with air,
And carved your body like a tree of earth.

This is the symbol that I shape of you;
Branching from the broad column of your flesh
Into the obdurate and fibrous mesh
Stubborn to break apart and stiff to hew;
Lost at your core a living skeleton
Like sharp roots pointing downward from the sun.

1938

FOR THE NAZIS

When you see red
it will be too late;
the night will be dead,
the sun will not wait;

say, can you see
what the sunrise will be?

When you command
the sea to stand still
at the safe edge of the sand,
do you think that it will?
say, do you know
where the high tide will go?

Call for your cannon,
call for your drum,
buzz with the airplane;
burst with the bomb;
you're up a tree now;
say, while you rave,
say, can you see now
the depth of your grave?

1944

MARGARET WALKER (1915–1998)

Born in Birmingham, Alabama, to a middle-class black family that moved to New Orleans a decade later. Walker first enrolled at New Orleans University. Then she met poet Langston Hughes, who encouraged her writing and advised her to go north to complete her education, which she did at Northwestern University. It was in Chicago, in 1936, that she met novelist and poet Richard Wright, about whom she would publish a critical biography fifty-two years later. She became a teacher and a novelist, and continued publishing poetry after the dramatic success of the poems of *For My People* (1942).

FOR MY PEOPLE

For my people everywhere singing their slave songs
repeatedly: their dirges and their ditties and their blues
and jubilees, praying their prayers nightly to an
unknown god, bending their knees humbly to an
unseen power;

For my people lending their strength to the years, to the
gone years and the now years and the maybe years,
washing ironing cooking scrubbing sewing mending
hoeing plowing digging planting pruning patching
dragging along never gaining never reaping never
knowing and never understanding;

For my playmates in the clay and dust and sand of Alabama
backyards playing baptizing and preaching and doctor
and jail and soldier and school and mama and cooking
and playhouse and concert and store and hair and Miss
Choomby and company;

For the cramped bewildered years we went to school to learn
to know the reasons why and the answers to and the
people who and the places where and the days when, in
memory of the bitter hours when we discovered we
were black and poor and small and different and nobody
cared and nobody wondered and nobody understood;

For the boys and girls who grew in spite of these things to
be man and woman, to laugh and dance and sing and
play and drink their wine and religion and success, to

marry their playmates and bear children and then die
of consumption and anemia and lynching;

For my people thronging 47th Street in Chicago and Lenox
Avenue in New York and Rampert Street in New
Orleans, lost disinherited dispossessed and happy
people filling the cabarets and taverns and other
people's pockets needing bread and shoes and milk and
land and memory and something—something all our own;

For my people walking blindly spreading joy, losing time
being lazy, sleeping when hungry, shouting when
burdened, drinking when hopeless, tied, and shackled
and tangled among ourselves by the unseen creatures
who tower over us omnisciently and laugh;

For my people blundering and groping and floundering in
the dark of churches and schools and clubs and
societies, associations and councils and committees and
conventions, distressed and disturbed and deceived and
devoured by money-hungry glory-craving leeches,
preyed on by facile force of state and fad and novelty, by
false prophet and holy believer;

For my people standing staring trying to fashion a better way
from confusion, from hypocrisy and misunderstanding,
trying to fashion a world that will hold all the people,
all the faces, all the adams and eves and their countless
generations;

Let a new earth rise. Let another world be born. Let a
bloody peace be written in the sky. Let a second
generation full of courage issue forth; let a people
loving freedom come to growth. Let a beauty full of
healing and a strength of final clenching be the pulsing
in our spirits and our blood. Let the martial songs be
written, let the dirges disappear. Let a race of men now
rise and take control.

1937

RUTH STONE (1915–2011)

Born in Roanoke, Virginia, Stone grew up in Indiana and Illinois, and was educated at the University of Illinois. Although she did not publish her first book until 1958 and withheld her next book until 1970, she nevertheless had a long and distinguished career. It was also, however, a career very much on the margins of the poetry establishment, about which "Some Things You'll Need to Know / Before You Join the Union" testifies with devastating wit. She went her own way, devoted more to writing her poetry than publishing it, courting few journals, living on a New England farm while serving occasionally as poet-in-residence at various universities, including the State University of New York at Binghamton, and all the while honing an intensely lyrical voice with a sharp edge of awareness about the politics of gender in America.

IN AN IRIDESCENT TIME

My mother, when young, scrubbed laundry in a tub,
She and her sisters on an old brick walk
Under the apple trees, sweet rub-a-dub.
The bees came round their heads, the wrens made talk.
Four young ladies each with a rainbow board
Honed their knuckles, wrung their wrists to red,
Tossed back their braids and wiped their aprons wet.
The Jersey calf beyond the back fence roared;
And all the soft day, swarms about their pet
Buzzed at his big brown eyes and bullish head.
Four times they rinsed, they said. Some things they starched,
Then shook them from the baskets two by two,
And pinned the fluttering intimacies of life
Between the lilac bushes and the yew:
Brown gingham, pink, and skirts of Alice blue.

1959

I HAVE THREE DAUGHTERS

I have three daughters
Like greengage plums.
They sat all day
Sucking their thumbs.
And more's the pity,
They cried all day,

Why doesn't our mother's brown hair
Turn gray?

I have three daughters
Like three cherries.
They sat at the window
The boys to please.
And they couldn't wait
For their mother to grow old.
Why doesn't our mother's brown hair
Turn to snow?

I have three daughters
In the apple tree
Singing Mama send Daddy
With three young lovers
To take them away from me.

I have three daughters
Like greengage plums,
Sitting all day
And sighing all day
And sucking their thumbs;
Singing, Mama won't you fetch and carry,
And Daddy, won't you let us marry,
Singing, sprinkle snow down on Mama's hair
And lordy, give us our share.

1970

POKEBERRIES

I started out in the Virginia mountains
with my grandma's pansy bed
and my Aunt Maud's dandelion wine.
We lived on greens and back-fat and biscuits.
My Aunt Maud scrubbed right through the linoleum.
My daddy was a northerner who played drums
and chewed tobacco and gambled.
He married my mama on the rebound.
Who would want an ignorant hill girl with red hair?
They took a Pullman up to Indianapolis
and someone stole my daddy's wallet.
My whole life has been stained with pokeberries.
No man seemed right for me. I was awkward

until I found a good wood-burning stove.
There is no use asking what it means.
With my first piece of ready cash I bought my own
place in Vermont; kerosene lamps, dirt road.
I'm sticking here like a porcupine up a tree.
Like the one our neighbor shot. Its bones and skin
hung there for three years in the orchard.
No amount of knowledge can shake my grandma out of me;
or my Aunt Maud; or my mama, who didn't just bite an apple
with her big white teeth. She split it in two.

1987

AMERICAN MILK

Then the butter we put on our white bread
was colored with butter yellow, a cancerous dye,
and all the fourth grades were taken by streetcar
to the Dunky Company to see milk processed; milk bottles
riding on narrow metal cogs through little doors that flapped.
The sour damp smell of milky-wet cement floors:
we looked through great glass windows at the milk.
Before we were herded back to the streetcar line,
we were each given a half pint of milk in tiny
milk bottles with straws to suck it up. In this way
we gradually learned about our country.

1987

FROM THE ARBORETUM

The bunya-bunya is a great louse that sucks.
From its center many limbs are fastened to the sky
which lies behind it placidly suffering.
At its bottom it wears the ruffles of a cancan girl.
Bird dung and nits drip with its resinous sweat.
Its forgotten threads underground are anaerobic
with the maximum strength of steel. For every stretch
upward it splits and bleeds—fingers grow out of fingers.
Rings of ants, bark beetles, sponge molds,
even cockroaches communicate in its armpits.
But it protests only with the voices of starlings,
their colony at its top in the forward brush.
To them it is only an old armchair, a brothel, the front porch.

1987

DROUGHT IN THE LOWER FIELDS

Steers are dumb like angels,
moony-eyed, and soft-calling
like channel bells
to sound the abyss,
the drop-off in the fog
that crows circle
and gliding buzzards
yearn down into with their small
red heads bent
looking for dead souls to pick.
Steers nod their heads, yes,
browsing the scalded grass,
they eat around the scarce
blue stars of chicory.

1987

SOME THINGS YOU'LL NEED TO KNOW BEFORE YOU JOIN THE UNION

I

At the poetry factory
body poems are writhing and bleeding.
An angry mob of women
is lined up at the back door
hoping for jobs.
Today at the poetry factory
they are driving needles through the poems.
Everyone's excited.
Mr. Po-Biz himself comes in from the front office.
He clenches his teeth.
"Anymore wildcat aborting out there," he hisses
"and you're all blacklisted."
The mob jeers.

II

The antiwar and human rights poems
are processed in the white room.
Everyone in there wears sterile gauze.
These poems go for a lot.
No one wants to mess up.
There's expensive equipment involved,
The workers have to be heavy,

very heavy.
These poems are packaged in cement.
You frequently hear them drop with a dull thud.

III

Poems are being shipped out
by freight car.
Headed up the ramp
they can't turn back.
They push each other along.
They will go to the packing houses.
The slaughter will be terrible,
an inevitable end of overproduction,
the poetry factory's GNP.
Their shelf life will be brief.

IV

They're stuffing at the poetry factory today.
They're jamming in images
saturated with *as* and *like*.
Lines are being stuffed to their limits.
If a line by chance explodes,
there's a great cheer.
However, most of them don't explode.
Most of them lie down and groan.

V

In the poetry factory
it's very hot.
The bellows are going,
the pressure is building up.
Young poems are being rolled out
ready to be cut.
Whistles are blowing.
Jive is rocking.
Barrels of thin words line the walls.
Fat words like links of sausages
hang on belts.
Floor walkers and straw bosses
take a coffee break.
Only the nervous apprentice
is anywhere near the machines
when a large poem

seems about to come off the assembly line.
"This is it," the apprentice shouts.
"Get my promotion ready!
APR, the quarterlies,
a chapbook, NEA,
a creative writing chair,
the poetry circuit, Yaddo!"
Inside the ambulance
as it drives away
he is still shouting,
"I'll grow a beard,
become an alcoholic,
consider suicide."

1987

THOMAS McGRATH (1916–1990)

Born on a farm near Sheldon, North Dakota, the grandchild of Irish Catholic homesteaders, McGrath was educated at the University of North Dakota, Louisiana State University, New College, and Oxford University, the latter as a Rhodes Scholar. He was in the U.S. Air Force in the Aleutian Islands during World War II, isolated from combat in a unit full of radicals feared by the high command. He moved to Hollywood on his return and married Alice Greenfield (McGrath), a communist organizer in Los Angeles who is the real social worker behind the heroine of Luis Valdez's play (and later film) *Zoot Suit*. In 1953, at the height of the long postwar inquisition that culminated in the McCarthy era, McGrath was teaching at Los Angeles State College when he was called before the House Un-American Activities Committee. Citing his constitutional guarantees of free speech and political association, guarantees the government swept aside, McGrath refused to answer the committee's questions about his own beliefs or to betray his friends. "Poets have been notorious non-cooperators where committees of this sort are concerned," he added, "I do not wish to bring dishonor upon my tribe." McGrath was fired from his teaching job and blacklisted as a result. A lifelong socialist and prairie populist, veteran of failed farms during the Great Depression, occasional welder and logger, McGrath then pieced together a living doing labor organizing, writing scripts for documentary films, and eventually, when the inquisition had run its course, teaching again. In 1975, he was investigated for possible third-degree murder in the shooting death of a Minnesota man; though the grand jury returned a no-charge verdict and he was not brought to trial, the incident hurt him deeply. Through it all he remained a revolutionary and an ironist, writing short poems notable not only for their rhetorical intricacy and political wit but also for their passionate commitment to justice and sanity. He would also write one of the great American book-length poem sequences, *Letter to an Imaginary Friend,* finally issued in its entirety posthumously in 1997.

DEEP SOUTH

Baton Rouge, 1940

These are savannas bluer than your dreams
Where other loves are fashioned to older music,
And the romantic in his light boat
Puts out among flamingos and water moccasins
Looking for the river that went by last year.

Even the angels wear confederate uniforms;
And when the magnolia blooms and the honeysuckle,

Golden lovers, brighter than the moon,
Read Catullus in the flaring light
Of the burning Negro in the open eye of midnight.

And the Traveller, moving in the hot swamps,
Where every human sympathy sends up the temperature,
Comes of a sudden on the hidden glacier,
Whose motives are blonder than Hitler's choir boys.

Here is the ambiguous tenderness of 'gators
Trumpeting their loves along a hundred miles
Of rivers writhing under trees like myths—
And human existence pursues the last,
The simple and desperate life of the senses.
Since love survives only as ironic legend—
Response to situations no longer present—
Men lacking dignity are seized by pride,
Which is the easy upper-class infection.

The masters are at home in this merciless climate
But deep in the caves of their minds some animal memory
Warns of the fate of the mammoth at the end of the ice-age;
As sleeping children a toy, they hug the last, fatal error,
But their eyes are awake and their dreams shake as with palsy.

***

Over Birmingham where the blast furnace flowers
And beyond the piney woods in cotton country,
Continually puzzling the pale aristocrats,
The sun burns equally white man and black.

The labor which they do makes more and more
Their brotherhood condition for their whole existence;
They mint their own light, and their fusing fires
Will melt at last these centuries of ice.

This is a nightmare nimble in the Big House,
Where sleepers are wakeful, cuddling their terror,
In the empty acres of their rich beds, dreaming
Of bones in museums, where the black boys yawn.

1940

CRASH REPORT

If perhaps you read in the paper somewhere
How Captain—or maybe Private—so and so—

Had been killed in Africa or India or even
The Aleutians—well, would you think him a hero?

It isn't important one way or another.
The guy is just as dead as Grant took Richmond.
In five years the flesh fails; five years and then
You can knock at his memory: nobody home.

For these heroes in handcuffs, out of War by Accident,
Never seem to wear well and anyway at best
Even the well dressed scarecrow or scapegoat
Possesses a limited survival value.

For instance, examine a case on record:
The dashing captain with the low-powered kite,
(It was crewed by a Christian Front mug from Yorkville
And somewhat overloaded with whisky and nurses)

—He crashed and was killed: wages of sin, etc.
While another man goes down over Paramashiru—
He wasn't joy-riding. But all is equal
In the book of Hearst's recording angel.

Yet not for us. We can recognize heroes
Before they are dead or fogged in with medals.
For heroes the hearse must he called for a reason.
It is not by accident their lives are given.

But for you, Gentle Reader, it doesn't matter a damn.
To you, real or phony, they're all the same.
And in the dead men's summers where they'll never feel the sun
It's of no importance. Everyone dies for your sins.

1944

FIRST BOOK OF GENESIS ACCORDING TO THE DIPLOMATS

On the first day they drowned the orphans,
The blue-eyed ones, in threes, in diplomats' pouches.
The dollar stood at four pounds of flesh in open market
And all markets were opened by the President,
Officially, on the first day.

The second day some opposition
Was begun by workers. These were all shot down
By students of the Radicals for Nixon movement.

Two million died in sin mortal and venial and
In hunger on the second day;

And were buried, noon, on the third day
In two speeches, given by the Secretary
Who said they were foreigners, et cetera. The Poet
Laureate was observed hustling, et cetera,
Officially, on the third day.

The fourth day was unofficial. Five
Officials of the Western Democracies were
Purchased, and some English peers. A brown rubber Bible
In a goldfish bowl was presented to a king.
The goldfish died on the fourth day.

The fifth day was the Apocalypse
Of Peoria. Armed invaders
Turned out to be a seal with a bicycle bell and two
Margarine golfballs in a birdcage. The Mayor
Had to resign on the fifth day.

On the sixth day Congress with a gun
At the taxpayer's head asked not to be provoked.
It wasn't. The Society of Atomic Widows made
The Statue of Liberty a charter member
Regretfully on the sixth day.

On the seventh day *Time* held out hope
That orphans with black-roofed mouths would not be drowned—
Or those in West Europe at least. Later the President
Took over the portfolio of Usury
And Wretchedness that seventh day.

But in the new week Congress could not be sure:
They had bought statesmen but would they stay bought?
They founded the feast of the Transformation of Liberals
But the very birds were beginning to rebel,
To sing a strange language,

And on the cold plateau of Spain, by the Mekong delta,
In hamlets on the tidy fields of France,
The accursed poor who can never be bought
Clothed with their flesh against the Pharoah's sword
A terrible infant, child of their desire.

1949

ARS POETICA: OR: WHO LIVES IN THE IVORY TOWER?

Perhaps you'd like a marching song for the embattled prolet-
Ariat, or a realistic novel, the hopeful poet
Said, or a slice of actual life with the hot red heart's blood running,
The simple tale of a working stiff, but better than Jack London?

Nobody wants your roundelay, nobody wants your sestina,
Said the housewife, we want Hedy Lamarr and Gable at the cinema,
Get out of my technicolor dream with your tragic view and your verses;
Down with iambic pentameter and hurray for Louella Parsons.

Of course you're free to write as you please, the liberal editor answered,
But take the red flags out of your poem—we mustn't offend the censor—
And change this stanza to mean the reverse, and you must tone down this passage;
Thank God for the freedom of the press and a poem with a message!

Life is lousy enough without you should put it into a sonnet,
Said the man in the street, so keep it out of the novel, the poem, the drama;
Give us a paean of murder and rape, or the lay of a willing maiden,
And to hell with the Bard of Avalon and to hell with Eliot Auden.

Recite the damn things all day long, get drunk on smoke come Sunday,
I respect your profession as much as my own, but it don't pay off when you're hungry;
You'll have to carry the banner instead—said the hobo in the jungle—
If you want to eat; and don't forget: it's my bridge you're sleeping under.

Oh it's down with art and down with life and give us another reefer—
They all said—give us a South Sea isle, where light my love lies dreaming;
And who is that poet come in off the streets with a look unleal and lour?

Your feet are muddy, you son-of-a-bitch, get out of our ivory
tower.

1949

A LITTLE SONG ABOUT CHARITY

(Tune of Matty Grove)°

The boss came around at Christmas—
Oh smiling like a lamb—
He made me a present of a pair of gloves
And then cut off my hands—
Oh and then cut off my hands.

The boss came around on my birthday
With some shoes of a rich man's brand.
He smiled like a priest and he cut off my feet
Then he said: "Go out and dance"—
Oh he said: "Go out and dance."

The boss came around on May Day.
He said: "You may parade."
Then his cops shot us down in the open street
And they clubbed us into jail—
Oh they clubbed us into jail.

The preacher says on Sunday:
"Turn ye the other cheek."
Don't turn it to the boss on Monday morn:
He may knock out all your teeth—
Oh he may knock out your teeth.

So listen to me workers:
When the boss seems kind and good
Remember that the stain on the cutting tool
Is nothing but your blood—
Oh it's nothing but your blood.

If you love your wife and daughters,
And if you love your sons,
And if you love the working class

---

epigraph: Matty Groves is an English folk ballad and is one of the Child Ballads collected by Francis James Child (1825–1896).

Then keep your love at home.
Don't waste it on the cockroach boss
But keep your love at home.

1949

AGAINST THE FALSE MAGICIANS

for Don Gordon

The poem must not charm us like a film:
See, in the war-torn city, that reckless, gallant
Handsome lieutenant turn to the wet-lipped blonde
(Our childhood fixation) for one sweet desperate kiss
In the broken room, in blue cinematic moonlight—
Bombers across that moon, and the bombs falling,
The last train leaving, the regiment departing—
And their lips lock, saluting themselves and death:
And then the screen goes dead and all go home . . .
Ritual of the false imagination.

The poem must not charm us like the fact:
A warship can sink a circus at forty miles,
And art, love's lonely counterfeit, has small dominion
Over those nightmares that move in the actual sunlight.
The blonde will not be faithful, nor her lover ever return
Nor the note be found in the hollow tree of childhood—
This dazzle of the facts would have us weeping
The orphaned fantasies of easier days.

It is the charm which the potential has
That is the proper aura for the poem.
Though ceremony fail, though each of your grey hairs
Help string a harp in the landlord's heaven,
And every battle, every augury,
Argue defeat, and if defeat itself
Bring all the darkness level with our eyes—
It is the poem provides the proper charm,
Spelling resistance and the living will,
To bring to dance a stony field of fact
And set against terror exile or despair
The rituals of our humanity.

1955

AFTER THE BEAT GENERATION

I.

What! All those years after the Annunciation at Venice
And no revolution in sights?
And how long since the lads
From West Stud Horse Texas and Poontang-on-the-Hudson
Slogged through the city of Lost Angels in the beardless years
Led by a cloud no bigger than an orgone box, whence issued—
Promising, promising, promising (and no revolution and no
Revolution in sight) issued the cash-tongued summons
Toward the guru of Big Sur and San Fran's stammering
Apocalypse?

I do not know how long this thing can go on!
—Waiting for Lefty, waiting for Godot, waiting for the heavenly fix.
In my way of counting, time comes in through my skin—
Blind Cosmos Alley, charismatic light
Of electric mustaches in the Deep Night of the Gashouse gunfire
From enormous imaginary loud cap pistols of infinitely small
caliber
Anarcholunacy—how long, in that light, to read what signposts?
When all that glows with a gem-like flame is the end of Lipton's
cigar?

II.

There ought to be other ways to skin this cat:
Journeys through the deep snow of a black book, bonefire, and
wormlight
To burn through the salty moss to the mark on the blazed tree
How long now since love out of a cloud of flesh
In Elysian Park stammered your secret name? Since Curtis
Zahn dipped his beard in the radioactive sea?
Since Rolfe went underground for the last time in that boneyard
On Santa Monica?
Bench marks.
Sea anchors of drowned guitars.
Alas, compañeros, have we not seen the imaginary travellers—
Whole boatloads of sensitive boy scouts aground in the dead river
Of the Lost Angels, and the coffee shops' simple malfeasance of
Light?
Hence it is required of us to go forward over the rubber bones
Of these synthetic rebels, over the tame poets

Who came to the Time's big table and the harp-shaped evergreen
swimming pools
To drink the waters of darkness.
In the Carbon 14 dating
We find the Naked Man: the starving: the Moon in the Penitentiary.

1963

ODE FOR THE AMERICAN DEAD IN ASIA

1.

God love you now, if no one else will ever,
Corpse in the paddy, or dead on a high hill
In the fine and ruinous summer of a war
You never wanted. All your false flags were
Of bravery and ignorance, like grade school maps:
Colors of countries you would never see—
Until that weekend in eternity
When, laughing, well armed, perfectly ready to kill
The world and your brother, the safe commanders sent
You into your future. Oh, dead on a hill,
Dead in a paddy, leeched and tumbled to
A tomb of footnotes. We mourn a changeling: you:
Handselled to poverty and drummed to war
By distinguished masters whom you never knew.

2.

The bee that spins his metal from the sun,
The shy mole drifting like a miner ghost
Through midnight earth—all happy creatures run
As strict as trains on rails the circuits of
Blind instinct. Happy in your summer follies,
You mined a culture that was mined for war:
The state to mold you, church to bless, and always
The elders to confirm you in your ignorance.
No scholar put your thinking cap on nor
Warned that in dead seas fishes died in schools
Before inventing legs to walk the land.
The rulers stuck a tennis racket in your hand,
An Ark against the flood. In time of change
Courage is not enough: the blind mole dies,
And you on your hill, who did not know the rules.

3.

Wet in the windy counties of the dawn
The lone crow skirls his draggled passage home:
And God (whose sparrows fall aslant his gaze,
Like grace or confetti) blinks and he is gone,
And you are gone. Your scarecrow valor grows
And rusts like early lilac while the rose
Blooms in Dakota and the stock exchange
Flowers. Roses, rents, all things conspire
To crown your death with wreaths of living fire.
And the public mourners come: the politic tear
Is cast in the Forum. But, in another year,
We will mourn you, whose fossil courage fills
The limestone histories: brave: ignorant: amazed:
Dead in the rice paddies, dead on the nameless hills.

1968

POEM AT THE WINTER SOLSTICE

Light falls slant on the long south slopes,
    On the pheasant-covert willow, the hawk-nest dark and foxes' hollow
As the year grows old.
                    Who will escape the cold?

                    These will endure
The scour of snow and the breakneck ice
    Where the print-scar mousetracks blur in the evergreen light
And the night-hunting high birds whirl—
All engines of feather and fur:
                    These will endure.

                    But how shall our pride,
Manwoman'schild, in the bone-chilling black frost born,
    Where host or hide
Who is bound in his orbit between iron and gold
    Robbed of his starry fire with the cold
Sewed in his side—
                    How shall he abide?

                    Bear him his gift,
    To bless his work,
Who, farming the dark on the love-worn stony plot,

The heaven-turning stormy rock of this share-crop world
His only brother warms and harms;
Who, without feathers or fur,
Faces the gunfire cold of the old warring
new
year—
Bless! Grant him gift and gear,
Against the night and riding of his need,
To seed the turning furrow of his light.

1983

ROBERT LOWELL (1917–1977)

Robert Lowell grew up in Boston, Massachusetts, as part of a family with a distinguished literary heritage. Poets James Russell Lowell and Amy Lowell were among his ancestors. This heritage no doubt made his own father's limitations—he was a business failure after his retirement from the U.S. Navy—seem more severe. Lowell enrolled at Harvard, much as the family expected, but after the first of his lifelong series of emotional breakdowns and periods of manic behavior, he transferred to Kenyon College in 1937. There he met poet and critic John Crowe Ransom, one of the leaders of American New Criticism, who introduced Lowell to preferences for rhetorically intricate and ironic poems. Lowell also broke with his Protestant family history by converting to Catholicism in 1940. Opposed to some of America's World War II policies, he served a year in prison as a conscientious objector.

Lowell's first books, biblical and apocalyptic in tone, gave way in *Life Studies* (1959) to a new style that would guarantee his reputation. Accompanied by an autobiographical essay and written in a far more open and personal style, the poems came to herald what would be called the "confessional" school of poetry. Yet from the outset of his career, Lowell had actually been drawn to a more complex subject—the intersection of public history and autobiographical experience. Though later work like *The Dolphin* (1973) would sometimes mine his personal experience remorselessly, his poems overall are a remarkable testament to how a reflective person lives and internalizes both the historical record and the public life of his time. The "confessional" label, which was more comfortable for critics who preferred poetry to be apolitical, has thus obscured the degree to which Lowell is a powerful critic of American culture and history. "Epilogue" is the final authored poem in his last book.

INAUGURATION DAY: JANUARY 1953°

The snow had buried Stuyvesant.°
The subways drummed the vaults. I heard
the El's° green girders charge on Third,
Manhattan's truss of adamant,
that groaned in ermine, slummed on want. . . .
Cyclonic zero of the word,
God of our armies, who interred

---

poem title: Dwight D. Eisenhower (1890–1969) was inaugurated as president of the United States in 1953. He had been supreme commander of the Allied Forces in World War II.

1. *Stuyvesant:* a statue honoring Peter Stuyvesant (1610–1672), the sometimes autocratic employee of the Dutch West India Company who was chief administrator for New Amsterdam (now New York City) from 1647 to 1664.

3. *El:* a subway train running on rails elevated above ground.

Cold Harbor's blue immortals, Grant!°
Horseman, your sword is in the groove!

Ice, ice. Our wheels no longer move.
Look, the fixed stars, all just alike
as lack-land atoms, split apart,
and the Republic summons Ike,°
the mausoleum in her heart.

1953

A MAD NEGRO SOLDIER CONFINED AT MUNICH°

"We're all Americans, except the Doc,
a Kraut DP,° who kneels and bathes my eye.
The boys who floored me, two black maniacs, try
to pat my hands. Rounds, rounds! Why punch the clock?

In Munich the zoo's rubble fumes with cats;
hoydens° with air-guns prowl the Koenigsplatz,
and pink the pigeons on the mustard spire.
Who but my girl-friend set the town on fire?

Cat-houses talk cold turkey to my guards;
I found my *Fraulein* stitching outing shirts
in the black forest of the colored wards—
lieutenants squawked like chickens in her skirts.

Her German language made my arteries harden—
I've no annuity from the pay we blew.
I chartered an aluminum canoe,
I had her six times in the English Garden.

Oh mama, mama, like a trolley-pole
sparking at contact, her electric shock—
the power-house!... The doctor calls our roll—
no knives, no forks. We file before the clock,

---

8. *Grant:* Ulysses S. Grant (1822–1885), who commanded the Union forces in the American Civil War, was also elected U.S. president. His tomb (and a statue honoring him) are in New York.

13. *Ike:* Eisenhower's nickname. "I like Ike" was a campaign slogan.

poem title: after a manic episode that took place while he was teaching in Europe in 1952, Lowell spent some weeks in the American military hospital in Munich, Germany. He was installed in a locked ward full of disturbed military personnel.

2. *DP:* displaced person.

6. *hoydens:* high-spirited young women.

and fancy minnows, slaves of habit, shoot
like starlight through their air-conditioned bowl.
It's time for feeding. Each subnormal boot-
black heart is pulsing to its ant-egg dole."

1959

COMMANDER LOWELL°

1887–1950

There were no undesirables or girls in my set,
when I was a boy at Mattapoisett°—
only Mother, still her Father's daughter.
Her voice was still electric
with a hysterical, unmarried panic,
when she read to me from the Napoleon book.°
Long-nosed Marie Louise°
Hapsburg in the frontispiece
had a downright Boston bashfulness,
where she grovelled to Bonaparte, who scratched his navel,
and bolted his food—just my seven years tall!
And I, bristling and manic,
skulked in the attic,
and got two hundred French generals by name,
From *A* to *V*—from Augereau to Vandamme.°
I used to dope myself asleep,
naming those unpronounceables like sheep.

Having a naval officer
for my Father was nothing to shout
about to the summer colony at "Matt."
He wasn't at all "serious,"
when he showed up on the golf course,
wearing a blue serge jacket and numbly cut

---

poem title: Lowell's elegy on his father.

2. *Mattapoisett:* town in Massachusetts.

6. *Napoleon book: Memoirs of Napoleon* by the Duchese d'Abrantes, a favorite of Lowell's mother, Charlotte. Napoleon Bonaparte (1769–1821), French general and emperor, a titanic figure in European history.

7. *Marie Louise:* Napoleon married Archduchess Marie Louise of Austria in 1809, after his earlier marriage to Josephine proved childless.

15. *Vandamme:* Pierre François Charles Augereau (1757–1816) and Dominique René Van damme (1770–1830) were military officers who served under Napoleon. Their careers mixed success and failure, though Augereau's in particular was compromised by personal failings. His record was tarnished by cruelty; as one writer put it, "he was tall and commanding, but his loud and vulgar behavior frequently betrayed the soldier of fortune."

white ducks he'd bought
at a Pearl Harbor commissariat . . .
and took four shots with his putter to sink his putt.
"Bob," they said, "golf's a game you really ought to know how to
play,
if you play at all."
They wrote him off as "naval,"
naturally supposed his sport was sailing.
Poor Father, his training was engineering!
Cheerful and cowed
among the seadogs at the Sunday yacht club,
he was never one of the crowd.

"Anchors aweigh," Daddy boomed in his bathtub,
"Anchors aweigh,"
when Lever Brothers offered to pay
him double what the Navy paid.
I nagged for his dress sword with gold braid,
and cringed because Mother, new
caps on all her teeth, was born anew
at forty. With seamanlike celerity,
Father left the Navy,
and deeded Mother his property.

He was soon fired. Year after year,
he still hummed "Anchors aweigh" in the tub—
whenever he left a job,
he bought a smarter car.
Father's last employer
was Scudder, Stevens and Clark, Investment Advisors,
himself his only client.
While Mother dragged to bed alone,
read Menninger,
and grew more and more suspicious,
he grew defiant.
Night after night,
à la clarté déserte de sa lampe,°
he slid his ivory Annapolis slide rule
across a pad of graphs—
piker speculations! In three years
he squandered sixty thousand dollars.

---

57. . . . *sa lampe:* (French) "by the empty brilliance of his lamp," from Stéphane Mallarmé's (1842–1898) poem "Brise Marine."

Smiling on all,
Father was once successful enough to be lost
in the mob of ruling-class Bostonians.
As early as 1928,
he owned a house converted to oil,
and redecorated by the architect
of St. Mark's° School. . . . Its main effect
was a drawing room, "longitudinal as Versailles,"°
its ceiling, roughened with oatmeal, was blue as the sea.
And once
nineteen, the youngest ensign in his class,
he was "the old man" of a gunboat on the Yangtze.°

1959

"TO SPEAK OF WOE THAT IS IN MARRIAGE"°

"It is the future generation that presses into being by means of these exuberant feelings and supersensible soap bubbles of ours."

SCHOPENHAUER°

"The hot night makes us keep our bedroom windows open.
Our magnolia blossoms. Life begins to happen.
My hopped up husband drops his home disputes,
and hits the streets to cruise for prostitutes,
free-lancing out along the razor's edge.
This screwball might kill his wife, then take the pledge.
Oh the monotonous meanness of his lust. . . .
It's the injustice . . . he is so unjust—
whiskey-blind, swaggering home at five.
My only thought is how to keep alive.
What makes him tick? Each night now I tie
ten dollars and his car key to my thigh. . . .
Gored by the climacteric of his want,
he stalls above me like an elephant."

1959

---

68. *St. Mark's:* an upper-crust Episcopalian boarding school in Southborough, Massachusetts, that Lowell was compelled to attend.

69. *Versailles:* a palace built for Louis XIII and XIV at the village of Versailles, fourteen miles southwest of Paris. Louis XV held court there in the eighteenth century.

73. *Yangtze:* the longest river in China.

poem title: in Geoffrey Chaucer's (1340–1400) *The Canterbury Tales,* the Wife of Bath opens her marriage stories with this line.

epigraph: *Schopenhauer:* Arthur Schopenhauer (1788–1860), German philosopher.

MAN AND WIFE

Tamed by *Miltown,*[o] we[o] lie on Mother's bed;
the rising sun in war paint dyes us red;
in broad daylight her gilded bed-posts shine,
abandoned, almost Dionysian.[o]
At last the trees are green on Marlborough Street,[o]
blossoms on our magnolia ignite
the morning with their murderous five days' white.
All night I've held your hand,
as if you had
a fourth time faced the kingdom of the mad[o]—
its hackneyed speech, its homicidal eye—
and dragged me home alive. . . . Oh my *Petite,*
clearest of all God's creatures, still all air and nerve:
you were in your twenties, and I,
once hand on glass
and heart in mouth,
outdrank the Rahvs[o] in the heat
of Greenwich Village, fainting at your feet—
too boiled and shy
and poker-faced to make a pass,
while the shrill verve
of your invective scorched the traditional South.[o]

Now twelve years later, you turn your back.
Sleepless, you hold
your pillow to your hollows like a child;
your old-fashioned tirade—
loving, rapid, merciless—
breaks like the Atlantic Ocean on my head.

1959

---

1. *Miltown:* a tranquilizer popular during the 1950s. The first lines also echo the opening lines of Book 2 of Milton's *Paradise Lost.* Satan's throne is now a marriage bed: "High on a throne of a royal state, which far / Outshone the wealth of Ormus and of Ind, / Or where the gorgeous East with richest hand / Showers on her kings barbaric pearl and gold, / Satan exhalted sat. . . ."

1. *we:* Lowell and his second wife, the critic Elizabeth Hardwick (1916–2007), whom he married in 1949.

4. *Dionysian:* according to Greek myth, Dionysus was the god of fertility and wine. The adjective suggests the frenzied, orgiastic festivals honoring him.

5. *Marlborough Street:* the Boston street on which the Lowells lived from 1955 to 1958.

10. *mad:* Lowell suffered periodic mental breakdowns.

17. *Rahvs:* American critic Philip Rahv (1908–1973) and his wife. Rahv was coeditor of *Partisan Review.*

22. *South:* Hardwick was born and raised in Lexington, Kentucky.

MEMORIES OF WEST STREET AND LEPKE°

Only teaching on Tuesdays, book-worming
in pajamas fresh from the washer each morning,
I hog a whole house on Boston's
"hardly passionate Marlborough Street,"°
where even the man
scavenging filth in the back alley trash cans,
has two children, a beach wagon, a helpmate,
and is a "young Republican."
I have a nine months' daughter,°
young enough to be my granddaughter.
Like the sun she rises in her flame-flamingo infants' wear.

These are the tranquillized *Fifties,*
and I am forty. Ought I to regret my seedtime?
I was a fire-breathing Catholic C. O.,°
and made my manic statement,
telling off the state and president, and then
sat waiting sentence in the bull pen
beside a Negro boy with curlicues
of marijuana in his hair.

Given a year,
I walked on the roof of the West Street Jail, a short
enclosure like my school soccer court,
and saw the Hudson River once a day
through sooty clothesline entanglements
and bleaching khaki tenements.
Strolling, I yammered metaphysics with Abramowitz,
a jaundice-yellow ("it's really tan")
and fly-weight pacifist,
so vegetarian,
he wore rope shoes and preferred fallen fruit.
He tried to convert Bioff and Brown,°

---

poem title: the West Street Jail in Manhattan, where Lowell spent ten days (before being transferred to the Federal Correctional Center at Danbury, Connecticut) in 1943 after he was sentenced to one year and one day for refusing to serve in the army; Louis " Lepke" Buchalter (1897–1944), a racketeer who headed Murder Incorporated, an association of criminals hired out as assassins, was a fellow prisoner. According to Ian Hamilton's biography *Robert Lowell* (1982), "Lepke says to [Lowell]: 'I'm in for killing. What are you in for?' 'Oh, I'm in for refusing to kill.' "

4. *"hardly passionate Marlborough Street":* a description by the novelist Henry James (1828–1911) of the street where Lowell lived from 1955 to 1958.

9. *daughter:* Harriet, daughter of Lowell and Elizabeth Hardwick.

14. *C.O.:* conscientious objector to war.

31. *Bioff and Brown:* William Bioff and George E. Brown were gangsters who sought to dominate the Hollywood labor scene. They were convicted of extortion in 1943. Brown had been convicted of pandering in 1922. Lowell could have assumed his audience would recognize the reference.

the Hollywood pimps, to his diet.
Hairy, muscular, suburban,
wearing chocolate double-breasted suits,
they blew their tops and beat him black and blue.

I was so out of things, I'd never heard
of the Jehovah's Witnesses.°
"Are you a C.O.?" I asked a fellow jailbird.
"No," he answered, "I'm a J.W."
He taught me the "hospital tuck,"°
and pointed out the T-shirted back
of *Murder Incorporated's* Czar Lepke,
there piling towels on a rack,
or dawdling off to his little segregated cell full
of things forbidden the common man:
a portable radio, a dresser, two toy American
flags tied together with a ribbon of Easter palm.
Flabby, bald, lobotomized,
he drifted in a sheepish calm,
where no agonizing reappraisal
jarred his concentration on the electric chair°—
hanging like an oasis in his air
of lost connections. . . .

1959

SKUNK HOUR°

(For Elizabeth Bishop)

Nautilus Island's° hermit
heiress still lives through winter in her Spartan cottage;
her sheep still graze above the sea.
Her son's a bishop. Her farmer
is first selectman° in our village;
she's in her dotage.

Thirsting for
the hierarchic privacy

---

37. *Jehovah's Witnesses:* members of a Christian religious sect who refuse to support a sovereign other than God (Jehovah) or to participate in war.

40. *hospital tuck:* tucking the ends of bedsheets tightly under a mattress; "hospital corners."

51. *electric chair:* Lepke was executed in March 1944.

poem title: written partly in response to Elizabeth Bishop's poem "The Armadillo," with its somewhat comparable short-line stanzas.

1. *Nautilus Island:* near Castine, Maine, where Lowell had a summer house.

5. *selectman:* official elected in a New England town to manage municipal affairs.

of Queen Victoria's century,°
she buys up all
the eyesores facing her shore,
and lets them fall.

The season's ill—
we've lost our summer millionaire,
who seemed to leap from an L. L. Bean°
catalogue. His nine-knot yawl°
was auctioned off to lobstermen.
A red fox stain covers Blue Hill.°

And now our fairy
decorator brightens his shop for fall;
his fishnet's filled with orange cork,
orange, his cobbler's bench and awl;
there is no money in his work,
he'd rather marry.

One dark night,
my Tudor Ford° climbed the hill's skull;
I watched for love-cars. Lights turned down,
they lay together, hull to hull,
where the graveyard shelves on the town....
My mind's not right.

A car radio bleats,
"Love, O careless Love...."° I hear
my ill-spirit sob in each blood cell,
as if my hand were at its throat....
I myself am hell;°
nobody's here—

only skunks, that search
in the moonlight for a bite to eat.

---

9. *century:* the nineteenth century. Alexandrina Victoria (1819–1901) was queen of Great Britain and Ireland from 1837 to 1901.

15. *L. L. Bean:* a mail-order company based in Freeport, Maine, specializing in sporting and camping equipment.

16. *yawl:* small sailboat.

18. *Blue Hill:* a Maine mountain near where Lowell lived. Lowell said the line was meant to describe the "rusty reddish color of autumn."

26. *Tudor Ford:* two-door Ford automobile.

32. *"Careless Love":* a popular American song of the period.

35. *hell:* "Which way I fly is Hell, myself am Hell," (IV. 75), Satan's words from *Paradise Lost* (1667) by John Milton (1608–1674).

They march on their soles up Main Street:
white stripes, moonstruck eyes' red fire
under the chalk-dry and spar spire
of the Trinitarian Church.

I stand on top
of our back steps and breathe the rich air—
a mother skunk with her column of kittens swills the garbage
    pail.
She jabs her wedge-head in a cup
of sour cream, drops her ostrich tail,
and will not scare.

1959

FOR THE UNION DEAD°

"Relinquunt Omnia Servare Rem Publicam."°

The old South Boston Aquarium stands
in a Sahara of snow now. Its broken windows are boarded.
The bronze weathervane cod has lost half its scales.
The airy tanks are dry.

Once my nose crawled like a snail on the glass;
my hand tingled
to burst the bubbles
drifting from the noses of the cowed, compliant fish.

My hand draws back. I often sigh still
for the dark downward and vegetating kingdom
of the fish and reptile. One morning last March,
I pressed against the new barbed and galvanized

fence on the Boston Common. Behind their cage,
yellow dinosaur steamshovels were grunting
as they cropped up tons of mush and grass
to gouge their underworld garage.

---

poem title: first published as "Colonel Shaw and the Massachusetts 54th" in the 1960 edition of Lowell's *Life Studies,* and then, with this revised title, as the title poem of his 1964 collection. Colonel Robert Gould Shaw (1837–1863) led the first African American regiment (of enlistees) in the American Civil War.

epigraph: Relinquunt . . .: (Latin), "They give up everything to serve the Republic," after the inscription on the bronze relief, a monument to Shaw and his men, sculpted by Augustus Saint-Gaudens (1848–1907), which stands at the edge of Boston Common, a public park across from the Boston State House. Lowell changed the subject of the Latin inscription to read "they," rather than "he," to honor all the men in the regiment more clearly.

Parking spaces luxuriate like civic
sandpiles in the heart of Boston.
A girdle of orange, Puritan-pumpkin colored girders
braces the tingling Statehouse,

shaking over the excavations, as it faces Colonel Shaw
and his bell-cheeked Negro infantry
on St. Gaudens' shaking Civil War relief,
propped by a plank splint against the garage's earthquake.

Two months after marching through Boston,
half the regiment was dead;
at the dedication,
William James° could almost hear the bronze Negroes breathe.

Their monument sticks like a fishbone
in the city's throat.
Its Colonel is as lean
as a compass-needle.

He has an angry wrenlike vigilance,
a greyhound's gentle tautness;
he seems to wince at pleasure,
and suffocate for privacy.

He is out of bounds now. He rejoices in man's lovely,
peculiar power to choose life and die—
when he leads his black soldiers to death,
he cannot bend his back.

On a thousand small town New England greens,
the old white churches hold their air
of sparse, sincere rebellion; frayed flags
quilt the graveyards of the Grand Army of the Republic.°

The stone statues of the abstract Union Soldier
grow slimmer and younger each year—
wasp-wasted, they doze over muskets
and muse through their sideburns. . .

---

28. *William James:* (1842–1910), philosopher and psychologist (and brother of Henry James), who at his "Oration at the Dedication of the Monument" in May 1897 said, "There on foot go the dark outcasts, so true to nature that one can almost hear them breathing as they march."

44. *Grand Army of the Republic:* an organization for Union and Confederate Civil War veterans.

Shaw's father wanted no monument
except the ditch,
where his son's body was thrown
and lost with his "niggers."°

The ditch is nearer.
There are no statues for the last war here;
on Boylston° Street, a commercial photograph
shows Hiroshima boiling

over a Mosler Safe,° the "Rock of Ages"
that survived the blast. Space is nearer.
When I crouch to my television set,
the drained faces° of Negro school-children rise like balloons.

Colonel Shaw
is riding on his bubble,
he waits
for the blessèd break.

The Aquarium is gone. Everywhere,
giant finned cars nose forward like fish;
a savage servility
slides by on grease.

1960

THE MOUTH OF THE HUDSON°

(For Esther Brooks)

A single man stands like a bird-watcher,
and scuffles the pepper and salt snow
from a discarded, gray
Westinghouse Electric cable drum.
He cannot discover America by counting
the chains of condemned freight-trains

---

52. *niggers:* a Confederate officer's epithet for Shaw's troops; on July 18, 1863, Shaw and most of his men were killed during an attack against Fort Wagner in South Carolina. The Confederates buried them in a common grave.

55. *Boylston:* a street in central Boston.

57. *Mosler Safe:* a brand of safe that was photographed as intact in Hiroshima after the United States dropped a nuclear bomb there in 1945. "Rock of Ages": a popular hymn written in 1775 by Augustus Montague Toplady (1740–1778).

60. *drained faces:* probably in relation to civil rights demonstrations supporting the desegregation of schools ordered by the U.S. Supreme Court's *Brown V. Board of Education of Topeka* decision of 1954.

poem title: the mouth of the Hudson River, at Lower New York Bay.

from thirty states. They jolt and jar
and junk in the siding below him.
He has trouble with his balance.
His eyes drop,
and he drifts with the wild ice
ticking seaward down the Hudson,
like the blank sides of a jig-saw puzzle.

The ice ticks seaward like a clock.
A Negro toasts
wheat-seeds over the coke-fumes°
of a punctured barrel.
Chemical air
sweeps in from New Jersey,
and smells of coffee.

Across the river,
ledges of suburban factories tan
in the sulphur-yellow sun
of the unforgivable landscape.

1964

JULY IN WASHINGTON

The stiff spokes of this wheel
touch the sore spots of the earth.

On the Potomac,° swan-white
power launches keep breasting the sulphurous wave.

Otters slide and dive and slick back their hair,
raccoons clean their meat in the creek.

On the circles, green statues ride like South American
liberators above the breeding vegetation—

prongs and spearheads of some equatorial
backland that will inherit the globe.

The elect, the elected . . . they come here bright as dimes,
and die dishevelled and soft.

---

16. *coke-fumes:* from burned coal or distilled petroleum.

3. *Potomac:* a major American river that passes through Washington, D.C., and runs to Chesapeake Bay.

We cannot name their names, or number their dates—
circle on circle, like rings on a tree—

but we wish the river had another shore,
some farther range of delectable mountains,

distant hills powdered blue as a girl's eyelid.
It seems the least little shove would land us there,

that only the slightest repugnance of our bodies
we no longer control could drag us back.

1964

THE MARCH I°

(For Dwight MacDonald)

Under the too white marmoreal Lincoln Memorial,
the too tall marmoreal Washington Obelisk,
gazing into the too long reflecting pool,
the reddish trees, the withering autumn sky,
the remorseless, amplified harangues for peace—
lovely to lock arms, to march absurdly locked
(unlocking to keep my wet glasses from slipping)
to see the cigarette match quaking in my fingers,
then to step off like green Union Army recruits
for the first Bull Run, sped by photographers,
the notables, the girls . . . fear, glory, chaos, rout . . .
our green army staggered out on the miles-long green fields,
met by the other army, the Martian, the ape, the hero,
his new-fangled rifle, his green new steel helmet.

1970

THE MARCH II

Where two or three were flung together, or fifty,
mostly white-haired, or bald, or women . . . sadly
unfit to follow their dream, I sat in the sunset
shade of our Bastille, the Pentagon,
nursing leg- and arch-cramps, my cowardly,
foolhardy heart; and heard, alas, more speeches,

---

poem title: a major demonstration against the Vietnam War, the peace march on the American military's headquarters at the Pentagon, took place in Washington, D.C., on October 21, 1967. Norman Mailer (1923–2007) describes Lowell's role in the events in *The Armies of the Night* (1967).

though the words took heart now to show how weak
we were, and right. An MP sergeant kept
repeating, "March slowly through them. Don't even brush
anyone sitting down." They tiptoed through us
in single file, and then their second wave
trampled us flat and back. Health to those who held,
health to the green steel head . . . to your kind hands
that helped me stagger to my feet, and flee.

1970

CENTRAL PARK°

Scaling small rocks, exhaling smog,
gasping at game-scents like a dog,
now light as pollen, now as white
and winded as a grounded kite—
I watched the lovers occupy
every inch of earth and sky:
one figure of geometry,
multiplied to infinity,
straps down, and sunning openly . . .
each precious, public, pubic tangle
an equilateral triangle,
lost in the park, half covered by
the shade of some low stone or tree.
The stain of fear and poverty
spread through each trapped anatomy,
and darkened every mote of dust.
All wished to leave this drying crust,
borne on the delicate wings of lust
like bees, and cast their fertile drop
into the overwhelming cup.

Drugged and humbled by the smell
of zoo-straw mixed with animal,
the lion prowled his slummy cell,°
serving his life-term in jail—
glaring, grinding, on his heel,
with tingling step and testicle . . .

---

poem title: *Central Park:* the large, 843-acre public park in Manhattan, opened in 1859, the first such landscaped park in the United States. A wonderful public space by day, it is notoriously dangerous at night, a daily transition the poem follows. Lowell has said that he wrote the poem when he was undergoing analysis and crossed the park every day on the way to his therapist.

23. *slummy cell:* at the time the poem was written, the Central Park Zoo was a cramped facility whose heavy cages gave animals little space.

Behind a dripping rock, I found
a one-day kitten on the ground—
deprived, weak, ignorant and blind,
squeaking, tubular, left behind—
dying with its deserter's rich
Welfare lying out of reach:
milk cartons, kidney heaped to spoil,
two plates sheathed with silver foil.

Shadows had stained the afternoon;
high in an elm, a snagged balloon
wooed the attraction of the moon.
Scurrying from the mouth of night,
a single, fluttery, paper kite
grazed Cleopatra's Needle,° and sailed
where the light of the sun had failed.
Then night, the night—the jungle hour,
the rich in his slit-windowed tower . . .
Old Pharaohs starving in your foxholes,
with painted banquets on the walls,
fists knotted in your captives' hair,
tyrants with little food to spare—
all your embalming left you mortal,
glazed, black, and hideously eternal,
all your plunder and gold leaf
only served to draw the thief . . .

We beg delinquents for our life.
Behind each bush, perhaps a knife;
each landscaped crag, each flowering shrub,
hides a policeman with a club.

1967

EPILOGUE

Those blessèd structures, plot and rhyme—
why are they no help to me now
I want to make
something imagined, not recalled?
I hear the noise of my own voice:

40. *Cleopatra's Needle:* a red granite obelisk, sixty-nine feet tall, that stands in Central Park near the Metropolitan Museum of Art at 82nd Street. Originally erected in Egypt about 1475 B.C., it was given to the United States in 1880. There is no actual historical connection to Cleopatra.

The painter's vision is not a lens,
it trembles to caress the light.
But sometimes everything I write
with the threadbare art of my eye
seems a snapshot,
lurid, rapid, garish, grouped,
heightened from life,
yet paralyzed by fact.
All's misalliance.
Yet why not say what happened?
Pray for the grace of accuracy
Vermeer° gave to the sun's illumination
stealing like the tide across a map
to his girl solid with yearning.
We are poor passing facts,
warned by that to give
each figure in the photograph
his living name.

1977

---

17. *Vermeer:* Jan Vermeer (1632–1675), Dutch painter renowned for his luminous portraits and interiors.

GWENDOLYN BROOKS (1917–2000)

Brooks was born in Topeka, Kansas. Her mother was a schoolteacher, her father a janitor. The family moved to Chicago almost immediately, and there Brooks spent most of her life. She attended Wilson Junior College in the mid-1930s, meanwhile meeting and being encouraged by James Weldon Johnson and Langston Hughes. She also wrote a poetry column for the *Chicago Defender.* In the following decade, she attended a poetry workshop where she read widely in modernist poetry, while also being schooled in traditional forms and meters; her first book, *A Street in Bronzeville*, appeared in 1945.

A key moment in her development came in 1967 when she attended the Black Writers Conference at Fisk University. Thereafter she became more active in the Chicago wing of the Black Arts Movement and switched from her New York publisher, Harper and Row, to Broadside Press in Detroit and then Third World Press in Chicago. Chicago's South Side black ghetto has always figured heavily in her work; she is in a way a poet of that neighborhood. Yet out of it came poems addressing the general status of race in America in a style that mixes international modernism with local experience. Brooks worked hard and successfully to reach a broad popular audience, but her poems are also deeply challenging. For years, she read them aloud with great success—using rhythm, emphasis, intonation, and strategic pauses to make them accessible—but close attention reveals a rhetorical intricacy that owes as much to high modernism as to populism. Even "We Real Cool," offered here in a captivating blackboard-style broadside version, only replicates street slang in its opening stanza. She invented a unique voice that speaks simultaneously from dispossession and from knowledge of the dominant high culture.

A SONG IN THE FRONT YARD

I've stayed in the front yard all my life.
I want a peek at the back
Where it's rough and untended and hungry weed grows.
A girl gets sick of a rose.

I want to go in the back yard now
And maybe down the alley,
To where the charity children play.
I want a good time today.

They do some wonderful things.
They have some wonderful fun.
My mother sneers, but I say it's fine
How they don't have to go in at quarter to nine.
My mother, she tells me that Johnnie Mae

Will grow up to be a bad woman.
That George'll be taken to Jail soon or late
(On account of last winter he sold our back gate.)

But I say it's fine. Honest, I do.
And I'd like to be a bad woman, too,
And wear the brave stockings of night-black lace
And strut down the streets with paint on my face.

1945

OF DE WITT WILLIAMS ON HIS WAY TO LINCOLN CEMETERY°

He was born in Alabama.
He was bred in Illinois.
He was nothing but a
Plain black boy.

Swing low swing low sweet sweet chariot.°
Nothing but a plain black boy.

Drive him past the Pool Hall.
Drive him past the Show.
Blind within his casket,
But maybe he will know.

Down through Forty-seventh Street:°
Underneath the L,°
And—Northwest Corner, Prairie,
That he loved so well.

Don't forget the Dance Halls—
Warwick and Savoy,
Where he picked his women, where
He drank his liquid joy.

Born in Alabama.
Bred in Illinois.
He was nothing but a
Plain black boy.

---

poem title: *Lincoln Cemetery:* an African American cemetery in Chicago.

5. *chariot:* from the African American spiritual *Swing Low, Sweet Chariot.*

11. *Forty-seventh Street:* the main street of Bronzeville, an African American neighborhood in Chicago.

12. *L:* the elevated railway.

Swing low swing low sweet sweet chariot.
Nothing but a plain black boy.

1945

GAY CHAPS AT THE BAR°

souvenir for Staff Sergeant Raymond Brooks° and every other soldier

GAY CHAPS AT THE BAR

. . . and guys I knew in the States, young officers, return from the front crying and trembling. Gay chaps at the bar in Los Angeles, Chicago, New York. . . .
LIEUTENANT WILLIAM COUCH
in the South Pacific

We knew how to order. Just the dash
Necessary. The length of gaiety in good taste.
Whether the raillery° should be slightly iced
And given green, or served up hot and lush.
And we knew beautifully how to give to women
The summer spread, the tropics, of our love.
When to persist, or hold a hunger off.
Knew white speech. How to make a look an omen.
But nothing ever taught us to be islands.
And smart, athletic language for this hour
Was not in the curriculum. No stout
Lesson showed how to chat with death. We brought
No brass° fortissimo,° among our talents,°
To holler down the lions° in this air.

STILL DO I KEEP MY LOOK, MY IDENTITY . . .

Each body has its art, its precious prescribed
Pose, that even in passion's droll contortions, waltzes,
Or push of pain—or when a grief has stabbed,

---

poem title: the poem is a sequence of twelve sonnets based in part on letters Brooks received from black soldiers in World War II, when the U.S. Army was still segregated; black soldiers thus risked their lives at the same time as they were structurally humiliated; the "bar" is not only a tavern but also the color bar and the bar between life and death.

dedication: *Raymond Brooks:* Brooks's brother.

3. *raillery:* good-natured teasing.

13. *brass:* alludes at once to a brass band, military brass (officers), and the adjective "brassy," or brazen.

13. *fortissimo:* very loudly.

13. *talents:* see Matthew 25.15–25 for the biblical story of the talents.

14. *lions:* airplanes (bombers).

Or hatred hacked—is its, and nothing else's.
Each body has its pose. No other stock
That is irrevocable, perpetual
And its to keep. In castle or in shack.
With rags or robes. Through good, nothing, or ill.
And even in death a body, like no other
On any hill or plain or crawling cot
Or gentle for the lilyless hasty pall
(Having twisted, gagged, and then sweet-ceased to
 bother),
Shows the old personal art, the look. Shows what
It showed at baseball. What it showed in school.

MY DREAMS, MY WORKS, MUST WAIT TILL AFTER HELL

I hold my honey and I store my bread
In little jars and cabinets of my will.
I label clearly, and each latch and lid
I bid, Be firm till I return from hell.
I am very hungry. I am incomplete.
And none can tell when I may dine again.
No man can give me any word but Wait,
The puny light. I keep eyes pointed in;
Hoping that, when the devil days of my hurt
Drag out to their last dregs and I resume
On such legs as are left me, in such heart
As I can manage, remember to go home,
My taste will not have turned insensitive
To honey and bread old purity could love.

LOOKING

You have no word for soldiers to enjoy
The feel of, as an apple, and to chew
With masculine satisfaction. Not "good-by!"
"Come back!" or "careful!" Look, and let him go.
"Good-by!" is brutal, and "come back!" the raw
Insistence of an idle desperation
Since could he favor he would favor now.
He will be "careful!" if he has permission.
Looking is better. At the dissolution
Grab greatly with the eye, crush in a steel
Of study—Even that is vain. Expression,
The touch or look or word, will little avail,
The brawniest will not beat back the storm
Nor the heaviest haul your little boy from harm.

PIANO AFTER WAR

On a snug evening I shall watch her fingers,
Cleverly ringed, declining to clever pink,
Beg glory from the willing keys. Old hungers
Will break their coffins, rise to eat and thank.
And music, warily, like the golden rose
That sometimes after sunset warms the west,
Will warm that room, persuasively suffuse
That room and me, rejuvenate a past.
But suddenly, across my climbing fever
Of proud delight—a multiplying cry.
A cry of bitter dead men who will never
Attend a gentle maker of musical joy.
Then my thawed eye will go again to ice.
And stone will shove the softness from my face.

MENTORS°

For I am rightful fellow of their band.
My best allegiances are to the dead.
I swear to keep the dead upon my mind,
Disdain for all time to be overglad.
Among spring flowers, under summer trees,
By chilling autumn waters, in the frosts
Of supercilious winter—all my days
I'll have as mentors those reproving ghosts.
And at that cry, at that remotest whisper,
I'll stop my casual business. Leave the banquet.
Or leave the ball—reluctant to unclasp her
Who may be fragrant as the flower she wears,
Make gallant bows and dim excuses, then quit
Light for the midnight that is mine and theirs.

THE WHITE TROOPS HAD THEIR ORDERS BUT THE NEGROES LOOKED LIKE MEN

They had supposed their formula was fixed.
They had obeyed instructions to devise
A type of cold, a type of hooded gaze.
But when the Negroes came they were perplexed.
These Negroes looked like men. Besides, it taxed
Time and the temper to remember those

---

poem title: Mentors: wise and trusted counselors or teachers.

Congenital° iniquities° that cause
Disfavor of the darkness. Such as boxed
Their feelings properly, complete to tags—
A box for dark men and a box for Other—
Would often find the contents had been scrambled.
Or even switched. Who really gave two figs?
Neither the earth nor heaven ever trembled.
And there was nothing startling in the weather.

FIRSTLY INCLINED TO TAKE WHAT IT IS TOLD

Thee sacrosanct,° Thee sweet, Thee crystalline,
With the full jewel wile° of mighty light—
With the narcotic milk of peace for men
Who find Thy beautiful center and relate
Thy round command, Thy grand, Thy° mystic good—
Thee like the classic quality of a star:
A little way from warmth, a little sad,
Delicately lovely to adore—
I had been brightly ready to believe.
For youth is a frail thing, not unafraid.
Firstly inclined to take what it is told,
Firstly inclined to lean. Greedy to give
Faith tidy and total. To a total God.
With billowing heartiness no whit° withheld.

"GOD WORKS IN A MYSTERIOUS WAY"°

But often now the youthful eye cuts down its
Own dainty veiling. Or submits to winds.
And many an eye that all its age had drawn its
Beam from a Book endures the impudence
Of modem glare that never heard of tact
Or timeliness, or Mystery that shrouds
Immortal joy: it merely can direct
Chancing feet across dissembling clods.
Out from Thy shadows, from Thy pleasant meadows,
Quickly, in undiluted light. Be glad, whose

---

91. *congenital:* existing at or before birth.

91. *iniquities:* acts of wickedness, injustice; these lines are an idiosyncratic condemnation of racism.

99. *sacrosanct:* sacred and inviolable, suggests the fusion of God and country.

100. *wile:* trickery, cunning.

103. *Thy:* the repetition suggests the Christian trinity, with "thy mystic good" being the Holy Ghost.

112. *whit:* particle.

poem title: an ironic adaptation of one of William Cowper's (1731–1800) *Olney Hymns* (1779): "God moves in mysterious ways."

Mansions are bright, to right Thy children's air.
If Thou be more than hate or atmosphere
Step forth in splendor, mortify our wolves.
Or we assume a sovereignty ourselves.

LOVE NOTE

I: SURELY

Surely you stay my certain own, you stay
My you. All honest, lofty as a cloud.
Surely I could come now and find you high,
As mine as you ever were; should not be awed.
Surely your word would pop as insolent
As always: "Why, of course I love you, dear."
Your gaze, surely, ungauzed° as I could want.
Your touches, that never were careful, what they were.
Surely—But I am very off from that.
From surely. From indeed. From the decent arrow
That was my clean naïveté and my faith.
This morning men deliver wounds and death.
They will deliver death and wounds tomorrow.
And I doubt all. You.° Or a violet.

LOVE NOTE

II: FLAGS

Still, it is dear defiance now to carry
Fair flags of you above my indignation,
Top, with a pretty glory and a merry
Softness, the scattered pound of my cold passion.
I pull you down my foxhole. Do you mind?
You burn in bits of saucy color then.
I let you flutter out against the pained
Volleys. Against my power crumpled and wan.°
You, and the yellow pert exuberance
Of dandelion days, unmocking sun;
The blowing of clear wind in your gay hair;
Love changeful in you (like a music, or
Like a sweet mournfulness, or like a dance,
Or like the tender struggle of a fan).

---

133. *ungauzed:* not wounded, not obscured; in what wars, we might ask, does a gaze amount to gauze?

140. *You:* America.

148. *wan:* unnaturally pale, weak.

THE PROGRESS

And still we wear our uniforms, follow
The cracked cry of the bugles, comb and brush
Our pride and prejudice, doctor the sallow
Initial ardor, wish to keep it fresh.
Still we applaud the President's voice and face.
Still we remark on patriotism, sing,
Salute the flag, thrill heavily, rejoice
For death of men who too saluted, sang.
But inward grows a soberness, an awe,
A fear, a deepening hollow through the cold.
For even if we come out standing up
How shall we smile, congratulate: and how
Settle in chairs? Listen, listen. The step
Of iron feet again. And again wild.

1945

WE REAL COOL

The Pool Players
Seven at the Golden Shovel

We real cool. We
Left school. We

Lurk late. We
Strike straight. We

Sing sin. We
Thin gin. We

Jazz June. We
Die soon.

1959

THE BALLAD OF RUDOLPH REED

Rudolph Reed was oaken.°
His wife was oaken too.
And his two good girls and his good little man
Oakened as they grew.

"I am not hungry for berries.
I am not hungry for bread.

---

1. *oaken:* both strong like an oak and brown like one.

But hungry hungry for a house
Where at night a man in bed

"May never hear the plaster
Stir as if in pain.
May never hear the roaches
Falling like fat rain.

"Where never wife and children need
Go blinking through the gloom.
Where every room of many rooms
Will be full of room.

"Oh my home may have its east or west
Or north or south behind it.
All I know is I shall know it,
And fight for it when I find it."

It was in a street of bitter white
That he made his application.
For Rudolph Reed was oakener°
Than others in the nation.

The agent's steep and steady stare
Corroded to a grin.
Why, you black old, tough old hell of a man,
Move your family in!

Nary a grin grinned Rudolph Reed,
Nary a curse cursed he,
But moved in his House. With his dark little wife,
And his dark little children three.

A neighbor would *look,* with a yawning eye
That squeezed into a slit.
But the Rudolph Reeds and the children three
Were too joyous to notice it.

For were they not firm in a home of their own
With windows everywhere
And a beautiful banistered stair
And a front yard for flowers and a back yard for grass?

---

23. *oakener:* more courageous, but also darker and more angry.

The first night, a rock, big as two fists.
The second, a rock big as three.
But nary a curse cursed Rudolph Reed.
(Though oaken as man could be.)

The third night, a silvery ring of glass.
Patience ached to endure.
But he looked, and lo! small Mabel's blood
Was staining her gaze so pure.

Then up did rise our Rudolph Reed
And pressed the hand of his wife,
And went to the door with a thirty-four
And a beastly butcher knife.

He ran like a mad thing into the night.
And the words in his mouth were stinking.
By the time he had hurt his first white man
He was no longer thinking.

By the time he had hurt his fourth white man
Rudolph Reed was dead.
His neighbors gathered and kicked his corpse.
"Nigger—" his neighbors said.

Small Mabel whimpered all night long,
For calling herself the cause.
Her oak-eyed mother did no thing
But change the bloody gauze.

1961

THE BLACKSTONE RANGERS°

I

As Seen by Disciplines°

There they are
Thirty at the corner.
Black, raw, ready.
Sores in the city
that do not want to heal.

---

poem title: the Blackstone Rangers are a Chicago teenage gang; Brooks conducted a creative writing class with some of the members. Blackstone Street is the eastern boundary of a Chicago black ghetto.

section head: *Disciplines:* law officers.

II

The Leaders

Jeff. Gene. Geronimo. And Bop.
They cancel, cure and curry.
Hardly the dupes of the downtown thing
the cold bonbon,
the rhinestone thing. And hardly
in a hurry.
Hardly Belafonte, King,
Black Jesus, Stokely, Malcolm X or Rap.
Bungled trophies.
Their country is a Nation on no map.

Jeff, Gene, Geronimo and Bop
in the passionate noon,
in bewitching night
are the detailed men, the copious men.
They curry, cure,
they cancel, cancelled images whose Concerts
are not divine, vivacious; the different tins
are intense last entries; pagan argument;
translations of the night.

The Blackstone bitter bureaus
(bureaucracy is footloose) edit, fuse
unfashionable damnations and descent;
and exulting, monstrous hand on monstrous hand,
construct, strangely, a monstrous pearl or grace.

III

Gang Girls

A Rangerette

Gang Girls are sweet exotics.
Mary Ann
uses the nutrients of her orient,
but sometimes sighs for Cities of blue and jewel
beyond her Ranger rim of Cottage Grove.°
(Bowery Boys, Disciples, Whip-Birds will
dissolve no margins, stop no savory sanctities.)

34. *Cottage Grove:* a street in the black ghetto.

Mary is
a rose in a whiskey glass.

Mary's
Februaries shudder and are gone. Aprils
fret frankly, lilac hurries on.
Summer is a hard irregular ridge.
October looks away.
And that's the Year!
                    Save for her bugle-love.
Save for the bleat of not-obese devotion.
Save for Somebody Terribly Dying, under
the philanthropy of robins. Save for her Ranger
bringing
an amount of rainbow in a string-drawn bag.
"Where did you get the diamond?" Do not ask:
but swallow, straight, the spirals of his flask
and assist him at your zipper; pet his lips
and help him clutch you.

Love's another departure.
Will there be any arrivals, confirmations?
Will there be gleaning?

Mary, the Shakedancer's child
from the rooming-flat, pants carefully, peers at
her laboring lover. . . .
                    Mary! Mary Ann!
Settle for sandwiches! settle for stocking caps!
for sudden blood, aborted carnival,
the props and niceties of non-loneliness—
the rhymes of Leaning.

1968

MALCOLM X

For Dudley Randall

Original.
Ragged-round.
Rich-robust.

He had the hawk-man's eyes.
We gasped. We saw the maleness.
The maleness raking out and making guttural the air
and pushing us to walls.

And in a soft and fundamental hour
a sorcery devout and vertical
beguiled the world.

He opened us—
who was a key,

who was a man.

1968

YOUNG AFRIKANS

of the furious

Who take Today and jerk it out of joint
have made new underpinnings and a Head.

Blacktime is time for chimeful
poemhood
but they decree a
jagged chiming now.

If there are flowers flowers
must come out to the road. Rowdy!—
knowing where wheels and people are,
knowing where whips and screams are,
knowing where deaths are, where the kind kills are.

As for that other kind of kindness,
if there is milk it must be mindful.
The milkofhumankindness must be mindful
as wily wines.
Must be fine fury.
Must be mega, must be main.

Taking Today (to jerk it out of joint)
the hardheroic maim the
leechlike-as-usual who use,
adhere to, carp, and harm.

And they await,
across the Changes and the spiraling dead,
our Black revival, our Black vinegar,
our hands, and our hot blood.

1970

THE BOY DIED IN MY ALLEY

Without my having known.
Policeman said, next morning,
"Apparently died Alone."
"You heard a shot?" Policeman said.
Shots I hear and Shots I hear.
I never see the dead.

The Shot that killed him yes I heard
as I heard the Thousand shots before;
careening tinnily down the nights
across my years and arteries.

Policeman pounded on my door.
"Who is it?" "POLICE!" Policeman yelled.
"A Boy was dying in your alley.
A Boy is dead, and in your alley.
And have you known this Boy before?"

I have known this Boy before.
I have known this Boy before, who
ornaments my alley.
I never saw his face at all.
I never saw his futurefall.
But I have known this Boy.

I have always heard him deal with death.
I have always heard the shout, the volley.
I have closed my heart-ears late and early.
And I have killed him ever.

I joined the Wild and killed him
with knowledgeable unknowing.
I saw where he was going.
I saw him Crossed. And seeing,
I did not take him down.

He cried not only "Father!"
but "Mother!
Sister!
Brother."

The cry climbed up the alley.
It went up to the wind.

It hung upon the heaven
for a long
stretch-strain of Moment.

The red floor of my alley
is a special speech to me.

1975

TO THOSE OF MY SISTERS WHO KEPT THEIR NATURALS

Never to look
a hot comb in the teeth.

Sisters!
I love you.
Because you love you.
Because you are erect.
Because you are also bent.
In season, stern, kind.
Crisp, soft—in season.
And you withhold.
And you extend.
And you Step out.
And you go back.
And you extend again.
Your eyes, loud-soft, with crying and
with smiles,
are older than a million years.
And they are young.
You reach, in season.
You subside, in season.
And All
below the richrough righttime of your hair.
You have not bought Blondine.
You have not hailed the hot-comb recently.
You never worshipped Marilyn Monroe.
You say: Farrah's hair is hers.
You have not wanted to be white.
Nor have you testified to adoration of that
state
with the advertisement of imitation
(*never* successful because the hot-comb is
laughing too.)

But oh the rough dark Other music!
the Real,
the Right.
The natural Respect of Self and Seal!
    Sisters!
Your hair is Celebration in the world!

1980

TO THE DIASPORA°

TO THE DIASPORA

you did not know you were Afrika

When you set out for Afrika
you did not know you were going.
Because
you did not know you were Afrika.
You did not know the Black continent
that had to be reached
was you.

I could not have told you then that some sun
would come,
somewhere over the road,
would come evoking the diamonds
of you, the Black continent—
somewhere over the road.
You would not have believed my mouth.

When I told you, meeting you somewhere close
to the heat and youth of the road,
liking my loyalty, liking belief,
you smiled and you thanked me but very little believed me.

Here is some sun. Some.
Now off into the places rough to reach.
Though dry, though drowsy, all unwillingly a-wobble,
into the dissonant and dangerous crescendo.
Your work, that was done, to be done to be done to be done.

---

poem title: the term "diaspora," which derives from a Greek word meaning "dispersion," originally referred only to the long exile of the Jews from the biblical homeland in Palestine. More recently, the term has been extended to apply to the historical experience of other peoples forced to leave their home countries, such as the Africans sold into slavery and brought to the New World.

MUSIC FOR MARTYRS

Steve Biko, killed in South Afrika
for loving his people

I feel a regret, Steve Biko.
I am sorry, Steve Biko.
    Biko the Emerger
laid low.

Now for the shapely American memorials.
The polished tears.
The timed tempest.
The one-penny poems.
The hollow guitars.
The joke oh jaunty.
The vigorous veal-stuffed voices.
The singings, the white lean lasses with streaming
yellow hair.
Now for the organized nothings.
Now for the weep-words.

Now for the rigid recountings
of your tracts, your triumphs, your tribulations.

A WELCOME SONG FOR LAINI NZINGA

Born November 24, 1975

Hello, little Sister.
Coming through the rim of the world.
We are here! to meet you and to mold and to maintain you.
With excited eyes we see you.
With welcoming ears we hear the
clean sound of new language.
The language of Laini-Nzinga.
We love and we receive you as our own.

TO BLACK WOMEN

Sisters,
where there is cold silence—
no hallelujahs, no hurrahs at all, no handshakes,
no neon red or blue, no smiling faces—
prevail.
Prevail across the editors of the world!

who are obsessed, self-honeying and self-crowned
in the seduced arena.

It has been a
hard trudge, with fainting, bandaging and death.
There have been startling confrontations.
There have been tramplings. Tramplings
of monarchs and of other men.

But there remain large countries in your eyes.
Shrewd sun.
The civil balance.
The listening secrets.

And you create and train your flowers still.

TO PRISONERS

I call for you cultivation of strength in the dark.
Dark gardening
in the vertigo cold.
In the hot paralysis.
Under the wolves and coyotes of particular silences.
Where it is dry.
Where it is dry.
I call for you
cultivation of victory Over
long blows that you want to give and blows you are going to get.

Over
what wants to crumble you down, to sicken
you. I call for you
cultivation of strength to heal and enhance
in the non-cheering dark,
in the many many mornings-after;
in the chalk and choke.

1981

WILLIAM BRONK (1918–1999)

William Bronk spent all his life in upstate New York, in the small town of Hudson Falls. He lived in the family home, a Victorian house, and managed the business, a retail fuel and building supply firm, that he inherited from his father, from 1945 until the mid-1970s. Bronk was born in Fort Edward, New York, and educated at Dartmouth. He served as an army historian during World War II and wrote *A History of the Eastern Defense Command and of the Defense of the Atlantic Coast of the United States in the Second World War* (1945). A critical book, *The Brother of Elysium* (1980), includes essays on several nineteenth-century American writers. Bronk's work has had a paradoxical thematic consistency throughout his career: he concentrates on how we construct knowledge of the world and yet his work disrupts our confidence in those very mental operations. Sometimes the topical focus is very specific, as in his poems about music, or the poems included here about the Mayan ruins, also the subject of his essays in *The New World* (1974). At other times, the topics are more abstractly epistemological or phenomenological, as in his poems about light. He avoided the poetry establishment for most of his life, meanwhile remaining one of the relatively few poets with a stable income. His career was an exceptionally focused one, with a wry intensity that is uniquely his own.

AT TIKAL

Mountains they knew, and jungle, the sun, the stars—
these seemed to be there. But even after they slashed
the jungle and burned it and planted the comforting corn,
they were discontent. They wanted the shape of things.
They imagined a world and it was as if it were there
—a world with stars in their places and rain that came
when they called. It closed them in. Stone by stone,
as they built this city, these temples, they built this world.
They believed it. This was the world, and they,
of course, were the people. Now trees make up
assemblies and crowd in the wide plazas. Trees
climb the stupendous steps and rubble them.
In the jungle, the temples are little mountains again.

It is always hard like this, not having a world,
to imagine one, to go to the far edge
apart and imagine, to wall whether in
or out, to build a kind of cage for the sake
of feeling the bars around us, to give shape to a world.
And oh, it is always a world and not the world.

1956

THE MAYAN GLYPHS UNREAD

Yes, the porpoises of course, it could
be of purport to talk to them. See what they say.
Indeed, what wouldn't we give? But the Mayans,—oh,
not but what I'd want to know, I would.
They were different from us in many ways. But we know
something about them, quite a bit in fact.
They were men, which makes me wonder could they have any more
to say to us than we have to say, ourselves,
to each other, or rather, could they have a better way
to say it that gets across? It seems to me
we all speak in undeciphered glyphs
as much as they do. OK. I'd like to know.
What's new with them? No, I'd try to talk
with anybody if I thought I could. You.
I'd try to talk to you. What do you know?

1969

I THOUGHT IT WAS HARRY

Excuse me. I thought for a moment you were someone I know.
It happens to me. One time at *The Circle in the Square*°
when it *was* still in the Square, I turned my head
when the lights went up and saw me there with a girl
and another couple. Out in the lobby, I looked
right at him and he looked away. I was no one he knew.
Well, it takes two, as they say, and I don't know what
it would prove anyway. Do we know who we are,
do you think? Kids seem to know. One time I asked
a little girl. She said she'd been sick. She said
she'd looked different and felt different. I said,
"Maybe it wasn't you. How do you know?"
"Oh, I was me," she said, "I know I was."

That part doesn't bother me anymore
or not the way it did. I'm nobody else
and nobody anyway. It's all the rest
I don't know. I don't know anything.
It hit me. I thought it was Harry when I saw you
and thought, "I'll ask Harry." I don't suppose
he knows, though. It's not that I get confused.
I don't mean that. If someone appeared and said,

---

2. *The Circle in the Square:* Broadway theater.

"Ask me questions," I wouldn't know where to start.
I don't have questions even. It's the way I fade
as though I were someone's snapshot left in the light.
And the background fades the way it might if we woke
in the wrong twilight and things got dim and grey
while we waited for them to sharpen. Less and less
is real. No fixed point. Questions fix
a point, as answers do. Things move again
and the only place to move is away. It was wrong:
questions and answers are what to be without
and all we learn is how sound our ignorance is.
That's what I wanted to talk to Harry about.
You looked like him. Thank you anyway.

1971

WHERE IT ENDS

The gentleness of the slant October light
cancels whatever else we might have thought.
It is a hard world, empty and cruel;
but this light, oh Jesus Christ! This light!

The maple leaves, passive in front of the house,
are laved in it, abandoned, green gone.
That nothing else should matter but this light.
Gentleness, gentleness, the light.

1975

LEFT ALONE

Left alone as it seems we often are,
we can determine parts of our lives and the lives
of some around us. More than that, we say
what the world may be, how it came about
and why. We give out truth. How great we are.

Something that doesn't mean to contravene
us, something that needn't even know we are there,
in going about its own procedures, sweeps
it all away: whatever we did or said.
Sweeps us away. We are beside the point.

No matter. Close beside. The seriousness
of desire is a voice that sings us up
and, in its singing, humbles whatever claims.

1993

ROBERT DUNCAN (1919–1988)

Born in Oakland, California, Duncan was adopted after his mother died in childbirth and given the name Robert Edward Symmes, but Duncan took his biological father's surname in 1941. He studied at the University of California at Berkeley from 1936 to 1938, spent some time in New York, and then returned to San Francisco, where he became a key figure in what came to be known as the "San Francisco Renaissance" and where he resided for the rest of his life. A conscientious objector during World War II, he studied at Berkeley again at the end of the 1940s, during which time he made early and courageous statements on behalf of gay rights. He was an active voice again in the antiwar movement of the 1960s, and for some years he declined to publish his poems, opting instead to circulate copies to a few friends. The painter Jess Collins (1923–2004) was his companion from 1951 until the end of his life. People interested in his work should seek out some of the beautiful holograph editions of his poems.

As the selections here demonstrate, Duncan excelled at both highly musical formal stanzas and at open form poems aimed at a field effect, which Duncan called a "grand collage." The two poems from "Passages" belong to an open-ended sequence that, unlike Pound's *Cantos,* was not designed to build to a decisive synthesis but rather to develop with history, Duncan's life, and his creative vision. Rich with literary and historical references, Duncan's sequence sides with love and against tyranny. His poetics is passionate and visionary, but aware of the compromising tendencies in the ecstasy it seeks, as a comparison of related elements in "The Torso" and "Up Rising" will suggest. Duncan's poetry manages to be both erudite and prophetic, both profoundly religious and erotic.

OFTEN I AM PERMITTED TO RETURN TO A MEADOW

as if it were a scene made-up by the mind,
that is not mine, but is a made place,

that is mine, it is so near to the heart,
an eternal pasture folded in all thought
so that there is a hall therein

that is a made place, created by light
wherefrom the shadows that are forms fall.

Wherefrom fall all architectures I am
I say are likenesses of the First Beloved
whose flowers are flames lit to the Lady.

She it is Queen Under The Hill
whose hosts are a disturbance of words within words
that is a field folded.

It is only a dream of the grass blowing
east against the source of the sun
in an hour before the sun's going down

whose secret we see in a children's game
of ring a round of roses told.

Often I am permitted to return to a meadow
as if it were a given property of the mind
that certain bounds hold against chaos,

that is a place of first permission,
everlasting omen of what is.

1960

MY MOTHER WOULD BE A FALCONRESS

My mother would be a falconress,
and I, her gay falcon treading her wrist,
would fly to bring back
from the blue of the sky to her, bleeding, a prize,
where I dream in my little hood with many bells
jangling when I'd turn my head.

My mother would be a falconress,
and she sends me as far as her will goes.
She lets me ride to the end of her curb
where I fall back in anguish.
I dread that she will cast me away,
for I fall, I mis-take, I fail in her mission.

She would bring down the little birds.
And I would bring down the little birds.
When will she let me bring down the little birds,
pierced from their flight with their necks broken,
their heads like flowers limp from the stem?

I tread my mother's wrist and would draw blood.
Behind the little hood my eyes are hooded.
I have gone back into my hooded silence,
talking to myself and dropping off to sleep.

For she has muffled my dreams in the hood she has made me,
sewn round with bells, jangling when I move.
She rides with her little falcon upon her wrist.
She uses a barb that brings me to cower.
She sends me abroad to try my wings
and I come back to her. I would bring down
the little birds to her
I may not tear into, I must bring back perfectly.

I tear at her wrist with my beak to draw blood,
and her eye holds me, anguisht, terrifying.
She draws a limit to my flight.
Never beyond my sight, she says.
She trains me to fetch and to limit myself in fetching.
She rewards me with meat for my dinner.
But I must never eat what she sends me to bring her.

Yet it would have been beautiful, if she would have carried me,
always, in a little hood with the bells ringing,
at her wrist, and her riding
to the great falcon hunt, and me
flying up to the curb of my heart from her heart
to bring down the skylark from the blue to her feet,
straining, and then released for the flight.

My mother would be a falconress,
and I her gerfalcon, raised at her will,
from her wrist sent flying, as if I were her own
pride, as if her pride
knew no limits, as if her mind
sought in me flight beyond the horizon.

Ah, but high, high in the air I flew.
And far, far beyond the curb of her will,
were the blue hills where the falcons nest.
And then I saw west to the dying sun—
it seemd my human soul went down in flames.

I tore at her wrist, at the hold she had for me,
until the blood ran hot and I heard her cry out,
far, far beyond the curb of her will •

to horizons of stars beyond the ringing hills of the world where
    the falcons nest
I saw, and I tore at her wrist with my savage beak.

I flew, as if sight flew from the anguish in her eye beyond her
sight,
sent from my striking loose, from the cruel strike at her wrist,
striking out from the blood to be free of her.

My mother would be a falconress,
and even now, years after this,
when the wounds I left her had surely heald,
and the woman is dead,
her fierce eyes closed, and if her heart
were broken, it is stilld •

I would be a falcon and go free.
I tread her wrist and wear the hood,
talking to myself, and would draw blood.

1968

THE TORSO PASSAGES 18

Most beautiful! the red-flowering eucalyptus,
the madrone, the yew

Is he . . .

So thou wouldst smile, and take me in thine arms
The sight of London to my exiled eyes
Is as Elysium to a new-come soul°

If he be Truth
I would dwell in the illusion of him

His hands unlocking from chambers of my male body

such an idea in man's image

rising tides that sweep me towards him

. . . *homosexual?*

and at the treasure of his mouth

pour forth my soul

4–6. *So . . . soul:* the italicized stanza is from the play *Edward II* (1590) by the British dramatist Chistopher Marlowe (1564–1593). These lines from the play's opening speech are spoken by Edward's young friend Gaveston, who is recalled from banishment when the king ascends to the throne. Gaveston is murdered in the course of the play.

his soul commingling

I thought a Being more than vast, His body leading
into Paradise, his eyes

quickening a fire in me, a trembling

hieroglyph: At the root of the neck

the clavicle, for the neck is the stem of the great artery
upward into his head that is beautiful

At the rise of the pectoral muscle,

the nipples, for the breasts are like sleeping fountains
of feeling in man, waiting above the beat of his heart,
shielding the rise and fall of his breath, to be
awakend

At the axis of his mid hriff

the navel, for in the pit of his stomach the chord from
which first he was fed has its temple

At the root of the groin

the pubic hair, for the torso is the stem in which the man
flowers forth and leads to the stamen of flesh in which
his seed rises

a wave of need and desire over taking me

cried out my name

(This was long ago; It was another life)

and said,

What do you want of me?

I do not know, I said. I have fallen in love. He
has brought me into heights and depths my heart
would fear without him. His look

pierces my side° • fire eyes •

---

42. *pierces my side:* the image of the wounded Christ is woven together here and in the next six lines, with references to man's fall, to Christ's incarnation and resurrection, and to human love and passion.

I have been waiting for you, he said:
I know what you desire

you do not yet know but through me •

And I am with you everywhere. In your falling

I have fallen from a high place. I have raised myself

from darkness in your rising

wherever you are

my hand in your hand seeking the locks, the keys

I am there. Gathering me, you gather

your Self •

For my Other is not a woman but a man

the King upon whose bosom let me lie.°

1968

UP RISING PASSAGES 25

Now Johnson° would go up to join the great simulacra of men,
Hitler and Stalin, to work his fame
with planes roaring out from Guam over Asia,
all America become a sea of toiling men
stirrd at his will, which would be a bloated thing,
drawing from the underbelly of the nation
such blood and dreams as swell the idiot psyche
out of its courses into an elemental thing
until his name stinks with burning meat and heapt honors

And men wake to see that they are used like things
spent in a great potlach, this Texas barbecue
of Asia, Africa, and all the Americas,

---

54. *King . . . lie:* a line from Marlowe, *Edward II.*

1. *Johnson:* Lyndon Baines Johnson (1908–1973), thirty-sixth president of the United States (1963–1969); his domestic accomplishments were overshadowed by his disastrous commitment to the Vietnam War. He was born and grew up in Texas.

And the professional military behind him, thinking
to use him as they thought to use Hitler
without losing control of their business of war,

But the mania, the ravening eagle of America
as Lawrence° saw him "bird of men that are masters,
lifting the rabbit-blood of the myriads up into . . ."
into something terrible, gone beyond bounds, or
As Blake° saw America in figures of fire and blood raging,
. . . in what image? the ominous roar in the air,
the omnipotent wings, the all-American boy in the cockpit
loosing his flow of napalm, below in the jungles
"any life at all or sign of life" his target, drawing now
not with crayons in his secret room
the burning of homes and the torture of mothers and fathers and
children,
their hair a-flame, screaming in agony, but
in the line of duty, for the might and enduring fame
of Johnson, for the victory of American will over its victims,
releasing his store of destruction over the enemy,
in terror and hatred of all communal things, of communion,
of communism •

has raised from the private rooms of small-town bosses and
businessmen,
from the council chambers of the gangs that run the great cities,
swollen with the votes of millions,
from the fearful hearts of good people in the suburbs turning the
savory meat over the charcoal burners and heaping their barbecue
plates with more than they can eat,
from the closed meeting-rooms of regents of universities and sessions
of profiteers

—back of the scene: the atomic stockpile; the vials of synthesized
diseases eager biologists have developt over half a century dreaming
of the bodies of mothers and fathers and children and hated rivals
swollen with new plagues, measles grown enormous, influenzas
perfected; and the gasses of despair, confusion of the senses, mania,
inducing terror of the universe, coma, existential wounds, that
chemists we have met at cocktail parties, passt daily and with a
happy "Good Day" on the way to classes or work, have workt to
make war too terrible for men to wage—

17. *Lawrence:* D. H. Lawrence (1885–1930), British novelist, poet, and essayist.
20. *Blake:* William Blake (1757–1827), British poet, painter, and visionary.

raised this secret entity of American's hatred of Europe, of Africa,
of Asia,
the deep hatred for the old world that had driven generations of
America out of itself,
and for the alien world, the new world about him, that might have
been Paradise
but was before his eyes already cleard back in a holocaust of burning
Indians, trees and grasslands,
reduced to his real estate, his projects of exploitation and profitable
wastes,

this specter that in the beginning Adams and Jefferson feard and knew
would corrupt the very body of the nation
and all our sense of our common humanity,
this black bile of old evils arisen anew,
takes over the vanity of Johnson;
and the very glint of Satan's eyes from the pit of the hell of
America's unacknowledged, unrepented crimes that I saw in
Goldwater's° eyes
now shines from the eyes of the President
in the swollen head of the nation.

1968

---

69. *Goldwater:* Barry Goldwater (1909–1997), conservative U.S. senator from Arizona, Lyndon Johnson's Republican opponent in the 1964 U.S. presidential elections.

BARBARA GUEST (1920–2006)

Born in Wilmington, North Carolina, and raised in California, Guest earned a B.A. in humanities in 1943 at UC Berkeley. She spent years in New York City, where she became involved with the New York School poets, including Frank O'Hara and John Ashbery. She was also well known for her book on the poet H.D., *Herself Defined: The Poet H.D. and Her World* (1984). Like the others in the New York School, Guest took issue with the closed-form New Critical aesthetics then dominating the academy. Her poetry was also influenced by the abstract expressionist and action painters of the 1950s and 1960s, as well as by surrealist poetry. Guest herself describes what it was like to come to maturity under the influence of surrealism: "In that creative atmosphere of magical rites, there was no recognized separation between the arts. . . . One could never again look at poetry as a locked kingdom. Poetry extended vertically, as well as horizontally. Never was it motionless within a linear structure." *Jacket* magazine adds: "Guest describes herself here as learning from the Surrealists how to make a poem move in ways other than by linear narrative: by introducing a more mobile, associative element into the poem, a sense of the 'magical' (or unrealistic) originating force from which the poem derived, and a blurring of boundaries among the poetic, musical, and visual (even plastic) arts." See *The Collected Poems of Barbara Guest* (2008).

from QUILTS

"COUCH OF SPACE"

Thought nest where secrets bubble
through the tucking, knowing what it's like outside,
drafts and preying beasts, midnight plunderers
testing your camp site and the aery demons, too,
waiting to plunge their icy fingers into your craw
and you crawl under, pull the quilt on top
making progress to the interior, soul's cell.

Following the channel through shallows
where footsteps tremble on quicksand squiggly
penmanship of old ladies, worms with cottony
spears, the light pillared the way trees crowd
with swallows and then a murmur in the ear
as deeper flows the water. The moon comes out
in old man dress thoughtfully casts an oar.

You float now tideless, secure in the rhythm
of stuffing and tying, edging and interlining,

bordered and hemmed; no longer unacquainted
you inhabit the house with its smooth tasks
sorted in scrap bags like kitchen nooks
the smelly cookery of cave where apples
ripen and vats flow domestic yet with schemes
of poetry sewed to educate the apron dawn.

Not exactly a hovel, not exactly a hearth;
"I think a taxi's like a little home," said
Marianne Moore,

this quilt's virago.

1980

WORDS

The simple contact with a wooden spoon and the word
recovered itself, began to spread as grass, forced
as it lay sprawling to consider the monument where
patience looked at grief, where warfare ceased
eyes curled outside themes to search the paper
now gleaming and potent, wise and resilient, word
entered its continent eager to find another as
capable as a thorn. The nearest possession would
house them both, they being then two might glide
into this house and presently create a rather larger
mansion filled with spoons and condiments, gracious
as a newly laid table where related objects might gather
to enjoy the interplay of gravity upon facetious hints,
the chocolate dish presuming an endowment, the ladle
of galactic rhythm primed as a relish dish, curved
knives, finger bowls, morsel carriages words might
choose and savor before swallowing so much was the
sumptuousness and substance of a rented house where words
placed dressing gowns as rosemary entered their scent
percipient as elder branches in the night where words
gathered, warped, then straightened, marking new wands.

1989

TWILIGHT POLKA DOTS

The lake was filled with distinguished fish purchased
at much expense in their prime. It was a curious lake, half salt,
wishing to set a tone of solitude edged with poetry.
This was a conscious body aware of shelves and wandering

rootlings, duty suggested it provide a scenic atmosphere
of content, a solicitude for the brooding emotions.

It despised the fish who enriched the waters. Fish with
their lithesome bodies, and their disagreeable concern
with feeding. They disturbed the water which preferred
the cultivated echoes of a hunting horn. Inside a
mercantile heart the lake dwelt on boning and deboning,
skin and sharpened eyes, a ritual search through
dependable deposits for slimier luxuries. The surface
presented an appeal to meditation and surcease.

Situated below the mountain, surrounded by aged trees,
the lake offered a picture appealing both to young and
mature romance. At last it was the visual choice of two
figures who in the fixity of their shared glance were
admired by the lake. Tactfully they ignored the lacustrine
fish, their gaze faltered lightly on the lapping
margins, their thoughts flew elsewhere, even beyond the
loop of her twisted hair and the accent of his poised tie-pin.

The scene supplied them with theatre, it was an evening
performance and the water understood and strained its
source for bugling echoes and silvered laments. The
couple referred to the lake without speech, by the turn
of a head, a hand waved, they placed a dignity upon the lake
brow causing an undercurrent of physical pleasure to
shake the water.

Until the letter fell. Torn into fragments the man tossed
it on the water, and the wind spilled the paper forward,
the cypress bent, the mountain sent a glacial flake.
Fish leapt. Polka dots now stippled the
twilight water and a superannuated gleam like a browned
autumnal stalk followed the couple where they shied in
the lake marsh grass like two eels who were caught.

1989

AARON KRAMER (1921–1997)

Among progressive modern American poets working with social and political themes and using traditional forms, Aaron Kramer may well be the single most accomplished figure. From his first protest poems, written in the mid-1930s when he was barely a teenager, through to his pointed critiques of the 1983 war in Grenada and Ronald Reagan's 1985 visit to Nazi graves in Bitburg, what stands out about Kramer's work is the musical character of his acts of political witness. Rhyme, meter, and traditional stanzaic forms in Kramer's poetry contain and direct anger, satire, and anguish about a century of singular violence. His 1937 poem "The Shoe-Shine Boy," published when Kramer was fifteen years old, is a definitive vignette about class. The speaker reports seeing "a child whose shoes looked old / Shining another's, till they shone like gold." From then on he would question exceptionalist claims about his country. The poem is notably also a deliberately ironic use of heroic couplets. Like Claude McKay, Kramer adopted traditional meters—favoring iambic trimeter, tetrameter, and pentameter—in part to install a radical politics within inherited rhythms. He wanted to radicalize root and branch of our literary tradition, not to abandon it for alternative forms.

The poems deploying these techniques in time would cluster around recurring themes and historical events. His first poems about exploited labor appeared in 1934; his last was published in 1995. His earliest poems about the suppression of freedoms in the United States date from 1938 and he continued writing them through the 1980s. Along with Edwin Rolfe, he is one of perhaps only two American writers to produce a series of poems about McCarthyism, from his satiric "The Soul of Martin Dies" (1940) to "Called In" (1980), his poem of outrage against those compelled to testify before the House Un-American Activities Committee. Over four decades he would repeatedly write poems about the Holocaust. Like a number of American poets who came of age in the 1930s, he wrote poems about the Spanish Civil War through much of his life. And, finally, he had a continuing interest in and commitment to testifying about African American history.

It is this last subject that occasioned what is perhaps his masterpiece—the twenty-six poems comprising the 1952 sequence "Denmark Vesey," about plans for an aborted 1822 slave revolt in Charleston, South Carolina. It is probably the single most ambitious and inventive poem about race ever written by a white American, and it is distinguished in part by Kramer's skill at negotiating the political relationship between form, sound, diction, and meaning. The first poem offers a hint of internal rhyme in Kramer's riveting definition of plantation agriculture—"acres rooted by uprooted hands"—and then gives the first full rhymes to slavery, as the founder of the Middle Passage gets the inspiration to kidnap African men, women, and children, then sees the idea become a thriving business, as "inspiration swiftly turned to gold. / The first shocked screams were muffled in the hold." In a typical Kramer strategy the hint of internal rhyme in the first poem is fulfilled in the second: "The sobs and moans cut through my bones." The line is spoken by the one white resident, the wife of a slave owner or auctioneer, who does hear. This poem, "Auction Block," is a brilliantly executed dialogue between her and her husband, with their respective statements differentiated in italics and roman type. The poem reinforces what will be a constant theme in the sequence: that white civilization is grounded not only in its indifference to the suffering it imposes on its darker brothers but also in a suppression of its own humanity. This theme builds until the devastating poem "Vesey's Nightmare," Vesey being the freed black who was the leader of the slaves. In his nightmare, delivered in off-rhymed five-beat couplets, white cannibals and vampires feed on black bodies and decorate themselves with human trophies—like ghouls elevated to positions of social prominence: "The lovely brocade their ladies wore / had once been Negro grandmothers' hair." The poem "Vesey Speaks to the Congregation" gives us Vesey's own bodily identification with the oppressed slaves in rhymed couplets: "my back is marked by your masters' whips; / and from your wounds my own blood drips." The reaction of the whites to intimations of revolt gets its own distinctive rhythm. In "The Legislators Vote," the relentless, lurching rhythm perfectly instantiates the legislature as an institutionalized lynch mob: "Fine them! Jail them! Bind them! Starve them! Brand them! Flail them!" Vesey finally warns the slaves not to hope for salvation from above: "You look for freedom in the sky? / Then chained you'll live and chained you'll die." "Turn all your sobs to battle-cries," Kramer urges, "cry freedom! freedom! and arise." It is a call to African Americans, but also a general rallying cry issued in the midst of McCarthyism. "Denmark Vesey" was issued in a small, privately published chapbook. It remained unavailable thereafter until Kramer's *Wicked Times: Selected Poems* (2004) was published. Kramer was born in Brooklyn, N.Y. He taught at Dowling College on Long Island for over thirty years.

DENMARK VESEY

THE KIDNAPPING

When the last Carolina brave lay still
by his beloved poplars, and his lawns
surrendered to the shadow of a stranger,
a new unholy Genesis began:
of acres rooted by uprooted hands. . . .

A voyager (whose name is not remembered)
showed in that time astounding business sense.
Sailing along the coast of Africa
he passed a hundred villages unknown
except to those who lived there; and one morning
or night he had a demon's inspiration:
why not seize quietly a stray child here,
a maiden bathing in the bay alone,
a strong-armed fellow dozing on the rocks—
and sell them to the planters overseas. . . .

That inspiration swiftly turned to gold.
The first shocked screams were muffled in the hold
of ships—and there in chains the kidnapped lay
while those who loved them wept, a world away.

What frantic thoughts stampeded through their brains
on that dark journey, while their hands and feet
lay numb and fevered in the grip of chains
among the rats there, in the stench and heat?

If sometimes a shrill cry upset the air
and reached the state-room, did the captain care,
or any of the crew, did they translate
their cargo's message of despair and hate?

Perhaps the free winds and the unbound waves
rendered the lamentation of the slaves
in language that the sky might understand:
"When will we see you, Sun—in what strange land?
For what vile purposes have we been torn
from all we knew and loved since we were born?"
But from the sky's red mouth no answer came.
—The port was reached; the cargo seemed quite tame. . . .

AUCTION BLOCK

Your lips are pale, your forehead's moist,
and your pulse is quick. . . .
    Not right, not right! a dreadful sight!
    Please take me home—I'm sick.

What sight? Was there some thing I missed?
Tell me what you mean!
The slaves were brought, and sold and bought,
It all went smooth and clean.

    A mother taken from her child!
    Husbands from their wives!
    —The sobs and moans cut through my bones
    more cruelly than knives. . . .

You like a rug in every room;
diamonds in your hair.
Without those blacks to bend their backs
your wrists would soon be bare.

They glared so when you named your price:
glared as if to say
A CLEVER TRADE! AND YET YOU'VE PAID
NOT HALF WHAT YOU SHALL PAY!

The whip will teach a sullen few;
chains will do for most;
and soon they'll come to call this "Home,"
forget their fathers' coast.

It may be so—and yet tonight
I'll not sleep a wink . . .
You'll sleep, my dear—and now, let's hear
no more of what you think!

PLANTATION SONG

How many days will it be,
oh how many days will it be?
I'll count them, Lord, I know how to count.
How many days will it be?

Master's alone with his gold,
old Master's alone with his gold.
He counts it, Lord, he knows how to count
more than his hands can hold.

Lady's gone shopping in town,
oh Lady's gone shopping in town.
She's counting, Lord, she knows how to count
jewels enough for a crown.

Overseer came with his whip,
mm, overseer came with his whip.
He counted, Lord, he knew how to count—
until my blood would drip.

How many days will it be,
oh how many days will it be?
I'll count them, Lord, I know how to count
until my hands go free.

REVOLT IN SANTO DOMINGO

The whip worked magic everywhere it fell;
the chains performed miraculously well;
the threat of starving cast a mighty spell.

But plundered veins swore to avenge their blood;
chained limbs at last their power understood;
a hunger grew more frantic than for food.

Santo Domingo was the first to learn
what comes to pass when feet may not return
to the beloved soil for which they yearn.

They crushed the whip that they'd been baptized with.
They broke the harness they had bent beneath,
and kicked it back into their masters' teeth.

And though the lords of Charleston raised a wall
to keep the news away, it was not tall
or thick enough—the news reached one and all.

SONG OF RETURNING SAILORS

We bring forbidden tidings
from harbors near and far:
of feet once bound together
that now unfettered are;

of joys like corpses buried
that rise up from their graves;
of slaves that now are masters,
of masters that are slaves.

We bring forbidden tidings
from harbors far and near—
and some will dance who hear it,
and some will die of fear.

THE PLANTER'S FRIGHT

Oh what a wringing of diamonded white hands!
Each year, each month new bells of ruin tolled.
The bedrock under Charleston seemed like sands—
the planters' voices all at once were old:

> It happened in Santo Domingo,
> then Mexico and Brazil:
> the weak have made themselves mighty
> and do whatever they will.
>
> They curse at all that was holy,
> make holy all that was cursed.

The wise old judges are sentenced,
the last-fed now eat first.

It happened in Venezuela,
then Cuba and Martinique:
the weak have made themselves mighty—
and the mighty—the mighty are weak!

REFUGEE RELIEF

Into the outstretched arms of New Orleans,
Richmond, and Charleston, ran the sobbing rich
spat out by nations that had outlawed chains. . . .
What tales they brought! what lessons they could teach
to those who still slept soundly!

Charleston planned
a benefit to buy new wigs and gowns
for those heroic Lords Without a Land.
Invited were the cream of nearby towns;
the loudest orchestra they could assemble
would lash the night with waltz and minuet;
the oldest wines would help their hearts forget
that more than music caused the walls to tremble. . . .

The shops were emptied of their choicest food,
that all might eat as much as they were able;
and for this banquet, a gigantic table
was ordered—of the rarest, sturdiest wood;
and who else could be called upon to build
a piece so sumptuous, but the most skilled
of Charleston's carpenters: the order came
to Denmark Vesey.
Do you know the name?

THE DENMARK VESEY SONG

Who rocked the cradle of Denmark Vesey?
Who taught him the names of trees?
In what hidden lake did he learn of his beauty?
Who kissed him at night but the breeze?

Do you know the name? have you heard the story?
He was fourteen summers old—

cradled in a slave-ship, kissed by a slave-whip,
his beauty bought and sold.

Do you know the name? have you heard the story?
He bought his liberty back—
but even in freedom he couldn't feel free
while chains bound those who were black.

Do you know the name? have you heard the story?
He won the planters' trust:
they hired his hammer, but night after night
he hammered their chains into dust.

CHARLESTON NOCTURNE

When Charleston shuts her thousand eyes
and rocks asleep the clamor,
she listens to the lullabies
of Denmark Vesey's hammer.

On beds of down, white ladies smile
to hear the hammer beating:
"At a table of the newest style
tomorrow we'll be eating!"

But slaves imagine other words,
and in their sleep smile often:
"Beat, hammer, beat! Nail down the boards!
Make slavery a coffin!"

THE MINUET

Through Col. Prioleau's majestic shutters,
music like wine poured into evening's cup,
until it overflowed along the gutters
where greedy coachmen stooped to lap it up.

"Sweet Maestro Franceschini! play that number
you wrote for Washington so long ago—
when you and I and Charleston were much younger . . .
The minuet, at least, before you go!"

And desperately there, with half-shut eyes,
the minuetting dowagers imagined
a time when lanterns told no brilliant lies,
when laughter wore the crown at every pageant;

when Charleston's men—who'd helped to make a king go—
came home and were anointed in his stead;

before the doom of Haiti and Domingo
reached like a nightmare into every bed. . . .

But they were pale, for all the pirouetting;
haggard and hushed, for all the boasts and toasts.
Even the young: past grieving, past forgetting,
performed their fathers' graceful dance like ghosts.

VESEY'S NIGHTMARE

It took Vesey long to fall asleep that night.
Over and over he heard the minuet;
till—tossing and turning—he fell into a dream.
It was Col. Prioleau's banqueting-room.

There stood the Colonel, bursting through his coat,
flanked by half the legislature of the State
all busily sampling and praising the food.
Instead of an ordinary meal, they had
young Negro bodies, baked to the bone.
Their fountain of wine was a Negro vein.

The lovely brocade their ladies wore
had once been Negro grandmothers' hair.
The gems that blinked on their arms like stars
were bright Negro eyes that had lately shed tears.

The drummer was beating a broad Negro chest,
and, instead of on trumpets, the trumpeters placed
thin lips on the hole of a Negro throat
that made a lament of the minuet.

Now lightly, now heavily, dancers caroused
on black children's faces: moaning and bruised—
while one slave kept bending to mop up the blood,
for which he received many pats on the head.

The Colonel smiled proudly up at his lamps:
they were Negro souls, which he'd bought for worn pants.
Now they saw Vesey—they were pointing at *him!*
"Not I!" he shrieked, and fled from the dream.

SUNDAY OFFERTORY PRAYER

We bring you, Lord, a week of wounds and worry—
put forth your loving arms and take them in.

We wished to fill your cups of offertory,
but better coin than hurt we did not win.

Put forth your arms, and take us in, and tell us
that at the end it will be otherwise—
that we'll yet reach your everlasting palace,
and claim for all our agonies a prize.

Breathe to our souls again the sacred promise!
Remind us of the Hell that you prepare
for those who've torn the love and laughter from us—
for those who now like fiends of Satan are.

Our veins run dry between the rows of cotton;
our years run out beneath a whip of hate.
Put forth your arms—too long we are forgotten—
too long we wait, oh Lord, too long we wait!

VESEY SPEAKS TO THE CONGREGATION

My leg is weak from the chains you wear;
my shoulders break at the load you bear;
my back is marked by your masters' whips;
and from your wound my own blood drips. . . .

> But when you bow, my beautiful sisters,
> ah brothers, when you bow and beg,
> my heart wears chains—for those who bought you
> have shackled you both heart and leg.

You look for freedom in the sky?
Then chained you'll live, and chained you'll die!
You seek in heaven the promised land?
Then lost is the promise of your hand!

> Israel whimpered once in bondage—
> who listened?—and who saw her bow?
> She cried aloud—and Pharaoh trembled!
> She rose—and what is Pharaoh now?

Like Israel, brothers, let us be:
wait not for God to set you free!

Turn all your sobs to battle-cries:
cry freedom! freedom! and arise. . . .

THE LEGISLATORS VOTE

The hot word, Liberty, rushed through their limbs
and gave their eyes a strange illumination
that could not go unnoticed. When they bowed
a pause came first, an ominous hesitation.
And when at work they hummed their Bible-hymns,
even the faintest note seemed somehow loud.

It was a bad year for the buyers of men.
Their merchandise would not stay on the shelves.
Their cotton spoiled untended in the sun.
Their forests grew more fugitives than trees.
Their mansions all at once were fortresses
in which they quakingly besieged themselves.

Some sold their lands and fled; but those who stayed
whipped twice as hard, to prove they still had power.
And when their legislature was assembled,
they roared to show that they were unafraid—
and Col. Prioleau, for at least an hour,
proved that his voice still rang and scarcely trembled:

"... In closing I have this to say:
take heed of how the black men pray!
Discover every whispered word!
Let every sigh be overheard!
Be careful when you see them laugh:
the joke may be our epitaph.
And when they bow too low, beware!
It is our burial they prepare."

"A law! a law! let's pass one now!"
"A Santo Domingo we'll never allow!"
"Look out for whisperers!" "Fine them!" "Jail them!"
"Bind them!" "Starve them!" "Brand them!" "Flail them!"
"Who dares to challenge the might of the slaver?"
"A law!" "Yes, a law!" "All those in favor—
say aye!" "AYE!!" "AYE!!" "Not one opposed?
Unanimously carried! Session is closed...."

A MEETING AT VESEY'S

Welcome, brothers, to my house
where lamps are not lit, where blinds are drawn,

where deeds instead of names will be known,
where friends greet friends with half a voice!

Beware of the informer moon!
Beware of trees that tell for a price!
Liberty now has no public place—
it is an outlaw in this town.

Brother Vesey, I am sent here by three hundred rebel slaves.
In your hands they rest their hope, and in your dream they place their lives.
Here are coins from harassed fingers—give them rifles in return!
Gabriel is what they call you—they are listening for the horn. . . .
Brother Vesey, I bring pennies, and a prayer from six plantations:
neither meat nor wine can fill us—we are hungry for munitions.
Do you need the angriest hundred? do you seek the most courageous?
Here's your list: my men are lions pacing back and forth in cages. . . .

Just like a wind with seeds to sow
whisper, whisper the word!
All through the cotton from row to row
whisper, whisper the word!
Wherever the whip has worked its woe
whisper, whisper the word!
Wherever no tears are left to flow
whisper, whisper the word!

Some will not answer though they're near you,
near enough to run and hide;
some, miles away, will hear you:
hear you and run to your side.
Some will rebuke and hound you,
hound you for the trouble you bring.
Some will put their arms around you
as though you are everything.

To all you know, wherever you go
whisper, whisper the word!
The trumpet of freedom is about to blow—
whisper, whisper the word!

TWO SLAVERS

There is a warning on the wind
that wakes me from my dreams at night:
"Your walls are doomed by angry eyes

that never shut—though yours be shut. . . .
In all your fields a frightful seed
has swelled, and burst, and taken root.
There'll be a harvest soon to reap
and underneath it you shall rot. . . ."

My slaves are secret as a great volcano
whose crater is too deep for eyes to know.
Alas for us who listen to such silence,
who watch for the first sign of wrath to show!
There'll be no sign, nor any sound of rumbling;
our doom will catch us dreaming in our beds.
The slaves will grow impatient of the secret
and pour their wrath like lava on our heads. . . .

PETER TELLS

"Why are there lights in all the rooms
and none of you asleep?"
"Peter has news to tell" "What news
so hot it cannot keep?"

"Take off your riding-boots, my dear,
and then come sit by me . . .
Now, Peter, let your master hear
the tale you told at tea!"

This morning, on my Sunday walk,
I passed along the Bay
and noticed much of busy talk
from which I kept away.

One whisperer went from crowd to crowd,
except where whites were by;
and when he came to where I stood
he looked me in the eye.

"You see that vessel, over there—
the one marked THIRTY-SIX?"
Then, leaning close against my ear,
he murmured: "All is fixed."

"What fixed?" I echoed. "Don't you know?
Haven't you heard the call?
The trumpet is about to blow—
next month our masters fall.

"Next month our limbs shake off the yoke—
come with us and be armed!"
"You wag an evil tongue," I spoke,
"to wish my master harmed."

I ran home quickly as I could,
and told my mistress all.
The devil strike that rascal dead
for wishing you to fall! . . .

"My dear, you're whiter than a ghost.
Here, take a bit of snuff!
Shall we allow a freedman's boast,
a word, to kill us off?"

"It is no boast—no idle word.
The state must hear this news.
Tomorrow, Peter, a reward—
my coat! no time to lose!"

IN THE WOODS

Vesey not here? *Not yet.*
He never was late before.
What message did you get?
The place and the time. No more.
Do you know what it's about?
Something about our Ned:
they say he's been found out.
Oh no! what dog betrayed?
They say a slaver's pet.
Such warning Vesey gave:
"Beware a bayonet
less than a petted slave!"
What now? *They'll make Ned speak.*
He'll blurt out Vesey's name.
If Vesey's wise he'll seek
in safer woods for game.
Maybe that's what he's done.
Maybe that's why he's late.
Better flee and live on
than stay, and die, and be great!
—Someone comes. *Who is he?*
Whose eye lights up the path?
It's Vesey. Denmark Vesey!
It is our Angel of Wrath.

BEFORE JULY!

Excuse me, brothers, for being late.
Patrolers blocked the city gate:
sniffing like hounds at every black
who tried to get out of Charleston or in.
If I had nothing to show but my skin
they'd have mocked me, too, and turned me back.

But I brought this box to hand the fools:
my good old box of carpenter's tools,
and a well-nailed fable to go with it:
you can thank a slaver's make-believe chair
for wheeling me through. . . . Oh brothers, take care!
The hounds are awake! the bonfires are lit!

The hounds are awake, that slept so sound;
they stretch their legs, and sniff at the ground. . . .
Believe me: if once they catch our scent
no fleetness of foot will be fleet enough—
the sharpest pike will not hold them off;
our moans will be their merriment.

Before the lips of the slaver part—
before he commands the hunt to start—
before the full-grown moon of July
gives us away—oh brothers, rise!
take hounds and hunters by surprise!
tear out their fangs, and let them die!

NED'S SILENCE

"'More time! more time!' You've *had* three days
and not a single name!
The days are running out for us
while you keep up your game.

"Last evening, and the night before,
you thought him weak enough."
—I've dealt with many stubborn men,
but never one so tough:

three hours we whipped him; but he bit
his lip, and made no sound.
We burnt his fingers till he writhed
in torment on the ground.

We held a lantern to his eyes;
we kicked him out of sleep;
we told him that his son would die,
and still he did not weep.

Now he sits hungry in the Hole,
with rats to call him brave—
soon he will pray, and soon he'll beg
like any other slave.

"Offer him liberty and gold
to give the plot away!
Don't let him die—we need the names!
I'll wait just one more day."

He sobbed this morning in his sleep. . . .
"An optimistic sign!"
I thank you for your confidence;
—tomorrow he'll be mine.

GOODBYE

There was a bend in the river
where weeping willows grew,
where the waves at night spoke softly,
and a wind from Africa blew
that only lovers knew.

"Why do you bring me, Denmark,
to our most holy place?
And why are my words, my kisses
not nimble enough to chase
the hardness from your face?

"This willow was my bridesmaid,
her shade our bridal bed;
the moon was our guest of honor
carousing overhead;
the waves declared us wed."

"Let these bear witness, darling,
these friends that know us well!
No matter how high the price is,
they'll not be coaxed to sell
the secret thing I tell:

"I lead a desperate legion
with doomsday in its hand.
Before the next moon blossoms
we who are branded will brand
this rotten-hearted land.

"Wait every night in the shadow,
as long as you can or care—
if I come at last to claim you
I'll bring you a crown to wear:
a crown fit for your hair.

"But if the next moon withers
without once showing my face
—go home; and when you hunger
for someone to embrace,
let Vengeance take my place. . . ."

There was a bend in the river
where weeping willows grew,
where the waves at night spoke softly,
and a wind from Africa blew
that only lovers knew.

THE NAME'S OUT

Upon the fourth night of his agony—
while Ned's tormentors hovered in amazement
over the last faint embers of his life—
they suddenly imagined that his lips
stirred for a moment.
"Stop the fire and ice!
He wants to speak."

Then, shutting all the windows
to keep away the noises of the night,
they put an ear close to his lips, and listened
until a sound crawled forth: his leader's name. . . .

That night the home of Vesey was surrounded
by a great noose of eyes—tighter and tighter—
while Vesey and his brothers, unaware,
worked busily inside.
A knock.
"Who is it?

Who beats so late against my door with fists?"
"OPEN!!"

"Oh brothers, I have feared such visit.
Smile and be silent while I burn the lists."

* * *

A guard stumbled into the State Troopers' House:
his helmet bashed in, and his tongue of no use.
They laid him out gently, and brought a wet cloth
to wash off the blood from his forehead and mouth.

"Who fixed you so prettily, lad?" asked the chief.
"Three killed . . . and two captured . . . I ran for my life . . .
"they leaped from the shadow . . . by sixes, by twelves . . .
they howled for our blood with the hunger of wolves. . . .

"In one hand a gun, in the other a pike . . .
a hymn on their lips . . . as they rose up and struck. . . ."
"Who were they? who fixed you so prettily, lad?"
"The legions . . . of Vesey . . . " he murmured, and died.

* * *

"Now listen to me," said the chief to the judge,
"You've acted your part like a star on the stage.
You've nodded politely, your smile has been fair.
Now take a low bow, and retire for the year!"

"I can't understand," said the judge to the chief.
"They said to go slowly—you told me yourself—
you hoped with more time to win over the list;
what names will you capture when Vesey's a ghost?"

"We hoped, yes, we hoped—but how foolish it was!
As foolish as hoping to hush him with laws. . . .
We ordered a river to turn into ice!
We ordered a rock to surrender its voice!

"We hoped, yes, we hoped—and we wasted our time:
from Vesey's own lips not a murmur will come.
His rifles—*they* speak to us—each has a tongue.
They call out the names and the list will be long."

The chief to the judge said, "Now listen to me:
I want Vesey hanged so a blind man can see.

Prepare the last speeches, and let them be brief!"
"I see what you mean," said the judge to the chief.

THE SENTENCE IS ANNOUNCED

The word of doom went through their bars
to spend the night beside them.
"My friends, if tears are in our eyes
we have no need to hide them.

"The warden's footstep fades away:
he cannot see us crying.
Alone we sit, with much to say
of living and of dying.

"As for myself, I call it mean
to hang in such bright weather;
but there are meaner ways to swing
than six true friends together.

"What does it matter if we be
remembered or forgotten . . .?
Ten thousand guns of liberty
we leave beneath the cotton.

"Ten thousand guns will sing our mass
when we no more can hear it—
and those who dread us in the flesh
may dread us more in spirit."

The word of doom went through their bars
to spend the night among them.
Get out, bleak word—you are not theirs!
Go haunt the ones who hang them!

THE WORD OF DOOM

Your banners, they dance so brightly!
Your bugles, they sound so pleased!
Has something happened to save you?
Was it The Wrath you seized?

Was it The Wrath of a People
you pushed at the point of a gun—
and sealed it up in a prison—
and doomed it to die with the sun?

If this is the prize you've taken,
make sure that the bars hold strong:
The Wrath of a People is restless,
it won't stay locked for long.

If this is the prize you've taken,
don't stop to celebrate!
Prepare great nooses and gallows
for The Wrath of a People is great.

But if the prize you've taken
is one man, only one,
watch out for The Wrath of a People:
it will come to claim its son.

THE HANGING

Many a lofty scaffold-work the carpenters had built,
but none in Charleston great enough for Denmark Vesey's guilt.

The city sent surveyors out, and finally they found
a hillock on the Lines that would be seen for miles around.

Here twenty men were set to work, the best that could be hired,
with twenty more to take their place as soon as they had tired.

They felled and trimmed gigantic trees to make the scaffold-frame;
they used great nails to keep it safe from any winds that came.

So loud a hammering at night! the children woke in wonder,
and mothers taught them that they heard no ordinary thunder.

At last the job was finished, and the carpenters were proud—
what scaffold ever had been high enough to hang a cloud?

The word flew everywhere, that on the second of July
whoever cared could come and see old Denmark Vesey die.

The crowd stood still when Vesey and his friends were marched outside—
then, somewhere, while the prayer was read, a Negro woman cried.

And when six silent upraised heads were circled by the noose,
through rows of mounted guards the people suddenly tore loose.

And when the sun made bright the eyes in Denmark Vesey's head,
the slavers could not easily believe that he was dead.

And when the sun was almost gone, the shadows of the dead
became so long, so dark and long, the slavers ran to bed.

And when the moon herself was hanged while rolling down the night,
the slavers locked their windows, and the doors they bolted tight.

And when through shutters they observed the silences in groups,
they sent a rider galloping to Washington for troops.

THE HAMMER AND THE LIGHT

Sometimes I've been too mournful
to fall asleep at night—
so tired and so mournful,
I couldn't sleep half the night—
then I'd sit by the window
and look out at Vesey's light.

His light was like a fire
getting ready to wake the town;
a sudden midnight fire
for the rotten streets of this town—
and my heart beat loud and angry
each time his hammer came down.

Last night I sat by the window,
patient as the stars in the sky—
I looked and I listened at the window
till the last star was gone from the sky.
This morning my sonny asked me:
"What happened to make you cry?

"You never would cry when they beat you,
though the whip cut through to the bone.
You just bit your lip when they beat you,
when you lay there, cut to the bone."
"I'm crying for a hammer that's quiet;
crying for a light that's gone.

"Without that light before me,
I can't seem to lift my feet.

Without that bright light before me,
the chains are back on my feet.
And without that angry hammer,
well, my heart doesn't want to beat."

My son said, "Buy me a hammer;
I'll beat all day and all night.
I'll make it the angriest hammer
that ever was heard in the night."
My son said, "Buy me a lantern—
I'll take good care of its light."

1952

RICHARD WILBUR (b. 1921)

Born in New York and raised in New Jersey, Wilbur was educated at Amherst College and Harvard. He served as a cryptographer during World War II, and was stationed in Africa, France, and Italy. Since then he has taught regularly, done successful translations of Molière, coauthored an operetta (*Candide,* 1957) with Lillian Hellman, and written two books of children's poetry. Taking the English metaphysical poets as his models in his own work, Wilbur has excelled at polished, witty, self-contained lyrics with formal stanzas and controlled metrics. He believes, as with his signature poem "Love Calls Us to the Things of This World," in spiritual impulses grounded in ordinary life. Yet the most ordinary things can, in the intense elegance of a civilizing gaze, become extraordinary. In "A Baroque Wall-Fountain in the Villa Sciarra" his language creates the secular, aesthetic miracle of Baroque water; the water itself seems to take on the Baroque style. The exquisite, sensuous, and precise description in the poem is Wilbur's version of the human potential for grace.

THE PARDON

My dog lay dead five days without a grave
In the thick of summer, hid in a clump of pine
And a jungle of grass and honeysuckle-vine.
I who had loved him while he kept alive

Went only close enough to where he was
To sniff the heavy honeysuckle-smell
Twined with another odor heavier still
And hear the flies' intolerable buzz.

Well, I was ten and very much afraid.
In my kind world the dead were out of range
And I could not forgive the sad or strange
In beast or man. My father took the spade

And buried him. Last night I saw the grass
Slowly divide (it was the same scene
But now it glowed a fierce and mortal green)
And saw the dog emerging. I confess

I felt afraid again, but still he came
In the carnal sun, clothed in a hymn of flies,
And death was breeding in his lively eyes.
I started in to cry and call his name,

Asking forgiveness of his tongueless head.
. . . I dreamt the past was never past redeeming:
But whether this was false or honest dreaming
I beg death's pardon now. And mourn the dead.

1950

A BAROQUE WALL-FOUNTAIN IN THE VILLA SCIARRA°

for Dore and Adja

Under the bronze crown
Too big for the head of the stone cherub whose feet
A serpent has begun to eat,
Sweet water brims a cockle° and braids down

Past spattered mosses, breaks
On the tipped edge of a second shell, and fills
The massive third below. It spills
In threads then from the scalloped rim, and makes

A scrim or summery tent
For a faun-ménage° and their familiar goose.
Happy in all that ragged, loose
Collapse of water, its effortless descent

And flatteries of spray,
The stocky god upholds the shell with ease,
Watching, about his shaggy knees,
The goatish innocence of his babes at play;

His fauness all the while
Leans forward, slightly, into a clambering mesh
Of water-lights, her sparkling flesh
In a saecular ecstasy, her blinded smile

Bent on the sand floor
Of the trefoil° pool, where ripple-shadows come

---

poem title: *Villa Sciarra:* a public park in Rome.

4. *cockle:* shell-shaped basin in the fountain.

10. *faun-ménage:* a faun household; in Roman mythology, fauns were rustic forest demons, companions of the shepherds, and the equivalents of the Greek Satyrs; they were half man and half goat.

22. *trefoil:* three-leaved.

And go in swift reticulum,°
More addling to the eye than wine, and more

Interminable to thought
Than pleasure's calculus. Yet since this all
Is pleasure, flash, and waterfall,
Must it not be too simple? Are we not

More intricately expressed
In the plain fountains that Maderna° set
Before St. Peter's—the main jet
Struggling aloft until it seems at rest

In the act of rising, until
The very wish of water is reversed,
That heaviness borne up to burst
In a clear, high, cavorting head, to fill

With blaze, and then in gauze
Delays, in a gnatlike shimmering, in a fine
Illumined version of itself, decline,
And patter on the stones its own applause?

If that is what men are
Or should be, if those water-saints display
The pattern of our areté,°
What of these showered fauns in their bizarre,

Spangled, and plunging house?
They are at rest in fullness of desire
For what is given, they do not tire
Of the smart of the sun, the pleasant water-douse

And riddled pool below,
Reproving our disgust and our ennui
With humble insatiety.
Francis,° perhaps, who lay in sister snow

---

23. *reticulum:* in an intricate, netlike pattern.

30. *Maderna:* Carlo Maderno (1556–1629), architect who helped design St. Peter's Basilica.

43. *areté:* Wilbur's note—a Greek word meaning roughly "virtue"; the combination of qualities that make for good character—excellence, valor, virtue.

52. *Francis:* St. Francis of Assisi (1182–1226), founder of the Franciscan Order of monks, who take vows of poverty, and patron saint of ecology.

Before the wealthy gate
Freezing and praising, might have seen in this
No trifle, but a shade of bliss—
That land of tolerable flowers, that state

As near and far as grass
Where eyes become the sunlight, and the hand
Is worthy of water: the dreamt land
Toward which all hungers leap, all pleasures pass.

1956

BEASTS

Beasts in their major freedom
Slumber in peace tonight. The gull on his ledge
Dreams in the guts of himself the moon-plucked waves below,
And the sunfish leans on a stone, slept
By the lyric water,

In which the spotless feet
Of deer make dulcet splashes, and to which
The ripped mouse, safe in the owl's talon, cries
Concordance. Here there is no such harm
And no such darkness

As the selfsame moon observes
Where, warped in window-glass, it sponsors now
The werewolf's painful change. Turning his head away
On the sweaty bolster, he tries to remember
The mood of manhood,

But lies at last, as always,
Letting it happen, the fierce fur soft to his face,
Hearing with sharper ears the wind's exciting minors,
The leaves' panic, and the degradation
Of the heavy streams.

Meantime, at high windows
Far from thicket and pad-fall, suitors of excellence
Sigh and turn from their work to construe again the painful
Beauty of heaven, the lucid moon
And the risen hunter,

Making such dreams for men
As told will break their hearts as always, bringing

Monsters into the city, crows on the public statues,
Navies fed to the fish in the dark
Unbridled waters.

1956

LOVE CALLS US TO THE THINGS OF THIS WORLD°

The eyes open to a cry of pulleys,
And spirited from sleep, the astounded soul
Hangs for a moment bodiless and simple
As false dawn.
Outside the open window
The morning air is all awash with angels.

Some are in bed-sheets, some are in blouses,
Some are in smocks: but truly there they are.
Now they are rising together in calm swells
Of halcyon° feeling, filling whatever they wear
With the deep joy of their impersonal breathing;

Now they are flying in place, conveying
The terrible speed of their omnipresence, moving
And staying like white water; and now of a sudden
They swoon down into so rapt a quiet
That nobody seems to be there.
The soul shrinks

From all that it is about to remember,
From the punctual rape of every blessèd day,
And cries,
"Oh, let there be nothing on earth but laundry,
Nothing but rosy hands in the rising steam
And clear dances done in the sight of heaven."

Yet, as the sun acknowledges
With a warm look the world's hunks and colors,
The soul descends once more in bitter love
To accept the waking body, saying now
In a changed voice as the man yawns and rises,

---

poem title: a quotation from St. Augustine (A.D. 354–430). Wilbur's note—"You must imagine the poem as occurring at perhaps seven-thirty in the morning; the scene is a bedroom high up in a city apartment building; outside the bedroom window, the first laundry of the day is being yanked across the sky and one has been awakened by the squeaking pulleys of the laundry-line."

10. *halcyon:* serene.

"Bring them down from their ruddy gallows;
Let there be clean linen for the backs of thieves;
Let lovers go fresh and sweet to be undone,
And the heaviest nuns walk in a pure floating
Of dark habits,
keeping their difficult balance."

1956

ADVICE TO A PROPHET

When you come, as you soon must, to the streets of our city,
Mad-eyed from stating the obvious,
Not proclaiming our fall but begging us
In God's name to have self-pity,

Spare us all word of the weapons, their force and range,
The long numbers that rocket the mind;
Our slow, unreckoning hearts will be left behind,
Unable to fear what is too strange.

Nor shall you scare us with talk of the death of the race.
How should we dream of this place without us?—
The sun mere fire, the leaves untroubled about us,
A stone look on the stone's face?

Speak of the world's own change. Though we cannot conceive
Of an undreamt thing, we know to our cost
How the dreamt cloud crumbles, the vines are blackened by frost,
How the view alters. We could believe,

If you told us so, that the white-tailed deer will slip
Into perfect shade, grown perfectly shy,
The lark avoid the reaches of our eye;
The jack-pine lose its knuckled grip

On the cold ledge, and every torrent burn
As Xanthus° once, its gliding trout

22. *Xanthus:* the name of the river that flowed through the plain of Troy. In the *Iliad* the river takes the form of the god Scamander, who objects to all the blood and bodies hurled into his domain in the course of the war. He causes the river to rise up, threatening to drown Achilles, but Hephaestus scolds Scamander and compels the river to return within its banks.

Stunned in a twinkling. What should we be without
The dolphin's arc, the dove's return,

These things in which we have seen ourselves and spoken?
Ask us, prophet, how we shall call
Our natures forth when that live tongue is all
Dispelled, that glass obscured or broken

In which we have said the rose of our love and the clean
Horse of our courage, in which beheld
The singing locust of the soul unshelled,
And all we mean or wish to mean.

Ask us, ask us whether with the worldless rose
Our hearts shall fail us; come demanding
Whether there shall be lofty or long standing
When the bronze annals of the oak-tree close.

1961

CHILDREN OF DARKNESS

If groves are choirs and sanctuaried fanes,
What have we here?
An elm-bole cocks a bloody ear;
In the oak's shadow lies a strew of brains.
Wherever, after the deep rains,

The woodlands are morose and reek of punk,
These gobbets grow—
Tongue, lobe, hand, hoof or butchered toe
Amassing on the fallen branch half-sunk
In leaf-mold, or the riddled trunk.

Such violence done, it comes as no surprise
To notice next
How some, parodically sexed,
Puff, blush, or gape, while shameless phalloi rise,
To whose slimed heads come carrion flies.

Their gift is not for life, these creatures who
Disdain to root,
Will bear no stem or leaf, no fruit,
And, mimicking the forms which they eschew,
Make it their pleasure to undo

All that has heart and fiber. Yet of course
What these break down
Wells up refreshed in branch and crown.
May we not after all forget that Norse
Drivel of Wotan's panicked horse,

And every rumor bred of forest-fear?
Are these the brood
Of adders? Are they devil's food,
Minced witches, or the seed of rutting deer?
Nowhere does water stand so clear

As in stalked cups where pine has come to grief;
The chanterelle
And cèpe are not the fare of hell;
Where coral schools the beech and aspen leaf
To seethe like fishes of a reef,

Light strikes into a gloom in which are found
Red disc, grey mist,
Gold-auburn firfoot, amethyst,
Food for the eye whose pleasant stinks abound,
And dead men's fingers break the ground.

Gargoyles is what they are at worst, and should
They preen themselves
On being demons, ghouls, or elves,
The holy chiaroscuro of the wood
Still would embrace them. They are good.

1976

MONA VAN DUYN (1921–2004)

Born in Waterloo, Iowa, Van Duyn was educated at the University of Northern Iowa and the University of Iowa. Typically a formalist poet, she often worked in long lines with varied meters. Sometimes taking up philosophical topics, she wrote about the commonplace events of ordinary life, as with "Toward a Definition of Marriage." She taught at Washington University.

TOWARD A DEFINITION OF MARRIAGE

I

It is to make a fill, not find a land.
Elsewhere, often, one sights americas of awareness,
suddenly there they are, natural and anarchic,
with plantings scattered but rich, powers to be harnessed—
but this is more like building a World's Fair island.
Somebody thought it could be done, contracts are signed,
and now all materials are useful, everything; sludge
is scooped up and mixed with tin cans and fruit rinds,
even tomato pulp and lettuce leaves are solid
under pressure. Presently the ground humps up and shows.
But this marvel of engineering is not all.
A hodgepodge of creatures (no bestiary would suppose
such an improbable society) are at this time
turned loose to run on it, first shyly, then more free,
and must keep, for self's sake, wiles, anger, much of their
spiney or warted nature, yet learn courtesy.

II

It is closest to picaresque, but essentially artless.
If there were any experts, they are dead, it takes too long.
How could its structure be more than improvising,
when it never ends, but line after line plods on,
and none of the ho hum passages can be skipped?
It has a bulky knowledge, but what symbol comes anywhere near
suggesting it? No, the notion of art won't fit it—
unless—when it's embodied. For digression there
is meaningful, and takes such joy in the slopes and crannies
that every bony gesture is generous, full,
all lacy with veins and nerves. There, the spirit
smiles in its skin, and impassions and sweetens to style.

So this comes to resemble a poem found in his notebooks
after the master died. A charred, balky man, yet one day
as he worked at one of those monuments, the sun guiled him,
and he turned to a fresh page and simply let play
his great gift on a small ground. Yellowed, unpublished,
he might have forgotten he wrote it. (All this is surmise.)
But it's known by heart now; it rounded the steeliest shape
to shapeliness, it was so loving an exercise.

III

Or, think of it as a duel of amateurs.
These two have almost forgot how it started—in an alley,
impromptu, and with a real affront. One thought,
"He is not me," and one, "She is not me,"
and they were coming toward each other with sharp knives
when someone saw it was illegal, dragged them away,
bundled them into some curious canvas clothing,
and brought them to this gym that is almost dark, and empty.
Now, too close together for the length of the foils,
wet with fear, they dodge, stumble, strike,
and if either finally thinks he would rather be touched
than touch, he still must listen to the clang and tick
of his own compulsive parrying. Endless. Nothing
but a scream for help can make the authorities come.
If it ever turns into more of a dance than a duel,
it is only because, feeling more skillful, one
or the other steps back with some notion of grace
and looks at his partner. Then he is able to find
not a wire mask for his target, but a red heart
sewn on the breast like a simple valentine.

IV

If there's a Barnum° way to show it, then think back
to a climax in the main tent. At the foot of the bleachers, a road
encloses the ringed acts; consider that as its design,
and consider whoever undertakes it as the whole parade
which, either as preview or summary, assures the public
hanging in hopeful suspense between balloons and peanutshells
that it's all worthwhile. The ponies never imagined
anything but this slow trot of ribbons and jinglebells.
An enormous usefulness constrains the leathery bulls

Barnum: P. T. Barnum (1810–1891), American showman and scam artist.

as they stomp on, and hardly ever run amuck.
The acrobats practiced all their lives for this easy
contortion, and clowns are enacting a necessary joke
by harmless zigzags in and out of line.
But if the procession includes others less trustworthy?
When they first see the circle they think some ignorant
cartographer has blundered. The route is a lie,
drawn to be strict but full, drawn so each going forth
returns, returns to a more informed beginning.
And still a familiar movement might tempt them to try it,
but since what they know is not mentioned in the tromboning
of the march, neither the day-long pace of caged
impulse, nor the hurtle of night's terrible box-cars,
they shrink in their stripes and refuse; other performers
drive them out and around with whips and chairs.
They never tame, but may be taught to endure
the illusion of tameness. Year after year their paws
pad out the false curve, and their reluctant parading
extends the ritual's claim to its applause.

V

Say, for once, that the start is a pure vision
like the blind man's (though he couldn't keep it, trees
soon bleached to familiar) when the bandage came off
and what a world could be first fell on his eyes.
Say it's when campaigns are closest to home
that farsighted lawmakers oftenest lose their way.
And repeat what everyone knows and nobody wants
to remember, that always, always expediency
must freckle the fairest wishes. Say, when documents,
stiff with history, go right into the council chambers
and are rolled up to shake under noses, are constantly read from,
or pounded on, or passed around, the parchment limbers;
and, still later, if these old papers are still being shuffled,
commas will be missing, ashes will disfigure a word;
finally thumbprints will grease out whole phrases, the clear prose
won't mean much; it can never be wholly restored.
Curators mourn the perfect idea, for it crippled
outside of its case. Announce that at least it can move
in the imperfect action, beyond the windy oratory,
of marriage, which is the politics of love.

1964

JACK KEROUAC (1922–1969)

Universally and internationally known for his fiction and for embodying the Beat movement, Kerouac is far less well known as a poet. "The Perfect Love of Mind Essence," from Kerouac's Buddhist phase, begins with a willfully prosaic passage, then shifts to a series of inventive couplets. Many of these rhymed couplets are haiku-like ("Water from the moon / Appears very soon"). Some have a distinctly Blakean character ("The child of delight / Rests in the night"). Others close in on visionary surrealism ("He never dies / Who has no eyes"). And some are closer to proverbs ("Unborn / No lamb shorn") or aphorisms ("Mind alone / Introduced the bone"). Some offer comic adaptations of unlikely diction ("Fire retires / When water admires"), and others are essentially absurdist ("Explaining in droves / To men in groves"). But all in varying ways embody the primary message: "There is no rain / Outside the brain" or "Wind in the trees / Is a mental breeze." We make a world out of names and the mental relationships they facilitate—foolish, loving, phantasmatic, fearful, or seemingly entirely material. We live among projections of values that are as fleeting as we ourselves. As he writes in another poem:

Life is like a dream,
You only think it's real
Cause you're born a sucker
For that kind of deal.

Kerouac also wrote hundreds of haiku during his career. One might compare his with those by Etheridge Knight. Kerouac's work in two registers. Some are satiric and radically Westernized. Others hew to a haiku tradition of meticulous description. The two groups are divided below.

THE PERFECT LOVE OF MIND ESSENCE:-

Mind Essence loves everything, because it
knows why everything is---
It loves everything because everything ends---
Mind Essence is like a little child,
It makes no discriminations at all,
All is the same and all's in the mind,
And all's to be loved as it stands,
All's to be loved as it falls.
The Karma is done
Mind Essence is one---
The wheel of thought
Is no more fought---
Differences of things

Are imaginary rings---
The child of delight
Rests in the night---
The mind of bliss
Is pure happiness---

He never dies
Who has no eyes
He never fears
Who has no ears
He never goes
Who has no nose---
He is never bawdy
Who has no body---

He is never hung
Who has no tongue---
There is no rain
Outside the brain---
Unborn,
No lamb shorn---
No crying
In essence undying

Sight is just dust,
Obey it must---
*

→

Mind alone
Introduced the bone.
*

Fire just feeds
On fiery deeds.
*

→

Only mind
The flame so kind.
*

Water from the moon
Appears very soon.
*

→

Mind is the sea
Made water agree.
*

Wind in the trees
Is a mental breeze.
*

→

Wind rose deep
From empty sleep.
*

Space in the ground
Was dirt by the pound
*

→

Devoid of space
Is the mind of grace.
*

Fire retires
When water admires

Fire inhibits
What earth admits

Fire and water
Bring earth a daughter

And space accepts
The green adepts

And wind responds
To magic wands
And men appear
With Dharma dear

Explaining in
droves
To men in
groves

"Not even alive
The Elements Five"

c. 1957

HAIKU

Gee last night—
dreamed
Of Harry Truman

When the moon sinks
down to the power line,
I'll go in

Crossing the football field,
Coming home from work
The lonely businessman

August moon—oh
I got a boil
On my thigh

The barn, swimming
In a sea
Of windblown leaves

Leaf dropping straight
Into the windless midnight:
The dream of change

2 traveling salesmen
passing each other
On a Western road

Woke up groaning
with a dream of a priest
Eating chicken necks

Swinging on delicate hinges
the Autumn Leaf
Almost off the stem

The trees, already
bent in the windless
Oklahoma plain

c. 1950–1965

JAMES DICKEY (1923–1997)

Born and raised in Atlanta, Georgia, and the surrounding area, Dickey was first a public figure as a high school football star. He did not decide to be a writer until after service in the air force in World War II and then enrollment at Vanderbilt University. Even then, he took up other occupations as well. He helped train pilots in the Korean War and worked as an advertising executive for Coca-Cola. Both in his poetry and in his widely successful novel, *Deliverance* (1970), he was fascinated by violent, definitive tests of selfhood. He could write poems glorifying combat, poems designed to shock readers with country sexuality, and, in the case of "Falling," a poem that celebrates a most transitory form of transcendence at the same time as it indulges in misogynist violence. Flamboyant in his personal style, he was at once a performer and an unforgettable writer.

THE SHEEP CHILD

Farm boys wild to couple
With anything   with soft-wooded trees
With mounds of earth   mounds
Of pinestraw   will keep themselves off
Animals by legends of their own:
In the hay-tunnel dark
And dung of barns, they will
Say   I have heard tell
That in a museum in Atlanta
Way back in a corner somewhere
There's this thing that's only half
Sheep   like a woolly baby
Pickled in alcohol because
Those things can't live   his eyes
Are open   but you can't stand to look
I heard from somebody who . . .

But this is now almost all
Gone. The boys have taken
Their own true wives in the city,
The sheep are safe in the west hill
Pasture   but we who were born there
Still are not sure. Are we,
Because we remember, remembered
In the terrible dust of museums?

Merely with his eyes, the sheep-child may

Be saying saying

I am here, in my father's house.
I who am half of your world, came deeply
To my mother in the long grass
Of the west pasture, where she stood like moonlight
Listening for foxes. It was something like love
From another world that seized her
From behind, and she gave, not lifting her head
Out of dew, without ever looking, her best
Self to that great need. Turned loose, she dipped her face
Farther into the chill of the earth, and in a sound
Of sobbing of something stumbling
Away, began, as she must do,
To carry me. I woke, dying,

In the summer sun of the hillside, with my eyes
Far more than human. I saw for a blazing moment
The great grassy world from both sides,
Man and beast in the round of their need,
And the hill wind stirred in my wool,
My hoof and my hand clasped each other,
I ate my one meal
Of milk, and died
Staring. From dark grass I came straight

To my father's house, whose dust
Whirls up in the halls for no reason
When no one comes piling deep in a hellish mild corner,
And, through my immortal waters,
I meet the sun's grains eye
To eye, and they fail at my closet of glass.
Dead, I am most surely living
In the minds of farm boys: I am he who drives
Them like wolves from the hound bitch and calf
And from the chaste ewe in the wind.
They go into woods into bean fields they go
Deep into their known right hands. Dreaming of me,
They groan they wait they suffer
Themselves, they marry, they raise their kind.

1967

FALLING

A 29-year-old stewardess fell . . . to her
death tonight when she was swept
through an emergency door that suddenly
sprang open . . . The body . . .
was found . . . three hours after the
accident.
— New York Times

The states when they black out and lie there rolling   when they turn
To something transcontinental   move by   drawing moonlight out
    of the great
One-sided stone hung off the starboard wingtip   some sleeper next to
An engine is groaning for coffee   and there is faintly coming in
Somewhere the vast beast-whistle of space. In the galley with its racks
Of trays   she rummages for a blanket   and moves in her slim tailored
Uniform to pin it over the cry at the top of the door. As though
    she blew

The door down with a silent blast from her lungs   frozen   she is black
Out finding herself   with the plane nowhere and her body taking by
    the throat
The undying cry of the void   falling   living   beginning to be
    something
That no one has ever been and lived through   screaming without
    enough air
Still neat   lipsticked   stockinged   girdled by regulation   her hat
Still on   her arms and legs in no world   and yet spaced also strangely
With utter placid rightness on thin air   taking her time   she holds it
In many places   and now, still thousands of feet from her death
    she seems
To slow   she develops interest   she turns in her maneuverable body

To watch it. She is hung high up in the overwhelming middle of things
    in her
Self   in low body-whistling wrapped intensely   in all her dark
    dance-weight
Coming down from a marvelous leap   with the delaying,
    dumfounding ease
Of a dream of being drawn   like endless moonlight to the harvest soil
Of a central state of one's country   with a great gradual warmth
    coming
Over her   floating   finding more and more breath in what she has
    been using

For breath   as the levels become more human   seeing clouds placed honestly
Below her left and right   riding slowly toward them   she clasps it all
To her and can hang her hands and feet in it in peculiar ways   and
Her eyes opened wide by wind, can open her mouth as wide   wider and suck
All the heat from the cornfields   can go down on her back with a feeling
Of stupendous pillows stacked under her   and can turn   turn as to someone
In bed   smile, understood in darkness   can go away   slant slide
Off tumbling   into the emblem of a bird with its wings half-spread
Or whirl madly on herself   in endless gymnastics in the growing warmth
Of wheatfields rising toward the harvest moon.   There is time to live
In superhuman health   seeing mortal unreachable lights far down seeing
An ultimate highway with one late priceless car probing it   arriving
In a square town   and off her starboard arm the glitter of water catches
The moon by its one shaken side   scaled, roaming silver   My God it is good
And evil lying in one after another of all the positions for love
Making   dancing   sleeping   and now cloud wisps at her no
Raincoat   no matter   all small towns brokenly brighter from inside
Cloud   she walks over them like rain   bursts out to behold a Greyhound
Bus shooting light through its sides   it is the signal to go straight
Down like a glorious diver   then feet first   her skirt stripped beautifully
Up   her face in fear-scented cloths   her legs deliriously bare   then
Arms out   she slow-rolls over   steadies out   waits for something great
To take control of her   trembles near feathers   planes head-down
The quick movements of bird-necks turning her head   gold eyes the insight-
eyesight of owls blazing into the hencoops   a taste for chicken overwhelming
Her   the long-range vision of hawks enlarging all human lights of cars
Freight trains   looped bridges   enlarging the moon racing slowly
Through all the curves of a river   all the darks of the midwest blazing
From above. A rabbit in a bush turns white   the smothering chickens
Huddle   for over them there is still time for something to live

With the streaming half-idea of a long stoop   a hurtling   a fall
That is controlled   that plummets as it wills   turns gravity
Into a new condition, showing its other side like a moon   shining
New Powers   there is still time to live on a breath made of nothing
But the whole night   time for her to remember to arrange her skirt
Like a diagram of a bat   tightly it guides her   she has this flying-skin
Made of garments   and there are also those sky-divers on TV   sailing
In sunlight   smiling under their goggles   swapping batons back
  and forth
And He who jumped without a chute and was handed one by a diving
Buddy. She looks for her grinning companion   white teeth   nowhere
She is screaming   singing hymns   her thin human wings spread out
From her neat shoulders   the air beast-crooning to her   warbling
And she can no longer behold the huge partial form of the world   now
She is watching her country lose its evoked master shape   watching
  it lose
And gain   get back its houses and peoples   watching it bring up
Its local lights   single homes   lamps on barn roofs   if she fell
Into water she might live   like a diver   cleaving   perfect   plunge

Into another   heavy silver   unbreathable   slowing   saving
Element: there is water   there is time to perfect all the fine
Points of diving   feet together   toes pointed   hands shaped right
To insert her into water like a needle   to come out healthily dripping
And be handed a Coca-Cola   there they are   there are the waters
Of life   the moon packed and coiled in a reservoir   so let me begin
To plane across the night air of Kansas   opening my eyes
  superhumanly
Bright to the dammed moon   opening the natural wings of my jacket
By Don Loper° moving like a hunting owl toward the glitter of water
One cannot just *fall   just tumble screaming all that time   one must use*
It   she is now through with all   through all   clouds   damp   hair
Straightened   the last wisp of fog pulled apart on her face like wool
  revealing
New darks   new progressions of headlights along dirt roads
  from chaos

And night   a gradual warming   a new-made, inevitable world of
  one's own
Country   a great stone of light in its waiting waters   hold   hold out
For water: who knows when what correct young woman must take up
  her body

Don Loper: (1906–1972), American fashion designer.

And fly   and head for the moon-crazed inner eye of midwest imprisoned
Water   stored up for her for years   the arms of her jacket slipping
Air up her sleeves to go   all over her? What final things can be said
Of one who starts out sheerly in her body in the high middle of night
Air   to track down water like a rabbit where it lies like life itself
Off to the right in Kansas? She goes toward   the blazing-bare lake
Her skirts neat   her hands and face warmed more and more by the air
Rising from pastures of beans   and under her   under chenille bedspreads
The farm girls are feeling the goddess in them struggle and rise brooding
On the scratch-shining posts of the bed   dreaming of female signs
Of the moon   male blood like iron   of what is really said by the moan
Of airliners passing over them at dead of midwest midnight   passing
Over brush fires   burning out in silence on little hills   and will wake
To see the woman they should be   struggling on the rooftree to become
Stars: for her the ground is closer   water is nearer   she passes
It   then banks   turns   her sleeves fluttering differently as she rolls
Out to face the east, where the sun shall come up from wheatfields she must
Do something with water   fly to it   fall in it   drink it   rise
From it   but there is none left upon earth   the clouds have drunk it back
The plants have sucked it down   there are standing toward her only
The common fields of death   she comes back from flying to falling
Returns to a powerful cry   the silent scream with which she blew down
The coupled door of the airliner   nearly nearly losing hold
Of what she has done   remembers   remembers the shape at the heart
Of cloud   fashionably swirling   remembers she still has time to die
Beyond explanation. Let her now take off her hat in summer air the contour
Of cornfields   and have enough time to kick off her one remaining
Shoe with the toes   of the other foot   to unhook her stockings
With calm fingers, noting how fatally easy it is to undress in midair
Near death   when the body will assume without effort any position
Except the one that will sustain it   enable it to rise   live
Not die   nine farms hover close   widen   eight of them separate, leaving
One in the middle   then the fields of that farm do the same   there is no
Way to back off   from her chosen ground   but she sheds the jacket
With its silver sad impotent wings   sheds the bat's guiding tailpiece

Of her skirt the lightning-charged clinging of her blouse the
  intimate
Inner flying-garment of her slip in which she rides like the holy ghost
Of a virgin sheds the long windsocks of her stockings absurd
Brassiere then feels the girdle required by regulations squirming
Off her: no longer monobuttocked she feels the girdle flutter shake
In her hand and float upward her clothes rising off her
  ascending
Into cloud and fights away from her head the last sharp dangerous
  shoe
Like a dumb bird and now will drop in SOON now will drop

In like this the greatest thing that ever came to Kansas down
  from all
Heights all levels of American breath layered in the lungs
  from the frail
Chill of space to the loam where extinction slumbers in corn tassels
  thickly
And breathes like rich farmers counting: will come among them after
Her last superhuman act the last slow careful passing of her hands
All over her unharmed body desired by every sleeper in his dream:
Boys finding for the first time their loins filled with heart's blood
Widowed farmers whose hands float under light covers to find
  themselves
Arisen at sunrise the splendid position of blood unearthly drawn
Toward clouds all feel something pass over them as she passes
Her palms over *her* long legs *her* small breasts and deeply between
Her thighs her hair shot loose from all pins streaming in the wind
Of her body let her come openly trying at the last second to land
On her back this is it THIS
                All those who find her impressed
In the soft loam gone down driven well into the image of her body
The furrows for miles flowing in upon her where she lies very deep
In her mortal outline in the earth as it is in cloud can tell nothing
But that she is there inexplicable unquestionable and remember
That something broke in them as well and began to live and die more
When they walked for no reason into their fields to where the whole
  earth
Caught her interrupted her maiden flight told her how to lie
  she cannot
Turn go away cannot move cannot slide off it and assume another
Position no sky-diver with any grin could save her hold her in
  his arms
Plummet with her unfold above her his wedding silks she can no
  longer

Mark the rain with whirling women that take the place of a dead wife
Or the goddess in Norwegian farm girls   or all the back-breaking whores
Of Wichita. All the known air above her is not giving up quite one
Breath   it is all gone   and yet not dead   not anywhere else
Quite   lying still in the field on her back   sensing the smells
Of incessant growth try to lift her   a little sight left in the corner
Of one eye   fading   seeing something wave   lies believing
That she could have made it   at the best part of her brief goddess
State   to water   gone in headfirst   come out smiling   invulnerable
Girl in a bathing-suit ad   but she is lying like a sunbather at the last
Of moonlight   half-buried in her impact on the earth   not far
From a railroad trestle   a water tank   she could see if she could
Raise her head from her modest hole   with her clothes beginning
To come down all over Kansas   into bushes   on the dewy sixth green
Of a golf course   one shoe   her girdle coming down fantastically
On a clothesline, where it belongs   her blouse on a lightning rod:

Lies in the fields   in *this* field   on her broken back as though on
A cloud she cannot drop through   while farmers sleepwalk without
Their women from houses   a walk like falling toward the far waters
Of life   in moonlight   toward the dreamed eternal meaning of their farms
Toward the flowering of the harvest in their hands   that tragic cost
Feels herself go   go toward   go outward   breathes at last fully
Not   and tries   less   once   tries   tries   AH,   GOD—

1981

DENISE LEVERTOV (1923–1997)

Born in Ilford, Essex, in England, Levertov was educated at home until she went briefly to ballet school and then trained to work as a nurse in London during World War II. Her father was a Jew who converted to Christianity and became an Anglican priest; her mother was Welsh. Levertov came to the United States in 1948. Since then, she served briefly as poetry editor for *The Nation,* and taught at several schools, including Stanford. Influenced by the English romantic poets early on, she increasingly began to be inspired by the open form poetry written by William Carlos Williams and other American poets, including Robert Creeley and Robert Duncan. That aesthetic combined with both a strong mystical bent and a long family tradition of political commitment. Her mother had worked with the League of Nations and on behalf of European refugees. Her father and sister protested Britain's indifference to the Spanish Republic's struggle with fascism. Years later, Levertov would write about nuclear war, compose a series of powerful poems about Vietnam, and, late in her career, address the Gulf War. Among her major achievements, however, is the haunting sequence of elegies to her sister Olga, reprinted here. Placing the Vietnam poems beside the elegies suggests a unifying spirituality, a belief in the sacred character of all life. Taken together, the poems also show Levertov's simultaneous commitment to open forms and careful craft.

THE ACHE OF MARRIAGE

The ache of marriage:

thigh and tongue, beloved,
are heavy with it,
it throbs in the teeth

We look for communion
and are turned away, beloved,
each and each

It is leviathan° and we
in its belly
looking for joy, some joy
not to be known outside it

8. *leviathan:* in the Old Testament, Jonah is swallowed by a leviathan, or great sea monster.

two by two in the ark° of
the ache of it

1964

OLGA POEMS

(Olga Levertoff, 1914–1964)

I

By the gas-fire, kneeling
to undress,
scorching luxuriously, raking
her nails over olive sides, the red
waistband ring—

(And the little sister
beady-eyed in the bed—
or drowsy, was I? My head
a camera—)

Sixteen. Her breasts
round, round, and
dark-nippled—

who now these two months long
is bones and tatters of flesh in earth.

II

The high pitch of
nagging insistence, lines
creased into raised brows—

Ridden, ridden—
the skin around the nails
nibbled sore—

You wanted
to shout the world to its senses,
did you?—to browbeat

12. *ark:* in the Book of Genesis, Noah build an ark, or boat, to save representatives of all species from the oncoming universal flood.

the poor into joy's
socialist republic—
What rage

and human shame swept you
when you were nine and saw
the Ley Street houses,
grasping their meaning as *slum.*
Where I, reaching that age,
teased you, admiring

architectural probity, circa
eighteen-fifty, and noted
pride in the whitened doorsteps.

Black one, black one,
there was a white
candle in your heart.

III

i

Everything flows
                she muttered into my childhood,
pacing the trampled grass where human puppets
rehearsed fates that summer,
stung into alien semblances by the lash of her will—
everything flows—
I looked up from my Littlest Bear's cane armchair
and knew the words came from a book
and felt them alien to me

but linked to words we loved
                from the hymnbook—*Time*
like an ever-rolling stream / bears all its sons away—

ii

Now as if smoke or sweetness were blown my way
I inhale a sense of her livingness in that instant,
feeling, dreaming, hoping, knowing boredom and zest like anyone
                else—

a young girl in the garden, the same alchemical square
I grew in, we thought sometimes

too small for our grand destinies—
But dread
was in her, a bloodbeat, it was against the rolling dark
oncoming river she raised bulwarks, setting herself
to sift cinders after early Mass all of one winter,

labelling her desk's normal disorder, basing
her verses on Keble's *Christian Year,* picking
those endless arguments, pressing on

to manipulate lives to disaster . . . To change,
to change the course of the river! What rage for order
disordered her pilgrimage—so that for years at a time

she would hide among strangers, waiting
to rearrange all mysteries in a new light.

iii

Black one, incubus—
she appeared
riding anguish as Tartars ride mares

over the stubble of bad years.

In one of the years
when I didn't know if she were dead or alive
I saw her in dream

haggard and rouged
lit by the flare
from an eel- or cockle-stand on a slum street—

was it a dream? I had lost

all sense, almost, of
who she was, what—inside of her skin,
under her black hair
dyed blonde—

it might feel like to be, in the wax and wane of the moon,
in the life I feel as unfolding, not flowing, the pilgrim years—

IV

On your hospital bed you lay
in love, the hatreds

that had followed you, a
comet's tail, burned out

as your disasters bred of love
burned out,
while pain and drugs
quarreled like sisters in you—

lay afloat on a sea
of love and pain—how you always
loved that cadence, 'Underneath
are the everlasting arms'—

all history
burned out, down
to the sick bone, save for

that kind candle.

V

i

In a garden grene whereas I lay—

you set the words to a tune so plaintive
it plucks its way through my life as through a wood.

As through a wood, shadow and light between birches,
gliding a moment in open glades, hidden by thickets of holly

your life winds in me. In Valentines
a root protrudes from the greensward several yards from its tree

we might raise like a trapdoor's handle, you said,
and descend long steps to another country

where we would live without father or mother
and without longing for the upper World. *The birds*
sang sweet, O song, *in the midst of the daye,*

and we entered silent mid-Essex churches on hot afternoons
and communed with the effigies of knights and their ladies

and their slender dogs asleep at their feet,
the stone so cold— *In youth*

is pleasure, in youth is pleasure.

ii

Under autumn clouds, under white
wideness of winter skies you went walking
the year you were most alone

returning to the old roads, seeing again
the signposts pointing to Theydon Garnon
or Stapleford Abbots or Greensted,

crossing the ploughlands (whose color I named *murple,*
a shade between brown and mauve that we loved
when I was a child and you

not much more than a child) finding new lanes
near White Roding or Abbess Roding; or lost in Romford's
new streets where there were footpaths then—

frowning as you ground out your thoughts, breathing deep
of the damp still air, taking
the frost into your mind unflinching.

How cold it was in your thin coat, your down-at-heel shoes—
tearless Niobe, your children were lost to you
and the stage lights had gone out, even the empty theater

was locked to you, cavern of transformation where all
had almost been possible.
How many books
you read in your silent lodgings that winter,
how the plovers transpierced your solitude out of doors with their strange cries
I had flung open my arms to in longing, once, by your side
stumbling over the furrows—

Oh, in your torn stockings, with unwaved hair,
you were trudging after your anguish
over the bare fields, soberly, soberly.

VI

Your eyes were the brown gold of pebbles under water.
I never crossed the bridge over the Roding, dividing
the open field of the present from the mysteries,
the wraiths and shifts of time-sense Wanstead Park held suspended,
without remembering your eyes. Even when we were estranged

and my own eyes smarted in pain and anger at the thought of you.
And by other streams in other countries; anywhere where the light
reaches down through shallows to gold gravel. Olga's
brown eyes. One rainy summer, down in the New Forest,
when we could hardly breathe for ennui and the low sky,
you turned savagely to the piano and sightread
straight through all the Beethoven sonatas, day after day—
weeks, it seemed to me. I would turn the pages some of the time,
go out to ride my bike, return—you were enduring in the
falls and rapids of the music, the arpeggios rang out, the rectory
trembled, our parents seemed effaced.
I think of your eyes in that photo, six years before I was born,
the fear in them. What did you do with your fear,
later? Through the years of humiliation,
of paranoia and blackmail and near-starvation, losing
the love of those you loved, one after another,
parents, lovers, children, idolized friends, what kept
compassion's candle alight in you, that lit you
clear into another chapter (but the same book) 'a clearing
in the selva oscura,
a house whose door
swings open, a hand beckons
in welcome'?°
                I cross
so many brooks in the world, there is so much light
dancing on so many stones, so many questions my eyes
smart to ask of your eyes, gold brown eyes,
the lashes short but the lids
arched as if carved out of olivewood, eyes with some vision
of festive goodness in back of their hard, or veiled, or shining,
unknowable gaze...

1964

WHAT WERE THEY LIKE?

1) Did the people of Vietnam
   use lanterns of stone?
2) Did they hold ceremonies
   to reverence the opening of buds?
3) Were they inclined to quiet laughter?
4) Did they use bone and ivory,
   jade and silver, for ornament?

---

175. *welcome:* Levertov's note—"the quoted lines—'a clearing / in the selva oscura, . . .'—are an adaption of some lines in 'Selva Oscura' by the late Louis MacNeice, a poem much loved by my sister, Olga."

5) Had they an epic poem?
6) Did they distinguish between speech and singing?

1) Sir, their light hearts turned to stone.
It is not remembered whether in gardens
stone lanterns illumined pleasant ways.
2) Perhaps they gathered once to delight in blossom,
but after the children were killed
there were no more buds.
3) Sir, laughter is bitter to the burned mouth.
4) A dream ago, perhaps. Ornament is for joy.
All the bones were charred.
5) It is not remembered. Remember,
most were peasants; their life
was in rice and bamboo.
When peaceful clouds were reflected in the paddies
and the water buffalo stepped surely along terraces,
maybe fathers told their sons old tales.
When bombs smashed those mirrors
there was time only to scream.
6) There is an echo yet
of their speech which was like a song.
It was reported their singing resembled
the flight of moths in moonlight.
Who can say? It is silent now.

1967

LIFE AT WAR

The disasters numb within us
caught in the chest, rolling
in the brain like pebbles. The feeling
resembles lumps of raw dough

weighing down a child's stomach on baking day.
Or Rilke said it, 'My heart . . .
Could I say of it, it overflows
with bitterness . . . but no, as though

its contents were simply balled into
formless lumps, thus
do I carry it about.'
The same war

continues.
We have breathed the grits of it in, all our lives,

our lungs are pocked with it,
the mucous membrane of our dreams
coated with it, the imagination
filmed over with the gray filth of it:

the knowledge that humankind,

delicate Man, whose flesh
responds to a caress, whose eyes
are flowers that perceive the stars,

whose music excels the music of birds,
whose laughter matches the laughter of dogs,
whose understanding manifests designs
fairer than the spider's most intricate web,

still turns without surprise, with mere regret
to the scheduled breaking open of breasts whose milk
runs out over the entrails of still-alive babies,
transformation of witnessing eyes to pulp-fragments,
implosion of skinned penises into carcass-gulleys.

We are the humans, men who can make;
whose language imagines *mercy,*
lovingkindness; we have believed one another
mirrored forms of a God we felt as good—

who do these acts, who convince ourselves
it is necessary; these acts are done
to our own flesh; burned human flesh
is smelling in Vietnam as I write.

Yes, this is the knowledge that jostles for space
in our bodies along with all we
go on knowing of joy, of love;

our nerve filaments twitch with its presence
day and night,
nothing we say has not the husky phlegm of it in the saying,
nothing we do has the quickness, the sureness,
the deep intelligence living at peace would have.

1967

ANTHONY HECHT (1923–2004)

Born in New York City and educated at Bard College and Columbia, Hecht served in Europe and Japan in the U.S. Army. He taught for a number of years at the University of Rochester and Georgetown University. Hecht wrote several books of criticism, including a study of W. H. Auden, and translated both classical and contemporary writers. Often learned and witty in his poetry, he has occasionally taken up more difficult subjects, as with the Holocaust poems "More Light! More Light!" and "The Book of Yolek." He was one of contemporary poetry's more elegant craftsmen, excelling in sustained technical ingenuity and willing to use the most complex traditional forms to tackle difficult subjects.

A HILL

In Italy, where this sort of thing can occur,
I had a vision once—though you understand
It was nothing at all like Dante's° or the visions of saints,
And perhaps not a vision at all. I was with some friends,
Picking my way through a warm sunlit piazza
In the early morning. A clear fretwork of shadows
From huge umbrellas littered the pavement and made
A sort of lucent shallows in which was moored
A small navy of carts. Books, coins, old maps,
Cheap landscapes and ugly religious prints
Were all on sale. The colors and noise
Like the flying hands were gestures of exultation,
So that even the bargaining
Rose to the ear like a voluble godliness.
And then, when it happened, the noises suddenly stopped,
And it got darker; pushcarts and people dissolved
And even the great Farnese Palace° itself
Was gone, for all its marble; in its place
Was a hill, mole-colored and bare. It was very cold,
Close to freezing, with a promise of snow.
The trees were like old ironwork gathered for scrap
Outside a factory wall. There was no wind,
And the only sound for a while was the little click
Of ice as it broke in the mud under my feet.
I saw a piece of ribbon snagged on a hedge,

3. *Dante:* Dante Alighieri (1265–1321), author of the *Divine Comedy.*
17. *Farnese Palace:* in Rome.

But no other sign of life. And then I heard
What seemed the crack of a rifle. A hunter, I guessed;
At least I was not alone. But just after that
Came the soft and papery crash
Of a great branch somewhere unseen falling to earth.

And that was all, except for the cold and silence
That promised to last forever, like the hill.

Then prices came through, and fingers, and I was restored
To the sunlight and my friends. But for more than a week
I was scared by the plain bitterness of what I had seen.
All this happened about ten years ago,
And it hasn't troubled me since, but at last, today,
I remembered that hill; it lies just to the left
Of the road north of Poughkeepsie;° and as a boy
I stood before it for hours in wintertime.

1967

"MORE LIGHT! MORE LIGHT!"°

for Heinrich Blücher and Hannah Arendt°

Composed in the Tower° before his execution
These moving verses, and being brought at that time
Painfully to the stake, submitted, declaring thus:
"I implore my God to witness that I have made no crime."

Nor was he forsaken of courage, but the death was horrible,
The sack of gunpowder failing to ignite.
His legs were blistered sticks on which the black sap
Bubbled and burst as he howled for the Kindly Light.°

And that was but one, and by no means one of the worst;
Permitted at least his pitiful dignity;
And such as were by made prayers in the name of Christ,
That shall judge all men, for his soul's tranquillity.

---

39. *Poughkeepsie:* town in New York State.

poem title: purportedly the dying words of German writer Johann Wolfgang von Goethe (1749–1832).

dedication: *Arendt:* (1906–1975), political philosopher who characterized Nazi SS leader Adolf Eichmann with the phrase "the banality of evil." Blücher, a philosophy professor, was her husband.

1. *Tower:* the Tower of London, a palace-fortress whose construction began in the eleventh century. From the fifteenth through the eighteenth centuries it was famous as a prison and place of execution. Hecht has explained that he had no single execution in mind: "the details are conflated from several executions, including Latimer and Ridley [Anglican bishops, for heresy, 1555] whose deaths at the stake are described by Foxe in *Acts and Monuments.* But neither of them wrote poems just before their deaths, as others did."

8. *Kindly Light:* from the nineteenth-century hymn "Lead, Kindly Light," which asks for mercy.

We move now to outside a German wood.°
Three men are there commanded to dig a hole
In which the two Jews are ordered to lie down
And be buried alive by the third, who is a Pole.

Not light from the shrine at Weimar° beyond the hill
Nor light from heaven appeared. But he did refuse.
A Lüger° settled back deeply in its glove.
He was ordered to change places with the Jews.

Much casual death had drained away their souls.
The thick dirt mounted toward the quivering chin.
When only the head was exposed the order came
To dig him out again and to get back in.

No light, no light in the blue Polish eye.
When he finished a riding boot packed down the earth.
The Lüger hovered lightly in its glove.
He was shot in the belly and in three hours bled to death.

No prayers or incense rose up in those hours
Which grew to be years, and every day came mute
Ghosts from the ovens, sifting through crisp air,
And settled upon his eyes in a black soot.

1967

THE BOOK OF YOLEK°

Wir haben ein Gesetz,
Und nach dem Gesetz soll er sterben.°

---

13. *a German wood:* near Buchenwald, the Nazi concentration camp. These 1944 events are detailed in *The Theory and Practice of Hell* (1958) by Eugen Kogon.

17. *shrine at Weimar:* the city where Goethe lived for some years.

19. *Lüger:* German military pistol.

poem title: Hecht's poem was inspired by Polish writer Hanna Mortkowicz Olczakowa's "Yanosz Korczak's Last Walk." Korczak (1879–1942), the pen name Henryk Goldszmit adopted after he began writing children's stories, was a pediatrician who became head of a large Jewish orphanage in Warsaw. When the Nazis came on August 5, 1942, to take the 200 orphanage children to their deaths in the Treblinka gas ovens, Korczak refused to abandon them. Instead, he led them in a procession, singing. "Yolek" is one of the children who was marched to his death that day. Hecht served with the U. S. 97th Infantry and participated in the liberation of Flossenburg, an annex of Buchenwald: "When we arrived . . . prisoners were dying at the rate of five hundred a day from typhus. . . . The place, the suffering, the prisoners' accounts were beyond comprehension. For years after I would wake shrieking."

epigraph: (German) "We have a law, and by that law he ought to die." From a translation of John 19:7 by German theologian and Protestant Reformation leader Martin Luther (1483–1546).

The dowsed coals fume and hiss after your meal
Of grilled brook trout, and you saunter off for a walk
Down the fern trail, it doesn't matter where to,
Just so you're weeks and worlds away from home,
And among midsummer hills have set up camp
In the deep bronze glories of declining day.

You remember, peacefully, an earlier day
In childhood, remember a quite specific meal:
A corn roast and bonfire in summer camp.
That summer you got lost on a Nature Walk;
More than you dared admit, you thought of home;
No one else knows where the mind wanders to.

The fifth of August, 1942.
It was morning and very hot. It was the day
They came at dawn with rifles to The Home
For Jewish Children, cutting short the meal
Of bread and soup, lining them up to walk
In close formation off to a special camp.

How often you have thought about that camp,
As though in some strange way you were driven to,
And about the children, and how they were made to walk,
Yolek who had bad lungs, who wasn't a day
Over five years old, commanded to leave his meal
And shamble between armed guards to his long home.

We're approaching August again. It will drive home
The regulation torments of that camp
Yolek was sent to, his small, unfinished meal,
The electric fences, the numeral tattoo,
The quite extraordinary heat of the day
They all were forced to take that terrible walk.

Whether on a silent, solitary walk
Or among crowds, far off or safe at home,
You will remember, helplessly, that day,
And the smell of smoke, and the loudspeakers of the camp.
Wherever you are, Yolek will be there, too.
His unuttered name will interrupt your meal.

Prepare to receive him in your home some day.
Though they killed him in the camp they sent him to,
He will walk in as you're sitting down to a meal.

1982

BOB KAUFMAN (1925–1986)

The introduction to Kaufman's selected poems tells us that he was born in New Orleans; his father, who was half African American and half Jewish, worked as a Pullman porter for the railroad that ran between New Orleans and Chicago. His mother, a black woman from an old Martinique family, the Vignes, was a schoolteacher. "His Jewish surname and Creole-like features," the introduction notes, "were shared with twelve brothers and sisters . . . Up until his death from emphysema in January of 1986, Kaufman was known as a mostly silent, wiry black man who walked the streets of San Francisco's North Beach district day and night, often appearing as a mendicant, madman, or panhandler. Yet various schools of American poetry have sung his praises." His working life began at sea; he was a cabin boy on the *Henry Gibbons*. Based in New York and San Francisco, he worked on Henry Wallace's 1948 Progressive Party presidential campaign, during which he was arrested and thrown into jail; early on he connected with the Beat poets and became one of the notable figures of the movement. At the end of the 1950s, City Lights Books issued three of his broadsides, including the widely read "Abominist Manifesto," whose fourteen points include these:

> *IN TIMES OF NATIONAL PERIL, ABOMINISTS, AS REALITY AMERICANS, STAND READY TO DRINK THEMSELVES TO DEATH FOR THEIR COUNTRY.*
>
> *ABOMINIST POETS, CONFIDENT THAT THE NEW LITERARY FORM "FOOT-PRINTISM" HAS FREED THE ARTIST OF OUTMODED RESTRICTIONS, SUCH AS: THE ABILITY TO READ AND WRITE, OR THE DESIRE TO COMMUNICATE, MUST BE PREPARED TO READ THEIR WORK AT DENTAL COLLEGES, EMBALMING SCHOOLS, HOMES FOR UNWED MOTHERS, INSANE ASYLUMS, USO CANTEENS, KINDERGARTENS, AND COUNTY JAILS. ABOMINISTS NEVER COMPROMISE THEIR REJECTIONARY PHILOSOPHY.*

Kaufman would declaim his poems and manifestoes at poetry readings and in other public places; often enough the police would arrest him. Eventually, he began to drink under the strain; back in New York he was arrested and given shock treatments against his will. After President Kennedy was shot, Kaufman took a vow of silence, maintaining it for a decade. Then he began writing again; the poems were rescued from a hotel fire by a friend and published as Kaufman's third book in 1981. By the end, he had been a Beat poet, a surrealist, a sound poet, a jazz poet, and a poet of black consciousness.

THE BIGGEST FISHERMAN

singular prints filed along damp banks,
supposed evidence of fouled strings, all,

breached dikes of teeth hewn agate statues
scaly echoes in eroded huts of slate and gristle.

mildewed toes of pastoral escapes, mossy charades,
cane towered blind, smooth blister on watern neck

angry glowing fish in eniwetok garments and pig tusks
alarmed horror of black croakers, finned hawks sinking.

collectors of fish teeth and souls of night vision demons
taxidermy fiesta of revolutionary aquatic holidays lost.

breeding hills of happy men, of no particular bent, or none,
condemned to undreamlike beauty of day to day to day to day,
deprived of night, ribbon bright streams die parched deaths
baked by fissioning waves of newly glowing fish.

1967

CROOTEY SONGO

DERRAT SLEGELATIONS, FLO GOOF BABER,
SCRASH SHO DUBIES, WAGO WAILO WAILO.
GEED BOP NAVA GLIED, NAVA GLIED NAVA,
SPLEERIEDER, HUYEDIST, HEDACAZ, AX—, O, O.

DEEREDITION, BOOMEDITION, SQUOM, SQUOM, SQUOM.
DEE BEETSTRAWIST, WAPAGO, LOCOEST, LOCORO, LO.
VOOMETEYEREEPETIOP, BOP, BOP, BOP, WHIPOLAT.

DEGET, SKLOKO, KURRITIF, PLOG, MANGI, PLOG MANGI,
CLOPO JAGO BREE, BREE, ASLOOPERED, AKINGO LABY.
ENGPOP, ENGPOP, BOP, PLOLO, PLOLO, BOP, BOP.

1967

NO MORE JAZZ AT ALACATRAZ°

No more jazz
At Alcatraz
No more piano
for Lucky Luciano
No more trombone
for Al Capone

---

poem title: *Alcatraz:* an island in California's San Francisco Bay, served as an American military prison from 1859 to 1934 and a maximum security federal prison thereafter, until it closed in 1963. Luciano (1897–1962), Capone (1899–1947), and Costello (1891–1973) were all organized crime figures, and Alcatraz inmates.

No more jazz
at Alcatraz
No more cello
for Frank Costello
No more screeching of the
Seagulls
As they line up for
Chow
No more jazz
At Alcatraz

c. 1963

from JAIL POEMS

1

I am sitting in a cell with a view of evil parallels,
Waiting thunder to splinter me into a thousand me's.
It is not enough to be in one cage with one self;
I want to sit opposite every prisoner in every hole.
Doors roll and bang, every slam a finality, bang!
The junkie disappeared into a red noise, stoning out his hell.
The odored wino congratulates himself on not smoking,
Fingerprints left lying on black inky gravestones,
Noises of pain seeping through steel walls crashing
Reach my own hurt. I become part of someone forever.
Wild accents of criminals are sweeter to me than hum of cops,
Busy battening down hatches of human souls; cargo
Destined for ports of accusations, harbors of guilt.
What do policemen eat, Socrates, still prisoner, old one?

2

Painter, paint me a crazy jail, mad water-color cells.
Poet, how old is suffering? Write it in yellow lead.
God, make me a sky on my glass ceiling. I need stars now,
To lead through this atmosphere of shrieks and private hells,
Entrances and exits, in . . . out . . . up . . . down, the civic seesaw.
Here—me—now—hear—me—now—always here somehow.

3

In a universe of cells—who is not in jail? Jailers.
In a world of hospitals—who is not sick? Doctors.
A golden sardine is swimming in my head.
Oh we know some things, man, about some things
Like jazz and jails and God.
Saturday is a good day to go to jail.

1959/1965

MAXINE KUMIN (1925–2014)

Kumin was born Maxine Winokur of Jewish parents in Philadelphia. She was educated at Radcliffe. She has written poetry, criticism, fiction, and more than twenty children's books, including four coauthored with Anne Sexton. She has taught at Tufts, the University of Massachusetts, and Princeton. Kumin spends much of her time in rural New Hampshire, where she raises horses. Although she has often written about middle-class suburban experience, seeking survival and continuity in the vestiges of nature it encompasses, she has also made harsh and witty appraisals of rural life. Her sharp irony, her New England settings, and her use of traditional forms make comparison with Frost both inevitable and reasonable. The easy linking of her with transcendentalism is less warranted, in part because Kumin rarely seeks lyrical transcendence of any kind, preferring stoical observation instead. She has also written sympathetically about women's lives and taken on public topics like famine, pollution, and nuclear war.

VOICES FROM KANSAS

The women of Wichita say they live in what
is casually known on both coasts as a flyover state.
The prairie wind here is constant in every season.
Sometimes it makes the sucking sound of ocean.
Sometimes it moans like an animal in heat.

In April, deliberate fires blacken great swatches
of cropland. Scarves of smoke darken the day
devouring briars and thistles and climbing vetches
before seedtime. Tractors draw threads to the edge of sky.
You learn to pull out and pass, say the Wichita women

whom distance has not flattened, who cruise at a cool
80 miles per hour toward the rolling-pin horizon
where oncoming headlights are visible more than a mile
away. Long hours at a stretch behind the wheel
they zoom up to Michigan to speak at a conference,

revisit a lover, drop in on old friends.
They will not be sequestered by space. Jo-El,
descended from Socialists, is saving the farm—
labor songs of her forebears, accompanied by dulcimer.
Lynn collects early photos of sodhouse homesteaders.

Mary Anne has got a sad history in her arms.
She is reconstructing her orphaned grandfather
in his sea of sheep, white blobs overspreading the plains,
his whole Scottish clan, ten siblings carried off together
in December of 1918 by a wildfire flu.
This tear-stained boy in the woolly fold, custodian
of his flock and her life, shines piercingly through.
As the grassland is rooted, so too are the Wichita women.
No absence among them may go unmarked into sleep.
Like wind in the wheat, the boundary blurs but keeps.

1992

SAGA

1. LIFE STYLE

Invincible begetters, assorted Scutzes
have always lived hereabouts in the woods
trapping beaver or fox, poaching enough
deer to get by on. Winters, they barricade
their groundsills with spoiled hay, which can ignite
from a careless cigarette or chimney spark.
In the fifties, one family barely got out
when the place lit up like the Fair midway at dark.

The singular name of Scutz, it is thought, derives
from *skuft,* Middle Dutch for the nape one is strung up by.
Hangmen or hanged, they led the same snug lives
in an Old World loft adjoining the pigsty
as now, three generations tucked in two
rooms with color tv, in the New.

2. LEISURE

The seldom-traveled dirt road by their door
is where, good days, the Scutzes take their ease.
It serves as living room, garage, *pissoir*
as well as barnyard. Hens scratch and rabbits doze
under cars jacked up on stumps of trees.

Someone produces a dozen bottles of beer.
Someone tacks a target to a tire
across the road and hoists it seductively
human-high. The Scutzes love to shoot.
Later, they line the empty bottles up.

The music of glassbreak gladdens them. The brute
sound of a bullet widening a rip
in rubber, the rifle kick, the powder smell
pure bliss. Deadeyes, the Scutzes lightly kill.

3. SHELTER

Old doors slanted over packing crates
shelter the Scutzes' several frantic dogs
pinioned on six-foot chains they haven't been
loosed from since January of '91
when someone on skis crept up in snow fog
and undid all of their catches in the night.

Each of the Scutzes' dogs has a dish or plate
to eat from, usually overturned in the dirt.
What do they do for water? Pray for rain.
What do they do for warmth? Remember when
they lay in the litter together, a sweet
jumble of laundry, spotted and stained.

O we are smug in the face of the Scutzes, we
who stroll past their domain, its aromas of ripe decay,
its casual discards mottled with smut and pee.
What do we neighbors do? Look the other way.

4. SELF-FULFILLING PROPHECY

If Lonnie Scutz comes back, he's guaranteed
free room and board in the State's crowbar hotel.
His girlfriend Grace, a toddler at her heels
and in her arms a grubby ten-month jewel,
looks to be pregnant again, but not his seed.
It's rumored this one was sired by his dad.

Towheads with skyblue eyes, they'll go to school
now and then, struggle to learn to read
and write, forget to carry when they add,
be mocked, kept back or made to play the fool
and soon enough drop out. Their nimble code,
hit first or get hit, supplants the Golden Rule.

It all works out the way we knew it would.
They'll come to no good end, the Scutzes' kids.

1992

OBLIVION

The dozen ways they did it—
off a bridge, the back of a boat,
pills, head in the oven, or
wrapped in her mother's old mink coat
in the garage, a brick on the accelerator,
the Cougar's motor thrumming
while she crossed over.

What they left behind—
the outline of a stalled novel, diaries,
their best poems, the note that ends
now will you believe me,
offspring of various ages, spouses
who cared and weep and yet
admit relief now that it's over.

How they fester, the old details
held to the light like a stained-glass icon
—the shotgun in the mouth, the string
from toe to trigger; the tongue
a blue plum forced between his lips
when he hanged himself in her closet—
for us it is never over

who raced to the scene, cut the noose,
pulled the bathtub plug on pink water,
broke windows, turned off the gas,
rode in the ambulance, only minutes later
to take the body blow of bad news.
We are trapped in the plot, every one.
Left behind, there is no oblivion.

2002

PANTOUM, WITH SWAN

for Carolyn Kizer

Bits of his down under my fingernails
a gob of his spit behind one ear
and a nasty welt where the nib of his beak
bit down as he came. It was our first date.

A gob of his spit behind one ear,
his wings still fanning. I should have known better,

I should have bitten him off on our first date.
And yet for some reason I didn't press charges;

I wiped off the wet. I should have known better.
They gave me the morning-after pill
and shook their heads when I wouldn't press charges.
The yolk that was meant to hatch as Helen

failed to congeal, thanks to the morning-after pill
and dropped harmlessly into the toilet
so that nothing became of the lost yolk, Helen,
Troy, wooden horse, forestalled in one swallow

flushed harmlessly away down the toilet.
The swan had by then stuffed Euripedes, Sophocles
—leaving out Helen, Troy, Agamemnon—
the whole house of Atreus, the rest of Greek tragedy,

stuffed in my head, every strophe of Sophocles.
His knowledge forced on me, yet Bird kept the power.
What was I to do with ancient Greek history
lodged in my cortex to no avail?

I had his knowledge, I had no power
the year I taught Yeats in a classroom so pale
that a mist enshrouded the ancient religions
and bits of his down flew from under my fingernails.

2002

WITH WILLIAM MEREDITH IN BULGARIA°

In the grim days of Zhivkov, President for Life,
you and I flew to Sofia in an old Russian Tupelov
where everyone smoked and coughed and spat
and over each window hung a little box marked
in English and Cyrillic *in case of emergency*
safety rope. Laughing, we said *sky hook,* but when
on landing they took away our passports and return
tickets, fear whistled down my throat. You,

ever equable, assured me that as our country's
goodwill ambassadors at the harvest festival
to honor Nikola Vaptsarov, we were safe as sunrise.
Vaptsar, they called him, this war-hero poet
and factory machinist martyred in the Resistance.

---

poem title: William Meredith (1919–2007), American poet.

Homegrown fascists dispatched him in 1942
but not before he flung the plume of revolution
at them. He survives as a park, boulevard, museum.

They bused us into his beloved mountains
where girls with fruit and flowers offered
ripe pears the size of platters, so succulent
that one bite sluiced our chins. Everyone
in peasant dress, all reds and greens, and endless
speeches. No one mentioned Vaptsarov's life story,
how his countrymen had hung him upside down
for hours and beaten him with rifle butts

before they assembled the firing squad. Because
you were gay and in the closet (this was the seventies)
you leaned your shoulder against mine in public
and squeezed my hand to stay awake through the rhetoric.
Nightly your new artist buddy Misha
hoped to be invited to your college.
Nightly we three drank to this with slivovitz
and Ludmilla, our interpreter, who did not drink,

who once had served for the Lord Mayor of London
and wanted help with amerikanski slang, raised
a dry glass. They took her from us the fourth day.
I said it was because we'd been too friendly.
You disagreed. Misha pulled away and fell silent.
Two more days of speeches, nights of parties
and then the hairpin turns back down the mountains
made queasier by hangovers. *The firing squad.*

And then the worms, Nikola wrote the night before
his execution. *I fell. Someone else will take my place.*
Balkan Airlines' engines throbbed, the door
was latched, we had already fastened our seatbelts
but how could we go? *Sit tight,* you said,
as if we could do anything else. The plane pulsed
angrily. The heavy seal gave way, a functionary galloped
down the aisle restoring our identities, our passports.

2010

DONALD JUSTICE (1925–2004)

Donald Justice was born in Miami and educated at Miami University, the University of North Carolina, and the University of Iowa. He taught for a number of years first at Iowa and then at the University of Florida. Several of the poets in this collection—including Jorie Graham, Mark Strand, and Charles Wright—are among his students. The selection here is designed as a miniature version of his career, beginning with witty and technically exquisite poems like "The Wall" and "An Old Fashioned Devil," then moving to a reflection on his own work in "Early Poems," and finally moving to the more open and meditative style of "Absences" and "Presences."

AN OLD-FASHIONED DEVIL

Who is it snarls our plow lines, wastes our fields,
Unbaits our hooks, and fishes out our streams?
Who leads our hunts to where the good earth yields
To marshlands, and we sink, but no one screams?
Who taught our children where the harlot lives?
They gnaw her nipples and they drain her pap,
Clapping their little hands like primitives,
With droll abandon bouncing on her lap.
Our wives may adore him; us he bores to tears.
Who cares if to our dry and yellowing grass
He strikes a match or two, then disappears?
It's only the devil on his flop-eared ass—
A beast too delicate to bear him well—
Come plodding by us on his way to hell.

1948

THE WALL

The wall surrounding them they never saw;
The angels, often. Angels were as common
As birds or butterflies, but looked more human.
As long as the wings were furled, they felt no awe.
Beasts, too, were friendly. They could find no flaw
In all of Eden: this was the first omen.
The second was the dream which woke the woman.
She dreamed she saw the lion sharpen his claw.
As for the fruit, it had no taste at all.
They had been warned of what was bound to happen.
They had been told of something called the world.

They had been told and told about the wall.
They saw it now; the gate was standing open.
As they advanced, the giant wings unfurled.

1960

EARLY POEMS

How fashionably sad those early poems are!
On their clipped lawns and hedges the snows fall.
Rains beat against the tarpaulines of their porches,
Where, Sunday mornings, the bored children sprawl,
Reading the comics before their parents rise.
—The rhymes, the meters, how they paralyze!

Who walks out through their streets tonight? No one.
You know these small towns, how all traffic stops
At ten, the corner street lamps gathering moths,
And mute, pale mannequins waiting in dark shops,
Undressed, and ready for the dreams of men.
—Now the long silence. Now the beginning again.

1967

PRESENCES

Everyone, everyone went away today.
They left without a word, and I think
I did not hear a single goodbye today.

And all that I saw was someone's hand, I think,
Thrown up out there like the hand of someone drowning,
But far away, too far to be sure what it was or meant.

No, but I saw how everything had changed
Later, just as the light had; and at night
I saw that from dream to dream everything changed.

And those who might have come to me in the night,
The ones who did come back but without a word,
All those I remembered passed through my hands like clouds—

Clouds out of the south, familiar clouds—
But I could not hold on to them, they were drifting away,
Everything going away in the night again and again.

1973

ABSENCES

It's snowing this afternoon and there are no flowers.
There is only this sound of falling, quiet and remote,
Like the memory of scales descending the white keys
Of a childhood piano—outside the window, palms!
And the heavy head of the cereus, inclining,
Soon to let down its white or yellow-white.

Now, only these poor snow-flowers in a heap,
Like the memory of a white dress cast down . . .
So much has fallen.
And I, who have listened for a step
All afternoon, hear it now, but already falling away,
Already in memory. And the terrible scales descending
On the silent piano; the snow; and the absent flowers
abounding.

1973

PAUL BLACKBURN (1926–1971)

Blackburn was born in St. Albans, Vermont. His parents separated when he was three, and he grew up with his mother's parents until his mother took him to New York's Greenwich Village when he was fourteen. After a stint in the army, he enrolled at New York University, but then transferred to the University of Wisconsin, where he started a correspondence with Ezra Pound, who was then incarcerated at St. Elizabeth's Hospital in Washington, and who encouraged Blackburn's poetry writing. In New York, Blackburn pursued an interest in Provençal troubadour poets, translating them into English. By the late 1950s, Blackburn was becoming known as a poet of city life, with poems that were both witty and observant about New York in particular. But he was also active in the antiwar and civil rights movements and regularly wrote poems about those issues as well. Meanwhile he was supporting himself with editing and translating jobs. All along he had also written culturally and epistemologically reflective poems about his travels abroad. "At the Well" is a strikingly contemporary and wittily challenging poem about otherness and colonialism. Blackburn died at age forty-four from cancer of the esophagus.

AT THE CROSSROAD

Close
but far

strayed into the half-cultivated country
of meditation
woven into it wholly
enlaced in the rare herbs of silence

another,
a lost stranger, our friend
asleep, perhaps nearly dead

Nite-stir of silence
Water runs beyond summer its gutters
Rustle of wind, light
Moonlight over it all

In the next field
the May ass screaming
drunk on the new hay

1957

AT THE WELL

Here we are, see?
in this village, maybe a camp
middle of desert, the
Maghreb, desert below Marrakesh°
standing in the street
simply.

Outskirts of the camp
at the edge of town, these riders
on camels or horses,
but riders, tribesmen, sitting
there on their horses.

They are mute. They are
hirsute, they are not
able to speak. If they
could the sound would be gutteral.
They cannot speak. They want
something.

I nor
you know what they want   .   They want
nothing.   They are beyond want.   They need
nothing.   They used to be slaves.   They
want something of us / of me / what
shall I say to them.

They have had their tongues cut out.
I have nothing to give them   ¿There is no
grace at the edge of my heart I would grant,
render them?   They want something, they
sit there on their horses.   Are there
children in the village I can give them.

My child's heart? Is it goods they want
as tribute. They have had their tongues
cut out. Can I offer them some sound
my mouth makes in the night? Can I
say they are brave, fierce,
implacable? that I would like to
join them?

---

4. *Marrakesh:* North African city in Morocco.

Let us go together

across the desert toward the
cities, let us
terrify the towns, the villages,
disappear among bazaars, sell our
camels, pierce our ears, for-
get that we are mute and drive
the princes out, take all the
slave-girls for ourselves?
What can I offer them.

They have appeared here on the edge of my soul.
I ask them what they want, they say
—You are our leader.   Tell us what
your pleasure is, we
want you.   They
say nothing.   They

are mute.   they are hirsute.   They
are the fathers I never had.   They are
tribesmen standing on the edge of town near
water, near the soul I must look into each
morning   .   myself.

Who are these wild men?
I scream:
—I want my gods!

I want my goods! I want
my reflection in the sun's pool at morning,
shade in the afternoon under the
date palms, I want and want!

What can I give them.
What tribe of nomads and wanderers am I continuation of, what
can I give my fathers?
What can I offer myself?

I want to see my own skin
at the life's edge, at the
life-giving water.   I want

to rise from the pool,
mount my camel and
be among the living, the other side of this village.

Come gentlemen,
wheel your mounts about.
There is nothing here .

1963/1970

FRANK O'HARA (1926–1966)

Born in Baltimore, Maryland, and raised in Grafton, Massachusetts, O'Hara served in the U.S. Navy in the South Pacific from 1944 to 1946. He was educated at Harvard and the University of Michigan, after which he served as associate curator at New York's Museum of Modern Art. He was also editor of *Art News*. Like John Ashbery, a friend and member of what came to be known as the New York School of poets, O'Hara mixes high and low cultural allusions with a certain effortless glee; he also manages abrupt shifts of tone that mimic the erratic, associational paths of a consciousness stimulated by external events and images. The poems skate easily over surfaces, light on objects, absorb variations in mood, and register the cultural and political temper of the times with a grace that makes them immensely pleasurable, but an oblique sense of tragedy also gives them a haunting gravity. As with the paintings he admired, O'Hara's poems are also chronicles of the process of their composition. He was often casual about his output, sometimes not even keeping copies of his poems; O'Hara's work survives today in part because he sent poems to friends that were later collected posthumously. Widely imitated, his voice remains exceptional. He was accidentally run over and killed by a jeep on New York's Fire Island.

from ALMA

Detroit was founded on the great near waterways next to Canada which was friendly and immediately gained for herself the appellation "the Detroit of Thermopylaes," a name which has stuck to this day wherever ballroom dancing is held in proper esteem. Let me remind you of that great wrist movement, the enjambement schizophrene, a particularly satisfying variation of which may be made by adding a little tomato paste. Great success. While in Detroit accused of starting the Chicago fire. Millions of roses from Russians. Alma had come a long way, she opened a jewelry shop, her name became a household word, she'd invented an arch-supporter.

How often she thought of her father! the castle, the kitchen-garden, the hollihocks and the mill stream beyond curving gently as a parenthesis. Many a bitter tear was shed by her on the boards of this theatre as she pondered the inscrutable meagerness of divine Providence, always humming, always shifting a little, never missing a beat. She guested one season at the height of her nostalgia with the Metropolitan Opera Ballet in *Salammbô;* her father seemed very close in all that oriental splendor of bamboo and hotel palms and stale sweat and bracelets, an engagement of tears. In the snow, in her white fox fur wraps, how more beautiful than Mary Garden!

1952

POEM

The eager note on my door said "Call me,
call when you get in!" so I quickly threw

a few tangerines into my overnight bag,
straightened my eyelids and shoulders, and

headed straight for the door. It was autumn
by the time I got around the corner, oh all
unwilling to be either pertinent or bemused, but
the leaves were brighter than grass on the sidewalk!

Funny, I thought, that the lights are on this late
and the hall door open; still up at this hour, a
champion jai-alai player like himself? Oh fie!
for shame! What a host, so zealous! And he was

there in the hall, flat on a sheet of blood that
ran down the stairs. I did appreciate it. There are few
hosts who so thoroughly prepare to greet a guest
only casually invited, and that several months ago.

1950

A STEP AWAY FROM THEM

It's my lunch hour, so I go
for a walk among the hum-colored
cabs. First, down the sidewalk
where laborers feed their dirty
glistening torsos sandwiches
and Coca-Cola, with yellow helmets
on. They protect them from falling
bricks, I guess. Then onto the
avenue where skirts are flipping
above heels and blow up over
grates. The sun is hot, but the
cabs stir up the air. I look
at bargains in wristwatches. There
are cats playing in sawdust.
On
to Times Square, where the sign
blows smoke over my head,° and higher
the waterfall pours lightly. A
Negro stands in a doorway with a
toothpick, languorously agitating.
A blonde chorus girl clicks: he

17. *head:* an advertising billboard in Times Square that puffs steam to simulate cigarette smoke.

smiles and rubs his chin. Everything
suddenly honks: it is 12:40 of
a Thursday.
Neon in daylight is a
great pleasure, as Edwin Denby[o] would
write, as are light bulbs in daylight.
I stop for a cheeseburger at JULIET'S
CORNER. Giulietta Masina, wife of
Federico Fellini, *è bell' attrice.*[o]
And chocolate malted. A lady in
foxes on such a day puts her poodle
in a cab.

There are several Puerto
Ricans on the avenue today, which
makes it beautiful and warm. First
Bunny died, then John Latouche,
then Jackson Pollock.[o] But is the
earth as full as life was full, of them?
And one has eaten and one walks,
past the magazines with nudes
and the posters for BULLFIGHT and
the Manhattan Storage Warehouse,
which they'll soon tear down. I
used to think they had the Armory
Show[o] there.
A glass of papaya juice
and back to work. My heart is in my
pocket, it is Poems by Pierre Reverdy.[o]

1956

THE DAY LADY DIED[o]

It is 12:20 in New York a Friday
three days after Bastille day,[o] yes

---

26. *Denby:* American poet (b. 1923).

30. . . . *attrice:* (Italian) "a beautiful actress." Fellini was a major Italian film director.

37–38. *Bunny, Latouche, Pollock:* Bunny (V. R. Lang, 1924–1956), a poet who directed the Poet's Theater in Cambridge, Massachusetts, and produced O'Hara's plays; Latouche (1917–1956) wrote lyrics for musicals; Pollock (1912–1956) famed founder of "action painting." All three were O'Hara's friends.

46. *Armory Show:* the famous 1913 show that introduced modem art to American audiences.

49. *Reverdy:* (1899–1960), French poet whose work O'Hara admired.

poem title: the poem honors the great blues and jazz singer Billie Holiday (1915–1959); the title inverts her nickname, "Lady Day," to announce its occasion.

2. *Bastille day:* July 14, French Independence day, celebrating the 1789 storming of the Bastille prison.

it is 1959 and I go get a shoeshine
because I will get off the 4:19 in Easthampton°
at 7:15 and then go straight to dinner
and I don't know the people who will feed me

I walk up the muggy street beginning to sun
and have a hamburger and a malted and buy
an ugly NEW WORLD WRITING to see what the poets
in Ghana are doing these days
                                        I go on to the bank
and Miss Stillwagon (first name Linda I once heard)
doesn't even look up my balance for once in her life
and in the GOLDEN GRIFFIN° I get a little Verlaine°
for Patsy° with drawings by Bonnard° although I do
think of Hesiod, trans. Richard Lattimore° or
Brendan Behan's° new play or *Le Balcon* or *Les Nègres*
of Genet,° but I don't, I stick with Verlaine
after practically going to sleep with quandariness

and for Mike I just stroll into the PARK LANE
Liquor Store and ask for a bottle of Strega and
then I go back where I came from to 6th Avenue
and the tobacconist in the Ziegfeld Theatre and
casually ask for a carton of Gauloises and a carton
of Picayunes,° and a NEW YORK POST with her face on it

and I am sweating a lot by now and thinking of
leaning on the john door in the 5 SPOT
while she whispered a song along the keyboard
to Mal Waldron° and everyone and I stopped breathing

1959

---

4. *Easthampton:* a town on Long Island's south shore, Long Island being east of Manhattan. The 4:19 is a scheduled train on the Long Island Railroad. Easthampton is near Southhampton, where O'Hara is heading for dinner. At the time the poem refers to, the Hamptons were still farming communities and reasonably priced places for New York City expatriates to live.

14. *Golden Griffin:* avant-garde New York bookstore.

14. *Verlaine:* Paul Verlaine (1844–1896), French poet.

15. *Patsy:* Patsy Southgate and Mike Goldberg, a painter, lived in Southhampton and were O'Hara's dinner companions.

15. *Bonnard:* Pierre Bonnard (1867–1947), a post-Impressionist French painter who illustrated Verlaine's *Parallelement* in 1902.

16. *Richard Lattimore:* published his translation of Greek poet Hesiod (c. 800 B.C.–c. 700 B.C.) in 1959.

17. *Brendan Behan:* (1923–1964), Irish playwright, whose 1958 play was *The Hostage*.

18. *Genet:* Jean Genet (1910–1968), French writer whose plays *Le Balcon* ("The Balcony") and *Les Nègres* ("The Blacks") were staged to much debate in the 1950s.

25. *Gauloises and Picayunes:* two brands of French cigarettes.

29. *Mal Waldron:* (b. 1924), Billie Holiday's pianist.

WHY I AM NOT A PAINTER

I am not a painter, I am a poet.
Why? I think I would rather be
a painter, but I am not. Well,

for instance, Mike Goldberg°
is starting a painting. I drop in.
"Sit down and have a drink" he
says. I drink; we drink. I look
up. "You have SARDINES in it."
"Yes, it needed something there."
"Oh." I go and the days go by
and I drop in again. The painting
is going on, and I go, and the days
go by. I drop in. The painting is
finished. "Where's SARDINES?"
All that's left is just
letters, "It was too much," Mike says.

But me? One day I am thinking of
a color: orange. I write a line
about orange. Pretty soon it is a
whole page of words, not lines.
Then another page. There should be
so much more, not of orange, of
words, of how terrible orange is
and life. Days go by. It is even in
prose, I am a real poet. My poem
is finished and I haven't mentioned
orange yet. It's twelve poems, I call
it ORANGES. And one day in a gallery
I see Mike's painting, called SARDINES.

1957

A TRUE ACCOUNT OF TALKING TO THE SUN AT FIRE ISLAND

The Sun woke me this morning loud
and clear, saying "Hey! I've been
trying to wake you up for fifteen
minutes. Don't be so rude, you are

---

4. *Goldberg:* (1924–2007), a painter with whom O'Hara collaborated. His silkscreen prints illustrate O'Hara's 1960 *Odes.*

only the second poet I've ever chosen
to speak to personally
so why
aren't you more attentive? If I could
burn you through the window I would
to wake you up. I can't hang around
here all day."
"Sorry, Sun, I stayed
up late last night talking to Hal."

"When I woke up Mayakovsky° he was
a lot more prompt" the Sun said
petulantly. "Most people are up
already waiting to see if I'm going
to put in an appearance."
I tried
to apologize "I missed you yesterday."
"That's better" he said. "I didn't
know you'd come out." "You may be
wondering why I've come so close?"
"Yes" I said beginning to feel hot
wondering if maybe he wasn't burning me
anyway.
"Frankly I wanted to tell you
I like your poetry. I see a lot
on my rounds and you're okay. You may
not be the greatest thing on earth, but
you're different. Now, I've heard some
say you're crazy, they being excessively
calm themselves to my mind, and other
crazy poets think that you're a boring
reactionary. Not me.
Just keep on
like I do and pay no attention. You'll
find that people always will complain
about the atmosphere, either too hot
or too cold too bright or too dark, days
too short or too long.

---

14. *Mayakovsky:* Vladimir Mayakofsky (1893–1930), one of the major Russian poets of the century. O'Hara's poem is inspired by Mayakofsky's poem "An Extraordinary Adventure Which Befell Vladimir Mayakofsky in a Summer Cottage" (1920), which is also constructed as a dialogue between the speaker and the sun. Mayakofsky had considerable influence on O'Hara's style.

If you don't appear
at all one day they think you're lazy
or dead. Just keep right on, I like it.

And don't worry about your lineage
poetic or natural. The Sun shines on
the jungle, you know, on the tundra
the sea, the ghetto. Wherever you were
I knew it and saw you moving. I was waiting
for you to get to work.

And now that you
are making your own days, so to speak,
even if no one reads you but me
you won't be depressed. Not
everyone can look up, even at me. It
hurts their eyes."
"Oh Sun, I'm so grateful to you!"

"Thanks and remember I'm watching. It's
easier for me to speak to you out
here. I don't have to slide down
between buildings to get your ear.
I know you love Manhattan, but
you ought to look up more often.
And
always embrace things, people earth
sky stars, as I do, freely and with
the appropriate sense of space. That
is your inclination, known in the heavens
and you should follow it to hell, if
necessary, which I doubt.
Maybe we'll
speak again in Africa, of which I too
am specially fond. Go back to sleep now
Frank, and I may leave a tiny poem
in that brain of yours as my farewell."

"Sun, don't go!" I was awake
at last. "No, go I must, they're calling
me."
"Who are they?"
Rising he said "Some
day you'll know. They're calling to you
too." Darkly he rose, and then I slept.

1958

ON SEEING LARRY RIVERS' *WASHINGTON CROSSING THE DELAWARE* AT THE MUSEUM OF MODERN ART°

Now that our hero has come back to us
in his white pants and we know his nose
trembling like a flag under fire,
we see the calm cold river is supporting
our forces, the beautiful history.

To be more revolutionary than a nun
is our desire, to be secular and intimate
as, when sighting a redcoat, you smile
and pull the trigger. Anxieties
and animosities, flaming and feeding

on theoretical considerations and
the jealous spiritualities of the abstract,
the robot? they're smoke, billows above
the physical event. They have burned up.
See how free we are! as a nation of persons.

Dear father of our country, so alive
you must have lied incessantly to be
immediate, here are your bones crossed
on my breast like a rusty flintlock,
a pirate's flag, bravely specific

and ever so light in the misty glare
of a crossing by water in winter to a shore
other than that the bridge reaches for.
Don't shoot until, the white of freedom glinting
on your gun barrel, you see the general fear.

1955

THINKING OF JAMES DEAN

Like a nickelodeon soaring over the island from sea to bay,
two pots of gold, and the flushed effulgence of a sky Tiepolo
and Turner had compiled in vistavision. Each panoramic second, of
his death. The rainbows canceling each other out, between martinis

---

poem title: Rivers (1923–2002) was an American artist who was born in New York. *Washington Crossing the Delaware* (1953) is the first of a series of ironic paintings about American history. An abstract expressionist as well as a predecessor of pop art, his paintings of the early 1950s often combine rigorous drawing with overlays of thin washes, giving them a fragmented appearance.

and the steak. To bed to dream, the moon invisibly scudding
under black-blue clouds, a stern Puritanical breeze pushing at
the house, to dream of roaches nibbling at my racing toenails,
great-necked speckled geese and slapping their proud heads

as I ran past. Morning. The first plunge in dolorous surf
and the brilliant sunlight declaring all the qualities of the world.
Like an ant, dragging its sorrows up and down the sand to find
a hiding place never, here where everything is guarded by dunes

or drifting. The sea is dark and smells of fish beneath its
silver surface. To reach the depths and rise, only in the sea;
the abysses of life, incessantly plunging not to rise to a face
of heat and joy again; habits of total immersion and the stance

victorious in death. And after hours of lying in nature, to nature,
and simulated death in the crushing waves, their shells and heart
pounding me naked on the shingle: had I died at twenty-four as he, but
in Boston, robbed of these suns and knowledges, a corpse more whole,

less deeply torn, less bruised and less alive, perhaps backstage
at the Brattle Theatre amidst the cold cream and the familiar lice
in my red-gold costume for a bit in *Julius Caesar,* would I be
smaller now in the vastness of light? a cork in the monumental

stillness of an eye-green trough, a sliver on the bleaching beach
to airplanes carried by the panting clouds to Spain. My friends
are roaming or listening to *La Bohème.* Precisely, the cold last swim
before the city flatters meanings of my life I cannot find,

squeezing me like an orange for some nebulous vitality, mourning
to the fruit ignorant of science in its hasty dying, kissing
its leaves and stem, exuding oils of Florida in the final glass of
pleasure. A leaving word in the sand, odor of tides: his name.

1955

JAMES MERRILL (1926–1995)

Born and raised in New York City, Merrill was the child of a founder of America's most famous brokerage firm. He was educated at Amherst College, a stay interrupted by a year's service in the U.S. infantry at the end of World War II. Thereafter he divided his time between Connecticut, Florida, and Greece, and devoted himself to a highly successful literary career. His poetry is poised, self-conscious, elegant, and witty; its manner owes perhaps as much to the stylistic polish of Proust's and James's fiction as to other poets. Thus it combines exacting attention to daily life with intricate literary allusiveness. At times, his irony almost masks the philosophical ambitions of texts like "Lost in Translation," but the poem nonetheless mounts a powerful reflection on the relations among history, memory, subjectivity, and experience. Merrill's earliest poems were so elegantly crafted and so preoccupied with transcendence that he acquired a reputation as a narrow aesthete, but he began to develop a more relaxed, conversational style in the early 1960s, eventually proving himself capable of taking up subjects like shopping malls and alcoholics' recovery programs that few aesthetes would risk. His book-length poetic epic *The Changing Light at Sandover* (1977–1982) is widely considered his masterpiece, though he produced supremely confident poetry in a wide variety of forms and meters. He also wrote novels and plays, and an especially beautiful memoir, *A Different Person* (1993).

AN URBAN CONVALESCENCE

Out for a walk, after a week in bed,
I find them tearing up part of my block
And, chilled through, dazed and lonely, join the dozen
In meek attitudes, watching a huge crane
Fumble luxuriously in the filth of years.
Her jaws dribble rubble. An old man
Laughs and curses in her brain,
Bringing to mind the close of *The White Goddess*.°

As usual in New York, everything is torn down
Before you have had time to care for it.
Head bowed, at the shrine of noise, let me try to recall
What building stood here. Was there a building at all?
I have lived on this same street for a decade.

8. *White Goddess:* (1948) book by British poet and critic Robert Graves; he argues that poetry has its inspirational goddess whose symbol is a crane, hence the pun on the mechanical crane above.

Wait. Yes. Vaguely a presence rises
Some five floors high, of shabby stone
—Or am I confusing it with another one
In another part of town, or of the world?—
And over its lintel into focus vaguely
Misted with blood (my eyes are shut)
A single garland sways, stone fruit, stone leaves,
Which years of grit had etched until it thrust
Roots down, even into the poor soil of my seeing.
When did the garland become part of me?
I ask myself, amused almost,
Then shiver once from head to toe,

Transfixed by a particular cheap engraving of garlands
Bought for a few francs long ago,
All calligraphic tendril and cross-hatched rondure,
Ten years ago, and crumpled up to stanch
Boughs dripping, whose white gestures filled a cab,
And thought of neither then nor since.
Also, to clasp them, the small, red-nailed hand
Of no one I can place. Wait. No. Her name, her features
Lie toppled underneath that year's fashions.
The words she must have spoken, setting her face
To fluttering like a veil, I cannot hear now,
Let alone understand.

So that I am already on the stair.
As it were, of where I lived,
When the whole structure shudders at my tread
And soundlessly collapses, filling
The air with motes of stone.
Onto the still erect building next door
Are pressed levels and hues—
Pocked rose, streaked greens, brown whites.
Who drained the pousse-café?°
Wires and pipes, snapped off at the roots, quiver.

Well, that is what life does. I stare
A moment longer, so. And presently
The massive volume of the world
Closes again.

---

46. *pousse-café:* after-dinner drink.

Upon that book I swear
To abide by what it teaches:
Gospels of ugliness and waste,
Of towering voids, of soiled gusts,
Of a shrieking to be faced
Full into, eyes astream with cold—

With cold?
All right then. With self-knowledge.

Indoors at last, the pages of *Time* are apt
To open, and the illustrated mayor of New York,
Given a glimpse of how and where I work,
To note yet one more house that can be scrapped.

Unwillingly I picture
My walls weathering in the general view.
It is not even as though the new
Buildings did very much for architecture.

Suppose they did. The sickness of our time requires
That these as well be blasted in their prime.
You would think the simple fact of having lasted
Threatened our cities like mysterious fires.

There are certain phrases which to use in a poem
Is like rubbing silver with quicksilver. Bright
But facile, the glamour deadens overnight.
For instance, how "the sickness of our time"

Enhances, then debases, what I feel.
At my desk I swallow in a glass of water
No longer cordial, scarcely wet, a pill
They had told me not to take until much later.

With the result that back into my imagination
The city glides, like cities seen from the air,
Mere smoke and sparkle to the passenger
Having in mind another destination

Which now is not that honey-slow descent
Of the Champs-Elysées,° her hand in his,

85. *Champs-Elysées:* famous Paris boulevard.

But the dull need to make some kind of house
Out of the life lived, out of the love spent.

1962

THE BROKEN HOME°

Crossing the street,
I saw the parents and the child
At their window, gleaming like fruit
With evening's mild gold leaf.

In a room on the floor below,
Sunless, cooler—a brimming
Saucer of wax, marbly and dim—
I have lit what's left of my life.

I have thrown out yesterday's milk
And opened a book of maxims.
The flame quickens. The word stirs.

Tell me, tongue of fire,
That you and I are as real
At least as the people upstairs.

My father,° who had flown in World War I,
Might have continued to invest his life
In cloud banks well above Wall Street and wife.
But the race was run below, and the point was to win.

Too late now, I make out in his blue gaze
(Through the smoked glass of being thirty-six)
The soul eclipsed by twin black pupils, sex
And business; time was money in those days.

Each thirteenth year he married. When he died
There were already several chilled wives
In sable orbit—rings, cars, permanent waves.
We'd felt him warming up for a green bride.

---

poem title: about the marital breakup of Merrill's parents; the poem is also constructed of sonnets, a formal home for poetic tradition, which are sometimes broken into unconventional units or rhymes.

15. *father:* Merrill's father, Charles E. Merrill, founded the brokerage firm now known as Merrill Lynch.

He could afford it. He was "in his prime"
At three score ten. But money was not time.

When my parents were younger this was a popular act:
A veiled woman would leap from an electric, wine-dark car
To the steps of no matter what—the Senate or the Ritz Bar—
And bodily, at newsreel speed, attack

No matter whom—Al Smith or José Maria Sert
Or Clemenceau°—veins standing out on her throat
As she yelled *War mongerer! Pig! Give us the vote!*,
And would have to be hauled away in her hobble skirt.°

What had the man done? Oh, made history.
Her business (he had implied) was giving birth,
Tending the house, mending the socks.

Always that same old story—
Father Time and Mother Earth,°
A marriage on the rocks.

One afternoon, red, satyr-thighed°
Michael, the Irish setter, head
Passionately lowered, led
The child I was to a shut door. Inside,

Blinds beat sun from the bed.
The green-gold room throbbed like a bruise.
Under a sheet, clad in taboos
Lay whom we sought, her hair undone, outspread,

And of a blackness found, if ever now, in old
Engravings where the acid bit.
I must have needed to touch it
Or the whiteness—was she dead?
Her eyes flew open, startled strange and cold.
The dog slumped to the floor. She reached for me. I fled.

---

34. *Clemenceau:* Alfred E. Smith (1873–1944), four times governor of New York and in 1928 the unsuccessful Democratic presidential candidate; Sert (1876–1945), the Spanish painter who decorated the lobby of New York City's Waldorf Astoria Hotel in 1930; Georges Clemenceau (1841–1929), premier of France during World War I.

36. *hobble skirt:* skirt fitting tightly below the knee.

41. *Father Time and Mother Earth:* according to Greek myth, the supreme god Cronus and the supreme goddess Gaea, overthrown by their son, Zeus.

43. *satyr-thighed:* lustful; Satyrs are goat-legged woodland deities of Greek myth.

Tonight they have stepped out onto the gravel.
The party is over. It's the fall
Of 1931. They love each other still.

She: Charlie, I can't stand the pace.
He: Come on, honey—why, you'll bury us all!

A lead soldier guards my windowsill:
Khaki rifle, uniform, and face.
Something in me grows heavy, silvery, pliable.

How intensely people used to feel!
Like metal poured at the close of a proletarian novel,°
Refined and glowing from the crucible,
I see those two hearts, I'm afraid,
Still. Cool here in the graveyard of good and evil,
They are even so to be honored and obeyed.

. . . Obeyed, at least, inversely. Thus
I rarely buy a newspaper, or vote.
To do so, I have learned, is to invite
The tread of a stone guest° within my house.

Shooting this rusted bolt, though, against him,
I trust I am no less time's child than some
Who on the heath impersonate Poor Tom°
Or on the barricades risk life and limb.

Nor do I try to keep a garden, only
An avocado in a glass of water—
Roots pallid, gemmed with air. And later,

When the small gilt leaves have grown
Fleshy and green, I let them die, yes, yes,
And start another. I am earth's no less.

A child, a red dog roam the corridors,
Still, of the broken home. No sound. The brilliant

---

66. *proletarian novel:* novels, especially during the 1930s, that offered political and social analyses of work; here, about iron and steel production.

74. *stone guest:* in the play *The Stone Feast* by French dramatist Molière (1622–1673), a stone statue representing the commander of Seville carries his murderer Don Juan into hell; in the opera *Don Giovanni* (1787), by the Austrian composer Wolfgang Amadeus Mozart (1756–1791), the commander returns as a statue to seek revenge against Don Giovanni.

77. *Poor Tom:* Edgar in Shakespeare's *King Lear,* who was disowned by his father, the Earl of Gloucester, gives himself this name when he wanders the heath pretending to be mad.

Rag runners halt before wide-open doors.
My old room! Its wallpaper—cream, medallioned
With pink and brown—brings back the first nightmares,
Long summer colds, and Emma, sepia-faced,
Perspiring over broth carried upstairs
Aswim with golden fats I could not taste.

The real house became a boarding school.
Under the ballroom ceiling's allegory
Someone at last may actually be allowed
To learn something; or, from my window, cool
With the unstiflement of the entire story,
Watch a red setter stretch and sink in cloud.

1966

WILLOWWARE CUP

Mass hysteria, wave after breaking wave
Blueblooded Cantonese upon these shores

Left the gene pool Lux-opaque and smoking
With dimestore mutants. One turned up today.

Plum in bloom, pagoda, blue birds, plume of willow—
Almost the replica of a prewar pattern—

The same boat bearing the gnat-sized lovers away,
The old bridge now bent double where her father signals

Feebly, as from flypaper, minding less and less.
Two smaller retainers with lanterns light him home.

Is that a scroll he carries? He must by now be immensely
Wise, and have given up earthly attachments, and all that.

Soon, of these May mornings, rising in mist, he will ask
Only to blend—like ink in flesh, blue anchor

Needled upon drunkenness while its destroyer
Full steam departs, the stigma throbbing, intricate—

Only to blend into a crazing texture.
You are far away. The leaves tell what they tell.

But this lone, chipped vessel, if it fills,
Fills for you with something warm and clear.

Around its inner horizon the old odd designs
Crowd as before, and seem to concentrate on you.

They represent, I fancy, a version of heaven
In its day more trouble to mend than to replace:

Steep roofs aslant, minutely tiled;
Tilted honeycombs, thunderhead blue.

1972

LOST IN TRANSLATION°

for Richard Howard

Diese Tage, die leer dir scheinen
und wertlos für das All,
haben Wurzeln zwischen, den Steinen
und trinken dort überall.°

A card table in the library stands ready
To receive the puzzle which keeps never coming.
Daylight shines in or lamplight down
Upon the tense oasis of green felt.
Full of unfulfillment, life goes on,
Mirage arisen from time's trickling sands
Or fallen piecemeal into place:
German lesson, picnic, see-saw, walk
With the collie who "did everything but talk"—
Sour windfalls of the orchard back of us.
A summer without parents is the puzzle,
Or should be. But the boy, day after day,
Writes in his Line-a-Day° *No puzzle.*

He's in love, at least. His French Mademoiselle,°
In real life a widow since Verdun,
Is stout, plain, carrot-haired, devout.
She prays for him, as does a curé in Alsace,°

---

poem title: Merrill is no doubt recalling Robert Frost's observation that poetry is that which is lost in translation. The epigraph then offers us a translation.

epigraph: *Diese Tage . . .*: from Ranier Maria Rilke's (1875–1926) translation of Paul Valéry's (1871–1945) poem "Palme." It may be translated into English as follows: "These days that you think empty / and worthless to the universe, / have roots among the stones / and drink from everywhere."

13. *Line-a-Day:* a name for a diary.

14. *Mademoiselle:* in this case a governess, widowed since the 1916 World War I Battle of Verdun.

17. *Alsace:* area in northeast France, on the German border; territory long contested by the two countries.

Sews costumes for his marionettes,
Helps him to keep behind the scene
Whose sidelit goosegirl, speaking with his voice,
Plays Guinevere° as well as Gunmoll° Jean.
Or else at bedtime in his tight embrace
Tells him her own French hopes, her German fears,
Her—but what more is there to tell?
Having known grief and hardship, Mademoiselle
Knows little more. Her languages. Her place.
Noon coffee. Mail. The watch that also waited
Pinned to her heart, poor gold, throws up its hands—
No puzzle! Steaming bitterness
Her sugars draw pops back into his mouth, translated:
"Patience, chéri. Geduld, mein Schatz."°
(Thus, reading Valéry the other evening
And seeming to recall a Rilke version of "Palme,"
That sunlit paradigm whereby the tree
Taps a sweet wellspring of authority,
The hour came back. Patience dans l'azur.°
Geduld im . . . Himmelblau? Mademoiselle.)

Out of the blue, as promised, of a New York
Puzzle-rental shop the puzzle comes—
A superior one, containing a thousand hand-sawn,
Sandal-scented pieces. Many take
Shapes known already—the craftsman's repertoire
Nice in its limitation—from other puzzles:
Witch on broomstick, ostrich, hourglass,
Even (surely not just in retrospect)
An inchling, innocently branching palm.
These can be put aside, made stories of
While Mademoiselle spreads out the rest face-up,
Herself excited as a child; or questioned
Like incoherent faces in a crowd,
Each with its scrap of highly colored
Evidence the Law must piece together.
Sky-blue ostrich? Likely story.
Mauve of the witch's cloak white, severed fingers

---

21. *Guinevere:* King Arthur's queen.

21. *Gunmoll:* a female gangster.

31. *"Patience, chéri. Geduld, mein Schatz":* "Patience, my dear," rendered in both French and German.

36. *Patience dans l'azur:* (French) "Patience in the blue," Valéry's description of the palm tree in his poem. "Geduld im . . . Himmelblau" proposes a German translation. That leads to Merrill's use of the American colloquialism "out of the blue" in the next line.

Pluck? Detain her. The plot thickens
As all at once two pieces interlock.

Mademoiselle does borders° —(Not so fast.
A London dusk, December last.
Chatter silenced in the library
This grown man reenters, wearing grey.
A medium. All except him have seen
Panel slid back, recess explored,
An object at once unique and common
Displayed, planted in a plain tole°
Casket the subject now considers
Through shut eyes, saying in effect:
"Even as voices reach me vaguely
A dry saw-shriek drowns them out,
Some loud machinery—a lumber mill?
Far uphill in the fir forest
Trees tower, tense with shock,
Groaning and cracking as they crash groundward.
But hidden here is a freak fragment
Of a pattern complex in appearance only.
What it seems to show is superficial
Next to that long-term lamination
Of hazard and craft, the karma that has
Made it matter in the first place.
Plywood. Piece of a puzzle." Applause
Acknowledged by an opening of lids
Upon the thing itself. A sudden dread—
But to go back. All this lay years ahead.)

Mademoiselle does borders. Straight-edge pieces
Align themselves with earth or sky
In twos and threes, naive cosmogonists
Whose views clash. Nomad inlanders meanwhile
Begin to cluster where the totem
Of a certain vibrant egg-yolk yellow
Or pelt of what emerging animal
Acts on the straggler like a trumpet call
To form a more sophisticated unit.
By suppertime two ragged wooden clouds
Have formed. In one, a Sheik with beard

---

57. *borders:* the word has multiple meanings here. Mademoiselle specializes in the borders of puzzles, but also crosses linguistic and national borders.

64. *tole:* lacquered or enameled metalware.

And flashing sword hilt (he is all but finished)
Steps forward on a tiger skin. A piece
Snaps shut, and fangs gnash out at us!
In the second cloud—they gaze from cloud to cloud
With marked if undecipherable feeling—
Most of a dark-eyed woman veiled in mauve
Is being helped down from her camel (kneeling)
By a small backward-looking slave or page-boy
(Her son, thinks Mademoiselle mistakenly)
Whose feet have not been found. But lucky finds
In the last minutes before bed
Anchor both factions to the scene's limits
And, by so doing, orient
Them eye to eye across the green abyss.
The yellow promises, oh bliss,
To be in time a sumptuous tent.

Puzzle begun I write in the day's space,
Then, while she bathes, peek at Mademoiselle's
Page to the curé: "... cette innocente mère,
Ce pauvre enfant, que deviendront-ils?"°
Her azure script is curlicued like pieces
Of the puzzle she will be telling him about.
(Fearful incuriosity of childhood!
"Tu as l'accent allemand,"° said Dominique.
Indeed. Mademoiselle was only French by marriage.
Child of an English mother, a remote
Descendant of the great explorer Speke,°
And Prussian father. No one knew. I heard it
Long afterwards from her nephew, a UN°
Interpreter. His matter-of-fact account
Touched old strings. My poor Mademoiselle,
With 1939° about to shake
This world where "each was the enemy, each the friend"
To its foundations, kept, though signed in blood,
Her peace a shameful secret to the end.)
"Schlaf wohl, chéri."° Her kiss. Her thumb
Crossing my brow against the dreams to come.

---

113. *"cette ... deviendront-ils"*: (French) "this innocent mother, this poor child, what will become of them?"

117. *"Tu ... allemand"*: (French) "You have a German accent."

120. *Speke:* John Hanning Speke (1827–1864), British explorer of Africa.

122. *UN:* United Nations.

125. 1939: World War II began when Germany invaded Poland in 1939.

129. *"Schlaf ... Cherie"*: (German, French) "Sleep well, my love."

This World that shifts like sand, its unforeseen
Consolidations and elate routine,
Whose Potentate had lacked a retinue?
Lo! it assembles on the shrinking Green.

Gunmetal-skinned or pale, all plumes and scars,
Of Vassalage the noblest avatars—
The very coffee-bearer in his vair
Vest° is a swart Highness, next to ours.

Kef° easing Boredom, and iced syrups, thirst,
In guessed-at glooms old wives who know the worst
Outsweat that virile fiction of the New:
"Insh'Allah,° he will tire—" "—or kill her first!"

(Hardly a proper subject for the Home,
Work of—dear Richard, I shall let *you* comb
Archives and learned journals for his name—
A minor lion attending on Gérôme.)°

While, thick as Thebes° whose presently complete
Gates close behind them, Houri and Afreet°
Both claim the Page.° He wonders whom to serve,
And what his duties are, and where his feet,

And if we'll find, as some before us did,
That piece of Distance deep in which lies hid
Your tiny apex sugary with sun,
Eternal Triangle, Great Pyramid!

Then Sky alone is left, a hundred blue
Fragments in revolution, with no clue
To where a Niche will open. Quite a task,
Putting together Heaven, yet we do.

---

138. *vair vest:* vest bordered with fur.

139. *Kef:* marijuana.

142. *Insh' Allah:* (Arabic) "If Allah wills."

146. *lion . . . Gérôme:* Jean Léon Gérôme (1824–1940), French painter of historical subjects. Also a pun referring to St. Jerome's kindness in pulling a thorn from a lion's paw.

147. *Thebes:* the ancient capital of Upper Egypt, situated on the Nile. Here "Thebes" is also a mispronunciation of "thieves."

148. *Houri and Afreet:* according to Arabian mythology, "Houri" are virgins given to those who enter paradise and "Afreet" are evil beings.

149. *Page:* a pun, referring both to a young male servant and to the printed page.

It's done. Here under the table all along
Were those missing feet. It's done.

The dog's tail thumping. Mademoiselle sketching
Costumes for a coming harem drama
To star the goosegirl. All too soon the swift
Dismantling. Lifted by two corners,
The puzzle hung together—and did not.
Irresistibly a populace
Unstitched of its attachments, rattled down.
Power went to pieces as the witch
Slithered easily from Virtue's gown.
The blue held out for time, but crumbled, too.
The city had long fallen, and the tent,
A separating sauce mousseline,°
Been swept away. Remained the green
On which the grown-ups gambled. A green dusk.
First lightning bugs. Last glow of west
Green in the false eyes of (coincidence)
Our mangy tiger safe on his bared hearth.

Before the puzzle was boxed and readdressed
To the puzzle shop in the mid-Sixties,°
Something tells me that one piece contrived
To stay in the boy's pocket. How do I know?
I know because so many later puzzles
Had missing pieces—Maggie Teyte's° high notes
Gone at the war's end, end of the vogue for collies,
A house torn down; and hadn't Mademoiselle
Kept back her pitiful bit of truth as well?
I've spent the last days, furthermore,
Ransacking Athens for that translation of "Palme."
Neither the Goethehaus° nor the National Library
Seems able to unearth it. Yet I can't
Just be imagining. I've seen it. Know
How much of the sun-ripe original
Felicity Rilke made himself forego
(Who loved French words—verger, mûr, parfumer)°

---

172. *mousseline:* a pun, referring both to a hollandaise cream sauce and to a sheet fabric made of muslin, the latter originally made in Iraq.

179. *mid-Sixties:* an approximate street address.

183. *Maggie Teyte:* (1888–1976), a British soprano who sang a number of French pieces.

189. *Goethehaus:* the name of a German library.

194. *verger, mûr, parfumer:* (French) "orchard, ripe, to scent."

In order to render its underlying sense.
Know already in that tongue of his
What Pains, what monolithic Truths
Shadow stanza to stanza's symmetrical
Rhyme-rutted pavement. Know that ground plan left
Sublime and barren, where the warm Romance
Stone by stone faded, cooled; the fluted nouns
Made taller, lonelier than life
By leaf-carved capitals in the afterglow.
The owlet umlaut° peeps and hoots
Above the open vowel. And after rain
A deep reverberation fills with stars.

Lost, is it, buried? One more missing piece?

But nothing's lost. Or else: all is translation
And every bit of us is lost in it
(Or found—I wander through the ruin of S°
Now and then, wondering at the peacefulness)
And in that loss a self-effacing tree,
Color of context, imperceptibly
Rustling with its angel,° turns the waste
To shade and fiber, milk and memory.

1976

---

204. *umlaut:* an accent mark in German, consisting of two dots placed above a vowel.
210. *ruin of S:* "S" is a lost love.
214. *Rustling with its angel*: Cf. Jacob *wrestling* with the angel in the Book of Genesis.

ALLEN GINSBERG (1926–1997)

Ginsberg was at once one of the major poets of the second half of the twentieth century and a public figure who entreated his country by way of his poetry to realize its full democratic potential. No one who saw and heard Ginsberg stand on a flatbed truck before thousands of U.S. Army troops at the Pentagon during the famous 1968 demonstration against the Vietnam War either could or would wish altogether to separate his work from its reception. With rifles bristling at him, Ginsberg read his Pentagon exorcism poem in defiance of imperialist military power and in a plea that the demons of war would quit the building. A rather modest poem, it nonetheless made for an unforgettable occasion. Yet Ginsberg was never actually militant or aggressive. Learned in Zen Buddhism and Western mysticism, his presence exuded rather an expansive and insistent gentleness.

He was born and grew up in New Jersey, but it was the emerging Beat generation in New York that shaped his vision and that he helped to define. He was educated at Columbia University, though his degree was delayed when he was expelled for what would now constitute no more than a prank: placing obscene messages on his grimy dormitory window to draw attention to the need to clean the room. More serious—as he became friends with William Burroughs, Jack Kerouac, and other figures in the Beat literary and drug scene—was his decision to let Herbert Huncke use his dorm room to store the stolen goods he employed to support his heroin habit. In exchange for avoiding prosecution, Ginsberg pleaded insanity and spent eight months in the Columbia Psychiatric Institute.

By then he had worked at a series of odd jobs, including service on merchant tankers. One day in Harlem, Ginsberg had an auditory vision of William Blake reading his poems aloud. He also soon met and was befriended by William Carlos Williams. Then he was on his way to San Francisco and the 1956 publication of *Howl and Other Poems*. Buoyed by the publicity accompanying an obscenity trial, "Howl" would become perhaps the most widely known poem of the era. Ginsberg had become a twentieth-century incarnation of Walt Whitman.

The mix of moods in his work would remain consistent throughout his career—prophetic, elegiac, ecstatic. He would write triumphant poems of political protest, lamentations about death, celebratory poems about homosexuality, and affirmations of visionary transformation. He chanted his poems to the accompaniment of finger cymbals, sang them with rock groups, and intoned them in a high resonant voice that made his poetry a form of contemporary prophecy.

LOVE POEM ON THEME BY WHITMAN

I'll go into the bedroom silently and lie down between the
    bridegroom and the bride,
those bodies fallen from heaven stretched out waiting naked and
    restless,
arms resting over their eyes in the darkness,

bury my face in their shoulders and breasts, breathing their skin,
and stroke and kiss neck and mouth and make back be open and
known,
legs raised up crook'd to receive, cock in the darkness driven
tormented and attacking
roused up from hole to itching head,
bodies locked shuddering naked, hot hips and buttocks screwed
into each other
and eyes, eyes glinting and charming, widening into looks and
abandon,
and moans of movement, voices, hands in air, hands between thighs,
hands in moisture on softened hips, throbbing contraction of bellies
till the white come flow in the swirling sheets,
and the bride cry for forgiveness, and the groom be covered with
tears of passion and compassion,
and I rise up from the bed replenished with last intimate gestures
and kisses of farewell—
all before the mind wakes, behind shades and closed doors in a
darkened house
where the inhabitants roam unsatisfied in the night,
nude ghosts seeking each other out in the silence.

1954

HOWL

(For Carl Solomon°)

I

I saw the best minds of my generation destroyed by madness,
starving hysterical naked,
dragging themselves through the negro streets at dawn looking for
an angry fix,°
angelheaded hipsters burning for the ancient heavenly connection°
to the starry dynamo in the machinery of night,
who poverty and tatters and hollow-eyed and high sat up smoking
in the supernatural darkness of cold-water flats floating across
the tops of cities contemplating jazz,

---

dedication: *Solomon:* (1928–1993), a fellow patient at the Columbia Psychiatric Institute in New York in 1949, who related his experiences in New York and Paris and shared books by Artaud and others with Ginsberg. At the time *Howl* was written, Ginsberg learned that Solomon had been admitted to a mental hospital again. As Ginsberg would write in the 1986 facsimile of *Howl,* he thought the dedication "a gesture of wild solidarity, a message into the asylum, a sort of hearts trumpet call." But the poem achieved wider fame than anyone could have anticipated, and Solomon, as a result, became virtually a mythical figure, inextricably linked to *Howl* ever thereafter. Solomon was an editor at Ace Books and later published *Mishaps, Perhaps* (1966) and *More Mishaps* (1968).

2. *angry fix:* Ginsberg's note—"Herbert Huncke cruised Harlem and Times Square at irregular hours, late forties, scoring junk"

3. *connection:* a pun linking spirituality and a drug connection.

who bared their brains to Heaven under the EL° and saw
Mohammedan angels° staggering on tenement roofs illuminated,
who passed through universities with radiant cool eyes
hallucinating Arkansas and Blake-light° tragedy among
the scholars of war,°
who were expelled° from the academies for crazy & publishing
obscene odes on the windows of the skull,
who cowered° in unshaven rooms in underwear, burning their
money in wastebaskets and listening to the Terror through the
wall,
who got busted in their pubic beards returning through Laredo°
with a belt of marijuana for New York,
who ate fire in paint hotels or drank turpentine in Paradise Alley,°
death, or purgatoried their torsos night after night
with dreams, with drugs, with waking nightmares, alcohol and cock
and endless balls,
incomparable blind streets of shuddering cloud and lightning in the
mind leaping toward poles of Canada & Paterson,° illuminating
all the motionless world of Time between,
Peyote° solidities of halls, backyard green tree cemetery dawns,
wine drunkenness over the rooftops, storefront boroughs of
teahead joyride neon blinking traffic light, sun and moon and
tree vibrations in the roaring winter dusks of Brooklyn, ashcan
rantings and kind king light of mind,
who chained themselves to subways for the endless ride from Battery°
to holy Bronx on benzedrine until the noise of wheels and

---

5. *El:* the elevated subway system in New York City and a Hebrew term for God.

5. *saw Mohammedan angels:* according to Ginsberg's note, this refers to poet Philip Lamantia's 1953 mystical experience.

6. *Blake-light:* Ginsberg experienced a mystical vision while reading the poetry of William Blake (1757–1827) in East Harlem in 1948.

6. *scholars of war:* Ginsberg's note—"During author's residence, 1944–1948, Columbia scientists helped split atoms for military power in secrecy. Subsequent military-industrial funding increasingly dominated university research."

7. *expelled:* Ginsberg was expelled from Columbia University in 1945 for drawing and writing obscenities on his dormitory windows.

8. *cowered . . . burning their money:* Ginsberg's note—"a Solomon anecdote."

9. *Laredo:* Texas city on the Mexican border.

10. *Paradise Alley:* Ginsberg's note—"a cold-water-flat courtyard on East 11th Street on New York's Lower East Side. The prototype of Jack Kerouac's (1922–1969) heroine in *The Subterraneans* (1958) lived there."

12. *Paterson:* New Jersey city where Ginsberg was born and later lived from 1950 to 1951, when he met poet William Carlos Williams (1946–1963) whose works include the long poem *Paterson.*

13. *Peyote:* a small Mexico and Texas cactus that is the source of the hallucinogen *mescaline,* used in Native American religious ceremonies and later adopted by the American counterculture. Ginsberg's note says that "tree vibrations" refers to his own first peyote experience.

14. *Battery:* Battery Park, at the southern end of Manhattan. "Battery to holy Bronx" marks the southern and northern ends of a New York City subway line. *Zoo*: the Bronx Zoo, at the northern end of a N.Y.C. subway line.

children brought them down shuddering mouth-wracked and battered bleak of brain all drained of brilliance in the drear light of Zoo,
who sank all night in submarine light of Bickford's° floated out and sat through the stale beer afternoon in desolate Fugazzis,° listening to the crack of doom on the hydrogen jukebox,
who talked continuously° seventy hours from park to pad to bar to Bellevue° to museum to the Brooklyn Bridge,
a lost battalion of platonic conversationalists jumping down the stoops off fire escapes off windowsills off Empire State out of the moon,
yacketayakking screaming vomiting whispering facts and memories and anecdotes and eyeball kicks and shocks of hospitals and jails and wars,
whole intellects disgorged in total recall for seven days and nights with brilliant eyes, meat for the Synagogue cast on the pavement,
who vanished into nowhere Zen New Jersey leaving a trail of ambiguous picture postcards of Atlantic City Hall,
suffering Eastern sweats and Tangerian bone-grindings° and migraines of China under junk-withdrawal in Newark's bleak furnished room,
who wandered around and around at midnight in the railroad yard wondering where to go, and went, leaving no broken hearts,
who lit cigarettes in boxcars boxcars boxcars racketing through snow toward lonesome farms in grandfather night,
who studied Plotinus Poe St. John of the Cross° telepathy and bop° kabbalah° because the cosmos instinctively vibrated at their feet in Kansas,
who loned it through the streets of Idaho seeking visionary indian angels who were visionary indian angels,
who thought they were only mad when Baltimore gleamed in supernatural ecstasy,

---

15. *Bickford's:* an all-night cafeteria on 42nd Street where Ginsberg mopped floors while a student at Columbia.

15. *Fugazzis:* a Greenwich Village bar on Sixth Avenue.

16. *talked continuously:* Ginsberg's note—"Ruth G., a young woman who knew both Solomon and Ginsberg and who one day talked for seventy-two hours in Washington Square until being committed to Bellevue. The phrase also evokes Cassady's nonstop monologues."

16. *Bellevue:* a New York public hospital with a psychiatric clinic.

21. *Tangerian-bone grindings:* Ginsberg's note refers us to details of beat writer William S. Burroughs's (1914–1997) heroin withdrawals in his *Letters to Allen Ginsberg 1953–1957* (1982). Tangiers is a coastal city in Morocco.

24. *Plotinus:* (205?–270), a Roman neo-Platonic philosopher; the poet and writer Edgar Allan Poe (1809–1849); *St. John of the Cross,* born Juan de Yepes y Alvaraz (1542–1591), a Spanish mystic poet.

24. *bop:* the bop style of jazz developed in the 1940s and 1950s.

24. *kabbalah:* the mystical tradition of interpreting Hebrew scripture.

who jumped in limousines with the Chinaman of Oklahoma on the impulse of winter midnight streetlight smalltown rain,
who lounged hungry and lonesome through Houston seeking jazz or sex or soup, and followed the brilliant Spaniard to converse about America and Eternity, a hopeless task, and so took ship to Africa,
who disappeared into the volcanoes of Mexico leaving behind nothing but the shadow of dungarees and the lava and ash of poetry scattered in fireplace Chicago,
who reappeared on the West Coast investigating the FBI in beards and shorts with big pacifist eyes sexy in their dark skin passing out incomprehensible leaflets,
who burned cigarette holes in their arms protesting the narcotic tobacco haze of Capitalism,
who distributed Supercommunist pamphlets in Union Square° weeping and undressing while the sirens of Los Alamos° wailed them down, and wailed down Wall,° and the Staten Island ferry also wailed,
who broke down crying in white gymnasiums naked and trembling before the machinery of other skeletons,
who bit detectives in the neck and shrieked with delight in policecars for committing no crime but their own wild cooking pederasty and intoxication,
who howled on their knees in the subway and were dragged off the roof waving genitals and manuscripts,
who let themselves be fucked in the ass by saintly motorcyclists,° and screamed with joy,
who blew and were blown by those human seraphim,° the sailors,° caresses of Atlantic and Caribbean love,
who balled in the morning in the evenings in rosegardens and the grass of public parks and cemeteries scattering their semen freely to whomever come who may,
who hiccuped endlessly trying to giggle but wound up with a sob behind a partition in a Turkish Bath when the blond & naked angel came to pierce them with a sword,°

---

32. *Union Square:* a neighborhood, park, and public square running from 14th to 21st Street in Manhattan. Often the site of workers' rallies and radical political protests.

32. *Los Alamos:* the New Mexico site for the research and development of the atomic bomb.

32. *Wall:* New York's financial district (Wall Street) and Jerusalem's Wailing Wall, thought to be part of the wall surrounding the temple of King Herod (73–4 B.C.) of Judea, where Jews have traditionally gathered for prayer.

36. *saintly motorcyclists:* Ginsberg's note directs us to Marlon Brando's film *The Wild Ones.*

37. *seraphim:* the highest order of angels.

37. *sailors:* Ginsberg's note—"The poet Hart Crane picked up sailors to love on Sand Street, Brooklyn, etc. Suffering alcoholic exhaustion and rejected by the crew on his last voyage, from Veracruz, Crane disappeared off the fantail of the Caribbean ship *Orizaba.*"

39. *sword:* refers to Lorenzo Bernini's (1598–1680) sculpture *The Ecstasy of St. Teresa,* which evokes an erotic religious vision by St. Teresa (1515–1582).

who lost their loveboys to the three old shrews of fate the one eyed shrew of the heterosexual dollar the one eyed shrew that winks out of the womb and the one eyed shrew° that does nothing but sit on her ass and snip the intellectual golden threads of the craftsman's loom,
who copulated ecstatic and insatiate with a bottle of beer a sweetheart a package of cigarettes a candle and fell off the bed, and continued along the floor and down the hall and ended fainting on the wall with a vision of ultimate cunt and come eluding the last gyzym of consciousness,
who sweetened the snatches of a million girls trembling in the sunset, and were red eyed in the morning but prepared to sweeten the snatch of the sunrise, flashing buttocks under barns and naked in the lake,
who went out whoring through Colorado in myriad stolen night-cars, N.C.,° secret hero of these poems, cocksman and Adonis° of Denver—joy to the memory of his innumerable lays of girls in empty lots & diner backyards, moviehouses' rickety rows, on mountaintops in caves or with gaunt waitresses in familiar roadside lonely petticoat upliftings & especially secret gas-station solipsisms° of johns, & hometown alleys too,
who faded out in vast sordid movies, were shifted in dreams, woke on a sudden Manhattan, and picked themselves up out of basements hungover with heartless Tokay° and horrors of Third Avenue iron dreams & stumbled to unemployment offices,
who walked all night with their shoes full of blood on the snowbank docks waiting for a door in the East River to open to a room full of steamheat and opium,
who created great suicidal dramas on the apartment° cliff-banks of the Hudson under the wartime blue floodlight of the moon & their heads shall be crowned with laurel in oblivion,
who ate the lamb stew of the imagination or digested the crab at the muddy bottom of the rivers of Bowery,°

---

40. *shrew:* shrews of fate; according to Roman myth, three goddesses of destiny who determine the course of human lives by spinning a line of thread until severing it at the point of death.

43. *N.C.:* Neal Cassady (1926–1968), Beat writer and friend of Ginsberg and Kerouac on whom Kerouac based the character Dean Moriarty in *On the Road* (1957).

43. *Adonis:* according to Greek myth, a handsome young man loved by Aphrodite, goddess of love.

43. *solipsisms:* philosophical theories by which only the self exists, so that all experience is subjective.

44. *Tokay:* a cheap, fortified Hungarian wine favored by alcoholic derelicts. Ginsberg refers us to Kerouac's accounts of drinking in New York in his letters.

46. *apartment:* high-rise apartment houses atop the cliffs of the Palisades along the Hudson River.

47. *Bowery:* the lower part of Third Avenue in New York City, frequented by derelicts and homeless people.

who wept at the romance of the streets with their pushcarts full of
onions and bad music,
who sat in boxes breathing in the darkness under the bridge, and
rose up to build harpsichords in their lofts,
who coughed on the sixth floor of Harlem crowned with flame
under the tubercular sky surrounded by orange crates of
theology,
who scribbled all night rocking and rolling over lofty incantations
which in the yellow morning were stanzas of gibberish,
who cooked rotten animals lung heart feet tail borsht° & tortillas
dreaming of the pure vegetable kingdom,
who plunged themselves under meat trucks looking for an egg,
who threw their watches off the roof to cast their ballot for
Eternity outside of Time, & alarm clocks fell on their heads
every day for the next decade,
who cut their wrists three times successively unsuccessfully, gave
up and were forced to open antique stores where they thought
they were growing old and cried,
who were burned alive in their innocent flannel suits on Madison
Avenue° amid blasts of leaden verse & the tanked-up clatter of
the iron regiments of fashion & the nitroglycerine shrieks of the
fairies of advertising & the mustard gas of sinister intelligent
editors, or were ran down by the drunken taxicabs of Absolute
Reality,
who jumped off the Brooklyn Bridge this actually happened and
walked away unknown and forgotten into the ghostly daze of
Chinatown soup alleyways & firetrucks, not even one free beer,
who sang out of their windows in despair, fell out of the subway
window, jumped in the filthy Passaic,° leaped on negroes, cried
all over the street, danced on broken wineglasses barefoot
smashed phonograph records of nostalgic European 1930s
German jazz finished the whiskey and threw up° groaning into
the bloody toilet, moans in their ears and the blast of colossal
steamwhistles,
who barreled down the highways of the past journeying to each
other's hotrod-Golgotha° jail-solitude watch or Birmingham
jazz incarnation,

---

52. *borsht:* Ginsberg's note—"Author's mother cooked lungen (lung stew) and Russian borscht (beet soup) when not eating nature-community vegetarian."

56. *Madison Avenue:* the traditional location of New York advertising agencies, whose conformist employees wore gray flannel suits as a uniform for success.

58. *Passaic:* the Passaic River, which flows past Paterson, New Jersey. The phrase "filthy Passaic" comes from William Carlos Williams's 1915 poem "The Wanderer."

58. *subway window . . . smashed records . . . threw up:* according to Ginsberg's note, these incidents come from the life of "William Cannastra, legendary late 1940s New York bohemian figure, life cut short by alcoholic accident, body balanced out of subway window, knocked against a pillar."

59. *Golgotha:* (Hebrew) "Place of a Skull": Calvary, the site of Jesus's crucifixion.

who drove crosscountry seventytwo hours to find out if I had a
    vision or you had a vision or he had a vision to find out
    Eternity,
who journeyed to Denver, who died in Denver,° who came back to
    Denver & waited in vain, who watched over Denver & brooded
    & loned in Denver and finally went away to find out the Time,
    & now Denver is lonesome for her heroes,
who fell on their knees in hopeless cathedrals praying for each
    other's salvation and light and breasts, until the soul illuminated
    its hair for a second,
who crashed through their minds in jail waiting for impossible
    criminals with golden heads and the charm of reality in their
    hearts who sang sweet blues to Alcatraz,
who retired° to Mexico to cultivate a habit, or Rocky Mount to
    tender Buddha or Tangiers to boys or Southern Pacific to the
    black locomotive or Harvard to Narcissus to Woodlawn° to the
    daisychain or grave,

who demanded sanity trials accusing the radio° of hypnotism &
    were left with their insanity & their hands & a hung jury,
who threw potato salad at CCNY° lecturers on Dadaism and
    subsequently presented themselves on the granite steps of the
    madhouse with shaven heads and harlequin speech of suicide,
    demanding instantaneous lobotomy,
and who were given instead the concrete void of insulin Metrazol°
    electricity hydrotherapy psychotherapy occupational therapy
    pingpong & amnesia,
who in humorless protest overturned only one symbolic pingpong
    table,° resting briefly in catatonia,
returning years later truly bald except for a wig of blood, and tears
    and fingers, to the visible madman doom of the wards of the
    madtowns of the East,

---

61. *Denver:* Ginsberg's note—"Lyric lines by Kerouac: 'Down in Denver, / Down in Denver, / All I did was die.' "

64. *who retired . . :* Burroughs lived in Mexico and Tangiers; Kerouac lived in Rocky Mount, North Carolina; Cassady worked for the Southern Pacific Railroad.

64. *Narcissus to Woodlawn:* according to Greek myth, Narcissus was a youth who fell in love with his own reflection in a pool; Naomi Ginsberg's window overlooked Woodlawn, a cemetery in the Bronx. She was Ginsberg's mother.

65. *accusing the radio:* alludes to Ginsberg's mother's paranoid fantasies.

66. *CCNY:* College of New York; *Dadaism:* an artistic and literary movement (1916–1922) emphasizing the irrational and the absurd. Carl Solomon writes, "My protest against the verbal, the rational and the acceptable took the form of disruption of a critical discussion of Mallarmé and other neo-dada clowning, which resulted in my incarceration in a psychiatric hospital in Manhattan."

67. *Metrazol:* brand name of pentylenetrazol, a drug used in shock therapy.

68. *overturned . . . pingpong table:* Ginsberg's note—"The incident of the Ping-Pong table is described by Solomon as a 'big burst anti-authoritarian rage on arrival at P.I. by me.' "

Pilgrim State's Rockland's and Greystone's° foetid halls, bickering
with the echoes of the soul, rocking and rolling in the midnight
solitude-bench dolmen-realms° of love, dream of life a
nightmare, bodies turned to stone as heavy as the moon,
with mother finally ******,° and the last fantastic book flung out
of the tenement window, and the last door closed at 4 A.M. and
the last telephone slammed at the wall in reply and the last
furnished room emptied down to the last piece of mental
furniture, a yellow paper rose twisted on a wire hanger in the
closet, and even that imaginary, nothing but a hopeful little bit
of hallucination—
ah, Carl, while you are not safe I am not safe, and now you're
really in the total animal soup of time—
and who therefore ran through the icy streets obsessed with a
sudden flash of the alchemy of the use of the ellipse the catalog
the meter & the vibrating plane,
who dreamt and made incarnate gaps in Time & Space through
images juxtaposed, and trapped the archangel of the soul
between 2 visual images and joined the elemental verbs and set
the noun and dash of consciousness together jumping with
sensation of Pater Omnipotens Aeterna Deus°
to recreate the syntax and measure of poor human prose and stand
before you speechless and intelligent and shaking with shame,
rejected yet confessing out the soul to conform to the rhythm of
thought in his naked and endless head,
the madman bum and angel beat in Time, unknown, yet putting
down here what might be left to say in time come after death,
and rose reincarnate in the ghostly clothes of jazz in the goldhorn
shadow of the band and blew the suffering of America's naked
mind for love into an eli eli lamma lamma sabacthani°
saxophone cry that shivered the cities down to the last radio
with the absolute heart of the poem of life butchered out of their
own bodies good to eat a thousand years.

---

70. *Pilgrim State's Rockland's and Greystone's:* hospitals for mentally ill patients near New York City. Solomon spent time at Pilgrim State and Rockland; his removal to Pilgrim State occasioned the poem's dedication. Ginsberg's mother, Naomi, institutionalized at Greystone since the late 1940s, died there in 1956.

70. *dolmen-realms:* dolmens are neolithic tombs consisting of a large, flat rock laid across upright rocks. Ginsberg's note—"Dolmens mark a vanished civilization, as Stonehenge or Greystone and Rockland monoliths."

71. *mother finally ******:* Ginsberg's draft reads "mother finally fucked." Ginsberg's note—"Author replaced letters with asterisks in final draft of poem to introduce appropriate level of uncertainty."

74. *Pater . . . Deus:* (Latin) "All-powerful Father, Eternal God," from a 1904 letter describing the power of nature by the French painter Paul Cézanne (1839–1906).

77. *eli . . . sabacthani:* (Aramaic) "My God, my God, why have you forsaken me?" Matthew 27:46, Jesus's last words on the Cross.

II

What sphinx° of cement and aluminum bashed open their skulls and ate up their brains and imagination?

Moloch!° Solitude! Filth! Ugliness! Ashcans and unobtainable dollars! Children screaming under the stairways! Boys sobbing in armies! Old men weeping in the parks!

Moloch! Moloch! Nightmare of Moloch! Moloch the loveless! Mental Moloch! Moloch the heavy judger of men!

Moloch the incomprehensible prison! Moloch the crossbone soulless jailhouse and Congress of sorrows! Moloch whose buildings are judgment! Moloch the vast stone of war! Moloch the stunned governments!

Moloch whose mind is pure machinery! Moloch whose blood is running money! Moloch whose fingers are ten armies! Moloch whose breast is a cannibal dynamo! Moloch whose ear is a smoking tomb!

Moloch whose eyes are a thousand blind windows! Moloch whose skyscrapers stand in the long streets like endless Jehovahs! Moloch whose factories dream and croak in the fog! Moloch whose smokestacks and antennae crown the cities!

Moloch whose love is endless oil and stone! Moloch whose soul is electricity and banks! Moloch whose poverty is the specter of genius! Moloch whose fate is a cloud of sexless hydrogen! Moloch whose name is the Mind!

Moloch in whom I sit lonely! Moloch in whom I dream Angels! Crazy in Moloch! Cocksucker in Moloch! Lacklove and manless in Moloch!

Moloch who entered my soul early! Moloch in whom I am a consciousness without a body! Moloch who frightened me out of my natural ecstasy! Moloch whom I abandon! Wake up in Moloch! Light streaming out of the sky!

Moloch! Moloch! Robot apartments! invisible suburbs! skeleton treasuries! blind capitals! demonic industries! spectral nations! invincible madhouses! granite cocks! monstrous bombs!

They broke their backs lifting Moloch to Heaven! Pavements, trees, radios, tons! lifting the city to Heaven which exists and is everywhere about us!

---

79. *sphinx:* mythical beast with a lion's body and a human head.

80. *Moloch:* Ginsberg's note—"Moloch, or Molech, the Canaanite fire god, whose worship was marked by parents' burning their children as propitiary sacrifice. 'And thou shalt not let any of thy seed pass through the fire to Molech' (Leviticus 18.21)."

Visions! omens! hallucinations! miracles! ecstasies! gone down the American river!
Dreams! adorations! illuminations! religions! the whole boatload of sensitive bullshit!
Breakthroughs! over the river! flips and crucifixions! gone down the flood! Highs! Epiphanies! Despairs! Ten years' animal screams and suicides! Minds! New loves! Mad generation! down on the rocks of Time!
Real holy laughter in the river! They saw it all! the wild eyes! the holy yells! They bade farewell! They jumped off the roof! to solitude! waving! carrying flowers! Down to the river! into the street!

III

Carl Solomon! I'm with you in Rockland
where you're madder than I am
I'm with you in Rockland
where you must feel very strange
I'm with you in Rockland
where you imitate the shade of my mother
I'm with you in Rockland
where you've murdered your twelve secretaries
I'm with you in Rockland
where you laugh at this invisible humor
I'm with you in Rockland
where we are great writers on the same dreadful typewriter
I'm with you in Rockland
where your condition has become serious and is reported on the radio
I'm with you in Rockland
where the faculties of the skull no longer admit the worms of the senses
I'm with you in Rockland
where you drink the tea of the breasts of the spinsters of Utica
I'm with you in Rockland
where you pun on the bodies of your nurses the harpies of the Bronx
I'm with you in Rockland
where you scream in a straightjacket that you're losing the game of the actual pingpong of the abyss
I'm with you in Rockland
where you hang on the catatonic piano the soul is innocent and immortal it should never die ungodly in an armed madhouse

I'm with you in Rockland
where fifty more shocks will never return your soul to its body
again from its pilgrimage to a cross in the void
I'm with you in Rockland
where you accuse your doctors of insanity and plot the Hebrew
socialist revolution against the fascist national Golgotha
I'm with you in Rockland
where you will split the heavens of Long Island and resurrect
your living human Jesus from the superhuman tomb
I'm with you in Rockland
where there are twentyfive thousand mad comrades all together
singing the final stanzas of the Internationale°
I'm with you in Rockland
where we hug and kiss the United States under our bedsheets
the United States that coughs all night and won't let us sleep
I'm with you in Rockland
where we wake up electrified out of the coma by our own souls'
airplanes roaring over the roof they've come to drop angelic
bombs the hospital illuminates itself imaginary walls
collapse O skinny legions run outside O starry-spangled
shock of mercy the eternal war is here O victory forget your
underwear we're free
I'm with you in Rockland
in my dreams you walk dripping from a sea-journey on the
highway across America in tears to the door of my cottage in
the Western night

1955–1956

A SUPERMARKET IN CALIFORNIA

What thoughts I have of you tonight, Walt Whitman, for I walked down the sidestreets under the trees with a headache self-conscious looking at the full moon.

In my hungry fatigue, and shopping for images, I went into the neon fruit supermarket, dreaming of your enumerations!

What peaches and what penumbras! Whole families shopping at night! Aisles full of husbands! Wives in the avocados, babies in the tomatoes! —and you, García Lorca, what were you doing down by the watermelons?

I saw you, Walt Whitman, childless, lonely old grubber, poking among the meats in the refrigerator and eyeing the grocery boys.

---

109. *Internationale:* the anthem of the international working class, *The Internationale* was written by Eugene Pottier in Paris in 1871 to celebrate the Paris Commune. It was later sung to celebrate a commitment to revolutionary socialism or communism; the Soviet anthem until 1944.

I heard you asking questions of each: Who killed the pork chops? What price bananas? Are you my Angel?

I wandered in and out of the brilliant stacks of cans following you, and followed in my imagination by the store detective.

We strode down the open corridors together in our solitary fancy tasting artichokes, possessing every frozen delicacy, and never passing the cashier.

Where are we going, Walt Whitman? The doors close in an hour. Which way does your beard point tonight?

(I touch your book and dream of our odyssey in the supermarket and feel absurd.)

Will we walk all night through solitary streets? The trees add shade to shade, lights out in the houses, we'll both be lonely.

Will we stroll dreaming of the lost America of love past blue automobiles in driveways, home to our silent cottage?

Ah, dear father, graybeard, lonely old courage-teacher, what America did you have when Charon° quit poling his ferry and you got out on a smoking bank and stood watching the boat disappear on the black waters of Lethe?

1955

WHO BE KIND TO

Be kind to your self, it is only one
    and perishable
of many on the planet, thou art that
one that wishes a soft finger tracing the
    line of feeling from nipple to pubes—
one that wishes a tongue to kiss your armpit,
    a lip to kiss your cheek inside your
    whiteness thigh—
Be kind to yourself Harry, because unkindness
    comes when the body explodes
napalm cancer and the deathbed in Vietnam
is a strange place to dream of   trees
    leaning over and angry American faces
grinning with sleepwalk terror over your
    last eye—
Be kind to yourself, because the bliss of your own
    kindness will flood the police tomorrow,
because the cow weeps in the field and the
    mouse weeps in the cat hole—

Charon: in Greek mythology, the ferryman of the dead.

Be kind to this place, which is your present
habitation, with derrick and radar tower
and flower in the ancient brook—
Be kind to your neighbor who weeps
solid tears on the television sofa,
he has no other home, and hears nothing
but the hard voice of telephones
Click, buzz, switch channel and the inspired
melodrama disappears
and he's left alone for the night, he disappears
in bed—
Be kind to your disappearing mother and
father gazing out the terrace window
as milk truck and hearse turn the corner
Be kind to the politician weeping in the galleries
of Whitehall, Kremlin, White House
Louvre and Phoenix City
aged, large nosed, angry, nervously dialing
the bald voice box connected to
electrodes underground converging thru
wires vaster than a kitten's eye can see
on the mushroom shaped fear-lobe under
the ear of Sleeping Dr. Einstein
crawling with worms, crawling with worms, crawling
with worms the hour has come—
Sick, dissatisfied, unloved, the bulky
foreheads of Captain Premier President
Sir Comrade Fear!
Be kind to the fearful one at your side
Who's remembering the Lamentations
of the bible
the prophecies of the Crucified Adam Son
of all the porters and char men of
Bell gravia—
Be kind to your self who weeps under
the Moscow moon and hide your bliss hairs
under raincoat and suede Levi's—
For this is the joy to be born, the kindness
received thru strange eyeglasses on
a bus thru Kensington,
the finger touch of the Londoner on your thumb,
that borrows light from your cigarette,
the morning smile at Newcastle Central
station, when longhair Tom blond husband

greets the bearded stranger of telephones—
the boom bom that bounces in the joyful
bowels as the Liverpool Minstrels of
CavernSink°
raise up their joyful voices and guitars
in electric Afric hurrah
for Jerusalem—
The saints come marching in, Twist &
Shout, and Gates of Eden are named
in Albion again
Hope sings a black psalm from Nigeria,
and a white psalm echoes in Detroit
and reechoes amplified from Nottingham to Prague
and a Chinese psalm will be heard, if we all
live out our lives for the next 6 decades—
Be kind to the Chinese psalm in the red transistor
in your breast—
Be kind to the Monk in the 5 Spot° who plays
lone chord-bangs on his vast piano
lost in space on a bench and hearing himself
in the nightclub universe—
Be kind to the heroes that have lost their
names in the newspaper
and hear only their own supplication for
the peaceful kiss of sex in the giant
auditoriums of the planet,
nameless voices crying for kindness in the orchestra,
screaming in anguish that bliss come true
and sparrows sing another hundred years
to white haired babes
and poets be fools of their own desire—O Anacreon
and angelic Shelley!
Guide these new-nippled generations on space
ships to Mars' next universe
The prayer is to man and girl, the only
gods, the only lords of Kingdoms of
Feeling, Christs of their own
living ribs—

---

67. *Liverpool Minstrels of Cavern Sink:* English rock band The Beatles performed nearly 300 times at Liverpool's Cavern Club.

81. *Monk in the 5 Spot:* American jazz musician Thelonious Monk (1917–1982) performed and recorded at New York's Five Spot Cafe, which Ginsberg frequented.

Bicycle chain and machine gun, fear sneer
& smell cold logic of the Dream Bomb
have come to Saigon, Johannesburg,
Dominica City, Phnom Penh, Pentagon
Paris and Lhasa—
Be kind to the universe of Self that
trembles and shudders and thrills
in XX Century,
that opens its eyes and belly and breast
chained with flesh to feel
the myriad flowers of bliss
that I Am to Thee—
A dream! a Dream! I don't want to be alone!
I want to know that I am loved!
I want the orgy of our flesh, orgy
of all eyes happy, orgy of the soul
kissing and blessing its mortal-grown
body,
orgy of tenderness beneath the neck, orgy of
kindness to thigh and vagina
Desire given with meat hand
and cock, desire taken with
mouth and ass, desire returned
to the last sigh!
Tonite let's all make love in London
as if it were 2001 the years
of thrilling god—
And be kind to the poor soul that cries in
a crack of the pavement because he
has no body—
Prayers to the ghosts and demons, the
lackloves of Capitals & Congresses
who make sadistic noises
on the radio—
Statue destroyers & tank captains, unhappy
murderers in Mekong & Stanleyville,
That a new kind of man has come to his bliss
to end the cold war he has borne
against his own kind flesh
since the days of the snake.

1965

RAIN-WET ASPHALT HEAT, GARBAGE CURBED CANS OVERFLOWING

I hauled down lifeless mattresses to sidewalk refuse-piles,
old rugs stept on from Paterson to Lower East Side filled with bed-bugs,
gray pillows, couch seats treasured from the street laid back on the street
—out, to hear Murder-tale, 3rd Street cyclists attacked tonite—
Bopping along in rain, Chaos fallen over City roofs,
shrouds of chemical vapour drifting over building-tops—
Get the *Times,* Nixon says peace reflected from the Moon,
but I found no boy body to sleep with all night on pavements 3 A.M.
home in sweating drizzle—
Those mattresses soggy lying by full five garbagepails—
Barbara, Maretta, Peter Steven Rosebud slept on these Pillows years ago,
forgotten names, also made love to me, I had these mattresses four years
on my floor—
Gerard, Jimmy many months, even blond Gordon later,
Paul with the beautiful big cock, that teenage boy that lived in
Pennsylvania,
forgotten numbers, young dream loves and lovers, earthly bellies—
many strong youths with eyes closed, come sighing and helping me
come—
Desires already forgotten, tender persons used and kissed goodbye
and all the times I came to myself alone in the dark dreaming of Neal or
Billy Budd
—nameless angels of half-life—heart beating & eyes weeping for lovely
phantoms—
Back from the Gem Spa, into the hallway, a glance behind
and sudden farewell to the bedbug-ridden mattresses piled soggy in dark
rain.

1969

FATHER DEATH BLUES°

Hey Father Death, I'm flying home
Hey poor man, you're all alone
Hey old daddy, I know where I'm going

Father Death, Don't cry any more
Mama's there, underneath the floor
Brother Death, please mind the store

---

poem title: composed in the air over Lake Michigan, "Father Death Blues" later became Part V of a poem sequence, "Don't Grow Old." Ginsberg set "Father Death Blues" to music and performed it at readings.

Old Aunty Death Don't hide your bones
Old Uncle Death I hear your groans
O Sister Death how sweet your moans

O Children Deaths go breathe your breaths
Sobbing breasts'll ease your Deaths
Pain is gone, tears take the rest

Genius Death your art is done
Lover Death your body's gone
Father Death I'm coming home

Guru Death your words are true
Teacher Death I do thank you
For inspiring me to sing this Blues

Buddha Death, I wake with you
Dharma Death, your mind is new
Sangha Death, we'll work it through

Suffering is what was born
Ignorance made me forlorn
Tearful truths I cannot scorn

Father Breath once more farewell
Birth you gave was no thing ill
My heart is still, as time will tell.

1976

SPHINCTER

I hope my good old asshole holds out
60 years it's been mostly OK
Tho in Bolivia a fissure operation
    survived the *altiplano*° hospital—
a little blood, no polyps, occasionally
    a small hemorrhoid
active, eager, receptive to phallus
    coke bottle, candle, carrot
    banana & fingers—
Now AIDS makes it shy, but still
    eager to serve—

---

altiplano: plateau in the Andes.

out with the dumps, in with the condom'd
        orgasmic friend—
still rubbery muscular,
        unashamed wide open for joy
But another 20 years who knows,
        old folks got troubles everywhere—
necks, prostates, stomachs, joints—
        Hope the old hole stays young
        till death, relax

1994

ROBERT CREELEY (1926–2005)

Creeley was born in Arlington, Massachusetts, near where he grew up on a small farm. As a young child he suffered two losses, that of his father and that of his left eye. He was raised by his mother, who worked as a public health nurse. Creeley enrolled at Harvard but took a leave to be an ambulance driver for the American Field Service toward the end of World War II. He was in the India-Burma area from 1944 to 1945. He returned to Harvard but left without his degree, taking up subsistence farming for a time in New Hampshire. A correspondence with poet Charles Olson, maintained while Creeley was in France and Spain, led him to Black Mountain College in North Carolina, where he completed his degree, began to teach, and edited the *Black Mountain Review*. He later spent time in New Mexico and Guatemala before taking a job in Buffalo for the rest of his career.

A thin, spare, compressed, and consistently minimalist verse became his signature style. Certainly the phrasing often seems conversational, though jazz is another continuing influence, but the progress of a poem is often interrupted by hesitation, sudden wonder, or disabling pain. Thus, in the end, it is consciousness's interior struggle with both self-reflection and exterior circumstances that explains his sometimes broken rhythms. William Carlos Williams was clearly a strong influence, both in form and subject matter, but a Williams poem flows smoothly, whereas a Creeley poem may choose to falter.

AFTER LORCA°

(for M. Marti)

The church is a business, and the rich
are the business men.
When they pull on the bells, the
poor come piling in and when a poor man dies, he has a
◁ wooden
cross, and they rush through the ceremony.

But when a rich man dies, they
drag out the Sacrament
and a golden Cross, and go *doucement, doucement*°
to to the cemetery.

---

poem title: Federico García Lorca (1898–1936), the premier poet of modern Spain, murdered by right-wing soldiers at the outset of the Spanish Civil War. See, for example, García Lorca's "Ode to the Most Holy Sacrament of the Altar."

9. *doucement:* (French) "sweetly."

And the poor love it
and think it's crazy.

1953

I KNOW A MAN

As I sd to my
friend, because I am
always talking,—John, I

sd, which was not his
name, the darkness sur-
rounds us, what

can we do against
it, or else, shall we &
why not, buy a goddamn big car,

drive, he sd, for
Christ's sake, look
out where yr going.

1954

THE FLOWER

I think I grow tensions
like flowers
in a wood where
nobody goes.

Each wound is perfect,
encloses itself in a tiny
imperceptible blossom,
making pain.

Pain is a flower like that one,
like this one,
like that one,
like this one.

1958

FOR LOVE

for Bobbie°

Yesterday I wanted to
speak of it, that sense above
the others to me
important because all

that I know derives
from what it teaches me.
Today, what is it that
is finally so helpless,

different, despairs of its own
statement, wants to
turn away, endlessly
to turn away.

If the moon did not . . .
no, if you did not
I wouldn't either, but
what would I not

do, what prevention, what
thing so quickly stopped.
That is love yesterday
or tomorrow, not

now. Can I eat
what you give me. I
have not earned it. Must
I think of everything

as earned. Now love also
becomes a reward so
remote from me I have
only made it with my mind.

Here is tedium,
despair, a painful
sense of isolation and
whimsical if pompous

---

dedication: Creeley's second wife.

self-regard. But that image
is only of the mind's
vague structure, vague to me
because it is my own.

Love, what do I think
to say. I cannot say it.
What have you become to ask,
what have I made you into,

companion, good company,
crossed legs with skirt, or
soft body under
the bones of the bed.

Nothing says anything
but that which it wishes
would come true, fears
what else might happen in

some other place, some
other time not this one.
A voice in my place, an
echo of that only in yours.

Let me stumble into
not the confession but
the obsession I begin with
now. For you

also (also)
some time beyond place, or
place beyond time, no
mind left to

say anything at all,
that face gone, now.
Into the company of love°
it all returns.

1962

---

63. *the company of love:* a quotation from Hart Crane's "The Broken Tower."

AMERICA

America, you ode for reality![1]
Give back the people you took.

Let the sun shine again
on the four corners of the world

you thought of first but do not
own, or keep like a convenience.

People are your own word, you
invented that locus and term.

Here, you said and say, is
where we are. Give back

what we are, these people you made,
us, and nowhere but you to be.

1969

AGE

Most explicit—
the sense of trap

as a narrowing
cone one's got

stuck into and
any movement

forward simply
wedges one more—

but where
or quite when,

even with whom,
since now there is no one

quite with you—Quite? Quiet?
English expression: *Quait?*

---

1. *ode for reality:* Creeley may be alluding to Whitman's famous description of the United States as "essentially the greatest poem" in the preface to *Leaves of Grass.*

Language of singular
impedance? A dance? An

involuntary gesture to
others *not* there? What's

wrong here? How
reach out to the

other side all
others live on as

now you see the
two doctors, behind

you, in mind's eye,
probe into your anus,

or ass, or bottom,
behind you, the roto-

rooter-like device
sees all up, concludes

"like a worn-out inner tube,"
"old," prose prolapsed, person's

problems won't do, must
cut into, cut out . . .

The world is a round but
diminishing ball, a spherical

ice cube, a dusty
joke, a fading,

faint echo of its
former self but remembers,

sometimes, its past, sees
friends, places, reflections,

talks to itself in a fond,
judgmental murmur,

alone at last.
I stood so close

to you I could have
reached out and

touched you just
as you turned

over and began to
snore not unattractively,

no, never less than
attractively, my love,

my love—but in this
curiously glowing dark, this

finite emptiness, *you, you, you*
are crucial, hear the

whimpering back of
the talk, the approaching

fears when I may
cease to be me, all

lost or rather lumped
here in a retrograded,

dislocating, imploding
self, a uselessness

talks, even if finally to no one,
talks and talks.

1988

ROBERT BLY (b. 1926)

Bly was born in Madison, a town in rural Minnesota, where he has lived most of his life. He was educated at St. Olaf's College and at Harvard, thereafter enrolling in the Writers' Workshop at the University of Iowa. From 1944 to 1946, Bly served in the Navy. In addition to his poetry, he has done a number of translations, including poetry by Neruda, Vallejo, and Rilke, and edited a continuing journal renamed after each decade—*The Fifties, The Sixties,* and so forth. Since then, he has been a leading figure in the men's movement, for which he has written successful manifestoes, including the widely read *Iron John* (1992).

Influences on his poetry include the poets he has translated and the seventeenth-century mystic Jakob Boehme. He has given intense poetry readings wearing masks, actively opposed the Vietnam War, and believes scientific rationalism has led us astray. He seeks deep images drawn from the unconscious and deploys them in relatively simple structures, believing that such subconscious or unconscious revelations can resist the dominant Cartesian logic of the Western world.

COUNTING SMALL-BONED BODIES

Let's count the bodies over again.

If we could only make the bodies smaller,
The size of skulls,
We could make a whole plain white with
  skulls in the moonlight!

If we could only make the bodies smaller,
Maybe we could get
A whole year's kill in front of us on a desk!

If we could only make the bodies smaller,
We could fit
A body into a finger-ring,
  for a keepsake forever.

1967

HEARING GARY SNYDER READ

SNYDER stands with his arms folded while he is introduced. He is short, definitely a small horse—though not a colt. He stands quietly, sure and trained; it will take a lot to make him shy. He would never leap sideways; he might jump back, but would leap ahead an instant later. His face has something of the lion too—the jaw curiously broad, the mouth very important. A line curls around each turned up valley-end, backing it up, into foothills. When he smiles widely, several other moats appear, one after the other, reaching far back into the gaunt cheekbones. As he reads, his eyes grow narrow and a bit slanted—it is eyes looking at something far away over the veldt grasses.

HE SPEAKS softly before the student audience, confident that he has much to say, and it is exactly what they need to know. He makes a few remarks about *Rip Rap* to start with. On certain mountainsides in the far west where one might want to build trails, an obsidian rock sheath is found, glassy, impossible for horses' hoofs to get a grip on. So smaller rocks have to be laid on it, but carefully. So he thought that words might be used that way, one slipped under the end of another, laid down on the glassy surface of some insight that one couldn't stand on otherwise.

HE READS a poem taken from a dream: he is with friends. A lion comes out behind his friends. When he hits it with a rock, it turns into a girl. "Hail to the goddess in the lion form who swims over a river."

SOMETIMES he tosses his head to the side, a kind of insignificant throw, as if to say, I am one of those floating, my lily pads are not connected to the bottom. After he finishes reading a poem, he smiles for a long time at the audience, partly of love for himself, and partly for the wonderful things he has said. He smiles actually because the poems he has written are tiny fragments of the universe, and *that* is wonderful. When he starts to read once more, he looks down—he does not have his poems by heart. They are thrown off from his life like feathers in a fight, or dropped off like hairs.

AS HE READS ON, and goes deeper into his poems, his face begins to shine. And where they go is deeper into wells of energy, male and female energy, what he calls Shiva energy! He says Shiva is still the god with the most living worshippers. He thinks that in the 1500 BC frieze the figure is Shiva, in a Yogi posture, with antlers coming from his head. He does not read as Creeley does to each person in the audience alone. Instead, as Snyder reads, an arm encloses the whole audience—it is a swirling motion, an energy that goes in a circle around the room, and returns to him. So everyone does have a relationship—not so much with him, as with a male-female core of energy in the universe. So that circular little globes of energy inside us are made larger as he reads.

YET HE somehow remains inside his own personality-body and can't escape. His comments are at times bookish in phrasing: "Kali, in her more benevolent aspect." When he reads some lines that permanently escape from bookishness, he swings his lion head firmly from side to side, swiftly, several times, and then swings his right foot backward for a moment and lets it fall.

1971

A. R. AMMONS (1926–2001)

Born in a farmhouse near Whiteville, North Carolina, the son of a tobacco farmer, Archie Randolph Ammons served on a Navy destroyer escort in World War II. He studied biology and chemistry at Wake Forest College in his home state and went on to literary studies at Berkeley. In 1964, after working for almost a decade as an executive at a glassmaking firm, he took a teaching job at Cornell University. The landscapes of the places where he has lived—from North Carolina to the south coast of New Jersey and finally to the hills and fields around Ithaca, New York—figure prominently in his poetry. Like Muriel Rukeyser before him, he makes heavy use of the colon in punctuation; it is a way of visualizing relationships of continuity, equivalence, and interdependence in the things he describes. His nature poems mix exact local representation with transcendental longings and moments of wit and irony; he is often compared to Emerson. From nature's mutability he leams a mental discipline of adaptability and a recognition that absolute demarcation is not offered to us by the world around us. Thus in "Corson's Inlet," very nearly his signature poem, he walks a changing shoreline with no inherent enclosures and celebrates its devotion to process. The book-length poem *Sphere* (1974) may be his masterpiece.

CORSONS INLET°

I went for a walk over the dunes again this morning
to the sea,
then turned right along
    the surf
            rounded a naked headland
            and returned

    along the inlet shore:

it was muggy sunny, the wind from the sea steady and high
crisp in the running sand,
          some breakthroughs of sun
   but after a bit

continuous overcast:

the walk liberating, I was released from forms,
from the perpendiculars,
          straight lines, blocks, boxes, binds

---

poem title: located on the south New Jersey shore.

of thought
into the hues, shadings, rises, flowing bends and blends
          of sight:

                    I allow myself eddies of meaning:
yield to a direction of significance
running
like a stream through the geography of my work:
    you can find
in my sayings
                swerves of action
                like the inlet's cutting edge:
          there are dunes of motion,
organizations of grass, white sandy paths of remembrance
in the overall wandering of mirroring mind:

but Overall is beyond me: is the sum of these events
I cannot draw, the ledger I cannot keep, the accounting
beyond the account:

in nature there are few sharp lines: there are areas of
primrose
          more or less dispersed;
disorderly orders of bayberry; between the rows
of dunes,
irregular swamps of reeds,
though not reeds alone, but grass, bayberry, yarrow, all . . .
predominantly reeds:

I have reached no conclusions, have erected no boundaries,
shutting out and shutting in, separating inside
          from outside: I have
          drawn no lines:
          as

manifold events of sand
change the dune's shape that will not be the same shape
tomorrow,

so I am willing to go along, to accept
the becoming
thought, to stake off no beginnings or ends, establish
          no walls:

by transitions the land falls from grassy dunes to creek
to undercreek: but there are no lines, though
change in that transition is clear
as any sharpness: but "sharpness" spread out,
allowed to occur over a wider range
than mental lines can keep:

the moon was full last night: today, low tide was low:
black shoals of mussels exposed to the risk
of air
and, earlier, of sun,
waved in and out with the waterline, waterline inexact,
caught always in the event of change:
a young mottled gull stood free on the shoals
and ate
to vomiting: another gull, squawking possession, cracked a crab,
picked out the entrails, swallowed the soft-shelled legs, a ruddy
turnstone running in to snatch leftover bits:

risk is full: every living thing in
siege: the demand is life, to keep life: the small
white blacklegged egret, how beautiful, quietly stalks and spears
the shallows, darts to shore
to stab—what? I couldn't
see against the black mudflats—a frightened
fiddler crab?

the news to my left over the dunes and
reeds and bayberry clumps was
fall: thousands of tree swallows
gathering for flight:
an order held
in constant change: a congregation
rich with entropy: nevertheless, separable, noticeable
as one event,
not chaos: preparations for
flight from winter,
cheet, cheet, cheet, cheet, wings rifling the green clumps,
beaks
at the bayberries
a perception full of wind, flight, curve,
sound:
the possibility of rule as the sum of rulelessness:
the "field" of action
with moving, incalculable center:

in the smaller view, order tight with shape:
blue tiny flowers on a leafless weed: carapace of crab:
snail shell:
pulsations of order
in the bellies of minnows: orders swallowed,
broken down, transferred through membranes
to strengthen larger orders: but in the large view, no
lines or changeless shapes: the working in and out, together
and against, of millions of events: this,
so that I make
no form
formlessness:

orders as summaries, as outcomes of actions override
or in some way result, not predictably (seeing me gain
the top of a dune,
the swallows
could take flight—some other fields of bayberry
could enter fall
berryless) and there is serenity:

no arranged terror: no forcing of image, plan,
or thought:
no propaganda, no humbling of reality to precept:

terror pervades but is not arranged, all possibilities
of escape open: no route shut, except in
the sudden loss of all routes:

I see narrow orders, limited tightness, but will
not run to that easy victory:
still around the looser, wider forces work:
I will try
to fasten into order enlarging grasps of disorder, widening
scope, but enjoying the freedom that
scope eludes my grasp, that there is no finality of vision,
that I have perceived nothing completely,
that tomorrow a new walk is a new walk.

1963

GRAVELLY RUN

I don't know somehow it seems sufficient
to see and hear whatever coming and going is,

losing the self to the victory
    of stones and trees,
of bending sandpit lakes, crescent
round groves of dwarf pine:

for it is not so much to know the self
as to know it as it is known
    by galaxy and cedar cone,
as if birth had never found it
and death could never end it:

the swamp's slow water comes
down Gravelly Run fanning the long
    stone-held algal
hair and narrowing roils between
the shoulders of the highway bridge:

holly grows on the hanks in the woods there,
and the cedars' gothic-clustered
    spires could make
green religion in winter bones:

so I look and reflect, but the air's glass
jail seals each thing in its entity:

no use to make any philosophies here:
    I see no
god in the holly, hear no song from
the snowbroken weeds: Hegel is not the winter
yellow in the pines: the sunlight has never
heard of trees: surrendered self among
    unwelcoming forms: stranger,
hoist your burdens, get on down the road.

1965

COON SONG

I got one good look
    in the raccoon's eyes
        when he fell from the tree
came to his feet
    and perfectly still
        seized the baying hounds
in his dull fierce stare,
    in that recognition all
        decision lost,

choice irrelevant, before the
battle fell
and the unwinding
of his little knot of time began:

Dostoevsky° would think
it important if the coon
could choose to
be back up the tree:
or if he could choose to be
wagging by a swamp pond,
dabbling at scuttling
crawdads:° the coon may have
dreamed in fact of curling
into the holed-out gall
of a fallen oak some squirrel
had once brought
high into the air
clean leaves to: but
reality can go to hell
is what the coon's eyes said to me:
and said how simple
the solution to my
problem is: it needs only
not to be: I thought the raccoon
felt no anger,
saw none; cared nothing for cowardice,
bravery; was in fact
bored at
knowing what would ensue:
the unwinding, the whirling growls,
exposed tenders,
the wet teeth—a problem to be
solved, the taut-coiled vigor
of the hunt
ready to snap loose:

you want to know what happened,
you want to hear me describe it,
to placate the hound's-mouth
slobbering in your own heart:

---

14. *Dostoevsky:* Russian novelist Fyodor Dostoevski (1821–1881).
21. *crawdads:* crayfish.

I will not tell you: actually the coon
possessing secret knowledge
pawed dust on the dogs
and they disappeared, yapping into
nothingness, and the coon went
down to the pond
and washed his face and hands and beheld
the world: maybe he didn't:
I am no slave that I
should entertain you, say what you want
to hear, let you wallow in
your silt: one two three four five:
one two three four five six seven eight nine ten:

(all this time I've been
counting spaces
while you were thinking of something else)
mess in your own sloppy silt:
the hounds disappeared
yelping (the way you would at extinction)
into—the order
breaks up here—immortality:
I know that's where you think the brave
little victims should go:
I do not care what
you think: I do not care what you think:
I do not care what you
think: one two three four five
six seven eight nine ten: here we go
round the here-we-go-round, the
here-we-go-round, the here-we-
go-round: coon will end in disorder at the
teeth of hounds: the situation
will get him:
spheres roll, cubes stay put: now there
one two three four five
are two philosophies:
here we go round the mouth-wet of hounds:

what I choose
is youse:
baby

1965

JAMES WRIGHT (1927–1980)

Born and raised in a steelworker's family in the steel town of Martins Ferry, Ohio, Wright joined the army after high school; he was sent to occupied Japan. After returning, he studied with John Crowe Ransom at Kenyon College and Theodore Roethke at the University of Washington, where he earned a Ph.D. He taught at the University of Minnesota, Hunter College, and the University of Delaware. In his first two books, Wright used regular meters and rhymes and often celebrated the social outsiders of the small towns and farms near where he grew up. "Saint Judas," on the other hand, from Wright's second book, is a portrait of another sort of outcast, Christ's betrayer. Then, on a Fulbright in Austria, he discovered the associative and sometimes partly surreal imagery of poets Georg Trakl and Theodor Storm. A visit to Robert Bly back in the United States helped give a name to this impulse and a rhetoric with which to bring it to realization—poetry of the "deep image." He adopted free-verse forms based on colloquial American speech and constructed as a series of evocative images leading toward moments of epiphany. "A Blessing" and "Lying in a Hammock" are notable examples. At the same time, some of his poems became more political, including some written in protest against the Vietnam War, and the outcasts he depicted were more often victims of American history.

SAINT JUDAS

When I went out to kill myself, I caught
A pack of hoodlums beating up a man.
Running to spare his suffering, I forgot
My name, my number, how my day began,
How soldiers milled around the garden stone
And sang amusing songs; how all that day
Their javelins measured crowds; how I alone
Bargained the proper coins, and slipped away.

Banished from heaven, I found this victim beaten,
Stripped, kneed, and left to cry. Dropping my rope
Aside, I ran, ignored the uniforms:
Then I remembered bread my flesh had eaten,
The kiss that ate my flesh. Flayed without hope,
I held the man for nothing in my arms.

1959

BEGINNING

The moon drops one or two feathers into the field.
The dark wheat listens.
Be still.

Now.
There they are, the moon's young, trying
Their wings.
Between trees, a slender woman lifts up the lovely shadow
Of her face, and now she steps into the air, now she is gone
Wholly, into the air.
I stand alone by an elder tree, I do not dare breathe
Or move.
I listen.
The wheat leans back toward its own darkness,
And I lean toward mine.

1963

AUTUMN BEGINS IN MARTINS FERRY, OHIO

In the Shreve High football stadium,
I think of Polacks nursing long beers in Tiltonsville,°
And gray faces of Negroes in the blast furnace at Benwood,°
And the ruptured° night watchman of Wheeling Steel,
Dreaming of heroes.

All the proud fathers are ashamed to go home.
Their women cluck like starved pullets,°
Dying for love.

Therefore,
Their sons grow suicidally beautiful
At the beginning of October,
And gallop terribly against each other's bodies.

1963

LYING IN A HAMMOCK AT WILLIAM DUFFY'S FARM IN PINE ISLAND, MINNESOTA

Over my head, I see the bronze butterfly,
Asleep on the black trunk,
Blowing like a leaf in green shadow.
Down the ravine behind the empty house,
The cowbells follow one another
Into the distances of the afternoon.
To my right,
In a field of sunlight between two pines,
The droppings of last year's horses

---

2. *Tiltonsville:* a town in eastern Ohio, north of Martins Ferry.

3. *Benwood:* a town south of Martins Ferry, the site of the Wheeling Steel Works.

4. *ruptured:* herniated.

7. *pullets:* young hens.

Blaze up into golden stones.
I lean back, as the evening darkens and comes on.
A chicken hawk floats over, looking for home.
I have wasted my life.

1963

A BLESSING

Just off the highway to Rochester, Minnesota,
Twilight bounds softly forth on the grass.
And the eyes of those two Indian ponies
Darken with kindness.
They have come gladly out of the willows
To welcome my friend and me.
We step over the barbed wire into the pasture
Where they have been grazing all day, alone.
They ripple tensely, they can hardly contain their happiness
That we have come.
They bow shyly as wet swans. They love each other.
There is no loneliness like theirs.
At home once more,
They begin munching the young tufts of spring in the darkness.
I would like to hold the slenderer one in my arms,
For she has walked over to me
And nuzzled my left hand.
She is black and white,
Her mane falls wild on her forehead,
And the light breeze moves me to caress her long ear
That is delicate as the skin over a girl's wrist.
Suddenly I realize
That if I stepped out of my body I would break
Into blossom.

1963

A CENTENARY ODE: INSCRIBED TO LITTLE CROW, LEADER OF THE SIOUX REBELLION IN MINNESOTA, 1862°

I had nothing to do with it, I was not here.
I was not born.
In 1862, when your hotheads
Raised hell from here to South Dakota,
My own fathers scattered into West Virginia
And southern Ohio.

---

poem title: crowded onto a reservation representing barely 10% of their tribal lands, their opportunities for hunting eliminated, the Sioux were at risk of starvation when a small group attacked a trading post and a farm. The sixty-year-old Little Crow led an unsuccessful attack on Fort Ridgely.

My family fought the Confederacy
And fought the Union.
None of them got killed.
But for all that, it was not my fathers
Who murdered you.
Not much.

I don't know
Where the fathers of Minneapolis finalized
Your flayed carcass.
Little Crow, true father
Of my dark America,
When I close my eyes I lose you among
Old lonelinesses.
My family were a lot of singing drunks and good carpenters.
We had brothers who loved one another no matter what they did.
And they did plenty.

I think they would have run like hell from your Sioux.
And when you caught them you all would have run like hell
From the Confederacy and from the Union
Into the hills and hunted for a few things,
Some bull-cat under the stones, a gar maybe,
If you were hungry, and if you were happy,
Sunfish and corn.

If only I knew where to mourn you,
I would surely mourn.

But I don't know.

I did not come here only to grieve
For my people's defeat.
The troops of the Union, who won,
Still outnumber us.
Old Paddy Beck, my great-uncle, is dead
At the old soldiers' home near Tiffen, Ohio.
He got away with every last stitch
Of his uniform, save only
The dress trousers.

Oh all around us,
The hobo jungles of America grow wild again.
The pick handles bloom like your skinned spine.
I don't even know where
My own grave is.

1971

JOHN ASHBERY (b. 1927)

Ashbery was born in Rochester, New York. He grew up on a farm in nearby Sodus and was educated at Harvard and Columbia. After a Fulbright fellowship took him to France, he stayed on and worked as an art critic for several newspapers and magazines, finally returning to become executive editor of *Art News* from 1965 to 1972. His long poem "Self-Portrait in a Convex Mirror" (1975) mixes critical analysis of a Renaissance painting by Parmigianino with reflections on his own mental process, though it lacks the cheerful surrealism and aggressive disjunctiveness of many of his shorter poems. In his early work, his approach sometimes seemed antirepresentational, with a focus on linguistic events and the structures of thought. As a result, he was often associated with abstract expressionist painting of the 1940s and 1950s. But as his witty incorporation of linguistic commonplaces and public speech was matched by the use of multiple references to popular culture, his work became more accessible and his project more distinctive. Rapid changes in focus and mood still marked his poems, but he was now questioning how a commodified world might shape human consciousness. He is thus perhaps the poet who has thought most deeply about the mental life that mass culture grants to us. In the process, he came to doubt the plausibility of any coherent selfhood or the credibility of a conventionally coherent narrative.

"THEY DREAM ONLY OF AMERICA"

They dream only of America
To be lost among the thirteen million pillars of grass:
"This honey is delicious
Though it burns the throat."

And hiding from darkness in barns
They can be grownups now
And the murderer's ash tray is more easily—
The lake a lilac cube.

He holds a key in his right hand.
"Please," he asked willingly.
He is thirty years old.
That was before

We could drive hundreds of miles
At night through dandelions.
When his headache grew worse we
Stopped at a wire filling station.

Now he cared only about signs.
Was the cigar a sign?
And what about the key?
He went slowly into the bedroom.

"I would not have broken my leg if I had not fallen
Against the living room table. What is it to be back
Beside the bed? There is nothing to do
For our liberation, except wait in the horror of it.

And I am lost without you."

1962

FARM IMPLEMENTS AND RUTABAGAS IN A LANDSCAPE°

The first of the undecoded messages read: "Popeye° sits in thunder,
Unthought of. From that shoebox of an apartment,
From livid curtain's hue, a tangram emerges: a country."
Meanwhile the Sea Hag was relaxing on a green couch: "How
    pleasant
To spend one's vacation *en la casa*° *de Popeye,"* she scratched
Her cleft chin's solitary hair. She remembered spinach

And was going to ask Wimpy if he had bought any spinach.
"M'love," he intercepted, "the plains are decked out in thunder
Today, and it shall be as you wish." He scratched
The part of his head under his hat. The apartment
Seemed to grow smaller. "But what if no pleasant
Inspiration plunge us now to the stars? *For this is my country."*

Suddenly they remembered how it was cheaper in the country.
Wimpy was thoughtfully cutting open a number 2 can of spinach
When the door opened and Swee'pea crept in. "How pleasant!"
But Swee'pea looked morose. A note was pinned to his bib.
    "Thunder
And tears are unavailing," it read. "Henceforth shall Popeye's
    apartment
Be but remembered space, toxic or salubrious, whole or scratched."

---

poem title: a spoof of titles traditionally given to landscape paintings. Ashbery was an editor of *Art News* and used to invent titles for imaginary paintings.

1. *Popeye* : all names in the poem are those of characters in the *Popeye* comic strip, created by Segar, which was later the basis of a series of animated films.

5. *en la casa de Popeye:* (Spanish) "in Popeye's house." When Ashbery wrote the poem, the strip was appearing in New York City only in the Spanish-language newspaper *El Diaró.* In an interview, Ashbery remarked, "I used to follow it also in French newspapers, where Popeye's dislocations of the English language are reproduced charmingly in French . . . I tend to dislocate the language myself."

Olive came hurtling through the window; its geraniums scratched
Her long thigh. "I have news!" she gasped. "Popeye, forced as you know to flee the country
One musty gusty evening, by the schemes of his wizened, duplicate father, jealous of the apartment
And all that it contains, myself and spinach
In particular, heaves bolts of loving thunder
At his own astonished becoming, rupturing the pleasant

Arpeggio° of our years. No more shall pleasant
Rays of the sun refresh your sense of growing old, nor the scratched
Tree-trunks and mossy foliage, only immaculate darkness and thunder."
She grabbed Swee'pea. "I'm taking the brat to the country."
"But you can't do that—he hasn't even finished his spinach,"
Urged the Sea Hag, looking fearfully around at the apartment.

But Olive was already out of earshot. Now the apartment
Succumbed to a strange new hush. "Actually it's quite pleasant
Here," thought the Sea Hag. "If this is all we need fear from spinach
Then I don't mind so much. Perhaps we could invite Alice the Goon over"—she scratched
One dug pensively— "but Wimpy is such a country
Bumpkin, always burping like that." Minute at first, the thunder

Soon filled the apartment. It was domestic thunder,
The color of spinach. Popeye chuckled and scratched
His balls: it sure was pleasant to spend a day in the country.

1970

MIXED FEELINGS

A pleasant smell of frying sausages
Attacks the sense, along with an old, mostly invisible
Photograph of what seems to be girls lounging around
An old fighter bomber, circa 1942 vintage.
How to explain to these girls, if indeed that's what they are,
These Ruths, Lindas, Pats and Sheilas
About the vast change that's taken place

25. *Arpeggio:* a chord whose notes are played in quick succession rather than simultaneously.

In the fabric of our society, altering the texture
Of all things in it? And yet
They somehow look as if they knew, except
That it's so hard to see them, it's hard to figure out
Exactly what kind of expressions they're wearing.
What are your hobbies, girls? Aw nerts,
One of them might say, this guy's too much for me.
Let's go on and out, somewhere
Through the canyons of the garment center
To a small café and have a cup of coffee.
I am not offended that these creatures (that's the word)
Of my imagination seem to hold me in such light esteem,
Pay so little heed to me. It's part of a complicated
Flirtation routine, anyhow, no doubt. But this talk of
The garment center? Surely that's California sunlight
Belaboring them and the old crate on which they
Have draped themselves, fading its Donald Duck insignia
To the extreme point of legibility.
Maybe they were lying but more likely their
Tiny intelligences cannot retain much information.
Not even one fact, perhaps. That's why
They think they're in New York. I like the way
They look and act and feel. I wonder
How they got that way, but am not going to
Waste any more time thinking about them.
I have already forgotten them
Until some day in the not too distant future
When we meet possibly in the lounge of a modern airport,
They looking as astonishingly young and fresh as when this picture
 was made
But full of contradictory ideas, stupid ones as well as
Worthwhile ones, but all flooding the surface of our minds
As we babble about the sky and the weather and the forests of
 change.

1975

STREET MUSICIANS

One died, and the soul was wrenched out
Of the other in life, who, walking the streets
Wrapped in an identity like a coat, sees on and on
The same corners, volumetrics, shadows
Under trees. Farther than anyone was ever
Called, through increasingly suburban airs
And ways, with autumn falling over everything:

The plush leaves the chattels in barrels
Of an obscure family being evicted
Into the way it was, and is. The other beached
Glimpses of what the other was up to:
Revelations at last. So they grew to hate and forget each other.

So I cradle this average violin that knows
Only forgotten showtunes, but argues
The possibility of free declamation anchored
To a dull refrain, the year turning over on itself
In November, with the spaces among the days
More literal, the meat more visible on the bone.
Our question of a place of origin hangs
Like smoke: how we picnicked in pine forests,
In coves with the water always seeping up, and left
Our trash, sperm and excrement everywhere, smeared
On the landscape, to make of us what we could.

1977

SYRINGA

Orpheus° liked the glad personal quality
Of the things beneath the sky. Of course, Eurydice was a part
Of this. Then one day, everything changed. He rends
Rocks into fissures with lament. Gullies, hummocks
Can't withstand it. The sky shudders from one horizon
To the other, almost ready to give up wholeness.
Then Apollo° quietly told him: "Leave it all on earth.
Your lute, what point? Why pick at a dull pavan few care to
Follow, except a few birds of dusty feather,
Not vivid performances of the past." But why not?
All other things must change too.
The seasons are no longer what they once were,
But it is the nature of things to be seen only once,
As they happen along, bumping into other things, getting along
Somehow. That's where Orpheus made his mistake.
Of course Eurydice vanished into the shade;
She would have even if he hadn't turned around.
No use standing there like a gray stone toga as the whole wheel

---

1. *Orpheus:* in Greek myth, Eurydice, wife of the singer and poet Orpheus, was bitten by a snake and died. The grief-stricken Orpheus plunged into Hades to bring her back. The music of his voice and lyre moved the gods of the underworld, and they granted his wish, but only on condition that he not look back at her until they reached the sunlight. In a moment of doubt, he looked back, and she was taken from him again, this time forever.

7. *Apollo:* in Greek myth, the son of Zeus and god of all the fine arts, of medicine, music, poetry, and eloquence; he gave Orpheus the lyre that he played so beautifully.

Of recorded history flashes past, struck dumb, unable to utter an
intelligent
Comment on the most thought-provoking element in its train.
Only love stays on the brain, and something these people,
These other ones, call life. Singing accurately
So that the notes mount straight up out of the well of
Dim noon and rival the tiny, sparkling yellow flowers
Growing around the brink of the quarry, encapsulates
The different weights of the things.
But it isn't enough
To just go on singing. Orpheus realized this
And didn't mind so much about his reward being in heaven
After the Bacchantes° had torn him apart, driven
Half out of their minds by his music, what it was doing to them.
Some say it was for his treatment of Eurydice.
But probably the music had more to do with it, and
The way music passes, emblematic
Of life and how you cannot isolate a note of it
And say it is good or bad. You must
Wait till it's over. "The end crowns all,"
Meaning also that the "tableau"
Is wrong. For although memories, of a season, for example,
Melt into a single snapshot, one cannot guard, treasure
That stalled moment. It too is flowing, fleeting;
It is a picture of flowing, scenery, though living, mortal,
Over which an abstract action is laid out in blunt,
Harsh strokes. And to ask more than this
Is to become the tossing reeds of that slow,
Powerful stream, the trailing grasses
Playfully tugged at, but to participate in the action
No more than this. Then in the lowering gentian sky
Electric twitches are faintly apparent first, then burst forth
Into a shower of fixed, cream-colored flares. The horses
Have each seen a share of the truth, though each thinks,
"I'm a maverick. Nothing of this is happening to me,
Though I can understand the language of birds, and
The itinerary of the lights caught in the storm is fully apparent to me.
Their jousting ends in music much
As trees move more easily in the wind after a summer storm
And is happening in lacy shadows of shore-trees, now, day after day."

---

30. *Bacchantes:* Thracian women who attacked Orpheus, while they were celebrating the orgies of Bacchus, and tore him to pieces; they were offended at his indifference to their advances.

But how late to be regretting all this, even
Bearing in mind that regrets are always late, too late!
To which Orpheus, a bluish cloud with white contours,
Replies that these are of course not regrets at all,
Merely a careful, scholarly setting down of
Unquestioned facts, a record of pebbles along the way.
And no matter how all this disappeared,
Or got where it was going, it is no longer
Material for a poem. Its subject
Matters too much, and not enough, standing there helplessly
While the poem streaked by, its tail afire, a bad
Comet screaming hate and disaster, but so turned inward
That the meaning, good or other, can never
Become known. The singer thinks
Constructively, builds up his chant in progressive stages
Like a skyscraper, but at the last minute turns away.
The song is engulfed in an instant in blackness
Which must in turn flood the whole continent
With blackness, for it cannot see. The singer
Must then pass out of sight, not even relieved
Of the evil burthen of the words. Stellification
Is for the few, and comes about much later
When all record of these people and their lives
Has disappeared into libraries, onto microfilm.
A few are still interested in them. "But what about
So-and-so?" is still asked on occasion. But they lie
Frozen and out of touch until an arbitrary chorus
Speaks of a totally different incident with a similar name
In whose tale are hidden syllables
Of what happened so long before that
In some small town, one indifferent summer.

1977

DAFFY DUCK IN HOLLYWOOD°

Something strange is creeping across me.
La Celestina° has only to warble the first few bars
Of "I Thought about You" or something mellow from

---

poem title: *Daffy Duck in Hollywood* is the title of a 1938 animated film by Tex Avery (1907–1980), who was also one of the creators of Bugs Bunny for the Warner Brothers studio. He developed a free-wheeling, violent, often surrealistic animation style for MGM cartoons in the 1940s.

2. *Celestina:* the title character in Spanish dramatist Fernando de Rojas's (1475–1538) play *Celestina* (1499, 1502). She is an elderly procuress and seller of love charms whose greed brings about her death.

Amadigi di Gaula° for everything—a mint-condition can
Of Rumford's Baking Powder,° a celluloid earring, Speedy
Gonzales,° the latest from Helen Topping Miller's° fertile
Escritoire,° a sheaf of suggestive pix on greige,° deckle-edged°
Stock—to come clattering through the rainbow trellis
Where Pistachio Avenue° rams the 2300 block of Highland
Fling Terrace. He promised he'd get me out of this one,
That mean old cartoonist,° but just look what he's
Done to me now! I scarce dare approach me mug's attenuated
Reflection in yon hubcap,° so jaundiced, so *déconfit*°
Are its lineaments—fun, no doubt, for some quack phrenologist's°
Fern-clogged waiting room, but hardly what you'd call
Companionable. But everything is getting choked to the point of
Silence. Just now a magnetic storm hung in the swatch of sky
Over the Fudds'° garage, reducing it—drastically—
To the aura of a plumbago-blue° log cabin on
A Gadsden Purchase° commemorative cover. Suddenly all is
Loathing. I don't want to go back inside any more. You meet
Enough vague people on this emerald traffic-island—no,
Not people, comings and goings, more: mutterings, splatterings,

---

4. *Amadigi di Gaula:* an opera by George Frederick Handel (1685–1759) first performed in 1715.

5. *Rumford's Baking Powder:* first produced in the mid-nineteenth century, it is presently manufactured by Hulman & Co. in Indiana. It was originally produced in Rumford, Rhode Island, a town near Providence named for its major industry, the Rumford Chemical Works. The co-inventor of Rumford's Baking Powder, Eben Horsford, had held the Rumford Chair of the Application of Science to the Useful Arts at Harvard. The chair was named after Count Rumford, actually the American Benjamin Thompson (1753–1814), who was granted a title in honor of services performed for the Duke of Bavaria.

6. *Speedy Gonzales:* a character from a Tex Avery cartoon, a mouse with a Spanish accent.

6. *Helen Topping Miller:* (1884–1960), a prolific author of popular historical novels from the late 1930s until her death. She concluded her career by publishing seven books with "Christmas" in the title, between 1954 and 1960, including *Christmas at Sagamore Hill with Theodore Roosevelt* and *Christmas at Monticello with Thomas Jefferson.*

7. *Escritoire:* a bureau, or combination bureau and bookcase, that includes a desk or writing surface.

7. *greige:* grayish beige.

7. *deckle-edged:* paper with a rough, untrimmed edge.

9. *Pistachio Avenue:* a real street in California and Arizona. Highland Fling Terrace is apparently not a real street, though there is a "Highland Fling Street" in a small town in Pennsylvania.

11. *cartoonist:* on the first level, a reference to Tex Avery, but there are many cartoonists in this poem, from Helen Topping Miller to John Milton, from those of us who might find a tin of baking powder collectable to the government that commemorated the Gadsden Purchase. Only the work of the Great Cartoonist above encompasses it all.

13. *me mug's . . . hubcap:* a sendup of Ashbery's poem "Self-Portrait in a Convex Mirror" delivered in Daffy Duck's diction.

13. *déconfit:* (French) flabbergasted.

14. *phrenologist:* one who studies the conformation of the skull as indicative of mental faculties and character traits.

18. *Fudd:* Elmer Fudd was the foil in the *Bugs Bunny* cartoons, expressing middle-class horror at Bugs's antics, meanwhile pronouncing his *rs* as *ws,* as in "that cwazy wabbit."

19. *plumbago-blue:* a purplish gray-blue.

20. *Gadsden Purchase:* an area In Arizona and New Mexico purchased from Mexico in 1853.

The bizarrely but effectively equipped infantries of happy-go-nutty
Vegetal jacqueries,° plumed, pointed at the little
White cardboard castle over the mill run. "Up
The lazy river, how happy we could be?"
How will it end? That geranium glow
Over Anaheim's° had the riot act read to it by the
Etna-size° firecracker that exploded last minute into
A *carte du Tendre*° in whose lower right-hand corner
(Hard by the jock-itch sand-trap that skirts
The asparagus patch of algolagnic° *nuits blanches*°) Amadis°
Is cozening the Princesse de Clèves° into a midnight micturition° spree
On the Tamigi° with the Wallets° (Walt, Blossom, and little
Skeezix) of a lamé barge "borrowed" from Ollie
Of the Movies' dread mistress of the robes. Wait!
I have an announcement! This wide, tepidly meandering,
Civilized Lethe° (one can barely make out the maypoles
And *châlets de nécessité*° on its sedgy shore) leads to Tophet,° that
Landfill-haunted, not-so-residential resort from which
Some travellers return! This whole moment is the groin
Of a borborygmic° giant who even now
Is rolling over on us in his sleep. Farewell bocages,
Tanneries, water-meadows. The allegory comes unsnarled
Too soon; a shower of pecky acajou° harpoons is
About all there is to be noted between tornadoes. I have

---

25. *jacqueries:* peasant revolts.

29. *Anaheim:* Orange County, California, city, site of Disneyland amusement park.

30. *Etna:* volcano in northeast Sicily.

31. *carte du Tendre:* allegorical map of the country of love, popular in seventeenth-century France.

33. *algolagnic:* characterized by sexual pleasure found in suffering or inflicting pain.

33. *nuits blanches:* (French) sleepless nights.

33. *Amadis:* a character in a Spanish chivalric romance by Garcia Ordonez de Montalvo; the story was adapted as an opera called *Amadis* by Jean-Baptiste Lully (1632–1687) in 1684 and again by Handel and others. Amadis falls in love with the Princess Oriane and eventually wins her hand through a series of heroic adventures. He would not have had much success with the Princess of Clèves.

34. *Princesse de Clèves:* title character in a novel *The Princess of Cleves* (1678) by Madame Marie de Lafayette (1634–1693); virtuous, but passionless, the princess disappoints her husband.

34. *micturition:* urination.

35. *Tamigi:* Italian name for the Thames River that flows through London.

35. *Wallets:* characters in the comic strip *Gasoline Alley*.

39. *Lethe:* in Greek mythology, the river of oblivion in the underworld; the dead drink from it to forget their earthly life.

40. *châlets de nécessité:* rustic "comfort stations."

40. *Tophet:* in the biblical book of Jeremiah, Tophet is a burial place associated with prophetic warnings of impending disaster.

43. *borborygmic:* producing rumbling sounds created by the movement of gas in the intestines.

46. *acajou:* wood (mahogany).

Only my intermittent life in your thoughts to live
Which is like thinking in another language. Everything
Depends on whether somebody reminds you of me.
That this is a fabulation, and that those "other times"
Are in fact the silences of the soul, picked out in
Diamonds on stygian° velvet, matters less than it should.
Prodigies of timing may be arranged to convince them
We live in one dimension, they in ours. While I
Abroad through all the coasts of dark destruction seek
Deliverance for us all,° think in that language: its
Grammar, though tortured, offers pavilions
At each new parting of the ways. Pastel
Ambulances scoop up the quick and hie them to hospitals.
"It's all bits and pieces, spangles, patches, really; nothing
Stands alone. What happened to creative evolution?"
Sighed Aglavaine.° Then to her Sélysette: "If his
Achievement is only to end up less boring than the others,
What's keeping us here? Why not leave at once?
I have to stay here while they sit in there,
Laugh, drink, have fine time. In my day
One lay under the tough green leaves,
Pretending not to notice how they bled into
The sky's aqua, the wafted-away no-color of regions supposed
Not to concern us. And so we too
Came where the others came: nights of physical endurance,
Or if, by day, our behavior was anarchically
Correct, at least by New Brutalism° standards, all then
Grew taciturn by previous agreement. We were spirited
Away *en bateau,*° under cover of fudge dark.
It's not the incomplete importunes, but the spookiness
Of the finished product. True, to ask less were folly, yet
If he is the result of himself, how much the better
For him we ought to be! And how little, finally,
We take this into account! Is the puckered garance° satin
Of a case that once held a brace of dueling pistols our
Only acknowledging of that color? I like not this,
Methinks, yet this disappointing sequel to ourselves

---

53. *stygian:* gloomy, deathly.

55–57. *While I/Abroad . . . Deliverance for us all:* quotes Satan in Book II (lines 463–465) of John Milton's (1608–1674) *Paradise Lost* (1667).

63. *Aglavaine:* title character in play *Aglavaine et Sélysette* (1896) by Belgian poet and dramatist Maurice Maeterlinck (1862–1949). Sélysette dies when she throws herself from a tower.

74. *New Brutalism:* 1950s architectural concept; its buildings often have large blocks of exposed concrete.

76. *en bateau:* (French) by boat.

81. *garance:* dark red.

Has been applauded in London and St. Petersburg. Somewhere
Ravens pray for us."
                    The storm finished brewing. And thus
She questioned all who came in at the great gate, but none
She found who ever heard of Amadis,
Nor of Stern Aureng-Zebe,° his first love. Some
There were to whom this mattered not a jot: since all
By defintion is completeness (so
In utter darkness they reasoned), why not
Accept it as it pleases to reveal itself? As when
Low skyscrapers from lower-hanging clouds reveal
A turret there, an art-deco escarpment here, and last perhaps
The pattern that may carry the sense, but
Stays hidden in the mysteries of pagination.
Not what we see but how we see it matters; all's
Alike, the same, and we greet him who announces
The change as we would greet the change itself.
All life is but a figment; conversely, the tiny
Tome that slips from your hand is not perhaps the
Missing link in this invisible picnic whose leverage
Shrouds our sense of it. Therefore bivouac we
On this great, blond highway, unimpeded by
Veiled scruples, worn conundrums. Morning is
Impermanent. Grab sex things, swing up
Over the horizon like a boy
On a fishing expedition. No one really knows
Or cares whether this is the whole of which parts
Were vouchsafed—once—but to be ambling on's
The tradition more than the safekeeping of it. This mulch for
Play keeps them interested and busy while the big,
Vaguer stuff can decide what it wants—what maps, what
Model cities, how much waste space. Life, our
Life anyway, is between. We don't mind
Or notice any more that the sky *is* green, a parrot
One, but have our earnest where it chances on us,
Disingenuous, intrigued, inviting more,
Always invoking the echo, a summer's day.

1977

PARADOXES AND OXYMORONS

This poem is concerned with language on a very plain level.
Look at it talking to you. You look out a window

---

90. *Aureng-Zebe:* noble savage hero of John Dryden's (1631–1700) tragedy *Aureng-zebe* (1675).

Or pretend to fidget. You have it but you don't have it.
You miss it, it misses you. You miss each other.

The poem is sad because it wants to be yours, and cannot.
What's a plain level? It is that and other things,
Bringing a system of them into play. Play?
Well, actually, yes, but I consider play to be

A deeper outside thing, a dreamed role-pattern,
As in the division of grace these long August days
Without proof. Open-ended. And before you know
It gets lost in the steam and chatter of typewriters.

It has been played once more. I think you exist only
To tease me into doing it, on your level, and then you aren't there
Or have adopted a different attitude. And the poem
Has set me softly down beside you. The poem is you.

1981

THE PROBLEM OF ANXIETY

Fifty years have passed
since I started living in those dark towns
I was telling you about.
Well, not much has changed. I still can't figure out
how to get from the post office to the swings in the park.
Apple trees blossom in the cold, not from conviction,
and my hair is the color of dandelion fluff.

Suppose this poem were about you—would *you*
put in the things I've carefully left out:
descriptions of pain, and sex, and how shiftily
people behave toward each other? Naw, that's
all in some book it seems. For you
I've saved the descriptions of chicken sandwiches,
and the glass eye that stares at me in amazement
from the bronze mantel, and will never be appeased.

1995

DULL MAUVE

Twenty miles away, in the colder
waters of the Atlantic, you gaze longingly
toward the coast. Didn't you once love someone
there? Yes, but it was only a cat, and I,
a manatee, what could I do? There are no rewards

in this world for pissing your life away, even
if it means you get to see forgotten icebergs
of decades ago peeling off from the mass
to dive under the surface, raising a
mountain of seething glass before they lunge back up
to start the unknown perilous journey
to the desolate horizon.

That was the way
I thought of each day when I was young, a sloughing-off,
both suicidal and imbued with a certain ritual grace.
Later, there were so many protagonists
one got quite lost, as in a forest of doppelgängers.
Many things were going on. And the moon, poised
on the ridge like an enormous, smooth grapefruit, understood
the importance of each and wasn't going
to make one's task any easier, though we loved her.

1995

A KIND OF CHILL

He had a brother in Schenectady°
but that was long, long ago. These days, crows
punch a time clock on a forgotten tract of land
not far from the Adirondacks. They keep fit
and in the swim with lists of what to do tomorrow:
cawing, regretting the past absolutely.
That spruces up the whole occasion
and energizes them in ways they never dreamed of.
His afternoon was on a roll,
and, as with anything else, he got sick of it.
No claims to adjust. No hovering in dark alleys
waiting for a priest, or the police,
most likely if this were the end of the fiscal year.

2007

SPOOKS RUN WILD

This is how curious. Some stuff got in from the terrace
and peed on common sense. This is how my days,
my nights are spent, in a crowded vacuum
overlooking last year's sinkhole. What I was about to say . . .
Oh forget it. The weather is untenable. I'll be on my way.

---

1. *Schenectady:* city in eastern New York State.

So spake an irritable urchin
to nothing in particular. Come on, I'll race you to the corner.
Nothing doing, he said, my calluses
are in an uproar. Besides, we had an agreement. Oh really? Yes,
about the triathlon. You were going to save me
at the end, take me home with you, feed me
tea and toasted cheese, tell me stories about a race of Titans
who once lived in these parts. Oh, if that's all. . .

So began a curious kind of friendship.
I saw him only twice more
before his untimely but merciful death.
Both times he said, What about the cheese?

2009

MARINE SHADOW

Just being washed out to sea, bashed around—
this impression, I mean this what you hear
is part of it. And quite useless. We're talking
non-fiction, which pours through at lunch time,
the whole stinking phenomenology wound into it
at the base of the stalk. From there it branches
out into other axioms and metaphors. Like,
I have a brand in Chicago. You'd better think about it.

Action figures take us just so far, to the edge
of the abyss. The fucking man swears by rifles.
The sparrow boys agreed. Everywhere that Mary went
dynasties collapsed amid gnashing teeth, and soon other
solvents reached the opposite shore, but this was only a test.
Time enough for the purple brine of consequences,
the tumbling package of breakers released by the breeze.
Cue bugle and castanets. This being more of an occasion
than that. It promised shy retribution. It's listing,
bungled. It can't, can it?

2012

WORDS TO THAT EFFECT

The drive down was smooth
but after we arrived things started to go haywire,
first one thing and then another. The days
scudded past like tumbleweed, slow then fast,
then slow again. The sky was sweet and plain.

You remember how still it was then,
a season putting its arms into a coat and staying unwrapped
for a long, a little time.

It was during the week we talked about deforestation.
How sad that everything has to change,
yet what a relief, too! Otherwise we'd only have
looking forward to look forward to.
The moment would be a bud
that never filled, only persevered
in a static trance, before it came to be no more.

We'd walked a little way in our shoes.
I was sure you'd remember how it had been
the other time, before the messenger came to your door
and seemed to want to peer in and size up the place.
So each evening became a forbidden morning
of thunder and curdled milk, though the invoices
got forwarded and birds settled on the periphery.

2012

GALWAY KINNELL (b. 1927)

Born in Providence, Rhode Island, Kinnell was educated at Princeton and the University of Rochester. He served in the U.S. Navy from 1945 to 1946 and then went on to do civil rights field work in Louisiana for the Congress on Racial Equality. Although he has written poems on contemporary topics, such as the use of the atomic bomb on Hiroshima and Nagasaki, the struggle for civil rights, and the long tragedy of the Vietnam War, he also has returned repeatedly and in different guises to take up the subject of transcendence in the midst of mortality, a concern apparent in both "The Porcupine" and "The Bear," both taken from his 1968 volume *Body Rags*. His first book, *What a Kingdom It Was* (1960), had a strong component of secularized Christianity, still apparent in the sacramental mood of the poems reprinted here. But now it is not so much oneness with God as oneness with nature and the primal rhythms of birth and death that the speaker seeks. His book-length poem sequence *The Book of Nightmares* (1978) is perhaps his masterpiece.

THE PORCUPINE

1

Fatted
on herbs, swollen on crabapples,
puffed up on bast and phloem,° ballooned
on willow flowers, poplar catkins, first
leafs of aspen and larch,
the porcupine
drags and bounces his last meal through ice,
mud, roses and goldenrod, into the stubbly high fields.

2

In character
he resembles us in seven ways:
he puts his mark on outhouses,
he alchemizes by moonlight,
he shits on the run,
he uses his tail for climbing,
he chuckles softly to himself when scared,
he's overcrowded if there's more than one of him per five acres,
his eyes have their own inner redness.

---

3. *bast and phloem:* technical names for parts of plants; bast is the woody outer layer of the stems of various plants; phloem is the food-conducting tissue of vascular plants.

3

Digger of
goings across floors, of hesitations
at thresholds, of
handprints of dread
at doorpost or window jamb, he would
gouge the world
empty of us, hack and crater
it
until it is nothing, if that
could rinse it of all our sweat and pathos.

Adorer of ax
handles aflow with grain, of arms
of Morris chairs, of hand
crafted objects
steeped in the juice of fingertips,
of surfaces wetted down
with fist grease and elbow oil,
of clothespins that have
grabbed our body-rags by underarm and crotch . . .

Unimpressed—bored—
by the whirl of the stars, by *these*
he's astonished, ultra-
Rilkean° angel!

for whom the true
portion of the sweetness of earth
is one of those bottom-heavy, glittering, saccadic°
bits
of salt water that splash down
the haunted ravines of a human face.

4

A farmer shot a porcupine three times
as it dozed on a tree limb. On
the way down it tore open its belly
on a broken
branch, hooked its gut,
and went on falling. On the ground

---

40. *Rilkean:* poet Ranier Maria Rilke (1875–1926) in his *Duino Elegies* described a hierarchy of beings from animals to angels.
43. *saccadic:* having to do with rapid eye movement.

it sprang to its feet, and
paying out gut heaved
and spartled through a hundred feet of goldenrod
before
the abrupt emptiness.

5

The Avesta°
puts porcupine killers
into hell for nine generations, sentencing them
to gnaw out
each other's hearts for the
salts of desire.

I roll
this way and that in the great bed, under
the quilt
that mimics this country of broken farms and woods,
the fatty sheath of the man
melting off,
the self-stabbing coil
of bristles reversing, blossoming outward—
a red-eyed, hard-toothed, arrow-stuck urchin
tossing up mattress feathers,
pricking the
woman beside me until she cries.

6

In my time I have
crouched, quills erected,
Saint
Sebastian° of the
scared heart, and been
beat dead with a locust club
on the bare snout.
And fallen from high places
I have fled, have
jogged
over fields of goldenrod,
terrified, seeking home,
and among flowers
I have come to myself empty, the rope

58. *Avesta:* the sacred text of ancient Persians.
79. *Saint Sebastian:* early Christian martyr.

strung out behind me
in the fall sun
suddenly glorified with all my blood.

7

And tonight I think I prowl broken
skulled or vacant as a
sucked egg in the wintry meadow, softly chuckling, blank
template of myself, dragging
a starved belly through the lichflowered acres,
where
burdock looses the arks of its seed
and thistle holds up its lost blooms
and rosebushes in the wind scrape their dead limbs
for the forced-fire
of roses.

1968

THE BEAR°

1

In late winter
I sometimes glimpse bits of steam
coming up from
some fault in the old snow
and bend close and see it is lung-colored
and put down my nose
and know
the chilly, enduring odor of bear.

2

I take a wolf's rib and whittle
it sharp at both ends
and coil it up
and freeze it in blubber and place it out
on the fairway of the bears.

And when it has vanished
I move out on the bear tracks,
roaming in circles
until I come to the first, tentative, dark
splash on the earth.

---

poem title: Hans Ruesch's *The Top of the World* is a source for the bear hunt story.

And I set out
running, following the splashes
of blood wandering over the world.
At the cut, gashed resting places
I stop and rest,
at the crawl-marks
where he lay out on his belly
to overpass some stretch of bauchy° ice
I lie out
dragging myself forward with bear-knives in my fists.

3

On the third day I begin to starve,
at nightfall I bend down as I knew I would
at a turd sopped in blood,
and hesitate, and pick it up,
and thrust it in my mouth, and gnash it down,
and rise
and go on running.

4

On the seventh day,
living by now on bear blood alone,
I can see his upturned carcass far out ahead, a scraggled,
steamy hulk,
the heavy fur riffling in the wind.
I come up to him
and stare at the narrow-spaced, petty eyes,
the dismayed
face laid back on the shoulder, the nostrils
flared, catching
perhaps the first taint of me as he
died.

I hack
a ravine in his thigh, and eat and drink,
and tear him down his whole length
and open him and climb in
and close him up after me, against the wind,
and sleep.

---

26. *bauchy:* uneasy, weak, without substance.

5

And dream
of lumbering flatfooted
over the tundra,
stabbed twice from within,
splattering a trail behind me,
splattering it out no matter which way I lurch,
no matter which parabola of bear-transcendence,
which dance of solitude I attempt,
which gravity-clutched leap,
which trudge, which groan.

6

Until one day I totter and fall—
fall on this
stomach that has tried so hard to keep up,
to digest the blood as it leaked in,
to break up
and digest the bone itself: and now the breeze
blows over me, blows off
the hideous belches of ill-digested bear blood
and rotted stomach
and the ordinary, wretched odor of bear,

blows across
my sore, lolled tongue a song
or screech, until I think I must rise up
and dance. And I lie still.

7

I awaken I think. Marshlights
reappear, geese
come trailing again up the flyway.°
In her ravine under old snow the dam-bear
lies, licking
lumps of smeared fur°
and drizzly eyes into shapes
with her tongue. And one
hairy-soled trudge stuck out before me,
the next groaned out,

80. *flyway:* migratory route.
83. *lumps . . . fur:* her cubs.

the next,
the next,
the rest of my days I spend
wandering: wondering
what, anyway,
was that sticky infusion, that rank flavor of blood, that poetry, by
which I lived?

1968

THE VOW

When the lover
goes, the vow though
broken remains, that
trace of eternity love
brings down among us
stays, to give
dignity to the suffering
and to intensify it.

1989

W. S. MERWIN (b. 1927)

Merwin was born in New York and raised first in Union City, New Jersey, and then in Scranton, Pennsylvania. He studied romance languages at Princeton University, where he worked with poet John Berryman and poet-critic R. P. Blackmur. It was at Princeton as well, in the midst of World War II, when some of his classmates were dying in Europe and the Pacific, that he began writing, but not publishing, poems of despair amid the violence of history. He would return to these themes again decades later, when the Vietnam War would come to seem a comprehensive figure for public life in America. His first published poems, however, made extensive use of mythology and displayed his mastery of traditional meter and form. Then in the 1960s, responding to the pressure of events, he adopted an open, unpunctuated form and a line closer to a unit of breath. Merwin was concerned about the destruction of natural life long before ecological awareness was common; now this deep-seated reverence was fused with rage at the carnage of a mindless and cynical war. Poems of prophesy and witness followed through the 1960s and 1970s, sometimes about the contemporary world and sometimes taking up earlier historical subjects. He also wrote haunting phenomenologies of loss and presence amidst emptiness. Throughout this time he maintained great wariness about institutional entanglements, preferring to support himself through translation and poetry readings rather than by taking a permanent teaching position. In addition to living in New York, he spent long periods in a farmhouse in the south of France, feeling a need to distance himself from America and its most intense city. He now makes his home on the island of Maui in Hawaii, among hundreds of rare tropical plants that he has preserved and cultivated. His prose poems and memoirs are as well regarded as his poems.

THE DRUNK IN THE FURNACE

For a good decade
The furnace stood in the naked gully, fireless
And vacant as any hat. Then when it was
No more to them than a hulking black fossil
To erode unnoticed with the rest of the junk-hill
By the poisonous creek, and rapidly to be added
To their ignorance,

They were afterwards astonished
To confirm, one morning, a twist of smoke like a pale
Resurrection, staggering out of its chewed hole,
And to remark then other tokens that someone,
Cosily bolted behind the eye-holed iron
Door of the drafty burner, had there established
His bad castle.

Where he gets his spirits
It's a mystery. But the stuff keeps him musical:
Hammer-and-anvilling with poker and bottle
To his jugged bellowings, till the last groaning clang
As he collapses onto the rioting
Springs of a litter of car-seats ranged on the grates,
To sleep like an iron pig.°

In their tar-paper church
On a text about stoke-holes that are sated never
Their Reverend lingers. They nod and hate trespassers.
When the furnace wakes, though, all afternoon
Their witless offspring flock like piped rats to its siren
Crescendo, and agape on the crumbling ridge
Stand in a row and learn.

1960

IT IS MARCH

It is March and black dust falls out of the books
Soon I will be gone
The tall spirit who lodged here has
Left already
On the avenues the colorless thread lies under
Old prices

When you look back there is always the past
Even when it has vanished
But when you look forward
With your dirty knuckles and the wingless
Bird on your shoulder
What can you write

The bitterness is still rising in the old mines
The fist is coming out of the egg
The thermometers out of the mouths of the corpses

At a certain height
The tails of the kites for a moment are
Covered with footsteps

Whatever I have to do has not yet begun

1967

21. *iron pig:* a crude slab poured from a smelting furnace.

CAESAR

My shoes are almost dead
And as I wait at the doors of ice
I hear the cry go up for him Caesar Caesar

But when I look out the window I see only the flatlands
And the slow vanishing of the windmills
The centuries draining the deep fields

Yet this is still my country
The thug on duty says What would you change
He looks at his watch he lifts
Emptiness out of the vases
And holds it up to examine

So it is evening
With the rain starting to fall forever

One by one he calls night out of the teeth
And at last I take up
My duty

Wheeling the president past banks of flowers
Past the feet of empty stairs
Hoping he's dead

1967

THE ROOM

I think all this is somewhere in myself
The cold room unlit before dawn
Containing a stillness such as attends death
And from a corner the sounds of a small bird trying
From time to time to fly a few beats in the dark
You would say it was dying it is immortal

1967

DECEMBER AMONG THE VANISHED

The old snow gets up and moves taking its
Birds with it

The beasts hide in the knitted walls
From the winter that lipless man
Hinges echo but nothing opens

A silence before this one
Has left its broken huts facing the pastures
Through their stone roofs the snow
And the darkness walk down

In one of them I sit with a dead shepherd
And watch his lambs

1967

FOR THE ANNIVERSARY OF MY DEATH

Every year without knowing it I have passed the day
When the last fires will wave to me
And the silence will set out
Tireless traveller
Like the beam of a lightless star

Then I will no longer
Find myself in life as in a strange garment
Surprised at the earth
And the love of one woman
And the shamelessness of men
As today writing after three days of rain
Hearing the wren sing and the falling cease
And bowing not knowing to what

1967

WHEN THE WAR IS OVER

When the war is over
We will be proud of course the air will be
Good for breathing at last
The water will have been improved the salmon
And the silence of heaven will migrate more perfectly
The dead will think the living are worth it we will know
Who we are
And we will all enlist again

1967

THE ASIANS DYING

When the forests have been destroyed their darkness remains
The ash the great walker follows the possessors
Forever
Nothing they will come to is real
Nor for long

Over the watercourses
Like ducks in the time of the ducks
The ghosts of the villages trail in the sky
Making a new twilight

Rain falls into the open eyes of the dead
Again again with its pointless sound
When the moon finds them they are the color of everything

The nights disappear like bruises but nothing is healed
The dead go away like bruises
The blood vanishes into the poisoned farmlands
Pain the horizon
Remains
Overhead the seasons rock
They are paper bells
Calling to nothing living

The possessors move everywhere under Death their star
Like columns of smoke they advance into the shadows
Like thin flames with no light
They with no past
And fire their only future

1967

FOR A COMING EXTINCTION

Gray whale
Now that we are sending you to The End
That great god
Tell him
That we who follow you invented forgiveness
And forgive nothing

I write as though you could understand
And I could say it
One must always pretend something
Among the dying
When you have left the seas nodding on their stalks
Empty of you
Tell him that we were made
On another day

The bewilderment will diminish like an echo
Winding along your inner mountains

Unheard by us
And find its way out
Leaving behind it the future
Dead
And ours

When you will not see again
The whale calves trying the light
Consider what you will find in the black garden
And its court
The sea cows the Great Auks the gorillas
The irreplaceable hosts ranged countless
And fore-ordaining as stars
Our sacrifices

Join your word to theirs
Tell him
That it is we who are important

1967

LOOKING FOR MUSHROOMS AT SUNRISE

for Jean and Bill Arrowsmith

When it is not yet day
I am walking on centuries of dead chestnut leaves
In a place without grief
Though the oriole
Out of another life warns me
That I am awake

In the dark while the rain fell
The gold chanterelles pushed through a sleep that was not mine
Waking me
So that I came up the mountain to find them

Where they appear it seems I have been before
I recognize their haunts as though remembering
Another life

Where else am I walking even now
Looking for me

1967

THE GARDENS OF ZUÑI°

The one-armed explorer°
could touch only half of the country
In the virgin half
the house fires give no more heat
than the stars
it has been so these many years
and there is no bleeding

He is long dead with his five fingers
and the sum of their touching
and the memory
of the other hand
his scout

that sent back no message
from where it had reached
with no lines in its palm
while he balanced
balanced
and groped on
for the virgin land

and found where it had been

1970

BEGINNING

Long before spring
king of the black cranes
rises one day
from the black
needle's eye
on the white plain
under the white sky

the crown turns
and the eye
drilled clear through his head

---

poem title: the Zuni River, which passes through the Zuni valley, is a tributary of the Colorado River in Arizona. The Zuni people, a Native American tribe with a unique language, settled the valley and built the Zuni pueblo there; there are now 10,000 tribal members.

1. *explorer:* John Wesley Powell (1834–1902), American geologist, ethnologist, and explorer who lost his right arm at the Civil War battle of Shiloh. He explored the canyons of the Colorado River, surveyed the arid high plains, and established the first definitive classification scheme for Native American languages.

turns
it is north everywhere
come out he says

come out then
the light is not yet
divided
it is a long way
to the first
anything
come even so
we will start
bring your nights with you

1970

THE HORSE

In a dead tree
there is the ghost of a horse
no horse
was ever seen near the tree
but the tree was born
of a mare
it rolled with long legs
in rustling meadows
it pricked its ears
it reared and tossed its head
and suddenly stood still
beginning to remember
as its leaves fell

1977

SUN AND RAIN

Opening the book   at a bright window
above a wide pasture   after five years
I find I am still standing   on a stone bridge
looking down with my mother at dusk into a river
hearing the current as hers   in her lifetime

now it comes to me   that that was the day
she told me of seeing my father   alive for the last time
and he waved her back from the door   as she was leaving
took her hand   for a while and said
nothing

at some signal
in a band of sunlight all the black cows   flow down the pasture
together
to turn uphill and stand   as the dark rain touches them

1983

BERRYMAN

I will tell you what he told me
in the years just after the war
as we then called
the second world war

don't lose your arrogance yet he said
you can do that when you're older
lose it too soon and you may
merely replace it with vanity

just one time he suggested
changing the usual order
of the same words in a line of verse
why point out a thing twice

he suggested I pray to the Muse
get down on my knees and pray
right there in the corner and he
said he meant it literally

it was in the days before the beard
and the drink but he was deep
in tides of his own through which he sailed
chin sideways and head tilted like a tacking sloop

he was far older than the dates allowed for
much older than I was he was in his thirties
he snapped down his nose with an accent
I think he had affected in England

as for publishing he advised me
to paper my wall with rejection slips
his lips and the bones of his long fingers trembled
with the vehemence of his view about poetry

he said the great presence
that permitted everything and transmuted it

in poetry was passion
passion was genius and he praised movement and invention

I had hardly begun to read
I asked how can you ever be sure
that what you write is really
any good at all and he said you can't

you can't you can never be sure
you die without knowing
whether anything you wrote was any good
if you have to be sure don't write

1983

DAYLIGHT

It is said that after he was seventy
Ingres° returned to the self-portrait
he had painted at twenty-four and he
went on with it from that far off though
there was no model and in the mirror
only the empty window and gray sky
and the light in which his hand was lifted
a hand which the eyes in the painting would not
have recognized at first raised in a way
they would never see whatever he might
bring to them nor would they ever see him
as he had come to be then watching them
there where he had left them and while he looked
into them from no distance as he thought
holding the brush in the day between them

2001

THE NAME OF THE AIR

It could be like that then the beloved
old dog finding it harder and harder
to breathe and understanding but coming
to ask whether there is something that can
be done about it coming again to
ask and then standing there without asking

2001

---

2. *Ingres:* Jean-Auguste-Dominique Ingres (1780–1867), French neoclassical painter.

FAR ALONG IN THE STORY

The boy walked on with a flock of cranes
following him calling as they came
from the horizon behind him
sometimes he thought he could recognize
a voice in all that calling but he
could not hear what they were calling
and when he looked back he could not tell
one of them from another in their
rising and falling but he went on
trying to remember something in
their calls until he stumbled and came
to himself with the day before him
wide open and the stones of the path
lying still and each tree in its own leaves
the cranes were gone from the sky and at
that moment he remembered who he was
only he had forgotten his name

2008

WORN WORDS

The late poems are the ones
I turn to first now
following a hope that keeps
beckoning me
waiting somewhere in the lines
almost in plain sight

it is the late poems
that are made of words
that have come the whole way
they have been there

2008

ANNE SEXTON (1928–1974)

Born Anne Gray Harvey in Newton, Massachusetts, the child of a wool merchant, Sexton and her family lived in the Boston suburbs and spent the summers on Squirrel Island, Maine. She married Alfred Sexton in 1948. Experiencing severe depression after her daughters were born in 1953 and 1955, she attempted suicide in 1956. Her doctor recommended writing poetry as an outlet for her feelings, and she attended Boston poetry workshops run by John Holmes and Robert Lowell. *To Bedlam and Part Way Back* (1960), her first book, was successful enough to send her on the poetry reading circuit, where intense and dramatic readings gave her a still larger following. She taught at Harvard, Radcliffe, and Boston University. She won a Pulitzer Prize in 1967, but she remained troubled and took her own life in 1974.

Though often grounded in personal experience and emotion, even her more confessional poems mix biographical truth with invention; moreover, they often address the generational conflicts women underwent as traditional roles were challenged and redefined in the 1950s and 1960s, at which point the personal became political. She also went on to write poetic versions of fairy tales and to produce revisionist poetic versions of biblical stores. Some of her female personas become visionary and mythic figures.

HER KIND

I have gone out, a possessed witch,
haunting the black air, braver at night;
dreaming evil, I have done my hitch
over the plain houses, light by light:
lonely thing, twelve-fingered,° out of mind.
A woman like that is not a woman, quite.
I have been her kind.

I have found the warm caves in the woods,
filled them with skillets, carvings, shelves,
closets, silks, innumerable goods;
fixed the suppers for the worms and the elves:
whining, rearranging the disaligned.
A woman like that is misunderstood.
I have been her kind.

I have ridden in your cart, driver,
waved my nude arms at villages going by,
learning the last bright routes, survivor

5. *twelve-fingered:* possession of a sixth finger per hand was once considered a sign of witchcraft.

where your flames still bite my thigh
and my ribs crack where your wheels wind.
A woman like that is not ashamed to die.
I have been her kind.

1960

THE TRUTH THE DEAD KNOW

For my mother, born March 1902, died March 1959
and my father, born February 1900, died June 1959

Gone, I say and walk from church,
refusing the stiff procession to the grave,
letting the dead ride alone in the hearse.
It is June. I am tired of being brave.

We drive to the Cape. I cultivate
myself where the sun gutters from the sky,
where the sea swings in like an iron gate
and we touch. In another country people die.

My darling, the wind falls in like stones
from the whitehearted water and when we touch
we enter touch entirely. No one's alone.
Men kill for this, or for as much.

And what of the dead? They lie without shoes
in their stone boats. They are more like stone
than the sea would be if it stopped. They refuse
to be blessed, throat, eye and knucklebone.

1962

AND ONE FOR MY DAME

A born salesman,
my father made all his dough
by selling wool to Fieldcrest, Woolrich and Faribo.

A born talker,
he could sell one hundred wet-down bales
of that white stuff. He could clock the miles and sales

and make it pay.
At home each sentence he would utter
had first pleased the buyer who'd paid him off in butter.

Each word
had been tried over and over, at any rate,
on the man who was sold by the man who filled my plate.

My father hovered
over the Yorkshire pudding and the beef:
a peddler, a hawker, a merchant and an Indian chief.

Roosevelt! Willkie!° and war!
How suddenly gauche I was
with my old-maid heart and my funny teenage applause.

Each night at home
my father was in love with maps
while the radio fought its battles with Nazis and Japs.

Except when he hid
in his bedroom on a three-day drunk,
he typed out complex itineraries, packed his trunk,

his matched luggage
and pocketed a confirmed reservation,
his heart already pushing over the red routes of the nation.

I sit at my desk
each night with no place to go,
opening the wrinkled maps of Milwaukee and Buffalo,

the whole U.S.,
its cemeteries, its arbitrary time zones,
through routes like small veins, capitals like small stones.

He died on the road,
his heart pushed from neck to back,
his white hanky signaling from the window of the Cadillac.

My husband,
as blue-eyed as a picture book, sells wool:
boxes of card waste, laps and rovings he can pull

---

16. *Wilkie:* Wendell Wilkie (1892–1944), American lawyer and Republican nominee for president in 1940.

to the thread
and say *Leicester, Rambouillet, Merino,*
a half-blood, it's greasy and thick, yellow as old snow.

And when you drive off, my darling,
Yes sir! Yes, sir! It's one for my dame,
your sample cases branded with my father's name,

your itinerary open,
its tolls ticking and greedy,
its highways built up like new loves, raw and speedy.

1962

JESUS ASLEEP

Jesus slept as still as a toy
and in His dream
He desired Mary.
His penis sang like a dog,
but He turned sharply away from that play
like a door slamming.
That door broke His heart
for He had a sore need.
He made a statue out of His need.
With His penis like a chisel
He carved the Pietà.°
At this death it was important to have only one desire.
He carved this death.
He was persistent.
He died over and over again.
He swam up and up a pipe toward it,
breathing water through His gills.
He swam through stone.
He swam through the godhead
and because He had not known Mary
they were united at His death,
the cross to the woman,
in a final embrace,
poised forever
like a centerpiece.

1972

---

11. *the Pietà:* subject in Christian art showing a sorrowful Mary cradling the dead body of Jesus.

JESUS RAISES UP THE HARLOT

The harlot squatted
with her hands over her red hair.
She was not looking for customers.
She was in a deep fear.
A delicate body clothed in red,
as red as a smashed fist
and she was bloody as well
for the townspeople were trying
to stone her to death.
Stones came at her like bees to candy
and sweet redheaded harlot that she was
she screamed out, *I never, I never.*
Rocks flew out of her mouth like pigeons
and Jesus saw this and thought to
exhume her like a mortician.

Jesus knew that a terrible sickness
dwelt in the harlot and He could lance it
with His two small thumbs.
He held up His hand and the stones
dropped to the ground like doughnuts.
Again He held up His hand
and the harlot came and kissed Him.
He lanced her twice. On the spot.
He lanced her twice on each breast,
pushing His thumbs in until the milk ran out,
those two boils of whoredom.
The harlot followed Jesus around like a puppy
for He had raised her up.
Now she forsook her fornications
and became His pet.
His raising her up made her feel
like a little girl again when she had a father
who brushed the dirt from her eye.
Indeed, she took hold of herself,
knowing she owed Jesus a life,
as sure-fire as a trump card.

1972

THE ROOM OF MY LIFE

Here,
in the room of my life
the objects keep changing.

Ashtrays to cry into,
the suffering brother of the wood walls,
the forty-eight keys of the typewriter
each an eyeball that is never shut,
the books, each a contestant in a beauty contest,
the black chair, a dog coffin made of Naugahyde,°
the sockets on the wall
waiting like a cave of bees,
the gold rug
a conversation of heels and toes,
the fireplace
a knife waiting for someone to pick it up,
the sofa, exhausted with the exertion of a whore,
the phone
two flowers taking root in its crotch,
the doors
opening and closing like sea clams,
the lights
poking at me,
lighting up both the soil and the laugh.
The windows,
the starving windows
that drive the trees like nails into my heart.
Each day I feed the world out there
although birds explode
right and left.
I feed the world in here too,
offering the desk puppy biscuits.
However, nothing is just what it seems to be.
My objects dream and wear new costumes,
compelled to, it seems, by all the words in my hands
and the sea that bangs in my throat.

1975

---

9. *Naugahyde:* vinyl-coated fabric designed to look like leather.

PHILIP LEVINE (b. 1928)

Born in Detroit, Michigan, and educated at Wayne State University, Levine later studied at Iowa with Robert Lowell and John Berryman. Along the way, he took a number of working-class jobs; those, and the ruined industrial landscape of Detroit, helped shape the settings and political loyalties of his poems. We can see that background most clearly in "Belle Isle, 1949" and "Fear and Fame," but it also underlies the slaughterhouse imagery of "Animals Are Passing From Our Lives" and the revolutionary transfiguration of vernacular language in what is very nearly his signature poem, "They Feed They Lion." For years, Levine has looked to modern Spanish poets for inspiration, and he has written a number of poems about the Spanish Civil War (including "Francisco, I'll Bring You Red Carnations"), often embodying his special sympathy for the Spanish anarchist movement. Although Levine's work is pervaded by an eloquent rage at injustice, it also reaches repeatedly for a visionary lyricism that Levine's subject matter makes uniquely his own.

FOR FRAN

She packs the flower beds with leaves,
Rags, dampened papers, ties with twine
The lemon tree, but winter carves
Its features on the uprooted stem.

I see the true vein in her neck
And where the smaller ones have broken
Blueing the skin, and where the dark
Cold lines of weariness have eaten

Out through the winding of the bone.
On the hard ground where Adam strayed,
Where nothing but his wants remain,
What do we do to those we need,

To those whose need of us endures
Even the knowledge of what we are?
I turn to her whose future bears
The promise of the appalling air,

My living wife, Frances Levine,
Mother of Theodore, John, and Mark,
Out of whatever we have been
We will make something for the dark.

1961

THE HORSE

for Ichiro Kawamoto, humanitarian,
electrician, & survivor of Hiroshima

They spoke of the horse alive
without skin, naked, hairless,
without eyes and ears, searching
for the stableboy's caress.
Shoot it, someone said, but they
let him go on colliding with
tattered walls, butting his long
skull to pulp, finding no path
where iron fences corkscrewed in
the street and bicycles turned
like question marks.
                                        Some fled and
some sat down. The river burned
all that day and into the
night, the stones sighed a moment
and were still, and the shadow
of a man's hand entered
a leaf.

                                The white horse never
returned, and later they found
the stable boy, his back crushed
by a hoof, his mouth opened
around a cry that no one heard.

They spoke of the horse again
and again; their mouths opened
like the gills of a fish caught
above water.

                                    Mountain flowers
burst from the red clay walls, and
they said a new life was here.
Raw grass sprouted from the cobbles
like hair from a deafened ear.

The horse would never return.

There had been no horse. I could
tell from the way they walked

testing the ground for some cold
that the rage had gone out of
their bones in one mad dance.

1963

ANIMALS ARE PASSING FROM OUR LIVES

It's wonderful how I jog
on four honed-down ivory toes
my massive buttocks slipping
like oiled parts with each light step.

I'm to market. I can smell
the sour, grooved block, I can smell
the blade that opens the hole
and the pudgy white fingers

that shake out the intestines
like a hankie. In my dreams
the snouts drool on the marble,
suffering children, suffering flies,

suffering the consumers
who won't meet their steady eyes
for fear they could see. The boy
who drives me along believes

that any moment I'll fall
on my side and drum my toes
like a typewriter or squeal
and shit like a new housewife

discovering television,
or that I'll turn like a beast
cleverly to hook his teeth
with my teeth. No. Not this pig.

1968

BELLE ISLE, 1949

We stripped in the first warm spring night
and ran down into the Detroit River
to baptize ourselves in the brine
of car parts, dead fish, stolen bicycles,
melted snow. I remember going under
hand in hand with a Polish highschool girl

I'd never seen before, and the cries
our breath made caught at the same time
on the cold, and rising through the layers
of darkness into the final moonless atmosphere
that was this world, the girl breaking
the surface after me and swimming out
on the starless waters towards the lights
of Jefferson Ave. and the stacks
of the old stove factory unwinking.
Turning at last to see no island at all
but a perfect calm dark as far
as there was sight, and then a light
and another riding low out ahead
to bring us home, ore boats maybe, or smokers
walking alone. Back panting
to the gray coarse beach we didn't dare
fall on, the damp piles of clothes,
and dressing side by side in silence
to go back where we came from.

1976

THEY FEED THEY LION

Out of burlap sacks, out of bearing butter,
Out of black bean and wet slate bread,
Out of the acids of rage, the candor of tar,
Out of creosote,° gasoline, drive shafts, wooden dollies,
They Lion grow.
Out of the gray hills
Of industrial barns, out of rain, out of bus ride,
West Virginia to Kiss My Ass, out of buried aunties,
Mothers hardening like pounded stumps, out of stumps,
Out of the bones' need to sharpen and the muscles' to stretch,
They Lion grow.

Earth is eating trees, fence posts,
Gutted cars, earth is calling in her little ones,
"Come home, Come home!" From pig balls,
From the ferocity of pig driven to holiness,
From the furred ear and the full jowl come
The repose of the hung belly, from the purpose
They Lion grow.

---

4. *creosote:* oily liquid obtained from coal tar and used as a wood preservative and disinfectant; it can cause severe neurological problems if inhaled.

From the sweet glues of the trotters°
Come the sweet kinks of the fist, from the full flower
Of the hams the thorax° of caves,
From "Bow Down" come "Rise Up,"
Come they Lion from the reeds of shovels,
The grained arm that pulls the hands,
They Lion grow.
From my five arms and all my hands,
From all my white sins forgiven, they feed,
From my car passing under the stars,
They Lion, from my children inherit,
From the oak turned to a wall, they Lion,
From they sack and they belly opened
And all that was hidden burning on the oil-stained earth
They feed they Lion and he comes.

1972

FRANCISCO, I'LL BRING YOU RED CARNATIONS

Here in the great cemetery
behind the fortress of Barcelona
I have come once more to see
the graves of my fallen.
Two ancient picnickers direct
us down the hill. "Durruti,"°
says the man, "I was on
his side." The woman hushes
him. All the way down
this is a city of the dead,
871,251 *difuntos*.°
The poor packed in tenements
a dozen high; the rich
in splendid homes or temples.
So nothing has changed
except for the single
unswerving fact: they are

---

19. *trotters:* cooked pig or sheep feet.

21. *thorax:* the chest cavity.

6. *Durruti:* Buenaventura Durruti (1896–1936), perhaps the most famous Spanish anarchist during the Spanish Civil War; he died while commanding a militia battallion on the Madrid front at University City on November 20, 1936, only four months after the war began. He remains to this day a potent symbol of the pure political revolutionary. For general information on the war, see the notes to Millay's "Say That We Saw Spain Die." For comments on the battles around Madrid, see the notes to Rolfe's "Elegia."

11. *difuntos:* (Spanish) "deceased."

all dead. Here is the Plaza
of San Jaime, here the Rambla
of San Pedro, so every death
still has a mailing address,
but since this is Spain
the mail never comes or
comes too late to be of use.
Between the cemetery and
the Protestant burial ground
we find the three stones
all in a row: Ferrer Guardia,°
B. Durruti, F. Ascaso,° the names
written with marking pens,
and a few circled A's and tributes
to the FAI° and CNT.°
For two there are floral
displays, but Ascaso faces
eternity with only a stone.
Maybe as it should be. He was
a stone, a stone and a blade,
the first grinding and sharpening
the other. Half his 36
years were spent in prisons
or on the run, and yet
in that last photograph

---

28. *Guardia:* Francisco Ferrer Guardia (1859–1909), famous Spanish anarchist educator executed by the state during the Tragic Week of July 1909, an outburst of rioting and church-burning triggered by popular resentment against the Moroccan War; the week raised before the privileged classes the specter of a proletarian revolution, a possibility that would haunt Spain's wealthy and galvanize its poor for decades.

29. *Ascaso:* Francisco Ascaso Budria (?–1936) was a leading anarchist figure in Catalonia. His brothers Domingo and Joaquín were also active in the movement. Ascaso had been a carpenter but evolved into a strike leader and political activist, one who believed in assassination as a political weapon. He was killed in the opening days of the Spanish Civil War, July 1936, fighting to put down the right-wing military rebellion in Barcelona. He was a reflective, capable leader, and his loss to Spanish anarchism was a substantial one.

32. *FAI:* (*Federación Anarquista Ibérica*), the group of theoreticians and activists who made up the ideological vanguard of Spanish anarchism. Its paramilitary cadres were responsible for some indiscriminate violence in the early days of the war. Historically somewhat at odds with the CNT, its position moderated enough so that its members came to hold positions of leadership in the CNT. Barcelona was its primary site of influence; its presence in Madrid was minimal. One of the major slogans of the CNT-FAI was "The war and revolution are inseparable."

32. *CNT:* (*Confederación Nacional del Trabajo*), founded in 1911, the CNT was one of the two important labor groups in Spain (the other was the UGT), both having around a million members. Often referred to as anarchist, the CNT practiced a form of syndicalism based in industrial unions and eschewed any belief that there could be anything but continuous class conflict between employers and workers. Independent of any political party, it often called on its members to boycott elections, but it was the absence of such a boycott that contributed to the electoral victory of the Popular Front in 1936. The CNT advocated a revolutionary strategy for winning the war and the revolution, a policy strenuously opposed by the Republican parties and especially by the communists.

taken less than an hour before
he died, he stands in a dark
suit, smoking, a rifle slung
behind his shoulder, and glances
sideways at the camera
half smiling. It is July 20,
1936, and before the darkness
falls a darkness will have
fallen on him. While
the streets are echoing
with victory and revolution,
Francisco Ascaso will take up
the hammered little blade
of his spirit and enter for
the last time the republics
of death. I remember
his words to a frightened
comrade who questioned
the wisdom of attack: "We
have gathered here to die, but we
don't have to die with dogs,
so go." Forty-one years
ago, and now the city stretches
as far as the eye can see,
huge cement columns like nails
pounded into the once green
meadows of the Llobregat.°
Your Barcelona is gone,
the old town swallowed
in industrial filth and
the burning mists of gasoline.
Only the police remain, armed
and arrogant, smiling masters
of the boulevards, the police
and your dream of the city
of God, where every man
and every woman gives
and receives the gifts of work
and care, and that dream

---

69. *Llobregat:* a region in Catalonia. Levine is invoking not just a place but also its revolutionary history. On September 3, 1931, the FAI called a general strike in Barcelona. In January 1932 miners on strike in the Pyrenean foothills occupied the surrounding townships and proclaimed a libertarian revolution. The following January, the FAI launched an insurrection that spread across eastern Spain, and in 1934 illegal strikes in the Llobregat potash mines were broken by mass detentions and firings.

goes on in spite of slums,
in spite of death clouds,
the roar of trucks, the harbor
staining the mother sea,
It goes on in spite of all
that mocks it. We have it here
growing in our hearts, as
your comrade said, and when
we give it up with our last
breaths someone will gasp
it home to their lives.
Francisco, stone, knife blade,
Single soldier still on
the run down the darkest
Street of all, we will be back
across an ocean and a continent
to bring you red carnations,
to celebrate the unbroken
promise of your life that
once was frail and flesh.

1979

FEAR AND FAME

Half an hour to dress, wide rubber hip boots,
gauntlets to the elbow, a plastic helmet
like a knight's but with a little glass window
that kept steaming over, and a respirator
to save my smoke-stained lungs. I would descend
step by slow step into the dim world
of the pickling tank and there prepare
the new solutions from the great carboys
of acids lowered to me on ropes—all from a recipe
I shared with nobody and learned from Frank O'Mera
before he went off to the bars on Vernor Highway
to drink himself to death. A gallon of hydrochloric
steaming from the wide glass mouth, a dash
of pale nitric to bubble up, sulphuric to calm,
metals for sweeteners, cleansers for salts,
until I knew the burning stew was done.
Then to climb back, step by stately step, the adventurer
returned to the ordinary blinking lights
of the swingshift at Feinberg and Breslin's
First-Rate Plumbing and Plating with a message
from the kingdom of fire. Oddly enough

no one welcomed me back, and I'd stand
fully armored as the downpour of cold water
rained down on me and the smoking traces puddled
at my feet like so much milk and melting snow.
Then to disrobe down to my work pants and shirt,
my black street shoes and white cotton socks,
to reassume my nickname, strap on my Bulova,
screw back my wedding ring, and with tap water
gargle away the bitterness as best I could.
For fifteen minutes or more I'd sit quietly
off to the side of the world as the women
polished the tubes and fixtures to a burnished purity
hung like Christmas ornaments on the racks
pulled steadily toward the tanks I'd cooked.
Ahead lay the second cigarette, held in a shaking hand,
as I took into myself the sickening heat to quell heat,
a lunch of two Genoa salami sandwiches and Swiss cheese
on heavy peasant bread baked by my Aunt Tsipie,
and a third cigarette to kill the taste of the others.
Then to arise and dress again in the costume
of my trade for the second time that night, stiffened
by the knowledge that to descend and rise up
from the other world merely once in eight hours is half
what it takes to be known among women and men.

1991

ON THE MEETING OF GARCÍA LORCA AND HART CRANE°

Brooklyn, 1929. Of course Crane's
been drinking and has no idea who
this curious Andalusian is, unable
even to speak the language of poetry.
The young man who brought them
together knows both Spanish and English,
but he has a headache from jumping
back and forth from one language
to another. For a moment's relief
he goes to the window to look
down on the East River, darkening
below as the early night comes on.
Something flashes across his sight,
a double vision of such horror

---

poem title: Federico García Lorca (1898–1936) is widely considered Spain's most important twentieth-century poet. He did visit New York and Cuba, which is the basis of Levine's speculative poem. Lorca was murdered by the fascists at the outbreak of the Spanish Civil War.

he has to slap both his hands across
his mouth to keep from screaming.
Let's not be frivolous, let's
not pretend the two poets gave
each other wisdom or love or
even a good time, let's not
invent a dialogue of such eloquence
that even the ants in your own
house won't forget it. The two
greatest poetic geniuses alive
meet, and what happens? A vision
comes to an ordinary man staring
at a filthy river. Have you ever
had a vision? Have you ever shaken
your head to pieces and jerked back
at the image of your young son
falling through open space, not
from the stern of a ship bound
from Vera Cruz to New York but from
the roof of the building he works on?
Have you risen from bed to pace
until dawn to beg a merciless God
to take these pictures away? Oh, yes,
let's bless the imagination. It gives
us the myths we live by. Let's bless
the visionary power of the human—
the only animal that's got it—,
bless the exact image of your father
dead and mine dead, bless the images
that stalk the corners of our sight
and will not let go. The young man
was my cousin, Arthur Lieberman,
then a language student at Columbia,
who told me all this before he died
quietly in his sleep in 1983
in a hotel in Perugia. A good man,
Arthur, he survived graduate school,
later came home to Detroit and sold
pianos right through the Depression.
He loaned my brother a used one
to compose his hideous songs on,
which Arthur thought were genius.
What an imagination Arthur had!

1995

ADRIENNE RICH (1929–2012)

Adrienne Rich grew up in Baltimore and was educated at Radcliffe College. After early work that had the controlled elegance and formality characteristic of some poets in the first years of the 1950s, she began to adapt the open forms that have been central to the American tradition since Whitman. Since then, she became one of the most widely read and influential poets of the second half of the twentieth century. That impact has grown not only from her poetry but also from a number of groundbreaking essays, including "When We Dead Awaken: Writing as Re-Vision" and "Compulsory Heterosexuality and Lesbian Existence."

Rich's position now is in many ways unique. She was our foremost contemporary feminist poet and an important theorist of the social construction of gender, but that dual status sometimes overshadows, and even obscures, the range of her most ambitious work. She wrote a number of unforgettable short poems, variously visionary, historical, political, and polemical. Some of these, along with longer poems like "Diving into the Wreck," have helped to define the personal and social understanding of a generation. Yet her many long poem sequences are inevitably more complex aesthetically and philosophically, and they demand extended reading and reflection.

It is in these poem sequences especially that her recurring topic of several decades—the relationship between individual experience, contemporary political and social life, and historical memory—receives its most innovative treatment. Devoted like so many other poets to understanding the burdens of national identity, she has tried to uncover at once the texture and the governing principles of the lesson Americans are least willing to learn: that we are intricately embedded in and shaped by social life. Other poets, to be sure, have dealt with the intersection of personal and public life. It was Robert Lowell's lifetime theme. But Rich is unusual in tracking these intersections with a keen sense for their temporal intricacy; in Rich social life and politics and the lives of earlier women (like that of Marie Curie in "Power") are registered on the pulses. Representing her adequately requires offering more than one of her poem sequences. We print most of "Shooting Script" and "Twenty-One Love Poems" in its entirety.

AUNT JENNIFER'S TIGERS

Aunt Jennifer's tigers prance across a screen,
Bright topaz denizens of a world of green.
They do not fear the men beneath the tree;
They pace in sleek chivalric certainty.

Aunt Jennifer's fingers fluttering through her wool
Find even the ivory needle hard to pull.
The massive weight of Uncle's wedding band
Sits heavily upon Aunt Jennifer's hand.

When Aunt is dead, her terrified hands will lie
Still ringed with ordeals she was mastered by.
The tigers in the panel that she made
Will go on prancing, proud and unafraid.

1951

from SHOOTING SCRIPT

PART I 11/69–2/70

1.

We were bound on the wheel of an endless conversation.

Inside this shell, a tide waiting for someone to enter.

A monologue waiting for you to interrupt it.

A man wading into the surf. The dialogue of the rock with the breaker.

•

The wave changed instantly by the rock; the rock changed by the wave returning over and over.

The dialogue that lasts all night or a whole lifetime.

A conversation of sounds melting constantly into rhythms.

A shell waiting for you to listen.

A tide that ebbs and flows against a deserted continent.

A cycle whose rhythm begins to change the meanings of words.

A wheel of blinding waves of light, the spokes pulsing out from where we hang together in the turning of an endless conversation.

The meaning that searches for its word like a hermit crab.

A monologue that waits for one listener.

An ear filled with one sound only.

A shell penetrated by meaning.

2.

Adapted from Mirza Ghalib°

Even when I thought I prayed, I was talking to myself; when I
found the door shut, I simply walked away.

We all accept Your claim to be unique; the stone lips, the
carved limbs, were never your true portrait.

Grief held back from the lips wears at the heart; the drop that
refused to join the river dried up in the dust.

Now tell me your story till the blood drips from your lashes. Any
other version belongs to your folklore, or ours.

•

To see the Tigris° in a water-drop . . . Either you were playing
games with me, or you never cared to learn the structure of my
language.

3.

The old blanket. The crumbs of rubbed wool turning up.

Where we lay and breakfasted. The stains of tea. The squares
of winter light projected on the wool.

You, sleeping with closed windows. I, sleeping in the silver
nitrate° burn of zero air.

Where it can snow, I'm at home; the crystals accumulating
spell out my story.

The cold encrustation thickening on the ledge.

The arrow-headed facts, accumulating, till a whole city is
taken over.

Midwinter and the loss of love, going comes before gone, over
and over the point is missed and still the blind will turns for
its target.

Section Note-*Ghalib:* Urdu poet Mirza Ghalib (1797–1869).

28. *Tigris:* river that runs through Turkey and Iraq.

35. *silver nitrate:* poisonous irritant, a soluble salt used in photography and as a germicide.

4.

In my imagination I was the pivot of a fresh beginning.

In rafts they came over the sea; on the island they put up those stones by methods we can only guess at.

If the vegetation grows as thick as this, how can we see what they were seeing?

It is all being made clear, with bulldozers, at Angkor Wat.°

The verdure was a false mystery; the baring of the stones is no solution for us now.

•

Defoliation progresses; concrete is poured, sheets of glass hauled overland in huge trucks and at great cost.

Here we never travailed, never took off our shoes to walk the final mile.

Come and look into this cellar-hole; this is the foundling of the woods.

Humans lived here once; it became sacred only when they went away.

5.

Of simple choice they are the villagers; their clothes come with them like red clay roads they have been walking.

The sole of the foot is a map, the palm of the hand a letter, learned by heart and worn close to the body.

They seemed strange to me, till I began to recall their dialect.

Poking the spade into the dry loam, listening for the tick of broken pottery, hoarding the brown and black bits in a dented can.

Evenings, at the table, turning the findings out, pushing them around with a finger, beginning to dream of fitting them together.

---

49. *Angkor Wat:* massive, richly sculpted twelfth-century temple in northern Cambodia, endangered during the Vietnam War.

Hiding all this work from them, although they might have helped
me.

Going up at night, hiding the tin can in a closet, where the
linoleum lies in shatters on a back shelf.

Sleeping to dream of the unformed, the veil of water pouring over
the wet clay, the rhythms of choice, the lost methods.

•

6.

You are beside me like a wall; I touch you with my fingers and
keep moving through the bad light.

At this time of year when faces turn aside, it is amazing that your
eyes are to be met.

A bad light is one like this, that flickers and diffuses itself along
the edge of a frontier.

No, I don't invest you with anything; I am counting on your
weakness as much as on your strength.

This light eats away at the clarities I had fixed on; it moves up
like a rodent at the edge of the raked paths.

Your clarities may not reach me; but your attention will.

It is to know that I too have no mythic powers; it is to see the
liability of all my treasures.

You will have to see all this for a long time alone.

You are beside me like a wall; I touch you with my fingers and
keep trying to move through the bad light.

PART II 3–7/70

9.

NEWSREEL

This would not be the war we fought in. See, the foliage is
heavier, there were no hills of that size there.

But I find it impossible not to look for actual persons known
to me and not seen since; impossible not to look for myself.

•

The scenery angers me, I know there is something wrong, the sun
is too high, the grass too trampled, the peasants' faces too broad,
and the main square of the capital had no arcades like those.

Yet the dead look right, and the roofs of the huts, and the crashed
fuselage burning among the ferns.

But this is not the war I came to see, buying my ticket, stumbling
through the darkness, finding my place among the sleepers and
masturbators in the dark.

I thought of seeing the General who cursed us, whose name they
gave to an expressway; I wanted to see the faces of the dead when
they were living.

Once I know they filmed us, back at the camp behind the lines,
taking showers under the trees and showing pictures of our girls.

Somewhere there is a film of the war we fought in, and it must
contain the flares, the souvenirs, the shadows of the netted brush,
the standing in line of the innocent, the hills that were not of
this size.

Somewhere my body goes taut under the deluge, somewhere I am
naked behind the lines, washing my body in the water of that war.

Someone has that war stored up in metal canisters, a memory he
cannot use, somewhere my innocence is proven with my guilt, but
this would not be the war I fought in.

10.

—for Valerie Glauber

They come to you with their descriptions of your soul.

They come and drop their mementos at the foot of your bed; their
feathers, ferns, fans, grasses from the western mountains.

•

They wait for you to unfold for them like a paper flower, a secret
springing open in a glass of water.

They believe your future has a history and that it is themselves.

They have family trees to plant for you, photographs of dead
children, old bracelets and rings they want to fasten onto you.

And, in spite of this, you live alone.

Your secret hangs in the open like Poe's purloined letter; their
longing and their methods will never let them find it.

Your secret cries out in the dark and hushes; when they start out
of sleep they think you are innocent.

You hang among them like the icon in a Russian play; living your
own intenser life behind the lamp they light in front of you.

You are split here like mercury on a marble counter, liquefying
into many globes, each silvered like a planet caught in a lens.

You are a mirror lost in a brook, an eye reflecting a torrent of
reflections.

You are a letter written, folded, burnt to ash, and mailed in an
envelope to another continent.

11.

The mare's skeleton in the clearing: another sign of life.

When you pull the embedded bones up from the soil, the flies
collect again.

The pelvis, the open archway, staring at me like an eye.

In the desert these bones would be burnt white; a green bloom grows
on them in the woods.

•

Did she break her leg or die of poison?

What was it like when the scavengers came?

So many questions unanswered, yet the statement is here and clear.

With what joy you handled the skull, set back the teeth spilt in the
grass, hinged back the jaw on the jaw.

With what joy we left the woods, swinging our sticks, miming the speech of noble savages, of the fathers of our country, bursting into the full sun of the uncut field.

12.

I was looking for a way out of a lifetime's consolations.

We walked in the wholesale district: closed warehouses, windows, steeped in sun.

I said: those cloths are very old. You said: they have lain in that window a long time.

When the skeletons of the projects° shut off the sunset, when the sense of the Hudson° leaves us, when only by loss of light in the east do I know that I am living in the west.

When I give up being paraphrased, when I let go, when the beautiful solutions in their crystal flasks have dried up in the sun, when the lightbulb bursts on lighting, when the dead bulb rattles like a seed-pod.

Those cloths are very old, they are mummies' cloths, they have lain in graves, they were not intended to be sold, the tragedy of this mistake will soon be clear.

Vacillant needles of Manhattan, describing hour & weather; buying these descriptions at the cost of missing every other point.

•

13.

We are driven to odd attempts; once it would not have occurred to me to put out in a boat, not on a night like this.

Still, it was an instrument, and I had pledged myself to try any instrument that came my way. Never to refuse one from conviction of incompetence.

A long time I was simply learning to handle the skiff; I had no special training and my own training was against me.

---

157. *projects:* large-scale housing complexes built for low-income families.
158. *Hudson:* river that flows past New York City to the Atlantic Ocean.

I had always heard that darkness and water were a threat.

In spite of this, darkness and water helped me to arrive here.

I watched the lights on the shore I had left for a long time; each
one, it seemed to me, was a light I might have lit, in the old days.

14.

Whatever it was: the grains of the glacier caked in the boot-cleats;
ashes spilled on white formica.

The death-col° viewed through power-glasses; the cube of ice melting
on stainless steel.

Whatever it was, the image that stopped you, the one on which you
came to grief, projecting it over & over on empty walls.

Now to give up the temptations of the projector; to see instead the
web of cracks filtering across the plaster.

To read there the map of the future, the roads radiating from the
initial split, the filaments thrown out from that impasse.

To reread the instructions on your palm; to find there how the
lifeline, broken, keeps its direction.

•

To read the etched rays of the bullet-hole left years ago in the
glass; to know in every distortion of the light what fracture is.

To put the prism in your pocket, the thin glass lens, the map
of the inner city, the little book with gridded pages.

To pull yourself up by your own roots; to eat the last meal in
your old neighborhood.

1970

TRYING TO TALK WITH A MAN

Out in this desert we are testing bombs,

that's why we came here.

---

182. *death-col:* a treacherous high mountain pass or depression in the crest of a ridge.

Sometimes I feel an underground river
forcing its way between deformed cliffs
an acute angle of understanding
moving itself like a locus of the sun
into this condemned scenery.

What we've had to give up to get here—
whole LP collections, films we starred in
playing in the neighborhoods, bakery windows
full of dry, chocolate-filled Jewish cookies,
the language of love-letters, of suicide notes,
afternoons on the riverbank
pretending to be children

Coming out to this desert
we meant to change the face of
driving among dull green succulents
walking at noon in the ghost town
surrounded by a silence

that sounds like the silence of the place
except that it came with us
and is familiar
and everything we were saying until now
was an effort to blot it out—
coming out here we are up against it

Out here I feel more helpless
with you than without you
You mention the danger
and list the equipment
we talk of people caring for each other
in emergencies—laceration, thirst—
but you look at me like an emergency

Your dry heat feels like power
your eyes are stars of a different magnitude
they reflect lights that spell out: EXIT
when you get up and pace the floor

talking of the danger
as if it were not ourselves
as if we were testing anything else.

1971

DIVING INTO THE WRECK

First having read the book of myths,
and loaded the camera,
and checked the edge of the knife-blade,
I put on
the body-armor of black rubber
the absurd flippers
the grave and awkward mask.
I am having to do this
not like Cousteau° with his
assiduous team
aboard the sun-flooded schooner
but here alone.

There is a ladder.
The ladder is always there
hanging innocently
close to the side of the schooner.
We know what it is for,
we who have used it.
Otherwise
it's a piece of maritime floss
some sundry equipment.

I go down.
Rung after rung and still
the oxygen immerses me
the blue light
the clear atoms
of our human air.
I go down.
My flippers cripple me,
I crawl like an insect down the ladder
and there is no one
to tell me when the ocean
will begin.

First the air is blue and then
it is bluer and then green and then
black I am blacking out and yet

---

9. *Cousteau:* Jacques Cousteau (1910–1997), French environmentalist, documentary filmmaker, and underwater explorer.

my mask is powerful
it pumps my blood with power
the sea is another story
the sea is not a question of power
I have to learn alone
to turn my body without force
in the deep element.

And now: it is easy to forget
what I came for
among so many who have always
lived here
swaying their crenellated° fans
between the reefs
and besides
you breathe differently down here.

I came to explore the wreck.
The words are purposes.
The words are maps.
I came to see the damage that was done
and the treasures that prevail.
I stroke the beam of my lamp
slowly along the flank
of something more permanent
than fish or weed

the thing I came for:
the wreck and not the story of the wreck
the thing itself and not the myth
the drowned face always staring
toward the sun
the evidence of damage
worn by salt and sway into this threadbare beauty
the ribs of the disaster
curving their assertion
among the tentative haunters.

This is the place.
And I am here, the mermaid whose dark hair
streams black, the merman in his armored body
We circle silently
about the wreck

---

48. *crenellated:* patterned with repeated notches or ridged indentations.

we dive into the hold.
I am she: I am he

whose drowned face° sleeps with open eyes
whose breasts still bear the stress
whose silver, copper, vermeil° cargo lies
obscurely inside barrels
half-wedged and left to rot
we are the half-destroyed instruments
that once held to a course
the water-eaten log
the fouled compass

We are, I am, you are
by cowardice or courage
the one who find our way
back to this scene
carrying a knife, a camera
a book of myths
in which
our names do not appear.

1972

TWENTY-ONE LOVE POEMS

I

Wherever in this city, screens flicker
with pornography, with science-fiction vampires,
victimized hirelings bending to the lash,
we also have to walk . . . if simply as we walk
through the rainsoaked garbage, the tabloid cruelties
of our own neighborhoods.
We need to grasp our lives inseparable
from those rancid dreams, that blurt of metal, those disgraces,
and the red begonia perilously flashing
from a tenement sill six stories high,
or the long-legged young girls playing ball
in the junior highschool playground.
No one has imagined us. We want to live like trees,
sycamores blazing through the sulfuric air,
dappled with scars, still exuberantly budding,
our animal passion rooted in the city.

---

78. *drowned face:* as in the carved female figureheads once placed on the prow of sailing ships.
80. *vermeil:* gilded silver, copper, or bronze.

II

I wake up in your bed. I know I have been dreaming.
Much earlier, the alarm broke us from each other,
you've been at your desk for hours. I know what I dreamed:
our friend the poet comes into my room
where I've been writing for days,
drafts, carbons, poems are scattered everywhere,
and I want to show her one poem
which is the poem of my life. But I hesitate,
and wake. You've kissed my hair
to wake me. *I dreamed you were a poem,*
I say, *a poem I wanted to show someone . . .*
and I laugh and fall dreaming again
of the desire to show you to everyone I love,
to move openly together
in the pull of gravity, which is not simple,
which carries the feathered grass a long way down the upbreathing
air.

III

Since we're not young, weeks have to do time
for years of missing each other. Yet only this odd warp
in time tells me we're not young.
Did I ever walk the morning streets at twenty,
my limbs streaming with a purer joy?
Did I lean from any window over the city
listening for the future
as I listen here with nerves tuned for your ring?
And you, you move toward me with the same tempo.
Your eyes are everlasting, the green spark
of the blue-eyed grass of early summer,
the green-blue wild cress washed by the spring.
At twenty, yes: we thought we'd live forever.
At forty-five, I want to know even our limits.
I touch you knowing we weren't born tomorrow,
and somehow, each of us will help the other live,
and somewhere, each of us must help the other die.

IV

I come home from you through the early light of spring
flashing off ordinary walls, the Pez Dorado,
the Discount Wares, the shoe-store. . . . I'm lugging my sack
of groceries, I dash for the elevator
where a man, taut, elderly, carefully composed

lets the door almost close on me.—*For god's sake hold it!*
I croak at him.—*Hysterical,*—he breathes my way.
I let myself into the kitchen, unload my bundles,
make coffee, open the window, put on Nina Simone°
singing *Here comes the sun*. . . . I open the mail,
drinking delicious coffee, delicious music,
my body still both light and heavy with you. The mail
lets fall a Xerox of something written by a man
aged 27, a hostage, tortured in prison:
My genitals have been the object of such a sadistic display
they keep me constantly awake with the pain . . .
Do whatever you can to survive.
You know, I think that men love wars . . .
And my incurable anger, my unmendable wounds
break open further with tears, I am crying helplessly,
and they still control the world, and you are not in my arms.

V

This apartment full of books could crack open
to the thick jaws, the bulging eyes
of monsters, easily: Once open the books, you have to face
the underside of everything you've loved—
the rack and pincers held in readiness, the gag
even the best voices have had to mumble through,
the silence burying unwanted children—
women, deviants, witnesses—in desert sand.
Kenneth tells me he's been arranging his books
so he can look at Blake and Kafka while he types;
yes; and we still have to reckon with Swift
loathing the woman's flesh while praising her mind,
Goethe's dread of the Mothers, Claudel vilifying Gide,°
and the ghosts—their hands clasped for centuries—
of artists dying in childbirth, wise-women charred at the stake,
centuries of books unwritten piled behind these shelves;
and we still have to stare into the absence
of men who would not, women who could not, speak
to our life—this still unexcavated hole
called civilization, this act of translation, this half-world.

---

58. *Nina Simone:* (1933–2003), American jazz vocalist and pianist.

80–83. *Blake . . . Gide:* William Blake (1757–1827), visionary British poet; Franz Kafka (1883–1924), Austrian novelist who described a threatening and incomprehensible world in a style of impeccable clarity; Jonathan Swift (1667–1745), Irish poet, essayist, novelist, and priest; Johann Wolfgang von Goethe (1749–1832,), German poet and novelist; Paul Claudel (1868–1955), French Roman Catholic dramatist and poet; Andre Gide (1869–1951), French novelist, critic, and playwright known for unconventional views on communism and homosexuality.

VI

Your small hands, precisely equal to my own—
only the thumb is larger, longer—in these hands
I could trust the world, or in many hands like these,
handling power-tools or steering-wheel
or touching a human face. . . . Such hands could turn
the unborn child rightways in the birth canal
or pilot the exploratory rescue-ship
through icebergs, or piece together
the fine, needle-like shards of a great krater-cup[o]
bearing on its sides
figures of ecstatic women striding
to the sibyl's den or the Eleusinian cave[o]—
such hands might carry out an unavoidable violence
with such restraint, with such a grasp
of the range and limits of violence
that violence ever after would be obsolete.

VII

What land of beast would turn its life into words?
What atonement is this all about?
—and yet, writing words like these, I'm also living.
Is all this close to the wolverines' howled signals,
that modulated cantata of the wild?
Or, when away from you I try to create you in words,
am I simply using you, like a river or a war?
And how have I used rivers, how have I used wars
to escape writing of the worst thing of all—
not the crimes of others, not even our own death,
but the failure to want our freedom passionately enough
so that blighted elms, sick rivers, massacres would seem
mere emblems of that desecration of ourselves?

VIII

I can see myself years back at Sunion,[o]
hurting with an infected foot, Philoctetes[o]
in woman's form, limping the long path,

---

99. *krater-cup:* a large vessel from Greek or Roman antiquity used to mix wine and water.

102. *cave:* Sibyl was a mythological figure who requested a thousand years of life but forgot to ask for youth as well; she finally hung from the ceiling of her cave or den, a shriveled figure in a bottle; cave: the Eleusinian cave was associated with ritual initiations and festivities observed by the people of ancient Athens.

120. *Sunion:* the summit at Cape Sounion in Greece contains the ruins of a temple.

121. *Philoctetes:* in Greek mythology he was bitten on the foot by a water snake during the Trojan War; the painful wound would not heal.

lying on a headland over the dark sea,
looking down the red rocks to where a soundless curl
of white told me a wave had struck,
imagining the pull of that water from that height,
knowing deliberate suicide wasn't my métier,
yet all the time nursing, measuring that wound.
Well, that's finished. The woman who cherished
her suffering is dead. I am her descendant.
I love the scar-tissue she handed on to me,
but I want to go on from here with you
fighting the temptation to make a career of pain.

IX

Your silence today is a pond where drowned things live
I want to see raised dripping and brought into the sun.
It's not my own face I see there, but other faces,
even your face at another age.
Whatever's lost there is needed by both of us—
a watch of old gold, a water-blurred fever chart,
a key. . . . Even the silt and pebbles of the bottom
deserve their glint of recognition. I fear this silence,
this inarticulate life. I'm waiting
for a wind that will gently open this sheeted water
for once, and show me what I can do
for you, who have often made the unnameable
nameable for others, even for me.

X

Your dog, tranquil and innocent, dozes through
our cries, our murmured dawn conspiracies
our telephone calls. She knows—what can she know?
If in my human arrogance I claim to read
her eyes, I find there only my own animal thoughts:
that creatures must find each other for bodily comfort,
that voices of the psyche drive through the flesh
further than the dense brain could have foretold,
that the planetary nights are growing cold for those
on the same journey who want to touch
one creature-traveler clear to the end;
that without tenderness, we are in hell.

XI

Every peak is a crater. This is the law of volcanoes,
making them eternally and visibly female.

No height without depth, without a burning core,
though our straw soles shred on the hardened lava.
I want to travel with you to every sacred mountain
smoking within like the sibyl stooped over her tripod,
I want to reach for your hand as we scale the path,
to feel your arteries glowing in my clasp,
never failing to note the small, jewel-like flower
unfamiliar to us, nameless till we rename her,
that clings to the slowly altering rock—
that detail outside ourselves that brings us to ourselves,
was here before us, knew we would come, and sees beyond us.

XII

Sleeping, turning in turn like planets
rotating in their midnight meadow:
a touch is enough to let us know
we're not alone in the universe, even in sleep:
the dream-ghosts of two worlds
walking their ghost-towns, almost address each other.
I've wakened to your muttered words
spoken light- or dark-years away
as if my own voice had spoken.
But we have different voices, even in sleep,
and our bodies, so alike, are yet so different
and the past echoing through our bloodstreams
is freighted with different language, different meanings—
though in any chronicle of the world we share
it could be written with new meaning
we were two lovers of one gender,
we were two women of one generation.

XIII

The rules break like a thermometer,
quicksilver spills across the charted systems,
we're out in a country that has no language
no laws, we're chasing the raven and the wren
through gorges unexplored since dawn
whatever we do together is pure invention
the maps they gave us were out of date
by years . . . we're driving through the desert
wondering if the water will hold out
the hallucinations turn to simple villages
the music on the radio comes clear—

neither *Rosenkavalier* nor *Götterdämmerung*°
but a woman's voice singing old songs
with new words, with a quiet bass, a flute
plucked and fingered by women outside the law.

XIV

It was your vision of the pilot
confirmed my vision of you: you said, *He keeps*
on steering headlong into the waves, on purpose
while we crouched in the open hatchway
vomiting into plastic bags
for three hours between St. Pierre and Miquelon.°
I never felt closer to you.
In the close cabin where the honeymoon couples
huddled in each other's laps and arms
I put my hand on your thigh
to comfort both of us, your hand came over mine,
we stayed that way, suffering together
in our bodies, as if all suffering
were physical, we touched so in the presence
of strangers who knew nothing and cared less
vomiting their private pain
as if all suffering were physical.

(The Floating Poem, Unnumbered)

Whatever happens with us, your body
will haunt mine—tender, delicate
your lovemaking, like the half-curled frond
of the fiddlehead fern in forests
just washed by sun. Your traveled, generous thighs
between which my whole face has come and come—
the innocence and wisdom of the place my tongue has found
    there—
the live, insatiate dance of your nipples in my mouth—
your touch on me, firm, protective, searching
me out, your strong tongue and slender fingers
reaching where I had been waiting years for you
in my rose-wet cave—whatever happens, this is.

---

200. *Götterdämmerung: Der Rosenkavalier* ("The Knight of the Rose," 1911), an opera by German composer Richard Strauss (1864–1949); *Götterdämmerung* ("The Twilight of the Gods," 1876), the fourth and final part of the operatic sequence *The Ring of the Nibelung* by German composer Richard Wagner (1813–1883).

209. *St. Pierre and Miquelon:* islands off the coast of Newfoundland, Canada, that belong to France.

XV

If I lay on that beach with you
white, empty, pure green water warmed by the Gulf Stream
and lying on that beach we could not stay
because the wind drove fine sand against us
as if it were against us
if we tried to withstand it and we failed—
if we drove to another place
to sleep in each other's arms
and the beds were narrow like prisoners' cots
and we were tired and did not sleep together
and this was what we found, so this is what we did—
was the failure ours?
If I cling to circumstances I could feel
not responsible. Only she who says
she did not choose, is the loser in the end.

XVI

Across a city from you, I'm with you,
just as an August night
moony, inlet-warm, seabathed, I watched you sleep,
the scrubbed, sheenless wood of the dressing-table
cluttered with our brushes, books, vials in the moonlight—
or a salt-mist orchard, lying at your side
watching red sunset through the screendoor of the cabin,
G minor Mozart on the tape-recorder,
falling asleep to the music of the sea.
This island of Manhattan is wide enough
for both of us, and narrow:
I can hear your breath tonight, I know how your face
lies upturned, the halflight tracing
your generous, delicate mouth
where grief and laughter sleep together.

XVII

No one's fated or doomed to love anyone.
The accidents happen, we're not heroines,
they happen in our lives like car crashes,
books that change us, neighborhoods
we move into and come to love.
Tristan und Isolde° is scarcely the story,

---

268. *Tristan und Isolde:* 1865 opera by Richard Wagner. Early in the opera they drink what Isolde thinks is a poison cup that is actually a love potion.

women at least should know the difference
between love and death. No poison cup,
no penance. Merely a notion that the tape-recorder
should have caught some ghost of us: that tape-recorder
not merely played but should have listened to us,
and could instruct those after us:
this we were, this is how we tried to love,
and these are the forces they had ranged against us,
and these are the forces we had ranged within us,
within us and against us, against us and within us.

XVIII

Rain on the West Side Highway,°
red light at Riverside:°
the more I live the more I think
two people together is a miracle.
You're telling the story of your life
for once, a tremor breaks the surface of your words.
The story of our lives becomes our lives.
Now you're in fugue across what some I'm sure
Victorian poet called the *salt estranging sea.*
Those are the words that come to mind.
I feel estrangement, yes. As I've felt dawn
pushing toward daybreak. Something: a cleft of light—?
Close between grief and anger, a space opens
where I am Adrienne alone. And growing colder.

XIX

Can it be growing colder when I begin
to touch myself again, adhesions pull away?
When slowly the naked face turns from staring backward
and looks into the present,
the eye of winter, city, anger, poverty, and death
and the lips part and say: *I mean to go on living?*
Am I speaking coldly when I tell you in a dream
or in this poem, *There are no miracles*?
(I told you from the first I wanted daily life,
this island of Manhattan was island enough for me.)
If I could let you know—
two women together is a work
nothing in civilization has made simple,

---

279. *West Side Highway:* it ran along Manhattan's West Side.
280. *Riverside:* street on Manhattan's Upper West Side.

two people together is a work
heroic in its ordinariness,
the slow-picked, halting traverse of a pitch
where the fiercest attention becomes routine
—look at the faces of those who have chosen it.

XX

That conversation we were always on the edge
of having, runs on in my head,
at night the Hudson° trembles in New Jersey light
polluted water yet reflecting even
sometimes the moon
and I discern a woman
I loved, drowning in secrets, fear wound round her throat
and choking her like hair. And this is she
with whom I tried to speak, whose hurt, expressive head
turning aside from pain, is dragged down deeper
where it cannot hear me,
and soon I shall know I was talking to my own soul.

XXI

The dark lintels, the blue and foreign stones
of the great round rippled by stone implements
the midsummer night light rising from beneath
the horizon—when I said "a cleft of light"
I meant this. And this is not Stonehenge°
simply nor any place but the mind
casting back to where her solitude,
shared, could be chosen without loneliness,
not easily nor without pains to stake out
the circle, the heavy shadows, the great light.
I choose to be a figure in that light,
half-blotted by darkness, something moving
across that space, the color of stone
greeting the moon, yet more than stone:
a woman. I choose to walk here. And to draw this circle.

1974–1976

313. *Hudson:* river that flows past New York City to the Atlantic Ocean.

327. *Stonehenge:* prehistoric monument in England constructed of twenty fifty-ton sandstone blocks.

POWER

Living   in the earth-deposits   of our history

Today a backhoe divulged   out of a crumbling flank of earth
one bottle   amber   perfect   a hundred-year-old
cure for fever   or melancholy   a tonic
for living on this earth   in the winters of this climate

Today I was reading about Marie Curie:°
she must have known she suffered   from radiation sickness
her body bombarded for years   by the element
she had purified
It seems she denied to the end
the source of the cataracts on her eyes
the cracked and suppurating skin   of her finger-ends
till she could no longer hold   a test-tube or a pencil

She died   a famous woman   denying
her wounds
denying
her wounds   came   from the same source as her power

1974

from AN ATLAS OF THE DIFFICULT WORLD

XIII. (DEDICATIONS)

I know you are reading this poem
late, before leaving your office
of the one intense yellow lamp-spot and the darkening window
in the lassitude of a building faded to quiet
long after rush-hour. I know you are reading this poem
standing up in a bookstore far from the ocean
on a grey day of early spring, faint flakes driven
across the plains' enormous spaces around you.
I know you are reading this poem
in a room where too much has happened for you to bear
where the bedclothes lie in stagnant coils on the bed
and the open valise speaks of flight
but you cannot leave yet. I know you are reading this poem

6. *Curie:* (1867–1934), Polish-born chemist whose work on radioactivity helped establish modern atomic science; the first woman to receive a Nobel Prize and the first person to receive it twice. Curie died of leukemia from long exposure to radiation.

as the underground train loses momentum and before running
up the stairs
toward a new kind of love
your life has never allowed.
I know you are reading this poem by the light
of the television screen where soundless images jerk and slide
while you wait for the newscast from the *intifada*.°
I know you are reading this poem in a waiting-room
of eyes met and unmeeting, of identity with strangers.
I know you are reading this poem by fluorescent light
in the boredom and fatigue of the young who are counted out,
count themselves out, at too early an age. I know
you are reading this poem through your failing sight, the thick
lens enlarging these letters beyond all meaning yet you read on
because even the alphabet is precious.
I know you are reading this poem as you pace beside the stove
warming milk, a crying child on your shoulder, a book in your
hand
because life is short and you too are thirsty.
I know you are reading this poem which is not in your language
guessing at some words while others keep you reading
and I want to know which words they are.
I know you are reading this poem listening for something, torn
between bitterness and hope
turning back once again to the task you cannot refuse.
I know you are reading this poem because there is nothing else
left to read
there where you have landed, stripped as you are.

1990–1991

BEHIND THE MOTEL

A man lies under a car half bare
a child plays bullfight with a torn cloth
hemlocks grieve in wraps of mist
a woman talks on the phone, looks in a mirror
fiddling with the metal pull of a drawer

She has seen her world wiped clean, the cloth
that wiped it disintegrate in mist
or dying breath on the skin of a mirror

20. *intifada:* mass protests organized by Palestinians against Israeli occupation of territory on the West Bank of the Jordan River.

She has felt her life close like a drawer
has awoken somewhere else, bare

He feels his skin as if it were mist
as if his face would show in no mirror
He needs some bolts he left in a vanished drawer
crawls out into the hemlocked world with his bare
hands, wipes his wrench on an oil-soaked cloth

stares at the woman talking into a mirror
who has shut the phone into the drawer
while over and over with a torn cloth
at the edge of hemlocks behind the bare
motel a child taunts a horned beast made from mist

2004

HOTEL

I dreamed the Finnish Hotel founded by Finns in an olden time
It was in New York had been there a long time
Finnish sea-captains had stayed there in their time
It had fallen on one then another bad time
Now restored it wished to be or seem of the olden time
The Finnish Hotel founded by Finns in an olden time

There was a perpendicular lighted sign along its spine:
THE FINNISH HOTEL and on the desk aligned
two lamps like white globes and a blond
wood lounge with curved chairs and a bar beyond
serving a clear icy liquor of which the captains had been fond
reputedly in the olden time

In the Finnish Hotel I slept on a mattress stuffed with straw
after drinking with a Finnish captain who regarded me with awe
saying, Woman who could put away that much I never saw
but I did not lie with him on the mattress, his major flaw
being he was a phantom of the olden time
and I a woman still almost in my prime

dreaming the Finnish Hotel founded by Finns in the olden time

2005

DEREK WALCOTT (b. 1930)

Born and raised on Saint Lucia in the Caribbean, Walcott also taught at Boston University for many years and thus frequently lived in the United States. He had a classical British education on Saint Lucia, not unlike the education Claude McKay had in Jamaica. The rhetorical heritage of the great British and Irish writers lends his work some of its high diction, but he is also engaged with his own island's bitter colonial history. He layers *Omeros* with both the high diction of his own education and the patois and West Indian English spoken on the Saint Lucia street. The multiple inheritances cannot be fully reconciled. Indeed, they are at once a gift and a wound. In fact, they are intertwined in Walcott's own ethnic history, as his grandfathers were Dutch and English whites, while his grandmothers were of African descent. In "A Far Cry from Africa," he asks, "How can I turn from Africa and live?" Yet, like McKay, he knows altogether embracing an African past is impossible. "Laventille" invokes the history of the slave trade to demonstrate that its historical burden remains contemporary. The rich mix of international and multicultural references in Walcott's work has perhaps its closest analogue in Melvin Tolson's "Libretto for the Republic of Liberia," also included in this anthology. Walcott was awarded the Nobel Prize in Literature in 1992.

A FAR CRY FROM AFRICA

A wind is ruffling the tawny pelt
Of Africa. Kikuyu,° quick as flies,
Batten upon the bloodstreams of the veldt.°
Corpses are scattered through a paradise.
Only the worm, colonel of carrion, cries:
"Waste no compassion on these separate dead!"
Statistics justify and scholars seize
The salients of colonial policy.
What is that to the white child hacked in bed?
To savages, expendable as Jews?

Threshed out by beaters,° the long rushes break
In a white dust of ibises° whose cries

---

2. *Kikuyu:* historically centered in the area around Mount Kenya, the Kikuyu are the major ethnic group in Kenya. They resisted the imposition of British colonial rule and the effort to award their farmland to white settlers in the first decades of the twentieth century, but the resistance largely failed. Then the Kenyan Land and Freedom Army, known as the Mau Mau, launched a major campaign against British rule in the early 1950s. Though defeated, the uprising eventually led to Kenyan independence in 1963.

3. *veldt:* African plains.

11. *beaters:* they flush game for hunters.

12. *ibises:* long-legged wading birds, objects of religious veneration in ancient Egypt.

Have wheeled since civilization's dawn
From the parched river or beast-teeming plain.
The violence of beast on beast is read
As natural law, but upright man
Seeks his divinity by inflicting pain.
Delirious as these worried beasts, his wars
Dance to the tightened carcass of a drum,
While he calls courage still that native dread
Of the white peace contracted by the dead.

Again brutish necessity wipes its hands
Upon the napkin of a dirty cause, again
A waste of our compassion, as with Spain,°
The gorilla wrestles with the superman.
I who am poisoned with the blood of both,
Where shall I turn, divided to the vein?
I who have cursed
The drunken officer of British rule, how choose
Between this Africa and the English tongue I love?
Betray them both, or give back what they give?
How can I face such slaughter and be cool?
How can I turn from Africa and live?

1956

LAVENTILLE°

[for V. S. Naipaul]°

To find the Western Path
Through the Gates of Wrath—
—Blake°

It huddled there
steel tinkling its blue painted metal air,
tempered in violence, like Rio's favelas,°

with snaking, perilous streets whose edges fell as
its Episcopal turkey-buzzards fall
from its miraculous hilltop

24. *Spain:* despite thousands of international volunteers coming to the aid of the Spanish Republic in the 1936–1939 Spanish Civil War, the fascists won the war with military assistance from Hitler and Mussolini.

poem title: *Laventille*: a crime ridden slum in the hills above Port of Spain, the capital of Trinidad and Tobago, it is also the creative center for the music of steel bands.

dedication: V. S. Naipaul (b. 1932), Trinidadian novelist.

epigraph: from William Blake's poem "Morning." Blake (1757–1827) was an English romantic poet and mystic.

3. *favelas:* hillside shantytowns overlooking Brazil's Rio de Janeiro.

shrine,
down the impossible drop
to Belmont, Woodbrook, Maraval, St. Clair°

that shine
like peddlers' tin trinkets in the sun.
From a harsh

shower, its gutters growled and gargled wash
past the Youth Centre, past the water catchment,
a rigid children's carousel of cement;

we climbed where lank electric
lines and tension cables linked its raw brick
hovels like a complex feud,

where the inheritors of the middle passage° stewed,
five to a room, still clamped below their hatch,
breeding like felonies,

whose lives revolve round prison, graveyard, church.
Below bent breadfruit trees
in the flat, coloured city, class

escalated into structures still,
merchant, middleman, magistrate, knight. To go downhill
from here was to ascend.

The middle passage never guessed its end.
This is the height of poverty
for the desperate and black;

climbing, we could look back
with widening memory
on the hot, corrugated-iron sea
whose horrors we all

shared. The salt blood knew it well,
you, me, Samuel's daughter, Samuel,
and those ancestors clamped below its grate.

---

9. *Belmont . . . . St. Clair:* Trinidad towns.

19. *middle passage:* the route of the slave trade. See Robert Hayden's poem "Middle Passage."

And climbing steeply past the wild
gutters, it shrilled
in the blood, for those who suffered, who were killed,

and who survive.
What other gift was there to give
as the godparents of his unnamed child?

Yet outside the brown annex of the church, the
stifling odour of bay rum and talc, the particular,
neat sweetness of the crowd distressed

that sense. The black, fawning verger,°
his bow tie akimbo, grinning, the clown-gloved
fashionable wear of those I deeply loved

once, made me look on with hopelessness and rage
at their new, apish habits, their excess
and fear, the possessed, the self-possessed;

their perfume shrivelled to a childhood fear
of Sabbath graveyards, christenings, marriages,
that muggy, steaming, self-assuring air

of tropical Sabbath afternoons. And in
the church, eyes prickling with rage,
the children rescued from original sin

by their Godfather since the middle passage,
the supercilious brown curate, who intones,
healing the guilt in these rachitic° bones,
twisting my love within me like a knife:
"across the troubled waters of this life . . ."

Which of us cares to walk
even if God wished
those retching waters where our souls were fished

for this new world? Afterwards, we talk
in whispers, close to death
among these stones planted on alien earth.

---

47. *verger:* a layperson who assists in Anglican services.
61. *rachitic:* deformed junction of ribs and cartilage seen in cases of rickets.

Afterwards,
the ceremony, the careful photograph
moved out of range before the patient tombs,

we dare a laugh,
ritual, desperate words,
born like these children from habitual wombs,

from lives fixed in the unalterable groove
of grinding poverty. I stand out on a balcony
and watch the sun pave its flat, golden path

across the roofs, the aerials, cranes, the tops
of fruit trees crawling downward to the city.
Something inside is laid wide like a wound,

some open passage that has cleft the brain,
some deep, amnesiac blow. We left
somewhere a life we never found,

customs and gods that are not born again,
some crib, some grille of light
clanged shut on us in bondage, and withheld

us from that world below us and beyond,
and in its swaddling cerements° we're still bound.

1965

THE FORTUNATE TRAVELLER

(For Susan Sontag)°

And I heard a voice in the midst of the four beasts say,
A measure of wheat for a penny,
and three measures of barley for a penny;
and see thou hurt not the oil and the wine.

—Revelation 6.6

I

It was in winter. Steeples, spires
congealed like holy candles. Rotting snow

---

89. *cerements:* grave cloth.

Dedication: Sontag (1933–2004), American cultural theorist, novelist, and filmmaker.

flaked from Europe's ceiling. A compact man,
I crossed the canal in a grey overcoat,
on one lapel a crimson buttonhole
for the cold ecstasy of the assassin.
In the square coffin manacled to my wrist:
small countries pleaded through the mesh of graphs,
in treble-spaced, Xeroxed forms to the World Bank°
on which I had scrawled the one word, MERCY;

I sat on a cold bench
under some skeletal lindens.°
Two other gentlemen, black skins gone grey
as their identical, belted overcoats,
crossed the white river.
They spoke the stilted French
of their dark river,
whose hooked worm, multiplying its pale sickle,°
could thin the harvest of the winter streets.
"Then we can depend on you to get us those tractors?"
"I gave my word."
"May my country ask you why you are doing this, sir?"
Silence.
"You know if you betray us, you cannot hide?"
A tug. Smoke trailing its dark cry.

At the window in Haiti, I remember
a gekko° pressed against the hotel glass,
with white palms, concentrating head.
With a child's hands. Mercy, monsieur. Mercy.
Famine sighs like a scythe
across the field of statistics and the desert
is a moving mouth. In the hold of this earth
10,000,000 shoreless souls are drifting.
Somalia:° 765,000, their skeletons will go under the tidal sand.

---

9. *World Bank:* major source of loans (and accompanying economic restrictions) for developing countries.

12. *lindens:* shade trees.

18. *Sickle:* a pun links the agricultural sickle with sickle-cell anemia.

27. *gekko:* small tropical lizard.

34. *Somalia:* East African country bordered by the Indian Ocean to the east and Ethiopia to the west. Italy and Britain each took control of parts of Somalia in the late nineteenth century, but armed resistance to colonial domination persisted. Divided for decades, the northern and southern regions united to form the Somali Republic under a civilian government in 1960, but Mohammed Siad Barre seized power and established a military dictatorship in 1969. That government too was overthrown after two decades, but Barre was still in power when Walcott wrote "The Fortunate Traveller." Warfare and famine have defined much of Somalia's history.

"We'll meet you in Bristol[o] to conclude the agreement?"
Steeples like tribal lances, through congealing fog
the cries of wounded church bells wrapped in cotton,
grey mist enfolding the conspirator
like a sealed envelope next to its heart.

No one will look up now to see the jet
fade like a weevil[o] through a cloud of flour.
One flies first-class, one is so fortunate.
Like a telescope reversed, the traveller's eye
swiftly screws down the individuals sorrow
to an oval nest of antic numerals,
and the iris, interlocking with this globe,
condenses it to zero, then a cloud.
Beetle-black taxi from Heathrow to my flat.
We are roaches,
riddling the state cabinets, entering the dark holes
of power, carapaced in topcoats,
scuttling around columns, signalling for taxis,
with frantic antennae, to other huddles with roaches;
we infect with optimism, and when
the cabinets crack, we are the first
to scuttle, radiating separately
back to Geneva, Bonn, Washington, London.

Under the dripping planes of Hampstead Heath,[o]
I read her letter again, watching the drizzle
disfigure its pleading like mascara. Margo,
I cannot bear to watch the nations cry.
Then the phone: "We will pay you in Bristol."
Days in fetid bedclothes swallowing cold tea,
the phone stifled by the pillow. The telly
a blue storm with soundless snow.
I'd light the gas and see a tiger's tongue.
I was rehearsing the ecstasies of starvation
for what I had to do. *And have not charity.*[o]

I found my pity, desperately researching
the origins of history, from reed-built communes

35. *Bristol:* British port city.
41. *weevil:* insect that infests grain.
58. *Hampstead Heath:* London park.
68. *charity:* I Corinthians 13:1—"Though I speak with the tongues of men and of angels, and have not charity, I am become as sounding brass, or a tinkling cymbal."

by sacred lakes, turning with the first sprocketed
water-driven wheels. I smelled imagination
among bestial hides by the gleam of fat,
seeking in all races a common ingenuity.
I envisaged an Africa flooded with such light
as alchemized the first fields of emmer wheat and barley,
when we savages dyed our pale dead with ochre,
and bordered our temples
with the ceremonial vulva of the conch
in the grey epoch of the obsidian adze.°
I sowed the Sahara with rippling cereals,
my charity fertilized these aridities.

What was my field? Late sixteenth century.
My field was a dank acre. A Sussex don,
I taught the Jacobean anxieties: *The White Devil.*°
Flamineo's torch startles the brooding yews.
The drawn end comes in strides. I loved my Duchess,°
the white flame of her soul blown out between
the smoking cypresses. Then I saw children pounce
on green meat with a rat's ferocity.

I called them up and took the train to Bristol,
my blood the Severn's° dregs and silver.
On Severn's estuary the pieces flash,
Iscariot's salary,° patron saint of spies.
I thought, who cares how many million starve?
Their rising souls will lighten the world's weight
and level its gull-glittering waterline;
we left at sunset down the estuary.

England recedes. The forked white gull
screeches, circling back.
Even the birds are pulled back by their orbit,
even mercy has its magnetic field.
Back in the cabin,
I uncap the whisky, the porthole
mists with glaucoma. By the time I'm pissed,

---

80. *adze:* an ancient cutting tool with a stone blade, today more commonly forged of steel.

85. *The White Devil:* tragedy by British playwright John Webster *(c. 1580–c. 1625).*

86–87. *Flamineo and the Duchess:* villain and heroine in *The White Devil.*

92. *Severn:* Bristol river.

94. *Iscariot's salary:* Judas's reward for betraying Jesus.

England, England will be
that pale serrated indigo on the sea-line.
"You are so fortunate, you get to see the world—"
Indeed, indeed, sirs, I have seen the world.
Spray splashes the portholes and vision blurs.

Leaning on the hot rail, watching the hot sea,
I saw them far off, kneeling on hot sand
in the pious genuflections of the locust,
as Ponce's armored knees crush Florida°
to the funeral fragrance of white lilies.

II

Now I have to come to where the phantoms live,
I have no fear of phantoms, but of the real.
The sabbath benedictions of the islands.
Treble clef of the snail on the scored leaf,
the Tantum Ergo° of black choristers
soars through the organ pipes of coconuts.
Across the dirty beach surpliced° with lace,
they pass a brown lagoon behind the priest,
pale and unshaven in his frayed soutane,
into the concrete church at Canaries;
as Albert Schweitzer° moves to the harmonium
of morning, and to the pluming chimneys,
the groundswell lifts *Lebensraum, Lebensraum.*°

Black faces sprinkled with continual dew—
dew on the speckled croton, dew
on the hard leaf of the knotted plum tree,
dew on the elephant ears of the dasheen.°
Through Kurtz's teeth, white skull in elephant grass,
the imperial fiction sings. Sunday
wrinkles downriver from the Heart of Darkness°
The heart of darkness is not Africa.

---

114. *Ponce . . . Florida:* Juan Ponce de Leon (1460–1521), Spanish conquistador who discovered Florida and sought to defeat the Indian tribes in the region.

120. *Tantum Ergo:* (Latin) "So much therefore," a line from a mass.

122. *supliced:* overlaid, as with a white ecclesiastical cloth.

126. *Schweitzer:* medical missionary (1875–1965) who played the harmonium in his jungle hospital.

128. *Lebensraum:* (German) "living room," the German motto for the goal of their World War II conquests.

132. *dasheen:* tropical plant.

135. *Heart of Darkness:* famous short novel by Joseph Conrad (1857–1924) in which the narrator goes on an African journey to meet the white adventurer Kurtz who has penetrated to the heart of human evil.

The heart of darkness is the core of fire
in the white center of the holocaust.
The heart of darkness is the rubber claw
selecting a scalpel in antiseptic light,
the hills of children's shoes outside the chimneys,
the tinkling nickel instruments on the white altar;
Jacob, in his last card, sent me these verses:
"Think of a God who doesn't lose His sleep
if trees burst into tears or glaciers weep.
So, aping His indifference, I write now,
not Anno Domini: After Dachau."°

III

The night maid brings a lamp and draws the blinds.
I stay out on the veranda with the stars.
Breakfast congealed to supper on its plate.

There is no sea as restless as my mind.
The promontories snore. They snore like whales.
Cetus, the whale, was Christ.
The ember dies, the sky smokes like an ash heap.
Reeds wash their hands of guilt and the lagoon
is stained. Louder, since it rained,
a gauze of sand flies hisses from the marsh.

Since God is dead, and these are not His stars,
but man-lit, sulphurous, sanctuary lamps,
it's in the heart of darkness of this earth
that backward tribes keep vigil of His Body,
in deya, lampion, and this bedside lamp.
Keep the news from their blissful ignorance.
Like lice, like lice, the hungry of this earth
swarm to the tree of life. If those who starve
like these rain-flies who shed glazed wings in light
grew from sharp shoulder blades their brittle vans
and soared toward that tree, how it would seethe—
ah, Justice! But fires
drench them like vermin, quotas
prevent them, and they remain
compassionate fodder for the travel book,
its paragraphs like windows from a train,
for everywhere that earth shows its rib cage

147. *Dachau:* the first of the Nazi concentration camps established in Germany.

and the moon goggles with the eyes of children,
we turn away to read. Rimbaud learned that.
Rimbaud,° at dusk,
idling his wrist in water past temples
the plumed dates still protect in Roman file,°
knew that we cared less for one human face
than for the scrolls in Alexandria's ashes,°
that the bright water could not dye his hand
any more than poetry. The dhow's° silhouette
moved through the blinding coinage of the river
that, endlessly, until we pay one debt,
shrouds, every night, an ordinary secret.

IV

The drawn sword comes in strides.
It stretches for the length of the empty beach;
the fishermen's huts shut their eyes tight.
A frisson° shakes the palm trees,
and sweats on the traveller's tree.
They've found out my sanctuary. Philippe, last night:
"It had two gentlemen in the village yesterday, sir,
asking for you while you was in town.
I tell them you was in town. They send to tell you,
there is no hurry. They will be coming back."

In loaves of cloud, *and have not charity,*
the weevil will make a sahara of Kansas,
the ant shall eat Russia.
Their soft teeth shall make, *and have not charity,*
the harvest's desolation,
and the brown globe crack like a begging bowl,
and though you fire oceans of surplus grain,
and have not charity,

still, through thin stalks,
the smoking stubble, stalks
grasshopper: third horseman,
the leather-helmed locust.

1981

---

177. *Rimbaud:* Arthur Rimbaud (1854–1891) lived his last decade in Africa.
179. *Roman file:* single file.
181. *ashes:* the Alexandrian library and the scrolls it housed were largely destroyed by fire in 47 B.C.
183. *dhow:* Arabian boat.
190. *frisson:* brief shudder.

from Omeros°

BOOK ONE

Chapter 1

I

"This is how, one sunrise, we cut down them canoes."
Philoctete° smiles for the tourists, who try taking
his soul with their cameras. "Once wind bring the news

to the *laurier-cannelles,*° their leaves start shaking
the minute the axe of sunlight hit the cedars,
because they could see the axes in our own eyes.

Wind lift the ferns. They sound like the sea that feed us
fishermen all our life, and the ferns nodded 'Yes,
the trees have to die.' So, fists jam in our jacket,

cause the heights was cold and our breath making feathers
like the mist, we pass the rum. When it came back, it
give us the spirit to turn into murderers.

I lift up the axe and pray for strength in my hands
to wound the first cedar. Dew was filling my eyes,
but I fire one more white rum. Then we advance."

For some extra silver, under a sea-almond,
he shows them a scar made by a rusted anchor,
rolling one trouser-leg up with the rising moan

---

poem title: Omeros:—modern Greek for Homer. *Omeros* is a book-length epic divided into seven "books" and sixty-four chapters. Set largely on the island of Saint Lucia, where Walcott was born and raised, the poem also includes descriptions of Walcott's experiences in such cities as Lisbon, London, Dublin, Rome, Toronto, and Brookline, Massachusetts, where Walcott was teaching at the time he wrote the poem. Walcott thus makes himself a character in the poem, which gives it a self-reflexive postmodern quality. The poem's predominant three-line form loosely echoes the *terza rima* form of Dante's *The Divine Comedy.* Saint Lucia's colonial history includes eighteenth-century warfare between France and England over the island's control. Indeed, control of the island changed so many times that it became known as "the Helen of the West Indies." Its location in the eastern Caribbean Sea on the boundary with the Atlantic Ocean gave it a strategic relationship to North America.

2. *Philoctete:* Walcott's character of this name (a wounded fisherman) alludes to the legend of the Greek hero Philoctetes. Philoctetes is the subject of Sophocles's play named after him; he is also mentioned in Homer's *Iliad.* There are multiple versions of the myth, but most have him as a Greek hero bitten by a snake on the way to the Trojan War. Exiled with his wound on the island of Lemnos, he survives, and the Greeks eventually return to Lemnos and enlist him in the war.

4. *laurier-cannelles:* plant native to Saint Lucia.

of a conch. It has puckered like the corolla
of a sea-urchin. He does not explain its cure.
"It have some things"—he smiles—"worth more than a dollar."

He has left it to a garrulous waterfall
to pour out his secret down La Sorcière,[o] since
the tall laurels fell, for the ground-dove's mating call

to pass on its note to the blue, tacit mountains
whose talkative brooks, carrying it to the sea,
turn into idle pools where the clear minnows shoot

and an egret stalks the reeds with one rusted cry
as it stabs and stabs the mud with one lifting foot.
Then silence is sawn in half by a dragonfly

as eels sign their names along the clear bottom-sand,
when the sunrise brightens the river's memory
and waves of huge ferns are nodding to the sea's sound.

Although smoke forgets the earth from which it ascends,
and nettles guard the holes where the laurels were killed,
an iguana hears the axes, clouding each lens

over its lost name, when the hunched island was called
"Iounalao," "Where the iguana is found."
But, taking its own time, the iguana will scale

the rigging of vines in a year, its dewlap fanned,
its elbows akimbo, its deliberate tail
moving with the island. The slit pods of its eyes

ripened in a pause that lasted for centuries,
that rose with the Aruacs[o] smoke till a new race
unknown to the lizard stood measuring the trees.

These were their pillars that fell, leaving a blue space
for a single God where the old gods stood before.
The first god was a gommier.[o] The generator

23. *La Sorcière:* (French) "the sorceress," St. Lucian mountain.
44. *Aruacs:* native people who once lived on St. Lucia.
48. *gommier:* gum tree.

began with a whine, and a shark, with sidewise jaw,
sent the chips flying like mackerel over water
into trembling weeds. Now they cut off the saw,

still hot and shaking, to examine the wound it
had made. They scraped off its gangrenous moss, then ripped
the wound clear of the net of vines that still bound it

to this earth, and nodded. The generator whipped
back to its work, and the chips flew much faster as
the shark's teeth gnawed evenly. They covered their eyes

from the splintering nest. Now, over the pastures
of bananas, the island lifted its horns. Sunrise
trickled down its valleys, blood splashed on the cedars,

and the grove flooded with the light of sacrifice.
A gommier was cracking. Its leaves an enormous
tarpaulin with the ridgepole gone. The creaking sound

made the fishermen leap back as the angling mast
leant slowly towards the troughs of ferns; then the ground
shuddered under the feet in waves, then the waves passed.

1990

GARY SNYDER (b. 1930)

Born in San Francisco and raised on a farm north of Seattle, Snyder was educated at Reed College, where he studied literature, Buddhist philosophy, and Native American mythology. He then worked as a logger and spent summers as a forest-fire lookout in Oregon, Washington, and California. Involved with the Beat writers in San Francisco in the mid-1950s, he made a major change in his life in 1956, moving to Japan to study Zen Buddhism. Except for some shipboard work, he remained there for twelve years. He had been through two failed marriages in the United States, but in Japan he met and married Masa Uehara, and that relationship survived until 1988. They returned to the United States in 1968, and a few years later Snyder built a home in a remote community in the foothills of the Sierra Nevada in California.

Although Snyder has adopted different forms over the years, he generally prefers a direct, simple diction over intricate metaphor and allusion. In "Riprap" he uses words like material objects to refine and teach us a mental discipline. One may hear Thoreau and Whitman behind such an impulse, along with his Zen studies, but the ecological imperative includes an anguish that we have fully earned only in our own century. Against the errors of industrial civilization Snyder sets not only a reverence for nature but also a vital celebration of human sexuality. More recently, Snyder has borrowed shamanistic effects from oral poetry and done more experimentation with field effects and the space of the page. He has taught college occasionally, most recently at the University of California at Davis.

RIPRAP°

Lay down these words
Before your mind like rocks.
        placed solid, by hands
In choice of place, set
Before the body of the mind
        in space and time:
Solidity of bark, leaf, or wall
        riprap of things:
Cobble of milky way,
        straying planets,
These poems, people,
        lost ponies with

---

poem title: riprap is an assemblage of broken stone put down to form a foundation in water or soft ground.

Dragging saddles—
        and rocky sure-foot trails.
The worlds like an endless
        four-dimensional
Game of *Go*.°
        ants and pebbles
In the thin loam, each rock a word
        a creek-washed stone
Granite: ingrained
        with torment of fire and weight
Crystal and sediment linked hot
        all change, in thoughts,
As well as things.

1959

BENEATH MY HAND AND EYE THE DISTANT HILLS. YOUR BODY

What my hand follows on your body
Is the line. A stream of love
    of heat, of light,   what my
    eye   lascivious
            licks
    over, watching
    far snow-dappled Uintah mountains°
Is that stream.
Of power.   what my
    hand curves over, following the line.
    "hip" and "groin"

Where "I"
    follow by hand and eye
    the swimming limit of your body.
As when vision idly dallies on the hills
Loving what it feeds on.
    soft cinder cones and craters;
    —Drum Hadley in the Pinacate°
      took ten minutes more to look again—
A leap of power unfurling:
      left,   right—right—

---

17. *Go:* an ancient Japanese game in which black and white stones are placed on a checkered board.

7. *Uintah:* mountain range in northeastern Utah.

18. *Pinacate:* California town.

My heart beat faster looking
 at the snowy Uintah mountains.

As my hand feeds on you
 runs down your side and curls beneath your hip.
oil pool; stratum; water—

What "is" within not known
 but feel it
 sinking with a breath
 pusht ruthless, surely, down.

Beneath this long caress of hand and eye
 "we" learn the flower burning,
 outward, from "below."

1968

I WENT INTO THE MAVERICK BAR

I went into the Maverick Bar
In Farmington, New Mexico.
And drank double shots of bourbon
 backed with beer.
My long hair was tucked up under a cap
I'd left the earring in the car.

Two cowboys did horseplay
 by the pool tables,
A waitress asked us
 where are you from?
a country-and-western band began to play
"We don't smoke Marijuana in Muskokie"
And with the next song,
 a couple began to dance.

They held each other like in High School dances
 in the fifties;
I recalled when I worked in the woods
 and the bars of Madras, Oregon.
That short-haired joy and roughness—
 America—your stupidity.
I could almost love you again.

We left—onto the freeway shoulders—
 under the tough old stars—

In the shadow of bluffs
I came back to myself,
To the real work, to
"What is to be done."°

1974

STRAIGHT-CREEK—GREAT BURN°

for Tom and Martha Burch

Lightly, in the April mountains—
Straight Creek,
dry grass freed again of snow
& the chicadees are pecking
last fall's seeds
fluffing tail in chilly wind,

Avalanche piled up cross the creek
and chunked-froze solid—
water sluicing under; spills out
rock lip pool, bends over,
braided, white, foaming,
returns to trembling
deep-dark hole.

Creek boulders show the flow-wear lines
in shapes the same
as running blood
carves in the heart's main
valve,

Early spring dry. Dry snow flurries;
walk on crusty high snow slopes
—grand dead burn pine—
chartreuse lichen as adornment
(a dye for wool)
angled tumbled talus° rock
of geosyncline° warm sea bottom
yes, so long ago.
"Once on a time,"

---

27. *What is to be done:* title of a 1902 book by Vladimir Lenin (1870–1924), leader of the 1917 Russian Revolution.

poem title: "burn" is a Scottish word for a running brook, though it can also refer to an area burned by a forest fire.

24. *talus:* rock debris under a cliff.

25. *geosyncline:* downward turning of the earth's crust.

Far light on the Bitteroots;°
scrabble down willow slide
changing clouds above,
shapes on glowing sun-ball
writhing, choosing
reaching out against eternal
azure—

us resting on dry fern and
watching

Shining Heaven
change his feather garments
overhead.

A whoosh of birds
swoops up and round
tilts back
almost always flying all apart
and yet hangs on!
together;

never a leader,
all of one swift

empty
dancing mind.

They arc and loop & then
their flight is done.
they settle down.
end of poem.

1974

AXE HANDLES

One afternoon the last week in April
Showing Kai how to throw a hatchet
One-half turn and it sticks in a stump.
He recalls the hatchet-head
Without a handle, in the shop
And go gets it, and wants it for his own.
A broken-off axe handle behind the door

28. *Bitteroots:* mountain range along the Idaho–Montana border.

Is long enough for a hatchet,
We cut it to length and take it
With the hatchet head
And working hatchet, to the wood block.
There I begin to shape the old handle
With the hatchet, and the phrase
First learned from Ezra Pound
Rings in my ears!
"When making an axe handle
        the pattern is not far off."
And I say this to Kai
"Look: We'll shape the handle
By checking the handle
Of the axe we cut with—"
And he sees. And I hear it again:
It's in Lu Ji's *Wên Fu,* fourth century
A.D. "Essay on Literature"—in the
Preface: "In making the handle
Of an axe
By cutting wood with an axe
The model is indeed near at hand."
My teacher Shih-hsiang Chen
Translated that and taught it years ago
And I see: Pound was an axe,
Chen was an axe, I am an axe
And my son a handle, soon
To be shaping again, model
And tool, craft of culture,
How we go on.

1983

GREGORY CORSO (1930–2001)

Born in New York City, Corso had a volatile life and career. His childhood was spent in a series of foster homes and sometimes on the street. To survive, he took up petty theft and ended up in prison from 1947 to 1950. On release, he worked as a manual laborer, an employee of the *San Francisco Examiner,* and a merchant seaman. In the mid-1950s, he became linked with the Beat writers and achieved some fame through his energetic poetry readings. He traveled widely in Europe and Mexico, often writing his irreverent, histrionic poems on the wing. Primarily a figure of the 1950s and 1960s, he continued to publish into the 1980s.

MARRIAGE

Should I get married? Should I be good?
Astound the girl next door with my velvet suit and faustus° hood?
Don't take her to movies but to cemeteries
tell all about werewolf bathtubs and forked clarinets
then desire her and kiss her and all the preliminaries
and she going just so far and I understanding why
not getting angry saying You must feel! It's beautiful to feel!
Instead take her in my arms lean against an old crooked tombstone
and woo her the entire night the constellations in the sky—

When she introduces me to her parents
back straightened, hair finally combed, strangled by a tie,
should I sit knees together on their 3rd degree sofa
and not ask Where's the bathroom?
How else to feel other than I am,
often thinking Flash Gordon° soap—
O how terrible it must be for a young man
seated before a family and the family thinking
We never saw him before! He wants our Mary Lou!
After tea and homemade cookies they ask What do you do for a
living?

Should I tell them? Would they like me then?
Say All right get married, we're losing a daughter
but we're gaining a son—
And should I then ask Where's the bathroom?

---

2. *faustus:* from Faust, the medieval alchemist who sold his soul to the devil in exchange for power and youth; subject of numerous literary works.

15. *Flash Gordon:* the science fiction comic strip and movie serial of the 1930s.

O God, and the wedding! All her family and her friends
and only a handful of mine all scroungy and bearded
just wait to get at the drinks and food—
And the priest! he looking at me as if I masturbated
asking me Do you take this woman for your lawful wedded wife?
And I trembling what to say say Pie Glue!
I kiss the bride all those corny men slapping me on the back
She's all yours, boy! Ha-ha-ha!
And in their eyes you could see some obscene honeymoon going
on—
Then all that absurd rice and clanky cans and shoes
Niagara Falls! Hordes of us! Husbands! Wives! Flowers!
Chocolates!
All streaming into cozy hotels
All going to do the same thing tonight
The indifferent clerk he knowing what was going to happen
The lobby zombies they knowing what
The whistling elevator man he knowing
The winking bellboy knowing
Everybody knowing! I'd be almost inclined not to do anything!
Stay up all night! Stare that hotel clerk in the eye!
Screaming: I deny honeymoon! I deny honeymoon!
running rampant into those almost climactic suites
yelling Radio belly! Cat shovel!
O I'd live in Niagara forever! in a dark cave beneath the Falls
I'd sit there the Mad Honeymooner
devising ways to break marriages, a scourge of bigamy
a saint of divorce—

But I should get married I should be good
How nice it'd be to come home to her
and sit by the fireplace and she in the kitchen
aproned young and lovely wanting my baby
and so happy about me she burns the roast beef
and comes crying to me and I get up from my big papa chair
saying Christmas teeth! Radiant brains! Apple deaf!
God what a husband I'd make! Yes, I should get married!
So much to do! like sneaking into Mr. Jones' house late at night
and cover his golf clubs with 1920 Norwegian books
Like hanging a picture of Rimbaud° on the lawnmower
like pasting Tannu Tuva° postage stamps all over the picket fence

---

63. *Rimbaud:* Arthur Rimbaud (1854–1891), French poet.

64. *Tannu Tuva:* Siberian republic in Russia on the Mongolian border.

like when Mrs Kindhead comes to collect for the Community
    Chest
grab her and tell her There are unfavorable omens in the sky!
And when the mayor comes to get my vote tell him
When are you going to stop people killing whales!
And when the milkman comes leave him a note in the bottle
Penguin dust, bring me penguin dust, I want penguin dust—

Yet if I should get married and it's Connecticut and snow
and she gives birth to a child and I am sleepless, worn,
up for nights, head bowed against a quiet window, the past behind me,
finding myself in the most common of situations a trembling man
knowledged with responsibility not twig-smear nor Roman coin
                                                                                soup—
O what would that be like!
Surely I'd give it for a nipple a rubber Tacitus°
For a rattle a bag of broken Bach° records
Tack Della Francesca° all over its crib
Sew the Greek alphabet on its bib
And build for its playpen a roofless Parthenon°

No, I doubt I'd be that kind of father
not rural not snow no quiet window
but hot smelly tight New York City
seven flights up, roaches and rats in the walls
a fat Reichian° wife screeching over potatoes Get a job!
And five nose running brats in love with Batman°
And the neighbors all toothless and dry haired
like those hag masses of the 18th century
all wanting to come in and watch TV
The landlord wants his rent
Grocery store Blue Cross Gas & Electric Knights of Columbus°
Impossible to lie back and dream Telephone snow, ghost parking—
No! I should not get married I should never get married!
But—imagine If I were married to a beautiful sophisticated woman

---

79. *Tacitus:* Cornelius Tacitus (c. A.D. 55–c. 117), Roman historian. Since *tacitus* means "silent" in Latin, a "rubber Tacitus" is also a pacifier.

80. *Bach:* Johann Sebastian Bach (1685–1750), German composer, one of the greatest in human history.

81. *Francesca:* Piero della Francesca (1420–1492), Italian Renaissance painter.

83. *Parthenon:* the principal building of the Athenian Acropolis in ancient Greece.

88. *Reichian:* after Wilhelm Reich (1897–1957), founder of a school of psychiatry.

89. *Batman:* American comic strip hero, the force for justice in fictional Gotham City.

94. *Knights of Columbus:* fraternal society of Roman Catholic men, founded in Columbus, Ohio, in 1882.

tall and pale wearing an elegant black dress and long black gloves
holding a cigarette holder in one hand and a highball in the other
and we lived high up in a penthouse with a huge window
from which we could see all of New York and ever farther on
clearer days
No, can't imagine myself married to that pleasant prison dream—

O but what about love? I forget love
not that I am incapable of love
it's just that I see love as odd as wearing shoes—
I never wanted to marry a girl who was like my mother
And Ingrid Bergman° was always impossible
And there's maybe a girl now but she's already married
And I don't like men and—
but there's got to be somebody!
Because what if I'm 60 years old and not married,
all alone in a furnished room with pee stains on my underwear
and everybody else is married! All the universe married but me!

Ah, yet well I know that were a woman possible as I am possible
then marriage would be possible—
Like SHE° in her lonely alien gaud waiting her Egyptian lover
so I wait—bereft of 2,000 years and the bath of life.

1960

BOMB

Budger of history Brake of time You Bomb
Toy of universe Grandest of all snatched-sky I cannot hate you
Do I hate the mischievous thunderbolt the jawbone of an ass
The bumpy club of One Million B.C. the mace the flail the axe
Catapult Da Vinci tomahawk Cochise flintlock Kidd dagger Rathbone
Ah and the sad desperate gun of Verlaine Pushkin Dillinger Bogart°
And hath not St. Michael a burning sword St. George a lance David a sling
Bomb you are as cruel as man makes you and you're no crueller than cancer

---

108. *Ingrid Bergman:* (1915–1982), Swedish actress whose American films included *Casablanca* and *Notorious.*

117. *SHE:* title character of H. Rider Haggard novel *She* (1887), who obtains eternal youth by bathing in a pillar of fire and then waits thousands of years for her lover to return.

5–6. *Bogart:* Leonardo Da Vinci (1452–1519), the Italian Renaissance genius whose work ranged from painting to weapons design; Cochise (d. 1874), American Apache chief who fiercely resisted white settlement on his ancestral lands; William (Captain) Kidd (c. 1645–1701), Scottish merchant and pirate; Basil Rathbone (1892–1967), film actor who played numerous villains as well as Sherlock Holmes; Paul Verlaine (1844–1896), French poet who shot the young poet Rimbaud in the wrist when their affair ended; Alexander Pushkin (1799–1837), Russian poet who killed a French royalist in a duel; John Dillinger (1903–1934), American gangster; Humphrey Bogart (1899–1957), American film actor who played both heroes and hoodlums.

All man hates you   they'd rather die by car-crash   lightning   drowning
Falling off a roof   electric-chair   heart-attack   old age   old age   O Bomb
They'd rather die by anything but you   Death's finger is free-lance
Not up to man whether you boom or not   Death has long since distributed its
categorical blue   I sing thee Bomb   Death's extravagance   Death's jubilee
Gem of Death's supremest blue   The flyer will crash   his death will differ
with the climber who'll fall   To die by cobra is not to die by bad pork
Some die by swamp   some by sea   and some by the bushy-haired man in the night
O there are deaths like witches of Arc°   Scarey deaths like Boris Karloff°
No-feeling deaths like birth-death   sadless deaths like old pain Bowery
Abandoned deaths   like Capital Punishment   stately deaths like senators
And unthinkable deaths like Harpo Marx°   girls on Vogue covers   my own
I do not know just how horrible Bombdeath is   I can only imagine
Yet no other death I know has so laughable a preview   I scope
a city   New York City   streaming   starkeyed   subway shelter
Scores and scores   A fumble of humanity   High heels bend
Hats whelming away   Youth forgetting their combs
Ladies not knowing what to do   with their shopping bags
Unperturbed gum machines   Yet dangerous 3rd rail
Ritz Brothers°   from the Bronx   caught in the A train
The smiling Schenley poster° will always smile
Impish Death   Satyr Bomb   Bombdeath
Turtles exploding over Istanbul
The jaguar's flying foot
soon to sink in arctic snow
Penguins plunged against the Sphinx
The top of the Empire State
arrowed in a broccoli field in Sicily
Eiffel shaped like a C in Magnolia Gardens
St. Sophia° peeling over Sudan
O athletic Death   Sportive Bomb
The temples of ancient times
their grand ruin ceased
Electrons   Protons   Neutrons
gathering Hesperean hair°
walking the dolorous golf of Arcady

---

17. *witches of Arc:* the French national heroine Joan of Arc (c. 1412–1431) was tried as a witch and condemned to death by the Inquisition.

17. *Karloff:* (1887–1969), American film actor known for his horror films.

20. *Marx:* (1888–1964), one of the Marx brothers film comedy team.

28. *Ritz Brothers:* zany comic trio, Al (1901–1965), Jim (1903–1985), and Harry (1906–1986), who were in many feature films.

29. *Schenley poster:* whiskey ad, perhaps seen on the "A train," a New York subway.

38. *St. Sophia:* (A.D. 537), the masterpiece of Byzantine architecture.

43. *Hesperean hair:* hair of the Amazons, who, in mythology, once inhabited Hesperia, a large island of Africa.

joining marble helmsmen
entering the final amphitheater
with a hymnody feeling of all Troys
heralding cypressean torches
racing plumes and banners
and yet knowing Homer with a step of grace
Lo the visiting team of Present
the home team of Past
Lyre and tuba together joined
Hark the hotdog soda olive grape
gala galaxy robed and uniformed
commissary   O the happy stands
Ethereal root and cheer and boo
The billioned all-time attendance
The Zeusian pandemonium
Hermes racing Owens°
the Spitball of Buddha
Christ striking out
Luther° stealing third
Planetarium Death   Hosannah Bomb
Gush the final rose   O Spring Bomb
Come with thy gown of dynamite green
unmenace Nature's inviolate eye
Before you the wimpled Past
behind you the hallooing Future   O Bomb
Bound in the grassy clarion air
like the fox of the tally-ho
thy field the universe thy hedge the geo
Leap Bomb   bound Bomb   frolic zig and zag
The stars a swarm of bees in thy binging bag
Stick angels on your jubilee feet
wheels of rainlight on your bunky seat
You are due and behold you are due
and the heavens are with you
hosannah incalescent glorious liaison
BOMB O havoc antiphony molten cleft BOOM
Bomb mark infinity a sudden furnace
spread thy multitudinous encompassed Sweep
set forth awful agenda
Carrion stars   charnel planets   carcass elements

---

60. *Hermes, Owens:* Hermes, Greek god, patron of messengers; Jesse Owens (1913–1980), U.S. Olympic athlete.

63. *Luther:* Martin Luther (1483–1546), German religious reformer and founder of the Reformation.

Corpse the universe   tee-hee finger-in-the-mouth hop
over its long long dead Nor
From thy nimbled matted spastic eye
exhaust deluges of celestial ghouls
From thy appellational womb
spew birth-gusts of great worms
Rip open your belly Bomb
from your belly outflock vulturic salutations
Battle forth your spangled hyena finger stumps
along the brink of Paradise
O Bomb   O final Pied Piper
both sun and firefly behind your shock waltz
God abandoned mock-nude
beneath His thin false-talc'd apocalypse
He cannot hear thy flute's
happy-the-day profanations
He is spilled deaf into the Silencer's warty ear
His Kingdom an eternity of crude wax
Clogged clarions untrumpet Him
Sealed angels unsing Him
A thunderless God   A dead God
O Bomb   thy BOOM His tomb
That I lean forward on a desk of science
an astrologer dabbling in dragon prose
half-smart about wars   bombs   especially bombs
That I am unable to hate what is necessary to love
That I can't exist in a world that consents
a child in a park   a man dying in an electric-chair
That I am able to laugh at all things
all that I know and do not know   thus to conceal my pain
That I say I am a poet and therefore love all man
knowing my words to be the acquainted prophecy of all men
and my unwords no less an acquaintanceship
That I am manifold
a man pursuing the big lies of gold
or a poet roaming in bright ashes
or that which I imagine myself to be
a shark-toothed sleep   a man-eater of dreams
I need not then be all-smart about bombs
Happily so   for if I felt bombs were caterpillars
I'd doubt not they'd become butterflies
There is a hell for bombs
They're there   I see them there
They sit in bits and sing songs
mostly German songs

and two very long American songs
and they wish there were more songs
especially Russian and Chinese songs
and some more very long American songs
Poor little Bomb that'll never be
an Eskimo song   I love thee
I want to put a lollipop
in thy furcal mouth
A wig of Goldilocks on thy baldy bean
and have you skip with me Hansel and Gretel
along the Hollywoodian screen
O Bomb in which all lovely things
moral and physical anxiously participate
O fairyflake plucked from the
grandest universe tree
O piece of heaven which gives
both mountain and anthill a sun
I am standing before your fantastic lily door
I bring you Midgardian°   roses   Arcadian° musk
Reputed cosmetics from the girls of heaven
Welcome me   fear not thy opened door
nor thy cold ghost's grey memory
nor the pimps of indefinite weather
their cruel terrestrial thaw
Oppenheimer is seated
in the dark pocket of Light
Fermi is dry in Death's Mozambique
Einstein° his mythmouth
a barnacled wreath on the moon-squid's head
Let me in   Bomb   rise from that pregnant-rat corner
nor fear the raised-broom nations of the world
O Bomb I love you
I want to kiss your clank   eat your boom
You are a paean   an acme of scream
a lyric hat of Mister Thunder
O resound thy tanky knees
BOOM   BOOM   BOOM   BOOM   BOOM
BOOM ye skies and BOOM ye suns

---

148. *Midgardian:* of Midgard, Middle Earth, the land where humans live, according to Norse mythology.

148. *Arcadian:* of Arcadia; in mythology, an ideal pastoral land.

154–157. *Oppenheimer . . . Einstein:* J. Robert Oppenheimer (1904–1967), physicist who directed the Manhattan Project laboratory in Los Alamos, New Mexico, where the atomic bomb was designed and built; Enrico Fermi (1901–1954), Nobel laureate physicist who helped develop the atomic bomb; Albeit Einstein (1879–1955), mathematical physicist whose theoretical work revised our understanding of the universe and who helped inspire the Manhattan Project.

BOOM BOOM ye moons ye stars BOOM
nights ye BOOM ye days ye BOOM
BOOM BOOM ye winds ye clouds ye rains
go BANG ye lakes ye oceans BING
Barracuda BOOM and cougar BOOM
Ubangi BANG orangoutang
BING BANG BONG BOOM bee bear baboon
ye BANG ye BONG ye BING
the tail the fin the wing
Yes Yes into our midst a bomb will fall
Flowers will leap in joy their roots aching
Fields will kneel proud beneath the halleluyahs of the wind
Pinkbombs will blossom Elkbombs will perk their ears
Ah many a bomb that day will awe the bird a gentle look
Yet not enough to say a bomb will fall
or even contend celestial fire goes out
Know that the earth will madonna the Bomb
that in the hearts of men to come more bombs will be born
magisterial bombs wrapped in ermine all beautiful
and they'll sit plunk on earth's grumpy empires
fierce with moustaches of gold

1958

ETHERIDGE KNIGHT (1931–1991)

Knight was born in Corinth, Mississippi. He dropped out of school in the eighth grade and joined the army in 1947. He was trained as a medical technician before being discharged in 1957 after receiving a serious shrapnel wound in Korea. Thereafter he battled drug and alcohol addiction, and was arrested for robbery in 1960. In prison he began to write, encouraged by poets Gwendolyn Brooks, Dudley Randall, and Sonia Sanchez. He published his first book in 1968, the year of his release from Indiana State Prison, and it made a general thematics out of contrasts between freedom and imprisonment. His poetry regularly combines traditional metrics with elements from African American culture. Knight continued to write and teach until his death from lung cancer.

HAIKU

1

Eastern guard tower
glints in sunset; convicts rest
like lizards on rocks.

4

To write a blues song
is to regiment riots
and pluck gems from graves.

9

Making jazz swing in
Seventeen syllables AIN'T
No square poet's job.

1968

HARD ROCK RETURNS TO PRISON FROM THE HOSPITAL FOR THE CRIMINAL INSANE

Hard Rock / was / "known not to take no shit
From nobody," and he had the scars to prove it:
Split purple lips, lumbed ears, welts above
His yellow eyes, and one long scar that cut

Across his temple and plowed through a thick
Canopy of kinky hair.

The WORD / was / that Hard Rock wasn't a mean nigger
Anymore, that the doctors had bored a hole in his head,
Cut out part of his brain, and shot electricity
Through the rest. When they brought Hard Rock back,
Handcuffed and chained, he was turned loose,
Like a freshly gelded stallion, to try his new status.
And we all waited and watched, like a herd of sheep,
To see if the WORD was true.

As we waited we wrapped ourselves in the cloak
Of his exploits: "Man, the last time, it took eight
Screws° to put him in the Hole."° "Yeah, remember when he
Smacked the captain with his dinner tray?" "He set
The record for time in the Hole—67 straight days!"
"Ol Hard Rock! man, that's one crazy nigger."
And then the jewel of a myth that Hard Rock had once bit
A screw on the thumb and poisoned him with syphilitic spit.

The testing came, to see if Hard Rock was really tame.
A hillbilly called him a black son of a bitch
And didn't lose his teeth, a screw who knew Hard Rock
From before shook him down and barked in his face.
And Hard Rock did *nothing.* Just grinned and looked silly,
His eyes empty like knot holes in a fence.

And even after we discovered that it took Hard Rock
Exactly 3 minutes to tell you his first name,
We told ourselves that he had just wised up,
Was being cool; but we could not fool ourselves for long,
And we turned away, our eyes on the ground. Crashed.
He had been our Destroyer,° the doer of things
We dreamed of doing but could not bring ourselves to do,
The fears of years, like a biting whip,
Had cut deep bloody grooves
Across our backs.

1968

---

17. *Screws:* prison guards.

17. *the Hole:* solitary confinement, typically a dark cell away from the rest of the prison population.

34. *Destroyer:* in part, an allusion to Ras the Destroyer, a figure in the Rastafarian religion.

THE IDEA OF ANCESTRY

I

Taped to the wall of my cell are 47 pictures: 47 black
faces: my father, mother, grandmothers (1 dead), grand-
fathers (both dead), brothers, sisters, uncles, aunts,
cousins (1st & 2nd), nieces, and nephews. They stare
across the space at me sprawling on my bunk. I know
their dark eyes, they know mine. I know their style,
they know mine. I am all of them, they are all of me;
they are farmers, I am a thief, I am me, they are thee.

I have at one time or another been in love with my mother,
1 grandmother, 2 sisters, 2 aunts (1 went to the asylum),
and 5 cousins. I am now in love with a 7-yr-old niece
(she sends me letters written in large block print, and
her picture is the only one that smiles at me).

I have the same name as 1 grandfather, 3 cousins, 3 nephews,
and 1 uncle. The uncle disappeared when he was 15, just took
off and caught a freight (they say). He's discussed each year
when the family has a reunion, he causes uneasiness in
the clan, he is an empty space. My father's mother, who is 93
and who keeps the Family Bible with everybody's birth dates
(and death dates) in it, always mentions him. There is no
place in her Bible for "whereabouts unknown."

2

Each fall the graves of my grandfathers call me, the brown
hills and red gullies of mississippi send out their electric
messages, galvanizing my genes. Last yr / like a salmon quitting
the cold ocean-leaping and bucking up his birthstream / I
hitchhiked my way from LA with 16 caps° in my pocket and a
monkey on my back. And I almost kicked it with the kinfolks.
I walked barefooted in my grandmother's backyard / I smelled the
old
land and the woods / I sipped cornwhiskey from fruit jars with the
men /
I flirted with the women / I had a ball till the caps ran out
and my habit came down. That night I looked at my grandmother
and split / my guts were screaming for junk / but I was almost

---

26. *caps:* heroin sold on the street in quantities appropriate for a fix.

contented / I had almost caught up with me.
(The next day in Memphis I cracked a croaker's crib° for a fix.)

This yr there is a gray stone wall damming my stream, and when the falling leaves stir my genes, I pace my cell or flop on my bunk and stare at 47 black faces across the space. I am all of them, they are all of me, I am me, they are thee, and I have no children to float in the space between.

1968

A POEM FOR MYSELF

(or Blues for a Mississippi Black Boy)

I was born in Mississippi;
I walked barefooted thru the mud.
Born black in Mississippi,
Walked barefooted thru the mud.
But, when I reached the age of twelve
I left that place for good.
Said my daddy chopped cotton
And he drank his liquor straight.
When I left that Sunday morning
He was leaning on the barnyard gate.
Left her standing in the yard
With the sun shining in her eyes.
And I headed North
As straight as the Wild Goose Flies,
I been to Detroit & Chicago
Been to New York city too.
I been to Detroit & Chicago
Been to New York city too.
Said I done strolled all those funky avenues
I'm still the same old black boy with the same old blues.
Going back to Mississippi
This time to stay for good
Going back to Mississippi
This time to stay for good—
Gonna be free in Mississippi
Or dead in the Mississippi mud.

1980

36. *croaker's crib:* drug seller's home.

FOR MALCOLM, A YEAR AFTER°

Compose for Red° a proper verse;
Adhere to foot and strict iamb;
Control the burst of angry words
Or they might boil and break the dam.
Or they might boil and overflow
And drench me, drown me, drive me mad.
So swear no oath, so shed no tear,
And sing no song blue Baptist sad.
Evoke no image, stir no flame,
And spin no yarn across the air.
Make empty anglo tea lace words—
Make them dead white and dry bone bare.

Compose a verse for Malcolm man,
And make it rime and make it prim.
The verse will die—as all men do—
But not the memory of him!
Death might come singing sweet like C,
Or knocking like the old folk say,
The moon and stars may pass away,
But not the anger of that day.

1966

TELEVISION SPEAKS

Television speaks:
"Blacks die on Soweto Streets!"
On Cape Cod, indolents
Buy "'burgers" and sticky sweets!

1969

FOR BLACK POETS WHO THINK OF SUICIDE

Black Poets should live—not leap
From steel bridges (like the white boys do).
Black Poets should live—not lay
Their necks on railroad tracks (like the white boys do).
Black Poets should seek—but not search too much
In sweet dark caves, nor hunt for snipe
Down psychic trails (like the white boys do).

---

poem title: Malcolm X (1925–1965), charismatic African American political and religious leader, assassinated in 1965; see the notes to Welton Smith's poem "Malcolm."

1. *Red:* Malcolm X's nickname.

For Black Poets belong to Black People. Are
The Flutes of Black Lovers. Are
The Organs of Black Sorrows. Are
The Trumpets of Black Warriors.
Let All Black Poets die as Trumpets,
And be buried in the dust of marching feet.

1969

SYLVIA PLATH (1932–1963)

Born in Boston, Massachusetts, Plath grew up in Winthrop. She was raised by her mother after her father died of complications from diabetes when she was eight. Plath was educated at Smith College and at Newnham College of Cambridge University. Even before attending college she was publishing poems and journalism; her academic and literary achievements, however, were in conflict with the traditional view of women's roles that prevailed in the 1950s, and she was unable to live comfortably with the contradictions. In 1953, after serving a month as a college guest editor at the New York fashion magazine *Mademoiselle,* she had a breakdown and was unwisely subjected to electric shock therapy. She then attempted suicide and was hospitalized for six months, events she later adapted for her novel *The Bell Jar* (1963). It was while in England two years later, from 1955 to 1956, that she met her husband, the poet Ted Hughes, who was for some time the controversial shepherd of her posthumous career.

Plath and Hughes came to the United States in 1957, and she taught at Smith for a year, also taking a poetry writing seminar offered by Robert Lowell at Boston University; Anne Sexton was enrolled as well. The couple returned to England in 1959 and she published her first book of poems the following year. The marriage was in difficulty, with each individual's ambitions sometimes putting them at odds with one another despite willingness to support the other's career. In the fall of 1962, after Plath learned that Hughes had been unfaithful, they separated.

It was a brutally cold winter and not easy to maintain a household. Yet the freedom enabled her to write. That fall, she began writing with an astonishing intensity, shaping nearly overwhelming emotions into flawlessly crafted poems. Into a crucible went details of her own life and the horrors of modern history; she fused them into a harrowing, ironic persona, an archetype of a modern woman in an ecstatic crisis of gendered self-recognition amidst the ruins of history. In a few short months, these astonishingly lucid poems—furious, sardonic, defiant, and exquisitely musical—established a benchmark against which every American poet wishing to tell a brutal truth would have to measure himself or herself. Then, apparently, she broke through into a kind of icy calm, or so some of the final poems suggest. In December, she moved from Devon to a London apartment with her two children. The whole experience had overwhelmed her, and she took her own life in February 1963. Much more than with male poets who committed suicide—Crane, Berryman, among others—critics have tended to read Plath's poems in the light of her death, as though she were writing against some inexorable deadline. Yet the poems are a personal and cultural triumph, not funeral ornaments. Her suicide comes afterward and tells us nothing about the poems, which are about all of us, not about her alone.

THE COLOSSUS°

I shall never get you put together entirely,
Pieced, glued, and properly jointed.
Mule-bray, pig-grunt and bawdy cackles
Proceed from your great lips.
It's worse than a barnyard.

Perhaps you consider yourself an oracle,
Mouthpiece of the dead, or of some god or other.
Thirty years now I have labored
To dredge the silt from your throat.
I am none the wiser.

Scaling little ladders with gluepots and pails of Lysol
I crawl like an ant in mourning
Over the weedy acres of your brow
To mend the immense skull-plates and clear
The bald, white tumuli° of your eyes.

A blue sky out of the Oresteia°
Arches above us. O father, all by yourself
You are pithy and historical as the Roman Forum.
I open my lunch on a hill of black cypress.
Your fluted bones and acanthine° hair are littered

In their old anarchy to the horizon-line.
It would take more than a lightning-stroke
To create such a ruin.
Nights, I squat in the cornucopia
Of your left ear, out of the wind,

Counting the red stars and those of plum-color.
The sun rises under the pillar of your tongue.
My hours are married to shadow.
No longer do I listen for the scrape of a keel
On the blank stones of the landing.

1959

---

poem title: the Colossus was a gigantic bronze statue of the Sun god Apollo, which stood at the harbor entrance of Rhodes, a Greek seaport; it was built about 280 B.C.

15. *tumuli:* ancient grave mounds.

16. *Oresteia:* a trilogy of plays (*Agamemnon, Libation Bearers,* and *Eumenides*) by the Greek tragic poet Aeschylus (c. 525–456 B.C.), in which lethal family violence passes from generation to generation.

20. *acanthine:* curved and piled like the leaves of the acanthus plant, a design used on the capitals of Corinthian columns in Greece.

THE BEE MEETING°

Who are these people at the bridge to meet me? They are the villagers—
The rector, the midwife, the sexton,° the agent for bees.°
In my sleeveless summery dress I have no protection,
And they are all gloved and covered, why did nobody tell me?
They are smiling and taking out veils tacked to ancient hats.

I am nude as a chicken neck, does nobody love me?
Yes, here is the secretary of bees with her white shop smock,
Buttoning the cuffs at my wrists and the slit from my neck to my knees.
Now I am milkweed silk, the bees will not notice.
They will not smell my fear, my fear, my fear.

Which is the rector now, is it that man in black?
Which is the midwife, is that her blue coat?
Everybody is nodding a square black head, they are knights in visors,
Breastplates of cheesecloth knotted under the armpits.
Their smiles and their voices are changing. I am led through a beanfield.

Strips of tinfoil winking like people,
Feather dusters fanning their hands in a sea of bean flowers,
Creamy bean flowers with black eyes and leaves like bored hearts.
Is it blood clots the tendrils are dragging up that string?
No, no, it is scarlet flowers that will one day be edible.

Now they are giving me a fashionable white straw Italian hat
And a black veil that molds to my face, they are making me one of them.
They are leading me to the shorn grove, the circle of hives.
Is it the hawthorn° that smells so sick?
The barren body of hawthorn, etherizing its children.

Is it some operation that is taking place?
It is the surgeon my neighbors are waiting for,

---

poem title: this is the first poem of a five-poem sequence—"The Bee Meeting," "The Arival of the Bee Box," "Stings," "The Swarm," and "Wintering."

3. *sexton:* a church caretaker, bellringer, and gravedigger.

3. *bees:* Plath's father, Otto Plath (1885–1940), was a biologist and author of *Bumble Bees and Their Ways* (1934). While living in Devon, England, she kept a hive of bees and attended meetings of the local beekeepers association.

25. *hawthorn:* a spring shrub of the rose family, with fragrant flowers and small red fruits.

This apparition in a green helmet,
Shining gloves and white suit.
Is it the butcher, the grocer, the postman, someone I know?

I cannot run, I am rooted, and the gorse° hurts me
With its yellow purses, its spiky armory.
I could not run without having to run forever.
The white hive is snug as a virgin,
Sealing off her brood° cells, her honey, and quietly humming.

Smoke rolls and scarves in the grove.
The mind of the hive thinks this is the end of everything.
Here they come, the outriders, on their hysterical elastics.°
If I stand very still, they will think I am cow-parsley,
A gullible head untouched by their animosity,

Not even nodding, a personage in a hedgerow.
The villagers open the chambers, they are hunting the queen.
Is she hiding, is she eating honey? She is very clever.
She is old, old, old, she must live another year, and she knows it.
While in their fingerjoint cells the new virgins

Dream of a duel they will win inevitably,
A curtain of wax dividing them from the bride flight,
The upflight of the murderess° into a heaven that loves her.
The villagers are moving the virgins, there will be no killing.
The old queen does not show herself, is she so ungrateful?

I am exhausted, I am exhausted—
Pillar of white in a blackout of knives.
I am the magician's girl who does not flinch.
The villagers are untying their disguises, they are shaking hands.
Whose is that long white box in the grove, what have they
    accomplished,
    why am I cold.

October 3, 1962

---

32. *gorse:* a spiny, yellow-flowered shrub.
36. *brood*: breeding.
39. *elastics:* the bees that left the hive return quickly.
49. *murderess:* the queen bee.

THE ARRIVAL OF THE BEE BOX

I ordered this, this clean wood box
Square as a chair and almost too heavy to lift.
I would say it was the coffin of a midget
Or a square baby
Were there not such a din in it.

The box is locked, it is dangerous.
I have to live with it overnight
And I can't keep away from it.
There are no windows, so I can't see what is in there.
There is only a little grid, no exit.

I put my eye to the grid.
It is dark, dark,
With the swarmy feeling of African hands
Minute and shrunk for export,
Black on black, angrily clambering.

How can I let them out?
It is the noise that appalls me most of all,
The unintelligible syllables.
It is like a Roman mob,
Small, taken one by one, but my god, together!

I lay my ear to furious Latin.
I am not a Caesar.
I have simply ordered a box of maniacs.
They can be sent back.
They can die, I need feed them nothing, I am the owner.

I wonder how hungry they are.
I wonder if they would forget me
If I just undid the locks and stood back and turned into a tree.
There is the laburnum,° its blond colonnades,
And the petticoats of the cherry.

They might ignore me immediately
In my moon suit and funeral veil.
I am no source of honey
So why should they turn on me?
Tomorrow I will be sweet God, I will set them free.

The box is only temporary.

October 4, 1962

---

29. *laburnum:* a European tree whose seed pods are poisonous.

STINGS

Bare-handed, I hand the combs.
The man in white smiles, bare-handed,
Our cheesecloth gauntlets neat and sweet,
The throats of our wrists brave lilies.
He and I

Have a thousand clean cells between us,
Eight combs of yellow cups,
And the hive itself a teacup,
White with pink flowers on it,
With excessive love I enameled it

Thinking 'Sweetness, sweetness'.
Brood cells gray as the fossils of shells
Terrify me, they seem so old.
What am I buying, wormy mahogany?
Is there any queen at all in it?

If there is, she is old,
Her wings torn shawls, her long body
Rubbed of its plush—
Poor and bare and unqueenly and even shameful.
I stand in a column

Of winged, unmiraculous women,
Honey-drudgers.°
I am no drudge
Though for years I have eaten dust
And dried plates with my dense hair.

And seen my strangeness evaporate,
Blue dew from dangerous skin.
Will they hate me,
These women who only scurry,
Whose news is the open cherry, the open clover?

It is almost over.
I am in control.
Here is my honey-machine,
It will work without thinking,
Opening, in spring, like an industrious virgin

22. *Honey-drudgers:* like the worker bees who make honey for the hive.

To scour the creaming crests
As the moon, for its ivory powders, scours the sea.
A third person is watching.
He has nothing to do with the bee-seller or with me.
Now he is gone

In eight great bounds, a great scapegoat.
Here is his slipper, here is another,
And here the square of white linen
He wore instead of a hat.
He was sweet,

The sweat of his efforts a rain
Tugging the world to fruit.
The bees found him out,
Molding onto his lips like lies,
Complicating his features.

They thought death was worth it, but I
Have a self to recover, a queen.
Is she dead, is she sleeping?
Where has she been,
With her lion-red body, her wings of glass?

Now she is flying
More terrible than she ever was, red
Scar in the sky, red comet
Over the engine that killed her—
The mausoleum, the wax house.

October 6, 1962

THE SWARM

Somebody is shooting at something in our town—
A dull pom, pom in the Sunday street.
Jealousy can open the blood,
It can make black roses.
Who are they shooting at?

It is you the knives are out for
At Waterloo, Waterloo, Napoleon,°

---

7. *Napoleon Bonaparte:* (1769–1821), French general and emperor, a titanic figure in European history. He was defeated at the Battle of Waterloo in 1815 and exiled on the island of Elba off the Italian coast.

The hump of Elba on your short back,
And the snow, marshaling its brilliant cutlery
Mass after mass, saying Shh!

Shh! These are chess people you play with,
Still figures of ivory.
The mud squirms with throats,
Stepping stones for French bootsoles.
The gilt and pink domes of Russia melt and float off

In the furnace of greed. Clouds, clouds.
So the swarm balls and deserts
Seventy feet up, in a black pine tree.
It must be shot down. Pom! Pom!
So dumb it thinks bullets are thunder.

It thinks they are the voice of God
Condoning the beak, the claw, the grin of the dog
Yellow-haunched, a pack-dog,
Grinning over its bone of ivory
Like the pack, the pack, like everybody.

The bees have got so far. Seventy feet high!
Russia, Poland and Germany!
The mild hills, the same old magenta
Fields shrunk to a penny
Spun into a river, the river crossed.

The bees argue, in their black ball,
A flying hedgehog, all prickles.
The man with gray hands stands under the honeycomb
Of their dream, the hived station
Where trains, faithful to their steel arcs,

Leave and arrive, and there is no end to the country.
Pom! Pom! They fall
Dismembered, to a tod° of ivy.
So much for the charioteers, the outriders, the Grand Army!
A red tatter, Napoleon!

The last badge of victory.
The swarm is knocked into a cocked straw hat.

38. *tod:* clump.

Elba, Elba, bleb° on the sea!
The white busts of marshals, admirals, generals
Worming themselves into niches.

How instructive this is!
The dumb, banded bodies
Walking the plank draped with Mother France's upholstery
Into a new mausoleum,
An ivory palace, a crotch pine.

The man with gray hands smiles—
The smile of a man of business, intensely practical.
They are not hands at all
But asbestos receptacles.
Pom! Pom! They would have killed *me*.'

Stings big as drawing pins!
It seems bees have a notion of honor,
A black intractable mind.
Napoleon is pleased, he is pleased with everything.
O Europe! O ton of honey!

October 7, 1962

WINTERING

This is the easy time, there is nothing doing.
I have whirled the midwife's extractor,°
I have my honey,
Six jars of it,
Six cat's eyes in the wine cellar,

Wintering in a dark without window
At the heart of the house
Next to the last tenant's rancid jam
And the bottles of empty glitters—
Sir So-and-so's gin.

This is the room I have never been in.
This is the room I could never breathe in.
The black bunched in there like a bat,
No light
But the torch and its faint

---

43. *bleb:* small blister.
2. *midwife's extractor:* tool used to remove honey from beehives.

Chinese yellow on appalling objects—
Black asininity. Decay.
Possession.
It is they who own me.
Neither cruel nor indifferent,

Only ignorant.
This is the time of hanging on for the bees—the bees
So slow I hardly know them,
Filing like soldiers
To the syrup tin

To make up for the honey I've taken.
Tate and Lyle keeps them going,
The refined snow.
It is Tate and Lyle° they live on, instead of flowers.
They take it. The cold sets in.

Now they ball in a mass,
Black
Mind against all that white.
The smile of the snow is white.
It spreads itself out, a mile-long body of Meissen,°

Into which, on warm days,
They can only carry their dead.
The bees are all women,
Maids and the long royal lady.
They have got rid of the men,

The blunt, clumsy stumblers, the boors.
Winter is for women—
The woman, still at her knitting,
At the cradle of Spanish walnut,
Her body a bulb in the cold and too dumb to think.

Will the hive survive, will the gladiolas
Succeed in banking their fires
To enter another year?
What will they taste of, the Christmas roses?
The bees are flying. They taste the spring.

October 9, 1962

---

29. *Tate and Lyle:* manufacturers of a commercial bee food and of syrup for people.

35. *Meissen:* a delicate porcelain ware originally made in Meissen, a German city on the Elbe River, in the eighteenth century.

DADDY°

You do not do, you do not do
Any more, black shoe
In which I have lived like a foot
For thirty years, poor and white,
Barely daring to breathe or Achoo.

Daddy, I have had to kill you.
You died before I had time—
Marble-heavy, a bag full of God,
Ghastly statue with one gray toe°
Big as a Frisco seal

And a head in the freakish Atlantic
Where it pours bean green over blue
In the waters off beautiful Nauset.°
I used to pray to recover you.
Ach, du.°

In the German tongue, in the Polish town°
Scraped flat by the roller
Of wars, wars, wars.
But the name of the town is common.
My Polack friend

Says there are a dozen or two.
So I never could tell where you
Put your foot, your root,
I never could talk to you.
The tongue stuck in my jaw.

It stuck in a barb wire snare.
Ich, ich, ich, ich,°

---

poem title: Plath's note—"The poem is spoken by a girl with an Electra complex [a tendency for a daughter to be attached to her father and hostile to her mother]. Her father died while she thought he was God. Her case is complicated by the fact that her father was also a Nazi and her mother very possibly part Jewish. In the daughter the two strains marry and paralyze each other—she has to act out the awful little allegory before she is free of it." Plath uses details from her own and her father's life, such as his German heritage, to invoke crucial moments of modern history and create s general figure of paternity that is no longer straightforwardly autobiographical. Plath's father was neither a Nazi nor a Nazi sympathizer; Plath was not Jewish. Yet both she and all of the rest of us are linked to the monstrous version of masculinity that fascism promoted.

9. *gray toe:* the result of diabetes-induced gangrene; Plath's father died from the disease.

13. *Nauset:* the Native American name for Eastham, Cape Cod, on the Massachusetts coast.

15. *Ach'du:* (German) "Ah, you."

16. *Polish town:* Grasbow, Poland, where Plath's father was born. He was of German descent.

27. *Ich . . . ich:* (German) "I, I, I, I."

I could hardly speak.
I thought every German was you.
And the language obscene

An engine, an engine
Chuffing° me off like a Jew.
A Jew to Dachau, Auschwitz, Belsen.°
I began to talk like a Jew.
I think I may well be a Jew.

The snows of the Tyrol,° the clear beer of Vienna
Are not very pure or true.
With my gipsy ancestress and my weird luck
And my Taroc pack° and my Taroc pack
I may be a bit of a Jew.

I have always been scared of *you,*
With your Luftwaffe,° your gobbledygoo.
And your neat mustache
And your Aryan° eye, bright blue.
Panzer-man,° panzer-man, O You—

Not God but a swastika°
So black no sky could squeak through.
Every woman adores a Fascist,
The boot in the face, the brute
Brute heart of a brute like you.

You stand at the blackboard,° daddy,
In the picture I have of you,
A cleft in your chin instead of your foot
But no less a devil for that, no not
Any less the black man who

---

32. *Chuffing:* chugging.

33. *Dachau, Auschwitz, Belsen:* Nazi concentration camps in Poland (Auschwitz) and Germany; the Germans murdered six million Jews—men, women, and children—during World War II, most of them at these and other death camps. This remains the largest and most elaborately mechanized program of genocide in human history.

36. *Tyrol:* Tirol, an Alpine region in Austria and northern Italy; the snow there is famous for being as pure as the beer in Vienna is clear.

39. *Taroc pack:* a variant of Tarot, ancient fortune-telling cards.

42. *Luftwaffe:* the German air force.

44. *Aryan:* in Nazi ideology, the "superior" race—blue-eyed, blond-haired Nordic people of German stock. Non-Aryans, including Jews, Blacks, Slavs, and Gypsies, were considered subhuman.

45. *Panzer:* (German) armor, especially the Nazi tank division in World War II.

46. *swastika:* the Nazi symbol.

51. *blackboard:* Plath's father taught biology at Boston University.

Bit my pretty red heart in two.
I was ten when they buried you.
At twenty I tried to die°
And get back, back, back to you.
I thought even the bones would do.

But they pulled me out of the sack,
And they stuck me together with glue.
And then I knew what to do.
I made a model of you,
A man in black with a Meinkampf° look

And a love of the rack and the screw.
And I said I do, I do.
So daddy, I'm finally through.
The black telephone's off at the root,
The voices just can't worm through.

If I've killed one man, I've killed two—
The vampire who said he was you
And drank my blood for a year,
Seven years, if you want to know.
Daddy, you can lie back now.

There's a stake in your fat black heart
And the villagers never liked you.
They are dancing and stamping on you.
They always *knew* it was you.
Daddy, daddy, you bastard, I'm through.

October 12, 1962

ARIEL°

Stasis in darkness.
Then the substanceless blue
Pour of tor° and distances.

God's lioness,
How one we grow,
Pivot of heels and knees!—The furrow

---

58. *I tried to die:* Plath first attempted suicide when she was home from college during summer break.

65. *Meinkampf:* German dictator Adolf Hitler's (1889–1945) early autobiography and manifesto *Mein Kampf* ("My Struggle," 1925) laid out his plans for world domination and detailed the political antagonisms and race hatred that would dominate his dictatorship when he came to power in 1933.

poem title: the name of the horse Plath rode in Devon, England, during the two years she lived there; a Hebrew name for Jerusalem meaning "lion of God"; and the name of the sprite of fire and air in Shakespeare's *The Tempest.*

3. *tor:* a high, craggy hill.

Splits and passes, sister to
The brown arc
Of the neck I cannot catch,

Nigger-eye
Berries cast dark
Hooks—

Black sweet blood mouthfuls,
Shadows.
Something else

Hauls me through air—
Thighs, hair;
Flakes from my heels.

White
Godiva,° I unpeel—
Dead hands, dead stringencies.

And now I
Foam to wheat, a glitter of seas.
The child's cry

Melts in the wall.
And I
Am the arrow,

The dew that flies
Suicidal, at one with the drive
Into the red

Eye, the cauldron of morning.

October 27, 1962

LADY LAZARUS°

I have done it again.
One year in every ten
I manage it—

20. *Godiva:* Lady Godiva, a noblewoman who supposedly rode naked on horseback through Coventry, England, in 1040 to get feudal obligations and taxes reduced.

poem title: in John 11. 39–44, Jesus raises Lazarus, the brother of Mary, from the dead; Plath is also linking her own suicide attempts with the biblical story and thus in some way saying that to live in our time is necessarily to rise from the dead.

A sort of walking miracle, my skin
Bright as a Nazi lampshade,°
My right foot

A paperweight,
My face a featureless, fine
Jew linen.

Peel off the napkin
O my enemy.
Do I terrify?—

The nose, the eye pits, the full set of teeth?
The sour breath
Will vanish in a day.

Soon, soon the flesh
The grave cave ate will be
At home on me

And I a smiling woman.
I am only thirty.
And like the cat I have nine times to die.

This is Number Three.
What a trash
To annihilate each decade.

What a million filaments.
The peanut-crunching crowd
Shoves in to see

Them unwrap me hand and foot—
The big strip tease.
Gentlemen, ladies

These are my hands
My knees.
I may be skin and bone,

Nevertheless, I am the same, identical woman.
The first time it happened I was ten.
It was an accident.

---

5. *lampshade:* in the World War II German death camps, the Nazis sometimes removed the skin of the people they killed and used it to make lampshades.

The second time I meant
To last it out and not come back at all.
I rocked shut

As a seashell.
They had to call and call
And pick the worms off me like sticky pearls.

Dying
Is an art, like everything else.
I do it exceptionally well.

I do it so it feels like hell.
I do it so it feels real.
I guess you could say I've a call.

It's easy enough to do it in a cell.
It's easy enough to do it and stay put.
It's the theatrical

Comeback in broad day
To the same place, the same face, the same brute
Amused shout:

'A miracle!'
That knocks me out.
There is a charge

For the eyeing of my scars, there is a charge
For the hearing of my heart—
It really goes.

And there is a charge, a very large charge
For a word or a touch
Or a bit of blood

Or a piece of my hair or my clothes.
So, so, Herr Doktor.°
So, Herr Enemy.

I am your opus,
I am your valuable,
The pure gold baby

---

65. *Herr Doktor:* (German) "Mr. Doctor."

That melts to a shriek.
I turn and burn.
Do not think I underestimate your great concern.

Ash, ash—
You poke and stir.
Flesh, bone, there is nothing there—

A cake of soap,
A wedding ring,
A gold filling.°

Herr God, Herr Lucifer
Beware
Beware.°

Out of the ash
I rise° with my red hair
And I eat men like air.

October 23–29, 1962

---

78. *soap / ring / filling:* the Nazis on occasion rendered the bodies of their victims into soap; they consistently removed all jewelry and gold fillings from teeth for themselves, sometimes hoarding it in foreign banks.

81. *Beware:* line 49 of Samuel Taylor Coleridge's (1772–1834) poem "Kubla Khan" reads "And all should cry, Beware! Beware!"

83. *I rise:* like the phoenix, a mythical bird that supposedly sets itself on fire and rises anew from its own ashes.

HENRY DUMAS (1934–1968)

Dumas was born in Sweet Home, Arkansas, where he spent the first ten years of his life. It was long enough to absorb gospel music and the folk traditions of the south. At that point he moved to Harlem, where he lived until joining the Air Force, a stint that included a year in the Middle East. All these experiences found a place in his poetry; "Son of Msippi" recalls his years in the south, while "Knees of a Natural Man" evokes the urban world of New York. He had spent some time at City College and at Rutgers, but never completed a degree. A stronger influence was no doubt his energetic civil rights work in the mid-1960s. In 1967, he took a job as a teacher and counselor at Southern Illinois University, where he met the poet Eugene Redmond. Only a year later, Dumas was gunned down in error by a New York City Transit policeman; it is to Redmond's posthumous editing that we owe his poems and short stories. Since most of Dumas's poetry was not published during his lifetime, the dates offered are speculative. We do, however, know that he was performing "Son of Msippi" and "Black Star Line" at poetry readings during the last year of his life.

SON OF MSIPPI

Up
from Msippi I grew.
(Bare walk and cane stalk
make a hungry belly talk.)
Up
from the river of death.
(Walk bare and stalk cane
make a hungry belly talk.)

Up
from Msippi I grew.
Up
from the river of pain.

Out of the long red earth dipping, rising,
spreading out in deltas and plains,
out of the strong black earth turning
over by the iron plough,

out of the swamp green earth dripping
with moss and snakes,

out of the loins of the leveed lands
muscling its American vein:

the great Father of Waters,
I grew
up,
beside the prickly boll of white,
beside the bone-filled Mississippi
rolling on and on,
breaking over,
cutting off,
ignoring my bleeding fingers.

Bare stalk and sun walk
I hear a boll-weevil talk
cause I grew
up
beside the ox and the bow,
beside the rock church and the shack row,
beside the fox and the crow,
beside the melons and maize,
beside the hound dog,
beside the pink hog,
flea-hunting,
mud-grunting,
cat-fishing,
dog pissing
in the Mississippi
rolling on and on,
ignoring the colored coat I spun
of cotton fibers.

Cane-sweat river-boat
nigger-bone floating.

Up from Msippi
I grew,
wailing a song with every strain.

Woman gone woe man too
baby cry rent-pause daddy flew.

c. 1967

KEF 24°

lay sixteen bales down in front on the plank
let me set and bay at the houndog moon

---

poem title: kef is a term for marijuana; Dumas has several poems in his "kef" series.

lay sixteen bales down of the cotton flank
pray with me brothers that the pink
boss dont sweat me too soon
beat my leg in a round nigger peg
lord have mercy on my black pole
lay sixteen bales in the even row
let me sweat and cuss my roustabout tune
lord have mercy on my shrinkin back
let me go with the jesus mule
lay sixteen bales for the warp and loom
beat a nigger down and bury his soul
boss dont sweat me too soon
pray with me brothers that I hold my cool
lord have mercy on this long black leg
let me ride on the jesus mule
lay sixteen bales of white fuzz down
lay sixteen tales of how I got around
lord have mercy on this sweat and stink
lord have mercy
lay sixteen bales
pray brothers
beat down
lord have
let me
lord lord
brothers
the houndog moon
howl jesus,
howl!

c. 1967

KEF 16

Down near the levee where the river once
broke through the sand and the dirt,

Down where the north fish drown in muddy
waters, where mountains become silt heaps,

I used to sit and throw out the wiggling worm,
as I dreamed of giant catfish asleep beneath

the blood.

c. 1967

FISH

Catfish niggerfish
low in the creek
Catfish blackfish
none all week

baitworm doughball
put your glad rags on
hook me a catfish ninefeet tall.

niggerspit catfish bit
only was a crawdad hole

good bait sent catfish went
must be fishin the whiteman's hole

c. 1967

KNEES OF A NATURAL MAN

(for Jay Wright)

my ole man took me to the fulton fish market
we walk around in the guts and the scales

my ole man show me a dead fish, eyes like throat spit
he say "you hongry boy?" i say "naw, not yet"

my ole man show me how to pick the leavings
he say people throw away fish that not rotten

we scaling on our knees back uptown on lenox
sold five fish, keepin one for the pot

my ole man copped a bottle of wine
he say, "boy, build me a fire out in the lot"

backyard cat climbin up my leg for fish
i make a fire in the ash can

my ole man come when he smell fish
frank williams is with him, they got wine

my ole man say "the boy cotch the big one"
he tell big lie and slap me on the head

i give the guts to the cat and take me some wine
we walk around the sparks like we in hell

my ole man is laughin and coughin up wine
he say "you hongry boy?" i say "naw, not yet"

next time i go to fulton fish market
first thing i do is take a long drink of wine

c. 1967

LOW DOWN DOG BLUES

Went to my baby's back door, my baby say she aint home
Yeah my baby holler she just aint home
But if you aint got no meat baby,
please throw your dog a bone

Standin in her back yard, my long tail tucked under
Standin in the back yard, my long tail tucked way under
Cryin so many tears, my baby think it's lightnin and thunder

Got them low down dog blues, people, my sniffer can't find
no bait
It's the low down dog blues, when your sniffer can't find
no bait
Just whinin for my baby to please open up her gate

Well, she aint heard my barkin, this dog better hit the trail
Yeah, guess a low down dog better hit the trail
That woman dont even care when a good dog wag his tail

c. 1967

BLACK STAR LINE°

My black mothers I hear them singing.

Sons, my sons,
dip into this river with your ebony cups
A vessel of knowledge sails under power.

---

poem title: the failed Black Star steamship line was founded by Marcus Garvey (1887–1940). Born in Jamaica, Garvey established the Universal Negro Improvement Association (UNIA) in 1914 and moved its offices to New York two years later. There he published the popular weekly newspaper *Negro World,* promoted his "back to Africa" movement that encouraged black people to form an independent nation in Africa, wrote poems and essays, and launched a number of failed capitalist ventures. Among them was his Black Star Line, which aimed to facilitate maritime trade between black nations. Garvey was convicted of mail fraud in 1923 after selling stock in the steamship line. Nonetheless, his message of pride and self-sufficiency helped inspire his people.

Study stars as well as currents.
Dip into this river with your ebony cups.

My black fathers I hear them chanting.

Sons, my sons,
let ebony strike the blow that launches the ship!
Send cargoes and warriors back to sea.
Remember the pirates and their chains of nails.
Let ebony strike the blow that launches this ship.
Make your heads not idle sails, blown about
by any icy wind like a tom page from a book.
Bones of my bones,
all you golden-black children of the sun,
lift up! and read the sky
written in the tongue of your ancestors.
It is yours, claim it.
Make no idle sails, my sons,
make heavy-boned ships that break a wave and pass it.
Bring back sagas from Songhay, Kongo, Kaaba,°
deeds and words of Malik, Toussaint,° Marcus,
statues of Mahdi° and a lance of lightning.
Make no idle ships.
Remember the pirates.
For it is the sea who owns the pirates,
not the pirates the sea.

My black mothers I hear them singing.

Children of my flesh,
dip into this river with your ebony cups.
A ship of knowledge sails unto wisdom.
Study what mars and what lifts up.
Dip into this river with your ebony cups.

c. 1967

---

20. *Songhay. . . Kaaba:* Songhay: West African state that rose to power in the latter part of the fifteenth century and commanded the trade routes of the Sahara. Kongo: African kingdom south of the River Congo that had considerable power from the fifteenth to the eighteenth century. Kaaba: the most sacred site in Islam, situated within the Great Mosque at Mecca in Saudi Arabia; it is a small building containing the Black Stone toward which Muslims turn when they pray.

21. *Toussaint:* Toussaint L'Ouverture (1746–1803), black revolutionary leader who joined an insurrection and ruled Haiti from 1797 until Napoleon sent a force that reconquered the island and reestablished slavery there.

22. *Mahdi:* (Arabic) "divinely guided one," the name given by Sunni Muslims to visionary leaders who galvanize the community.

PEAS

Peas in the pod
peas in my gut
peas in the belly roll
doing the strut.
Blackeyes over
blackeyes down
blackeyes browneyes going to town

c. 1967

YAMS

I made a yamship for my belly with my spoon
and sweet riding jelly bread kept me til noon.

c. 1967

AMIRI BARAKA (LEROI JONES) (1934–2014)

Born Everett Leroy Jones to a middle-class family in Newark, New Jersey, the son of a postal employee and a social worker, Baraka was educated at Rutgers, Howard, and Columbia Universities. His work and his system of beliefs have gone through several distinct phases. In the late 1950s and early 1960s, he was active among Beat writers on New York's Lower East Side, writing his own poetry and plays and editing two period magazines, *Yugen* and *Floating Bear.* Yet he was also increasingly impatient with what he saw as the political irrelevance of the Beats and the gradualism of the civil rights movement. In Baraka, the Beats' scorn for materialism was gradually being transformed into a more aggressive and politically focused critique of capitalism. Race was also becoming more central to his view of American culture. His center of operations moved from the Lower East Side to Harlem, and he became a founding figure of the Black Arts Movement of the late 1960s and early 1970s. "Black Art" was essentially the *ars poetica* of the movement. He had first published as LeRoi Jones; now he was Amiri Baraka. For several years he was a stunningly forceful advocate of black cultural nationalism, but by 1975 he was finding its racial exclusivity confining. He thus embraced the revolutionary forms of international socialism. Baraka's poetry, plays, and essays have been defining documents for African American culture for nearly four decades. His view of Christianity in "When We'll Worship Jesus," a poem that should be read aloud, may be compared with that of Langston Hughes in "Goodbye Christ" and contrasted with that of Carolyn Rodgers.

SOS

Calling black people
Calling all black people, man woman child
Wherever you are, calling you, urgent, come in
Black People, come in, wherever you are, urgent, calling
you, calling all black people
calling all black people, come in, black people, come on in.

1969

BLACK ART°

Poems are bullshit unless they are
teeth or trees or lemons piled
on a step. Or black ladies dying
of men leaving nickel hearts
beating them down. Fuck poems
and they are useful, wd they shoot

poem title: "Black Art" became virtually an *ars poetica* for the Black Arts Movement.

come at you, love what you are,
breathe like wrestlers, or shudder
strangely after pissing. We want live
words of the hip world live flesh &
coursing blood. Hearts Brains
Souls splintering fire. We want poems
like fists beating niggers out of Jocks
or dagger poems in the slimy bellies
of the owner-jews.° Black poems to
smear on girdlemamma mulatto bitches
whose brains are red jelly stuck
between 'lizabeth taylor's toes. Stinking
Whores! We want "poems that kill."
Assassin poems, Poems that shoot
guns. Poems that wrestle cops into alleys
and take their weapons leaving them dead
with tongues pulled out and sent to Ireland. Knockoff
poems for dope selling wops or slick halfwhite
politicians Airplane poems. rrrrrrrrrrrrrrrrrr
rrrrrrrrrrrrrr. . . . tuhtuhtuhtuhtuhtuhtuhtuhtuhtuh
. . . . rrrrrrrrrrrrrr. . . . Setting fire and death to
whities ass. Look at the Liberal
Spokesman for the jews clutch his throat
& puke himself into eternity. . . . rrrrrrrr
There's a negroleader pinned to
a bar stool in Sardi's eyeballs melting
in hot flame. Another negroleader
on the steps of the white house one
kneeling between the sheriff's thighs
negotiating cooly for his people.
Aggh . . . stumbles across the room . . .
Put it on him, poem. Strip him naked
to the world! Another bad poem cracking
steel knuckles in a jewlady's mouth
Poem scream poison gas on beasts in green berets
Clean out the world for virtue and love,
Let there be no love poems written
until love can exist freely and

---

15. *owner-jews:* although the import of this passage can be minimized as rhetoric directed against Jewish businessmen in black communities, the fact is that anti-Semitism was a frequent feature of Black Arts poetry. Virtually every participating poet wrote at least one anti-Semitic poem, and some wrote more, though the level of virulence varied considerably. For Baraka it was partly personal; he had been close to Jewish poet Allen Ginsberg during his Beat period, and now he was disavowing both the cultural and the personal connections. But for others the Jews were a convenient scapegoat, as well as a way to revile whites without risking broader cultural consequences.

cleanly. Let Black People understand
that they are the lovers and the sons
of lovers and warriors and sons
of warriors Are poems & poets &
all the loveliness here in the world

We want a black poem. And a
Black World.
Let the world be a Black Poem
And Let All Black People Speak This Poem
Silently

or LOUD

1969

WHEN WE'LL WORSHIP JESUS

We'll worship Jesus
When jesus do
Somethin
When jesus blow up
the white house
or blast nixon down
when jesus turn out congress
or bust general motors to
yard bird motors
jesus we'll worship jesus
when jesus get down
when jesus get out his yellow lincoln
w/the built in cross stain glass
window & box w/black peoples
enemies we'll worship jesus when
he get bad enough to at least scare
somebody—cops not afraid
of jesus
pushers not afraid
of jesus, capitalists racists
imperialists not afraid
of jesus shit they makin money
off jesus
we'll worship jesus when mao
do, when toure does
when the cross replaces Nkrumah's°

26. *Nkrumah:* (1909–1972), leader of Ghana from 1951 to 1966 and founding member of the Organization of African Unity.

star
Jesus need to hurt some a our
enemies, then we'll check him
out, all that screaming and hollering
& wallering and moaning talkin bout
jesus, jesus, in a red
check velvet vine + 8 in. heels
jesus pinky finger
got a goose egg ruby
which actual bleeds
jesus at the apollo°
doin splits and helpin
nixon trick niggers
jesus w/his one eyed self
tongue kissing johnny carson
up the behind
jesus need to be busted
jesus need to be thrown down and whipped
till something better happen
jesus aint did nothing for us
but kept us turned toward the
sky (him and his boy allah
too, need to be checkd
out!)
we'll worship jesus
when he get a boat load of ak-47s
and some dynamite
and blow up abernathy robotin
for gulf
jesus need to be busted
we ain't gonna worship nobody
but niggers gettin up off
the ground
not gon worship jesus
unless he just a tricked up
nigger somebody named
outside his race
need to worship yo self fo
you worship jesus
need to bust jesus (+ check
out his spooky brother
allah while you heavy

°*Apollo:* theater in Harlem, New York.

on the case)
cause we ain gon worship jesus
we aint gon worship
jesus
we aint gon worship
jesus
not till he do somethin
not till he help us
not til the world get changed
and he ain, jesus ain, he cant change the world
we can change the world
we can struggle against the forces of backwardness, we can
change the world
we can struggle against our selves, our slowness, our connection
with
the oppressor, the very cultural aggression which binds us to
our enemies
as their slaves.
we can change the world
we aint gonna worship jesus cause jesus dont exist
xcept in song and story except in ritual and dance, except in
slum stained
tears or trillion dollar opulence stretching back in history, the
history
of the oppression of the human mind
we worship the strength in us
we worship our selves
we worship the light in us
we worship the warmth in us
we worship the world
we worship the love in us
we worship our selves
we worship nature
we worship ourselves
we worship the life in us, and science, and knowledge, and
transformation
of the visible world
but we aint gonna worship no jesus
we aint gonna legitimize the witches and devils and spooks and
hobgoblins
the sensuous lies of the rulers to keep us chained to fantasy and
illusion
sing about life, not jesus
sing about revolution, not no jesus
stop singing about jesus,

sing about, creation, our creation, the life of the world and
    fantastic
nature how we struggle to transform it, but dont victimize our
    selves by
distorting the world
stop moanin about jesus, stop sweatin and crying and stompin
    and dyin for jesus
unless thats the name of the army we building to force the land
    finally to
change hands. And lets not call that jesus, get a quick
    consensus, on that,
lets damn sure not call that black fire muscle
    no invisible psychic dungeon
no gentle vision strait jacket, lets call that peoples army, or
    wapenduzi or
        simba
wachanga, but we not gon call it jesus, and not gon worship
    jesus, throw
jesus out yr mind. Build the new world out of reality, and new
    vision
we come to find out what there is of the world
to understand what there is here in the world!
to visualize change, and force it.
we worship revolution

1972

N. SCOTT MOMADAY (b. 1934)

Born in Lawton, Oklahoma, Momaday is well known as a poet, novelist (*House Made of Dawn* and *The Way to Rainy Mountain*), painter, playwright, and storyteller. Although his work is centered in Native American culture and history, he has written poems about a variety of subjects, including those about nature partly shaped by a Native American vision. His literary influences are still wider, as is apparent when he writes in rhymed syllablics. Some of his literary works include his line drawings and paintings, which have been exhibited a number of times. Long the most highly acclaimed Native American literary figure, his work has inspired a generation of younger artists. He is an enrolled member of the Kiowas, a Native American people who once made their homes across the southern plains of the American west. Educated primarily at the University of New Mexico and Stanford, from which he received a Ph.D., he teaches at the University of Arizona and is a member of the Kiowa Gourd Dance Society. His author's note for *In the Presence of the Sun: Stories and Poems* (1992) concludes, "He walks long distances, and he rides an Appaloosa mare named 'Ma'am.' At his best he cooks. He is justly famous for a recipe named 'The Washita Crossing Soup,' the ingredients of which are, in his words, 'simple, sacred, and secret.' He is a bear."

PLAINVIEW: 3°

The sun appearing: a pendant
of clear cutbeads, flashing;
a drift of pollen and glitter
lapping and overlapping night;
a prairie fire.

1976

BUTEO REGALIS°

His frailty discrete, the rodent turns, looks.
What sense first warns? The winging is unheard,
Unseen but as distant motion made whole,
Singular, slow, unbroken in its glide.
It veers, and veering, tilts broad-surfaced wings.
Aligned, the span bends to begin the dive
And falls, alternately white and russet,°
Angle and curve, gathering momentum.

1974

---

poem title: No. 3 in a sequence of four "Plainview" poems.

poem title: (Latin), the scientific name for the Ferruginous Hawk, a large (two-foot-long) hawk of the North American plains; habitually soars in high, wide circles in search of its prey. *Regalis* means "regal"; the *buteo* family includes hawks and eagles.

7. *white and russet:* the dominant colors, respectively, of the underside and back of the hawk.

CROWS IN A WINTER COMPOSITION

This morning the snow,
The soft distances
Beyond the trees
In which nothing appeared—
Nothing appeared.
The several silences,
Imposed one upon another,
Were unintelligible.

I was therefore ill at ease
When the crows came down,
Whirling down and calling,
Into the yard below
And stood in a mindless manner
On the gray, luminous crust,
Altogether definite, composed,
In the bright enmity of my regard,
In the hard nature of crows.

1976

CARRIERS OF THE DREAM WHEEL

This is the Wheel of Dreams°
Which is carried on their voices,
By means of which their voices turn
And center upon being.
It encircles the First World,
This powerful wheel.
They shape their songs upon the wheel
And spin the names of the earth and sky,
The aboriginal names.
They are old men, or men
Who are old in their voices,
And they carry the wheel among the camps,
Saying: Come, come,
Let us tell the old stories,
Let us sing the sacred songs.

1976

---

1. *Dreams:* dreams or visions are central to the religious and spiritual life of many Native American peoples. They reveal the existence of and give access to a spirit world that has continuity with this one. Actively sought both in sleep and through ritual fasting, dreams grant powers that are central to the social life of the dreamer. Foundational dreams are sometimes transmitted through kinship groups during special ceremonies. Among the Plains Indians, dreamers used special objects and painted designs, often kept in sacred bundles, to hold the power granted them in dreams.

RINGS OF BONE

There were rings of bone
on the bandoliers of old men dancing.

Then, in the afternoon stippled with leaves
and the shadows of leaves,
the leaves glistened
and their shine shaped the air.

Now the leaves are dead.
Cold comes upon the leaves
and they are crisped upon the stony ground.
Webs of rime, like leaves, fasten on the mould,
and the wind divides and devours the leaves.

Again the leaves have more or less to do
with time. Music pervades the death of leaves.
The leaves clatter like the rings of bone
on the bandoliers of old men dancing.

1990

THE STALKER

Sampt'e drew the string back and back until he
felt the bow wobble in his hand, and he let the
arrow go. It shot across the long light of the
morning and struck the black face of a stone in the
meadow; it glanced then away towards the west,
limping along in the air; and then it settled down
in the grass and lay still. Sampt'e approached; he
looked at it with wonder and was wary; honestly he
believed that the arrow might take flight again;
so much of his life did he give into it.

1976

from THE COLORS OF NIGHT

PURPLE°

There was a man who killed a buffalo bull to no
purpose, only he wanted its blood on his hands. It
was a great, old, noble beast, and it was a long
time blowing its life away. On the edge of the night
the people gathered themselves up in their grief

---

poem title: "Purple" is the seventh poem in an eight-poem sequence, *The Colors of Night.*

and shame. Away in the west they could see the hump
and spine of the huge beast which lay dying along
the edge of the world. They could see its bright
blood run into the sky, where it dried, darkening,
and was at last flecked with flakes of light.

1976

THE BURNING

In the numb, numberless days
There were disasters in the distance,
Strange upheavals. No one understood them.
At night the sky was scored with light,
For the far planes of the planet buckled and burned.
In the dawns were intervals of darkness
On the scorched sky, clusters of clouds and eclipse,
And cinders descending.
Nearer in the noons
The air lay low and ominous and inert.
And eventually at evening, or morning, or midday,
At the sheer wall of the wood,
Were shapes in the shadows approaching,
Always, and always alien and alike.
And in the foreground the fields were fixed in fire,
And the flames flowered in our flesh.

1976

DECEMBER 29, 1890°

WOUNDED KNEE CREEK

In the shine of photographs
are the slain, frozen and black

on a simple field of snow.
They image ceremony:

---

poem title: the date of the Wounded Knee Massacre. In 1890, people on the Lakota Sioux reservations were near starvation; promised increases in government rations had materialized as cuts. Desperate for relief, thousands gathered in the badlands of the Pine Ridge Reservation to call for the return of their ancestors and the buffalo through the religious ceremonies of the Ghost Dance. Frightened by the ceremonies, area whites succeeded in bringing half the entire U.S. Army to the reservations. In response, the Ogalallas and Lakotas began returning home. Then legendary leader Sitting Bull was murdered, and one returning band led by Chief Big Foot fled toward the Pine Ridge Agency. They surrendered to the Seventh Cavalry, which proceeded to train four rapid-fire Hotchkiss cannons on the band camped along Wounded Knee Creek. Then the soldiers got drunk. The next morning, in the midst of disarming the Sioux, a weapon discharged, and immediately the Hotchkiss cannons began firing explosive shells into the Indian camp. As the women and children fled, individual soldiers pursued and murdered them. Medals for bravery were awarded the troops. The poem partly describes a photograph taken after the massacre.

women and children dancing,
old men prancing, making fun.

In autumn there were songs, long
since muted in the blizzard.

In summer the wild buckwheat
shone like fox fur and quillwork,

and dusk guttered on the creek.
Now in serene attitudes

of dance, the dead in glossy
death are drawn in ancient light.

1992

THE SHIELD THAT CAME BACK°

Turning Around tested his son Yellow Grass. "You must kill thirty scissortails and make me a fan of their feathers."

"Must I make the whole fan?" asked Yellow Grass. "Must I do the beadwork too?" Yellow Grass had never made a fan.

"Yes. You must do the beadwork too—blue and black and white and orange."

"Those are the colors of your shield," said Yellow Grass.

Yellow Grass fretted over the making of his father's fan, but when at last it was finished it was a fine, beautiful thing, the feathers tightly bunched and closely matched, their sheen like a rainbow—yet they could be spread wide in a disc, like a shield. And the handle was beaded tightly. The blue and black and white and orange beads glittered in every light. And there was a long bunch of doeskin fringes at the handle's end.

When Turning Around saw the fan he said nothing, but he was full of pride and admiration. Then he went off on a raiding expedition to the Pueblo country, and there he was killed. After that, Yellow Grass went among the Pueblos and redeemed his father's shield. But the fan could not be found.

When he was an old man Yellow Grass said to his grandson Handsome Horse, "You see, the shield was more powerful than the fan, for the shield came back and the fan did not. Some things,

---

poem title: from *In the Presence of the Sun: A Gathering of Shields,* a sequence of eighteen poems and prose poems. Among the Plains Indians, a shield was typically made of buffalo hide and carefully decorated; each one is a unique work of art. As Momaday writes, "only in a limited sense can the shield rightly be considered armor . . . above all the shield is medicine. . . . In a real sense the Plains warrior *is* his shield. It is his personal flag, the realization of his vision and name, the object of his holiest quest."

if they are very powerful, come back. Remember that. For us, in this camp, that is how to think of the world,"

1992

THE SNOW MARE

In my dream, a blue mare loping,
Pewter on a porcelain field, away.
There are bursts of soft commotion
Where her hooves drive in the drifts,
And as dusk ebbs on the plane of night,
She shears the web of winter,
And on the far, blind side
She is no more. I behold nothing,
Wherein the mare dissolves in memory,
Beyond the burden of being.

2011

TO AN AGED BEAR

Hold hard this infirmity.
It defines you. You are old.

Now fix yourself in summer,
In thickets of ripe berries,

And venture towards the ridge
Where you were born. Await there

The setting sun. Be alive
To that old conflagration

One more time. Mortality
Is your shadow and your shade.

Translate yourself to spirit;
Be present on your journey.

Keep to the trees and waters.
Be the singing of the soil.

1999

A BENIGN SELF-PORTRAIT

A mirror will suffice, no doubt.
The high furrowed forehead,

The heavy-lidded Asian eyes,
The long-lobed Indian ears.
Brown skin beginning to spot,
Of an age to bore and be bored.
I turn away, knowing too well
My face, my expression
For all seasons, my half-smile.

Birds flit about the feeder,
The dog days wane, and I
Observe the jitters of leaves
And the pallor of the ice-blue beyond.
I read to find inspiration. I write
To restore candor to the mind.
There are raindrops on the window,
And a peregrine wind gusts on the grass.
I think of my old red flannel shirt,
The one I threw away in July.
I would like to pat the warm belly of a
Beagle or the hand of a handsome woman.
I look ahead to cheese and wine,
And a bit of Bach, perhaps,
Or Schumann on the bow of Yo-Yo Ma.

I see the mountains as I saw them
When my heart was young.
But were they not a deeper blue,
shimmering under the fluency of skies
Radiant with crystal light? Across the way
The yellow land lies out, and standing stones
Form distant islands in the field of time.
There is a stillness on this perfect world,
And I am content to settle in its hold.
I turn inward on a wall of books.
They are old friends, even those that
Have dislodged my dreams. One by one
They have shaped the thing I am.

These are the days that swarm
Into the shadows of legend. I ponder.
And when the image on the glass
Is refracted into the prisms of the past
I shall remember: my parents speaking
Quietly in a warm familiar room, and
I bend to redeem an errant, broken doll.

My little daughter, her eyes brimming
With love, beholds the ember of my soul.
There is the rattle of a teacup, and
At the window and among the vines,
The whir of a hummingbird's wings.
In the blue evening, in another room,
There is the faint laughter of ghosts,
And in a tarnished silver frame, the
likeness of a boy who bears my name.

2012

MARK STRAND (b. 1934)

Born on Prince Edward Island, Canada, of American parents, Strand moved regularly as a child whenever his salesman father was relocated. Strand was educated at Antioch College and at several universities—Yale, Florence, and Iowa. He has taught at Utah, Johns Hopkins, and in the University of Chicago's Committee on Social Thought, and served as poetry editor of *The New Republic*. In addition to his poetry, he has written a book on the painter Edward Hopper as well as short stories and books for children. A book-length poem in fifty-five sections, *Dark Harbor* (1993) relates a mental journey through memories and into the afterlife. He often manages a surprisingly controlled use of surreal imagery in poems focused on absence and loss. Recent work has encompassed prose poetry.

THE PREDICTION

That night the moon drifted over the pond,
turning the water to milk, and under
the boughs of the trees, the blue trees,
a young woman walked, and for an instant

the future came to her:
rain falling on her husband's grave, rain falling
on the lawns of her children, her own mouth
filling with cold air, strangers moving into her house,

a man in her room writing a poem, the moon drifting into it,
a woman strolling under its trees, thinking of death,
thinking of him thinking of her, and the wind rising
and taking the moon and leaving the paper dark.

1970

WHERE ARE THE WATERS OF CHILDHOOD?

See where the windows are boarded up,
where the gray siding shines in the sun and salt air
and the asphalt shingles on the roof have peeled or fallen off,
where tiers of oxeye daisies float on a sea of grass?
That's the place to begin.

Enter the kingdom of rot,
smell the damp plaster, step over the shattered glass,
the pockets of dust, the rags, the soiled remains of mattress,

look at the rusted stove and sink, at the rectangular stain
on the wall where Winslow Homer's° *Gulf Stream* hung.

Go to the room where your father and mother
would let themselves go in the drift and pitch of love,
and hear, if you can, the creak of their bed,
then go to the place where you hid.

Go to your room, to all the rooms whose cold, damp air you
 breathed,
to all the unwanted places where summer, fall, winter, spring,
seem the same unwanted season, where the trees you knew
 have died
and other trees have risen. Visit that other place
you barely recall, that other house half hidden.

See the two dogs burst into sight. When you leave,
they will cease, snuffed out in the glare of an earlier light.
Visit the neighbors down the block; he waters his lawn,
she sits on her porch, but not for long.
When you look again they are gone.

Keep going back, back to the field, flat and sealed in mist.
On the other side, a man and a woman are waiting;
they have come back, your mother before she was gray,
your father before he was white.

Now look at the North West Arm, how it glows a deep
 cerulean blue.
See the light on the grass, the one leaf burning, the cloud
that flares. You're almost there, in a moment your parents
will disappear, leaving you under the light of a vanished star,
under the dark of a star newly born. Now is the time.

Now you invent the boat of your flesh and set it upon the
 waters
and drift in the gradual swell, in the laboring salt.
Now you look down. The waters of childhood are there.

1978

10. *Homer:* (1836–1910), American painter noted for naturalistic treatment of maritime subjects.

AUDRE LORDE (1934–1992)

Lorde was born and raised in New York City as the child of West Indian immigrants, She was educated at Hunter College, also spending a year at the National University of Mexico. For more than a decade she was head librarian at Town School Library in New York. Then, in 1968, she published her first volume of poetry and spent a transformative year as poet in residence at historically black Tougaloo College in Mississippi. Her next book, *Cables to Rage* (1970), acknowledged her homosexuality. Thereafter she would call herself "a black feminist lesbian mother poet," and her work began to combine intimate self-reflection and political prophecy. The result is protest poetry focused at once on personal and social transformation.

Her nonfiction prose has also had wide impact, from her account of her struggle with cancer in *The Cancer Journals* (1980) to her fictionalized autobiography *Zami* (1982) and her collection of essays *Sister Outsider* (1984).

from COAL

I

is the total black, being spoken
from the earth's inside.
There are many kinds of open
how a diamond comes into a knot of flame
how sound comes into a word, coloured
by who pays what for speaking.

Some words are open like a diamond
on glass windows
singing out within the passing crash of sun
Then there are words like stapled wagers
in a perforated book,—buy and sign and tear apart—
and come whatever wills all chances
the stub remains
an ill-pulled tooth with a ragged edge.
Some words live in my throat
breeding like adders. Others know sun
seeking like gypsies over my tongue
to explode through my lips
like young sparrows bursting from shell.
Some words
bedevil me.

Love is a word, another kind of open.
As the diamond comes into a knot of flame

I am Black because I come from the earth's inside
now take my word for jewel in the open light.

1976

SISTERS IN ARMS

The edge of our bed was a wide grid
where your fifteen-year-old daughter was hanging
gut-sprung on police wheels
a cablegram nailed to the wood
next to a map of the Western Reserve
I could not return with you to bury the body
reconstruct your nightly cardboards
against the seeping Transvaal° cold
I could not plant the other limpet mine
against a wall at the railroad station
nor carry either of your souls back from the river
in a calabash upon my head
so I bought you a ticket to Durban°
on my American Express
and we lay together
in the first light of a new season.

Now clearing roughage from my autumn garden
cow sorrel   overgrown rocket gone to seed
I reach for the taste of today
the *New York Times* finally mentions your country
a half-page story
of the first white south african killed in the "unrest"
Not of Black children massacred at Sebokeng
six-year-olds imprisoned for threatening the state
not of Thabo Sibeko, first grader, in his own blood
on his grandmother's parlor floor
Joyce, nine, trying to crawl to him
shitting through her navel
not of a three-week-old infant, nameless
lost under the burned beds of Tembisa
my hand comes down like a brown vise over the marigolds
reckless through despair
we were two Black women touching our flame
and we left our dead behind us
I hovered   you rose   the last ritual of healing

8. *Transvaal:* at the time Lorde wrote the poem, a province of South Africa; one-third of it consists of a high plateau.

13. *Durban:* Lorde's note—"Indian Ocean seaport and resort in Natal Province, S.A."

"It is spring," you whispered
"I sold the ticket for guns and sulfa
I leave for home tomorrow"
and wherever I touch you
I lick cold from my fingers
taste rage
like salt from the lips of a woman
who has killed too often to forget
and carries each death in her eyes
your mouth a parting orchid
"Someday you will come to *my* country
and we will fight side by side?"

Keys jingle in the door ajar threatening
whatever is coming belongs here
I reach for your sweetness
but silence explodes like a pregnant belly
into my face
a vomit of nevers.

Mmanthatisi° turns away from the cloth
her daughters-in-law are dyeing
the baby drools milk from her breast
she hands him half-asleep to his sister
dresses again for war
knowing the men will follow.
In the intricate Maseru° twilights
quick sad vital
she maps the next day's battle
dreams of Durban sometimes
visions the deep wry song of beach pebbles
running after the sea.

1986

OUTLINES

I

What hue lies in the slit of anger
ample and pure as night
what color the channel
blood comes through?

---

54. *Mmanthatisi:* Lorde's note—"warrior queen and leader of the Tlokwa (Sotho) people during the *mfecane* (crushing), one of the greatest crises in southern African history. The Sotho now live in the Orange Free State, S.A."

60. *Maseru:* Lorde's note—"scene of a great Tlokwa battle and now the capital of Lesotho."

A Black woman and a white woman
charter our courses close
in a sea of calculated distance
warned away by reefs of hidden anger
histories rallied against us
the friendly face of cheap alliance.

Jonquils through the Mississippi snow
you entered my vision
with the force of hurled rock
defended by distance and a warning smile
fossil tears   pitched over the heart's wall
for protection
no other women
grown beyond safety
come back to tell us
whispering
past the turned shoulders
of our closest
we were not the first
Black woman white woman
altering course to fit our own journey.

In this treacherous sea
even the act of turning
is almost fatally difficult
coming around full face
into a driving storm
putting an end to running
before the wind.

On a helix of white
the letting of blood
the face of my love
and rage
coiled in my brown arms
an ache in the bone
we cannot alter history
by ignoring it
nor the contradictions
who we are.

II

A Black woman and a white woman
in the open fact of our loving

with not only our enemies' hands
raised against us
means a gradual sacrifice
of all that is simple
dreams
where you walk the mountain
still as a water-spirit
your arms lined with scalpels
and I hide the strength of my hungers
like a throwing knife in my hair.

Guilt wove through quarrels like barbed wire
fights in the half forgotten schoolyard
gob of spit in a childhood street
yet both our mothers once scrubbed kitchens
in houses where comfortable women
died a separate silence
our mothers' nightmares
trapped into familiar hatred
the convenience of others drilled into their lives
like studding into a wall
they taught us to understand
only the strangeness of men.

To give   but not beyond what is wanted
to speak   as well as to bear
the weight of hearing
Fragments of the word wrong
clung to my lashes like ice
confusing my vision with a crazed brilliance
your face   distorted into grids
of magnified complaint
our first winter
we made a home outside of symbol
learned to drain the expansion tank together
to look beyond the agreed-upon disguises
not to cry each other's tears.

How many Februarys
shall I lime this acid soil
inch by inch
reclaimed through our gathered waste?
from the wild onion shoots of April
to mulch in the August sun
squash blossoms   a cement driveway

kale and tomatoes
muscles etch the difference
between I need and forever.

When we first met
I had never been
for a walk in the woods

III

light catches two women on a trail
together   embattled by choice
carving an agenda with tempered lightning
and no certainties
we mark tomorrow
examining every cell of the past
for what is useful   stoked by furies
we were supposed to absorb by forty
still we grow   more precise with each usage
like falling stars or torches
we print code names upon the scars
over each other's resolutions
our weaknesses   no longer hateful.

When women make love
beyond the first exploration
we meet each other   knowing
in a landscape
the rest of our lives
attempts to understand.

IV

Leaf-dappled the windows lighten
after a battle that leaves our night in tatters
and we two glad to be alive   and tender
the outline of your ear pressed on my shoulder
keeps a broken dish from becoming always.

We rise to dogshit   dumped on our front porch
the brass windchimes from Sundance stolen
despair offerings of the 8 A.M. News
reminding us we are still at war
and not with each other

"give us 22 minutes and we will give you the world . . ."
and still we dare
to say we are committed
sometimes without relish.

Ten blocks down the street
a cross is burning
we are a Black woman and a white woman
with two Black children
you talk with our next-door neighbors
I register for a shotgun
we secure the tender perennials
against an early frost
reconstructing a future we fuel
from our living   different precisions
In the next room a canvas chair
whispers beneath your weight
a breath of you between laundered towels
the flinty places that do not give.

V

Your face upon my shoulder
a crescent of freckle over bone
what we share   illuminates what we do not
the rest is a burden of history
we challenge
bearing each bitter piece to the light
we hone ourselves upon each other's courage
loving
as we cross the mined bridge   fury
tuned like a Geiger counter

to the softest place.
One straight light hair on the washbasin's rim
difference
intimate as a borrowed scarf
the children arrogant as mirrors
our pillows' mingled scent
this grain of our particular days
keeps a fine sharp edge
to which I cling like a banner
in a choice of winds

seeking an emotional language
in which to abbreviate time.

I trace the curve of your jaw
with a lover's finger
knowing the hardest battle
is only the first
how to do what we need for our living
with honor and in love
we have chosen each other
and the edge of each other's battles
the war is the same
if we lose
someday women's blood will congeal
upon a dead planet
if we win
there is no telling.

1986

CALL

Holy ghost woman
stolen out of your name
Rainbow Serpent
whose faces have been forgotten
Mother   loosen my tongue or adorn me
with a lighter burden
Aido Hwedo° is coming.

On worn kitchen stools and tables
we are piecing our weapons together
scraps of different histories
do not let us shatter
any altar
she who scrubs the capitol toilets, listening
is your sister's youngest daughter
gnarled Harriet's anointed
you have not been without honor
even the young guerrilla has chosen
yells as she fires into the thicket
Aido Hwedo is coming.

---

7. *Aido Hwedo:* Lorde's note—"the Rainbow Serpent; also a representation of all ancient deities who must be worshipped but whose names and faces have been lost in time."

I have written your names on my cheekbone
dreamed your eyes flesh my epiphany
most ancient goddesses hear me
enter
I have not forgotten your worship
nor my sisters
nor the sons of my daughters
my children watch for your print
in their labors
and they say Aido Hwedo is coming.

I am a Black woman turning
mouthing your name as a password
through seductions self-slaughter
and I believe in the holy ghost
mother
in your flames beyond our vision
blown light through the fingers of women
enduring warring
sometimes outside your name
we do not choose all our rituals
Thandt Modise winged girl of Soweto
brought fire back home in the snout of a mortar
and passes the word from her prison cell whispering
Aido Hwedo is coming.

Rainbow Serpent who must not go
unspoken
I have offered up the safety of separations
sung the spirals of power
and what fills the spaces
before power unfolds or flounders
in desirable nonessentials
I am a Black woman stripped down
and praying
my whole life has been an altar
worth its ending
and I say Aido Hwedo is coming.

I may be a weed in the garden
of women I have loved
who are still
trapped in their season

but even they shriek
as they rip burning gold from their skins
Aido Hwedo is coming.

We are learning by heart
what has never been taught
you are my given   fire-tongued
Oya   Seboulisa   Mawu   Afrekete
and now we are mourning our sisters
lost to the false hush of sorrow
to hardness and hatchets and childbirth
and we are shouting
Rosa Parks° and Fannie Lou Hamer°
Assata Shakur° and Yaa Asantewa
my mother and Winnie Mandela° are singing
in my throat
the holy ghosts' linguist
one iron silence broken
Aido Hwedo is calling
calling
your daughters are named
and conceiving
Mother   loosen my tongue
or adorn me
with a lighter burden
Aido Hwedo is coming.

Aido Hwedo is coming.

Aido Hwedo is coming.

1986

---

71. *Parks:* (1913–2005), jailed in Montgomery, Alabama, for refusing to give up her bus seat to a white rider in December 1955, she helped start the contemporary civil rights movement and later protested South African apartheid.

71. *Hamer:* (1917–1977), American civil rights activist and politician.

72. *Assata Shakur:* (b. 1947), African American activist who has lived in Cuba in political asylum since 1984.

73. *Mandela:* (1936–2013), South African activist; at the time Lorde wrote the poem she was married to imprisoned leader Nelson Mandela.

KATHLEEN FRASER (b. 1935)

Kathleen Fraser grew up in Oklahoma, Colorado, and California, graduating from Occidental College, then working in New York as an editorial assistant for *Mademoiselle* for a time before taking up her writing and teaching career full time. While teaching at San Francisco State University from 1972 to 1992, she directed the Poetry Center and founded the American Poetry Archives. Fraser was cofounder and coeditor of the feminist poetics newsletter *(HOW)ever.* From 1983 to 1991, Fraser published and edited *HOW(ever)* as "a journal focused on innovative writing by contemporary women and neglected texts by American modernist women writers." Barbara Guest, Frank O'Hara, Lorine Niedecker, and George Oppen are among her influences. She now divides her time between San Francisco and Rome. Fraser has long been committed to the experimental tradition. She commented at one point that it was Charles Olson's "declared move away from the narcissistically probing, psychological defining of self—so seductively explored by Sylvia Plath, Anne Sexton and Robert Lowell in the early and mid-1960s, and by their avid followers for at least a generation after—that provided a major alternative ethic of writing for women poets. While seriously committed to gender consciousness, a number of us carried an increasing skepticism towards any fixed rhetoric of the poem, implied or intoned. We resisted the prescription of authorship as an exclusively unitary proposition—the essential 'I' positioned as central to the depiction of reflectivity. As antidote to a mainstream poetics that enthusiastically embraced those first dramatic 'confessional' poems, Olson (in "PROJECTIVE VERSE") had already proposed 'getting rid of the lyrical interference of the individual ego.'"

IN COMMEMORATION OF THE VISIT OF FOREIGN COMMERCIAL REPRESENTATIVES TO JAPAN, 1947

for Bob Glück

PRELIMINARY WORDS

In language, you once hovered. Now you are the hunched body holding the blue oar, so useless in waves. Before I knew your plan, I had already purchased the picture book I called "mine," with its memoir of brown sand extending so casually its territories.

My ignorance in this cannot be excused, yet everything in that room offered itself to me: it was the Foreign Representative who finally caught my eye, between brass hinges. You knew my weakness but sent me there anyway; wanting screens, and you had inscribed the invitation on thick, creamy paper you thought might provide a solution for despair.

Abruptly, just as I stretched out my hand, the mountain presented its snow and deep blue slope, the Foreign Representative's delicate breast. If we can talk about distance, I would propose that series of thatched roofs, the faded hem of the boatman's blue jacket.

Away, my page is one inch longer than at home, with narrower margins; my brush unused, except in commemoration.

I imagine each scratch on the glass pillow to be a person, waiting.

THE GENERAL HEADQUARTERS OF THE ALLIED POWERS

Beginning from the perspective of the personal, you surprised me with your concrete buddha and dark woolen coats of young European style. How those diminished shadows of trees subtracted us from winter. Badly tinted sky does not represent the "traveler's dream." In your twelve letters, I read a different set of requirements and expectations: our powers linked by windows.

Now our ambitions grow sharper with each darkening rectangle: buildings both dry and thick with steam. Blue water makes its ally with unnatural embankments, yet bodies cling to the edges, and one can see a pair of white trousers in motion, caught with the same swift closure as the black car behind it. I must confess, I had expected the cliches of my childhood and miss them, although I understand your discomfort on hearing this. I draw an ideogram to show you what I mean.

I count on you to translate, as your training requires.

YOMEI MON, THE ELABORATELY CARVED GATE OF THE NOTED TOKUGAWA SHOGUNATE MAUSOLEUM AT NIKKO, REPRESENTING "ONE OF THE FINEST JAPANESE CARVINGS AND LACQUER DECORATIONS"

What can be represented by this "finest carving" which is too exhaustive to retain? Our guide has proposed a second look at garish green-and-pink petals, as if to raise his glass in a toast to our arrival and departure. One struggles to find words, yet feels the soft diminishing of oxygen. The monumental divests memory of its pockets on foreign soil, where time is a cloud made solid with carving. I am blinded by my bad faith or lack of appropriate counsel.

Yet this elaboration of gold fell short of sight, as we entered the gate. Thoughts of death, while normally disturbing, seemed "notable," instead, as if an excess of enameled color, banded by red, could justify any harsh loss.

Ashes, scattered on water or under trees, was my family's solution, although now I cannot find my father or my sister and have no specific location for my grief. If their ashes and bits of bone were here, in little painted boxes, would my thoughts arrive in calmer progression?

JAPAN'S "WORLD-FAMOUS" MT. FUJI

One thing appears to be certain. We stand gazing from separate windows in the same hotel. You note the white veins of snow and the pale crusts yet remaining on the near slopes. I think of the Foreign Representative's delicate breast, before confusion came into its dark silk, and economy staged itself, as you might expect, in the popular guises of fame and reform. This drift of quince so close to the hotel window, branching an historical calm—has it changed you into a person someone might banish from sight, for lack of a perfect description? You travel by yellow boat, the April sun is rigorous and punctual; it casts a gloss on every surface, spreading another mountain through the barely moving inches of grey sea. You imagine yourself at diplomatic attention, even choose your trousers and jacket with a longing for precision, while I import a suspect leisure, having served on another occasion.

Now my wish comes and goes with the sun's rigor, expanding and diminishing as if I were one of those white buildings at the foot of the mountain, still read by afternoon light which may fade in an hour, and return.

ASHI-NO-KO (LAKE ASHI), ON THE TOP OF HAKONE, A "FAMOUS HOTSPRING RESORT"

Commas, necessarily magnified, curve inside walls, separating rice-paper screens from oxygen. One can consider private matters in silence, give over entirely to the skin's necessity, the water's sulfurous fumes. *A towel, please,* I might have said, if you'd been with me. These learned modesties soon fall before the tremor of red roofs lining the port. The architectural jump creates false pleasure. A colonial banner flaps in the wind like washing hung along the inner court. My tea soothes entirely, in spite of premonitions, and the Foreign Representative tucks the layerings of embroidered silk in the creases of her folded knees and thighs. She hands me the fine-haired brush and a stick of ink, with a little water. I think of drawing you a letter, because words are slipping and faltering under foot. I paint a path of stones which you will recognize, one at a time, as you attempt to extend your influence from those dormer windows, so clearly positioned for their view of flagpoles just at the lake's edge.

Decisions are being taken among the allied powers which, later, will be regretted.

TORO HATCHO, "ONE OF THE MOST PICTURESQUE POOLS IN JAPAN" (WAKAYAMA PREFECTURE)

I am taken on a boat just wide enough for myself and the boatman, unless we should encounter your party at one of the crossways. Then I would wave to you, hoping to separate you from commerce and modernity, indicating another seat in the boat. Can you feel a drifting like sleep, re-shaping the first idea we were given when they sent us here? While I am not alarmed, I wish to compare these recent days, and the views of water so amply restored to each morning's rising. A certain formality beckons and forbids.

Blue shines up, from between the rafts. I watch the backs of the pole-men pushing their load to the next town. They call out to my boatman, wave a fish and laugh and beckon to us. Their bare toes curve with the wood.

No buildings, for miles now. Only shoals of rock and sharply dropping embankments, leading in no direction I recognize. I look back, chinking of our first meeting and the later dream where you were a woman and I was a man. Now that we have exchanged boundaries and blood types, it is easier. If I do not see you at the impasse, I will understand your message and return to the hotel lobby.

HIROSAKI CASTLE, IN NORTHEASTERN JAPAN, A "TYPICAL CITADEL" OF THE FEUDAL LORDS

"Be a flame for them to pass through," you advised me.

GOJU.NO.TO (FIVE-STORIED PAGODA), IN THE KIMOMIZU DERA ("NOTED KWANNON TEMPLE"), IN KYOTO, ONE OF THE TWENTY-FIVE SACRED TEMPLES IN JAPAN

This red will swallow, this temple surround.

Trees lean and persist, worn thin by wind. Bark, leaf and nub salute the small man in gathered cotton trousers with garden shears, now trimming, now bending back a foreign branch. And his father. And his father, before him.

ITSUKUSHIMA SHRINE, IN THE INLAND SEA, "ONE OF THE BEST KNOWN SCENIC SPOTS IN JAPAN"

I've lost sight of where you are journeying, because of the planned charm of "best-known scenery" and weather's unplanned damage to certainty. I could remain here until your return, watching the flicker of silver fins without economic plan or commercial gain. The ordinary is my altar. I think of you holding up your favorite tea-cup, inviting me to commemorate the line of blue hill behind the red gate.

For the first time, I refer to your letter and read your ambivalence, no, your wish to note each change of heart and the substitution of *path* for *daughter,* animal love for speculative representation.

MT. ZAO SKIING GROUNDS, IN NORTHEASTERN JAPAN

If white equals mystery and snow equals death, how am I to understand the two bent figures in black on the ski slope? I choose the one with his shadow intact and hope that it's you, for lack of binoculars. Your form appears admirable and the shadow to your right, entirely severed and autonomous except at the feet. From this perspective, a diagonal gash of blue sky gives geometric relief to a moment so perfectly caught it might slip into fiction. I could "go on" about the snow-covered trees but decisions are hovering like already memorized language. You are needed by the allied powers who require your shadow ability. I'm tapping the air between us and hoping you can hear me. Do not depend on the former treaty or visual aids. Here is the list you sent me:

"rough, smooth, dark, blond, rich, middle class, tender, cruel, narcissist, altruist, east, west"

No one is "alike," and neither are you, though joined at the feet with your daytime abilities.

DAIBUTSU, IN KAMAKURA, THE GIANT BRONZE BUDDHA IMAGE, RISING FORTY FEET HIGH

I think that SCALE must be the shadow of domination. I cannot look. (Or is it, *You don't want to.*)

ARASHIYAMA, IN KYOTO, NOTED FOR ITS CHERRY BLOSSOMS AND AUTUMN LEAVES

Again, the human. A silly heart for Sunday—today, hands inside of hands, the procession of covered boats rocking from side-to-side in their slow pace down the river. Your "daughter" holding her paper parasol painted with falcons and Lily wagging her tail and limping along the left bank of the Arashiyama, flowing over—almost—with melted snow . . . such patient and difficult lovers.

You leap to the boat, a little drunk, and I am your ally in pines and grilled sea bass. I have not booked the return trip due to a seasonal error. The errand you sent me on, also the Foreign Representative arriving for tea and the multiple bodies of water in my life are discrete but not conclusive arrangements. What was once a refusal lingers, as if pine needles had broken and spread their scent on the skin—a new ideogram I am trying to paint, whenever I lift my brush.

NIJUBASHI, THE "FAMOUS DOUBLE ARCH BRIDGE, THE GATEWAY" TO THE IMPERIAL PALACE

Tunneling forward cowards the awaited arch at the opposite end, the mind *does* see, then the eye—following yearning—grabs hold of space and watches it expand until the curved frame is lost, the opening regained.

We observe the double arch of Nijubashi through this split-second lens so that reflections of imperial design may curve and flash as if we were looking for ourselves in the moving plaits of water, the solidity of human desire all equal and held intact for our reference and imagined stability. How tiny we are, seen from there. How calm, the unsevered branches of silver and green, the lush and edible yellow fruit of the ginkgos about to pierce their coverings and burst through.

Because we opened the same book, we are bound by these ties of silk, particularly at the gateway.

1988

CHARLES WRIGHT (b. 1935)

Born in 1935 in Pickwick Dam, Tennessee, educated at Davidson College, the University of Iowa's Writers' Workshop, and the University of Rome, Wright is currently a professor in the writing program at the University of Virginia. Wright's interest in poetry was quickened by a tour of duty in the U.S. Army Intelligence Service in Italy in 1957. He became an admirer of Ezra Pound and Italian poets like Eugenio Montale whose work he translated in 1979, and Cesare Pavese, whose rich sonority his own poetic line carries over into English. He also has a stronger interest than many of his contemporaries in working through the symbols and concepts of the Judeo-Christian religious tradition. Wright composes as if he were in the line of imagist poets, specializing in fragments that gain their authority from their startling juxtapositions. But his language has a musical dimension matched by few contemporaries. So extravagantly sumptuous are his blendings of sight and sound—and sometimes so little anchored to incident—that it is with reluctance that one leaves the world of the poem to a reality that may seem diminished by comparison.

SPIDER CRYSTAL ASCENSION

The spider, juiced crystal and Milky Way, drifts on his web through
    the night sky
And looks down, waiting for us to ascend . . .

At dawn he is still there, invisible, short of breath, mending his net.

All morning we look for the white face to rise from the lake like a
    tiny star.
And when it does, we lie back in our watery hair and rock.

1984

CLEAR NIGHT

Clear night, thumb-top of a moon, back-lit sky.
Moon-fingers lay down their same routine
On the side deck and the threshold, the white keys and the black
    keys.
Bird hush and bird song. A cassia flower falls.

I want to be bruised by God.
I want to be strung up in a strong light and singled out.
I wanted to be stretched, like music wrung from a dropped seed.
I want to be entered and picked clean.

And the wind says, "What?" to me.
And the castor beans, with their little earrings of death, say "What?"
to me.
And the stars start out on their cold slide through the dark.
And the gears notch and the engines wheel.

1977

HOMAGE TO PAUL CÉZANNE°

At night, in the fish-light of the moon, the dead wear our white
shirts
To stay warm, and litter the fields.
We pick them up in the mornings, dewy pieces of paper and scraps
of cloth.
Like us, they refract themselves. Like us,
They keep on saying the same thing, trying to get it right.
Like us, the water unsettles their names.

Sometimes they lie like leaves in their little arks, and curl up at the
edges.
Sometimes they come inside, wearing our shoes, and walk
From mirror to mirror.
Or lie in our beds with their gloves off
And touch our bodies. Or talk
In a corner. Or wait like envelopes on a desk.

They reach up from the ice plant.
They shuttle their messengers through the oat grass.
Their answers rise like rust on the stalks and the spidery leaves.

We rub them off our hands.

•

Each year the dead grow less dead, and nudge
Close to the surface of all things.
They start to remember the silence that brought them there.
They start to recount the gain in their soiled hands.

Their glasses let loose, and grain by grain return to the river bank.
They point to their favorite words

---

poem title: Cézanne: (1839–1906), French painter. Considered by some the greatest post-Impressionist painter, his work with cubic masses and architectonic lines set the stage for the partial abstraction of the Cubist movement. Noted for both landscapes and portraits.

Growing around them, revealed as themselves for the first time:
They stand close to the meanings and take them in.

They stand there, vague and without pain,
Under their fingernails an unreturnable dirt.
They stand there and it comes back,
The music of everything, syllable after syllable

Out of the burning chair, out of the beings of light.
It all comes back.
And what they repeat to themselves, and what they repeat to themselves,
Is the song that our fathers sing.

•

In steeps and sighs,
The ocean explains itself, backing and filling
What spaces it can't avoid, spaces
In black shoes, their hands clasped, their eyes teared at the edges:
We watch from the high hillside,
The ocean swelling and flattening, the spaces
Filling and emptying, horizon blade
Flashing the early afternoon sun.

The dead arc constant in
The white lips of the sea.
Over and over, through clenched teeth, they tell
Their story, the story each knows by heart:
Remember me, speak my name.
When the moon tugs at my sleeve,
When the body of water is raised and becomes the body of light,
Remember me, speak my name.

•

The dead are a cadmium blue.
We spread them with palette knives in broad blocks and planes.

We layer them stroke by stroke
In steps and ascending mass, in verticals raised from the earth.

We choose, and layer them in,
Blue and a blue and a breath,

Circle and smudge, cross-beak and buttonhook,
We layer them in. We squint hard and terrace them line by line.

And so we are come between, and cry out,
And stare up at the sky and its cloudy panes,

And finger the cypress twists.
The dead understand all this, and keep in touch,

Rustle of hand to hand in the lemon trees,
Flags, and the great sifts of anger

To powder and nothingness.
The dead are a cadmium blue, and they understand.

•

The dead are with us to stay.
Their shadows rock in the back yard, so pure, so black,
Between the oak tree and the porch.

Over our heads they're huge in the night sky.
In the tall grass they turn with the zodiac.
Under our feet they're white with the snows of a thousand years.

They carry their colored threads and baskets of silk
To mend our clothes, making us look right,
Altering, stitching, replacing a button, closing a tear.
They lie like tucks in our loose sleeves, they hold us together.

They blow the last leaves away.
They slide like an overflow into the river of heaven.
Everywhere they are flying.

The dead are a sleight and a fade
We fall for, like flowering plums, like white coins from the rain
Their sighs are gaps in the wind.

•

The dead are waiting for us in our rooms,
Little globules of light
In one of the far corners, and close to the ceiling, hovering,
  thinking our thoughts.

Often they'll reach a hand down,
Or offer a word, and ease us out of our bodies to join them in
  theirs.
We look back at our other selves on the bed.

We look back and we don't care and we go.

And thus we become what we've longed for,
                                        past tense and otherwise,
A BB, a disc of light,
                        song without words.
And refer to ourselves
In the third person, seeing that other arm
Still raised from the bed, fingers like licks and flames in the boned air.

Only to hear that it's not time.
Only to hear that we must re-enter and lie still, our arms at rest at our sides.
The voices rising around us like mist

And dew, *it's all right, it's all right, it's all right . . .*

•

The dead fall around us like rain.
They come down from the last clouds in the late light for the last time
And slip through the sod.

They lean uphill and face north.
                                        Like grass,
They bend toward the sea, they break toward the setting sun.

We filigree and we baste.
But what do the dead care for the fringe of words,
Safe in their suits of milk?
What do they care for the honk and flash of a new style?

And who is to say if the inch of snow in our hearts
Is rectitude enough?

Spring picks the locks of the wind.
High in the night sky the mirror is hauled up and unsheeted.
In it we twist like stars.

Ahead of us, through the dark, the dead
Are beating their drums and stirring the yellow leaves.

•

We're out here, our feet in the soil, our heads craned up at the
sky,
The stars streaming and bursting behind the trees.

At dawn, as the clouds gather, we watch
The mountain glide from the east on the valley floor,
Coming together in starts and jumps.
Behind their curtain, the bears
Amble across the heavens, serene as black coffee . . .

Whose unction can intercede for the dead?
Whose tongue is toothless enough to speak their piece?

What we are given in dreams we write as blue paint,
Or messages to the clouds.
At evening we wait for the rain to fall and the sky to clear.
Our words are words for the clay, uttered in undertones,
Our gestures salve for the wind.

We sit out on the earth and stretch our limbs,
Hoarding the little mounds of sorrow laid up in our hearts.

1981

MARY OLIVER (b. 1935)

Born in Maple Heights, Ohio, near Cleveland, Oliver attended both Ohio State University and Vassar College. She lived for many years in Provincetown, Massachusetts. In addition to many volumes of poetry and prose poetry, she has written a book on prosody, *A Poetry Handbook*, as well as *Blue Pastures*, a collection of essays. She has recently taught at Sweet Briar College in Virginia, Duke University, and Bennington College. The social world appears infrequently in Oliver's poetry, for she is above all a poet of nature. In her capacity for exquisitely precise description and in her fascination with nature's indifferent, animate life, she recalls Roethke's early work. Her sense of awe and revelation, however, more fully echoes Hopkins and Jeffers. At moments when nature's sheer difference produces a sense of self-knowledge, a kind of ecstasy arises that is her special signature.

THE MORNING WALK

There are a lot of words meaning thanks.
Some you can only whisper.
Others you can only sing.
The pewee whistles instead.
The snake turns in circles.
The beaver slaps his tail
on the surface of the pond.
The deer in the pinewoods stamps his hoof.
Goldfinches shine as they float through the air.
A person, sometimes, will hum a little Mahler.°
Or put arms around old oak tree,
Or take out lovely pencil and notebook to find a few
touching, kissing words.

1997

AT GREAT POND

At Great Pond
the sun, rising,
scrapes his orange breast
on the thick pines,
and down tumble
a few orange feathers into

°*Mahler:* (1860–1911), Austrian composer and conductor.

the dark water.
On the far shore
a white bird is standing
like a white candle—
or a man, in the distance,
in the clasp of some meditation—
while all around me the lilies
are breaking open again
from the black cave
of the night.
Later, I will consider
what I have seen—
what it could signify—
what words of adoration I might
make of it, and to do this
I will go indoors to my desk—
I will sit in my chair—
I will look back
into the lost morning
in which I am moving, now,
like a swimmer,
so smoothly,
so peacefully,
I am almost the lily—
almost the bird vanishing over the water
on its sleeves of night.

1997

BLACK SNAKE THIS TIME

lay
under the oak trees
in the early morning,
in a half knot,

in a curl,
and, like anyone
catching the runner at rest,
I stared

at that thick black length
whose neck, all summer,
was a river,
whose body was the same river—

whose whole life was a flowing—
whose tail could lash—
who, footless, could spin
like a black tendril and hang

upside down in the branches
gazing at everything
out of seed-shaped red eyes
as it swung to and fro,

the tail making its quick sizzle,
the head lifted
like a black spout.
Was it alive?

Of course it was alive.
This was the quick wrist of early summer,
when everything was alive.
Then I knelt down, I saw

that the snake was gone—
that the face, like a black bud,
had pushed out of the broken petals
of the old year, and it had emerged

on the hundred hoops of its belly,
the tongue sputtering its thread of smoke,
the work of the pearl-colored lung
never pausing, as it pushed

from the chin,
from the crown of the head,
leaving only an empty skin
for the mice to nibble and the breeze to blow

as over the oak leaves and across the creek
and up the far hill it had gone,
damp and shining in the starlight
like a rollicking finger of snow.

1997

JAYNE CORTEZ (1936–2012)

Born in Fort Huachuca, Arizona, Cortez grew up in the Watts ghetto of Los Angeles, but spent most of her adult life in the New York City area. Her first books combine politics, music, and surrealism, but more musical and performative elements emerged during her marriage to jazz musician Ornette Coleman and after her directorship (1964–1970) of the Watts Repertory Theatre Company in Los Angeles. Her band, "The Firespitters," accompanied her performances and powerful poetry recordings, which sometimes made use of an almost mesmerizing chanting style. As one critic writes, hearing "her most volatile poems is akin to listening to a Greek chorus rebuke the cosmos." See her *Coagulations: New and Selected Poems* (1984).

I AM NEW YORK CITY

i am new york city
here is my brain of hot sauce
my tobacco teeth my
   mattress of bedbug tongue
legs apart   hand on chin
   war on the roof   insults
pointed fingers   pushcarts
my contraceptives all

look at my pelvis blushing

i am new york city of blood
police and fried pies
i rub my docks red with grenadine
and jelly madness in a flow of tokay°
my huge skull of pigeons
my seance of peeping toms
my plaited ovaries excuse me
this is my grime my thigh of
steelspoons and toothpicks
   i imitate no one

i am new york city
of the brown spit and soft tomatoes
give me my confetti of flesh
   my marquee of false nipples

---

13. *tokay:* sweet wine.

my sideshow of open beaks
  in my nose of soot
in my ox bled eyes
in my ear of saturday night specials

i eat ha ha hee hee and ho ho

i am new york city
never change never sleep never melt
my shoes are incognito
cadavers grow from my goatee
look i sparkle with shit with wishbones
my nickname is glue-me

take my face of stink bombs
my star spangled banner of hot dogs
take my beer can junta
my reptilian ass of footprints
and approach me through life
approach me through death
approach me through my widow's peak
through my split ends my
asthmatic laugh approach me
through my wash rag
half ankle half elbow
massage me with your camphor tears
salute the patina and concrete
of my rat tail wig
face up face down piss
into the bite of our handshake

i am new york city
my skillet-head friend
my fat-bellied comrade
citizens
break wind with me

1973

DO YOU THINK

Do you think this is a sad day
  a sad night
full of tequila full of el dorado°
  full of banana solitudes

---

3. *el dorado:* both wine and the legend of a New World city of gold.

And my chorizo° face a holiday for knives
  and my arching lips a savannah for cuchifritos°
and my spit curls a symbol for you
  to overcharge overbill oversell me
these saints these candles
  these dented cars loud pipes
no insurance and no place to park
  because my last name is Cortez

Do you think this is a sad night
  a sad day

And on this elevator
  between my rubber shoes
in the creme de menthe of my youth
  the silver tooth of my age
the gullah° speech of my one trembling tit
full of tequila full of el dorado
  full of banana solitudes you tell me
i use more lights more gas
  more telephones more sequins more feathers
more iridescent headstones
  you think i accept this pentecostal church
in exchange for the lands you stole

And because my name is Cortez
  do you think this is a revision
of flesh studded with rivets
  my wardrobe clean
the pick in my hair
  the pomegranate in my hand
14th street delancey street 103rd street
  reservation where i lay my skull
the barrio° of need
  the police state in ashes
drums full of tequila full of el dorado
  full of banana solitudes say:

Do you really think time speaks english
  in the men's room

1973

---

5. *chorizo:* sausage.

6. *cuchifritos:* fried pork skin and other pork-based dishes.

19. *gullah:* Creole language centered in the South Carolina and Georgia low country, related to Jamaican patois and other dialects.

35. *barrio:* (Spanish) neighborhood, as in Spanish Harlem in New York City. In Central America it often refers to a slum.

LUCILLE CLIFTON (1936–2010)

Clifton was born Thelma Louise Sayles in Depew, New York, where her mother worked in a laundry and her father in a steel mill. She attended Howard University and Fredonia State Teachers College, though she left before finishing a degree to devote herself to her writing. Supporting herself as an actor in the 1950s, marrying Fred Clifton in 1958, and working for a time as a claims clerk in Buffalo, New York, Clifton meanwhile began to refine the minimalist poetic style—a compressed free verse lyric, often untitled, with a short iambic trimeter line—that would unify her diverse subject matter. She published her first book of poems in 1969 after poet Robert Hayden entered her work into a poetry contest. She was interested in all of America's historic victims, including both black people and Native Americans, and was consistently eloquent about the special character of women's lives. She was also deeply religious and her poem sequences about biblical subjects—here represented by "brothers," a remarkable dialogue with Satan—have been particularly inventive. She also wrote both poetry and fiction for children, as well as a history of her family ancestry, *Generations* (1976), that begins with her great-great-grandmother being kidnapped and sold into slavery.

I AM ACCUSED OF TENDING TO THE PAST

i am accused of tending to the past
as if i made it,
as if i sculpted it
with my own hands. i did not.
this past was waiting for me
when i came,
a monstrous unnamed baby,
and i with my mother's itch
took it to breast
and named it
History.
she is more human now,
learning language everyday,
remembering faces, names and dates.
when she is strong enough to travel
on her own, beware, she will.

1991

at the cemetery, walnut grove plantation, south carolina, 1989

among the rocks
at walnut grove
your silence drumming
in my bones,
tell me your names.

nobody mentioned slaves
and yet the curious tools
shine with your fingerprints.
nobody mentioned slaves
but somebody did this work
who had no guide, no stone,
who moulders under rock.

tell me your names,
tell me your bashful names
and i will testify.

the inventory lists ten slaves
but only men were recognized.

among the rocks
at walnut grove
some of these honored dead
were dark
some of these dark
were slaves
some of these slaves
were women
some of them did this
honored work.
tell me your names
foremothers, brothers,
tell me your dishonored names.
here lies
here lies
here lies
here lies
hear

1991

reply

FROM A LETTER WRITTEN TO DR. W.E.B. DUBOIS BY ALVIN BORGQUEST OF CLARK UNIVERSITY IN MASSACHUSETTS AND DATED APRIL 3, 1905.

"We are pursuing an investigation here on the subject of crying as an expression of the emotions, and should like very much to learn about its peculiarities among the colored people. We have been referred to you as a person competent to give us information on the subject. We desire especially to know about the following salient aspects: 1. Whether the Negro sheds tears . . ."

reply

he do
she do
they live
they love
they try
they tire
they flee
they fight
they bleed
they break
they moan
they mourn
they weep
they die
they do
they do
they do

1991

the message of crazy horse°

i would sit in the center of the world,
the Black Hills hooped around me and
dream of my dancing horse. my wife

---

poem title: Crazy Horse (Tasunke Witko, 1840–1877), Ogalalla Sioux Chief, born in South Dakota. He defeated General George Armstrong Custer at the Battle of Little Bighorn (1876) and was widely considered the greatest Sioux military leader, though personally he was rather shy and introspective. He was killed by a guard in a scuffle at Fort Robinson, Nebraska.

was Black Shawl who gave me the daughter
i called They Are Afraid Of Her.
i was afraid of nothing

except Black Buffalo Woman.
my love for her i wore
instead of feathers. i did not dance

i dreamed. i am dreaming now
across the worlds. my medicine is strong.
my medicine is strong in the Black basket
of these fingers. i come again through this

Black Buffalo woman. hear me;
the hoop of the world is breaking.
fire burns in the four directions.
the dreamers are running away from the hills.
i have seen it. i am crazy horse.

1987

poem to my uterus

you uterus
you have been patient
as a sock
while i have slippered into you
my dead and living children
now
they want to cut you out
stocking i will not need
where i am going
where am i going
old girl
without you
uterus
my bloody print
my estrogen kitchen
my black bag of desire
where can i go
barefoot
without you
where can you go
without me

1991

to my last period

well girl, goodbye,
after thirty-eight years.
thirty-eight years and you
never arrived
splendid in your red dress
without trouble for me
somewhere, somehow.

now it is done,
and i feel just like
the grandmothers who,
after the hussy has gone,
sit holding her photograph
and sighing, *wasn't she*
beautiful? wasn't she beautiful?

1991

brothers

(being a conversation in eight poems between an aged Lucifer and God, though only Lucifer is heard. The time is long after.)

I

invitation

come coil with me
here in creation's bed
among the twigs and ribbons
of the past. i have grown old
remembering this garden,
the hum of the great cats
moving into language, the sweet
fume of the man's rib
as it rose up and began to walk.
it was all glory then,
the winged creatures leaping
like angels, the oceans claiming
their own. let us rest here a time
like two old brothers
who watched it happen and wondered
what it meant.

2

how great Thou art

listen, You are beyond
even Your own understanding.
that rib and rain and clay
in all its pride,
its unsteady dominion,
is not what You believed
You were,
but it is what You are;
in Your own image as some
lexicographer supposed.
the face, both he and she,
the odd ambition, the desire
to reach beyond the stars
is You. all You, all You
the loneliness, the perfect
imperfection.

3

as for myself

less snake than angel
less angel than man
how come i to this
serpent's understanding?
watching creation from
a hood of leaves
i have foreseen the evening
of the world.
as sure as she,
the breast of Yourself
separated out and made to bear,
as sure as her returning,
i too am blessed with
the one gift you cherish;
to feel the living move in me
and to be unafraid.

4

in my own defense

what could i choose
but to slide along behind them,

they whose only sin
was being their father's children?
as they stood with their backs
to the garden,
a new and terrible luster
burning their eyes,
only You could have called
their ineffable names,
only in their fever
could they have failed to hear.

5

the road led from delight

into delight. into the sharp
edge of seasons, into the sweet
puff of bread baking, the warm
vale of sheet and sweat after love,
the tinny newborn cry of calf
and cormorant and humankind.
and pain, of course,
always there was some bleeding,
but forbid me not
my meditation on the outer world
before the rest of it, before
the bruising of his heel, my head,
and so forth.

6

"the silence of God is God."
—Carolyn Forché

tell me, tell us why
in the confusion of a mountain
of babies stacked like cordwood,
of limbs walking away from each other,
of tongues bitten through
by the language of assault,
tell me, tell us why
You neither raised Your hand
nor turned away, tell us why
You watched the excommunication of
that world and You said nothing.

7

still there is mercy, there is grace

how otherwise
could i have come to this
marble spinning in space
propelled by the great
thumb of the universe?
how otherwise
could the two roads
of this tongue
converge into a single
certitude?
how otherwise
could i, a sleek old
traveler,
curl one day safe and still
beside You
at Your feet, perhaps,
but, amen, Yours.

8

". . . . . is God"

so.
having no need to speak
You sent Your tongue
splintered into angels.
even i,
with my little piece of it
have said too much.
to ask You to explain
is to deny You.
before the word
You were.
You kiss my brother mouth.
the rest is silence.

1993

SUSAN HOWE (b. 1937)

Howe was born to Irish-American parents in Boston. She was educated as a painter at the Boston Museum of Fine Arts and exhibited her work in several group shows in New York. In the course of working on collages and then on performance pieces, she became interested in poetry and gradually made writing her career. She began to teach at the State University of New York at Buffalo in 1991. In addition to her poetry, she has written important critical books, including *My Emily Dickinson* (1985) and *The Birth-Mark: Unsettling the Wilderness in American Literary History* (1993).

Often grouped with the L=A=N=G=U=A=G=E poets because she shares with them a lineage that goes back at least to Gertrude Stein, Howe is also very much an experimental writer with her own unique project. More than most of her contemporaries, she has used the archive of American history to fashion linguistically complex contemporary reflections on national identity. "The Falls Fight" and "Hope Atherton's Wanderings" are the first two (of three) sections of a long poem titled *Articulation of Sound Forms in Time.* The sections reprinted here recast the equivalent of a seventeenth-century American captivity narrative as a linguistic journey. The foray into language is like a foray into the wilderness. One must be led astray linguistically, succumb to the wilderness of strange words—some English, some Native American—become lost, be captured, abandon familiar syntax, in order to find oneself finally at home. The linguistic rite of passage in turn becomes an analogue for the necessary structure of a proper American story of exploration and settlement, in which the conqueror's will to mastery gives way to immersion in the wild overgrowth of words.

from ARTICULATION OF SOUND FORMS IN TIME

from seaweed said nor repossess rest
scape esaid

I

THE FALLS FIGHT

Land! Land! Hath been the idol of many in New England!
INCREASE MATHER°

Just after King Philip's War so-called by the English and shortly before King William's War or Governor Dudley's War called the War of the Spanish Succession by Europeans, Deerfield was the northern most colonial settlement in the Connecticut

---

Epigraph: Mather: (1639–1723), American Puritan theologian whose publications include *Remarkable Providences* (1684), *History of the War with the Indians* (1676), and *Cases of Conscience Concerning Witchcraft* (1693). He was less agitated about witchcraft than his son Cotton was.

River Valley. In May 1676 several large bands of Indians had camped in the vicinity. The settlers felt threatened by this gathering of tribes. They appealed to Boston for soldiers, and a militia was sent out to drive away Squakeags, Pokomtucks, Mahicans, Nipmunks, and others. The standing forces were led by Captain Turner of Boston. Captain Holyoke brought a contingent from Springfield; Ensign Lyman, a group from Northampton. Sergeants Kellog and Dickinson led the militia from Hadley. Benjamin Wait and Experience Hinsdale were pilots.

"The Reverend Hope Atherton, minister of the gospel, at Hatfield, a gentleman of publick spirit, accompanied the army."

The small force of 160 men marched from Hatfield on May 17, shortly before nightfall. They passed the river at Cheapside where they were heard by an Indian sentinel who aroused his people. Indians searched the normal fording place but the colonial militia had missed it by accident. Finding no footprints they assumed the sentry had been deceived by the noise of moose passing along the river. The colonial troops continued on their way until they happened on an unguarded Nipmunk, Squakeag, Pokomtuck, or Mahican camp. This they immediately attacked by firing into the wigwams. Wakened from sleep the frightened inhabitants thought they were being raided by Mohawks. The chronicler writes: "They soon discovered their mistake but being in no position to make an immediate defense were slain on the spot, some in their surprise ran directly to the river, and were drowned; others betook themselves to their bark canoes, and having in their confusion forgot their paddles, were hurried down the falls and dashed against the rocks. In this action the enemy by their own confession, lost 300, women and children included."

What the historian doesn't say is that most of the dead were women and children.

Only one white man was killed at what came to be called *The Falls Fight.* Indian survivors soon rallied neighboring bands and when they realized that the English force was only a small one, they pursued and harassed the victorious retreating army. Now thirty-seven soldiers were killed and several more wounded. The solders were retreating because they had run out of ammunition. The retreat soon became a rout. About twenty members of the militia stood their ground and fired at the pursuing Native Americans who were crossing the river. After a hard skirmish they rejoined the body of the now surrounded army, and together they fought their way ten miles back to safety. Except for Hope Atherton and seven or eight others who were somehow separated from their fellows. These Christian soldiers soon found themselves lost. After hiding in the woods for several days some of them came to the Indians and offered to surrender on the condition that their lives would be spared. But the Squakeags, Nipmunks, Pokomtucks, or Mahicans, instead of giving them quarter, covered each man with dry thatch. Then they set the thatch on fire and ordered each soldier to run. When one covering of thatch was burnt off, another was added, and so these colonists continued running, until, Indians later told the historian: "Death delivered them from their hands."

Prophesie is Historie antedated;
and History is Postdated Prophesie.
JOHN COTTON

In our culture Hope is a name we give women. Signifying desire, trust, promise, does her name prophetically engender pacification of the feminine?

Pre-revolution Americans viewed America as the land of Hope.

"The Reverend Hope Atherton, minister of the gospel, at Hatfield, a gentleman of publick spirit, accompanied the army."

Hope's baptism of fire. No one believed the Minister's letter. He became a stranger to his community and died soon after the traumatic exposure that has earned him poor mention in a seldom opened book.

Hope's literal attributes. Effaced background dissolves remotest foreground. Putative author, premodern condition, presently present what future clamors for release?

Hope's epicene name draws its predetermined poem in.

I assume Hope Atherton's excursion for an emblem foreshadowing a Poet's abolished limitations in our demythologized fantasy of Manifest Destiny.

EXTRACT FROM A *LETTER* (DATED JUNE 8, 1781) OF STEPHEN WILLIAMS TO PRESIDENT STYLES:

"In looking over my papers I found a copy of a paper left by the Rev. Hope Atherton, the first minister of Hatfield, who was ordained May 10th, 1670. This Mr. Atherton went out with the forces (commanded by Capt. Turner, captain of the garrison soldiers, and Capt. Holyoke of the county militia) against the Indians at the falls above Deerfield, in May, 1676. In the fight, upon their retreat, Mr. Atherton was unhorsed and separated from the company, wandered in the woods some days and then got into Hadley, which is on the east side of the Connecticut River. But the fight was on the west side. Mr. Atherton gave account that he had offered to surrender himself to the enemy, but they would not receive him. Many people were not willing to give credit to this account, suggesting he was beside himself. This occasioned him to publish to his congregation and leave in writing the account I enclose to you. I had the paper from which this is copied, from Jonathan Wells, Esq., who was in the fight and lived afterward at Deerfield and was immediately acquainted with the *Indians* after the war. *He* did himself inform *me* that the *Indians* told *him* that after the fall fight, a little man with a black coat and without any hat, came toward them, but they were afraid and ran from him, thinking it was the Englishman's God, etc., etc."

II

HOPE ATHERTON'S WANDERINGS

Prest try to set after grandmother
revived by and laid down left ly
little distant each other and fro
Saw digression hobbling driftwood

forage two rotted beans & etc.
Redy to faint slaughter story so
Gone and signal through deep water
Mr. Atherton's story Hope Atherton

Clog nutmeg abt noon
scraping cano muzzell
foot path sand and so
gravel rubbish vandal
horse flesh ryal tabl
sand enemys flood sun
Danielle Warnare Servt
Turner Falls Fight us
Next wearer April One

Soe young mayde in March or April laught
who was lapd M as big as any kerchief
as like tow and beg grew bone and bullet
Stopt when asleep so Steven boy companion
Or errant Socoquis if you love your lives
War closed after Clay Gully hobbling boy
laid no whining trace no footstep clue
"Deep water" he *must* have crossed over

Who was lapt R & soe grew bone & bullet
as like tow and as another scittuation
Stopt when Worshp Steven boy companion
Abt noon and abt sun come Country Farm
Follow me save me thither this winter
Capt. Turner little horn of powder
Medfield Clay Gully hobbling boy
Sixteen trace no wanton footstep rest
Soe struck fire set the woods on fire

Two blew bird eggs plat
Habitants before dark

Little way went mistook awake
abt again Clay Gully
espied bounds to leop over
Selah cithera Opynne be
5 rails high houselot Cow
Kinsmen I pray you hasten
Furious Nipnet Ninep Ninap
little Pansett fence wth ditch
Clear stumps grubbing ploughing
Clearing the land

Antagonists lay level direction
Logic hail um bushell forty-seven
These letters copy for shoeing
was alarum by seaven bold some
Lady Ambushment signed three My
excuse haste Nipmunk to my loues
Dress for fast Stedyness and Sway
Shining at the site of Falls Jump
Habitants inning the corn & Jumps

Rash catastrophe deaf evening
Bonds loosd catcht sedge environ
Extinct ordr set tableaux
hay and insolent army
Shape of so many comfortless
And deep so deep as my narrative
our homely manner and Myself
Said "matah" and "chirah"
Pease of all sorts and best
courtesy in every place
Whereat laughing they went away

---

rest chondriacal lunacy

velc cello viable toil

quench conch uncannunc

drumm amonoosuck ythian

---

scow aback din

flicker skaeg ne

barge quagg peat

~~sieve catacomb~~

stint chisel sect

Otherworld light into fable
Best plays are secret plays

Mylord have maize meadow

have Capes Mylord to dim

barley Sion beaver Totem

W'ld bivouac by vineyard

Eagle aureole elses thend

Impulsion of a myth of beginning
The figure of a far-off Wanderer

Grail face of bronze or brass
Grass and weeds cover the face

Colonnades of rigorous Americanism
Portents of lonely destructivism

Knowledge narrowly fixed knowledge
Whose bounds in theories slay

Talismanic stepping-stone children
brawl over pebble and shallow

Marching and counter marching
Danger of roaming the woods at random

Men whet their scythes go out to mow
Nets tackle weir birchbark

Mowing salt marshes and sedge meadows

Body perception thought of perceiving (half-thought

chaotic architect repudiate line Q confine lie link realm

circle a euclidean curtail theme theme toll function coda

severity whey crayon so distant grain scalp gnat carol

omen Cur cornice zed primitive shad sac stone fur bray

tub epoch too tall fum alter rude recess emblem sixty key

Epithets young in a box told as you fly

Posit gaze level diminish lamp and asleep(selv)cannot see

is notion most open apparition past Halo view border redden

possess remote so abstract life are lost spatio-temporal hum

Maoris empirical Kantian a little lesson concatenation up

tree fifty shower see step shot Immanence force to Mohegan

blue glare(essence)cow bed leg extinct draw scribe upside
even blue(A)ash-tree fleece comfort(B)draw scribe sideup

Posit gave level diminish lamp and asleep(selv)cannot see

MoheganToForceImmanenceShotStepSeeShowerFiftyTree

UpConcatenationLessonLittleAKantianEmpiricalMaoris

HumTemporal-spatioLostAreLifeAbstractSoRemotePossess

ReddenBorderViewHaloPastApparitionOpenMostNotion *is*

blue glare(essence)cow bed leg extinct draw scribe   sideup
even blue(A)ash-tree fleece comfort(B)draw scribe   upside

Loving Friends and Kindred:—

When I look back

So short in charity and good works

We are a small remnant

of signal escapes wonderful in themselves

We march from our camp a little

and come home

Lost the beaten track and so

River section dark all this time

We must not worry

how few we are and fall from each other

More than language can express

Hope for the artist in America & etc

This is my birthday

These are the old home trees

1987

MICHAEL S. HARPER (b. 1938)

Born in Brooklyn, New York, to parents who were a postal worker and a medical stenographer, Harper moved to Los Angeles with his family in 1951. While at Los Angeles City College, then State College, in the late 1950s, he worked in the post office and met a number of articulate black coworkers blocked from more challenging employment. Finally settling on a writing career, he attended the Iowa Writers' Workshop, the only black writer in his class; he was forced to live in segregated housing. Soon after that he met the legendary jazz saxophonist and composer John Coltrane; their friendship had a profound impact on Harper's writing, making him perhaps the contemporary black writer whose poetry has the most original and intricate relation to music. He has worked out a wide range of techniques to make his poetry, which must be read aloud, musical, from the use of subtle irregular repetition and varying line lengths, to the more obvious placement of blues refrains. The lines are also rhythmically paced in surprising ways, with lines meant to be read rapidly mixed effectively with lines designed to be lingered over and read slowly. Meanwhile, his subject matter mixes strong acts of witness to America's racist history with wrenching accounts of family tragedy. The two counterpoint one another in such a way as to make individual lives mythic in their very specificity and history verified and lived in the pulse of individual experience. Harper has taught at Brown University since 1971.

SONG: *I WANT A WITNESS*

Blacks in frame houses
call to the helicopters,
their antlered arms
spinning; jeeps pad
these glass-studded streets;
on this hill are tanks painted gold.

Our children sing
spirituals of *Motown*,°
idioms these streets suckled
on a southern road.
This scene is about power,
terror, producing

8. *Motown:* American record company.

love and pain and pathology;
in an army of white dust,
blacks here to *testify*
and *testify,* and *testify,*
and *redeem,* and *redeem,*
in black smoke coming,
as they wave their arms,
as they wave their tongues.

1972

BLUE RUTH: AMERICA

I am telling you this:
the tubes in your nose,
in the esophagus,
in the stomach;
the small balloon
attached to its end
is your bleeding gullet;
yellow in the canned
sunshine of gauze,
stitching, bedsores,
each tactoe cut
sewn back
is America:
I am telling you this:
history is your own heartbeat.

1971

BROTHER JOHN

Black man:
I'm a black man;
I'm black; I am—
A black man; black—
I'm a black man;
I'm a black man;
I'm a man; black—
I am—

Bird, buttermilk bird—
smack, booze and bitches

I am Bird
baddest nightdreamer
on sax in the ornithology-world
I can fly—higher, high, higher—
I'm a black man;
I am; I'm a black man—

Miles, blue haze,
Miles high, another bird,
more Miles, mute,
Mute Miles, clean,
bug-eyed, unspeakable,
Miles, sweet Mute,
sweat Miles, black Miles;
I'm a black man;
I'm black; I am;
I'm a black man—

Trane, Coltrane; John Coltrane;
it's tranetime; chase the Trane;
it's a slow dance;
it's the Trane
in Alabama; acknowledgment,
a love supreme,
it's black Trane; black;
I'm a black man; I'm black;
I am; I'm a black man—

Brother John, Brother John
plays no instrument;
he's a black man; black;
he's a black man; he is
Brother John; Brother John—

I'm a black man; I am;
black; I am; I'm a black
man; I am; I am;
I'm a black man;
I'm a black man;
I am; I'm a black man;
I am:

1970

AMERICAN HISTORY

Those four black girls blown up
in that Alabama church°
remind me of five hundred
middle passage° blacks,
in a net, under water
in Charleston harbor
so *redcoats*° wouldn't find them.
Can't find what you can't see
can you?

1970

WE ASSUME: ON THE DEATH OF OUR SON, REUBEN MASAI HARPER

We assume
that in 28 hours,
lived in a collapsible isolette,
you learned to accept pure oxygen
as the natural sky;
the scant shallow breaths
that filled those hours
cannot, did not make you fly—
but dreams were there
like crooked palmprints on
the twin-thick windows of the nursery
in the glands of your mother.

We assume
the sterile hands
drank chemicals in and out
from lungs opaque with mucus,
pumped your stomach,
eeked the bicarbonate in
crooked, green-winged veins,
out in a plastic mask;

---

2. *Alabama church:* in 1963, civil rights opponents killed four black girls when they exploded a bomb in a Birmingham, Alabama, church.

4. *middle passage:* the name of the route slave ships took across the Atlantic Ocean from Africa to North or South America.

7. *redcoats:* British soldiers during the colonial period of American history.

A woman who'd lost her first son
consoled us with an angel gone ahead
to pray for our family—
gone into that sky
seeking oxygen,
gone into autopsy,
a fine brown powdered sugar,
a disposable cremation:

We assume
you did not know we loved you.

1970

REUBEN, REUBEN

I reach from pain
to music great enough
to bring me back,
swollenhead, madness,
lovefruit, a pickle of hate
so sour my mouth twicked
up and would not sing;
there's nothing in the beat
to hold it in
melody and turn human skin;
a brown berry gone
to rot just two days on the branch;
we've lost a son,
the music, *jazz*, comes in.

1970

DEATHWATCH

Twitching in the cactus
hospital gown, a loon
on hairpin wings,
she tells me how
her episiotomy°
is perfectly sewn
and doesn't hurt

5. *episiotomy:* surgical procedure to widen the vaginal opening during childbirth.

while she sits in a pile
of blood
which once cleaned
the placenta
my third son should be in.
She tells me how early
he is, and how strong,
like his father,
and long, like a black-
stemmed Easter rose
in a white hand.

Just under five pounds
you lie there, a collapsed
balloon doll, burst in your
fifteenth hour, with the face
of your black father,
his fingers, his toes,
and eight voodoo
adrenalin holes in
your pinwheeled hair-lined
chest; you witness
your parents sign the autopsy
and disposal papers
shrunken to duplicate
in black ink
on white paper
like the country
you were born in,
unreal, asleep,
silent, almost alive.

This is a dedication
to our memory
of three sons—
two dead, one alive—
a reminder of a letter
to Du Bois°
from a student
at Clark—on behalf
of his whole history class.

---

43. *Du Bois:* W. E. B. Du Bois (1868–1963), African American writer and activist; also see Lucille Clifton's poem "Reply" (p. 472).

The class is confronted
with a question,
and no one—
not even the professor—
is sure of the answer:
"Will you please tell us
whether or not it is true
that negroes
are not able to cry?"

America needs a killing.
America needs a killing.
Survivors will be human.

1970

DEAR JOHN, DEAR COLTRANE°

a love supreme, a love supreme
a love supreme, a love supreme

Sex fingers toes
in the marketplace
near your father's church°
in Hamlet, North Carolina°—
witness to this love
in this calm fallow
of these minds,
there is no substitute for pain:
genitals gone or going,
seed burned out,
you tuck the roots in the earth,
turn back, and move
by river through the swamps,
singing: *a love supreme, a love supreme;*
what does it all mean?
Loss, so great each black

---

poem title: John Coltrane (1926–1967) was the premier jazz saxophonist of his generation and an influential avant-garde jazz composer. He wrote "A Love Supreme," a four-part composition, in response to a spiritual experience in 1957, which led him to stop using heroin and alcohol; it was recorded in 1964.

3. *father's church:* Coltrane's grandfather, who lived in the family home, was minister of St. Stephens AME Zion Church in Hamlet.

4. *Hamlet, North Carolina:* Coltrane's birthplace.

woman expects your failure
in mute change, the seed gone.
You plod up into the electric city—
your song now crystal and
the blues. You pick up the horn
with some will and blow
into the freezing night:
a love supreme, a love supreme—

Dawn comes and you cook
up the thick sin 'tween
impotence and death, fuel
the tenor sax cannibal
heart, genitals and sweat
that makes you clean—
a love supreme, a love supreme—

Why you so black?
cause I am
why you so funky?
cause I am
why you so black?
cause I am
why you so sweet?
cause I am
why you so black?
cause I am
a love supreme, a love supreme:

So sick
you couldn't play *Naima,*°
so flat we ached
for song you'd concealed
with your own blood,
your diseased liver gave
out its purity,
the inflated heart
pumps out, the tenor kiss,
tenor love:
a love supreme, a love supreme—
a love supreme, a love supreme—

1970

---

44. *Naima:* a Coltrane composition recorded in 1959, the name of his first wife.

ISHMAEL REED (b. 1938)

A versatile, unpredictable, and frequently iconoclastic figure, Reed has written nine novels, edited several anthologies, written songs and operas, and recorded some of the poetry from his five books of poems. He was born in Chattanooga, Tennessee, and raised in Buffalo, New York. He enrolled at the State University of New York at Buffalo, but left to do civil rights and community reporting for a Buffalo newspaper. While there he met Malcolm X and decided to move to New York in 1962, where he worked at numerous jobs, joined a writing workshop, and produced his first novel. In 1967, he moved to California, first to Berkeley and then Oakland. In 1976, he was cofounder of the multiethnic Before Columbus Foundation.

I AM A COWBOY IN THE BOAT OF RA

The devil must be forced to reveal any such physical evil (potions, charms, fetishes, etc.) still outside the body and these must be burned.
(Rituale Romanum, published 1947, endorsed by the coat-of-arms and introductory letter from Francis Cardinal Spellman°)

I am a cowboy in the boat of Ra,°
sidewinders in the saloons of fools
bit my forehead   like   O
the untrustworthiness of Egyptologists
who do not know their trips. Who was that
dog-faced° man? they asked, the day I rode
from town.

School marms with halitosis° cannot see
the Nefertiti° fake chipped on the run by slick

---

epigraph: *Spellman:* (1889–1967), conservative Catholic archbishop and cardinal of New York.

1. *Ra:* the Egyptian creator god and sun god, also known as Re and as Amun-Re, often depicted as a falcon wearing the sun disc on its head, or as a human figure with a ram's head. In some cults he is a double god—Ra by day and Osiris, god of the underworld, by night. The *boat* of Ra draws in multiple associations, starting with the boats included in Egyptian tombs to carry the body and spirit of dead Pharaohs and extending to the slave ships under the control of white masters that brought blacks to the Americas.

6. *dog-faced:* Anubis, the Egyptian mortuary god, takes the form of a black dog or a jackal. "Who was that masked man?" is a recurrent line from the *Lone Ranger* radio drama, comic strip, and television series.

8. *halitosis:* here a sign of cultural incapacitation; folks with "bad breath" cannot play the saxophone and are not hip to either the dominant culture's deceptions or the alternative knowledge the poem synthesizes.

9. *Nefertiti:* fourteenth-century B.C. Egyptian queen, consort of Pharaoh Akhenaton; her image is best known from the sculptured head found at Amarna in 1912, chipped and removed by Germans, and now in the Berlin Museum.

germans, the hawk behind Sonny Rollins'° head or
the ritual beard of his axe; a longhorn winding
its bells thru the Field of Reeds.

I am a cowboy in the boat of Ra. I bedded
down with Isis,° Lady of the Boogaloo,° dove
down deep in her horny, stuck up her Wells-Far-ago°
in daring midday getaway. 'Start grabbing the
blue',° I said from top of my double crown.°

I am a cowboy in the boat of Ra. Ezzard Charles°
of the Chisholm Trail.° Took up the bass but they
blew off my thumb.° Alchemist in ringmanship but a
sucker for the right cross.

I am a cowboy in the boat of Ra. Vamoosed from
the temple i bide my time. The price on the wanted
poster was a-going down, outlaw alias copped° my stance
and moody greenhorns were making me dance; while my mouth's
shooting iron got its chambers jammed.

I am a cowboy in the boat of Ra. Boning-up in
the ol West i bide my time. You should see

---

10. *Rollins:* (b. 1929), American jazz tenor-saxophonist. The "hawk behind Sonny Rollins' head" does more than allude to hawk-headed Egyptian gods; it is a specific reference to Coleman Hawkins (1901–1969), who was Rollins's predecessor in a hard style of saxophone playing. In jazz slang your "axe" is your musical instrument; practicing, in the same lingo, is "woodshedding." The "longhorn" invokes both the famous breed of cattle in the Old West and the saxophone. The "bell" is both a cowbell and the saxophone's expanded mouth. The "field of reeds" in the stanza's last line doubles as a musical reference (a saxophone has a reed in the mouthpiece) and a reference to the bullrushes at the edge of Egypt's Nile River where Moses was found.

14. *Isis:* Egyptian mother goddess; she impregnated herself from Osiris's corpse as he was entering the underworld to become its ruler.

14. *Boogaloo:* popular dance style of the 1960s. In black English, "to boogaloo" came to mean "to dance" or "to fool around, usages that white racists tried to appropriate as a slur, when "boogaloo" became a way of referring to a black person.

15. *Wells-Far-ago:* play on Wells Fargo, a stage company in the American West, and a "farrago," a word whose multiple meanings are all in play here: a mixed fodder for cattle; an apparently irrational assemblage of references (the poem); a staged event of mixed fact and fancy designed to deceive (American culture).

17. *blue:* perhaps includes an allusion to Rollins's well-known piece "Blue Seven."

17. *double crown:* at once the combined crown of Ammon and Ra of rival Egyptian cults and the double crowns of music and poetry.

18. *Ezzard Charles:* (1922–1975), African American prizefighter who was heavyweight champion of the world from 1949 to 1951.

19. *Chisholm Trail:* route in the American Old West used to drive cattle from Texas to Kansas.

20. *thumb:* one cannot play the bass without a thumb.

24. *copped:* originally, "stole or took unfairly"; now in black English "understood," or assumed a manner or attitude.

me pick off these tin cans whippersnappers. I
write the motown° long plays for the comeback of
Osiris. Make them up when stars stare at sleeping
steer out here near the campfire. Women arrive
on the backs of goats and throw themselves on
my Bowie.°

I am a cowboy in the boat of Ra. Lord of the lash,
the Loup Garou° Kid. Half breed son of Pisces and
Aquarius.° I hold the souls of men in my pot. I do
the dirty boogie° with scorpions. I make the bulls
keep still and was the first swinger to grape the taste.

I am a cowboy in his boat. Pope Joan° of the
Ptah° Ra. C/mere a minute willya doll?
Be a good girl and
bring me my Buffalo horn of black powder
bring me my headdress of black feathers
bring me my bones of Ju-Ju° snake
go get my eyelids of red paint.
Hand me my shadow

I'm going into town after Set°

I am a cowboy in the boat of Ra

---

30. *motown:* Detroit-based, black-owned record company that came to prominence in the 1960s and was the first really successful incursion of a black sensibility into the rock and roll scene.

34. *Bowie:* large knife, here phallic.

36. *Loup Garou:* (French) werewolf. "Loup Garou" also rhymes with the name of Lash LaRue, star of a series of western films, such as *The Black Lash* (1952) and *Law of the Lash* (1947), whose work is invoked in the previous phrase, "Lord of the lash." LaRue, who also appeared in a comic book series, used a whip to disarm villains. Finally, under a slightly different spelling, Loop Garoo is the whip-wielding cowboy protagonist of Reed's novel *Yellow Back Radio Broke-Down* (1969).

37. *Pisces and Aquarius*: the twelfth and eleventh signs of the zodiac, a zone of fixed stars that marks the apparent courses of the sun, moon, and planets about the earth.

38. *boogie:* several meanings are in play. Boogie (or boogie-woogie) is a percussive style of playing blues on the piano, as well as a jitterbug dance performed to the same music; it is also disparaging slang for a black person. To "boogie" is also to dance or to have sexual intercourse; hence the phrase "do the dirty boogie." The poem's account of struggles over meaning encompasses language, myth, and history.

40. *Pope Joan:* apocryphal female pope said to have served in the ninth century. One of the dedicatees of Reed's novel *Yellow Back Radio Broke-Down.*

41. *Ptah:* Egyptian creator god and god of craftsmen, a rival claimant with Ra as senior figure in the pantheon.

45. *Ju-Ju:* a charm or spell used to ward off evil spirits.

48. *Set:* Egyptian god of chaos and adversity, sometimes depicted as a man with the head of an animal, who murdered his brother Osiris. In the poem the word also invokes a musical set.

look out Set here i come Set
to get Set to sunset Set
to unseat Set to Set down Set

usurper of the Royal couch
imposter RAdio of Moses' bush°
party pooper O hater of dance
vampire outlaw of the milky way

1972

OAKLAND BLUES

Well it's six o'clock in Oakland
and the sun is full of wine
I say, it's six o'clock in Oakland
and the sun is red with wine
We buried you this morning, baby
in the shadow of a vine

Well, they told you of the sickness
almost eighteen months ago
Yes, they told you of the sickness
almost eighteen months ago
You went down fighting, daddy. Yes
You fought Death toe to toe

O, the egrets fly over Lake Merritt
and the blackbirds roost in trees
O, the egrets fly over Lake Merritt
and the blackbirds roost in trees
Without you little papa
what O, what will become of me

O, it's hard to come home, baby
To a house that's still and stark
O, it's hard to come home, baby
To a house that's still and stark
All I hear is myself
thinking
and footsteps in the dark

1988

---

54. *Moses' bush:* the burning bush, described in the book of Exodus, out of which God spoke to Moses, who led the Jewish people out of Egyptian slavery, a role both poetry and music fill for American blacks in the poem.

LAWSON FUSAO INADA (b. 1938)

Born in Fresno, California, as a child Inada spent World War II in a concentration camp with his family. In a period of racist hysteria, constitutional guarantees were set aside, and Japanese Americans were interned for the duration of the war. He would later write of the experience in *Before the War: Poems as They Happened* (1971). Lawson was then educated at Berkeley and Fresno State College, followed by studies in creative writing at the University of Iowa and the University of Oregon. He teaches at Southern Oregon State College. While maintaining the strong political perspective of *Before the War,* he has also taken up other subjects, as "Listening Images" and its epigrammatic portraits of jazz artists suggests.

LISTENING IMAGES

LESTER YOUNG°

Yes, clouds do have
The smoothest sound.

BILLIE HOLIDAY°

Hold a microphone
Close to the moon.

CHARLIE PARKER°

Rapids to baptism
In one blue river.

COLEMAN HAWKINS°

A hawk for certain,
But as big as a man.

Young: tenor saxophonist Lester Young (1909–1959) played airy, melodic lines in the upper register of his horn.

Holiday: with her enormous emotional range, Billie Holiday (1915–1959) transformed any song she vocalized, from the Tin Pan Alley ditties that were thrust before her as commercial ventures to the haunting works she composed herself.

Parker: alto saxophonist Charlie Parker (1920–1955), one of the inventors of bebop, was notable for the speed with which he played.

Hawkins: tenor saxophonist Coleman "Hawk" Hawkins (1901–1969) dominated small groups with his inventive harmonies and deep burly tone.

BEN WEBSTER°

Such fragile moss
In a massive tree.

LOUIS ARMSTRONG°

Just dip your ears
And taste the sauce.

ROY ELDRIDGE°

Get in the car.
Start the engine.

DIZZY GILLESPIE°

Gusts of gusto
Sweep the desert.

MILES DAVIS°

3 valves, tubing . . .
How many feelings?

CLIFFORD BROWN°

A fine congregation
This spring morning.

ART TATUM°

Innumerable dew,
A splendid web.

Webster: tenor saxophonist Ben Webster (1909–1973) ornamented his solos with elaborate filigrees and a dramatic vibrato.

Armstrong: jazz pioneer and trumpeter Louis Armstrong (1900–1975) was raised in New Orleans; his "Struttin' with Some Barbecue" was a hit of the 1920s.

Eldridge: the solid and substantial trumpet solos of Roy Eldridge (1911–1989) graced numerous big bands of the 1930s and 1940s.

Gillespie: (1917–1993), a trumpet virtuoso and bebop innovator, Gillespie was the rare musician whose performances were swept with humor.

Davis: especially on ballads recorded in the 1950s, the trumpet playing of Miles Davis (1926–1991) has been likened to "a man walking on eggshells" (Ira Gitler).

Brown: trumpeter and composer of the resplendent "Joy Spiring," Clifford Brown (1930–1956) died suddenly, his immense promise unrealized.

Tatum: Art Tatum (1909–1956) demonstrated his complete command of the piano by producing solos that were beehives of harmonic activity.

BUD POWELL°

The eye, and then
The hurricane.

THELONIOUS MONK°

Always old, always new,
Always déjà vu.

COUNT BASIE°

Acorns on the roof—
Syncopated oakestra.

DUKE ELLINGTON°

Stars, stripes, united
States of Ellington.

GENE AMMONS
CHU BERRY
DON BYAS
EDDIE DAVIS
HERSCHEL EVANS
PAUL GONSALVES
DEXTER GORDON
WARDELL GRAY
RAHSAAN KIRK
HANK MOBLEY
CHARLIE ROUSE
SONNY STITT°

Mountain mist,
Monumental totem.

Powell: the right hand of pianist Bud Powell (1924–1966) strung out lanky boppish lines that his left hand interrupted with irregular and dissonant chords.

Monk: (1917–1982), his unpredictable piano improvisations blended dissonant avant-garde harmonies with a down home, percussive rhythm.

Basie: well-known orchestra leader William "Count" Basie (1904–1984) punctuated the ending of his understated piano solos with short staccato notes.

Ellington: (1899–1974), his compositions were concerto-like showcasings of stars in the orchestra he took on the road across America.

Stitt: from "Gene Ammons" to "Sonny Stitt," this alphabetical list of tenor saxophonists from a range of different backgrounds over a number of generations—the earliest born in 1909 (Evans), the latest in 1936 (Kirk)—dramatizes the variety of jazz.

JOHN COLTRANE°

Sunrise golden
At the throat.

ERIC DOLPHY°

Coming across quick
Deer in the forest.

DELTA BLUES°

They broke bottles
Just to get the neck.

SON HOUSE°

A lone man plucking
Bolts of lightning.

KANSAS CITY SHOUTERS°

Your baby leaves you on the train.
You stand and bring it back again.

BIG JOE TURNER°

Big as laughter, big as rain,
Big as the big public domain.

1993

Coltrane: John Coltrane (1926–1967) was a singularly innovative tenor and soprano saxophonist.

Dolphy: alto saxophonist, bass clarinetist, and flutist Eric Dolphy (1928–1964) was a player of remarkable fluency.

Blues: blues performers from the Mississippi Delta played "bottleneck" guitar, extracting a plaintive wail from the instrument by sliding a broken bottleneck, worn on the little finger of the left hand, up and down the neck of a guitar unconventionally tuned in thirds and fifths.

House: a blues guitarist and vocalist brought up in a religious household, Eddie "Son" House Jr. (1902–1988) was torn between the ministry and the secular desires of the popular performer.

Shouters: the Kansas City Shouters were deep-voiced male vocalists from the southwest in the 1930s and 1940s who sang their blues with triumphant authority and power.

Turner: the rhythm-and-blues recording of "Shake, Rattle and Roll" by Kansas City Shouter Big Joe Turner (1911–1985) became a commercial success after it was adapted by Bill Haley and His Comets.

ROBERT PINSKY (b. 1940)

Born in Long Branch, New Jersey, Pinsky was educated at Rutgers and Stanford Universities. In California, he worked with poet-critic Ivor Winters and earned a Ph.D. He has taught at several schools, translated Dante's *Inferno,* and published both criticism and poetry. Pinsky generally uses regular stanzas and traditional forms, modifying them when he wishes. He has drawn both from his own experience and, as with "The Unseen" and "Shirt," from modern history, balancing a will to reason with spiritual inclinations.

DYING

Nothing to be said about it, and everything—
The change of changes, closer or further away:
The Golden Retriever next door, Gussie, is dead,

Like Sandy, the Cocker Spaniel from three doors down
Who died when I was small; and every day
Things that were in my memory fade and die.

Phrases die out: first, everyone forgets
What doornails are; then after certain decades
As a dead metaphor, *"dead as a doornail"* flickers

And fades away. But someone I know is dying—
And though one might say glibly, "everyone is,"
The different pace makes the difference absolute.

The tiny invisible spores in the air we breathe,
That settle harmlessly on our drinking water
And on our skin, happen to come together

With certain conditions on the forest floor
Or even a shady corner of the lawn—
And overnight the fleshy, pale stalks gather,

The colorless growth without a leaf or flower;
And around the stalks, the summer grass keeps growing
With steady pressure, like the insistent whiskers

That grow between shaves on a face, the nails
Growing and dying from the toes and fingers
At their own humble pace, oblivious

As the nerveless moths, that live their night or two—
Though like a moth a bright soul keeps on beating,
Bored and impatient in the monster's mouth.

1984

THE UNSEEN

In Krakow° it rained, the stone arcades and cobbles
And the smoky air all soaked one penetrating color
While in an Art Nouveau° café, on harp-shaped chairs,

We sat making up our minds to tour the death camp.°
As we drove there the next morning past farms
And steaming wooden villages, the rain had stopped

Though the sky was still gray. A young guide explained
Everything we saw in her tender, hectoring° English:
The low brick barracks; the heaped-up meticulous

Mountains of shoes, toothbrushes, hair; one cell
Where the Pope° had prayed and placed flowers; logbooks,
Photographs, latrines—the whole unswallowable

Menu of immensities. It began drizzling again,
And the way we paused to open or close the umbrellas,
Hers and ours, as we went from one building to the next,

Had a formal, dwindled feeling. We felt bored
And at the same time like screaming Biblical phrases.
I am poured out like water; Thine is the day and

Thine also the night; I cannot look to see
My own right hand . . . I remembered a sleep-time game,
A willed dream I had never thought of by day before:

I am there; and granted the single power of invisibility,
Roaming the camp at will. At first I savor my mastery
Slowly by creating small phantom diversions,

---

1. *Krakow:* city in southern Poland.

3. *Art Noveau:* decorating style that; originated in the late nineteenth century, characterized by sinuous lines and foliate forms.

4. *death camp:* Auschwitz, a Nazi concentration camp just west of Krakow; more than a million Jews were murdered there during World War II.

8. *hectoring:* brow-beating.

11. *Pope:* John Paul II (1920–2005), pope from 1978 to 2005.

Then kill kill kill kill, a detailed and strangely
Passionless inward movie: I push the man holding
The crystals° down from the gas chamber roof, bludgeon

The pet collie of the Commandant's children
And in the end flush everything with a vague flood
Of fire and blood as I drift on toward sleep

In a blurred finale, like our tour's—eddying
In a downpour past the preserved gallows where
The Allies hung the Commandant, in 1947.

I don't feel changed, or even informed—in that,
It's like any other historical monument; although
It is true that I don't ever at night any more

Prowl rows of red buildings unseen, doing
Justice like an angry god to escape insomnia. And so,
O discredited Lord of Hosts, your servant gapes

Obediently to swallow various doings of us, the most
Capable of all your former creatures—we have
No shape, we are poured out like water, but still

We try to take in what won't be turned from in despair:
As if, just as we turned toward the fumbled drama
Of the religious art shop window to accuse you

Yet again, you were to slit open your red heart
To show us at last the secret of your day and also,
Because it also is yours, of your night.

1984

SHIRT

The back, the yoke, the yardage. Lapped seams,
The nearly invisible stitches along the collar
Turned in a sweatshop by Koreans or Malaysians

Gossiping over tea and noodles on their break
Or talking money or politics while one fitted
This armpiece with its overseam to the band

---

27. *crystals:* cyanide crystals, causing death by asphixiation; administered by the Germans in rooms holding scores of victims, with friends and family members aware of each other dying.

Of cuff I button at my wrist. The presser, the cutter,
The wringer, the mangle. The needle, the union,
The treadle, the bobbin. The code. The infamous blaze

At the Triangle° Factory in nineteen-eleven.
One hundred and forty-six died in the flames
On the ninth floor, no hydrants, no fire escapes—

The witness in a building across the street
Who watched how a young man helped a girl to step
Up to the windowsill, then held her out

Away from the masonry wall and let her drop.
And then another. As if he were helping them up
To enter a streetcar, and not eternity.

A third before he dropped her put her arms
Around his neck and kissed him. Then he held
Her into space, and dropped her. Almost at once

He stepped to the sill himself, his jacket flared
And fluttered up from his shirt as he came down,
Air filling up the legs of his gray trousers—

Like Hart Crane's Bedlamite, "shrill shirt ballooning."
Wonderful how the pattern matches perfectly
Across the placket and over the twin bar-tacked

Corners of both pockets, like a strict rhyme
Or a major chord. Prints, plaids, checks,
Houndstooth, Tattersall, Madras. The clan tartans

Invented by mill-owners inspired by the hoax of Ossian,°
To control their savage Scottish workers, tamed
By a fabricated heraldry: MacGregor,

Bailey, MacMartin. The kilt, devised for workers
To wear among the dusty clattering looms.
Weavers, carders, spinners. The loader,

---

10. *Triangle:* on March 25, 1911, a fire swept through the Triangle Shirtwaist Company in the Greenwich Village section of New York City. It was a sweatshop where the mostly women workers produced poorly paid piecework in a building without fire escapes or other safety provisions. The fire consumed 146 workers, trapped in part by management's decision to restrict breaks by keeping the doors locked. It was one of the nation's worst industrial tragedies.

31. *Ossian:* legendary Gaelic bard and warrior.

The docker, the navvy. The planter, the picker, the sorter
Sweating at her machine in a litter of cotton
As slaves in calico headrags sweated in fields:

George Herbert,° your descendant is a Black
Lady in South Carolina, her name is Irma
And she inspected my shirt. Its color and fit

And feel and its clean smell have satisfied
Both her and me. We have culled its cost and quality
Down to the buttons of simulated bone.

The buttonholes, the sizing, the facing, the characters
Printed in black on neckband and tail. The shape,
The label, the labor, the color, the shade. The shirt.

1990

VENI, CREATOR SPIRITUS

Blessed is He who came to Earth as a Bull°
And ravished our virgin mother and ran with her
Astride his back across the plains and mountains
Of the whole world. And when He came to Ocean,
He swam across with our mother on his back.
And in His wake the peoples of the world
Sailed trafficking in salt, oil, slaves and opal.
Hallowed be His name, who blesses the nations:
From the Middle Kingdom, gunpowder and Confucius.
From Europe, Dante and the Middle Passage.
Shiva° is His lieutenant, and by His commandment
Odysseus brought the palm tree to California,
Tea to the Britons, opium to the Cantonese.
Horses, tobacco, tomatoes and gonorrhea
Coursed by His will between Old Worlds and New.
In the Old Market where children once were sold,
Pirated music and movies in every tongue,
Defying borders as Algebra trans-migrated
From Babylon to Egypt. At His beck

---

40. *Herbert:* (1593–1633) English metaphysical poet and clergyman whose poem "The Collar" includes the refrain "I will abroad," suggesting travel to the New World.

1. *Bull:* Zeus came to earth in the form of a white bull, abducted the Phoenician princess Europa, and raped her.

11. *Shiva:* Hindu god with a third eye in his forehead, often depicted as destroying demons.

Empire gathers, diffuses, and in time disperses
Into the smoky Romance of its name.
And after the great defeat in Sicily°
When thousands of Athenians were butchered
Down in the terrible quarries, and many were bound
And branded on the face with a horse's head,
Meaning *this man is a slave,* a few were spared
Because they could recite new choruses
By the tragedian Euripides,° whose works
And fame had reached to Sicily—as willed
By the Holy One who loves blood sacrifice
And burnt offerings, commerce and the Arts.

2007

---

22. *defeat in Sicily:* a disastrous Athenian Military expedition to Sicily (415 BC to 413 BC) was the turning point in the Peloponnesian war. Athens lost two hundred ships and thousands of soldiers.

28. *Euripides:* (c. 480–406 BC), one of the three great tragedians of classical Athens.

WELTON SMITH (1940–2006)

Smith, who was born in Houston, Texas, is the author of *Penetration* (1972), a collection of poems, and *The Roach Riders*, a play. His poem sequence "Malcolm," which was included in the historic 1968 Black Arts collection *Black Fire: An Anthology of Afro-American Writing*, edited by Larry Neal and Amiri Baraka, is one of a number of elegies written after Malcolm X was killed in 1965. Its tonal shifts help make it one of the most memorable and one of the more inventive poems to come out of the Black Arts Movement.

MALCOLM°

Malcolm

i cannot move
from your voice.
there is no peace
where i am. the wind
cannot move
hard enough to clear the trash
and far away i hear my screams.

the lean, hard-bone face
a rich copper color.
the smile. the
thin nose and broad
nostrils. Betty—in the quiet
after midnight. your hand
soft on her back. you kiss
her neck softly
below her right ear.
she would turn
to face you and arch up—
her head moving to your chest.

---

poem title: Malcolm X (1925–1965), charismatic African American political and religious leader, assassinated at a rally in 1965. Born Malcolm Little, his family's house in Michigan was burned by the Ku Klux Klan, his father murdered, and his mother institutionalized. A petty criminal and drug user, he converted to the Nation of Islam in prison, changed his last name to "X," showing that he regarded "Little" as a vestige of slavery, and educated himself. After prison, he became a minister in the church and an increasingly public figure, arguing (contrary to Martin Luther King's nonviolence) for black separatism and violence for self-defense. Watched by the FBI and often demonized by the white press, he was killed after he broke with the Nation of Islam. Coauthor of *The Autobiography of Malcolm X* (1965), he is an enduring cultural icon and symbol of black pride.

her arms sliding
round your neck. you breathe deeply.
it is quiet, in this moment
you knew
what it was all about.

your voice
is inside me; i loaned
my heart in exchange
for your voice.

in harlem, the long
avenue blocks. the miles
from heart to heart.
a slobbering emaciated man
once a man of god sprawled
on the sidewalk. he clutches
his bottle. pisses on himself
demands you respect him
because his great grandmother
was one-eighth cherokee.
in this moment, you knew.

in berkeley the fat
jewess moves the stringy brown
hair from her face saying
she would like to help you—
give you some of her time.
you knew.
in birmingham "get a move
on you, girl, you bet'not
be late for sunday school."
not this morning—
it is a design, you knew.

sometimes
light plays on my eyelashes
when my eyes
are almost closed—
the chrome blues and golds
the crimson and pale
ice green the swift movements
of lights through my lashes—
fantastic—

the sound of mecca
inside you. you knew.

the man
inside you; the men
inside you fought.
fighting men inside you
made a frenzy
smelling like shit.
you reached into yourself—
deep—and scooped your frenzy
and rolled it to a slimy ball
and stretched your arm back
to throw

now you pace the regions
of my heart. you know
my blood and see
where my tears are made.
i see the beast
and hold my frenzy;
you are not lonely—
in my heart there are many
unmarked graves.

THE NIGGA SECTION

slimy obscene creatures. insane
creations of a beast. you
have murdered a man. You
have devoured me. you
have done it with precision
like the way you stand green
in the dark sucking pus
and slicing your penis
into quarters—stuffing
shit through your noses.
you rotten motherfuckin bastards
murder yourselves again and again
and call it life. you have made
your black mother to spread
her legs   wide
you have crawled in mucous
smeared snot in your hair
let machines crawl up your cock

rammed your penis into garbage disposals
spread your gigantic ass from
one end of america to the other
and peeped from under your legs
and grinned a gigantic white grin
and called all the beasts
to fuck you hard in the ass
you have fucked your fat black mothers
you have murdered malcolm
you have torn out your own tongue
you have made your women
to grow huge dicks you
have stuffed me into your mouth
and slobbered my blood
in your grinning derangement.
your are the dumbest thing
on the earth   the slimiest
most rotten thing in the universe
you motherfuckin germ
you konk-haired blood suckin punks
you serpents of pestilence you
samboes you green witches nawing the heads of infants
you rodents you whores
you sodomites you fat
slimy cockroaches crawling to your
holes with bits of malcolm's flesh
i hope you are smothered
in the fall of a huge yellow moon.

INTERLUDE

we never spent time in the mountains
planting our blood in the land planting
our blood in the dirt planting our blood
in the air   we never walked together
down Fillmore or Fifth Avenue
down Main Street together
Friend we never sat together as guests
at a friend's table   Friend
we never danced together as men
in a public park   Friend we never
spent long mornings fishing or laughed
laughed falling all down into the dirt
laughed rolling in the dirt   holding
our stomachs laughing rolling   our mouths

wide open   huge fat laughter
our black bodies shaking   Friend
we never laughed like that together

SPECIAL SECTION FOR THE NIGGAS ON THE LOWER EASTSIDE OR: INVENT THE DIVISOR AND MULTIPLY

you are the lice
of the lower eastside
you are deranged imitators
of white boys acting out a
fucked-up notion of the mystique
of black suffering. uptown
they believe they are niggas
here you have explanations—
psychological, cultural, sociological,
epistomological, cosmological, political,
economic, aesthetic, religious, dialectical,
existential, jive-ass bullshit explanation
for being niggas   you are
deranged slobbering punks lapping in the
ass of a beast
in the bars you recite
slave rebellions you recite egypt
you recite timbuktu you stand
on your head and whine anger
you are frauds   trying to legitimatize
what they say you are
you are jive revolutionaries
who will never tear this house down
you are too terrified of cold
too lazy to build another house

you lick every cranny in tompkins square
you slurp every gutter from river to river
you are gluttons devouring
every cunt in every garbage can on avenue b
you hope to find
an eighty ton white woman
with a cock big enough
to crawl inside
you don't just want a white woman
you want to be a white woman
you are concubines of a beast
you want to be lois lane, audrey hepburn, ma perkins, lana

turner, jean harlow, kim stanley, may west, marilyn
monroe, sophie tucker, betty crocker, tallulah bankhead,
judy canova, shirley temple, and trigger
you frauds: with your wire-rim glasses and double-breasted
pin striped coats, and ass choaker pants
you sing while your eyes are scraped from their sockets
you dance while flares are rammed into your ears
you jive mercenary frauds
selling nappy hair for a party invitation
selling black   for a part in a play
selling black   for a ride in a rolls
selling black   for a quick fuck
selling black   for two lines on page 6,000 in the new york
times
selling babies in birmingham for a smile in the den

turn white you jive motherfucker   and ram the bomb up
your ass.

INTERLUDE

screams
screams
malcolm
does not hear my screams
screams
betty
does not hear my screams
screams scraping my eyes
screams from the guns
screams
screams
the witches ecstasy
screams screams
ochs sulzberger oppenheimer
ecstasy luce ecstasy johnson
galbraith kennedy ecstasy
franco ecstasy bunche
ecstasy king ecstasy salazar rowan ecstasy
screams
screams
in my nights in st. louis
screams in my nights
screams

screams in the laughter of children
screams in the black faces
schlesinger lodge ecstasy conant ecstasy
stengel nimitz ecstasy screams
screams in my head screams
screams six feet deep.

THE BEAST SECTION

i don't think it important
to say you murdered malcolm
or that you didn't murder malcolm
i find you vital and powerful
i am aware that you use me
but doesn't everyone
i am comfortable in your house
i am comfortable in your language
i know your mind   i have an interest
in your security. your civilization
compares favorably with any known
your power is incomparable
i understand why you would destroy
the world rather than pass it to lesser
people. i agree completely.
aristotle tells us in the physics
that power and existence are one
all i want is to sit quietly
and read books and earn
my right to exist. come—
i've made you a fantastic dish
you must try it, if not now
very soon.

1968

WILLIAM HEYEN (b. 1940)

Through the course of a long and productive career, William Heyen has regularly returned to the Holocaust as a subject. Thus we open this selection from his work with his frequently anthologized poem "Riddle." But in many ways his most remarkable achievement is the book-length poem sequence *Crazy Horse in Stillness* (1996), which consists of a 464-poem "dialogue" between the great Ogalala Lakota war chief Crazy Horse (c. 1840–1877) and General George Armstrong Custer (1839–1877), all leading up to the June 1876 Battle of the Little Bighorn when Custer and all the troops under his command were defeated and killed. Custer and Crazy Horse do not actually meet in Heyen's book, but each speaks in poems that embody his cultural or personal perspective, and the result is a compelling confrontation between different worldviews. Heyen's success at entering the American Indian world is among very few such poems in the history of modem poetry. Heyen, I should add, read and approved this effort to present the imaginative core of the book.

Heyen was born in Brooklyn, New York, and educated at the State University of New York at Brockport and Ohio State University before taking up a thirty-year teaching career at SUNY–Brockport.

RIDDLE

From Belsen a crate of gold teeth,
from Dachau a mountain of shoes,
from Auschwitz a skin lampshade.
Who killed the Jews?

Not I, cries the typist,
not I, cries the engineer,
not I, cries Adolf Eichmann,
not I, cries Albert Speer.

My friend Fritz Nova lost his father—
a petty official had to choose.
My friend Lou Abrahms lost his brother.
Who killed the Jews?

David Nova swallowed gas,
Hyman Abrahms was beaten and starved.
Some men signed their papers,
and some stood guard,

and some herded them in,
and some dropped the pellets,

and some spread the ashes,
and some hosed the walls,

and some planted the wheat,
and some poured the steel,
and some cleared the rails,
and some raised the cattle.

Some smelled the smoke,
some just heard the news.
Were they Germans? Were they Nazis?
Were they human? Who killed the Jews?

The stars will remember the gold,
the sun will remember the shoes,
the moon will remember the skin.
But who killed the Jews?

1991

from CRAZY HORSE IN STILLNESS

FORCES

Crazy Horse & Custer rode through one another
emerging on the other side.
This happened in a warp of starlight
too long ago in the future to predict

or remember. For each of them,
it was as though a wind made of locusts
the size of particles of pollen, or smaller,
atoms, or smaller, had swept them

together, the exchange being . . . inevitable,
necessary, good. Crazy Horse wore
a breastplate in the shape of a butterfly,
Custer a red cravat, but these were insubstantial,

pure. The starlight wrinkles. Their horses
blink, separate, & reassemble. Then, here,
the two warriors pause to estimate their final
destinations, mount, & ride on.

WHITE & GOLD

Curly & his friend Lone Bear found a white man dead.
In a sack hung around the neck, two stones

of the yellow stuff. He'd seen hundreds of these people
headed over the mountains. Some came back, some
got trapped in snow & ate one another, these whites.

ONE WORLD

At a small pond ringed by willows & twilight,
Crazy Horse, who had not slept for how many days,
stared into his face filled with frogspawn,
with stars. So, that was where the dead lived,
& waited, there behind his eyes. He'd never again

worry where he would spend eternity, this now, as long
as one Lakota lived to contain the world. . . .
His horse snuffled from its tether in the willows—
they'd return to the village, & fall awake,
& dream the stars in the pond, the spawn in the stars.

BONE & VELVET

In defense or warning, the bull elk emits a low whistle.
Custer heard in it the soft natural "E" of the organ,
& practiced the note himself until he could almost feel
in his forehead the first bulbous beginnings of horn.

MOTHER

Crazy Horse saw a woman so enormous in belly
she seemed to carry all the Lakota,
all the world.

He liked thinking of this: rivers from source to egress, hills
ever blossoming forth, herds swelling in her
until their birth.

THE COUNT

Crazy Horse counted cottonwood leaves along the river,
realizing one leaf for each buffalo,
& those just appearing in the spring of this dream

were calves being born. If he could keep the trees
from the whites, the herds would thunder,
so he watched the buffalo trees until their colors

wavered dark & light in the running wind. . . .
If he could keep his rootedness, there,
he could shade his people, here.

SURVEYORS

Indians pegged their own tipis, but these whites set sticks everywhere
as though staking a huge invisible tent to cover
all the land.

ROT

Flesh side up, skins were stretched, scraped, shaved thin,
rubbed with a mixture of tallow & brains,
left for sun & wind to dry, then

the best robe painted & given back to the hunting grounds. Over time,
earth accepted the robe: maggots & insects,
then mice & small birds,

then raptors that took these, & then the sky. In the end, the last
patches of fur vanished downward into that place
where the herds were conceived.

V

An arrow of geese passed over the village,
& then another. The children pointed,
waved their arms, clucked & honked,
then arrowed & ran out over the grass,

laughing. Crazy Horse closed his eyes:
up there, stretching his neck forward, his legs
tucked up under his belly, beating his wings,
he'd reach safety, sweeping his people behind him.

RESOLVE, 1876

Custer watched blocks of ice unclog the river,
spring reaching even here. The Sioux,
as they had for centuries, would soon travois
their flimsy villages toward the migrating herds,
but this year something new in the equation,
he himself & his 7th. He'd corner the enemy

on their hunting grounds, & break them,
& run them in, without reservation.

TREATY

Said Custer, Here's how it's going down:
we'll ration water to the fish first come,
first served; grass to the buffalo by rank;
sky to the hawks one windgust at a time.
Keep your people quiet and in single file.
For any trouble, you'll sacrifice a child
a minute for as many of your moons
as ever bled your dirty women. Keep
questions to yourself, and call me friend.

SNOWBIRDS

Custer saw snow dotted with bodies . . . birds
frozen to death a few days before . . . the squall
merciless against even indigenous creatures.
His Arikara scouts gathered bagfuls

for later plucking, a winter harvest, not unusual,
even expected: the Great Mystery possessed
invisible arrows numerous as snowflakes until
birds opened their eyes in the bellies of the people.

THE SLOWING

White Bull, Rain-in-the-Face, Flat Hip & Brave Bear
all thought they might have killed Custer.
Red Horse said an unidentified Santee killed Custer.
Yes, all these, but maybe Sitting Bull's dream

of soldiers falling headfirst into his campfires
killed Custer. Yes, but maybe Crazy Horse's trance
slowed Custer down, slowed him down at last
to slower than slow motion for the kill.

THE PAPER IT'S WRITTEN ON

At the millisecond of death, he is still on his horse.
A bullet has severed his brain-stem, & he is dead,

but in this instant even he does not know this.
The last strobe of consciousness is passing out of him.
Dead in the saddle, his dead body still on auto
before he disassembles, his horse unaware of his limbo,
he is the treaty imposed & signed with smoke & x's.

THE TOOTH

After the beheading, they found
the one gold tooth in Custer's mouth.
They propped open his jaws,

cut away his upper lip,
& looked into the tooth in firelight.
It was like a small television

tuned to the news, & a white man
in a white suit was already
stepping down onto the moon.

WAKAN TANKA

For a time after the battle dust assumed
the form of a white buffalo grazing the dead.

DISEQUILIBRIUM

When only a thousand buffalo were left alive on the plains,
one old bull hid inside a tree, crossed its growth rings
inward toward dead heartwood where it somehow knew
it would have to live. Each year the tree added a ring,

& each year the buffalo receded further toward its future.
Meanwhile, from beyond the riverbank where the tree lived,
soldiers were galloping toward him with politicians
& lawyers & dozers & cement trucks on their shoulders.

ECLIPSE

The men run out
& shoot arrows at the animal
eating the moon.

1996

JUDY GRAHN (b. 1940)

Born and raised in Chicago until her parents, a cook and a photographer's assistant, moved to New Mexico, Grahn graduated from San Francisco State University and remained in the Bay Area thereafter. Early on she worked as a waitress, a short-order cook, a barmaid, an artist's model, a typesetter, and a nurse's aide. A serious illness led to a coma, but she recovered. Then she became both a writer and an activist, helping to found one of the first women's presses, working for prisoners' and welfare rights groups, participating in anti-rape campaigns, and advocating on behalf of gay rights. She writes feminist, political, and lesbian poems distinguished at once by their strong cultural analysis and by their verbal and musical inventiveness. The musical changes rung in poems like "Plainsong" are as important to their message as any direct statements the poems make. Grahn has also written stories and essays.

I HAVE COME TO CLAIM MARILYN MONROE'S BODY

I have come to claim
Marilyn Monroe's° body
for the sake of my own.
dig it up, hand it over,
cram it in this paper sack.
hubba. hubba. hubba.
look at those luscious
long brown bones, that wide and crusty
pelvis, ha HA, oh she wanted so much to be serious

but she never stops smiling now.
Has she lost her mind?

Marilyn, be serious—they're taking
your picture, and they're taking the pictures
of eight young women in New York City
who murdered themselves for being pretty
by the same method as you, the very
next day, after you!
I have claimed their bodies too,
they smile up out of my paper sack
like brainless cinderellas.

---

2. *Monroe:* (1926–1962), American movie actress whose films include *River of No Return* (1954), *Bus Stop* (1956), and *Some Like it Hot* (1959); she became both a sex symbol and, after her suicide, a symbol of the terrible psychological price Hollywood stardom and American culture as a whole can exact from women.

the reporters are furious, they're asking
me questions
what right does a woman have
to Marilyn Monroe's body? and what
am I doing for lunch? They think I
mean to eat you. Their teeth are lurid
and they want to pose me, leaning
on the shovel, nude. Dont squint.
But when one of the reporters comes too close
I beat him, bust his camera
with your long, smooth thigh
and with your lovely knucklebone
I break his eye.

Long ago you wanted to write poems;
Be serious, Marilyn
I am going to take you in this paper sack
around the world, and
write on it: — the poems of Marilyn Monroe —
Dedicated to all princes,
the male poets who were so sorry to see you go,
before they had a crack at you.
They wept for you, and also
they wanted to stuff you
while you still had a little meat left
in useful places;
but they were too slow.

Now I shall take them my paper sack
and we shall act out a poem together:
"How would you like to see Marilyn Monroe,
in action, smiling, and without her clothes?"
We shall wait long enough to see them make familiar faces
and then I shall beat them with your skull.
hubba. hubba. hubba. hubba. hubba.
Marilyn, be serious
Today I have come to claim your body for my own.

1970

VIETNAMESE WOMAN SPEAKING TO AN AMERICAN SOLDIER

Vietnamese woman speaking
to an American soldier

Stack your body
on my body
make
        life
make children play
in my jungle hair
make rice flare into my sky like
whitest flak
the whitest flash
my eyes have
        burned out
looking
press your swelling weapon
here
between us   if you
push it quickly I should
    come
to understand your purpose
what you bring us
what you call it
there
in your country

1970

CAROL

Carol and
her crescent wrench
work bench
wooden fence
wide stance
Carol and her
pipe wrench
pipe smoke
pipe line
high climb
smoke eyes
chicken wire
Carol and her
hack saw
well worn
torn back
bad spine
never-mind
timberline

clear mind
Carol and her
hard glance
stiff dance
clean pants
bad ass
lumberjack's
wood ax
Carol and her
big son
shot gun
lot done
not done
never bored
do more
do less
try to rest
Carol and her
new lands
small hands
big plans
Carol and her
long time
out shine
worm gear
warm beer
quick tears
dont stare
Carol is another
queer
chickadee
like me, but Carol does
everything
better
if you let her.

1972

PLAINSONG°

Slowly: a plainsong from an older
woman to a younger woman

---

poem title: monophonic chants used in some Christian liturgies.

am I not   olden olden olden
it is unwanted.

wanting, wanting
am I not   broken
stolen   common

am I not crinkled cranky poison
am I not glinty-eyed and frozen

am I not   aged
shaky   glazing
am I not   hazy
guarded   craven

am I not   only
stingy   little
am I not   simple
brittle   spitting

was I not   over
over   ridden?

it is a long story
will you be proud to be my version?

it is unwritten.

writing, writing
am I not   ancient
raging   patient

am I not   able
charming   stable
was I not   building
forming   braving

was I not   ruling
guiding   naming
was I not   brazen
crazy   chosen

even the stones would do my bidding?

it is a long story
am I not proud to be your version?

it is unspoken.

speaking, speaking
am I not elder
berry
brandy

are you not wine before you find me
in your own beaker?

do you not turn away your shoulder?
have I not shut my mouth against you?

are you not shamed to treat me meanly
when you discover you become me?
are you not proud that you become me?

I will not shut my mouth against you.
do you not turn away your shoulder.
we who brew in the same bitters
that boil us away
we both need stronger water.

we're touched by a similar nerve.

I am new like your daughter.
I am the will, and the riverbed
made bolder
by you—my oldest river—
you are the way.

are we not olden, olden, olden.

1972

THE WOMAN WHOSE HEAD IS ON FIRE

the woman whose head is on fire
the woman with a noisy voice
the woman with too many fingers
the woman who never smiled once in her life
the woman with a boney body
the woman with moles all over her

the woman who cut off her breast
the woman with a large bobbing head
the woman with one glass eye

the woman with broad shoulders
the woman with calloused elbows
the woman with a sunken chest
the woman who is part giraffe

the woman with five gold teeth
the woman who looks straight ahead
the woman with enormous knees
the woman who can lick her own clitoris
the woman who screams on the trumpet
the woman whose toes grew together
the woman who says I am what I am

the woman with rice under her skin
the woman who owns a machete
the woman who plants potatoes
the woman who murders the kangaroo
the woman who stuffs clothing into a sack
the woman who makes a great racket
the woman who fixes machines
the woman whose chin is sticking out
the woman who says I will be

the woman who carries laundry on her head
the woman who is part horse
the woman who asks so many questions
the woman who cut somebody's throat

the woman who gathers peaches
the woman who carries jars on her head
the woman who howls
the woman whose nose is broken
the woman who constructs buildings
the woman who has fits on the floor
the woman who makes rain happen
the woman who refuses to menstruate

the woman who sets broken bones
the woman who sleeps out on the street
the woman who plays the drums
the woman who is part grasshopper
the woman who herds cattle
the woman whose will is unbending
the woman who hates kittens

the woman who escaped from the jailhouse
the woman who is walking across the desert
the woman who buries the dead
the woman who taught herself writing
the woman who skins rabbits
the woman who believes her own word
the woman who chews bearskin
the woman who eats cocaine
the woman who thinks about everything

the woman who has the tatoo of a bird
the woman who puts things together
the woman who squats on her haunches
the woman whose children are all different   colors

singing   i am the will of the woman
                 the woman
                 my will is unbending

when She-Who-moves-the-earth will turn over
when She Who moves, the earth will turn over.

1972

CAROLYN M. RODGERS (1941–2010)

Carolyn Rodgers grew up in Chicago's South Side, where her intellectual and political vision was shaped in part by the Organization of Black African Culture and by poet Gwendolyn Brooks. Her poetry of the late 1960s voices the revolutionary nationalism of the Black Arts Movement, but in a free-verse style with street slang that some of the male leaders of the movement found inappropriate for a woman. Even in these early poems, moreover, she registers notable tension between her revolutionary program and African American culture's more traditional commitments. In the 1970s, the period emphasized in this selection, she broke with her earlier militancy and emphasized her family heritage and the church's foundational role in her life. Rodgers was educated at Roosevelt University and the University of Chicago. She also wrote short stories and influential literary criticism.

HOW I GOT OVAH

i can tell you
about them
i have shaken rivers
out of my eyes
i have waded eyelash deep
have crossed rivers
have shaken the water weed out
of my lungs
have swam for strength
pulled by strength
through waterfalls with electric beats
i have bore the shocks
of water deep deep
waterlogs are my bones
i have shaken the water free of my hair
have kneeled on the banks
and kissed my ancestors of the dirt
whose rich dark root fingers rose up reached out
grabbed and pulled me rocked me cupped me
gentle strong and firm
carried me
made me swim for strength
cross rivers
though i shivered
was wet was cold
and wanted to sink down
and float as water, yea—

i can tell you.
i have shaken rivers
out of my eyes.

1975

AND WHEN THE REVOLUTION CAME

(for Rayfield and Lillie and the whole rest)

and when the revolution came
the militants said
niggers wake up
you got to comb yo hair
the natural way
            and the church folks say oh yeah? sho 'nuff . . .
and they just kept on going to church
gittin on they knees and praying
and tithing and building and buying

and when the revolution came
the militants said
niggers you got to change
the way you dress
and the church folk say oh yeah?
            and they just kept on going to church
with they knit suits and flowery bonnets
and gittin on they knees and praying
and tithing and building and buying

and when the revolution came
the militants said
you got to give up
white folks and the
            church folk say oh yeah? well?
never missed what we never had
and they jest kept on going to church
with they nice dresses and suits and
praying and building and buying

and when the revolution came
the militants say you got to give up
pork and eat only brown rice and
health food and the
            church folks said uh hummmm
and they just kept on eating they chitterlings and
going to church and praying and tithing and
building and buying

and when the revolution came
the militants said
all you church going niggers
got to give up easter and christmas
and the bible
cause that's the white man's religion
and the church folks said well well well well well

and then the militants said we got to
build black institutions where our children
call each other sister and brother
and can grow beautiful, black and strong and grow in black grace
and the church folks said yes, lord Jesus we been calling each other
sister and brother a long time

and the militants looked around
after a while and said hey, look at all
these fine buildings we got scattered throughout
the black communities some of em built wid schools and nurseries
who do they belong to?

and the church folks said, yeah.
we been waiting fo you militants
to realize that the church is an eternal rock
now why don't you militants jest come on in
we been waiting for you
we can show you how to build
anything that needs building
and while we're on our knees, at that.

1975

MAMA'S GOD

mama's God never was no white man.
her My Jesus, Sweet Jesus never was neither.
the color they had was the color of
her aches and trials, the tribulations of her heart
mama never had no saviour that would turn
his back on her because she was black
when mama prayed, she knew who she
was praying to and who she was praying to
didn't and ain't got
no color.

1975

ROBERT HASS (b. 1941)

Born in San Francisco and raised in San Rafael, California, Hass was educated at St. Mary's College and at Stanford University, where he received a Ph.D. In addition to four books of poetry, he has written criticism and translated European poets into English, including several volumes by Czeslaw Milosz. He has also published *The Essential Haiku: Versions of Basho, Buson, and Issa* (1994) and has taught at several schools, including Buffalo and Berkeley. Unlike poets who hope to redeem the ordinary by finding the poetic in it, Hass sometimes begins with the poetic—a radiant detail, a moment of loveliness—and works to show its relevance to daily life. Yet as the poems included here show, he is also deeply concerned with the struggle to live both morally and aesthetically and with the ways history and culture challenge such an effort. He has written about Vietnam, about Native Americans, about the American working class, and about the collapse of American cities. These concerns are unified by a recurring interest in the relationship between language and material reality and by a meditative sadness of tone that pervades much of his work.

RUSIA EN 1931

The archbishop° of San Salvador is dead, murdered by no one knows
who. The left says the right, the right says provocateurs.

But the families in the barrios sleep with their children beside them and
a pitchfork, or a rifle if they have one.

And posterity is grubbing in the footnotes to find out who the bishop is,

or waiting for the poet to get back to his business. Well, there's this:

her breasts are the color of brown stones in moonlight, and paler in
moonlight.

And that should hold them for a while. The bishop is dead. Poetry
proposes no solutions: it says justice is the well water of the city of
Novgorod,° black and sweet.

---

1. *archbishop:* Oscar Romero (1917–1980), Roman Catholic archbishop in El Salvador, murdered on March 24, 1980, while saying mass in San Salvador. An outspoken advocate of human rights, he was killed because of his support of the poor and his criticism of El Salvador's right-wing government. When Hass reprinted his poem in *Human Wishes* (1989) he noted that it had since become clear Romero was killed by right-wing death squads.

11. *Novgorod:* in western Russia, one of its oldest cities, it was ruled by Alexander Nevsky from 1238 to 1263, after which it rivaled Moscow until being laid waste by Czar Ivan IV in 1570; rebuilt, it was later captured by the Germans in World War II and held by them for several years.

César Vallejo° died on a Thursday. It might have been malaria, no one
is sure; it burned through the small town of Santiago de Chuco in
an Andean valley in his childhood; it may very well have flared in
his veins in Paris on a rainy day;

and nine months later Osip Mandelstam° was last seen feeding off
the garbage heap of a transit camp near Vladivostok.

They might have met in Leningrad in 1931,° on a corner; two men
about forty; they could have compared gray hair at the temples, or
compared reviews of *Trilce* and *Tristia* in 1922.

What French they would have spoken! And what the one thought
would save Spain killed the other.°

"I am no wolf by blood," Mandelstam wrote that year. "Only an equal
could break me."

And Vallejo: "Think of the unemployed. Think of the forty million
families of the hungry. . . ."

1989

A STORY ABOUT THE BODY

The young composer, working that summer at an artist's colony, had watched her for a week. She was Japanese, a painter, almost sixty, and he thought he was in love with her. He loved her work, and her work was like the way she moved her body, used her hands, looked at him directly when she made amused and considered answers to his questions. One night, walking back from a concert, they came to her door and she turned to him and said, "I think you would like to have me. I would like that too, but I must tell you that I have had a double mastectomy," and when he didn't understand, "I've lost both my breasts." The radiance that he had carried around in his belly and

---

12. *Vallejo:* (1892–1938), Peruvian poet and novelist, born in the Andean town of Santiago de Chuco. *Trilce* (1922) was a volume of his radical experimental poetry, some of it written in a Peruvian prison. He lived in Paris from 1923 to 1931, when he was deported, and moved to Spain, where he joined the Communist Party. He became active in the antifacist movement when the Spanish Civil War broke out.

16. *Mandelstam:* (1891–1938), Russian modernist poet and literary critic, whose second volume of poetry, *Tristia* (1922) was attacked by Communist Party critics because its author was reluctant to espouse the revolution in his work. A proposed 1933 volume of collected works was withdrawn when he refused to meet censors' demands for cuts. The following year he was arrested for writing an epigram on Stalin and reading it to friends. After a few years of exile, he returned to Moscow but was arrested again and died in custody at a transit camp near Vladivostok.

18. *Leningrad in 1931:* Vallejo made trips to Russia in 1928, 1929, and 1931; it was hypothetically possible for him to have met Mandelstam.

22. *other:* "What the one [Vallejo] thought would save Spain killed the other [Mandelstam]." The subject of the sentence is communism.

chest cavity—like music—withered very quickly, and he made himself look at her when he said, "I'm sorry. I don't think I could." He walked back to his own cabin through the pines, and in the morning he found a small blue bowl on the porch outside his door. It looked to be full of rose petals, but he found when he picked it up that the rose petals were on top; the rest of the bowl—she must have swept them from the corners of her studio—was full of dead bees.

1989

FORTY SOMETHING

She says to him, musing, "If you ever leave me,
and marry a younger woman and have another baby,
I'll put a knife in your heart." They are in bed,
so she climbs onto his chest, and looks directly
down into his eyes. "You understand? Your heart."

1996

SONNET

A man talking to his ex-wife on the phone.
He has loved her voice and listens with attention
to every modulation of its tone. Knowing
it intimately. Not knowing what he wants
from the sound of it, from the tendered civility.
He studies, out the window, the seed shapes
of the broken pods of ornamental trees.
The kind that grow in everyone's garden, that no one
but horticulturists can name. Four arched chambers
of pale green, tiny vegetal proscenium arches,
a pair of black tapering seeds bedded in each chamber.
A wish geometry, miniature, Indian or Persian,
lovers or gods in their apartments. Outside, white,
patient animals, and tangled vines, and rain.

1996

LYN HEJINIAN (b. 1941)

Lyn Hejinian was born in Alameda, California, in the San Francisco Bay Area, and educated at Harvard. She was editor of Tuumba Press from 1976 to 1984, when it pioneered in issuing a series of fifty Language poet chapbooks. She has also been coeditor of *Poetics Journal* for over twenty years. What Juliana Spahr said of one of Hejinian's earlier books certainly applies to the poem sequence *The Distance* as well: "Hejinian's work often demonstrates how poetry is a way of thinking, a way of encountering and constructing the world, one endless utopian moment even as it is full of failures." In much of her work, Hejinian explores how language constructs the self. Language, as she has put it, "is an order of reality itself and not a mere mediating medium." Thus any attempt at autobiography, as her signature book *My Life* demonstrates, will be riddled with erasure and endlessly branching connotation. Hejinian teaches poetics at UC–Berkeley.

from MY LIFE

A PAUSE, A ROSE, SOMETHING ON PAPER

A moment yellow, just as four years later, when my father returned home from the war, the moment of greeting him, as he stood at the bottom of the stairs, younger, thinner than when he had left, was purple—though moments are no longer so colored. Somewhere, in the background, rooms share a pattern of small roses. Pretty is as pretty does. In certain families, the meaning of necessity is at one with the sentiment of pre-necessity. The better things were gathered in a pen. The windows were narrowed by white gauze curtains which were never loosened. Here I refer to irrelevance, that rigidity which never intrudes. Hence, repetitions, free from all ambition. The shadow of the redwood trees, she said, was oppressive. The plush must be worn away. On her walks she stepped into people's gardens to pinch off cuttings from their geraniums and succulents. An occasional sunset is reflected on the windows. A little puddle is overcast. If only you could touch, or, even, catch those gray great creatures. I was afraid of my uncle with the wart on his nose, or of his jokes at our expense which were beyond me, and I was shy of my aunt's deafness who was his sister-in-law and who had years earlier fallen into the habit of nodding, agreeably. Wool station. See lightning, wait for thunder. Quite mistakenly, as it happened. Long time lines trail behind every idea, object, person, pet, vehicle, and event. The afternoon happens, crowded and therefore endless. Thicker, she agreed. It was a tic, she had the habit, and now she bobbed like my toy plastic bird on the edge of its glass, dipping into and recoiling from the water. But a word is a bottomless pit. It became magically pregnant and one day split open, giving birth to a stone egg, about as big as a football. In May when the lizards emerge from the stones, the stones turn gray, from green. When daylight moves, we delight in distance. The waves rolled over our stomachs, like spring rain over an orchard slope. Rubber bumpers on rubber cars. The resistance on sleeping to being asleep. In every country is a word which attempts the sound of cats, to match an inisolable portrait in the clouds to a din in the air. But the constant noise is not an omen of music to come. "Everything is a question of sleep," says Cocteau, but he forgets the shark, which does not. Anxiety is vigilant. Perhaps initially, even before one can talk, restlessness is already conventional, establishing the incoherent border which will later separate events from experience. Find a drawer that's not filled up. That we sleep plunges our work into the dark. The ball was lost in a bank of myrtle. I was in a room with the particulars of which a later nostalgia might be formed, an indulged childhood. They are sitting in wicker chairs, the legs of which have sunk unevenly into the ground, so that each is sitting slightly tilted and their postures make adjustment for that. The cows warm their own barn. I look at them fast and it gives the illusion that they're moving. An "oral history" on paper. *That* morning this morning. I say it about the psyche because it is not optional. The overtones are a denser shadow in the room characterized by its habitual readiness, a form of charged waiting, a perpetual attendance, of which I was thinking when I began the paragraph, "So much of childhood is spent in a manner of waiting."

1980, 1987

from THE DISTANCE

III

Great cumulous clouds hang overhead
One moment and terns
Another. It is always safe
To predict variability. The light
On my face is cold and yet I often feel
Heat. Perhaps we are all small suns.
The sunflower in its pot on deck doesn't think
So. It turns
Frantically
But not to us
As the *Distance* rides the sea and sends the sun
Sliding
Violently into all the compass corners.
Am I compassionate? Or is it from some other species of
  enthusiasm
That I give a thumbs-up
As the *Distance* slows so as to pass
Gently through a flock of floating seabirds? Their kind must be
Persistent and have been here long
Before the first human flutterings
Whose persistence has brought us
Here to no end
Unless an anomaly can be termed an end.

XIX

The woman who sets sail will cross
Reefs, science is the practice of unknowing, and given
Enough time every circumstance will betray
What it promised
To guarantee—these
Are, as I've discovered, inconclusive, uninhibited
Observations—all as allegorical
As the rooster's "cock-a-doodle-do"
Which I can accurately quote but in no way understand.
All in all
There is very little containment in the universe
Except what's temporarily contained in the bodies
Of things as presence
Or in animate bodies as life. The sea
Is never silent—it subjects one to sound—that's the only name I
    know
For the distance. It has noisy spans.
They *rumble* and *splash* as the ropes *pong*
Against the stanchions, the decks *roar*
With cold. I know these words.
My thoughts are dead without them.

XXIV

We have a concept of justice
Despite the fact that asymmetry is ubiquitous
And constantly throws things off-balance. But then
We are a tilted species
Dipping and lunging forward, swinging our baskets
Of eggs, stuck to our shadows
Which gravity in turn sticks to life
Throughout the long days that night disarrays.
The fog is taking shape, it is forming
Gulls and longshoremen, dolphins and cities
It sweeps from a sliding circle
Whose circumference lies beyond the edges of the field
Of vision by which we are engulfed. It leaps
From under a sheet and mumbles a sound that might have been a
    word—
It was probably not. It is late
Afternoon before it hesitates. It says something
Inseparable from what it doesn't say
But of course that would be the case—we're talking about music.

A buzzer goes off.
Dawn is drawn.
And this is a dawn advancing impressions
At sea. Advance. The excitement curls up
As if around a pin or a lost stick,
Walking and otherwise. But one can't reserve it
Anymore than one can reserve one's place at sea
Though we've selected the sea
As have the clouds. The shadows of the clouds fall
On the *Distance*
Which they stick to the sea.

XXX

We are surrounded by immobilized projections.
The sails slat and the rigging drips
Into a reflecting sea. We can easily forget
Whether it is night or day that is thrust forward
Whether we are awake or asleep. Our mappings are as arbitrary
As words—they are mere estimates, juttings, externalizations.
Experts say that the emotions begin
And end in the body
Equally inescapable and capable of escape
But like Mercator we have cast them
With straight meridians and arcing parallels
Though the results chime inconclusively with what we see.
Good bones and waves and weights all slide into the status of
    reasons
And slip away again. Only the *Distance*
Blinded by the fog hardly dares to move. Decisions draw
A blank. Sasha is pale. I feel calm.
Detached.
Frozen.
Hardly alive.
But that's normal, no cause for alarm
Which I wouldn't sound even if I could. I am here.
Hardily alive, then
Alive, hard at it,
That is. Yes.
The stanchions are humming. I put my hand on the shrouds, face
Forward, and hear
Radio signals, a voice, then
Music, now speaking
"The episode herself," "a rise

In worker output rolling"
"Per hour the rule"
"Unsung"—
Drifting imprecisely.

XXXII

Every traveler's tale unfolds
Along the rising and falling contours
And over the edges
Written around the map
Of the tale folded into it. We are exposed. There is nothing here
But exposure. Every wave, even as it curls over the light, produces
 exposure,
Every thought is crossed by its own frame of illimitable
Transient foam. Exposure produces the blanks on the map
Which are as blindingly bright as the white light that the sun casts
Through the translucent mist
And that is the source of vision. The sun
Is always prejudiced in favor of appearances—change,
 eventfulness
And destination. One cannot die invisibly
In its presence.

XXXVII

We have no Prospero° to wreck us
And turn us into mules with dazzling haunches
Or geese in a saga sung to lyres
Around a fire blazing over buried treasure
On land we don't remember coming to.
The future has acquired the habit of waiting to reveal itself.
History should come next, as if it were a wind
That could make us happy.

2008

120. *Prospero:* protagonist of Shakespeare's *The Tempest.*

SHARON OLDS (b. 1942)

Olds was born in San Francisco and educated at Stanford and Columbia, earning a Ph.D. at the latter. She grew up in a conservative religious family for which the thought was the moral equivalent of the deed; thoughts themselves, therefore, were to be self-policed. The project of becoming a writer has for her been partly one of unlearning that family lesson; she has trained herself to take risks and take up subjects other poets have ignored. A short, outrageously witty poem "The Pope's Penis" is perhaps the most notorious instance of that, but in the more ambitious poems reprinted here she has also enlarged our sense of what it is possible to do in poetry.

For some years Olds has taught poetry workshops in the Graduate Creative Writing Program at New York University, while helping to run NYU's workshop program at Goldwater Hospital, a 900-bed public hospital for the severely physically disabled, on New York's Roosevelt Island. She has published numerous volumes of poetry, whose focus is alternately historical, as with "Ideographs" and "Photograph of the Girl," and personal, as with "The Waiting" and "His Father's Cadaver." Yet in both cases her central subjects are death and sexuality or regeneration, or the relations between the two, as in "Photograph of the Girl." While she is regularly admired for her candor, the praise pales before the singularly uncompromising, even harrowing, quality of her vision. In the intricacy of her attention to subjects we would rather repress, and in the unsparing negotiation of her own feelings, she surpasses even Plath. *The Father* (1992), from which "The Waiting" is taken, is a daughter's book-length poetic chronicle of her father's death from cancer, unflinching in its recitation of her ambivalence and his physical deterioration. One reviewer described it as "something close to a spiritual ordeal for the reader." Fully understanding Olds's work requires recognizing how the public and private poems underwrite one another and make each other possible. While she was writing *The Father,* in fact, she was simultaneously composing a still-unpublished poem sequence on World War II. Sometimes the public and the private explicitly interpenetrate, as in her short poem "Japanese-American Farmhouse, California, 1942." The poem describes the abandoned, looted former home of World War II Japanese American internees, then ends with what strikes us as a stunning indictment of her family: "I as born, that day, near there, / in wartime, of ignorant people." But of course the ignorance typifies not only her family but most of the country. On the other hand, "Ideographs" and "Portrait of the Girl" respond to fairly well known photographs but do not aim to replace a prose historical account; instead the poems teach us how one responsible consciousness can respond to public events. Finally, "Known to Be Left" and "Left-Wife Goose" are taken from her 2012 book *Stag's Leap,* which explores the disintegration of her thirty-year marriage.

THE POPE'S PENIS

It hangs deep in his robes, a delicate
clapper at the center of a bell.
It moves when he moves, a ghostly fish in a

halo of silver seaweed, the hair
swaying in the dark and the heat—and at night,
while his eyes sleep, it stands up
in praise of God.

1987

IDEOGRAPHS

(a photograph of China, 1905)

The small scaffolds, boards in the form of
ideographs, the size of a person,
lean against a steep wall of
dressed stone. One is the simple
shape of a man. The man on it
is asleep, his arms nailed to the wood.
No timber is wasted; his fingertips
curl in at the very end of the plank
as a child's hands open in sleep.
The other man is awake—he looks
directly at us. He is fixed to a more
complex scaffold, a diagonal cross-piece
pointing one arm up, one down,
and his legs are bent, the spikes through his ankles
holding them up off the ground,
his knees cocked, the folds of his robe flowing
sideways as if he were suspended in the air
in flight, his naked leg bared.
They are awaiting execution, tilted against the wall
as you'd prop up a tool until you needed it.
They'll be shouldered up over the crowd and
carried through the screaming. The sleeper will wake.
The twisted one will fly above the faces, his
garment rippling.
Here there is still the backstage quiet,
the dark at the bottom of the wall, the props
leaning in the grainy half-dusk.
He looks at us in the silence. He says
Save me, there is still time.

1984

PHOTOGRAPH OF THE GIRL

The girl sits on the hard ground,
the dry pan of Russia, in the drought

of 1921,° stunned,
eyes closed, mouth open,
raw hot wind blowing
sand in her face. Hunger and puberty are
taking her together. She leans on a sack,
layers of clothes fluttering in the heat,
the new radius of her arm curved.
She cannot be not beautiful, but she is
starving. Each day she grows thinner, and her bones
grow longer, porous. The caption says
she is going to starve to death that winter
with millions of others. Deep in her body
the ovaries let out her first eggs,
golden as drops of grain.

1984

THINGS THAT ARE WORSE THAN DEATH

(for Margaret Randall)

You are speaking of Chile,
of the woman who was arrested
with her husband and their five-year-old son.
You tell how the guards tortured the woman, the man, the child,
in front of each other,
"as they like to do."
Things that are worse than death.
I can see myself taking my son's ash-blond hair in my fingers,
tilting back his head before he knows what is happening,
slitting his throat, slitting my own throat
to save us that. Things that are worse than death:
this new idea enters my life.
The guard enters my life, the sewage of his body,
"as they like to do." The eyes of the five-year-old boy, Dago,
watching them with his mother. The eyes of his mother
watching them with Dago. And in my living room as a child,
the word, Dago. And nothing I experienced was worse than death,
life was beautiful as our blood on the stone floor
to save us that—my son's eyes on me,
my eyes on my son—the ram-boar on our bodies
making its look at our old enemy and bow in welcome,
gracious and eternal death
who permits departure.

1984

---

3. *1921:* as many as five million people lost their lives in the drought and resulting famine.

THE WAITING

No matter how early I would get up
and come out of the guest room, and look down the hall,
there between the wings of the wing-back chair
my father would be sitting, his head calm
and dark between the wings. He sat
unmoving, like something someone has made,
his robe fallen away from his knees,
he sat and stared at the swimming pool
in the dawn. By then, he knew he was dying,
he seemed to approach it as a job to be done
which he knew how to do. He got up early
for the graveyard shift. When he heard me coming down the
hall, he would not turn—he had
a way of holding still to be looked at,
as if a piece of sculpture could sense
the gaze which was running over it—
he would wait with that burnished, looked-at look until
the hem of my nightgown came into view,
then slew his eyes up at me, without
moving his head, and wait, the kiss
came to him, he did not go to it.
Now he would have some company
as he tried to swallow an eighth of a teaspoon
of coffee, he would have his child to give him
the cup to spit into, his child to empty it—
I would be there all day, watch him nap,
be there when he woke, sit with him
until the day ended, and he could get back into
bed with his wife. Not until the next
dawn would he be alone again, night-
watchman of matter, sitting, facing
the water—the earth without form, and void,
darkness upon the face of it, as if
waiting for his daughter.

1995

HIS FATHER'S CADAVER

The old man had always wanted
to end up there, on the chrome table,
the Medical School Dissection Room
on that island in the North Atlantic

his heaven. So his only child signed the papers—
son, M.D. He knew that the students
would start with a butterfly incision,
cutting the body down the center, lifting
the skin of the chest and the abdomen up
and out to the sides. He had heard the high
neutral scream of the bone-saw, he knew
they would pry back the ribs to get at the heart.
He knew the pattern they followed, he had done it himself—
chest, abdomen, head, hands,
feet. They would stand there, the medical students,
day after day, around his father,
one doing a knee, one
the bowels, the scalp, the eye, the face.
This is what his father had wanted,
to throw himself bodily into the hospital like a
roe-fish thrown back, to enter his students
directly, as knowledge—
so the wreckage could be seen as good, even
his chest, which might look gnawed, his jaws
shining through as they removed his lips,
even the pool of slurry like the fish factory—
and every week his son had some idea
where they might be, as those at home
will chart the route of Arctic explorers,
the pins on the map moving in
through the cold toward the center. He knew if it got
too crowded at the gurney, someone would take
the brain over to another table
to separate it, into its parts, like a
god his father would move, piece
by piece, out into the world. At night,
they would cover everything with plastic bags,
the veins and arteries lying fanned out
across the back of the hand—by day they were
murmuring Latin, memorizing the old man.
For six months, from two thousand miles,
the son follows it, with occasional horror,
with respect, the long dismantling
of that man who used to grease him down
and lower him into the Bay of Fundy°
to check on his wave machine, which he hoped

45. *Bay of Fundy:* in eastern Canada.

would harness the power of the sea, that man who had
delivered him, his palm waiting under
the head when it came forth, trusting
himself, best, to touch, first,
the mortal boy they had made.

1995

KNOWN TO BE LEFT

If I pass a mirror, I turn away,
I do not want to look at her,
and she does not want to be seen. Sometimes
I don't see exactly how to go on doing this.
Often, when I feel that way,
within a few minutes I am crying, remembering
his body, or an area of it,
his backside often, a part of him
just right now to think of, luscious, not too
detailed, and his back turned to me.
After tears, the chest is less sore,
as if some goddess of humanness
within us has caressed us with a gush of tenderness.
I guess that's how people go on, without
knowing how. I am so ashamed
before my friends—to be known to be left
by the one who supposedly knew me best,
each hour is a room of shame, and I am
swimming, swimming, holding my head up,
smiling, joking, ashamed, ashamed,
like being naked with the clothed, or being
a child, having to try to behave
while hating the terms of your life. In me now
there's a being of sheer hate, like an angel
of hate. On the badminton lawn, she got
her one shot, pure as an arrow,
while through the eyelets of my blouse the no-see-ums
bit the flesh no one seems now
to care to touch. In the mirror, the torso
looks like a pinup hives martyr,
or a cream pitcher speckled with henbit and pussy-paws,
full of the milk of human kindness
and unkindness, and no one is lining up to drink.
But look! I am starting to give him up!
I believe he is not coming back. Something

has died, inside me, believing that,
like the death of a crone in one twin bed
as a child is born in the other. Have faith,
old heart. What is living, anyway,
but dying.

2012

LEFT-WIFE GOOSE

Hoddley, Poddley, Puddles and Fogs,
Cats are to Marry the Poodle Dogs;
Cats in Blue Jackets and Dogs in Red Hats,
What Will Become of the Mice and Rats?
        Had a trust fund, had a thief in,
        Had a husband, could not keep him.
Fiddle-Dee-Dee, Fiddle-Dee-Dee,
The Fly Has Left the Humble-Bee.
They Went to the Court, and Unmarried Was She:
The Fly Has Left the Humble-Bee.
        Had a sow twin, had a reap twin,
        Had a husband, could not keep him.
In Marble Halls as White as Milk,
Lined with a Skin as Soft as Silk,
Within a Fountain Crystal-Clear,
A Golden Apple Doth Appear.
No Doors There Are to This Stronghold
Yet Robbers Break In and Steal the Gold.
        Had an egg cow, had a cream hen,
        Had a husband, could not keep him.
Formed Long Ago, Yet Made Today,
Employed While Others Sleep;
What Few Would Like to Give Away,
Nor Any Wish to Keep.
        Had a nap man, had a neap man,
        Had a flood man, could not keep him.
Ickle, Ockle, Blue Bockle,
Fishes in the Sea.
If You Want a Left Wife,
Please Choose Me.
        Had a safe of 4X sheepskin,
        Had a brook brother, could not keep him.
Inter, Mitzy, Titzy, Tool,
  Ira, Dura, Dominee,

Oker, Poker, Dominocker,
Out Goes Me.
  Had a lamb, slung in keepskin,
  Had some ewe-milk, in it seethed him.
There Was an Old Woman Called Nothing-at-All,
Who Lived in a Dwelling Exceedingly Small;
A Man Stretched His Mouth to the Utmost Extent,
And Down at One Gulp House and Old Woman Went.
  Had a rich pen, had a cheap pen,
  Had a husband, could not keep him.
Put him in this nursery shell,
And here you keep him very well.

2012

LOUISE GLÜCK (b. 1943)

Born in New York City and raised on Long Island, Glück was educated at Sarah Lawrence College and Columbia. She lives in Plainfield, Vermont, but has taught at a number of schools, including Columbia University and Williams College. Glück's 1994 volume of essays, *Proofs and Theories,* includes remarks on the autobiographical overtones of a number of her early poems, which were often dark portraits of family and childhood. Those poems sometimes opted to transform personal experience by integrating it with mythic allusions, a technique given a perhaps more witty and ambitious realization in *Meadowlands* (1996), a book-length poem sequence from which eight of the poems here are taken. *Meadowlands* chronicles a contemporary marriage in crisis with characters taken from Homer's *Odyssey,* including Odysseus's wife, Penelope, and the witch Circe, who turned Odysseus's crew into animals and delayed him on his return voyage to Ithaca after the Trojan War. Indeed, it is simultaneously a rereading of the classical text and a contemporary story; neither has absolute priority. The fusion of the two perspectives lets her speakers at once be oracular and ordinary. Also see her *Collected Poems* (2012).

THE DROWNED CHILDREN

You see, they have no judgment.
So it is natural that they should drown,
first the ice taking them in
and then, all winter, their wool scarves
floating behind them as they sink
until at last they are quiet.
And the pond lifts them in its manifold dark arms.

But death must come to them differently,
so close to the beginning.
As though they had always been
blind and weightless. Therefore
the rest is dreamed, the lamp,
the good white cloth that covered the table,
their bodies.

And yet they hear the names they used
like lures slipping over the pond:
What are you waiting for
come home, come home, lost
in the waters, blue and permanent.

1980

VESPERS

You thought we didn't know. But we knew once,
children know these things. Don't turn away now—we inhabited
a lie to appease you. I remember
sunlight of early spring, embankments
netted with dark vinca. I remember
lying in a field, touching my brother's body.
Don't turn away now; we denied
memory to console you. We mimicked you, reciting
the terms of our punishment. I remember
some of it, not all of it: deceit
begins as forgetting. I remember small things, flowers
growing under the hawthorn tree, bells
of the wild scilla. Not all, but enough
to know you exist: who else had reason to create
mistrust between a brother and sister but the one
who profited, to whom we turned in solitude? Who else
would so envy the bond we had then
as to tell us it was not earth
but heaven we were losing?

1992

VESPERS

More than you love me, very possibly
you love the beasts of the field, even,
possibly, the field itself, in August dotted
with wild chicory and aster:
I know. I have compared myself
to those flowers, their range of feeling
so much smaller and without issue; also to white sheep,
actually gray: I am uniquely
suited to praise you. Then why
torment me? I study the hawkweed,
the buttercup protected from the grazing herd
by being poisonous: is pain
your gift to make me
conscious in my need of you, as though
I must need you to worship you,
or have you abandoned me
in favor of the field, the stoic lambs turning
silver in twilight; waves of wild aster and chicory shining
pale blue and deep blue, since you already know
how like your raiment it is.

1992

THE WILD IRIS

At the end of my suffering
there was a door.

Hear me out: that which you call death
I remember.

Overhead, noises, branches of the pine shifting.
Then nothing. The weak sun
flickered over the dry surface.

It is terrible to survive
as consciousness
buried in the dark earth.

Then it was over: that which you fear, being
a soul and unable
to speak, ending abruptly, the stiff earth
bending a little. And what I took to be
birds darting in low shrubs.

You who do not remember
passage from the other world
I tell you I could speak again: whatever
returns from oblivion returns
to find a voice:

from the center of my life came
a great fountain, deep blue
shadows on azure seawater.

1992

from MEADOWLANDS

PENELOPE'S SONG

Little soul, little perpetually undressed one,
do now as I bid you, climb
the shelf-like branches of the spruce tree;
wait at the top, attentive, like
a sentry or look-out. He will be home soon;
it behooves you to be
generous. You have not been completely
perfect either; with your troublesome body
you have done things you shouldn't

discuss in poems. Therefore
call out to him over the open water, over the bright water
with your dark song, with your grasping,
unnatural song—passionate,
like Maria Callas.° Who
wouldn't want you? Whose most demonic appetite
could you possibly fail to answer? Soon
he will return from wherever he goes in the meantime,
suntanned from his time away, wanting
his grilled chicken. Ah, you must greet him,
you must shake the boughs of the tree
to get his attention,
but carefully, carefully, lest
his beautiful face be marred
by too many falling needles.

QUIET EVENING

You take my hand; then we're alone
in the life-threatening forest. Almost immediately

we're in a house; Noah's
grown and moved away; the clematis after ten years
suddenly flowers white.

More than anything in the world
I love these evenings when we're together,
the quiet evenings in summer, the sky still light at this hour.

So Penelope took the hand of Odysseus,
not to hold him back but to impress
this peace on his memory:

from this point on, the silence through which you move
is my voice pursuing you.

PARABLE OF THE KING

The great king looking ahead
saw not fate but simply
dawn glittering over
the unknown island: as a king
he thought in the imperative—best
not to reconsider direction, best

---

14. *Callas:* (1923–1977), American operatic soprano.

to keep going forward
over the radiant water. Anyway,
what is fate but a strategy for ignoring
history, with its moral
dilemmas, a way of regarding
the present, where decisions
are made, as the necessary
link between the past (images of the king
as a young prince) and the glorious future (images
of slave girls). Whatever
it was ahead, why did it have to be
so blinding? Who could have known
that wasn't the usual sun
but flames rising over a world
about to become extinct?

PARABLE OF THE HOSTAGES

The Greeks are sitting on the beach
wondering what to do when the war ends. No one
wants to go home, back
to that bony island; everyone wants a little more
of what there is in Troy, more
life on the edge, that sense of every day as being
packed with surprises. But how to explain this
to the ones at home to whom
fighting a war is a plausible
excuse for absence, whereas
exploring one's capacity for diversion
is not. Well, this can be faced
later; these
are men of action, ready to leave
insight to the women and children.
Thinking things over in the hot sun, pleased
by a new strength in their forearms, which seem
more golden than they did at home, some
begin to miss their families a little,
to miss their wives, to want to see
if the war has aged them. And a few grow
slightly uneasy: what if war
is just a male version of dressing up,
a game devised to avoid
profound spiritual questions? Ah,
but it wasn't only the war. The world had begun
calling them, an opera beginning with the war's

loud chords and ending with the floating aria of the sirens.
There on the beach, discussing the various
timetables for getting home, no one believed
it could take ten years to get back to Ithaca;
no one foresaw that decade of insoluble dilemmas—oh
  unanswerable
affliction of the human heart: how to divide
the world's beauty into acceptable
and unacceptable loves! On the shores of Troy,
how could the Greeks know
they were hostage already: who once
delays the journey is
already enthralled; how could they know
that of their small number
some would be held forever by the dreams of pleasure,
some by sleep, some by music?

CIRCE'S POWER

I never turned anyone into a pig.
Some people are pigs; I make them
look like pigs.

I'm sick of your world
that lets the outside disguise the inside.

Your men weren't bad men;
undisciplined life
did that to them. As pigs,

under the care of
me and my ladies, they
sweetened right up.

Then I reversed the spell,
showing you my goodness
as well as my power. I saw

we could be happy here,
as men and women are
when their needs are simple. In the same breath,

I foresaw your departure,
your men with my help braving
the crying and pounding sea. You think

a few tears upset me? My friend,
every sorceress is
a pragmatist at heart; nobody

sees essence who can't
face limitation. If I wanted only to hold you

I could hold you prisoner.

CIRCE'S GRIEF

In the end, I made myself
known to your wife as
a god would, in her own house, in
Ithaca, a voice
without a body: she
paused in her weaving, her head turning
first to the right, then left
though it was hopeless of course
to trace that sound to any
objective source: I doubt
she will return to her loom
with what she knows now. When
you see her again, tell her
this is how a god says goodbye:
if i am in her head forever
I am in your life forever.

REUNION

When Odysseus has returned at last
unrecognizable to Ithaca and killed
the suitors swarming the throne room,
very delicately he signals to Telemachus
to depart: as he stood twenty years ago,
he stands now before Penelope.
On the palace floor, wide bands of sunlight turning
from gold to red. He tells her
nothing of those years, choosing to speak instead
exclusively of small things, as would be
the habit of a man and woman long together:
once she sees who he is, she will know what he's done.
And as he speaks, ah,
tenderly he touches her forearm.

TELEMACHUS' BURDEN

Nothing
was exactly difficult because
routines develop, compensations
for perceived
absences and omissions. My mother
was the sort of woman
who let you know she was suffering and then
denied that suffering since in her view
suffering was what slaves did; when
I tried to console her,
to relieve her misery, she
rejected me. I now realize
if she'd been capable of honesty
she would have been
a Stoic. Unfortunately
she was a queen, she wanted it understood
at every moment she had chosen
her own destiny. She would have had to be
insane to choose that destiny. Well,
good luck to my father, in my opinion
a stupid man if he expects
his return to diminish
her isolation; perhaps
he came back for that.

1996

BEFORE THE STORM

Rain tomorrow, but tonight the sky is clear, the stars shine.
Still, the rain's coming,
maybe enough to drown the seeds.
There's a wind from the sea pushing the clouds;
before you see them, you feel the wind.
Better look at the fields now,
see how they look before they're flooded.

A full moon. Yesterday, a sheep escaped into the woods,
and not just any sheep—the ram, the whole future.
If we see him again, we'll see his bones.

The grass shudders a little; maybe the wind passed through it.
And the new leaves of the olives shudder in the same way.

---

poem title: *Telemachus:* son of Odysseus and Penelope.

Mice in the fields. Where the fox hunts,
tomorrow there'll be blood in the grass.
But the storm—the storm will wash it away.

In one window, there's a boy sitting.
He's been sent to bed—too early,
in his opinion. So he sits at the window—

Everything is settled now.
Where you are now is where you'll sleep, where you'll wake up in the morning.
The mountain stands like a beacon, to remind the night that the earth exists,
that it mustn't be forgotten.

Above the sea, the clouds form as the wind rises,
dispersing them, giving them a sense of purpose.

Tomorrow the dawn won't come.
The sky won't go back to being the sky of day; it will go on as night,
except the stars will fade and vanish as the storm arrives,
lasting perhaps ten hours altogether.
But the world as it was cannot return.

One by one, the lights of the village houses dim
and the mountain shines in the darkness with reflected light,

No sound. Only cats scuffling in the doorways.
They smell the wind: time to make more cats.
Later, they prowl the streets, but the smell of the wind stalks them.
It's the same in the fields, confused by the smell of blood,
though for now only the wind rises; stars turn the field silver.

This far from the sea and still we know these signs.
The night is an open book.
But the world beyond the night remains a mystery.

2009

A VILLAGE LIFE

The death and uncertainty that await me
as they await all men, the shadows evaluating me
because it can take time to destroy a human being,
the element of suspense
needs to be preserved—

On Sundays I walk my neighbor's dog
so she can go to church to pray for her sick mother.

The dog waits for me in the doorway. Summer and winter
we walk the same road, early morning, at the base of the escarpment.
Sometimes the dog gets away from me—for a moment or two,
I can't see him behind some trees. He's very proud of this,
this trick he brings out occasionally, and gives up again
as a favor to me—

Afterward, I go back to my house to gather firewood.

I keep in my mind images from each walk:
monarda growing by the roadside;
in early spring, the dog chasing the little gray mice,

so for a while it seems possible
not to think of the hold of the body weakening, the ratio
of the body to the void shifting,

and the prayers becoming prayers for the dead.

Midday, the church bells finished. Light in excess:
still, fog blankets the meadow, so you can't see
the mountain in the distance, covered with snow and ice.

When it appears again, my neighbor thinks
her prayers are answered. So much light she can't control her happiness—
it has to burst out in language. *Hello,* she yells, as though
that is her best translation.

She believes in the Virgin the way I believe in the mountain,
though in one case the fog never lifts.
But each person stores his hope in a different place.

I make my soup, I pour my glass of wine.
I'm tense, like a child approaching adolescence.
Soon it will be decided for certain what you are,
one thing, a boy or girl. Not both any longer.
And the child thinks: I want to have a say in what happens.
But the child has no say whatsoever.

When I was a child, I did not foresee this.

Later, the sun sets, the shadows gather,
rustling the low bushes like animals just awake for the night.

Inside, there's only firelight. It fades slowly;
now only the heaviest wood's still
flickering across the shelves of instruments.
I hear music coming from them sometimes,
even locked in their cases.

When I was a bird, I believed I would be a man.
That's the flute. And the horn answers,
when I was a man, I cried out to be a bird.
Then the music vanishes. And the secret it confides in me
vanishes also.

It's the window, the moon is hanging over the earth,
meaningless but full of messages.

Its dead, it's always been dead,
but it pretends to be something else,
burning like a star, and convincingly, so that you feel sometimes
it could actually make something grow on earth.

If there's an image of the soul, I think that's what it is.

I move through the dark as though it were natural to me,
as though I were already a factor in it.
Tranquil and still, the day dawns.
On market day, I go to the market with my lettuces.

2009

MICHAEL PALMER (b. 1943)

Born and raised in New York City, Palmer was educated at Harvard and lived on the East Coast before moving to San Francisco. The most lyrical of the well-known writers associated with L=A=N=G=U=A=G=E poetry—he is sometimes considered one of the movement's precursors—Palmer shares their interest in fragmented and disjunctive narrativity, depersonalized speakers, and investigations of how language works as an independent system of meanings. But musicality and wit, along with a regular haunting by vestigial narrativity, distinguish his work from many others in the movement. Similarly, he shares their interest in philosophy and critical theory, but has a stronger surrealist component in his poetry. Several of his books include poem sequences. Palmer has taught occasionally and collaborated on several projects with dancers and artists, including writing numerous dance scenarios for Margaret Jenkins Dance Company and books with the painters Irving Petlin and Sandro Chia.

SONG OF THE ROUND MAN

for Sarah when she's older

The round and sad-eyed man puffed cigars as if
he were alive. Gillyflowers
to the left of the apple, purple bells to the right

and a grass-covered hill behind.
I am sad today said the sad-eyed man
for I have locked my head in a Japanese box

and lost the key.
I am sad today he told me
for there are gillyflowers by the apple

and purple bells I cannot see.
Will you look at them for me
he asked, and tell me what you find?

I cannot I replied
for my eyes have grown sugary and dim
from reading too long by candlelight.

Tell me what you've read then
said the round and sad-eyed man.
I cannot I replied

for my memory has grown tired and dim
from looking at things that can't be seen
by any kind of light

and I've locked my head in a Japanese box
and thrown away the key.
Then I am you and you are me

said the sad-eyed man as if alive.
I'll write you in where I should be
between the gillyflowers and the purple bells

and the apple and the hill
and we'll puff cigars from noon till night
as if we were alive.

1981

ALL THOSE WORDS

All those words we once used for things but have now discarded in order to come to know things. There in the mountains I discovered the last tree or the letter A. What it said to me was brief, "I am surrounded by the uselessness of blue falling away on all sides into fields of bitter wormwood, all-heal and centaury. If you crush one of these herbs between your fingers the scent will cling to your hand but its particles will be quite invisible. This is a language you cannot understand." Dismantling the beams of the letter tree I carried them one by one down the slope to our house and added them to the fire. Later over the coals we grilled red mullets flavored with oil, pepper, salt and wild oregano.

1984

I HAVE ANSWERS TO ALL OF YOUR QUESTIONS

for C. E.

I have answers to all of your questions. My name is the word for wall, my head is buried in that wall. When I leap over that wall I think of my head, I can assure you. And into the garden: paradise—broken bottles, tractor tires, shattered adjectives (fragments of a wall). The sky beyond on fire, this is true. The hills beyond a glinting gold, also true. And you married to that clown, that ape, that gribbling assassin of light. Your daughters will avenge you. And into the garden: paradise—the soldiers, their rifles, their boots, their eyes narrowed, searching for a lost head. Or a stolen head? The head of a pornographer. There, I've said it. Pink nipples grow hard as she brushes them with her lips. Moans can be heard coming from poems—poems you, Senator, want desperately to read but will not let yourself, since you are a citizen, proud and erect. And out of the head laughter, tears, tiny bubbles of spit. It is a head from another century, the last one or the next.

1988

FIFTH PROSE

Because I'm writing about the snow not the sentence
Because there is a card—a visitor's card—and on that card there are words of ours arranged in a row

and on those words we have written house, we have written leave this house, we
have written be this house, the spiral of a house, channels through this house

and we have written The Provinces and The Reversal and something called the Human Poems
though we live in a valley on the Hill of Ghosts

Still for many days the rain will continue to fall
A voice will say Father I am burning

Father I've removed a stone from a wall, erased a picture from that wall,
a picture of ships—cloud ships—pressing toward the sea

words only
taken limb by limb apart

Because we are not alive not alone
but ordinary extracts from the tablets

Hassan the Arab and his wife
who did vaulting and balancing

Coleman and Burgess, and Adele Newsome
pitched among the spectators one night

Lizzie Keys
and Fred who fell from the trapeze

into the sawdust and
wasn't hurt at all

and Jacob Hall the rope-dancer
Little Sandy and Sam Sault

Because there is a literal shore, a letter that's blood-red
Because in this dialect the eyes are crossed or quartz

seeing swimmer and seeing rock
statue then shadow

and here in the lake
first a razor then a fact

1988

AUTOBIOGRAPHY

(for Poul Borum)

All clocks are clouds.
Parts are greater than the whole.°
A philosopher is starving in a rooming house, while it rains outside.
He regards the self as just another sign.°
Winter roses are invisible.
Late ice sometimes sings.

A and *Not-A* are the same.°
My dog does not know me.
Violins, like dreams, are suspect.
I come from Kolophon, or perhaps some small island.
The strait has frozen, and people are walking—a few skating—
across it.
On the crescent beach, a drowned deer.

A woman with one hand, her thighs around your neck.
The world is all that is displaced.°
Apples in a stall at the streetcorner by the Bahnhof, pale yellow to
blackish red.
Memory does not speak.
Shortness of breath, accompanied by tinnitus.
The poet's stutter and the philosopher's.

The self is assigned to others.
A room from which, at all times, the moon remains visible.
Leningrad cafe: a man missing the left side of his face.

---

2. *whole:* the notion that the whole is greater than the sum of its parts is central to dialectical thinking in Hegel, Marx, and gestalt theory; a competing view, that the sum of the parts equals the whole, pervades analytic thought.

4. *sign:* the notion that the self is a construct of signs is a commonplace structuralist claim.

7. *same:* this line contradicts a standard law of logic.

14. *displaced:* Cf. the famous formulation in *Tractatus Logico-philosophicus* (1921) by Austrian philosopher Ludwig Wittgenstein (1899–1951): "The world is everything that is the case."

Disappearance of the sun from the sky above Odessa.
True description of that sun.°
A philosopher lies in a doorway, discussing the theory of colors

with himself
the theory of self with himself, the concept of number, eternal return,° the sidereal pulse
logic of types, Buridan° sentences, the *lekton.*
Why now that smoke off the lake?
Word and thing are the same.°
Many times white ravens have I seen.

That all planes are infinite, by extension.
She asks, Is there a map of these gates?
She asks, Is this the one called Passages, or is it that one to the west?
Thus released, the dark angels converse with the angels of light.
They are not angels.
Something else.

1995

---

23. *sun:* see "A True Account of Talking to the Sun at Fire Island" by Frank O'Hara in the present volu me, itself based in part on an earlier poem by Russian poet Vladimir Mayakovsky (1894–1930).

26. *eternal return:* a doctrine in the work of German philosopher Friedrich Nietzsche (1844–1900).

28. *types, Buridan:* British philosopher Bertrand Russell (1872–1970) developed a theory of types to solve certain logical problems. Jean Buridan was a fourteenth-century French philosopher who explored the logic of equivalent choices.

30. *same:* the line evokes a Renaissance theory of meaning, one that structuralism has rejected.

PAUL VIOLI (1944–2011)

Born in New York City, raised on Long Island, and educated at Boston University, Violi was managing editor of *Architectural Forum*, worked on various special projects for Universal Limited Art Edition, and taught at several colleges, including New York University. He published eight books of poetry since the 1970s. "Index" is not his only poem that textualizes apparently innocent linguistic contexts. "Errata" achieves similar results with an invented errata page. "Marina" makes a socially unstable poem out of real or imagined boats' names. "Tanka" and "A Moveable Snack" show his black humor with its typical concision.

INDEX

Hudney, Sutej IX, X, XI, 7, 9, 25, 58, 60, 61, 64
  Plates 5, 10, 15
  Childhood 70, 71
  Education 78, 79, 80
  Early relationship with family 84
  Enters academy, honors 84
  Arrest and bewilderment 85
  Formation of spatial theories 90
  "Romance of Ardoy, The" 92
  Second arrest 93
  Early voyages, life in the Pyrenees 95
  Marriage 95
  Abandons landscape painting 96
  Third arrest 97
  Weakness of character, inconstancy 101
  First signs of illness, advocation of celibacy 106, 107
  Advocates abolishment of celibacy 110
  Expulsion from Mazar 110
  Collaborations with Fernando Gee 111
  Composes lines beginning: "Death, wouldst that I had died /
    While thou wert still a mystery." 117
  Consequences of fame, violent rows, professional disputes 118, 119
  Disavows all his work 120
  Bigamy, scandals, illness, admittance of being "easily crazed, like
    snow." 128
  Theories of perspective published 129
  Birth of children 129
  Analysis of important works:
      Wine glass with fingerprints
      Nude on a blue sofa

The drunken fox trappers
Man wiping tongue with large towel
Hay bales stacked in a field
Self portrait
Self portrait with cat
Self portrait with frozen mop
Self portrait with belching duck 135
Correspondence with Cecco Angolieri 136
Dispute over attribution of lines: "I have as large supply of
evils / as January has not flowerings." 137
Builds first greenhouse 139
Falling-out with Angolieri 139
Flees famine 144
Paints *Starved cat eating snow* 145
Arrested for selling sacks of wind to gullible peasants 146
Imprisonment and bewilderment 147
Disavows all his work 158
Invents the collar stay 159
Convalescence with third wife 162
Complains of "a dense and baleful wind blowing the words I
write off the page." 165
Meets with Madam T. 170
Departures, mortal premonitions, "I think I'm about to snow." 176
Disavows all his work 181
Arrest and pardon 182
Last days 183
Last words 184, 185, 186, 187, 188, 189, 390

1982

TANKA

Where the blossoms fall
like snow on the dock
bring fifty thousand in cash

or you'll never see
your baby again

1993

A MOVABLE SNACK

A ruckus outside the church after the reading starts.
Then they shoulder their way through the double doors,
laughing, a forced, snarling laughter. Two of them, thin but

tough, tough but worn-out. About forty, stubble beard, bootcamp crewcuts, and long coats; dirty hands and hard, weathered faces. A store-bought container of rice pudding. They are eating rice pudding with switch-blades. Drunk, sour, they lean over the table with Poetry Project flyers spread under a roll of tickets. The wind blows the doors open. It's cold. Globs drop: glop. You can't fit much rice pudding on a switchblade. They're shivering, their coats hang like wrecked tents. They want to know: "Is Burroughs° reading here tonight?"

1993

Burroughs: William Burroughs (1914–1997), American writer and artist.

THOMAS JAMES (1946–1974)

Thomas James was born Thomas Edward Bojeski in Joliet, Illinois, the city in which he lived most of his life. The obvious predecessor who was his inspiration was Sylvia Plath. As a reviewer writes in the *Boston Review* years later, "like the *Ariel* sequence, James's poems fondle and embroider the delicate veil between life and death." James died in 1974 at his own hand at the age of twenty-seven, just after the first publication of his only book, *Letters to a Stranger.* In the years since, it has become deeply admired in poetry workshops across the country, but it was more an underground classic than an object of critical attention. According to Lucie Brock-Broido, until it was reprinted years later, it "existed in hundreds and hundreds of xeroxed copies across the country, a small underground railroad of reading for young poets." Edward Hirsch describes it as "a book of dark intensities and deeply felt connections, both haunted and haunting, at once brooding, sensual and lucid. . . . The voice in these poems—painfully lonely and filled with longing, estranged and religious—has stayed with me for more than twenty years. It deserves to be remembered." Brock-Broido remarks about "Mummy of a Lady Named Jemutesonekh" that the "poem is a soliloquy in the voice of a young girl from Thebes in the year 1051 BC as she is being mummified according to *The Egyptian Book of the Dead.* For all the physical violence of the process, her descriptions are luminous, romantic, graphically and magically sensual."

MUMMY OF A LADY NAMED JEMUTESONEKH XXI DYNASTY

My body holds its shape. The genius is intact.
Will I return to Thebes? In that lost country
The eucalyptus trees have turned to stone.
Once, branches nudged me, dropping swollen blossoms,
And passionflowers lit my father's garden.
Is it still there, that place of mottled shadow,
The scarlet flowers breathing in the darkness?

I remember how I died. It was so simple!
One morning the garden faded. My face blacked out.
On my left side they made the first incision.
They washed my heart and liver in palm wine—
My lungs were two dark fruit they stuffed with spices.
They smeared my innards with a sticky unguent
And sealed them in a crock of alabaster.

My brain was next. A pointed instrument
Hooked it through my nostrils, strand by strand.

A voice swayed over me. I paid no notice.
For weeks my body swam in sweet perfume.
I came out scoured. I was skin and bone.
They lifted me into the sun again
And packed my empty skull with cinnamon.

They slit my toes; a razor gashed my fingertips.
Stitched shut at last, my limbs were chaste and valuable,
Stuffed with paste of cloves and wild honey.
My eyes were empty, so they filled them up,
Inserting little nuggets of obsidian.
A basalt scarab wedged between my breasts
Replaced the tinny music of my heart.

Hands touched my sutures. I was so important!
They oiled my pores, rubbing a fragrance in.
An amber gum oozed down to soothe my temples.
I wanted to sit up. My skin was luminous,
Frail as the shadow of an emerald.
Before I learned to love myself too much,
My body wound itself in spools of linen.

Shut in my painted box, I am a precious object.
I wear a wooden mask. These are my eyelids,
Two flakes of bronze, and here is my new mouth,
Chiseled with care, guarding its ruby facets.
I will last forever. I am not impatient—
My skin will wait to greet its old complexions.
I'll lie here till the world swims back again.

When I come home the garden will be budding,
White petals breaking open, clusters of night flowers,
The far-off music of a tambourine.
A boy will pace among the passionflowers,
His eyes no longer two bruised surfaces.
I'll know the mouth of my young groom, I'll touch
His hands. Why do people lie to one another?

1973

DISSECTING A PIG

I

I have kept you in a laboratory jar
Comfortable as the château of your mother.

Blind, you squinted at me from the shelf
For two whole days,
And then I hoisted you, knuckles and all,
Out of your glassed-in belly.

I delivered you into the hard light
Clean as a son of God.

II

One day, your eyes slammed shut like doors.
You were the one that never went to market.
Your snout is moon-colored. I remember the time
I watched a sow get butchered.
She screamed like a woman in labor.
I couldn't look away.

Her heart kept right on pumping its bruised pistons;
The cut throat sent a jet of red to the ceiling.

III

The sun ricochets off my scalpel
As I open your throat.
I slice you like a ham,
Inching meticulously across your belly.
You take it all in stride;
You do not even smile.

You are a strongbox broken open. Suddenly
I am aware of your valuable possessions.

IV

Someone has filled your veins with plastic
So that you do not bleed or make a sound.
Your lungs have given out
Like two deflated life preservers.
You are full of a silence.
I move about you almost reverently.

You were baptized in formaldehyde
Before I brought you to this strange autopsy.

V

Here is your heart, fished out of the wreckage,
Inflated, mapped with ink-blue arteries,
And not at all as dreadful as I imagined.
I will hang it on a silver chain
And wear it under my clothing like an amulet
Of humming muscle, like a crucifix.

It will tap my ribs in secret for a month
Before it turns into a thin black angel.

1973

RON SILLIMAN (b. 1946)

Born in Pasco, Washington, Silliman grew up in Albany, California, just north of Berkeley. He was educated at Merritt College, San Francisco State University, and the University of California at Berkeley. He has worked as an organizer in prisoner and tenant movements, as well as a lobbyist, teacher, and college administrator. In the 1970s, he first edited *Labyrinth* for the Committee for Prisoner Humanity and Justice and then edited the *Tenderloin Times* for San Francisco's Central City Hospital House. For several years he was executive editor of *Socialist Review,* and since then has worked in the computer industry in Pennsylvania as a marketing communications specialist. A leading poet and theorist of the L=A=N=G=U=A=G=E poetry movement, author of the theoretical work *The New Sentence* (1987), and editor of the movement's most ambitious anthology, *In the American Tree* (1986), he has often used formal experiments to help us see how language functions as an autonomous system and shapes our understanding of the world. Silliman's work is also notable for its humor, its social conscience, and for its interest in the relationship between ordinary experience and narrativity. He often grounds his projects in his deliberate experiments; thus *Ketjak,* from which we reprint opening and closing sections, is a prose poem constructed of expanding paragraphs. The first paragraph has one sentence, while the second contains that sentence plus another; the third paragraph uses the two previous sentences, sometimes subtly altered, and adds two more; the fourth includes the previous four but adds four new sentences, and so forth. The previous sentences are uncannily altered by new contexts, and the reader is compelled to focus on sentence creation and the mutability of meaning.

from KETJAK°

Revolving door.

Revolving door. A sequence of objects which to him appears to be a caravan of fellaheen, a circus, begins a slow migration to the right vanishing point on the horizon line.

Revolving door. Fountains of the financial district. Houseboats beached at the point of low tide, only to float again when the sunset is reflected in the water. A sequence of objects which to him appears to be a caravan of fellaheen, a circus, camels pulling wagons of bear cages, tamed ostriches in toy hats, begins a slow migration to the right vanishing point on the horizon line.

Revolving door. First flies of summer. Fountains of the financial district spout. She was a unit in a bum space, she was a damaged child. Dark brown houseboats beached

---

poem title: *Ketjak* is a book-length sequence of twelve prose poems.

at the point of low tide—men atop their cabin roofs, idle, play a dobro, a jaw's harp, a 12-string guitar—only to float again when the sunset is reflected in the water. I want the grey-blue grain of western summer. A cardboard box of wool sweaters on top of the book case to indicate Home. A sequence of objects, silhouettes, which to him appears to be a caravan of fellaheen, a circus, dromedaries pulling wagons bearing tiger cages, tamed ostriches in toy hats, begins a slow migration to the right vanishing point on the horizon line.

Revolving door. Earth science. Fountains of the financial district spout soft water in a hard wind. How the heel rises and the ankle bends to carry the body from one stair to the next. She was a unit in a bum space, she was a damaged child. The fishermen's cormorants wear rings around their necks to keep them from swallowing, to force them to surrender the catch. Dark brown houseboats beached at the point of low tide—men atop their cabin roofs, idle, play a dobro, a jaw's harp, a 12 string guitar—only to float again when the sunset is reflected in the water. Silverfish, potato bugs. What I want is the gray-blue grain of western summer. The nurse, by a subtle shift of weight, moves in front of the student in order to more rapidly board the bus. A cardboard box of wool sweaters on top of the book case to indicate Home. A day of rain in the middle of June. A sequence of objects, silhouettes, which to him appears to be a caravan of fellaheen, a circus, dromedaries pulling wagons bearing tiger cages, fringed surreys, tamed ostriches in toy hats, begins a slow migration to the right vanishing point on the horizon line. We ate them.

Revolving door. The garbage barge at the bridge. Earth science. Resemblance. Fountains of the financial district spout soft water in a hard wind. The bear flag in the plaza. How the heel rises and the ankle bends to carry the body from one stair to the next. A tenor sax is a toy. She was a unit in a bum space, she was a damaged child, sitting in her rocker by the window. I'm unable to find just the right straw hat. The fishermen's cormorants wear rings around their necks to keep them from swallowing, to force them to surrender the catch. We drove through fields of artichokes. Dark brown houseboats beached at the point of low tide—men atop their cabin roofs, idle, play a dobro, a jaw's harp, a 12 string guitar—only to float again when the sunset is reflected in the water of Richardson Bay. Write this down in a green notebook. Silverfish, potato bugs. A tenor sax is a weapon. What I want is the gray-blue grain of western summer. Mention sex. The nurse, by a subtle redistribution of weight, shift of gravity's center, moves in front of the student of oriental porcelain in order to more rapidly board the bus. Awake, but still in bed, I listen to cars pass, doors, birds, children are day's first voices. A cardboard box of wool sweaters on top of the bookcase to indicate Home. Attention is all. A day of rain in the middle of June. Modal rounders. A sequence of objects, silhouettes, which to him appears to be a caravan of fellaheen, a circus, dromedaries pulling wagons bearing tiger cages, fringed surreys, tamed ostriches in toy hats, begins a slow migration to the right vanishing point on the horizon line. The implications of power within the ability to draw a single, vertical straight line. Look at that room filled with fleshy babies. We ate them.

Revolving door. How will I know when I make a mistake. The garbage barge at the bridge. The throb in the wrist. Earth science. Their first goal was to separate the workers from their means of production. He bears a resemblance. A drawing of a Balinese spirit with its face in its stomach. Fountains of the financial district spout soft water in a hard wind. In a far room of the apartment I can hear music and a hammer. The bear flag in the black marble plaza. Rapid transit. How the heel rises and the ankle bends to carry the body from one stair to the next. The desire for coffee. A tenor sax is a toy. Snow is remarkable to one not accustomed to it. She was a unit in a bum space, she was a damaged child, sitting in her rocker by the window. The formal beauty of a back porch. I'm unable to find just the right straw hat. He hit the bricks, took a vacation, got rolled up, popped, as they say. The fishermen's cormorants wear rings around their necks to keep them from swallowing, to force them to surrender their catch. She had only the slightest pubic hair. We drove through fields of artichokes. Feet, do your stuff. Dark brown houseboats beached at the point of low tide—men atop their cabin roofs, idle, play a dobro, a jaw's harp, a 12 string guitar—only to float again when the sunset is reflected in the water of Richardson Bay. Frying yellow squash in the wok. Write this down in a green notebook. Television in the 1950s. Silverfish, potato bugs. We stopped for hot chocolate topped with whipped cream and to discuss the Sicilian Defense. A tenor sax is a weapon. The Main Library was a grey weight in a white rain. What I want is the gray-blue grain of western summer. Subtitles lower your focus. Mention sex, fruit. Drip candles kept atop old, empty bottles of wine. The young nurse in sunglasses, by a subtle redistribution of weight, shift of gravity's center, moves in front of the black student of oriental porcelain in order to more rapidly board the bus home, before all the seats are taken. Are pears form. Awake, but still in bed, I listen to cars pass, doors, birds, children are day's first voices. Eventually the scratches became scabs. A cardboard box of wool sweaters on top of the bookcase to indicate Home. Bedlingtons were at first meant to hunt rats in coal mines. Attention is all. He knew how to hold an adz. A day of rain in the middle of June. The gamelan is not simple. Modal rounders. A sequence of objects, silhouettes, which to him appears to be a caravan of fellaheen, a circus, dromedaries pulling wagons bearing tiger cages, fringed surreys, tamed ostriches in toy hats, begins a slow migration to the right vanishing point on the horizon line. Slag iron. The implicit power within the ability to draw a single, vertical straight line. That was when my nose began to peel. Look at that room filled with fleshy babies, incubating. A tall glass of tawny port. We ate them.

1978

from SUNSET DEBRIS

Can you feel it? Does it hurt? Is this too soft? Do you like it? Do you like this? Is this how you like it? Is it alright? Is he there? Is he breathing? Is it him? Is it near? Is it hard? Is it cold? Does it weigh much? Is it heavy? Do you have to carry it far? Are those hills? Is this where we get off? Which one are you? Are we there yet? Do we need to bring sweaters? Where is the border between blue and green? Has the mail come? Have you come yet? Is it perfect bound? Do you prefer ballpoints? Do you know which insect you most resemble? Is it the red one? Is that your hand? Want to go out? What about dinner? What does it cost? Do you speak English? Has he found his voice yet? Is this anise or is it fennel? Are you high yet? Is your throat sore? Can't you tell dill weed when you see it? Do you smell something burning? Do you hear a ringing sound? Do you hear something whimpering, mewing, crying? Do we get there from here? Does the ink smear? Does the paper get yellow and brittle? Do you prefer soft core? Are they on their way to work? Are they feeling it? Are they locked out? Are you pessimistic? Are you hard? Is that where you live? Is the sink clogged? Have the roaches made a nest in the radio? Are the cats hungry, thirsty, tired? Does he need to have a catheter? Is he the father? Are you a student at the radio school? Are you afraid to fail? Are you in constant fear of assassination? Why has the traffic stopped? Why does blue fade into green? Why didn't I go back to Pasco and become a cop? Why does water curl into the drain in different directions on either side of the equator? Why does my ankle throb? Why do I like it when I pop my knuckles? Is that a bald spot? It that an ice cap? Is that a birth mark? Will the fog burn off soon? Are her life signs going to stabilize? Can you afford it? Is it gutted? What is it that attracts you to bisexual women? Does it go soggy in the milk? Do people live there? Is there a limit? Did it roll over when it went off the road? Will it further class struggle? Is it legible? Do you feel that it's private? Does it eat flies, worms, children? Is it nasty? Can you get tickets? Do you wear sunglasses out of a misplaced sense of increased privacy? Do you derive pleasure from farts in the bath? Is there an erotic element to picking your nose? Have you a specific conceptualization of ear wax? What am I doing here? How do the deaf sing? How is it those houses will burn in the rain? What is the distance to Wall Drugs? Why do they insist on breaking the piñata? Is penetration of the labia sufficient to support a conviction? Is it a distraction to be aware of the walls? Is it bigger than a breadbox? Which is it? When you skydive, do your ears pop? Do you bruise? Did the bridge rust? Is your life clear to you? How will you move it? Will you go easy on the tonic please? Do you resent your parents? Was your childhood a time of great fear? Is that the path? Do the sandpipers breed here? Is that what you want? Have your cramps come? Do you tend to draw words instead of write them? Do you have an opinion about galvanized steel? Who was John Deere? Are you trapped by your work? Would you like to explore that quarry? Is it the form of a question? Where is Wolf Grade? Are your legs sore? Is that a bottle neck? Who is the Ant Farm? Where did she learn to crawl like that? Is the form of the dance the dancer or the space she carves? Can we go home now? Who was that masked man? Does he have an imagination? Will he use it? Is it obvious? Is it intentional? Is it possible? Is it hot? Why did the mirror fog up? What is the context of discourse? What is the premise of the man asking passersby if they have change for a dollar? Who took my toothbrush? What made her choose to get back into the life? What is the cause of long fingers? What is the role of altered, stretched canvas on wood supports, hung from a wall? Why do they seem so focused, intent, on their way to work? What makes you needle happy? Why does he keep large bills in his shirt pocket? How do you locate the cross-hairs of your bitterness? What was it about shouting, mere raised voices, that caused him always to go out of control? Do you hear that hum? Is there damage? Is the answer difficult or hard? Is each thing needful? If there was a rip in my notebook, how would you know it? What makes you think you have me figured out? Why do my eyes water, devoid of emotion? What is the difference between a film and a movie? Do you want sugar? Why does my mood correspond to the weather? How do you get down to the beach? Is the act distinct from the object? What did you put in the coffee? Did your ears pop? Would you prefer to watch the condos burn? Where do the verbs go? Will you ever speak to the issue of cholesterol? What is a psychotropic? Does pleonasm scare you? Kledomania? Who leads the low-riders? What is the relation between any two statements? Is anything as tight as anal penetration? Will we stop soon? Will we continue? Where are those sirens coming from? Is it necessary? Is it off-white? Is a legitimate purpose served in limiting access? Will this turn out to be the last day of summer? Will you give up, give out, over? Why is sarcasm so often the final state of marriage? Is this the right exit? Have you received a security clearance? What do you think of when I say "red goose shoes"?

1986

THE CHINESE NOTEBOOK

1. Wayward, we weigh words. Nouns reward objects for meaning. The chair in the air is covered with hair. No part is in touch with the planet.

2. Each time I pass the garage of a certain yellow house, I am greeted with barking. The first time this occurred, an instinctive fear seemed to run through me. I have never been attacked. Yet I firmly believe that if I opened the door to the garage I should confront a dog.

3. Chesterfield, sofa, divan, couch—might these items refer to the same object? If so, are they separate conditions of a single word?

4. My mother as a child would call a potholder a "boppo," the term becoming appropriated by the whole family, handed down now by my cousins to their own children. Is it a word? If it extends, eventually, into general usage, at what moment will it become one?

5. Language is, first of all, a political question.

6. I wrote this sentence with a ballpoint pen. If I had used another would it have been a different sentence?

7. This is not philosophy, it's poetry. And if I say so, then it becomes painting, music or sculpture, judged as such. If there are variables to consider, they are at least partly economic—the question of distribution, etc. Also differing critical traditions. Could this be good poetry, yet bad music? But yet I do not believe I would, except in jest, posit this as dance or urban planning.

8. This is not speech. I wrote it.

9. Another story, similar to 2: until well into my twenties the smell of cigars repelled me. The strong scent inevitably brought to mind the image of warm, wet shit. That is not, in retrospect, an association I can rationally explain. Then I worked as a legislative advocate in the state capitol and was around cigar smoke constantly. Eventually the odor seemed to dissolve. I no longer noticed it. Then I began to notice it again, only now it was an odor I associated with suede or leather. This was how I came to smoke cigars.

10. What of a poetry that lacks surprise? That lacks form, theme, development? Whose language rejects interest? That examines itself without curiosity? Will it survive?

11. Rose and maroon we might call red.

12. Legalistic definitions. For example, in some jurisdictions a conviction is not present, in spite of a finding of guilt, without imposition of sentence. A suspension of sentence, with probation, would not therefore be a conviction. This has substantial impact on teachers' credentials, or the right to practice medicine or law.

13. That this form has a tradition other than the one I propose, Wittgenstein,° etc., I choose not to dispute. But what is its impact on the tradition proposed?

14. Is Wittgenstein's contribution strictly formal?

15. Possibility of a poetry analogous to the paintings of Rosenquist°—specific representational detail combined in non-objective, formalist systems.

16. If this were theory, not practice, would I know it?

17. Everything here tends away from an aesthetic decision, which, in itself, is one.

18. I chose a Chinese notebook, its thin pages not to be cut, its six redline columns which I turned 90°, the way they are closed by curves at both top and bottom, to see how it would alter the writing. Is it flatter, more airy? The words, as I write them, are larger, cover more surface on this two-dimensional picture plane. Shall I, therefore, tend toward shorter terms—impact of page on vocabulary?

19. Because I print this, I go slower. Imagine layers of air over the planet. One closer to the center of gravity moves faster, while the one above it tends to drag. The lower one is thought, the planet itself the object of the thought. But from space what is seen is what filters through the slower outer air of representation.

---

13. *Wittgenstein:* Ludwig Wittgenstein (1889–1951), Austrian-born philosopher.
15. *Rosenquist:* James Rosenquist (b. 1933), American painter.

20. Perhaps poetry is an activity and not a form at all. Would this definition satisfy Duncan?°

21. Poem in a notebook, manuscript, magazine, book, reprinted in an anthology. Scripts and contexts differ. How could it be the same poem?

22. The page intended to score speech. What an elaborate fiction that seems!

23. As a boy, riding with my grandparents about Oakland or in the country, I would recite such signs as we passed, directions, names of towns or diners, billboards. This seems to me now a basic form of verbal activity.

24. If the pen won't work, the words won't form. The meanings are not manifested.

25. How can I show that the intentions of this work and poetry are identical?

26. Anacoluthia, parataxis°—there is no grammar or logic by which the room in which I sit can be precisely recreated in words. If, in fact, I were to try to convey it to a stranger, I'd be inclined to show photos and draw a floor map.

27. Your existence is not a condition of this work. Yet, let me, for a moment, posit it. As you read, other things occur to you. You hear the drip of a faucet, or there's music on, or your companion gives a sigh that represents a poor night's sleep. As you read, old conversations reel slowly through your mind, you sense your buttocks and spine in contact with the chair. All of these certainly must be a part of the meaning of this work.

28. As students, boys and girls the age of ten, we would write stories and essays, reading them to the class if the teacher saw fit. The empty space of blank paper seemed to propose infinite dimensions. When the first term was fixed, the whole form readily appeared. It seemed more a question of finding the writing than of creating it. One day a student—his name was Jon Arnold—read an essay in which he described our responses to hearing him read it. It was then I knew what writing meant.

29. Mallard, drake—if the words change, does the bird remain?

30. How is it possible that I imagine I can put that chair into language? There it sits, mute. It knows nothing of syntax. How can I put it into something it doesn't inherently possess?

---

20. *Duncan:* Robert Duncan, American poet. Other poets mentioned who are included in *Anthology of American Poetry* are not identified.

26. *Anacoluthia, parataxis:* Anacoluthia: the failure to complete a sentence according to the structural plan by which it was started; used deliberately, it is a recognized figure of speech. Parataxis: a style in which there are few linking terms between juxtaposed clauses or sentences.

31. "Terminate with extreme prejudice." That meant kill. Or "we had to destroy the village in order to save it." Special conditions create special languages. If we remain at a distance, their irrationality seems apparent, but, if we came closer, would it?

32. The Manson° family, the SLA.° What if a group began to define the perceived world according to a complex, internally consistent, and precise (tho inaccurate) language? Might not the syntax itself propel their reality to such a point that to our own they could not return? Isn't that what happened to Hitler?

33. A friend records what she hears, such as a lunatic awaiting his food stamps, speaking to those who also wait in line, that "whether or not you're good people, that's what I can't tell." As if such acts of speech were clues to the truth of speech itself.

34. They are confused, those who would appropriate Dylan or Wittgenstein—were there ever two more similar men?—, passing them off as poets?

35. What now? What new? All these words turning in on themselves like the concentric layers of an onion.

36. What does it mean: "saw fit"?

37. Poetry is a specific form of behavior.

38. But test it against other forms. Is it more like a drunkenness than filling out an absentee ballot? Is there any value in knowing the answer to this question?

39. Winter wakens thought, much as summer prods recollection. Ought poetry to be a condition of the seasons?

40. What any of us eventually tries—to arrive at some form of "bad" writing (e.g., 31–34?) that would be one form of "good" poetry. Only when you achieve this will you be able to define what it is.

41. Speech only tells you the speaker.

42. Analogies between poetry and painting end up equating page and canvas. Is there any use in such fiction?

43. Or take the so-called normal tongue and shift each term in a subtle way. Is this speech made new or mere decoration?

---

32. *Manson:* Charles Manson (b. 1934), American mass murderer; his "family" was the cult group who carried out murders on his command in the late 1960s.

32. *SLA:* the Symbionese Liberation Army, a radical, anticapitalist, terrorist organization operating in the United States in the mid-1970s; their most famous act was the kidnapping of heiress Patricia Hearst in 1974.

44. Poets of the syntagmeme, poets of the paradigm.

45. The word in the world.

46. Formal perception: that this section, because of the brevity of the foregoing two, should be extensive, commenting, probing, making not aphorisms but fine distinctions, one sentence perhaps of a modular design, verbs in many clauses like small houses sketched into the mountainsides of a grand Chinese landscape, noting to the mind as it passes the gears and hinges of the design, how from the paradigm "large, huge, vast, great, grand," the term was chosen, by rhyme, anticipate "landscape," time itself signaled by the repetition.

47. Have we come so very far since Sterne or Pope?°

48. Language as a medium attracts me because I equate it with that element of consciousness which I take to be intrinsically human. Painting or music, say, might also directly involve the senses, but by ordering external situations to provoke specific (or general) responses. Do I fictionalize the page as form not to consider it as simply another manifestation of such "objective" fact? I have known writers who thought they could make the page disappear.

49. Everything you hear in your head, heart, whole body, when you read this, is what this is.

50. Ugliness v. banality. Both, finally, are attractive.

51. Time is one axis. Often I want to draw it out, to make it felt, a thing so slow that slight alterations (long v. short syllables, etc., clusters of alliteration . . .) magnify, not line (or breath) but pulse, the blood in the muscle.

52. Etymology in poetry—to what extent is it hidden (i.e., present and felt, but not consciously perceived) and to what extent lost (i.e., not perceived or felt, or, if so, only consciously)? The Joycean tradition here is based on an analytic assumption which is not true.

53. Is the possibility of publishing this work automatically a part of the writing? Does it alter decisions in the work? Could I have written that if it did not?

54. Increasingly I find object art has nothing new to teach me. This is also the case for certain kinds of poetry. My interest in the theory of the line has its limits.

55. The presumption is: I can write like this and "get away with it."

---

47. *Sterne or Pope:* Lawrence Sterne (1713–1768) and Alexander Pope (1688–1744), Irish novelist and British poet, respectively.

56. As economic conditions worsen, printing becomes prohibitive. Writers posit less emphasis on the page or book.

57. "He's content just to have other writers think of him as a poet." What does this mean?

58. What if there were no other writers? What would I write like?

59. Imagine meaning rounded, never specific.

60. Is it language that creates categories? As if each apple were a proposed definition of a certain term.

61. Poetry, a state of emotion or intellect. Who would believe that? What would prompt them to do so? Also, what would prompt them to abandon this point of view?

62. The very idea of margins. A convention useful to fix forms, perhaps the first visual element of ordering, preceding even the standardization of spelling. What purpose does it have now, beyond the convenience of printers? Margins do not seem inherent in speech, but possibly that is not the case.

63. Why is the concept of a right-hand margin so weak in the poetry of western civilization?

64. Suppose I was trying to explain a theory of the margin to a speaker of Mandarin or Shasta—how would I justify it? Would I compare it to rhyme as a sort of decision? Would I mention the possibility of capitalizing the letters along the margin? If I wanted, could I work "backwards" here, showing how one could posit nonspoken acrostics vertically at the margin and justify its existence from that? What if the person to whom I was explaining this had no alphabet, no writing, in his native tongue?

65. Saroyan and, more completely, Grenier° have demonstrated that there is no useful distinction between language and poetry.

66. Under certain conditions any language event can be poetry. The question thus becomes one of what are these conditions.

67. By the very act of naming—The Chinese Notebook—one enters into a process as into a contract. Yet each section, such as this, needs to be invented, does not automatically follow from specific prior statements. However, that too could be the case.

---

65. *Saroyan . . . Grenier:* William Saroyan (1908–1981) and Robert Grenier (b. 1941), American novelist and American experimental poet, respectively.

68. I have never seen a theory of poetry that adequately included a subtheory of choice.

69. There is also the question of work rhythms and habits. When I was a boy, after each dinner I would place the family typewriter—it was ancient and heavy—atop the kitchen table, typing or writing furiously—it was almost automatic writing—until it was time to go to bed. Later, married, I still wrote in the evening, as though unable to begin until each day's information reached a certain threshold which I could gauge by fatigue. All throughout these years, I could not work on a given piece beyond one sitting—a condition I attributed to my attention span—, although on occasion "one sitting" could extend to 48 hours. Since then there has been a shift. I have lately been writing in notebooks, over extended periods (in one instance, five months), and in the morning, often before breakfast and at times before dawn. Rather than the fatigue of digested sense data, the state of mind I work in is the empty-headed clarity which follows sleep.

70. This work lacks cunning.

71. An offshoot of projectivist theory was the idea that the form of the poem might be equivalent to the poet's physical self. A thin man to use short lines and a huge man to write at length. Kelly, etc.

72. Antin's° theory is that in the recent history of progressive forms (himself, Schwerner, Rothenberg, MacLow, Higgins, the Something Else writers et al), it has become clear that only certain domains yield "successful" work. But he has not indicated what these domains are, nor sufficiently defined success.

73. A social definition of a successful poet might be anyone who has a substantial proportion of his or her work generally available, so that an interested reader can, without knowing the writer, grasp, in broad terms at least, the scope of the whole.

74. If this bores you, leave.

75. What happened to fiction was a shift in public sensibility. The general reader no longer is apt to identify with a character in a story, but with its author. Thus the true narrative element is the development of the form. The true drama of, say, Mailer's *Armies of the Night,*° is the question: will this book work? In film, an even more naturally narrative medium than prose, this condition is readily apparent.

76. If I am correct that this is poetry, where is its family resemblance to, say, *The Prelude*?° Crossing the Alps.

---

72. *Antin:* David Antin (b. 1932), American poet known for his improvisational "talk" poems.
75. *Mailer*: Norman Mailer (1923–2007), American novelist.
76. *Prelude:* long poem by British poet William Wordsworth (1770–1850).

77. The poem as code or fad. One you must "break," while the other requires the decision of whether or not to follow.

78. Is not-writing (and here I don't mean discarding or revising) also part of the process?

79. I am continually amazed at how many writers are writing the poems they believe the person they wish they were would have written.

80. What if writing was meant to represent all possibilities of thought, yet one could or would write only in certain conditions, states of mind?

81. I have seen poems thought or felt to be dense, difficult to get through, respaced on the page, two dimensional picture plane, made airy, "light." How is content altered by this operation?

82. Certain forms of "bad" poetry are of interest because inept writing blocks referentiality, turning words and phrases in on themselves, an autonomy of language which characterizes the "best" writing. Some forms of sloppy surrealism or pseudo-beat automatic writing are particularly given to this.

83. Designated art sentence.

84. One can use the inherent referentiality of sentences very much as certain "pop" artists used images (I'm thinking of Rauschenberg, Johns,° Rosenquist, etc.) to use as elements for so-called abstract composition.

85. Abstract v. concrete, a misleading vocabulary. If I read a sentence (story, poem, whatever unit) of a fight, say, and identify with any spectator or combatant, I am having a vicarious experience. But if I experience, most pronouncedly, this language as event, I am experiencing that fact directly.

86. Impossible to posit the cat's expectations in words. Or Q's example—the mouse's fear of the cat is counted as his believing true a certain English sentence. If we are to speak of things, we are proscribed, limited to the external, or else create laughable and fantastic fictions.

87. Story of a chimpanzee taught that certain geometrical signs stood for words, triangle for bird, circle for water, etc., when presented with a new object, a duck, immediately made up the term "water bird."

---

84. *Rauschenberg, Johns:* Jasper Johns (b. 1930) and Robert Rauschenberg (1925–2005), American painters.

88. That writing was "speech" "scored." A generation caught in such mixed metaphor (denying the metaphor) as that. That elaboration of technical components of the poem carried the force of prophecy.

89. Is any term now greater than a place-holder? Any arrangement of weighted squares, if ordered by some shared theory of color, could be language.

90. What do nouns reveal? Conceal?

91. The idea of the importance of the role of the thumb in human evolution. Would I still be able to use it if I did not have a word for it? Thought it simply a finger? What evidence do I have that my right and left thumbs are at least roughly symmetrical equivalents? After all I don't really use my hands interchangeably, do I? I couldn't write this with my left hand, or if I did learn to do so, it would be a specific skill and would be perceived as that.

92. Perhaps as a means of containing meaning outside of the gallery system, the visual arts have entered into a period where the art itself exists in a dialectic, in the exchange between worker, critic and worker. Writing stands in a different historical context. Fiction exists in relation to a publishing system, poetry to an academic one.

93. At Berkeley, when I was a student, graduate students in the English Department liked to think of themselves as "specialized readers."

94. What makes me think that form exists?

95. One possibility is my ability to "duplicate" or represent it. As a child, I could fill in a drawing as tho it and color existed.

96. I want these words to fill the spaces poems leave.

97. The assumption is, language is equal if not to human perception per se, then to what is human about perception.

98. Good v. bad poetry. The distinction is not useful. The whole idea assumes a shared set of articulatable values by which to make such a judgment. It assumes, if not the perfect poem, at least the theory of limits, the most perfect poem. How would you proceed to make such a distinction?

99. Those who would excerpt or edit miss the point.

100. "When I look at a blank page it's never blank!" Prove or disprove this statement.

101. Before you can accept the idea of fiction, you have to admit everything else.

102. "The only thing language can change is language." Ah, but to the extent that we act on our thoughts, we act on their syntax.

103. The order of this room is subject-verb-predicate.

104. Put all of this another way: can I use language to change myself?

105. Once I wrote some stories for an elementary school text. I was given a list of words from which to work, several hundred terms proposed to me as the information range of any eight year old. This included no verbs of change.

106. "Time is the common enemy."

107. Concepts of past and future precede an ability to conceive of the sentence.

108. Subjects hypnotized to forget the past and future wrote words at random intervals about the page.

109. So-called non-referential language when structured non-syntactically tends to disrupt time perception. Once recognized, one can begin to structure the disruption. Coolidge,° for example, in *The Maintains,* uses line, stanza and repetition. Ashbery's *Three Poems,* not referential but syntactical, does not alter time.

110. The flaw of non-referentiality is that words are derived. They do not exist prior to their causes. Even when the origins are not obvious or are forgotten. The root, for example, of *denigrate* is *Negro.* Words only become non-referential through specific context. A condition as special (i.e., not universal or "ordinary") as the poem perceived as speech scored for the page.

111. When I was younger, the argument was whether, when you stripped the poem of all inessentials, you were left finally with a voice or with an image. Now it seems clear that the answer is neither. A poem, like any language, is a vocabulary and a set of rules by which it is processed.

112. But if the poem/language equation is what we have been seeking, other questions nevertheless arise. For example, are two poems by one poet two languages or, as Zukofsky argues, only one? But take specifics—*Catullus, Mantis, Bottom, "A"-12*—are these not four vocabularies with four sets of rules?

113. Compare sections 26 and 103.

---

109. *Coolidge:* Clark Coolidge (b. 1939), American poet.

114. If four poets took a specific text from which to derive the terms of a poem, what I call a "vocab," and by prior agreement each wrote a sestina, that would still be four languages and not one, right?

115. A hill with two peaks, or two hills. If I grant that the language alters one's perception, and if it follows naturally that, depending on which perception one "chooses," one acts differently, becomes used to different paths, thinks of certain people as neighbors and others not, and that such acts collectively will alter the hill (e.g., one peak becomes middle-class, residential, while the other slips into ghettohood later to be cleared off for further "development" which might include leveling the top of the peak to make it useable industrial space)—If I grant the possibility of this chain, is not the landscape itself a consequence of language? And isn't this essentially the history of the planet? Can one, in the context of such a chain, speak of what we know of as the planet as existing prior to language?

116. This jumps around. It does not have an "argument."

117. Paris is in France. Also, Paris has five letters. So does France. But so do Ghana, China, Spain. How should I answer "Why is Paris Paris?"

118. The question within the question. To which does the question mark refer? If one question mark is lost, where does its meaning go? How is it possible for punctuation to have multiple or non-specific references?

119. In what way is this like prose? In what way is this unlike it?

120. Only esthetic consistency constitutes content (Yates' proposition regarding music). Applied to writing one arrives at the possibility of a "meaningful" poetry as the sum of "meaningless" poems.

121. But consistency demands a perception of time. Thus, if we accept the proposition, we tacitly approve some definition of poetry as a specific time construct.

122. There is no direction. There is only distance.

123. What is the creative role of confusion in any work?

124. At times, my own name is simply a gathering of letters. Very distant.

125. Words relate to the referred world much the way each point in a line can be said to describe a curve.

126. The sun variously rises each morning. We, variously, attempt to relate that. No single way is exact, yet everyone knows what we mean.

127. The words are not "out there."

128. By the time you admit the presence of verbs, you have already conceded all of the assumptions.

129. The historical attention of the arts to madness is a question of what happens if you redefine the language.

130. Content is only an excuse, something to permit the writing to occur, to trigger it. Would a historian looking for information about Massachusetts fishing colonies have much use for *Maximus?*° To say yes is to concede that in order to like, say, Pound, you'd have to *agree* with him, no?

131. *Sad is faction.* That sounds alone are not precise meaning (in the referential sense) means that before the listener can recognize content he/she must first have the perception of the presence of words.

132. But if one denies the possibility of referentiality, how does *sad is faction* differ from *satisfaction?* How do we know this?

133. "Post-syntactical" implies that syntax was a historical period of language, not a condition inherent in it. Rather than seeing language as a universe whose total set cannot be dealt with until all its conditions are brought into play, this designation opts for an easy and incorrect solution. Occasionally, it has been used in such a fashion as to assert some sort of competition with "syntactical" writing, with the supposedly-obvious presumption that, being later in language's various conditions, it is more advanced. Such a view distorts the intentions and functions of abandoning syntactical and even paratactical modes.

134. Terms, out of context, inevitably expand and develop enlarged inner conditions, the large field of the miniaturists.

135. Eigner's° work, for example. The early writings resemble a late Williams/early Olson mode, discursive syntax, which becomes in later works increasingly a cryptic notation until now often words in a work will float in an intuitive vocabulary—space, their inner complexities expanded so that words are used like the formal elements in abstract art.

136. To move away from the individualist stance in writing I first began to choose vocabularies for poems from language sources that were not my own, science texts, etc. Then I began to develop forms which opt away from the melodic dominant line

---

130. *Maximus:* the major poem sequence by Charles Olson.
135. *Eigner:* Larry Eigner (1927–1996), American poet.

of the past several decades, using formal analogies taken from certain Balinese and African percussive and ensemble musics, as well as that of Steve Reich.

137. The concept that the poem "expresses" the poet, vocally or otherwise, is at one with the whole body of thought identified as Capitalist Imperialism.

138. If poetry is to be perfect, it cannot be all-knowing. If it is to be all-knowing, it cannot be perfect.

139. I began writing seriously a decade ago and was slow to learn. For years I was awkward, sloppy, given to overstatement, the sentimental image, the theatrical resolution. Yet, subtracting these, I am amazed at the elements, all formal and/or conceptual, which have remained constants. It is those who tell me who I am.

140. The presumption of the logical positivists that "the relation between language and philosophy is closer than, as well as essentially different from, that between language and any other discipline," would upset most poets. Three answers seem possible: (1) the logical positivists are wrong, (2) poetry and philosophy are quite similar and perhaps ought to be considered different branches of a larger category, (3) poetry is not a discipline, at least in the sense of the special definition of the logical positivists. I reject the third alternative as not being true for any except those poets whose work lacks all sense of definition. This leaves me with two possible conclusions.

141. Why is this work a poem?

142. One answer: because certain information is suppressed due to what its position in the sequence would be.

143. But is it simply a question of leaving out?

144. It is our interpretation of signs, not their presence (which, after all, could be any series of random marks on the page, sounds in the air), that makes them referential.

145. There are writers who would never question the assumptions of non-objective artists (Terry Fox, say, or even Stella or the late Smithson)° who cannot deal with writing in the same fashion. Whenever they see certain marks on the page, they always presume that something *besides* those marks is also present.

146. On page 282 of *Imaginations,* Williams writes "This is the alphabet," presents the typewriter keyboard, except that where the s should be there appears a second *e*. Whether this was "in error" or not, it tells us everything about the perception of language.

---

145. *Stella . . . Smithson:* Frank Stella (b. 1936), Robert Smithson (1938–1973), American painters.

147. The failure of Williams to go beyond his work of *Spring and All* and the *Great American Novel* seems to verify Bergmann's° assertion that nominalism inevitably tends toward (deteriorates into?) representationalism.

148. Konkretism was a very narrow base on which to build a literature. Futurism of the Russian school, especially the *zaum*° works of the Group 41, is the true existing body of experimental literature with which contemporary writers have to work.

149. What is it that allows me to identify this as a poem, Wittgenstein to identify his work as technical philosophy, Brockman's *Afterwords* to be seen as Esalen-oriented metaphysics, and Kenner's° piece on Zukofsky literary criticism?

150. But is it a distortion of poetry to speak of it like this? How might I define poetry so as to be able to identify such distortions?

151. Can one even say, as have Wellek and Warren,° that literature (not even here to be so specific as to identify the poem to the exclusion of other modes) is first of all words in a sequence? One can point to the concretist tradition as a partial refutation, or one can point to the great works of Grenier, *A Day at the Beach* and *Sentences,* where literature occurs within individual words.

152. Possibly, if one approached it cautiously, one could hope to make notations, provisional definitions of poetry. For example, one might begin by stating that it is any language act—not necessarily a sequence of terms—which makes no other formal assertion other than it is poetry. This would permit the exclusion of Kosuth and Wittgenstein, but the inclusion of this.

153. But how, if it does not state it, does a work make a formal assertion? Certain structural characteristics such as line, stanza, etc. are not always present. Here is where one gets into Davenport's position regarding Ronald Johnson,° to say that one is a poet who has written no poems, per se.

154. Performance as a form is only that. As always, the intention of the creator defines the state in which the work is most wholly itself, so that it is possible that a talking piece, say, could be said to be a poem. But formally its ties are closer to other arts than to the tradition of poetry. I have, in the last year, heard talking pieces that were proposed as poetry, as music and as sculpture. Each, in all major respects, resembled the

---

147. *Bergmann:* Gustav Bergmann (1906–1987), Austrian philosopher.

148. *zaum:* a variety of Cubo-futurist experiments with transsense language (*zaum*) flourished in Russia in the 1910s–1920s.

149. *Kenner:* Hugh Kenner (1923–2003), American literary critic, an early advocate of Ezra Pound's poetry.

151. *Wellek and Warren:* René Wellek (1903–1995) and Austin Warren, American literary critics who coauthored an influential textbook, *Theory of Literature* (1949).

153. *Johnson:* (1935–1998), American poet.

late period of Lenny Bruce or perhaps Dick Cavett.° The form of the talking piece, its tradition, was always stronger than the asserted definition. Nor is the talking piece the only nontraditional (if, in fact, it is that at all) mode to run into this problem. Some of the visualists, e.g., Kostelanetz, have utilized film for their poems, but the poem is readily lost in this transfer. What one experiences in its presence is the fact of film.

155. Why did I write "As always, the intention of the creator defines the state in which the work is most wholly itself"? Because it is here and here only where one can "fix" a work into a given state (idea, projective process, text, affective process, impression), an act which is required, absolutely, before one can place the work in relation to others, only after which can one make judgments.

156. What if I told you I did not really believe this to be a poem? What if I told you I did?

157. Periodically one hears that definitions are unimportant, or, and this implicitly is more damning, "not interesting." I reject this, taking all language events to be definitions or, if you will, propositions.

158. I find myself not only in the position of arguing that all language acts are definitions and that they nonetheless are not essentially referential, but also that this is not a case specifically limited to an "ideal" or "special" language (such as one might argue poetry to be), but is general, applicable to all.

159. If, at this point, I was to insert 120 rhymed couplets, would it cause definitions to change?

160. Lippard° (*Changing*, p. 206) argues against a need for a "humanistic" visual arts, but makes an exception for literature, which "as a verbal medium, demands a verbal response." One wonders what, precisely, is meant by that? Is it simply a question of referentiality posed in vague terms? Or does it mean, as I suspect she intended it to, that language, like photography, is an ultimately captive medium? If so, is the assertion correct? It is not.

161. It becomes increasingly clear that the referential origin of language and its syntactical (or linguistic, or relational) meaning is the contradiction (if it is one) that is to be understood if we are to accept a poetics of autonomous language.

162. If I could make an irrefutable argument that non-referential language does exist (besides, that is, those special categories, such as prepositions or determiners), would I include this in it? Of course I would.

---

154. *Cavett:* Lenny Bruce (1925–1966), American satiric stand-up comic; Dick Cavett (b. 1936), American comic and television talk show host.

160. *Lippard:* Lucy Lippard, American art critic.

163. What you read is what you read.

164. Make a note in some other place, then transfer it here. Is it the same note?

165. I want form to be perceivable but not consequent to referred meaning. Rather, it should serve to move that element to the fore- or back-brain at will.

166. Form that is an extension of referred meaning stresses that meaning's relation to the individual, voice or image as extension of self, emphasizes one's separateness from others. What I want, instead, is recognition of our connectedness.

167. A writing which is all work, technical procedure, say a poem derived from a specific formula, is of interest for this fact alone.

168. Words in a text like states on a map: meaning is commerce.

169. One type of criticism would simply describe the formal features of any given work, demonstrate its orderliness with the implicit purpose of, from this, deducing the work's intention. A comparison, then, of the intention to the work (and, secondarily, to other works of identical or similar intention), would provide grounds for a judgment.

170. Is it possible for a work to conceal its intention?

171. But if the intention is always to be arrived at deductively, will not the work always be equal to it? Would we be able to recognize a work which had not met the writer's original intention?

172. Perhaps this poem could be said to be an example of the condition described in 171.

173. Is it possible for intentions to be judged, good or malevolent, right or otherwise? This brings us into the realm of political and ethical distinctions?

174. In recent years, criticism has played a dynamic role in the evolution of the visual arts, but not in writing. Theory, much of it unsound, even mystical, on the part of writers, has had more impact. A possible explanation: criticism is applied theory, useful only if it is rigorous in its application, which has been impossible given the loose and vague standards characteristic of so much recent writing, while theory can be used suggestively, which it has been regardless of the mystifications present.

175. A poem written in pen could never have been written in pencil.

176. When I was younger, I was so habituated to the typewriter as a tool and to the typewritten page as a space, that, even when I worked from notebooks, the poems transposed back into a typewritten text tended to perfectly fill the page.

177. Deliberately determining the way one writes, determines much of what will be written.

178. If I were to publish only parts of this, sections, it would alter the total proposition.

179. How far will anything extend? Hire dancers dressed as security personnel to walk about an otherwise empty museum, then admit the public. Could this be poetry if I have proposed it as such? If so, what elements could be altered or removed to make it not poetry? E.g., hire not dancers but ordinary security personnel. But if the answer is "no," if any extension, thing, event, would be poetry if proposed as such, *what* would poetry, the term, mean?

180. Possibly poetry is a condition applicable to any state of affairs. What would constitute such a condition? Would it be the same or similar in all instances? Could it be identified, broken down? Does it have anything to do with the adjectival form "poetic"?

181. If one could propose worrying as one form of poetry, what in the worrying would be the poem?

182. Or could one have poetry without the poem? Is it possible that these two states do not depend on the presence (relational as it is) of each other? Give examples.

183. Why is it language characterizes the man?

184. Or I meant, possibly, why is it that language characterizes man?

185. Is it language?

186. Context—against the text. Literally a circumstance where meaning is not obvious simply by the presence of terms in a specific sequence. Remove 185 from this text: "it" in 185 then means either "this writing" or some "other" event. But in the notebook as it is, the sentence must mean "Is it language that characterizes (the) man?" Is the same sentence in two contexts one or two sentences? If it is one, how can we assign it differing meanings? If it is two, there could never literally be repetition.

187. Alimentary, my dear Watson.

188. But if poetry were a 'system'—not necessarily a single system, but if for any individual it was—then one could simply plug in the raw data and out would flow 'poetry,' not necessarily poems.

189. Is this not what Robert Kelly° does?

---

189. *Kelly:* (b. 1935), American poet.

190. It was Ed van Aelstyn who, in his linguistics course, planted the idea (1968) that the definition of a language was also a definition of any poem: a vocabulary plus a set of rules through which to process it. What did I think poetry was before that?

191. But does the vocabulary include words which do not end up in the finished text? If so, how would we know which words they are?

192. A friend, a member of the Old Left, challenges my aesthetic. How, he asks, can one write so as not to "communicate"? I, in turn, challenge his definitions. It is a more crucial lesson, I argue, to learn how to experience language directly, to tune one's senses to it, than to use it as a mere means to an end. Such use, I point out, is, in bourgeois life, common to all things, even the way we "use" our friends. Some artists (Brecht is the obvious example) try to focus such "use" to point up all the alienation, to present a bourgeois discourse "hollowed out." But language, so that it is experienced directly, moves beyond any such exercise in despair, an unalienated language. He wants an example. I give him Grenier's

thumpa
thumpa
thumpa
thump

pointing out how it uses so many physical elements of speech, how it is a speech that only borders on language, how it illumines that space. He says "I don't understand."

193. Determiners, their meaning.

194. Each sentence is new born.

195. Traditionally, poetry has been restrictive, has had no room for the appositive.

196. I imagine at times this to be discourse. Sometimes it is one voice, sometimes many.

197. Language on walls. Graffiti, "fuk speling," etc. As a boy I rode with my Grandparents about town, learning to read by reading all the signs aloud. I am still apt to do this.

198. This sentence is that one.

199. "This in which," i.e., the world in its relations. What is of interest is *not* the objectification, but relativity: Einstein's "What time does the station get to the train?"

200. Imagine the man who liked de Kooning° out of a fondness for women.

201. There is no way in language to describe the experience of knowing my hand.

---

200. *de Kooning:* Willem de Kooning (1904–1997), American artist known for his vibrant, hugely distorted portraits of women.

202. I was chased, running through a forest. Because I knew the names of the plants I could run faster.

203. The formal considerations of indeterminacy are too few for interest to extend very far, even when posed in other terms—"organic" etc. But organic form is strict, say, 1:1:2:3:5:8:13:21. . . . What is the justification for strict form (Xenakis'° music, for example) which cannot be perceived? Is there an aesthetic defense for the hidden?

204. Presence and absence. This axis is form's major dimension.

205. Are 23 and 197 the same or different?

206. A paper which did not absorb fluids well, a pencil that was blunt or wrote only faintly. These would determine the form of the work. Now, when I set out on a piece, choice of instrument and recorder (notebook, typing paper, etc.) are major concerns. I am apt to buy specific pens for specific pieces.

207. Words to locate specific instance—personalism, localism. Quality of a journal to what this or that one does. "Another hard day of gossip."

208. Any writer carries in his or her head a set, what 'the scene' is, its issues, etc. So often little or no overlap at all, but how it defines what anyone does!

209. The day is wrappt in its definitions, this room is.

210. Whether one sees language as learned or inherent determines, in part, what one does with it. The 'organic' sentence (truncated, say, by breath, or thought's diversions) versus the sentence as an infinitely plastic (I don't mean this in the pejorative sense) one, folding, unfolding, extending without limit. Dahlberg or Faulkner.°

211. Absolutely normal people. Would their writing be any different?

212. Information leaks through these words. Each time I use them new things appear.

213. Values are vowels.

214. A language of one consonant, one vowel, various as any.

215. Like eyesight, our minds organizing what we 'see' before we even see it. As tho I did not know about oranges, tho I had eaten them all my life. Each time I ate one I would not know what taste to expect.

---

203. *Xenakis:* Iannis Xenakis (1922–2001), Romanian-born Greek musical composer who has organized musical compositions by computer.

210. *Dahlberg or Faulkner:* Edward Dahlberg (1900–1977) and William Faulkner (1897–1962), American novelists.

216. I do not read to 'read of the world,' but for the pleasure in the act of reading.

217. The ocean's edge is a mantra. Strollers, bathers, dogs, gulls. Its great sound. The smell of salt. Sun's sheen on water. But there is no way to repeat this in language. Anything we say, descriptively, is partial. At best one constructs an aesthetic of implication. One can, however, make of the language itself a mantra. But this is not the ocean.

218. Buildup, resolution. What have these to do with the writing?

219. Just as doubt presumes a concept of certainty, non-referentiality presumes knowledge of the referential. Is this a proof?

220. When I return here to ideas previously stated, that's rhyme.

221. Any piece I write precludes the writing of some other piece. As this work is the necessary consequence of previous writings, called poems, so it will also create necessities, ordering what follows. I take this as absolute verification of its poemhood.

222. Language hums in the head, secretes words.

223. This is it.

1986

from TONER°

Meet my personality.
A deaf man's whistle
could seem inexact.
                        I don't
            want to get my
feathers hot.
Bag lady stands in

                    A phone booth
out of the rain.
First dot, best dot.
Death of
            Porky the Pig.
Already the jaws
of narrative open.

---

volume title: *Toner* is a book-length poem consisting of 199 stanzas.

On the street
a woman
returns the man's leer,
involuntary grimace.
Static
storms the intercom.
A reduction in species

Simplifies planet.
Tongue pressed
to third rail.
The way the new el
undeckles the margin
between suburb and sky.
After a walk in the rain

Cuffs damp for hours.
Shapeless mass in express lane
checkout counter.
Now when I hear
someone on the bus talking
I turn
to see

If anyone is there
to listen.
Write first
and ask questions after,
exact trace
of anxiety
does not "make the man"

Lumber yard
surrounded by condos:
its days are numbered.
People gasp,
mouse loose on the train.
Top Stars Tell How They Died,
see inside. Multiples weep

To see the space about them—
vacant lots
stretching
not forever but to the freeway,
not vacant

but each
holding a cement foundation

Visible to infrared
poised in night sky.
Anthropomorphic,
                    the president grins
across a screen filled with snow,
                    unattended
in the tavern corner,

The hard sound of billiards
banging together.
                    Ice melts
settling in the tall glass
about the clear plastic straw,
model
        for offshore drilling.

I'm in touch with my emotions,
in search of a tourniquet,
            event at which
life narrows
to the Final Four.
Pull string here
                says Band-Aid's

Wax paper wrapper
                    but instead
                the red string
just slides out.
Woodpecker walks up
trunk of the pine.
Windmill breaks up broadcast transmission.

Economists conduct thought experiment
for a society of two islands
containing one individual each.
        Man struggles
to move
        from wheelchair
to auto.

                    Extra-wide briefcase
indicates salesman,

stewardess' luggage in portable dolly.
                    Fumbles with his walkman
at the end of the tape.
Escalator's steady hum
dissolves in the muzak:

Soft repetitive bell
sends plainclothes security staff
sprinting to department store exit.
       We have nothing
to form
but form
       itself,

The social queues up
                    like children
at the end of recess
in the rain.
       A nurse
with bruised knees, lawyer's
belly strains dull shirt,

Tie open wide.
             The line waits
for the previous show to let out.
Who watches the watchmen?
Far across the bay
I see the city rise,
                 hazy,

Verticals without depth.
Throat sore from indoor heat,
                          old prof
shambles across the quad,
                 that verb
mere predication.
Left-handed woman writes in margin

Of casebook.
           Library book
dust jacket
           encased in plastic.
Four men in 1914,
three at Columbia
determine American literary canon.

Pronounce that canyon.
She said I said
                    in my sleep
the same word
          over and over
"Dama,"
whatever that means.

          Large-boned woman,
freckled,
her hair in thick braids,
asleep on the train.
                              Year that
some men thought it hip
to shave sideburns

1992

ADRIAN C. LOUIS (b. 1946)

Born and raised in Nevada, Louis is an enrolled member of the Lovelock Paiute Indian tribe. He was educated at Brown University, where he also went on to receive an M.A. in creative writing. A former journalist, he edited four tribal newspapers and was a founder of the Native American Press Association. Since 1999, he has taught English at Minnesota State University in Marshall. Louis, who writes both poetry and fiction, is at the forefront of a new generation of Native American writers. Having abandoned the celebratory lyricism of some of his predecessors, he opts instead to tell harsh truths about both white and Indian cultures. Frank about alcoholism, frank about self-pity, he also displays an articulate bitterness about the humiliation and demoralization his people continue to suffer. His primary focus is not the past but the present life of Native Americans, but it is a present at once redolent with history and destabilized by moments of magical revelation. Louis thereby discovers uncanny instances of transfiguration amidst loss and the ordinary routines of daily life. Like Sherman Alexie, his work mixes uncompromising social criticism with an unforgettable irony, but Louis is unique in turning that irony on himself as often as he turns it on the world around him.

DUST WORLD

for Sherman Alexie

I.

Whirlwinds of hot autumn dust
paint every foolish hope dirty.
I stand in the impudent ranks of the poor
and scream for the wind to abate.
Prayers to Jesus might be quicker
than these words from blistered hands
and liquor, but the death wind
breaks the lines to God.
I have no sylvan glades of dreams,
just dust words
for my people dying.

II.

With pupil-dilated *putti* in arms
three teenaged mothers
on the hood of a '70 Chevy
wave at me like they know me.

Inside the video rental
a small fan ripples sweat
and scatters ashes upon two young attendants
practicing karate kicks and ignoring me
because they're aware I could dust
their wise asses individually or collectively.
They're products of Pine Ridge° High
which means they would have had two strikes
against them even if they did graduate
and these two clowns never did.
I guess they're almost courting me,
in a weird macho way almost flirting,
because I'm fatherly, half buzzed-up,
and have biceps as thick as their thighs.
Heyyyy . . . ever so softly,
this is the whiskey talking now.

III.

With pupils dilated and beer in hand
three teenaged mothers court frication
more serious than their sweet Sioux butts
buffing the hood of their hideous car.
When I glide my new T-bird°
out of the video store parking lot
they wave like they really know me.
One of the girls, beautiful enough
to die for except for rotten teeth
smiles and I suck in my gut
and lay some rubber.
I cruise through a small whirlwind
of lascivious regrets
and float happily through the dark streets
of this sad, welfare world.
This is the land that time forgot.
Here is the Hell the white God gave us.

---

22. *Pine Ridge:* town in South Dakota; nearby is the Pine Ridge Indian Reservation, home of the Ogalala Lakota holy man Black Elk (1863–1950). This Sioux reservation was the focus of a major effort by the U.S. Federal Bureau of Investigation (FBI) to suppress the American Indian Movement (AIM), which was founded in 1968. It culminated in a seventy-one-day 1973 FBI siege of the Wounded Knee hamlet on the Pine Ridge Reservation, near the site, as it happened, of the infamous Wounded Knee massacre of 1890, when nearly 300 Lakota men, women, and children were slaughtered by U.S. cavalry. In the three years following the siege, the FBI fostered the murder of more than sixty AIM members on the reservation.

36. *T-bird:* a popular automobile, the Thunderbird, whose name coopts a Native American symbol for commercial purposes; in Louis's fallen, postmodern world he drives the car with a strong sense of irony.

The wind from the Badlands° brings
a chorus of chaos and makes everything dirty.
I meander past my house and stop briefly
before driving back to where
the young girls are.
I park my car and re-enter the store.
The two young boys are still dancing
like two cats in mid-air, snarling, clawless
and spitting. No harm done.
I stare them down and place two cassettes,
both rated X, on the counter.
It's Friday night and I'm forty years old
and the wild-night redskin
parade is beginning.

1992

WAKINYAN°

Puppy Luppy, our super sleek black Lab
was missing for two days, running
with the pack after a Spaniel in heat
and because the day was warm, we walked
down to the pow-wow grounds° by the creek
to look for that goofy boy.
We had a lot of money and love invested
in him and he'd never been out for two days.
We sat in the shade of the squaw cooler
underneath the boughs of rusted pines
for a minute to catch our breath
before we headed for the tick-infested creek.
It had snowed heavily a week earlier so
it must have been the heat that brought
the opening buds of the cottonwoods and willows
and the spider-like ticks who, once attached,
would turn to big, green grapes on my dogs.

Wakinyan, the thunder beings, kicked us
in the crotch before we got to the creek.
The sky turned violet, lightning cracked
and crackled sideways, not up and down.
Rain slapped down so hard, for an instant

---

49. *Badlands:* a barren but beautiful region of southwest South Dakota, marked by steep eroded hills and gullies; east of the Black Hills, traditional birthplace of the Sioux nation.

poem title: *Wakinyan,* a Lakota Sioux word for thunder. Mythically, a "thunder spirit" or "thunder being."

5. *pow-wow grounds:* see the annotation to Sherman Alexie's "No. 9."

I heard strains of Junior Wells° at a Chicago
nightspot twenty years past.
That didn't last long. The rain hardened
into hail and we ran past the music in my mind
and huddled in a large clump of wild cherry.
Broken bottles, buried frogs, and reason rushed
all around us in swollen rivulets of rain and hail.
The thunder beings had driven us to humanity.
Inside the thicket across from us were two winos,
coats thickened by greasepuke and woodsmoke,
shivering with shivering eyes.
It was early spring and the day was sweating wet.
God had emerged for the first time since creation
and had decided to show his magnificent mirth.
Four Indians in a bush were being pelted
by golf ball-sized pellets of ice.
We laughed aloud and the two winos did too.
We stared at them in silence and they stared
back with yellow, empty eyes.
We quickly left the bush and entered the storm.
Pain is easier to deal with than spirits.

1989

WITHOUT WORDS

Farewell from this well is impossible.
Man is composed mainly of water.
I lower a frayed rope into the depths and hoist
the same old Indian tears to my eyes.
The liquid is pure and irresistible.
We have nothing to live for, nothing to die for.
Each day we drink and decompose into a different flavor.
Continuity is not fashionable
and clashing form is sediment
obscuring the bottom of thirst.
The parched and cracking mouths
of our Nations do not demand
a reason for drinking
so across America
we stagger and stumble with contempt for the future
and with no words of pride for our past.

1989

---

23. *Junior Wells:* a Chicago-based blues artist.

COYOTE NIGHT°

A flat tire ten miles
east of Pine Ridge
just past the Wounded Knee° turnoff.
I disembark into Siberia°
looking for Zhivago.
A non-stopping semi whines away
into a state of exhaustion.
This winter night is held
in silence as if a giant squid
fell upon the land and froze.
Scraggly pines try to feel
up the miserable moon.
Snapping twigs signal
sneaking-up coyotes.
Here there are no distant
garbage trucks,
no all-night neon.
I click the safety off my .22 Llama
and light a cigar.
Coyote eyes float
in deep-ass blackness.
Coyote eyes float
in deep-ass blackness.
Coyote eyes gloat
in black glass glee
and I laugh and return to my car.
It drives pretty good
on three tires.

1992

---

poem title: refers both to the small, wolflike carnivorous animal native to many areas of the continent and to Coyote, perhaps the most well known and pan-Indian figure in Native American mythology. Coyote figures in creation stories and in numerous more recent tales. A North American version of the trickster figure, Coyote is creative, wily, lecherous, and a master of disguise. He can take many shapes and intervenes in human affairs, sometimes positively and sometimes mischievously.

3. *Wounded Knee:* See the notes to N. Scott Momaday's poem "December 29, 1890" and to Louis's poem "Dust World."

4. *Siberia:* vast, 500-million-square-mile region in northern Russia and Asia; its northernmost reaches are open, frozen tundra.

HOW VERDELL AND DR. ZHIVAGO° DISASSEMBLED THE SOVIET UNION

"You are the blessing in a stride towards perdition when living sickens more than sickness itself."
—Boris Pasternak°

Last year, before cruising to the warehouse
near the old Moccasin Factory,
Verdell and I stopped at the bootlegger
for a quick belt to cinch
his stomach full of fears.
He said the pint of rotgut whiskey
tasted worse than gangrene
but it did the job and choked silent
the raging world around him.
We meandered through tons
of remaindered and donated tomes,
a tax-deductible donation
to destitute savages, these boxed words
were stacked from concrete floor
to rusted sheet-metal roof.
Buzzed-up and warmed by his whiskey,
Verdell came upon four cartons
of Pasternak's *Doctor Zhivago*
and became transfixed by the flaming
scarlet fake leather covering.

But I saw dead ikons of the past
in cardboard and glory on the grandest scale.
Deep in Holy Mother Russia
marching through the bitter snow

I saw peasant armies mouthing
death songs while
not knowing where
their souls would go.

We lugged those four cartons of *Zhivago*
bound in leatherette
to his puke-stained Plymouth.
That spring, without an ounce of shame
and some pride, Verdell related how

---

poem title: *Zhivago:* title character from the Russian writer Boris Pasternak's 1957 novel, *Dr. Zhivago.*

epigraph: *Pasternak:* (1890–1960) Russian poet and novelist whose most famous work is the novel *Doctor Zhivago* (1957).

he had liked the Russian story,
but he said he ran out of firewood
during the last blizzard of March
and his hungry woodstove
vaporized Yurii Andreievich,
sweet Lara, and those eerie blue wolves
howling at snowbound Varykino.
Again and again, Verdell burned the books
until the cast iron glowed a deep, dark red
and the way he figured it, the heat
from his woodstove melted the glue
of the Soviet Union that spring.

1995

WANBLI GLESKA° WIN

Eagle woman:
Wanbli Gleska Win.
Distant and unseen
in the air the piercing
whistle of an eagle taunts.

It's been six months
since you shut the door
of your flesh to me and I miss
your calm brown strength,
your high-cholesterol cooking,
the fragrant down beneath your wings
and that snake-eating beak
between your Sioux thighs.

1995

LOOKING FOR JUDAS

Weathered gray, the wooden walls
of the old barn soak in the bright
sparkling blood of the five-point mule
deer I hang there in the moonlight.
Gutted, skinned, and shimmering in eternal
nakedness, the glint in its eyes could
be stolen from the dry hills of Jerusalem.
They say before the white man
brought us Jesus, we had honor.
They say when we killed the Deer People,

poem title: Wanbli Gleska, for the Lakota Sioux spotted Eagle, which may not be a literal being.

we told them their spirits
would live in our flesh.
We used bows of ash, no spotlights, no rifles,
and their holy blood became ours.
Or something like that.

1995

A COLOSSAL AMERICAN COPULATION

for Scarecrow

They say there's a promise
coming down that dusty road.
They say there's a promise coming
down that dusty road, but I don't see it.
So, fuck the bluebird of happiness.
Fuck the men who keep their dogs chained.
Fuck the men who molest their daughters.
Ditto the men who wrap their dicks
in the Bible and then claim the right
to speak for female reproductive organs.
Likewise the men who hunt coyotes.
And the whining farmers who get paid
for not growing corn and wheat.
The same to the *National Enquirer.*°
Also Madonna° (Santa Evita, indeed).
Yes, add the gutless Tower of Babel
that they call the United Nations.
Fuck every gangbanger in America.
Fuck furiously the drive-by shooters,
the carjack thugs, the Colombian coke° cartels.
And the ghost of Richard Milhous Nixon.°
Okay, add the yuppie-hillbillies who mess up
the powerspray carwash when they come down
from the hills with half the earth clinging
to their new four-wheel drives.
Fuck my neighbor who beats his kids.
And my other neighbor who has plastic

---

14. *National Enquirer:* a tabloid (sensationalist) U.S. newspaper.

15. *Madonna:* (b. 1959), American pop singer and actress who played the part of Eva Peron in the movie musical *Evita.*

20. *coke:* cocaine.

21. *Nixon:* (1913–1994), thirty-seventh U.S. president (1969–1974), forced to resign as evidence accumulated of his complicity in the Watergate cover-up and various abuses of federal and presidential power. His early career was built on active red-baiting during the McCarthy period.

life-sized deer in his front yard.
And Tommy's Used Cars in Chadron, Neb.

Fuck my high school coach for not starting
me in the '64 State Championship game.
Fuck the first bar I puked in.
That first cigarette I ever smoked.
That first pussy I ever touched.
Fuck it again, Sam.
And that know-it-all Larry King°
and his stupid suspenders.
Fuck the Creative Writing programs
and all the Spam poets they hatch.
And the air that blew Marilyn Monroe's°
dress up over her waist.
Fuck you very, very much.
Fuck the Bureau of Indian Affairs.
The ATF° for the Waco° massacre.
And sissy boy George Will.°
And Sam Donaldson's° wig.
Fuck the genocidal Serb soldiers;°
may their nuts roast in napalm hell.
Fuck all the booze I ever drank. Yes, include
the hair of the dog that bit me for
more than twenty drunken years.

Fuck a duck!
And the '60s and all that righteous reefer.
Fuck James Dean° and his red jacket.
John Wayne° and the gelding
American horse he rode in on.

---

36. *King:* (b. 1933) radio/television talk show host.

40. *Monroe:* (1926–1962), American movie actress; the poem refers to a scene in the film *Some Like It Hot* (1959).

44. *ATF:* Alcohol, Tobacco, and Firearms, a U.S. federal agency.

44. *Waco:* Texas town that was the site of an April 1993 FBI assault on the compound of the Branch Davidian religious sect. Thirty-three members of the cult died, most from the resulting fire.

45. *Will:* (b. 1941), a conservative television commentator and political columnist for the U.S. magazine *Newsweek.*

46. *Donaldson:* (b. 1933), television reporter for the American Broadcasting Company (ABC); he is noted for shamelessly injecting opinion into purportedly objective news reports.

47. *Serb soldiers:* responsible for mass murders of Muslim civilians in the former Republic of Yugoslavia in the 1990s.

54. *Dean:* American movie actor. See the annotation to Sherman Alexie's "Tourists."

55. *Wayne:* American movie actor noted for his Indian-fighting westerns. See the annotation to Louise Erdrich's "Dear John Wayne."

The IRA° and their songs and bombs.
All the Gila monsters in Arizona.
Bob Dylan° for leading me astray
for three misty, moping decades.
My gall bladder for exploding.
Fuck *The Waste Land* by T. S. Eliot
and all those useless allusions.
Fuck war in every form and all other clichés.
Fuck, no, double-fuck the Vietnam War.
Every cruel act I ever committed.
Every random act of kindness.
And the undertaker who will gaze
upon my dead and naked flesh
and wince at my lack of tattoos.
Fuck O. J. Simpson° and his Ginsus.
Fuck Jesse Helms,° and when he dies,
wormfuck him good in his grave.
Fuck the prairie dogs.
The mosquitoes.
The immaturity of MTV.°
Those Monster Trucks.
Mother Teresa.° Jesus, just kidding.
The Information Superhighway.
F*U*C*K the L*A*N*G*U*A*G*E poets
and fuck rodeo cowboys in their chapped
and bony butts and boots.
Fuck the gutless Guardsmen
who were at Kent State;° may they still
have night horrors after all these years.

Fuck all those, who because of this and that
and a touch of cowardice on my part,

---

57. *IRA:* Irish Republican Army, revolutionary political and terrorist group seeking an end to British rule in Northern Ireland.

59. *Dylan:* (b. 1941), American folk singer and composer who was hugely influential in the counterculture in the 1960s and 1970s. Louis may feel that the message in songs like "The Times They Are A-Changin'" (1963) was untrue.

71. *Simpson:* (b. 1947), a famous American athlete—he was a running back for the Buffalo Bills football team—and then movie actor. He made television commercials, including one for Ginsu carving knives. He was later tried, but acquitted, for murdering his former wife.

72. *Helms:* archconservative U.S. senator from North Carolina.

76. *MTV:* television station devoted to rock music videos.

78. *Teresa:* (1910–1997), Roman Catholic nun and missionary.

84. *Kent State:* on May 4, 1970, Ohio National Guard troops opened fire on students at Kent State University who were protesting the U.S. invasion of Cambodia. Four students were killed and eleven wounded.

I neglected here to name.
Fuck Alzheimer's Disease.
And all the things my woman
cannot remember.
Fuck all the things my woman
cannot comprehend.
And time. It only confuses her.
Fuck dog spelled backwards.
And fucking. We don't do it anymore.
And death. Almost an afterthought.
Fuck it. Fuck it short and tall.
Fuck it big and small.
Fuck it all.
Fucking A. Fuck me.
Never mind. I'm already fucked.

They say there's a promise
coming down that dusty road.
They say there's a promise coming down
that dusty road, but I don't see it.

1997

PETROGLYPHS OF SERENA°

Poets behave impudently towards their experiences: they exploit them.
—Friedrich Nietzsche°

In Yellowbird's Store, the tart tinge
of something sour boggles my nose.
Overpriced cans of Spaghetti-Os
and Spam on the sad shelves
are powdered with Great Plains dust.
In Yellowbird's Store, winter people
are hooked up to video poker
machines for brief transfusions.
The faint whispers of dreams and desires
fade with each coin thrown away.
Some Indians prefer gambling to making love.
Not me. I love to graze on the sparse, black
cornsilk in the valleys of the Sioux
and it will be my downfall.

---

poem title: petroglyphs, carvings or drawings on rocks, including ancient forms of symbolic and ritual representation among Native American peoples.
epigraph: *Nietzsche:* (1844–1900), German philosopher.

Six-twenty in the morning. These Dakota stars
are as blanched as dead minnows floating
on a garish pink and blue sea of daybreak.
I shake my head, light a Marlboro,
and scope my wife getting dressed.
She can't cook worth a damn,
is incredibly and increasingly forgetful.
But she loves me and treats me as good
as a recovering drunk deserves.
Nevertheless, I'm thinking of the wondrous
and drool-making beauty of my student Serena
who is flunking but would get an A-plus
and my fuzzy soul if she asked.

Unlike parched Christ on his cross,
my mouth was watering.
Sitting on the front porch, I saw the snot
yellow moon dishevel two Kleenex clouds.
A clichéd stray dog down by the creek
was alternating keys of hunger and horror.
It would soon be suppertime.
I fired up a smoke and sucked it greedily.
The dancing coal lost itself
in the star blanket of night.
In the house my tired wife
was frying venison steaks.
My mouth was watering,
but I wasn't hungry at all.
I was dreaming of Serena.
Dark Serena with her broken English.
Wild-ass Serena and our Indian dance
of self-destruction.

Friday is a blistering prairie day.
105-degree heat will dissolve the will
of the people and tonight you'll see all hues
of brown swarming over this dusty soil.
Many of these people will be scarred.
Some of them will be magna cum laude
graduates of the S.D.° State Pen.
Some will be young and lost for the first
time and some will be old and dying.

52. *S.D.:* South Dakota.

All will be thirsty. Parched and tough.
Tonight there is bound to be trouble.
I can hardly wait. Lord,
how lust becomes me.
I will be there and so will Serena.

The old people said bad spirits blew in
with the west wind and would not leave
no matter how much they prayed.
The old people said the air was bad.
Death danced through the front doors
of many houses that winter, and finally
spring sent children wild upon the earth.
Death ran from the sharp glee in their eyes.
Death ran from the sex breath of summer.
Finally, Serena was with me.
We were naked, biting each other hard
and the air, oh, the air was good
and I drank it in without
the slightest cough of guilt.

And then it was winter again.
Oh, man, a desperate Dakota winter.
Our neighbors shot a starving deer
behind their HUD° house
and butchered it in their front yard.
They wrapped large pieces in Hefty° bags
and stored them in the trunk
of their broken-down '72 Olds.
In February they ran out of wood so they
burned chunks of old tires in the woodstove.
Their children went to school smudged
and smelling like burnt rubber.
A typical hard-ass Dakota winter.
All across the Rez, wild Indians
shiver-danced around woodstoves
and howled the most wondrous songs
of brilliant poverty.

Lust comes with a darkblood price.
This is how darkness comes to me.
Serena's late for speech class as usual.

---

77. *HUD:* Housing and Urban Development, a federal agency.
79. *Hefty:* a brand of large plastic garbage bag.

Everyone's done their demos but her:
Ain't got none. I'm sorry, but
I just come from working
on a friend's brokedown car.
Then said (in a sly-shy-sneaky kind of way)
she could demo how to clean a carburetor.
Outside in the bed of her pickup.
Well... Okay. (What the hell could I say?)
So the whole class trudges
out upon the jagged-ice earth.
It's dark, crazy, she has no flashlight, so
I let her use my new white plastic one.
She GUMS-OUT the carb. Slaps in a new kit.
We're all freezing ass. This is Indian education?
Above, the nosey, twinkling stars are giggling.
I give her a C for effort. Would've been higher,
but she decorated my new flashlight
with big, fat greaseprints. I tell you now that
the next week I hear she's drunk-rolled
a car and is dead, just like that—dead,
so I buy a new flashlight.
A red one.
I take a drive through the deserted Badlands
late at night and stop.
I turn on the old flashlight she used
and toss it in some sage beside the road.
It glows in my rearview mirror
for miles before it finally vanishes.

The old people were moving slowly
through the cold air like exhausted swimmers
fighting the tides of a lung-raping sea.
But, the sun had its high beams on
and near the creek children were laughing
and moving as fast as spit on a hot woodstove.
Grandfather, it was a good day to pray.
Grandfather, it was a good day to pray
that the young would somehow get to be old.
Above all, it was a good day to die.
I did not know her family that well so
I watched her burial from a distance.
Old Indian... trick.
Middle-aged Indian... trick.

About a year after Serena
died in the car wreck
I saw her again—sort of spooky, but
ghost sightings are common around here.
Spirits come and go, to and fro.
She was with some strange-looking Skins,°
drove a different car, and looked puzzled,
half-angry when I waved at her.
Acted like she didn't know me.
Kind of gave me a kiss-my-butt look
and then flipped me the bird.
I shrugged and did the same back to her.
Her car was filled with buffalo heads,
stampeding the ghost road
to White Clay.

Driving the sheet-ice reservation roads,
ground blizzards whirl and blind. Underneath
all, something paleolithic begs fidelity.
It is something deep inside the hardened fist
of almost every Indian man I know.
It is not an unquenchable thirst to live
free from red tape and plastic.
Brothers, you know it is not trickster
dreams or buffalo visions.
It isn't self-determination or the good red road.
It is the unending whisper of the ancestors.
It is that simple urge to scalp a white man.
I think it has something to do with love.
The sweet, sweet squeak
of blade hitting headbone.
The snapdance of sinew
yanked awry.

Near here, over by those dead cottonwoods, is
where I picked up the lady hitchhiker last winter.
Oh, she laughed and talked Skin sexy
after I gave her a cigarette and a beer.
Near Wolf Creek turnoff I glanced
over to where she was sitting.
She'd vanished. The seat was empty.

---

141. *Skins:* slang, an abbreviation for "Redskin."

My heart beat brilliant.
I began to sweat and then shook
like lemon Jell-O.°
Up the road, I saw a deer dash past.
Its eyes were smiling, and a cigarette
dangled from its red-painted lips.
Its eyes were Serena's.

Newly minted leaves sparkle
on the giant cottonwoods.
It's the first pow-wow of the season.
They say even a white man can listen closely
and understand how the drum is our heart.
It pounds and pulses these words through
the blood of our Indian Nations:
"We have survived. Yes, we have survived.
Look at us dancing. Look at us laughing.
God damn you *wasicus*, we'll always survive!"
Yes, they say *even* a white man can listen closely
and understand how the drum is our heart.

The sign here on this bar used to say
NO INDIANS ALLOWED but that wasn't true.
Hey, we know that was not true at all.
Here, the white traders made a fortune
taking savage souls in payment
for pints of whiskey and wine.
Here, countless stumbling Skins entered
the gates of the Fire Water World.
If you listen closely, you can hear their ghosts
winging and whimpering through
the dark skies of this dying America.
Brothers, I swear to Christ on his cross
if you open your mouth, you can taste
their rain of ghost tears.

We are all hiding from the truth.
Our children have no respect
because their parents cannot connect
the values of the ancient chiefs
to the deadly grief that welfare brings.
We're reaping the womb's reward of mutant
generations who stumbled toward dismembering

---

177. *Jell-O:* gelatin dessert.

the long and sometimes senile span between you,
Great Spirit, and your artwork, man.
The question is, can the children be saved?
And if so, then why? Will they ever be whole
or do we just add them to the dark days
of casualties from Sand Creek°
to Ira Hayes?°

I mean, do we catalogue them
in the first grade and then sit back
and wait, afraid that one will be dead
in a car wreck at ten? That one has a room
reserved at the state pen?
That one will flunk out of college
a total of eight times over a ten-year slate
and then will take his life after stabbing
his kids, his dad, his wife?
That one will have six children,
none from the same man,
and all will carry their mom's surname?
That one will move to a city and drink
so much that his heart will forget
the prayer of human touch?
That one will write their story
and end it as if it were
a lousy job he just quit
without searching
for a space to inject
the slightest hint of grace?

What we never say is that when we hit
rock-bottom, we can still drop farther.
She said back in the old days
we took care of our elders.
There was no AFDC,° no food stamps.
We had gardens, we hunted.

---

220. *Sand Creek:* November 29, 1864, Colorado massacre of over seventy Cheyennes and Arapahos who thought themselves under U.S. Army protection. Many of the bodies were mutilated by either the 125 regular army troops or the 700 Colorado volunteers who attacked them.

221. *Ira Hayes:* (1923–1955), a media-created Native American (Pima) hero of World War II. He was one of six marines to restage the February 1945 flag raising on the newly captured South Pacific island of Iwo Jima. The photograph brought him fame he could not tolerate. He returned home to find the Pimas still lacked sufficient water for their farms, and he began to drink. The Indian Relocation Program moved him to Chicago, which proved equally unsuccessful. He returned home, where he froze to death in 1955.

247. *AFDC:* Aid to Families of Dependent Children, a federal program.

We respected our parents
and we weren't afraid of work.
In the old days, men did not beat
their women for no reason.
In the old days, children had two parents.
Yes, in the old days life was better.
In the old days I was young and in love,
she said with a shrug . . . so I kissed her.
On Serena's mother's old,
cracked fullblood lips
I kissed her ever so softly.

Inside this shack the restless spirit
of a woman will put on a faded shawl
and take a kerosene lamp
from atop a battered bureau.
She will open the door and float
through the chilled air to the outhouse.
She will spread the light into all the corners
making sure no spiders lurk.
Then she will sing to herself and dream
of running water and porcelain.
That is what this spirit will do. I know.
She is the grandmother
of us all.

Wanbli Gleska Wi (Thalia) said
old-time Lakota call it *wasigla.*
A woman must mourn for a full year
to pay respect to the spirit of the departed.
Not supposed to leave the house,
have to wear black,
can't go shopping or go pow-wow.
Just stay home and mourn.
When a woman is spirit-keeping or
ghost-keeping, she can't make sudden
moves—especially with her hands.
Can't disturb the air.
And has to put out food
at each meal to feed the spirit.
One full year, Serena's younger sister
Thalia said in my motel room.
Must never offend the spirits, Thalia said.

Must *never* offend the spirits, Thalia said,
or bad shit will happen to you.
Traditional Indian wisdom, she said.
What goes around comes around
or should it be
what comes around goes around?
You don't believe that, do you? I asked.
Nothing bad would happen to me.
I laughed and got undressed,
safe and guilt-free
in the snug, smug darkness
of lust.

1997

JESUS FINDS HIS GHOST SHIRT

Somewhere along the Via Dolorosa
Jesus noticed Mary was AWOL.
Further steps were uncalled for.
His carpenter's heart exploded.
An ejaculation, a quicksilver
burst of evanescence, birthed
stars so fragile that tears
seemed quite pointless.
He put down his burden
and went to his car at the curb.
Rummaging around the backseat
he found evidence that made all obvious:
a checkbook, deposits from unknown johns,
too many rolls of unopened LifeSavers,
plenty of cherry lip balm, and cheap
condoms in tawdry Day-Glo shades.
And a soft shirt of fringed deerskin
which puzzled him so deeply
that he felt compelled to put it on
and rise from the dead.

2006

YUSEF KOMUNYAKAA (b. 1947)

Komunyakaa is an African American poet who was born in Bogalusa, Louisiana, the son of a carpenter. He grew up in Louisiana and was educated at the University of Colorado, Colorado State University, and the University of California at Irvine. Long interested in the relationship between jazz and poetry, he has coedited two volumes on the subject. From 1965 to 1967 he served a tour of duty in South Vietnam, where he was an information specialist and editor of the military newspaper *Southern Cross*; he won a bronze star, but it was not until more than a decade after returning from the war that he would begin writing poems about the experience. This would lead to *Dien Cai Dau* (1988), almost certainly the best Vietnam poems by an American veteran of the war. This book-length sequence, from which "Tu Do Street," "Prisoners," and "Communiqué" are reprinted, continually returns to the war's racial tensions and its racial constitution. White and black troops from America's working class and its underclass were drafted to kill a colored enemy indistinguishable from Vietnam's civilian population. The only redemption we can now ask, Komunyakaa's poems demonstrate, grows out of admitting the racial structures we have previously repressed. Both in poems like "Tu Do Street" and in "Work" Komunyakaa becomes especially eloquent when he takes on unpopular or awkward topics. He often manages to combine violent subject matter and strong narrative conflicts with notably rich imagery. The poems as a result can be both harsh and musical. His selected poems, *Neon Vernacular,* won the Pulitzer Prize in 1994. Komunyakaa has taught at several universities, including Indiana, Washington, Harvard, and Princeton.

TU DO STREET°

Music divides the evening.
I close my eyes & can see
men drawing lines in the dust.
America pushes through the membrane
of mist & smoke, & I'm a small boy
again in Bogalusa.° *White Only*
signs & Hank Snow.° But tonight
I walk into a place where bar girls
fade like tropical birds. When

---

poem title: *Tu Do Street:* a busy warren of bars, brothels, and bistros at the center of Saigon, capital of South Vietnam and American Army headquarters during the Vietnam War, 1956–1975.

6. *Bogalusa:* the Louisiana town where Komunyakaa grew up.

7. *Hank Snow:* (1914–1999), Canadian country singer who moved to the United States in 1948 and joined Nashville's *Grand Ole Opry* program in 1950.

I order a beer, the mama-san
behind the counter acts as if she
can't understand, while her eyes
skirt each white face, as Hank Williams°
calls from the psychedelic jukebox.
We have played Judas where
only machine-gun fire brings us
together. Down the street
black GIs hold to their turf also.
An off-limits sign pulls me
deeper into alleys, as I look
for a softness behind these voices
wounded by their beauty & war.
Back in the bush at Dak To°
& Khe Sanh,° we fought
the brothers of these women
we now run to hold in our arms.
There's more than a nation
inside us, as black & white
soldiers touch the same lovers
minutes apart, tasting
each other's breath,
without knowing these rooms
run into each other like tunnels
leading to the underworld.

1988

PRISONERS

Usually at the helipad
I see them stumble-dance
across the hot asphalt
with crokersacks over their heads,
moving toward the interrogation huts,
thin-framed as box kites
of sticks & black silk
anticipating a hard wind
that'll tug & snatch them

---

13. *Hank Williams:* (1923–1953), American composer, vocalist, guitarist; one of the greatest stars and most influential composers of country music, his classic songs include "Your Cheatin' Heart."

23. *Dak To*: a city in northwest South Vietnam that was the site of one of the most violent battles of the war in November 1967; its airfield was attacked again in February 1968.

24. *Khe Sanh:* site of U.S. Marine base in northernmost South Vietnam near the Laotian border; attacked by North Vietnamese Army on January 21, 1968, and kept under seige until April 7.

out into space. I think
some must be laughing
under their dust-colored hoods,
knowing rockets are aimed
at Chu Lai°—that the water's
evaporating & soon the nail
will make contact with metal.
How can anyone anywhere love
these half-broken figures
bent under the sky's brightness?
The weight they carry
is the soil we tread night & day.
Who can cry for them?
I've heard the old ones
are the hardest to break.
An arm twist, a combat boot
against the skull, a .45
jabbed into the mouth, nothing
works. When they start talking
with ancestors faint as camphor
smoke in pagodas, you know
you'll have to kill them
to get an answer.
Sunlight throws
scythes against the afternoon.
Everything's a heat mirage; a river
tugs at their slow feet.
I stand alone & amazed,
with a pill-happy door gunner
signaling for me to board the Cobra.
I remember how one day
I almost bowed to such figures
walking toward me, under
a corporal's ironclad stare.
I can't say why.
From a half-mile away
trees huddle together,
& the prisoners look like
marionettes hooked to strings of light.

1988

---

14. *Chu Lai:* a northern coastal town fifty miles south of Danang in South Vietnam; in 1965 it was the site of the first major U.S. amphibious operation since 1958; a huge American base was established there.

COMMUNIQUÉ

Bob Hope's° on stage, but we want the Gold Diggers,°
want a flash of legs

through the hemorrhage of vermilion, giving us
something to kill for.

We want our hearts wrung out like rags & ground down
to Georgia dust

while Cobras° drag the perimeter, gliding along the sea,
swinging searchlights

through the trees. The assault & battery of hot pink
glitter erupts

as the rock 'n' roll band tears down the night—caught
in a safety net

of brightness, The Gold Diggers convulse. White legs
shimmer like strobes.

The lead guitarist's right foot's welded to his wah-wah.
"I thought you said

Aretha° was gonna be here." "Man, I don't wanna see
no Miss America."

"There's Lola." The sky is blurred by magnesium flares
over the fishing boats.

"Shit, man, she looks awful white to me." We duck
when we hear the quick

metallic hiss of the mountain of amplifiers struck by
a flash of rain.

After the show's packed up & gone, after the choppers
have flown out backwards,

---

1. *Hope:* (1903–2003), American entertainer and comedian who made trips overseas to entertain American troops in World War II, the Korean War, and, as here, in the Vietnam War.

1. *Gold Diggers:* a ten-to twelve-member female dance troup that was a summer replacement for the *The Dean Martin Show* on American television in 1968, 1969, and 1970.

7. *Cobra:* brand of helicopter gun ship.

17. *Aretha:* Aretha Franklin (1942–), American soul singer.

after the music & colors have died slowly in our heads,
& the downpour's picked up,

we sit holding our helmets like rain-polished skulls.

1988

THE DOG ACT

I'm the warm-up act.
I punch myself in the face
across the makeshift stage.
Fall through imaginary trapdoors.
Like the devil, I turn cartwheels
& set my hair afire.
Contradiction, the old barker
drunk again on these lights
& camaraderie. The white poodles,
Leo, Camellia, St. John, & Anna,
leap through fiery hoops
to shake my hand.
I make a face
that wants to die
inside me.
"Step right up ladies & gentlemen,
see the Greatest Show on Earth,
two-headed lions, seraphim,°
unicorns, satyrs, a woman
who saws herself in half."
I can buckdance till I am
in love with the trapeze artist.
Can I have your attention now?
I'm crawling across the stagefloor
like a dog with four broken legs.
You're supposed to jump up
& down now, laugh & applaud.

1979

THE NAZI DOLL

It sits lopsided
in a cage. Membrane.

---

18. *seraphim:* the highest order of angels; unicorns: fabled creatures, a horse with a single spiraled horn growing from its head, often symbolizing virginity; satyrs: in Greek mythology, licentious woodland creatures, half man, half goat, with goat's pointed ears, legs, and short horns.

Vertebra. This precious, white
ceramic doll's brain

twisted out of a knob of tungsten.
It bleeds a crooked smile

& arsenic sizzles in the air.
Its eyes an old lie.

Its bogus tongue, Le Diable.°
Its lampshade of memory.

Guilt yahoos, benedictions
in its Cro-Magnon° skull

blossom, a flurry of fireflies,
vowels of rattlesnake beads.

Its heart hums the song of dust
like a sweet beehive.

1979

FOG GALLEON

Horse-headed clouds, flags
& pennants tied to black
Smokestacks in swamp mist.
From the quick green calm
Some nocturnal bird calls
Ship ahoy, ship ahoy!
I press against the taxicab
Window. I'm back here, interfaced
With a dead phosphorescence;
The whole town smells
Like the world's oldest anger.
Scabrous residue hunkers down under
Sulfur & dioxide, waiting
For sunrise, like cargo
On a phantom ship outside Gaul.°
Cool glass against my cheek

---

9. *Le Diable:* the devil.

12. *Cro-Magnon:* prehistoric human being.

15. *Gaul*: ancient region of western Europe, corresponding roughly to present-day France and Belgium; the Romans extended the designation to include northern Italy.

Pulls me from the black schooner
On a timeless sea—everything
Dwarfed beneath the papermill
Lights blinking behind the cloudy
Commerce of wheels, of chemicals
That turn workers into pulp
When they fall into vats
Of steamy serenity.

1993

WORK

I won't look at her.
My body's been one
Solid motion from sunrise,
Leaning into the lawnmower's
Roar through pine needles
& crabgrass. Tiger-colored
Bumblebees nudge pale blossoms
Till they sway like silent bells
Calling. But I won't look.
Her husband's outside Oxford,
Mississippi, bidding on miles
Of timber. I wonder if he's buying
Faulkner's ghost, if he might run
Into Colonel Sartoris°
Along some dusty road.
Their teenage daughter & son sped off
An hour ago in a red Corvette
For the tennis courts,
& the cook, Roberta,
Only works a half day
Saturdays. This antebellum house
Looms behind oak & pine
Like a secret, as quail
Flash through branches.
I won't look at her. Nude
On a hammock among elephant ears
& ferns, a pitcher of lemonade

---

14. *Faulkner:* William Faulkner (1897–1962), American novelist who lived in Oxford, Mississippi; Colonel John Sartoris (1873–1924) is a Faulkner character in *Sartoris* (1929) and *The Unvanquished* (1938) from the series of novels set in the fictitious county modeled after Faulkner's own.

Sweating like our skin.
Afternoon burns on the pool
Till everything's blue,
Till I hear Johnny Mathis°
Beside her like a whisper.
I work all the quick hooks
Of light, the same unbroken
Rhythm my father taught me
Years ago: *Always give*
A man a good day's labor.
I won't look. The engine
Pulls me like a dare.
Scent of honeysuckle
Sings black sap through mystery,
Taboo, law, creed, what kills
A fire that is its own heart
Burning open the mouth.
But I won't look
At the insinuation of buds
Tipped with cinnabar.°
I'm here, as if I never left,
Stopped in this garden,
Drawn to some Lotus-eater.° Pollen
Explodes, but I only smell
Gasoline & oil on my hands,
& can't say why there's this bed
Of crushed narcissus°
As if gods wrestled here.

1993

31. *Mathis:* (b. 1935), American popular singer, concentrating on haunting ballads; hits include "Misty" (1959) and "The Twelfth of Never" (1961).

47. *cinnabar:* vivid red to reddish-orange color.

50. *Lotus-eater:* in Greek mythology, one of a group of people who fed on the lotus plant and lived in a drugged, indolent state of pleasure.

54. *narcissus:* spring flowering bulbs with white or yellow flowers having cup-shaped or trumpet-shaped central crowns; in Greek mythology, Narcissus was a youth who pined away infatuated with his own image in a pool of water and was transformed into the flower bearing his name.

AI (1947–2010)

Born Florence Anthony in Albany, Texas, Ai did not learn her real father's identity until she was sixteen. Then she learned she had a Japanese American father; her mother was black, Irish, and Choctaw Indian. She took the name "Ai," which means "love" in Japanese, to signal her heritage. Ai's childhood was spent in a variety of cities, including Tucson, Los Angeles, and San Francisco. She was educated at the University of Arizona and the University of California at Irvine. Although she wrote short lyrics on both intimate and public historical topics, as "Twenty-Year Marriage" and "The German Army, Russia, 1943" demonstrate, her specialty was the dramatic monologue, sometimes in the voices of invented personas, sometimes in the person of named public figures. Her speakers included Marilyn Monroe, Leon Trotsky, Emiliano Zapata, John F. Kennedy, Joseph McCarthy, the Atlanta child murderer, and an anonymous *Kristallnacht* survivor. Some are corrupted seekers of power who try to justify themselves fruitlessly; others have been consumed by different appetites. Her language is vivid but rather matter-of-fact and unadorned. Indeed, the voices of her speakers sometimes acquire an almost deadpan, driven passion. She was obsessed, throughout her career, with the intersecting subjects of death, sex, history, and religion. Her poems seek to lay bare the most violent inner motives we have and the meaning of the desire behind them. Like Plath, she sought a way to write without holding anything back. In the process, especially when taking up real people and events, she showed us one thing we might not have known poetry was uniquely suited to do—speak brutal truths about public life with a clarity no other discourse can muster.

THE ROOT EATER

The war has begun
and I see the Root Eater bending,
shifting his hands under the soil
in search of the arthritic knuckles of trees.
I see dazed flower stems
pushing themselves back into the ground.
I see turnips spinning endlessly
on the blunt, bitten-off tips of their noses.
I see the Root Eater going home on his knees,
full of the ripe foundations of things,
longing to send his seed up through his feet
and out into the morning

but the stumps of trees heave themselves forward
for the last march

and the Root Eater waits,
knowing he will be shoved, rootless,
under the brown, scaly torso of the rock.

1967

TWENTY-YEAR MARRIAGE

You keep me waiting in a truck
with its one good wheel stuck in the ditch,
while you piss against the south side of a tree.
Hurry. I've got nothing on under my skirt tonight.
That still excites you, but this pickup has no windows
and the seat, one fake leather thigh,
pressed close to mine is cold.
I'm the same size, shape, make as twenty years ago,
but get inside me, start the engine;
you'll have the strength, the will to move,
I'll pull, you push, we'll tear each other in half.
Come on, baby, lay me down on my back.
Pretend you don't owe me a thing
and maybe we'll roll out of here,
leaving the past stacked up behind us;
old newspapers nobody's ever got to read again.

1973

THE GERMAN ARMY, RUSSIA, 1943

For twelve days,
I drilled through Moscow ice
to reach paradise,
that white tablecloth, set with a plate
that's cracking bit by bit
like the glassy air, like me,
I know I'll fly apart soon,
the pieces of me so light they float.
The Russians burned their crops,
rather than feed our army.
Now they strike us against each other like dry rocks
and set us on fire with a hunger
nothing can feed.
Someone calls me and I look up.
It's Hitler.
I imagine eating his terrible, luminous eyes.
Brother, he says.
I stand up, tie the rags tighter around my feet.

I hear my footsteps running after me,
but I am already gone.

1979

THE TESTIMONY OF J. ROBERT OPPENHEIMER°

A Fiction

When I attained enlightenment,
I threw off the night like an old skin.
My eyes filled with light
and I fell to the ground.
I lay in Los Alamos,
while at the same time,
I fell
toward Hiroshima,
faster and faster,
till the earth,
till the morning
slipped away beneath me.
Some say when I hit
there was an explosion,
a searing wind that swept the dead before it,
but there was only silence,
only the soothing baby-blue morning
rocking me in its cradle of cumulus cloud,
only rest.
There beyond the blur of mortality,
the roots of the trees of Life and Death,
the trees William Blake called Art and Science,
joined in a kind of Gordian knot
even Alexander couldn't cut.

To me, the ideological high wire
is for fools to balance on with their illusions.
It is better to leap into the void.
Isn't that what we all want anyway?—
to eliminate all pretense

---

poem title: Oppenheimer (1904–1967) was a to physicist who, in 1942, joined the World War II Manhattan Project to develop an atomic bomb. From 1943 to 1945 he directed the laboratory in Los Alamos, New Mexico, where the bomb was designed, built, and (at a remote site) tested, and, as a result, he became known internationally as "the father of the atomic bomb." When the test succeeded, he is reported to have recalled a line from the *Bhaghavad Gita:* "I am become death, destroyer of worlds." In 1945, he was one of a panel of scientists who recommended the bomb's use against Japan. After initially opposing research on a hydrogen bomb in 1951, he ran afoul of McCarthyism and lost his security clearance in 1953.

till like the oppressed who in the end
identifies with the oppressor,
we accept the worst in ourselves
and are set free.

In high school, they told me
all scientists
start from the hypothesis "what if"
and it's true.
What we as a brotherhood lack in imagination
we make up for with curiosity.
I was always motivated
by a ferocious need to know.
Can you tell me, gentlemen,
that you don't want it too?—
the public collapse,
the big fall smooth as honey down a throat.
Anything that gets you closer
to what you are.
Oh, to be born again and again
from that dark, metal womb,
the sweet, intoxicating smell of decay
the imminent dead give off
rising to embrace me.

But I could say anything, couldn't I?
Like a bed we make and unmake at whim,
the truth is always changing,
always shaped by the latest
collective urge to destroy.
So I sit here,
gnawed down by the teeth
of my nightmares.
My soul, a wound that will not heal.
All I know is that urge,
the pure, sibylline intensity of it.
Now, here at parade's end
all that matters:
our military in readiness,
our private citizens
in a constant frenzy of patriotism
and jingoistic pride,
our enemies endless,
our need to defend infinite.

Good soldiers,
we do not regret or mourn,
but pick up the guns of our fallen.
Like characters in the funny papers,
under the heading
"Further Adventures of the Lost Tribe,"
we march past the third eye of History,
as it rocks back and forth
in its hammock of stars.
We strip away the tattered fabric
of the universe
to the juicy, dark meat,
the nothing beyond time.
We tear ourselves down atom by atom,
till electron and positron,
we become our own transcendent annihilation.

1986

WENDY ROSE (b. 1948)

Rose was born in Oakland, California, of Hopi and Miwok ancestry. She attended Contra Costa College and the University of California at Berkeley and since then has taught Native American Studies at several colleges, including the University of California at Berkeley. She is an anthropologist, poet, and artist, and has served as the editor of *American Indian Quarterly*. She presently teaches at Fresno City College and sometimes writes under the pseudonym Chiron Khanshendel. "Truganinny" is partly an effort to venture beyond Native American experience and reach out to identity struggles experienced by other outcast groups.

TRUGANINNY

"Truganinny, the last of the Tasmanians,° had seen the stuffed and mounted body of her husband and it was her dying wish that she be buried in the outback or at sea for she did not wish her body to be subjected to the same indignities. Upon her death she was nevertheless stuffed and mounted and put on display for over eighty years."

Paul Coe, Australian Aborigine Activist, 1972

You will need
to come closer
for little is left
of this tongue
and what I am saying
is important.

I am
the last one.

I whose nipples
wept white mist
and saw so many
dead daughters
their mouths empty and round
their breathing stopped
their eyes gone gray.

---

epigraph: *Tasmanians:* one of the geographically defined groups of Aborigines who were the native inhabitants of Australia; Tasmania, an island separated from the Australian mainland by the Bass Strait. The Australian government forced the remaining Tasmanians to move to Flinders Island in 1831, and the last full-blooded member, Truganinny, died there in 1876.

Take my hand
black into black
as yellow clay
is a slow melt
to grass gold
of earth

and I am melting
back to the Dream.

Do not leave
for I would speak,
I would sing
another song.

Your song.

They will take me.
Already they come;
even as I breathe
they are waiting for me
to finish my dying.

We old ones
take such
a long time.

Please
take my body
to the source of night,
to the great black desert
where Dreaming was born.
Put me under
the bulk of a mountain
or in the distant sea,
put me where
they will not
find me.

1985

TIMOTHY STEELE (b. 1948)

Timothy Steele was born in Burlington, Vermont, and educated at Stanford and Brandeis. Partly because of his early commitment to meter and rhyme when free verse dominated the contemporary scene—and partly because he has theorized the formal choices available to poets in his critical book *Missing Measures: Modern Poetry and the Revolt against Meter* (1990)—Steele has become a leading figure in the loosely defined New Formalist movement. Steele also wrote a textbook, *All the Fun's in How You Say a Thing: An Explanation of Meter and Versification* (1999). He teaches at California State University, Los Angeles. As the poems here demonstrate, his interests range from the California urban landscape to historical subjects. "April 27, 1937" deals with the bombing of Guernica during the Spanish Civil War.

DAYBREAK, BENEDICT CANYON

Thick fog has filled the canyon overnight
And turned it to a sea of milky gray:
The steep-sloped chaparral and streets below
Are drowned from view; hilltops across the way
Form a low-lying archipelago
Upon the fog's smothering gulfs and shoals.
The scene, in the uncertain predawn light,
Recalls those Chinese landscapes on silk scrolls

In which mists haunt ravines, and clouds surround
Remote peaks fading to remoter skies.
The scene suggests, too, the apocalypse
The earth may suffer if sea levels rise.
This very deck could be a ghostly ship's
And I a lone survivor, cast by fate
Out on a flood as lifeless and profound
As the one Noah had to navigate.

Yet soon this world's specifics will revive
And banish fanciful analogies.
Some mourning doves, on airily whistling wings,
Will light in canyon-overhanging trees;
Damp breeze will test the tensile strength of strings,
Jeweled and soaking, that a spider's spun;
Cars snaking up along Mulholland Drive
Will flash their windshields at the rising sun.

The fog will drain; the canyon will evince
Toyon, buckthorn, and yucca, and restore
The ceanothus thickets that hide deer;
Houses will surface on the canyon floor.
The only ocean will be south of here
And glimpsed through a green hollow in a ridge,
Pacific in its sunny sparks and glints
Beyond San Pedro's Vincent Thomas Bridge.

2006

APRIL 27, 1937

General Ludendorff,° two years before,
Had pushed the concept in his *Total War,*
And so it seemed a perfect time to see
If one could undermine an enemy
By striking its civilian population.
This proved a most effective innovation,
As the defenseless ancient Basque town learned:
Three-quarters of its buildings bombed and burned,
Its children and young wives were blown to bits
Or gunned down, when they fled, by Messerschmitts.
Shocked condemnations poured forth from the press,
But Franco° triumphed; and, buoyed by success,
The Luftwaffe° would similarly slam
Warsaw and Coventry and Rotterdam.

Berlin cheered these developments; but two
Can play such games—and usually do—
No matter how repellent or how bloody.
And Churchill° was, as always, a quick study
And would adopt the tactic as his own,
Sending the RAF to blitz Cologne.
Devising better ways to carpet-bomb
(Which later were employed in Vietnam),
The Allies, in a show of aerial might,
Incinerated Dresden in a night
That left the good and evil to their fates,
While back in the untorched United States
Others approved an even darker plan
To coax a prompt surrender from Japan.

Ludendorff: Erich Ludendorff (1865–1937), German general.
Franco: Francisco Franco (1892–1975), Spanish dictator.
Luftwaffe: German branch of air warfare.
Churchill: Winston Churchill (1874–1965), prime minister of the United kingdom.

That day in Spain has taught us, to our cost,
That there are lines that never should be crossed;
The ignorance of leaders is not bliss
If they're intent on tempting Nemesis.
Each day we rise, and each day life goes on:
An author signs beneath a colophon;
Trucks carry freight through waves of desert heat;
A bat cracks, a crowd rises to its feet;
Huge jets lift to the sky, and, higher yet,
Float satellites that serve the Internet.
But still, despite our cleverness and love,
Regardless of the past, regardless of
The future on which all our hopes are pinned,
We'll reap the whirlwind, who have sown the wind.

2006

ALBERT GOLDBARTH (b. 1948)

Albert Goldbarth was born in Chicago and educated at the University of Illinois at Chicago and the University of Iowa. He taught for a decade at the University of Texas at Austin and now teaches at Wichita State University in Kansas. His poems are rich with the history of the language and manage to extract both dark and witty meaning from that very history. The erudition on display is both dazzling and compulsive, and the unsteady line between the two impulses provides part of the pleasure of his work.

SWAN

Not just as individuals, but also as a couple, they
were so demure . . . no, not "demure" exactly, but a sort
of gracious quietude attended them, and *then*
at the end—and everyone remembers the night of alternating
operatic solos of confession over drinks at The Italian Gardens—
something seized them, something like a sudden lyricism
so demanding of its vessels, that it used them up.
The Greeks of course said the same of the swan: its whole life,
mute; and then that single one-hour flower of fine
coloratura. What's a Geiger counter if not an ear
for how the ticking death-song of uranium echoes faintly
over time? "I heard" the speaker says in a novel of Clifford Simak's
"the tiny singing of the tiny lightbulb and I knew
by the singing that it was on the verge of burning out."

2003

COINAGES: A FAIRY TALE

On May 1, 1947, when *airlift* barely existed, my father
lay down beside my mother. He wasn't my father
yet, she wasn't my mother, not technically, the late sun
played the scales of light on the lake at Indian Lodge State Park,
and *rocket-booster* was new by a year, and *thruway*
only by two, and *sputnik*° waited somewhere
in the clouded-over swales of the future and, beyond it,
pixel, rolfing, homeboy floated
in a *cyberspace* too far-removed and conceptual
even to be defined by cloud. He stroked her. She stirred
in her veil of slumber—when was the last time

6. *Sputnik:* the first artificial Earth Satellite, launched by the Soviet Union in 1957.

anyone "slumbered," except in a poem?—but didn't wake.
Not that he wanted to wake her: only to stay
in contact with this singular, corporeal thing they'd made
of themselves amid the chenille and gas heat of the room.
It would be night soon. It would be dusk, and then
the dreamy, let's say the oneiric, nighttime.
Macrobiotic would come into being, *fractal, rock-and-roll.*
The first reported use of *twofer, LP, fax* is 1948.
Spelunker°, 1946, and *cybernetics, TV, vitamin B*-12 were
newfangled, still as if with the glister
of someone's original utterance on them. Others,
say, the *kit bag* that they'd lazily left open near the radio, as in
"pack up your troubles in your ol' kit bag and smile,
darn you, smile"—were even now
half-insubstantial, like a remnant
foxfire glimmering richly over a mound of verbal mulch.
Wingding, riffraff, tittle-tattle: holding even. I'm not saying
vocabulary is people, or anything easily
equational like that—although surely
we've all known a generation going *naught* and *o'er* and *nary*
that disappeared with its language. How
was the pulse of *boogie-woogie* doing? *demesne?*° *lapsarian?*
He looked out the window—as solid by now with darkness
as a tile trivet. Obsidian. Impenetrable.
He looked *at* it—or *through* it—or looked crystal-ball-like *into* it
at himself, and tried to practice things he'd been wanting to say.
Outside, in an invisible ripple, *eleemosynary*° faded
further from the fundament of human use—and *farrier*°
and *haberdasher* and *lyre* and *tocsin° and arras* and *yore.*
When was the last time a liar dissembled, the cressets° were lit,
the nefarious were vilified? My father said "Albert"
—that was the name they'd decided on, for a boy. He breathed it
into the night, into the turning invisible
bingo drum of give-and-take out there, where *radar* was new
and dynastic, and *transistor* was equally sturdy,
and *aerosporin,* and the brave new world of *Xerox* and *laser* and *virtual reality*
held initiating breath in abeyance, somewhere

---

20. *Spelunker:* one who explores caves.

33. *demesne:* land controlled by a lord of the manor.

38. *eleemosynary:* relating to or supported by charity.

39. *farrier:* one who specializes in trimming and shoeing horses' hooves.

40. *tocsin:* an alarm bell or ringing one.

41. *cressets:* oil-filled cups lit as beacons.

yonder in future time. "Albert"—it had been his father's name.
My mother opened her eyes now, she was sprawled in a daringly brief,
but sensibly flannel, nightie—exactly
under the ceiling fan, that turned like the oars of rowers
who keep circling over some fabulous discovery below.
That's what my father thought: it was fabulous! *They*
were fabulous! And he was terrified,
too; he knew that over the dark hills in the dark night,
varlets waited, and scurrilous knaves, and goons and racketeers,
he knew the darkness spewed forth villainy and predation the way
a spoiled cheese frothed maggots—after all,
he'd searched out bodies in the coal mine
with a thin wood lathe they'd issued him for feeling through
the seepage, and he'd lounged around the poolrooms
where the ward boss and his thick, pomaded cronies
held their shabby court. By this, and by the other signs
a body ages into itself, he understood the emptiness
in everything, he understood it long before
neutrino and *pulsar* and *chaos theory* would be
the current buzz, and simply standing there
in his half-price Florsheim wingtip brogues he'd polished
to an onyx shine, he understood a man and a woman
clatter for the casual amusement of the gods
like pea gravel flung in an oil drum. All this,
and a sense of grandiosity, of flame and aching sweetness
in the coils of him, and of the Milky Way he'd touched increasingly
alive in her skin . . . all this, and more, was asking him, now,
to be brought into speech, on May 1, 1947,
at Indian Lodge State Park. He swallowed,
and was silent, and shook, until she saw
and asked what was the matter.
He didn't have the words.

1995

1400

Saps, and the anal grease of an otter, and pig's blood,
and the crushed-up bulbous bodies of those insects
that they'd find so thickly gathered on barnyard excrement
it makes a pulsing rind, and oven soot, and the oil
that forms in a flask of urine and rotting horseflesh,
and the white of an egg, and charcoal, and the secret
watery substance in an egg, and spit-in-charcoal
in a sluggish runnel of gray they mixed

with the harvested scum of a bloated tomato,
and steamed plant marrows beaten to a paste,
and orange clay, and auburn clay, and clay bespangled
with the liquid pearl of fish scales stirred in milt,
and suet, and glue boiled out of a hoof,
and ash, and grape-like clusters of fat grabbed
out of a chicken carcass and dried in the sun
until it became inert and yet still pliable, and lime,
and the pulp of the cherry, and the pulp of the cherry
immersed in egg, and coral in a powder,
and silver flake, and fig, and pollen, and dust, and beeswax,
and an iridescence scraped with infinite care
from the wings of hundreds of tiny flying things,
and salted iridescence, and human milk, and ores,
and gall, and stains expressed from teas, and gobs of squeeze-off
from the nettings of cheese, and rouge, and kohl,
and luster, and oyster, and lees: and so from these
they made their paints: and then
their Gods and their saints.

2009

C. D. WRIGHT (b. 1949)

Born and raised in the Ozark Mountains of Arkansas, C(arolyn) D. Wright is the daughter of a judge and a court reporter. She received her first degree from Memphis State University and completed her education at the University of Arkansas. She has remained in touch with her roots. She remains the poet laureate of Arkansas's Boone County and organized a traveling exhibit about the state in the mid-1990s. Some of her short, unsparing lyrics retell stories of her experience in the south, though she also has wider investments in populist politics and has written a number of linguistically experimental prose poems. Indeed, among linguistically experimental poets, at times it seems she alone actually builds accessible political commitment into her poetry. "Over Everything," reprinted here as part of *Just Whistle,* is adapted from a passage near the end of John Hersey's *Hiroshima* (1946), pp. 91–92. Her book-length poem sequence, *One Big Self: Prisoners of Louisiana,* a collaboration with photographer Deborah Luste, manages to mix reportorial revelations about the Louisiana prison system with the moral and epistemological uncertainties inherent in linguisticality. Wright has published several critical essays and essays on poetics as well as numerous volumes of poetry. Along with poet Forrest Gander, she runs Lost Roads Publishers. She teaches at Brown University.

OBEDIENCE OF THE CORPSE

The midwife puts a rag in the dead woman's hand,
takes the hairpins out.

She smells apples,
wonders where she keeps them in the house.
Nothing is under the sink
but a broken sack of potatoes
growing eyes in the dark.

She hopes the mother's milk is good a while longer,
and the woman up the road is still nursing.
But she remembers the neighbor
and the dead woman never got along.

A limb breaks,
She knows it's not the wind.
Somebody needs to set out some poison.

She looks to see if the woman wrote down any names,
finds a white shirt to wrap the baby in.

It's beautiful she thinks
like snow nobody has walked on.

1979

from JUST WHISTLE

THE BODY, ALIVE, NOT DEAD BUT DORMANT, like a cave that has stopped growing, stirred up, awakened, waked, woke itself altogether up, arose to a closed set of words, *I wish you wouldn't wear your panties to bed,* the body, on its flat feet, breaking into sweat, breaking into rivers, unbent at five and one-half feet, having slept, as if in a boat, where the hair on its legs continued to curl long and gold, where its papers were stored, more or less dry, in a can, where whatever grew tired or useless fell off, fell away, having been not dead, but dormant, living, slept as if in a boat, oarless, unmoored, sand pouring out of a canvas bag,

BECAUSE CONDITIONS ARE IDEAL FOR CROWING the singers flock to this spot. They rageth they seizeth they penetrateth and maketh us to lie down by the roaring waters. By day they take the longstem roses to our backdoor. They secure us to trellises. They whip us breathless. This includes the pool painter whose hands are perpetually blue. Aquatic. Transbluent. One hand signs the blued canvas of our body. Other hands. Cigaretted. Hired hands. Dripping paint on the plush carpet. They set a different set of teeth to each teat. Spit like grasshoppers. In the eden of their woods, dogs glom. Warm winds stir them up. They let the flightless birds peck our feet. We hold mirrors. Bloody our lip under the rent in the backdoor. They crow us for the quick and the dead and on the third day they rise and crow us again. Very soon now we can return to our life of wonder and regret.

AND NOTHING. The body slept under the bow two nights. Propped up with an oar. Cocked its gnarly head and listened to sheet metal music. Birds swooped down on it. The rock on its chest getting bigger. The wind told secondhand lies, more lies. It felt a breeze enter its vestibule. The flesh had begun to grow over the elastic in its panties like bark over fencing. Several of its fingers fell off, fell away. Oh well. It would not end up like the others. In a typing pool. Splitting gizzards. If necessary a prosthesis could be fashioned out of lime, hair, and dung. It could still crow.

THE CORPSE WAS IN THE BED. On its back. The eyes were slipping back into the head. The lids were shutting down. Entrance to vast funnel of silence. It was dressed in a white shirt and white shorts. There was very little blood. A few bottles of beer. Chicken wings on the end table.

ON THE MORN OF

The body would shut its eyes like blinds
letting the nearly even lines of light
steal away from its sheets,
straight gold hair astreaming there;
it would close like a glass door, an ear, arms

To be folded without crossing:
it would seal its lips on the forest
and let the teeth impress themselves in the skin
of its fruit, feast upon the marl
of the other body like a wilderness. To wit:

Its whistling world would be not harmed.

Let the record show the body
has never made such plaintive claims before
except in the wake, the wake of.

A PARTITION SEPARATES IT FROM OTHER BODIES: a calm is coming: the promise of calm is calming: the body a yellow and blue canvas: swollen: distended: yellow and blue mixed gives green: the other body wipes the leavings from the swollen distended body: not a word on the armadillo: the gorgeous god is set upon an aureola: loveblinded: they are: in the country: it is: golden: of the blind: they are: kings

OVER EVERYTHING: up through the wreckage of the body, in its troughs, and along its swells, tangled among its broken veins, climbing on its swollen limbs: a blanket of fresh, vivid, lush, optimistic green; the verdancy rising even from the foundations of its ruins. Weeds already amid the bruises, and wildflowers bloomed among its bones. Everywhere were bluets and Spanish bayonets, goosefoot, morning glories and daylilies, purslane and clotbur and panic grass and feverfew. Especially in a circle at the center, sickle senna grew in extraordinary regeneration, not only standing among the blown remnants of the same plant but

pushing up in new places, among distended folds and through
rents in the flesh. It actually seemed as if a load of sickle senna
had been dropped. On the eighth day . . .

1993

SONG OF THE GOURD

In gardening I continued to sit on my side of the car: to drive whenever possible at the usual level of distraction: in gardening I shat nails glass contaminated dirt and threw up on the new shoots: in gardening I learned to praise things I had dreaded: I pushed the hair out of my face: I felt less responsible for one man's death one woman's long-term isolation: my bones softened: in gardening I lost nickels and ring settings I uncovered buttons and marbles: I lay half the worm aside and sought the rest: I sought myself in the bucket and wondered why I came into being in the first place: in gardening I turned away from the television and went around smelling of offal the inedible parts of the chicken: in gardening I said excelsior: in gardening I required no company I had to forgive my own failure to perceive how things were: I went out barelegged at dusk and dug and dug and dug: I hit rock my ovaries softened: in gardening I was protean as in no other realm before or since: I longed to torch my old belongings and belch a little flame of satisfaction: in gardening I longed to stroll farther into soundlessness: I could almost forget what happened many swift years ago in arkansas: I felt like a god from down under: chthonian: in gardening I thought this is it body and soul I am home at last: excelsior: praise the grass: in gardening I fled the fold that supported the war: only in gardening could I stop shrieking: stop: stop the slaughter: only in gardening could I press my ear to the ground to hear my soul let out an unyielding noise: my lines softened: I turned the water onto the joyfilled boychild: only in gardening did I feel fit to partake to go on trembling in the last light: I confess the abject urge to weed your beds while the bittersweet overwhelmed my daylilies: I summoned the courage to grin: I climbed the hill with my bucket and slept like a dipper in the cool of your body: besotted with growth; shot through by green

1996

ONLY THE CROSSING COUNTS.

It's not how we leave one's life. How go off
the air. You never know, do you. You think you're ready
for anything; then it happens, and you're not. You're really
not. The genesis of an ending, nothing
but a feeling, a slow movement, the dusting
of furniture with a remnant of the revenant's shirt.
Seeing the candles sink in their sockets; we turn
away, yet the music never quits. The fire kisses our face.
O phthisis, O lotharian dead eye, no longer

will you gaze on the baize of the billiard table. No more
shooting butter dishes out of the sky. Scattering light.
Between snatches of poetry and penitence you left
the brumal wood of men and women. Snow drove
the butterflies home. You must know
how it goes, known all along what to expect,
sooner or later . . . the faded cadence of anonymity.
Frankly my dear, frankly my dear, frankly

2005

UNTIL WORDS TURN TO MOSS.

This was all roses, here, where an overblown house crowns
the hill, the whole field, roses, all the way to the end;
when the rosarian died, the partition of roses
began. We've come out of nowhere, literally,
nowhere, autumnal towns marked for destruction
by a phantom hand; houses held underwater, every bed
a sunken tub, tools drowned between rows, every keyhole
caulked; clouds hallucinating girls asleep on a wedge
of wedding cake; the white rose, among the greatest of liars,
beginning to show the debilitating effects of fame;
the ever-popular blaze placates a vase; the bad sons
of thunder beating back a strand of light; someone
who knows nothing apart from the rain
standing on a chair in muddy legs; the roses
blown into their cumulonimbi,
and someone whose glove is recovered, a face
that doesn't come clear, a face drawn under an umbrella,
beautiful, charcoal, beautiful, like words
that never get old, the sons of thunder beating

2005

WHAT WOULD OPPEN SAY,

What would Oppen say, he would say, "It is difficult now to speak of poetry—." And for twenty-five years he did not—from 1934–1958—so abstemious was he in his relationship to his commitment to social change and so absolutist in his relationship to his art that he could not yield to programmatic ideals.

So, what does it mean *now* to sequester oneself for the single purpose of exploring the limits of one's language *in our time* when the accords of nations with respect to the fate of millions, with respect to the very viability of the world, are deemed anachronisms, that is, irrelevant by a handful of political hacks, war criminals, and profiteers who are more or less recognized as being in rightful control. *Now* that Max Weber's definition of *state* is the only fitting one: "a human community that (successfully) claims the monopoly of the legitimate use of physical force within a given territory." Period.

So, which is it *now, in our time, our only time,* an act of resignation, self-interest, or refusal to abdicate the language to the most powerful to write a poem that may or may not make the most minimal public appearance, and if it does, may or may not directly address the crises of our time.

The time has come to loot to hew and Eden, writes Marjorie Milligan, an obscure Providence poet. I take her line as a call to words. I submit that pressing the demands of the word forward is pertinent, urgent, a requirement even. The happiness that belongs to all of us has been stolen by the few, declared Rigoberta Menchú. I can't accept this outcome. I will not. Notwithstanding scale—

2005

DEAR DYING TOWN,

The food is cheap; the squirrels are black; the box factories have all moved offshore; the light reproaches us, and our coffee is watered down, but we have an offer from the Feds to make nerve gas; the tribe is lobbying hard for another casino; the bids are out to attract a nuclear dump; and there's talk of a supermax—

In the descending order of your feelings
Please identify your concerns

P.S.: Remember Susanville, where Restore the Night Sky has become the town cry.

2002

JESSICA HAGEDORN (b. 1949)

Born in Manila and raised in the Philippines before coming to the United States, Hagedorn is known as a novelist, a performance artist, a poet, and a playwright. Her 1993 collection *Danger and Beauty* gathers poems, stories, and memoirs. It is dedicated to poet Kenneth Rexroth, who first published her in 1973 when she was living in San Francisco, two years before she formed a band, the West Coast Gangster Choir. A few years later she moved to New York, where she read poems to music, worked as program coordinator for the St. Mark's Poetry Project, wrote the screenplay for the film *Fresh Kill* (1994), and created performance art pieces like *Mango Tango* and *Airport Music.* Hagedorn has taught in the graduate playwriting program at the Yale School of Drama and in the creative writing program at Columbia University. She currently teaches at Long Island University in Brooklyn.

MING THE MERCILESS°

dancing on the edge/of a razor blade
ming/king of the lionmen
sing/bring us to the planet
of no return . . .

king of the lionmen
come dancing in my tube
sing, ming, sing . . .
blink sloe-eyed phantasy
and touch me where
there's always hot water
in this house

o flying angel
o pterodactyl
your rocket glides
like a bullet

you are the asian nightmare
the yellow peril
the domino theory
the current fashion trend

---

poem title: the wily Emperor Ming was the implacable but stylish villain of Alex Raymond's *Flash Gordon* science fiction comic strip and popular movie serials, *Flash Gordon* (1936), *Flash Gordon's Trip to Mars* (1938), and *Flash Gordon Conquers the Universe* (1940), noted for their futuristic sets and nonstop action. With his flamboyant art deco costume and its high collars, Ming is an unforgettable presence. His name is presumably borrowed from the Ming dynasty (1368–1644) in China.

ming, merciless ming,
come dancing in my tube
the silver edges of your cloak
slice through my skin
and king vulgar's cardboard wings
flap-flap in death
(for you)

o ming, merciless ming,
the silver edges of your cloak
cut hearts in two
the blood red dimensions
that trace american galaxies

you are the asian nightmare
the yellow peril
the domino theory
the current fashion trend

sing, ming, sing . . .
whistle the final notes
of your serialized abuse
cinema life
cinema death
cinema of ethnic prurient interest

o flying angel
o pterodactyl
your rocket glides
like a bullet
and touches me where
there's always hot water
in this house

1985

CHARLES BERNSTEIN (b. 1950)

Charles Bernstein was born in New York City and educated at Harvard. He teaches at the University of Pennsylvania. In 2010, he observed about his work, "It's true that, on the one hand, I mock and destabilize the foundation of a commitment to lyric poetry as an address toward truth or toward sincerity. But, on the other hand, if you're interested in theory as a stable expository mode of knowledge production or critique moving toward truth, again, I should be banned from your republic. (I've already been banned from mine.) My vacillating poetics of poems and essays is a serial practice, a play of voices." His poetry, as others have said, "combines the language of politics, popular culture, advertising, literary jargon, corporate-speak, and myriad others to show the ways in which language and culture are mutually constructive and interdependent." Bernstein puts it at once more playfully and more aggressively: "I want to engage the materials of the culture, derange them as they have deranged me, sound them out, as they sound me out." He has long stood against what he calls "official verse culture," with its "restricted vocabulary, neutral and univocal tone in the guise of voice or persona, grammar-book syntax, received conceits, static and unitary form." All this has been designed to enhance "the priestly function of the poet." Instead he offers "the comic and bathetic, the awkward and railing: to be grounded horizontally in the social and not vertically in the ethers." His characteristic intermixing of threat and humor is evident in all the poems here.

YOU

Time wounds all heals, spills through
with echoes neither idea nor lair
can jam. The door of your unfolding
starts like intervening vacuum, lush
refer to accidence or chance of
lachrymose fixation made
mercurial as the tors in crevice lock
dried up like river made the rhymes
to know what ocean were unkempt
or hide's detain the wean of
hide's felicity depend.

1983

from FOREIGN BODY SENSATION

"I am especially interested in the treatment of depression. With my Lord and Savior Jesus Christ at the center of my life, I have found real Joy and Purpose in dedicating myself to the Truth of His Teaching as Written in the Bible. What gives the job its excitement is working with Stan Richards, a nationally recognized creative wizard: *Adweek* recently named our agency among the eight most creative in the U.S. I moved into this area after six years in the aerospace industry, which I entered after early retirement from a career as a venture capitalist and real estate developer. This has been a stimulating opportunity for my work on late Pleistocene and early Holocene environmental changes. Pat is currently in Sri Lanka helping organize sera collection for leprosy patients. Nowadays, being a husband, father, homeowner, and Jew keeps me both busy and satisfied. I find myself immersed in a foreign but also satisfyingly tangible world of container shipping. I still find the labor movement to be the (imperfect) representative of workers' interests, and the necessary base from which the realization of class structure in economic and social life is explained and organized into coherent, worker-oriented politics. It wasn't long before I found myself in the company of a spiritual adept who teaches the most profound way of transcendence of every kind of self-possession. Left the firm and freelanced in stained glass. I studied hula seriously in Hawaii and taught Hawaiian dance locally, forming a group to hire out for bar mitzvahs and luaus. To my knowledge this is a unique occurrence, of great spiritual and cultural significance. My work has taken me into the area of robotics and industrial automation. For several years I worked in insurance, specializing in kidnap and expropriation coverage. A professional interest has been in the area of domestic violence; I love the work and feel strongly about violent crime. For a while, I served in the Peace Corps in Guatemala as a nurse working with cancer patients. After two years in Met State, I became increasingly eager to work with severely disturbed children. I am beginning to dabble in writing screenplays, humor, and poetry. What time is left I devote to coursework at the Divinity School, where I am studying for the priesthood. It seems I have done other things also, but maybe not. I guess I. In the future, I look forward to the private practice of pathology. Just when that will occur is uncertain. I am now administering substances to others to alter or obliterate their consciousness. The break is wonderful. Though nothing has educated me as well as watching my father walk the picket line in a strike that was eventually broken."

1987

THE KIWI BIRD IN THE KIWI TREE

I want no paradise only to be
drenched in the downpour of words, fecund
with tropicality. Fundament beyond
relation, less 'real' than made, as arms
surround a baby's gurgling: encircling
mesh pronounces its promise (not bars
that pinion, notes that ply). The tailor tells
of other tolls, the seam that binds, the trim,
the waste. & having spelled these names, move on
to toys or talcums, skates & scores. Only
the imaginary is real—not trumps
beclouding the mind's acrobatic versions.
The first fact is the social body,
one from another, nor needs no other.

1991

RIDDLE OF THE FAT FACED MAN

None guards the moor where stands
Receipt of scorn, doting on doddered
Mill as fool compose compare, come
Fair padre to your pleated score
Mind the ducks but not the door
Autumnal blooms have made us snore

1991

THE BOY SOPRANO

Daddy loves me this I know
Cause my granddad told me so
Though he beats me blue and black
That's because I'm full of crap

My mommy she is ultra cool
Taught me the Bible's golden rule
Don't talk back, do what you're told
Abject compliance is as good as gold

The teachers teach the grandest things
Tell how poetry's words on wings
But wings are for Heaven, not for earth
Want my advice: hijack the hearse

2001

JORIE GRAHAM (b. 1950)

Jorie Graham's poems often begin *in media res*. The reader is refused a position of mastery in relation to the text. We struggle to get our bearing in a Graham poem because that is the condition of consciousness and of our embedding in language. Her poetry is not designed to repair that condition or offer us consolations for enduring it. As one critic has written, she "discovers in her narrative the critical or pivotal moment: she then slows the action to expose its perilous eventual consequences." Her long lines are frequently units of perception or representation, but then typographical elements—from parentheses to ellipses to dashes—intervene to disrupt the flow of logic. "History" and "From the New World," two poems engaged with Holocaust memory and understanding, embody the oblique and troubled relation with history that Graham believes is the only one possible. Graham was born in New York City, raised and educated in Italy and France. She attended the Sorbonne in Paris and later studied at New York University and the Iowa Writers' Workshop. She taught at the workshop before leaving to join the faculty at Harvard.

HISTORY

Into whose ear the deeds are spoken. The only
listener. So I believed
he would remember everything, the murmuring trees,
the sunshine's zealotry, its deep
unevenness. For history
is the opposite
of the eye
for whom, for instance, six million bodies in portions
of hundreds and
the flowerpots broken by a sudden wind stand as
equivalent. What more
is there
than fact? *I'll give ten thousand dollars to the man*
who proves the holocaust really
occurred said the exhausted solitude
in San Francisco
in 1980. Far in the woods
in a faded photograph
in 1942 the man with his own
genitalia in his mouth and hundreds of
slow holes
a pitchfork has opened
over his face
grows beautiful. The ferns and deepwood

lilies catch
the eye. Three men in ragged uniforms
with guns keep laughing
nervously. They share the day
with him. A bluebird
sings. The feathers of the shade touch every inch
of skin—the hand holding down the delicate gun,
the hands holding down the delicate
hips. And the sky
is visible between the men, between
the trees, a blue spirit
enveloping
anything. Late in the story, in northern Italy,
a man cuts down some trees for winter
fuel. We read this in the evening
news. Watching the fire burn late
one night, watching it change and change, a hand
grenade,
lodged in the pulp the young tree
grew around, explodes, blinding the man, killing
his wife. Now who
will tell the children
fairytales? The ones where simple
crumbs over the forest
floor endure
to help us home?

1983

FROM THE NEW WORLD

Has to do with the story about the girl who didn't die
in the gas chamber, who came back out asking
for her mother. Then the moment—the next coil—where the guard,
Ivan, since the 50's an autoworker in Cleveland,
orders a man on his way in to rape her.
Then the narrowing, the tightening, but not in hunger, no,—the
witness

recollecting this on the stand somewhere in Israel in
February 87 should You be keeping
track. Has to do with her coming back out? Asking for her mother?
Can you help me in this?
Are you there in your stillness? Is it a real place?
God knows I too want the poem to continue,

want the silky swerve into shapeliness
and then the click shut
and then the issue of sincerity, the glossy diamond-backed
skin—will you buy me, will you take me home. . . . About the one
who didn't die, her face still there on the new stalk of her body as the
doors open,

the one who didn't like a relentless treble coming back out
right here into the thing we call
daylight but which is what now, unmoored?
The one time I knew something about us
though I couldn't say what

my grandmother then already ill
took me by the hand asking to be introduced.
And then *no, you are not Jorie—but thank you for*
saying you are. No. I'm sure. I know her you
see. I went into the bathroom, locked the door.
Stood in front of the mirrored wall—

not so much to see in, not looking up at all in fact,
but to be held in it as by a gas,
the thing which was me there in its chamber. Reader,
they were all in there, I didn't look up,
they were all in there, the coiling and uncoiling
billions,

the about-to-be-seized,
the about to be held down,

the about to be held down, bit clean, shaped,
and the others, too, the ones gone back out, the ending
wrapped round them,
hands up to their faces why I don't know,

and the about-to-be stepping in,
one form at a time stepping in as if to stay clean,
stepping over something to get into here,
something there on the floor now dissolving,
not looking down but stepping up to clear it,

and clearing it,
stepping in.
Without existence and then with existence.
Then into the clearing as it clamps down
all round.
Then into the fable as it clamps down.

We put her in a Home, mother paid.
We put him in a Home, mother paid.
There wasn't one that would take both of them we
could afford.
We were right we put him down the road it's all
there was,
there was a marriage of fifty years, you know this
they never saw each other again,
paralyzed on his back the last few years
he bribed himself a private line, he rigged the phone so he

could talk, etcetera, you know this,
we put her in X, she'd fallen out we put her back in,
there in her diaper sitting with her purse in her hands all day every
day, asking can I go now,
meaning him, meaning the
apartment by then long since let go, you know this

don't you, shifting wind sorting and re-sorting the stuff, flesh,
now the sunstruck field beyond her window,
now her hands on the forties sunburst silver
clasp, the white patent-leather pocketbook—
I stood there. Let the silver down all over my shoulders.

The sink. The goldspeck formica. The water
uncoiling.
Then the click like a lock being tried.
Then the hollow caressing the back of my neck.
Then the whole thing like a benediction you can't
shake off,

and the eyes unfastening, nervous, as if they smelled something up there
and had to go (don't wait for me), the
eyes lifting, up into the decoration, the eyes
looking. Poor thing.

As if real. As if *in* the place.
    The twitch where the eyes meet the eyes.
A blush.
    You see it's not the matter of her coming back out

alive, is it?
    It's the asking-for. The please.
Isn't it?
    Then the man standing up, the witness, screaming it's him it's him

I'm sure your Honor I'm sure. Then Ivan coming up to him
    and Ivan (you saw this) offering his hand, click, whoever
he is, and the old man getting a dial-tone, friend,
    and old whoever clicking and unclicking the clasp, the
silver knobs,
    shall we end on them? a tracking shot? a

close-up on the clasp a two-headed beast it turns out
    made of silvery
leaves? Where would you go now? *Where*
    screaming it's him it's
him? At the point where she comes back out something begins, yes,
    something new, something completely
new, but what—there underneath the screaming—what?

Like what, I wonder, to make the bodies come on, to make
    room,

like what, I whisper,

like which is the last new world, *like, like,* which is the thin

young body (before it's made to go back in) whispering *please.*

1991

RAY A. YOUNG BEAR (b. 1950)

An enrolled member of the Mesquakie Nation of central Iowa, Ray Young Bear grew up on the tribal lands near Tama. He is not only a poet and a novelist but also a performing artist. With his wife Stella, whose bead work is depicted on the cover of *The Invisible Musician* (1990), he founded the Black Eagle Child Dance Troupe, for which Young Bear plays drums. Under the Woodland Singers title, they have recorded traditional Native American songs. Young Bear has taught at several schools, including the University of Iowa; he also writes essays and editorials for the *Des Moines Sunday Register.* His poetry frequently takes up contemporary subjects in the light of our historical inheritance and in the context of Native American mythology.

IN VIEWPOINT: POEM FOR 14 CATFISH AND THE TOWN OF TAMA, IOWA°

into whose world do we go on living?
the northern pike and the walleye fish
thaw in the heat of the stove.
it wasn't too long ago
when they swam under the water,
sending bursts of water and clouds
of mossy particles from their gills,
camouflaging each other's route—
unable to find the heart to share
the last pockets of sunlight
and oxygen,
stifled by the inevitable
realization that the end is near
when man-sized fish slowly tumble up
from their secretive pits.
i, and many others, have an unparalleled
respect for the iowa river even though
the ice may be four to five feet thick,
but the farmers and the local whites
from the nearby town of tama and surrounding
towns, with their usual characteristic

poem title: Tama, a town in central Iowa, is near lands where the Mesquakie (Red Earth People) make their home today. In the seventeenth century, the Mesquakie tribe lived on the southern shore of Lake Superior in what is now Wisconsin, generally moving to the prairies to hunt in the winter. Toward the end of the eighteenth century, the encroachment of white settlers forced them to move south to the Mississippi River in Iowa and Illinois. A few decades later, they were compelled to move again, this time to a reservation in Kansas, but in the mid-nineteenth century a group of them pooled their resources to purchase land near Tama. Through much of their history, they remained committed to self-determination and resistance to assimilation.

ignorance and disregard, have driven noisily
over the ice and across our lands
on their pickups and snowmobiles,
disturbing the dwindling fish
and wildlife—
and due to their
own personal greed and self-displeasure
in avoiding the holes
made by tribal spearfishermen in
search of food (which would die
anyway because of the abnormal weather),
the snowmobilers ran and complained like
a bunch of spoiled and obnoxious children
to the conservation officer, who, with
nothing better to do along with a deputy
sheriff and a highway patrolman, rode out
to tribal land and arrested the fishermen
and their catfish.

with a bit of common sense,
and with a thousand other places
in the vast state of iowa to play toys
with their snowmobiles in, and with the winter
snow in well overabundance, they could have gone
elsewhere, but with the same 17th century
instincts they share with their own town's
drunken scums who fantasize like ritual
each weekend of finally secluding and beating
a lone indian's face into a bloody pulp,
they're no different except for the side
of railroad tracks they were born on
and whatever small town social
prominence they were born into.
it is the same attitude shared by lesser
intelligent animals who can't adapt
and get along with their environmental
surroundings.

undaunted, they gladly take our money
into their stores and banks, arrest
at whim our people—
deliberately overcharge us,
have meetings and debates as
to how much they should be paid to educate
our young.

why the paved streets as indicated
in their application for government funds
will benefit the indians.
among them, a dentist jokes and makes claims
about indian teeth he extracted solely
for economics.

the whites will pick and instigate
fights, but whenever an indian is provoked
into a defensive or verbal stand
against their illiterates,
or because he feels that he has been
unjustly wronged for something he has been
doing long before their spermatozoa set
across the atlantic (polluting and bloating
the earth with herbicides and insecticides),
troops of town police, highway patrolmen,
and assorted vigilantes storm through
indian-populated taverns, swinging
their flashlights and nervously holding on
to the bulbous heads of their nightclubs
with their sweaty hands, hoping
and anxiously waiting for someone
to trigger their archaic desires.
state conservation officers enter
our houses without permission,
opening and taking the meat and the skins
of our food from our cooking shacks
and refrigerators.
sometimes a mayor or two will deem it necessary
to come out and chase us and handcuff us over
our graveyards. the town newspaper overpublishes
any wrong or misdeed done by the indian
and the things which are significantly
important to the tribe as well as to the town,
for the most, ends up in the last pages,
after filling its initial pages
with whatever appeals to them as
being newsworthy and relevant indian
reading material.
unfortunately, through all of this,
some of *our* own people we hire, elect,
or appoint become so infected and obsessed
with misconceptions and greed, that they

forget they are there for the purpose
of helping us, not to give themselves
and each other's families priorities
in housing, education, and jobs.

altogether, it's pathetic seeing the town
and seeing mature uniformed and suited men
being led astray by its own scum, hiring
and giving morale to its own offspring scum
to make it right for all other scums
to follow.

they can't seem to leave us alone.
until they learn that the world and time
has moved on regardless of whether they still
believe and harbor antiquated ideas and notions
of being superior because of their pale light skin
alone, and until they learn that in their paranoia
to compare us to their desensitized lives,
they will never progress into what they
themselves call a community,
or even for the least,
a human.

1980

IT IS THE FISH-FACED BOY WHO STRUGGLES

it is the fish-faced boy who straggles
with himself beside the variant rivers
that his parents pass on their horse
and wagon. he sees the brilliant river.
at times it turns invisible and he sees
fish he has never seen before.
once, somewhere here he had dreamt
of a wild pig killing his mother and
sister. it chased him into the river
and he swam to the other side and stood
on the beach, wiping the water from his face.
two others came and encircled him.
the dream ended under the river
where he walked into a room
full of people dressed in sacks.
the morning wind chilled his languid body.
he peered out again. birds hopped along
the frosted grass. he remembered what

the submerged people said to him when
he walked into the room: we've been
expecting you.
large glistening fins filled
his eyes with the harsh sunlight.
he felt his lungs expanding.
the ribs from his body tilted
at an angle away from the ground.
the fish in the river, a spectacle.
he sat back against the rocking
sideboards of the wagon.
he noticed his father's black hat
and his mother's striped wool blanket
bouncing in the ride.

as they crossed the iron bridge
he felt the tension from his body
subside, fog from the openings
in the river drifted into the swamps.
the road led them through a forest.
he thought of invisibility.
the web between the bone spines of the fish
were intercrossed with incandescent fiber.
their jaws sent bursts of water
down to the river bottom.
clouds of mud and sediment
settled beside white needlepoint teeth.
he could faintly hear the barking of dogs.
he knew they were nearing home
from the permeating scent
of the pinetrees. it occurred to him
that the trees and the scent were an
intrinsic part of the seasons.
these were moments when he questioned
his existence. for awhile he pictured
awkwardly dressed people. they were standing
motionless beside long tables.
the impression was, they were ready
to eat but there was no food.
he had seen the long tables somewhere.
the wagon stopped. his father stepped
down from the wagon and carried him
into the summer house. it was warm inside.
huge poles which supported the roof

stood in dark brown color absorbing
the constant smoke from the fire.
far ahead in time, his grandson
would come down from the lavender hills
with the intention of digging out the poles
to carry on the memory under a new roof.

he knew it was the next day
when he woke. he could hear the chickens
shuffling about. it was no longer warm.
the daylight dissipated as it came in
through the hole in the center
of the roof.
he turned on his side
and bumped into a small tin bucket.
he reached over and drew it close.
at first smell,
he couldn't define it, but gradually
as he slushed it around, he recognized
his vomit. yesterday's food.
suspended above the door
was a dried head of a fish.
its face a shield. the rainbow-colored
eyes. the teeth were constructed
with blue stone. he knew its symbols
represented a guardian.
white painted thorns and barbs stuck
out from its gills. lines of daylight
rushed through the cracks in the walls.
the smoke-darkened poles were ornately
decorated. the door moved against the force
of the centered breeze. the cool odor
of the pinetrees chilled his entire body.
he pulled his thin blanket closer to him
and he attempted to walk to the door.
for each step he took, he forgot
through the next one. he could faintly
distinguish what sounded like the cracking
of ice over the flapping of wings.

his father stood above the ice
with a spear in his arms. his eyes affixed
to the opening. the giant fish swam by
piled on top of one another. some were

luminous. others swam so close together
they resembled clouds. there were even
a few who quickly swallowed what looked
like intestines. the ones who had their
mouths closed led long streamers
of this substance and it camouflaged
whoever followed behind. these were the fish
who represented a power and a belief.
the season was coming sooner than
anyone had anticipated.
the people in the hills
completely forgot their ceremonies
yet you saw them everywhere, here, to observe.
the women were along the banks
of the river tying long straps
of leather around the deer hooves
on their feet.
the men in their dried speckled
fish heads hummed as they scraped blue
curls of ice with their stone teeth.
small children covered each mark
on the ice. fresh water was refilled.
underneath, the fish swung their tails
side to side, alert.
the women in their deer hooves
walked onto the ice.
the men in their fish heads
began to sing and the small children
after drinking what remained of the water
ran ahead pointing out the giant fish.

1980

CAROLYN FORCHÉ (b. 1950)

Forché was born in Detroit; her father was a tool and die maker, while her mother was a journalist. She studied both international relations at Michigan State University and creative writing at Bowling Green State University. From 1978 to 1980 she worked as a reporter and human rights activist in El Salvador; "The Colonel" describes a meeting with a Salvadoran military officer. She went on to spend time in South Africa. She has thus been interested both in the impact of U.S. diplomacy and in local revolutionary movements. In addition to her poetry, she has done translations and edited a groundbreaking international anthology about political oppression, *Against Forgetting* (1993). She teaches at Georgetown University.

THE COLONEL

What you have heard is true. I was in his house. His wife carried a tray of coffee and sugar. His daughter filed her nails, his son went out for the night. There were daily papers, pet dogs, a pistol on the cushion beside him. The moon swung bare on its black cord over the house. On the television was a cop show. It was in English. Broken bottles were embedded in the walls around the house to scoop the kneecaps from a man's legs or cut his hands to lace. On the windows there were gratings like those in liquor stores. We had dinner, rack of lamb, good wine, a gold bell was on the table for calling the maid. The maid brought green mangoes, salt, a type of bread. I was asked how I enjoyed the country. There was a brief commercial in Spanish. His wife took everything away. There was some talk then of how difficult it had become to govern. The parrot said hello on the terrace. The colonel told it to shut up, and pushed himself from the table. My friend said to me with his eyes: say nothing. The colonel returned with a sack used to bring groceries home. He spilled many human ears on the table. They were like dried peach halves. There is no other way to say this. He took one of them in his hands, shook it in our faces, dropped it into a water glass. It came alive there. I am tired of fooling around he said. As for the rights of anyone, tell your people they can go fuck themselves. He swept the ears to the floor with his arm and held the last of his wine in the air. Something for your poetry, no? he said. Some of the ears on the floor caught this scrap of his voice. Some of the ears on the floor were pressed to the ground.

1978

THE MUSEUM OF STONES

This is your museum of stones, assembled in matchbox and tin,
collected from roadside, culvert, and viaduct,
battlefield, threshing floor, basilica, abattoir,°
stones loosened by tanks in the streets

3. *abbatoir:* slaughterhouse.

of a city whose earliest map was drawn in ink on linen,
schoolyard stones in the hand of a corpse,
pebble from Apollinaire's° *oui,*
stone of the mind within us
carried from one silence to another,
stone of cromlech and cairn, schist and shale, hornblende,
agate, marble, millstones, and ruins of choirs and shipyards,
chalk, marl, and mudstone from temples and tombs,
stone from the silvery grass near the scaffold,
stone from the tunnel lined with bones,
lava of the city's entombment,
chipped from lighthouse, cell wall, scriptorium,°
paving stones from the hands of those who rose against the army,
stones where the bells had fallen, where the bridges were blown,
those that had flown through windows and weighted petitions,
feldspar, rose quartz, slate, blueschist, gneiss, and chert,
fragments of an abbey at dusk, sandstone toe
of a Buddha mortared at Bamiyan,°
stone from the hill of three crosses and a crypt,
from a chimney where storks cried like human children,
stones newly fallen from stars, a stillness of stones, a heart,
altar and boundary stone, marker and vessel, first cast, lode, and hail,
bridge stones and others to pave and shut up with,
stone apple, stone basil, beech, berry, stone brake,
stone bramble, stone fern, lichen, liverwort, pippin, and root,
concretion of the body, as blind as cold as deaf,
all earth a quarry, all life a labor, stone-faced, stone-drunk
with hope that this assemblage, taken together, would become
a shrine or holy place, an ossuary, immovable and sacred,
like the stone that marked the path of the sun as it entered the human dawn.

2007

THE LIGHTKEEPER

A night without ships. Foghorns called into walled cloud, and you
still alive, drawn to the light as if it were a fire kept by monks,
darkness once crusted with stars, but now death-dark as you sail inward.

---

7. *Apollinaire:* Guillaume Apollinaire (1880–1918), French modernist poet.

16. *scriptorium:* a room in medieval European monasteries devoted to the copying of manuscripts by monastic scribes.

22. *Bamiyan:* monumental statues of standing Buddhas carved into the side of a cliff in the Bamiyan valley in the Hazarajat region of central Afghanistan between A.D. 507 and 554 were dynamited and destroyed by the Taliban in 2001.

Through wild gorse and sea wrack, through heather and torn wool
you ran, pulling me by the hand, so I might see this for once in my life:
the spin and spin of light, the whining of it, light in search of the lost,
there since the era of fire, era of candles and hollow-wick lamps,
whale oil and solid wick, colza and lard, kerosene and carbide,
the signal fires lighted on this perilous coast in the Tower of Hook.°
You say to me stay awake, be like the lensmaker who died with his
lungs full of glass, be the yew in blossom when bees swarm, be
their amber cathedral and even the ghosts of Cistercians° will be kind
to you.
In a certain light as after rain, in pearled clouds or the water beyond,
seen or sensed water, sea or lake, you would stop still and gaze out
for a long time. Also when fireflies opened and closed in the pines,
and a star appeared, our only heaven. You taught me to live like this.
That after death it would be as it was before we were born. Nothing
to be afraid. Nothing but happiness as unbearable as the dread
from which it comes. Go toward the light always, be without ships.

2010

MORNING ON THE ISLAND

The lights across the water are the waking city.
The water shimmers with imaginary fish.
Not far from here lie the bones of conifers
washed from the sea and piled by wind.
Some mornings I walk upon them,
bone to bone, as far as the lighthouse.
A strange beetle has eaten most of the trees.
It may have come here on the ships playing
music in the harbor, or it was always here, a winged
jewel, but in the past was kept still by the cold
of a winter that no longer comes.
There is an owl living in the firs behind us but he is white,
meant to be mistaken for snow burdening a bough.
They say he is the only owl remaining. I hear him at night
listening for the last of the mice and asking *who* of no other owl.

2010

---

9. *Hook:* Hook Lighthouse (also known as Hook Head Lighthouse) is a building situated at the tip of the Hook Peninsula in County Wexford, Ireland. It is one of the oldest lighthouses in the world.

12. *Cisterians:* a Roman Catholic religious order of monks and nuns.

ANDREW HUDGINS (b. 1951)

Andrew Hudgins was born in Killeen, Texas, as part of a military family, which entailed relocating through the south repeatedly while he was growing up. Some of that comes through in his verse autobiography *The Glass Hammer: A Southern Childhood* (1994). His essay collection *The Glass Anvil* (1997) takes up both his personal poetics and the complexities of childhood memory. Hudgins was educated at Huntingdon College, the University of Alabama, and the University of Iowa. He teaches at Ohio State University.

The three poems reprinted here are all from *After the Lost War: A Narrative* (1988), a series of dramatic monologues supposedly in the voice of Georgia poet and Confederate soldier Sidney Lanier, but as Hudgins points out in the preface to the book, "the voice of these poems will be unfamiliar to anyone who knows the writings of this historical figure." Nonetheless, Hudgins offers some details about Lanier's life. Born in Macon, Georgia, in 1842, he joined the Macon Volunteers and fought in the Civil War Battle of Chancellorsville. Later, when aboard the English blockade runner *Lucy,* he was captured and confined under brutal conditions at Fort Lookout. His health broken and suffering from tuberculosis, Lanier staggered home through the Carolinas. He eventually taught at Johns Hopkins before his death in 1881.

AT CHANCELLORSVILLE

THE BATTLE OF THE WILDERNESS

He was an Indiana corporal
shot in the thigh when their line broke
in animal disarray. He'd crawled
into the shade and bled to death.
My uniform was shabby with
continuous wear, worn down to threads
by the inside friction of my flesh on cloth.
The armpit seams were rotted through
and almost half the buttons had dropped off.
My brother said I should remove
the Yank's clean shirt: "From now on, Sid,
he'll have no use for it." Imagining
the slack flesh shifting underneath
my hands, the other-person stink
of that man's shirt, so newly his,
I cursed Clifford from his eyeballs to
his feet. I'd never talked that way before
and didn't know I could. When we returned,
someone had beat me to the shirt.

So I had compromised my soul
for nothing I would want to use —
some knowledge I could do without.
Clifford, thank God, just laughed. It was good
stout wool, unmarked by blood.
By autumn, we wore so much blue
we could have passed for New York infantry.

1988

THE SUMMER OF THE DROUGHT

He wasn't right. We all knew that. His head
bulged oddly on the left above his eye
and he'd eat anything that he could cram
into his mouth. Once, at the creek, I saw
him catching polliwogs and slurping them
out of his palms. I made him stop, of course,
and walked him home, but later he sneaked back,
and Mary saw him down there eating clay.
Then, in the summer of the drought, the streams
dried up, and he crawled underneath my house
to cool down in the dark. I'm guessing now.
He found a wasp nest, grabbed it from the brace,
and stuffed the boiling lump into his mouth.
At least that's what I figure must have happened.
He never talked again. And coming through
the floor beneath my feet, his scream was high
and thin, like flimsy metal being ground.
I was sitting at the table, drinking tea.
The air was heavy with the scent of sulphur
and lilac. I felt it vibrate through my feet.
The human whine of metal being ground.

1988

HE IMAGINES HIS WIFE DEAD

I'd just leapt quickly to the curb
to keep from being run down by a horse,
when suddenly I understood my wife might die,
and since that time I've thought of little else,
as if the threatened mind is trying
to keep from being taken by surprise.
And worse, it tries to find the benefits:
the joys of flirting and games of courtship —
all things I loved but have no use for now.

How can I blame the mind? It wants to live
and will be ruthless to that end,
as a plant that's moved into a darkened room
will drop the lower, inessential leaves
to keep the growing tip alive. But the heart
depends on more than blood. It needs a cause.
I left my dull heart beating when I slept,
and found it beating when I woke
to Mary smiling oddly in her fever
as she lay tangled in the sweaty sheets.
Her eyes, unfocused and afraid,
were a blue I'd never seen in eyes before,
as if a jay were caught inside her head
and through her eyes I saw it leaping back and forth
and trying to extend its bright blue wings.
It scared me more than prison camp or war.
My Mary is my only love
that's not a subterfuge for death.

1988

GARRETT KAORU HONGO (b. 1951)

Born in Volcano, Hawaii, of Japanese American parents, Hongo grew up on the North Shore of Oahu and later in California. His father was an electrician and his mother a personnel analyst. He was educated at Pomona College, the University of Michigan, and the University of California at Irvine. He was the founding director of a Seattle theater group called the Asian Exclusion Act. In addition to his own poems, he has edited several books, written a collaborative book, *The Buddha Bandits Down Highway 99* (1978), with Alan Lau and Lawson Inada, and written a memoir called *Volcano* (1995). He teaches at the University of Oregon. His work has often aimed at recovering his distinctive bicultural history, ranging from poems about his childhood in Los Angeles to poems like "Ancestral Graves, Kahuku" that recover his Japanese American heritage. "Kubota to Miguel Hernández in Heaven, Leup, Arizona, 1942" is the opening poem from a seven-poem sequence, "The Wartime Letters of Hideo Kubota," in Hongo's 2011 collection *Coral Road.* The sequence is written in the voice of a Japanese American held in a World War II internment camp.

ANCESTRAL GRAVES, KAHUKU°

(for Edward Hirsch)

Driving off Kam Highway along the North Shore,
    past the sugar mill,
Rusting and silent, a haunt for crows
    and the quick mongoose,
Cattle egrets and papaya trees in the wet fields
    wheeling on their muddy gears;

We turn left, *makai*° towards the sea,
    and by the old "76,"
Its orange globe a target for wind
    and the rust, and the bleeding light;
Down a chuckholed gravel road
    between state-built retirement homes
And the old village of miscellaneous shotguns
    overgrown with vines, yellow *hau* flowers,
And the lavish hearts and green embroidery of bougainvillaea
    stitching through their rotting screens.

---

poem title: Kahuku Point is on the north side of the island of Oahu, Hawaii.

4. *makai:* "towards the sea," as the poem says; in Hawaii directions are often given as "toward the mountains" or "toward the sea."

At the golf course, built by Castle & Cooke
    by subscription, 60 some years ago,
We swing past Hole No. 7 and its dying grass
    worn by generations of the poor
And losing out to the traps and dunes
    pushing in from the sea.

It's a dirt road, finally,
    two troughs of packed earth
And a strip of bermuda all the way
    to the sandy point
Where, opposite the homely sentinels
    of three stripped and abandoned cars
Giving in to the rain and its brittle decay,
    a wire fence
Opens to the hard scrabble of a shallow beach
    and the collapsing stones
And the rotting stakes,
    o-kaimyō° for the dead,
Of this plantation-tough
    cemetery-by-the-sea.

We get out, and I guide you,
    as an aunt did once for me,
Over the drying tufts and patchy carpeting
    of temple moss
Yellowing in the saline earth,
    pointing out,
As few have in any recent time,
    my family graves
And the mayonnaise jars empty of flowers,
    the broken saucers
Where rice cakes and mandarins were stacked,
    the weather-smoothed
Shards of unglazed pots for sand and incense
    and their chowders of ash.

The wind slaps through our clothes
    and kicks a sand-cloud
Up to our eyes, and I remember
    to tell you

---

17. *o-kaimyō:* posthumous Buddhist names.

how the *tsunami* in '46 took out
over half the gravesites,
Tore through two generations,
most of our dead
Gone in one night, bones and tombstones
up and down the beach,
Those left, half-in, half-out of the broken cliff
harrowed by the sea.

I remember to say that the land,
what's left of it,
Still belongs to the growers,
the same as built the golf course,
Who own, even in death,
those they did in life,
And that the sea came then
through a vicious tenderness
Like the Buddha's, reaching
from his lotus-seat
And ushering all the lost and incapable
from this heaven to its source.

I read a few names—
this one's the priest,
His fancy stone scripted with ideograms
carved almost plain by the wind now,
And this one, Yaeko, my grandfather's sister
who bedded down one night
In the canefields and with a Scotsman
and was beaten to death
For the crime—
a hoe handle they say—
Struck by her own father,
mythic and unabsolved.

Our shame is not her love,
whether idyll or rape
Behind the green shrouds and whispering tassels
of sugar cane,
Not is it the poor gruel of their daily lives
or the infrequent
Pantomime of worship they engaged in
odd Saturdays;
It is its effacement, the rough calligraphy
on rotting wood

Worn smooth and illegible,
    the past
Like a name whispered in a shallow grave
    just above tideline
That speaks to us in a quiet woe
    without forgiveness
As we move off, back toward our car,
    the grim and constant
Muttering from the sea
    a cool sutra in our ears.

1988

KUBOTA TO MIGUEL HERNÁNDEZ IN HEAVEN, LEUPP, ARIZONA, 1942°

The sun travels slowly from over the top of this adobe stockade
And, when I finally wake and pull my face to the bars
At my window, I see a gray light filling in the shadows
Between the mess and guard quarters
And among river stones on the sides of the central well.
Horses snort and whinny far off from the corral I cannot see,
And a line of burros shuffles by, led by a single Navajo
Dressed in khaki-colored clothes from the trading post.
I've been here two months now, can name the hills
Surrounding this plateau of piñon pines—words I learned
From the guards and other prisoners, Japanese like me
Swept up in the days after the attack on Pearl Harbor.
The guards won't say what our crime is, rarely address us,
But I overhear them sometimes, saying the names of mountains,
Nearby towns, complaining about food and us "Japs."
They won't say if we'll be let go. The interrogators come
Every few days and ask about our hobbies back home—
Studying poetry, working the shortwave radio at night,
And me, how I go night fishing for *kumu* on Kahuku Point.
What landed me here was I used to go torching,
Wrapping the kerosene-soaked rags on bamboo poles,
Sticking them into the sand inside the lagoon,
And then go light them with a flick from my Zippo.
The fish come in from outside the reef,
Schooling to the light, and me I catch enough
To feed my neighbors—Portagee, Hawaiian, Chinee, and all—

---

poem title: Spanish poet Miguel Hernández died in a fascist prison in 1942. He had been an active supporter of the Spanish Republic.

Eating good for days after, like New Year's in early December.
For this they say I'm signaling submarines offshore,
Telling the Japanese navy the northernmost landfall on the island.
That's a lie. They ask when—I tell them. They ask where—I tell them.
How many fish?—I tell them same every time. No change my answer.
But how can you transform your sorrow into poems, Miguel?
To think of your wife and infant son with only onions to eat,
While you sing your lullabies from your cell in Alicante?
Is it cold for you, Miguel? With only the dark to wrap yourself in?
It is warm, even hot here on Navajo land in northern Arizona,
Where your poems descend to me in the moon's sweet, silver light
As it rises over the Mogollon Plateau these summer evenings.
They say that your sentence was death for writing poetry,
That you celebrated the Republic and the commoners.
I celebrated only my family and the richness of the sea.
My sentence, therefore, is only eternity to wait, not knowing,
Imagining *everything,* imagining nothing—
My wife taking in boarders, doing their laundry and sewing,
My children growing more trivial by the day
Without word where I have been taken,
Whether I will be returned or simply have vanished
Into the unwritten history of our country.
Your suffering tells me to be patient, Miguel,
To think of your song of sweet onions lulling your baby,
Even in his hunger, to a peaceful sleep,
While the wars of our time, and their ignorant ministrations,
Go on shedding their black, tyrannical light into the future.

2011

RITA DOVE (b. 1952)

Born in Akron, Ohio, Dove was educated at Miami University in Ohio, the University of Tübingen in Germany, and the University of Iowa. She teaches at the University of Virginia. History and myth are frequent subjects. A book-length poem sequence, *Thomas and Beulah* (1986), presents her maternal grandparents' family history in the broad context of African American migration north after reconstruction. *Mother Love* (1995) is a contemporary retelling of the story of Demeter and Persephone.

PARSLEY°

I. THE CANE FIELDS

There is a parrot imitating spring
in the palace, its feathers parsley green.
Out of the swamp the cane appears

to haunt us, and we cut it down. El General
searches for a word; he is all the world
there is. Like a parrot imitating spring,

we lie down screaming as rain punches through
and we come up green. We cannot speak an R—
out of the swamp, the cane appears

and then the mountain we call in whispers *Katalina.*°
The children gnaw their teeth to arrowheads.
There is a parrot imitating spring.

El General has found his word: *perejil.*
Who says it, lives. He laughs, teeth shining
out of the swamp. The cane appears

in our dreams, lashed by wind and streaming.
And we lie down. For every drop of blood
there is a parrot imitating spring.
Out of the swamp the cane appears.

poem title: Dove's note:—"On October 2, 1957, Rafael Trujillo (1891–1961), dictator of the Dominican Republic, ordered 20,000 blacks killed because they could not pronounce the letter 'r' in *perejil*, the Spanish word for parsley."

10. *Katalina:* in other words, "Katarina," because they cannot pronounce "r."

2. THE PALACE

The word the general's chosen is parsley.
It is fall, when thoughts turn
to love and death; the general thinks
of his mother, how she died in the fall
and he planted her walking cane at the grave
and it flowered, each spring stolidly forming
four-star blossoms. The general

pulls on his boots, he stomps to
her room in the palace, the one without
curtains, the one with a parrot
in a brass ring. As he paces he wonders
Who can I kill today. And for a moment
the little knot of screams
is still. The parrot, who has traveled

all the way from Australia in an ivory
cage, is, coy as a widow, practising
spring. Ever since the morning
his mother collapsed in the kitchen
while baking skull-shaped candies
for the Day of the Dead,° the general
has hated sweets. He orders pastries
brought up for the bird; they arrive

dusted with sugar on a bed of lace.
The knot in his throat starts to twitch;
he sees his boots the first day in battle
splashed with mud and urine
as a soldier falls at his feet amazed—
how stupid he looked!—at the sound
of artillery. *I never thought it would sing*
the soldier said, and died. Now

the general sees the fields of sugar
cane, lashed by rain and streaming.
He sees his mother's smile, the teeth
gnawed to arrowheads. He hears
the Haitians sing without R's

39. *Day of the Dead:* All Soul's Day, November 1. In Latin America, a procession honoring the dead is decked out with elaborately decorated skulls, coffins, and skeletons, along with flowers, candles, and food.

as they swing the great machetes:
Katalina, they sing, *Katalina*,

mi madle, mi amol en muelte.° God knows
his mother was no stupid woman; she
could roll an R like a queen. Even
a parrot can roll an R! In the bare room
the bright feathers arch in a parody
of greenery, as the last pale crumbs
disappear under the blackened tongue. Someone

calls out his name in a voice
so like his mother's, a startled tear
splashes the tip of his right boot.
My mother, my love in death.
The general remembers the tiny green sprigs
men of his village wore in their capes
to honor the birth of a son. He will
order many, this time, to be killed

for a single, beautiful word.

1983

RECEIVING THE STIGMATA°

There is a way to enter a field
empty-handed, your shoulder
behind you and air tightening.

The kite comes by itself,
a spirit on a fluttering string.

Back when people died for
the smallest reasons, there was
always a field to walk into.
Simple men fell to their knees
below the radiant crucifix
and held out their palms

in relief. Go into the field
and it will reward. Grace

---

57. *mi madle . . . :* the italicized line in the next stanza translates the phrase.
poem title: crucifixion wounds received by Jesus.

is a string growing straight
from the hand. Is
the hatchet's shadow on the
rippling green.

1983

JIMMY SANTIAGO BACA (b. 1952)

Born in Sante Fe, New Mexico, of Chicano and Apache Indian descent, but abandoned at age two, Baca lived part of the time with a grandparent. By his fifth birthday, his father was dead of alcoholism, his mother had been murdered by her new husband, and Baca was in an orphanage. He escaped at age eleven and lived on the street, moving on to drugs and alcohol. Soon he was convicted on a drug charge, though he may not have been guilty. He wrote the poems in his first book, *Immigrants in Our Own Land* (1979), while he was in prison, where he had taught himself to read. While there, he received forced shock treatments and spent four years in isolation. More recently, he has lived on a small farm outside Albuquerque, New Mexico, and traveled doing poetry readings. His other work includes the screenplay for *Bound by Honor* and the book *Working in the Dark: Reflections of a Poet of the Barrio* (1992). His book-length poem sequence *Martin & Meditations on the South Valley* (1989) is a southwestern narrative journey in which the main character is restored by contacts with land and heritage.

MI TÍO BACA EL POETA DE SOCORRO°

Antonio Ce De Baca
chiseled on stone chunk gravemarker,
propped against a white wooden cross.
Dust storms faded the birth and death numbers.
Poet de Socorro,
whose poems roused *la gente*
to demand their land rights back,
'til one night—that terrible night,
hooves shook your earthen-floor
one-room adobe, lantern flame
flickered shadowy omens on walls,
and you scrawled across the page,
"*¡Aqui vienen! ¡Aqui vienen!*
Here they come!"
Hooves clawed your front yard,
guns glimmering blue
angrily beating at your door.
                    You rose.
Black boots scurried round four adobe walls,
trampling flower beds.

---

poem title: (Spanish) "My Uncle Baca the Poet from Socorro"; Socorro is a city located on the Rio Grande in Socorro County, New Mexico.

They burst through the door.
It was a warm night, and carried the scent
of their tobacco, sulphur, and leather.
Faces masked in dusty hankies,
men wearing remnants of Rinche uniforms,
arms pitchforked you out,
where arrogant young boys on horses
held torches and shouted,
"Shoot the Mexican! Shoot him!"
Saliva flew from bits
as horses reared from you,
while red-knuckled recruits held reins tight,
drunkenly pouring whiskey over you,
kicking you up the hill by the yucca,
where you turned, and met the scream
of rifles with your silence.

Your house still stands.
Black burnt tin covers window openings,
weeds grow on the dirt roof
that leans like an old man's hand
on a cane *viga*. . . .
I walk to the church a mile away,
a prayer on my lips bridges
years of disaster between us.
Maybe things will get better.
Maybe our struggle to speak and be
as we are, will come about.
For now, I drink in your spirit, Antonio,
to nourish me as I descend
into dangerous abysses of the future.
I came here this morning
at 4:30 to walk over my history.
Sat by the yucca, and then imagined you again,
walking up to me
face sour with tortuous hooks
pulling your brow down in wrinkles,
cheeks weary with defeat,
face steady with implacable dignity.
The softness in your brown eyes
said you could take no more.
You will speak with the angels now.
I followed behind you to the church,
your great bulky field-working shoulders
lean forward in haste

as if angels really did await us.
Your remorseful footsteps
in crackly weeds
sound the last time
I will hear and see you. Resolve is engraved
in each step. I want to believe
whatever problems we have, time will take
its course, they'll be endured and consumed.
Church slumps on a hill, somber and elegant.
After you, I firmly pull the solid core door back.
You kneel before La Virgen De Guadalupe,
bloody lips moving slightly,
your great gray head poised in listening,
old jacket perforated with bloody bullet holes.
I close the door, and search the prairie,
considering the words *faith, prayer* and *forgiveness,*
wishing, like you, I could believe them.

1989

THE PAINTERS

The painters paint over my shoes,
over my heart, over my face,
their brushes sweep across,
across, trying to blend me in
with everything else.

In gluey clumsiness,
the moon unsticks itself and rises
leaving a trail of yellow footsteps,
through the soot and grime.
Bells drip blue iron notes
down the streets,
and the wind sticks to tree branches,
heavy with smog,
like wet bristles of a brush
dipped in black paint;
the dumb hardened boughs
ladder up splinteringly
scraping the sky.
Chipped leaves peel off
and beat themselves
on dull dark doors of the city.

With the acrid-smelling stuff
of my soul,
I rub the roots and
I rub and rub,
and slowly the old burnish
of an autumn leaf draws out,
roots begin to move,
and I hold a fistful of earth
in my palm,
and accept my uniqueness,
my exile, from the painters.

1990

ALBERTO RÍOS (b. 1952)

Alberto Alvaro Ríos was born in the city of Nogales, Arizona, on the Mexican border. His mother was British and his father Mexican. Ríos was educated at University of Arizona and now teaches at Arizona State University. His poetry has been set to music in a cantata by James DeMars called "Toto's Say" and also adapted to both dance and popular music. As "Madre Sofía" demonstrates, there is a distinctive strain of magical realism in his work, something he is adept at sustaining in verse narratives. Ríos's short story "Eyes Like They Say the Devil Has" takes up the same childhood visit to a gypsy fortune teller. Ríos is equally well known for his fiction and for *Capirotada: A Nogales Memoir* (1999). His work presents one of the most vital imaginative accounts of life on the border between Mexico and the United States.

MADRE SOFÍA

My mother took me because she couldn't
wait the second ten years to know.
This was the lady rumored to have been
responsible for the box-wrapped baby
among the presents at that wedding,
but we went in, anyway, through the curtains.
Loose jar-top, half turned
and not caught properly in the threads
her head sat mimicking its original intention
like the smile of a child hitting himself.
Central in that head grew unfamiliar poppies
from a face mahogany, eyes half yellow
half gray at the same time, goat and fog,
slit eyes of the devil, his tweed suit, red
lips, and she smelled of smoke, cigarettes,
but a diamond smoke, somehow; I inhaled
sparkles, I could feel them, throat, stomach.
She did not speak, and as a child
I could only answer, so that together
we were silent, cold and wet, dry and hard:
from behind my mother pushed me forward.
The lady put her hand on the face
of a thin animal wrap, tossing that head
behind her to be pressured incredibly
as she sat back in the huge chair and leaned.
And then I saw the breasts as large as her
head, folded together, coming out of her dress
as if it didn't fit, not like my mother's.

I could see them, how she kept them
penned up, leisurely, in maroon feed bags,
horse nuzzles of her wide body,
but exquisitely penned up
circled by pearl reins and red scarves.
She lifted her arm, but only with the tips
of her fingers motioned me to sit opposite.
She looked at me but spoke to my mother
words dark, smoky like the small room,
words coming like red ants stepping occasionally
from a hole on a summer day in the valley,
red ants from her mouth, her nose, her ears,
tears from the corners of her cinched eyes.
And suddenly she put her hand full on my head
pinching tight again with those finger tips
like a television healer, young Oral Roberts°
half standing, quickly, half leaning
those breasts swinging toward me
so that I reach with both my hands to my lap
protecting instinctively whatever it is
that needs protection when a baseball is thrown
and you're not looking but someone yells,
the hand, then those breasts coming toward me
like the quarter-arms of the amputee Joaquín
who came back from the war to sit
in the park, reaching always for children
until one day he had to be held back.
I sat there, no breath, and could see only
hair around her left nipple, like a man.
Her clothes were old.
Accented, in a language whose spine had been
snapped, she whispered the words of a city
witch, and made me happy, alive like a man:
The future will make you tall.

1982

WHAT HAPPENED TO ME

A boy rides a horse after school
On a warm day and clear,
And on one day he does not hear
The call, one day does not come home.

---

44. *Oral Roberts:* (1918–2009) American religious leader.

The day is not less usual,
Not different from any other,
That particular day when now his mother
Cannot coolly bathe him, or comb him,
Or kiss his face, his hands, cannot
Fool this boy so easily about things.
The day is not different when he brings
Home nothing, though his hands are full.
On a warm day and clear
A boy rides a horse after school.
He is a small boy, still,
But the horse is big.
The world is there and this
Is its animal, and this,
His stepping off, is the getting on
The horse of the ground that will take him.

2002

ANITA ENDREZZE (b. 1952)

Endrezze was born in Long Beach, California, of Yaqui and European ancestry. An artist as well as a poet and short story writer, her paintings and illustrations have been reproduced in a number of publications and been exhibited both in the United States and in Europe. She has also written a novel for children. She has worked part time for Washington State as a poet-in-residence, and has edited newsletters for the Spokane chapter of the Audubon Society and the Indian Artists Guild. Her books include *At the Helm of Twilight* (1992) and *The Humming of Stars and Bees* (1998). *Throwing Fire at the Sun* (2000) is an account of her family and tribal history told in paintings, poetry, legend, fact, and family memories. As the poems reprinted here suggest, she has been unusually successful at finding linguistic equivalents of Native American views of nature.

RETURN OF THE WOLVES

All through the valley, the people are whispering:
the wolves are returning, returning
to the narrow edge of our fields, our dreams.
They are returning the cold to us.
They are wearing the crowns of ambush,
offering the rank and beautiful snow-shapes
of dead sheep, an old man too deep in his cups,
the trapper's gnawed hands, the hunter's tongue.
They are returning the whispers of our lovers,
whose promises are less enduring than the wolves.

Their teeth are carving the sky into delicate antlers,
carving dark totems full of moose dreams: meadows
where light grows with the marshgrass and water
is a dark wolf under the hoof.
Their teeth are carving our children's names
on every trail, carving night into a different bone—
one that seems to be part of my body's long memory.

Their fur is gathering shadows, gathering
the thick-teethed white-boned howl of their tribe,
gathering the broken-deer smell of wind
into their longhouse of pine and denned earth,
gathering me also, from my farmhouse
with its golden light and empty rooms, to the cedar
(that also howls its woody name to the cave of stars),
where I am silent as a bow unstrung
and my scars are not from loving wolves.

1988

BIRDWATCHING AT FAN LAKE

Our blue boat drifts
on the flat-shelled water.

In my lap: the red Book of Birds,
genesis of egg and feather

in the leavened air, begetting
the moist nests of osprey

and the mallard that floats
like bread on the water.

Around the lake are dark crowns
of granite and tall reeds with eyes

that burn gold in afternoon sun.
We eat salt crackers, green apples,

round cheese. On the shore,
a woman bends for a bright towel,

a white horse chews on wood.
The creek sings: *dribblestone*

pebblelarvae. The red faces
of salamanders are wise

under the green bracken.
Waxwings sing to a chokecherry sun,

their throats shrill glass whistles.
We check our lists, compare.

Mine has notes like: the birds fly
into the white corridor of the sky.

Or: does the ruffed grouse's drumming
enter into the memories of trees?

Lately, we've talked less, been less
sure of each other. Love, why

travel this far to find rarity
and remain silent

in the curved wing of our boat?
Your hand on the oar is enough

for me to think of love's migration
from the intemperate heart to halcyon soul.

You point to a kingfisher,
whose eggs are laid on fish bones.

The fish are fin to the fisher's crest.
On a rocky beach, a kildeer keens,

orange-vested children pull up canoes,
camp smoke nests on the leafy water.

You take my hand and call it *wing*.
Sunlight is reborn in the heart

of the wild iris. Its purple shadows
sway over the root-dark fish.

Look: the long-necked herons
in the green-billed water

are pewter. Their wet-ash wings wear
medallions of patience. We drift on,

buoyed by the tiny currents between us,
the light long-legged, the wind

full of hearts that beat quick
and strong.

1988

LA MORENA AND HER BEEHIVE HAIRDO

1965–1970

The Dark One sported a beehive hairdo
where she once hid her brother Alfonso.
His girlfriend had a husband who carried a switchblade
pretty as a butterfly in his back pocket.
Alfonso camped out in La Morena's dusky hair
until the coast was clear, at least as far as San Pedro.
Then he vamoosed to Tucson

where he married a young hairdresser
from the Yaqui barrio.

Without any family responsibilities, La Morena felt light-headed.
She changed her name again. *Old Lady.* It was the sixties, man,
and she was everyone's old lady. She really dug those long-haired vets
from Nam.° She wore granny boots and long paisley dresses
and carried a small baggie of white horse
in her leather fringed purse. Everyone called her
Indian Princess and said Cher° looked just like her.
She slept around, sniffing like a coyote
at every dude's balls, snorting coke up a straw
until she saw red stars galloping around her heart
and herds of tiny white horses dying in nights of Black Velvet.°

I won't ask her if she remembers. It was real
but it wasn't true. She was living in someone else's mandala
because it was on the top-ten chart. Somewhere
along the way she lost herself. It's the Yaqui Way
of Knowledge by Carlos Coyote-Peyote.
When we found Jesus, we held out our palms
for coins, Bibles, good-looking Indian boys.
She was my sister. Kneel down, little sister, she said.
And we did, down in front of altars of bees
and tubes of pale lipstick, crosses made of lovers' bodies,
broken shoes, floods of moons, Janis Joplin,° rowdy measures
of life. Those summers, slab dancing and picking up guys,
were the best times, she says, the *best.* When she was young
and I was just beginning my own story, my own howling
at the American moon.

2000

---

13. *Nam:* Vietnam.
16. *Cher:* (b. 1946), American singer and actress.
20. *Black Velvet:* Canadian whiskey.
31. *Janis Joplin:* (1943–1970). American singer-songwriter.

ANA CASTILLO (b. 1953)

Castillo was born and grew up in Chicago of Aztec and Mexican ancestry. She was educated at Northern Illinois University and the University of Chicago, thereafter earning a Ph.D. at the University of Bremen. In both high school and college, Castillo was active in the Chicano movement and began writing political poems about ethnic experience. Known for both her novels and her poetry, she has often explored the politics of sexuality. She has worked as associate editor for *Third Woman Magazine* and *Humanizarte* and has taught at San Francisco State University, the University of New Mexico, and Mount Holyoke College. She lives in Albuquerque, New Mexico.

SEDUCED BY NATASSJA KINSKI°

I always had a thing for Natassja Kinski.
My Sorbonne clique and I went to see her latest film. Giant
billboards all over Paris: Natassja—legs spread, her
lover's face lost in between.
I watched *Paris, Texas*° twice, living with
the eternal memory of those lips
biting into a fleshy strawberry in *Tess*.°
Thank you, Roman Polanski.

Long after I have gotten over Natassja Kinski,
I am with a Chicago clique on holiday. I am an atom now,
in constant, ungraspable flux, when my Bulgarian scarf is
pulled off my neck. It is Natassja Kinski.

She has removed her KGB° black-leather coat; bottom of
the ocean eyes are working me, and yes, that mouth . . .

When we dance, I avoid her gaze.
I am trying every possible way to escape eyes,
mouth, smile, determination, scarf pulling me

---

poem title: Kinski is a German-born (1959) actress. Ephraim Katz's *Film Encyclopedia* describes her as a "radiantly sensual, full-lipped, gray-green-eyed star of international films."

5. *Paris, Texas:* 1984 film directed by Wim Wenders.

7. *Tess:* 1979 film directed by Roman Polanski.

13. *KGB:* the security service of the Soviet Union; it enforced political discipline at home and conducted espionage abroad.

closer, cheap wine, strobe light, dinner invitation,
"Come home with me. It's all for fun," she says.

I dance with her friends again. I am a tourist in my
hometown, and the girls are showing me a good time.
I think *I'll leave with someone else.*
But she finds me at a table in the dark.
"What do you want, my money?" I ask. She reminds, cockily,
that she has more money than I do. I am a poet, everybody
does. And when we dance, I am a strawberry, ripened and
bursting, devoured, and she has won.

We assure each other, the next day, neither of us has
ever done anything like that before.

By Sunday night, we don't go out for dinner as planned.
Instead, over a bottle of champagne,
Natassja wants me forever. Unable to bear that mouth,
sulking, too sad for words, I whisper: "*te llevaré conmigo.*"°
As if I ever had a choice.

1991

HUMMINGBIRD HEART
(MARCEL AT SIX)

Hummingbird heart
with hummingbird hands.
Such a tentative rush
toward petal and scent.
The smallest child
with the grandest of hearts
takes it all in.

1990

---

33. *te llevaré conmigo*: (Spanish) "I'll take you with me," which carries connotations of "I'll be with you always" or "I'll carry you in my heart."

MARK DOTY (b. 1953)

Born in Tennessee, the son of an army engineer, Doty has taught at Sarah Lawrence College, the M.F.A. program at Vermont College, the University of Utah, and the University of Houston. He now teaches at Rutgers University. In addition to his poetry, he is the author of a 1981 critical study of James Agee and of *Heaven's Coast* (1996), a memoir of his partner Wally Roberts's death from AIDS. Frightened by his emerging sexual identity, Doty married hastily at age eighteen but was divorced after graduating from Drake University in Iowa. While a temporary office worker in Manhattan, he studied creative writing at Goddard College. He also met Roberts, a department store window dresser, and lived with him for twelve years. While Doty has written about a variety of urban subjects, the specificity and variety of his poems about gay life—with their frankness, their substantial cultural resonance, their wit, their political insight, and their metaphoric inventiveness—make them his major contribution to American poetry to date. He did not, however, so much start out to write political poetry as to write about his own life, but the life of a gay man in America proved political. Doty has a rich and complex relation to the work of several other American poets, including Hart Crane. In Crane's case, one might say that Doty has set out to write the poems Crane himself could not have written in his own time.

HOMO WILL NOT INHERIT

Downtown anywhere and between the roil
of bathhouse steam—up there the linens of joy
and shame must be laundered again and again,

all night—downtown anywhere
and between the column of feathering steam
unknotting itself thirty feet above the avenue's

shimmered azaleas of gasoline,
between the steam and the ruin
of the Cinema Paree (marquee advertising

its own milky vacancy, broken showcases sealed,
ticketbooth a hostage wrapped in tape
and black plastic, captive in this zone

of blackfronted bars and bookstores
where there's nothing to read
but longing's repetitive texts,

where desire's unpoliced, or nearly so)
someone's posted a xeroxed headshot
of Jesus: permed, blonde, blurred at the edges

as though photographed through a greasy lens,
and inked beside him, in marker strokes:
HOMO WILL NOT INHERIT. *Repent* & *be saved.*

I'll tell you what I'll inherit: the margins
which have always been mine, downtown after hours
when there's nothing left to buy,

the dreaming shops turned in on themselves,
seamless, intent on the perfection of display,
the bodegas and offices lined up, impenetrable:

edges no one wants, no one's watching. Though
the borders of this shadow-zone (mirror and dream
of the shattered streets around it) are chartered

by the police, and they are required,
some nights, to redefine them. But not now, at twilight,
permission's descending hour, early winter darkness

pillared by smoldering plumes. The public city's
ledgered and locked, but the secret city's boundless;
from which do these tumbling towers arise?

I'll tell you what I'll inherit: steam,
and the blinding symmetry of some towering man,
fifteen minutes of forgetfulness incarnate.

I've seen flame flicker around the edges of the body,
pentecostal, evidence of inhabitation.
And I have been possessed of the god myself,

I have been the temporary apparition
salving another, I have been his visitation, I say it
without arrogance, I have been an angel

for minutes at a time, and I have for hours
believed—without judgement, without condemnation—
that in each body, however obscured or recast,

is the divine body—common, habitable—
the way in a field of sunflowers
you can see every bloom's

the multiple expression
of a single shining idea,
which is the face hammered into joy.

I'll tell you what I'll inherit:
stupidity, erasure, exile
inside the chalked lines of the police,

who must resemble what they punish,
the exile you require of me,
you who's posted this invitation

to a heaven nobody wants.
You who must be patrolled,
who adore constraint, I'll tell you

what I'll inherit, not your pallid temple
but a real palace, the anticipated
and actual memory, the moment flooded

by skin and the knowledge of it,
the gesture and its description
—do I need to say it?—

the flesh *and* the word. And I'll tell you,
you who can't wait to abandon your body,
what you want me to, maybe something

like you've imagined, a dirty story:
Years ago, in the baths,
a man walked into the steam,

the gorgeous deep indigo of him gleaming,
solid tight flanks, the intricately ridged abdomen—
and after he invited me to his room,

nudging his key toward me,
as if perhaps I spoke another tongue
and required the plainest of gestures,

after we'd been, you understand,
worshipping a while in his church,
he said to me, *I'm going to punish your mouth.*

I can't tell you what that did to me.
My shame was redeemed then;
I won't need to burn in the afterlife.

It wasn't that he hurt me,
more than that: the spirit's transactions
are enacted now, here—no one needs

your eternity. This failing city's
radiant as any we'll ever know,
paved with oily rainbow, charred gates

jeweled with tags, swoops of letters
over letters, indecipherable as anything
written by desire. I'm not ashamed

to love Babylon's scrawl.° How could I be?
It's written on my face as much as on
these walls. This city's inescapable,

gorgeous, and on fire. I have my kingdom.

1995

THE EMBRACE

You weren't well or really ill yet either;
just a little tired, your handsomeness
tinged by grief or anticipation, which brought
to your face a thoughtful, deepening grace.

I didn't for a moment doubt you were dead.
I knew that to be true still, even in the dream.
You'd been out—at work maybe?—
having a good day, almost energetic.

We seemed to be moving from some old house
where we'd lived, boxes everywhere, things

97. *scrawl:* Daniel 5 describes the writing on a palace wall that Daniel interpreted as a condemnation of Babylon's king Belshazzar.

in disarray: that was the *story* of my dream,
but even asleep I was shocked out of narrative

by your face, the physical fact of your face:
inches from mine, smooth-shaven, loving, alert.
Why so difficult, remembering the actual look
of you? Without a photograph, without strain?

So when I saw your unguarded, reliable face,
your unmistakable gaze opening all the warmth
and clarity of you—warm brown tea—we held
each other for the time the dream allowed.

Bless you. You came back, so I could see you
once more, plainly, so I could rest against you
without thinking this happiness lessened anything,
without thinking you were alive again.

1998

HARRYETTE MULLEN (b. 1953)

Mullen was born in Florence, Alabama, and grew up in Fort Worth, Texas. She was educated at the University of Texas and the University of California at Santa Cruz. She has taught at Cornell University and now teaches at UCLA. She has written both poems and prose poems since publishing her first book, *Tree Tall Woman*, in 1981. Her prose poems, which grow out of the Language poetry movement, wittily display human motivation with a linguistic basis.

from TRIMMINGS

Akimbo bimbos, all a jangle. Tricked out trinkets, aloud galore. Gimcracks, a stack. Bang and a whimper. Two to tangle. It's a jungle.

Punched in like slopwork. Mild frump and downward drab. Slipshod drudge with chance of dingy morning slog. Tattered shoulders, frayed eyes, a dowdy gray. Frowzy in a slatternly direction.

Animal pelts, little minks, skins, tail. Fur flies. Pet smitten, smooth beaver strokes. Muff, soft, 'like rabbits.' Fine fox stole, furtive hiding. Down the road a pretty fur piece.

Opens up a little leg, some slender, high exposure. Splits a chic sheath, tight slit. Buy another peek experience, price is slashed. Where tart knife, scoring, minced a sluttish strut. Laughing splits the seams. Teeth in a gash, letting off steam.

A fish caught, pretty fish wiggles for a while. A caught fish squirms. A freshly licked fish sighs. Gapes with holes for eyes. A wiggling fish flashes its display. A pattern over whiteness. Bareness comes with coverage for peeking through holes to see flesh out of water. Cold holes where eyes go. The sea is cold. Her body of foam, some frothy Venus. Or strayed mermaid, tail split, bleeds into the sea. With brand new feet walks unsteady on land, each step an ache.

Her ribbon, her slender is ribbon when to occupy her hands a purse is soft. Wondering where to hang the keys the moon is manicured. Her paper parasol and open fan become her multiplication of a rib which is connected and might start a fire for cooking. Who desires crisp vegetables, she opens for the climate. A tomato isn't hard. It splits in heat, easy. It's seasonal. Once in a while there is heat, and several flowers are perennials. Roses shining with greengold leaves and bright threads. Some threads do wilt after starching. She has done the starching and the bleaching. She has pink too and owns earrings. Would never be shamed by pearls. A subtle blush communicates much. White peeks out, an eyelet in a storm.

1991

from S*PeRM**K*T

Aren't you glad you use petroleum? Don't wait to be told you explode. You're not fully here until you're over there. Never let them see you eat. You might be taken for a zoo. Raise your hand if you're sure you're not.

Kills bugs dead. Redundancy is syntactical overkill. A pinprick of peace at the end of the tunnel of a nightmare night in a roach motel. Their noise infects the dream. In black kitchens they foul the food, walk on our bodies as we sleep over oceans of pirate flags. Skull and crossbones, they crunch like candy. When we die they will eat us, unless we kill them first. Invest in better mousetraps. Take no prisoners on board ship, to rock the boat, to violate our beds with pestilence. We dream the dream of extirpation. Wipe out a species, with God on our side. Annihilate the insects. Sterilize the filthy vermin.

A daughter turned against the grain refuses your gleanings, denies your milk, soggy absorbency she abhors. Chokes on your words when asked about love. Never would swallow the husks you're allowed. Not a spoonful gets down what you see of her now. Crisp image from disciplined form. Torn hostage ripening out of hand. Boxtop trophy of war, brings to the table a regimen from hell. At breakfast shuts out all nurturant murmurs. Holds against you the eating for two. Why brag of pain a body can't remember? You pretend once again she's not lost forever.

Off the pig, ya dig? He squeals, grease the sucker. Hack that fatback, pour the pork. Pig out, rib the fellas. Ham it up, hype the tripe. Save your bacon, bring home some. Sweet dreams pigmeat. Pork belly futures, larded accounts, hog heaven. Little piggish to market. Tub of guts hog wilding. A pig of yourself, high on swine, cries all the way home. Streak a lean gets away cleaner than Safeway chitlings. That's all, folks.

Ad infinitum perpetual infants goo. Pastel puree of pure pink bland blue-eyed babes all born a cute blond with no chronic colic. Sterile eugenically cloned rows of clean rosy dimples and pamper proof towhead cowlicks. Adorable babyface jars. Sturdy innocent in the pink, out of the blue packs disposing durable superabsorbent miracle fibers. As solids break down, go to waste, a land fills up dead diapers with funky halflife.

Flies in buttermilk. What a fellowship. That's why white milk makes yellow butter. Homo means the same. A woman is different. Cream always rises over split milk. Muscle men drink it all in. Awesome teeth and wholesale bones. Our cows are well adjusted. The lost family album keeps saying cheese. Speed readers skim the white space of this galaxy.

1992

LOUISE ERDRICH (b. 1954)

Born in Little Falls, Minnesota, Erdrich grew up in the town of Wahpeton, North Dakota, near the Minnesota border and the Turtle Mountain Reservation. She is an enrolled member of the Turtle Mountain Chippewa tribe of North Dakota; her mother is of French-Chippewa descent, and for many years her grandfather was tribal chair of the reservation. Her parents were Bureau of Indian Affairs educators; both taught at the boarding school in Wahpeton. Erdrich was educated at Dartmouth College and Johns Hopkins; she has taught poetry in prisons and edited a Native American newspaper. In addition to publishing two books of poetry, *Jacklight* (1984) and *Baptism of Fire* (1989), she has written a number of novels and short stories. Her novels include *Love Medicine* (1984), *The Bingo Palace* (1991), and *The Round House* (2012).

INDIAN BOARDING SCHOOL: THE RUNAWAYS°

Home's the place we head for in our sleep.
Boxcars stumbling north in dreams
don't wait for us. We catch them on the run.
The rails, old lacerations that we love,
shoot parallel across the face and break
just under Turtle Mountains.° Riding scars
you can't get lost. Home is the place they cross.

The lame guard strikes a match and makes the dark
less tolerant. We watch through cracks in boards
as the land starts rolling, rolling till it hurts
to be here, cold in regulation clothes.
We know the sheriff's waiting at midrun
to take us back. His car is dumb and warm.
The highway doesn't rock, it only hums
like a wing of long insults. The worn-down welts
of ancient punishments lead back and forth.

All runaways wear dresses, long green ones,
the color you would think shame was. We scrub
the sidewalks down because it's shameful work.

poem title: a number of military style boarding schools for Indian children were established by U.S. government policy in the mid-nineteenth century. It was part of a plan to forcibly assimilate the next generation of Native Americans into white culture. Visits home were severely restricted to prevent the children from reverting to Indian lifestyles, and use of native languages was often prohibited. Many of the institutions were financed by unpaid student labor. Meanwhile, medical care at the schools was exceedingly poor, food was insufficient, and hundreds of the children died of disease. The schools were widely used through the 1930s.

6. *Turtle Mountains:* in North Dakota, site of a Chippewa Indian reservation.

Our brushes cut the stone in watered arcs
and in the soak frail outlines shiver clear
a moment, things us kids pressed on the dark
face before it hardened, pale, remembering
delicate old injuries, the spines of names and leaves.

1984

DEAR JOHN WAYNE°

August and the drive-in picture is packed.
We lounge on the hood of the Pontiac
surrounded by the slow-burning spirals they sell
at the window, to vanquish the hordes of mosquitoes.
Nothing works. They break through the smoke screen for blood.

Always the lookout spots the Indians first,
spread north to south, barring progress.
The Sioux or some other Plains bunch
in spectacular columns, ICBM missiles,
feathers bristling in the meaningful sunset.

The drum breaks. There will be no parlance.
Only the arrows whining, a death-cloud of nerves
swarming down on the settlers
who die beautifully, tumbling like dust weeds
into the history that brought us all here
together: this wide screen beneath the sign of the bear.

The sky fills, acres of blue squint and eye
that the crowd cheers. His face moves over us,
a thick cloud of vengeance, pitted
like the land that was once flesh. Each rut,
each scar makes a promise: *It is*
not over, this fight, not as long as you resist.

Everything we see belongs to us.

A few laughing Indians fall over the hood
slipping in the hot spilled butter.
The eye sees a lot, John, but the heart is so blind.

---

poem title: Wayne (1907–1979), American film actor and icon, one of the most widely known performers in westerns and films about World War II. He was launched into stardom shooting Indians in *Stagecoach* (1939) and consumed by racial hatred for them in *The Searchers* (1956); in between, as a cavalry officer in several films, Indians are merely a problem for him to control.

Death makes us owners of nothing.
He smiles, a horizon of teeth
the credits reel over, and then the white fields

again blowing in the true-to-life dark.
The dark films over everything.
We get into the car
scratching our mosquito bites, speechless and small
as people are when the movie is done.
We are back in our skins.

How can we help but keep hearing his voice,
the flip side of the sound track, still playing:
Come on, boys, we got them
where we want them, drunk, running.
They'll give us what we want, what we need.
Even his disease was the idea of taking everything.
Those cells, burning, doubling, splitting out of their skins.

1984

THE FENCE

Then one day the gray rags vanish
and the sweet wind rattles her sash.
Her secrets bloom hot. I'm wild for everything.
My body is a golden armor around my unborn child's body,
and I'll die happy, here on the ground.
I bend to the mixture of dirt, chopped hay,
grindings of coffee from our dark winter breakfasts.
I spoon the rich substance around the acid-loving shrubs.
I tear down last year's drunken vines,
pull the black rug off the bed of asparagus
and lie there, knowing by June I'll push the baby out
as easily as seed wings fold back from the cotyledon.°
I see the first leaf already, the veined tongue
rigid between the thighs of the runner beans.
I know how the shoot will complicate itself
as roots fill the trench.
Here is the link fence, the stem doubling toward it,
and something I've never witnessed.
One moment the young plant trembles on its stalk.
The next, it has already gripped the wire.

12. *Cotyledon:* curled leaf in a seed pod.

Now it will continue to climb, dragging rude blossoms
to the other side
until in summer fruit like green scimitars,
the frieze of vines, and then the small body
spread before me in need
drinking light from the shifting wall of my body,
and the fingers, tiny stems wavering to mine,
flexing for the ascent.

1989

LORNA DEE CERVANTES (b. 1954)

Lorna Dee Cervantes was born in San Francisco of Chicana and Native American (Chumash) heritage. For many years she taught at University of Colorado and edited the Chicana/o journal *MANGO*, which was the first to publish Sandra Cisneros, Jimmy Santiago Baca, and Alberto Ríos, all poets included in the present collection. Her work has long evoked the dynamics of race, sex, class, and economics in Latino culture, with a special emphasis on the impact of the dominant culture on the lives of Latina women and on the forms of resistance they have devised.

REFUGEE SHIP

Like wet cornstarch, I slide
past my grandmother's eyes. Bible
at her side, she removes her glasses.
The pudding thickens.

Mama raised me without language.
I'm orphaned from my Spanish name.
The words are foreign, stumbling
on my tongue. I see in the mirror
my reflection: bronzed skin, black hair.

I feel I am a captive
aboard the refugee ship.
The ship that will never dock.
El barco que nunca atraca.°

1981

POEMA PARA LOS CALIFORNIOS MUERTOS°

Once a refuge for Mexican Californios . . .
—PLAQUE OUTSIDE A RESTAURANT
IN LOS ALTOS, CALIFORNIA, 1974.

These older towns die
into stretches of freeway.
The high scaffolding cuts a clean cesarean
across belly valleys and fertile dust.
What a bastard child, this city

13. *El barco . . .* : (Spanish), translates the previous line.
poem title: (Spanish) "Poem for Dead Californians."

lost in the soft
llorando de las madres.°
Californios moan like husbands of the raped,
husbands de la tierra,
tierra la madre.°

I run my fingers
across this brass plaque.
Its cold stirs in me a memory
of silver buckles and spent bullets,
of embroidered shawls and dark rebozos.
Yo recuerdo los antepasados muertos.
Los recuerdo en la sangre,
la sangre fértil.°

What refuge did you find here,
ancient Californios?
Now at this restaurant nothing remains
but this old oak and an ill-placed plaque.
Is it true that you still live here
in the shadows of these white, high-class houses?
Soy la hija pobrecita
pero puedo maldecir estas fantasmas blancas.
Las fantasmas tuyas deben aquí quedarse,
solas las tuyas.°

In this place I see nothing but strangers.
On the shelves there are bitter antiques,
yanqui remnants
y estos no de los Californios.°
A blue jay shrieks
above the pungent odor of crushed
eucalyptus and the pure scent
of rage.

1981

---

7. *ilorando . . . :* (Spanish) "crying of mothers."

9–10. *husbands . . . :* (Spanish) "husbands of the earth, mother earth."

16–18. *Yo recuerdo . . . :* (Spanish) "I remember dead ancestors. I remember them in the blood, fertile blood."

25–28. *Soy la hija . . . :* (Spanish) "I am the poor daughter. Yet I can curse the white ghosts. Your ghosts, only your ghosts, must remain here."

32. *y estos no . . . :* (Spanish) "these not referring to the Californians."

STARFISH

They were lovely in the quartz and jasper sand
As if they had created terrariums with their bodies
On purpose; adding sprigs of seaweed, seashells,
White feathers, eel bones, miniature
Mussels, a fish jaw. Hundreds; no—
Thousands of baby stars. We touched them,
Surprised to find them soft, pliant, almost
Living in their attitudes. We would dry them, arrange them,
Form seascapes, geodesics . . . We gathered what we could
In the approaching darkness. Then we left hundreds of
Thousands of flawless five-fingered specimens sprawled
Along the beach as far as we could see, all massed
Together: little martyrs, soldiers, artless suicides
In lifelong liberation from the sea. So many
Splayed hands, the tide shoveled in.

1981

SANDRA CISNEROS (b. 1954)

Born in Chicago to working-class parents—her father was an upholsterer, her mother a factory worker—Cisneros spent her early years shuttling between the United States and her father's family home in Mexico City. After studying at the Iowa Writers' Workshop at the University of Iowa, she settled in Texas in a house on the San Antonio River, though she has also been a writer-in-residence at the University of Michigan and the University of California at Irvine. Her published work includes not only poetry but also experimental collections of fiction and sketches. *The House on Mango Street* (1983) and *Woman Hollering Creek and Other Stories* (1991) are her most famous works of fiction.

LITTLE CLOWN, MY HEART

Little clown, my heart,
Spangled again and lopsided,
Handstands and Peking pirouettes,
Backflips snapping open like
A carpenter's hinged ruler,

Little gimp-footed hurray,
Paper parasol of pleasures,
Fleshy undertongue of sorrows,
Sweet potato plant of my addictions,

Acapulco cliff-diver *corazón*,°
Fine as an obsidian dagger,
Alley-oop and here we go
Into the froth, my life,
Into the flames!

1994

10. *corazón:* (Spanish) "heart."

THYLIAS MOSS (b. 1954)

Born Thylias Rebecca Brasier into a working-class family in Cleveland, Ohio, Moss's mother was a maid and her father was a recapper for the Cardinal Tire Company. She enrolled at Syracuse University but left when she found the racial tension there unpleasant. She married John Moss in 1973, raised two sons, and then returned to school, earning degrees from Oberlin College in 1981 and the University of New Hampshire in 1983. Her professors encouraged her writing but they were also unprepared for its political anger. Nevertheless she published her first book in 1983 and since then has taught at Phillips Academy in Andover, Massachusetts, and now teaches at the University of Michigan. She has continued to write poems of great passion about her family experience and about American history, but she is equally at home writing about the intensity of religious conviction, about all forms of cultural mystification, and about the critical moments of human life. She is often almost theatrically inventive with both diction and sound in her work. In addition to her poetry, she has written a memoir, *Tale of a Sky-Blue Dress* (1998).

FULLNESS

One day your place in line will mean the
Eucharist has run out. All because you waited
your turn. Christ's body can be cut into only
so many pieces. One day Jesus will be eaten up.
The Last Supper won't be misnamed. One day the
father will place shavings of his own blessed fingers
on your tongue and you will get back in line for
more. You will not find yourself out of line again.
The bread will rise inside you. A loaf of tongue.
Pumpernickel liver. You will be the miracle.
You will feed yourself five thousand times.

1990

THERE WILL BE ANIMALS

There will be animals to teach us
what we can't teach ourselves.

There will be a baboon who is neither stupid nor clumsy
as he paints his mandrill face for the war being waged
against his jungle.

There will he egrets in a few thousand years
who will have evolved without plumes so we cannot take them.

There will be ewes giving and giving their wool
compensating for what we lack in humility.

There will be macaws with short arched bills
that stay short because they talk without telling lies.

Mackerel will continue to appear near Cape Hatteras each spring
and swim north into Canadian waters so there can be continuity.

There will be penguins keeping alive Hollywood's golden era.

The chaparral cock will continue to outdistance man
twisting and turning on a path unconcerned with shortcuts.

Coffin fly dun will leave the Shawsheen River
heading for the lights of Lawrence. What they see in 48 hours
makes them adults who will fast for the rest of their short lives,
mating once during the next hour and understanding everything
as they drop into a communal grave three feet thick with family
reaching the same conclusions.

The coast horned lizard still won't be found
without a bag of tricks; it will inflate and the first
of six million Jewfish will emerge from its mouth.
We will all be richer.

John Dory will replace John Doe
so the nameless among us will have Peter's thumbmark
on their cheek
and the coin the saint pulled from their mouths
in their pockets. Then once and for all
we will know it is no illusion:
The lion lying with the lamb, the grandmother
and Little Red Riding Hood
walking out of a wolf named Dachau.

1990

THE LYNCHING

They should have slept, would have
but had to fight the darkness, had
to build a fire and bathe a man in
flames. No

other soap's as good when
the dirt is the skin. Black since

birth, burnt by birth. His father
is not in heaven. No parent

of atrocity is in heaven. My father chokes
in the next room. It is night, darkness
has replaced air. We are white like
incandescence

yet lack light. The God in my father
does not glow. The only lamp
is the burning black man. Holy
burning, holy longing, remnants of

a genie after greed. My father
baptizes by fire same as
Jesus will. Becomes a holy ghost when
he dons his sheet, a clerical collar

out of control, Dundee Mills percale,
fifty percent cotton, dixie, confederate
and fifty percent polyester, man-made, manipulated,
unnatural, mulatto fiber, warp

of miscegenation.
After the bath, the man is hung as if
just his washed shirt, the parts
of him most capable of sin removed.

Charred, his flesh is bark, his body
a trunk. No sign of roots. I can't leave
him. This is limbo. This is the life after
death coming if God is an invention as were

slaves. So I spend the night, his thin moon-begot
shadow as mattress; something smouldering
keeps me warm. Patches of skin fall onto me
in places I didn't know needed mending.

1991

INTERPRETATION OF A POEM BY FROST

A young black girl stopped by the woods,
so young she knew only one man: Jim Crow
but she wasn't allowed to call him Mister.
The woods were his and she respected his boundaries

even in the absence of fence.
Of course she delighted in the filling up
of his woods, she so accustomed to emptiness,
to being taken at face value.
This face, her face eternally the brown
of declining autumn, watches snow inter the grass,
cling to bark making it seem indecisive
about race preference, a fast-to-melt idealism.
With the grass covered, black and white are the only options,
polarity is the only reality; corners aren't neutral
but are on edge.
She shakes off snow, defiance wasted
on the limited audience of horse.
The snow does not hypnotize her as it wants to,
as the blond sun does in making too many prefer daylight.
She has promises to keep,
the promise that she bear Jim no bastards,
the promise that she ride the horse only as long
as it is willing to accept riders,
the promise that she bear Jim no bastards,
the promise to her face that it not be mistaken as shadow,
and miles to go, more than the distance from Africa to Andover
more than the distance from black to white
before she sleeps with Jim.

1991

AMBITION

A boy says his father wants to be a Smurf°
and no one can top that; no one else there has
ambition that comes close to that. Only his father
wants to be a Smurf.

His mother holds her shock still; no teen marriage here,
there was long engagement and shacking up long
before the license; she knew what was necessary to know
about this man: His lack of criminal past, his dislike
of physical solutions, the cycles of his preferences
that she has matched with three wardrobes and wigs.
This, however, he kept from her, would share only with
a son, his deepest desire his sex with her won't betray

1. *Smurfs:* a Saturday morning American television cartoon show for children that ran from 1981 to 1990, chronicling the adventures of a group of little blue humanoids living peaceably in a forest; their enemy Gargamel sought unsuccessfully to capture them.

in an elfin blue boundary. With her he is in love;
with the Smurf, he is deeper in himself.

Any moment could bring loss of anything. She is prepared
for theft of his heart by, she'd like to think, another woman,
or even better, a vehicular finishing by bus, car, truck, plane,
Harley, yacht or Hummer.° A random act of God comforts.
Even fantasy can be robber.

Falling in love is not something done once then
the ability forsaken; part of what brought them together
was the time of morning, their vulnerability
when something so bright was starting, warming them
separately and together. So far, morning has arrived every day
and he could again be with a stranger when the sun
is at that identical angle that made him notice he wasn't alone.

Not that there need be hierarchy of loss, but the worst to her
is his new pride originating from his manhood, not from
the hermaphroditic entity that results from the influence
of marriage; a masculine, feminine merger that frightens
in its disrespect of boundaries on which order depends.
He is a man thoroughly, she notices, as he fingers
his Adam's apple; his face will not stay smooth, the beard invincible
even as it forfeits jet for a white haunting of masculinity he enjoys,
now praises wondering how he could love anything unlike this
and why he did not date the bearded lady he spent
all his quarters on; at least then he'd know
what the influence of beard is in a kiss.

It's more than that now; emptied of infatuation, left with
the aftermath of youth, it's beard he loves and testicle
and he wants the world to know of his epiphany, but still ruled
by fairness, first he tells his wife who's been hurt by impotence,
hurt by endometriosis, hurt by infertility, and the promises technology
can't make fast enough to help her, the cracking open of her own
genes,
their reorganization while she's under general anesthetic sleeping
a hundred years, waking alone too old for a life
hers only through science. It's beard he loves and testicle.

Who knows what logically follows Smurf
even knowing the logic of arriving at Smurf? Blue

18. *Harley:* a popular American motorcycle; Hummer: a large, four-wheel jeep first developed for the military.

as if offspring of a sky at last inspired as it has been inspiring.
Theirs is genealogy shared with Tinker Bell;° indeed,
they have never tasted meat and are considered delicacy
by the animated villain who has never tasted Smurf,
not even a cool blue lick.

Never mind her injury; look at the benefit for the child
she knows she'll keep. He has never felt more pride,
more connection to his father. No more doubting paternal love
now that the father wants his identity based on
something the son understands.

1998

CRYSTALS

In 1845 Dr. James Marion Sims° had seen it many times,
vesico-vaginal fistula, abnormal passageway
between bladder and vagina through which urine leaks
almost constantly if the fistula is large

as it tends to become after those pregnancies
not quite a year apart in Anarcha° and her slave
friends Lucy, Betsey. *If you can just fix this*
the girl said, probably pregnant again, her vulva inflamed,
her thighs caked with urinary salts; from the beginning
he saw his future in those crystals.

Society women sometimes had this too, a remaking of the vulva,
more color, pustules like decorations of which women
were already fond: beads, cultured pearls of pus, status.
Perhaps the design improves in its greater challenge to love
and fondle even in the dark except that there is pain,
inability to hold water.

---

51. *Tinker Bell:* the miniature winged sprite in the children's novel *Peter Pan* (1904) by Scottish writer Sir James Matthew Barrie (1860–1937). *Peter Pan* was later revived as a musical and a cartoon.

1. *Sims:* (1813–1883), American gynecologist who practiced medicine in Montgomery, Alabama, and gained attention through his investigations of vesicovaginal fistula (fistula, or abnormal channel, connecting the urinary bladder with the vagina) in the 1840s, during which he invented the Sims's speculum. Under slavery, he was able to conduct surgical experiments (without anesthesia) on black women's bodies in ways he could not have done with white patients. He later investigated sterility, attributing barrenness in marriage to women, and subjected them to painful therapies, such as the surgical incision of the neck of the uterus; he changed his views in a 1869 paper that revealed defects in sperm could be responsible for sterility.

6. *Anarcha:* Moss's note— "Although the implication is that Anarcha, her actual name, was or had been pregnant, there is not yet evidence of her pregnancies, suggesting that her fistula had some other cause, such as horseback riding. However, among those multiparas [women who have given birth twice or more], especially enslaved multiparas, who develop these fistulas, repeated childbirth is often the cause." Anarcha was subjected to a series of operations over a period of years; Sims successfully closed Anarcha's fistula in the thirtieth operation.

He tried to help Anarcha first, drawing on what
he was inventing: frontier ingenuity and gynecology,
and operated thirty times, using a pewter teaspoon
that he reshaped, bent and hammered for each surgery,
no sterilant but spit, while she watched; it became
his famous duck-bill speculum too large and sharp
to be respectful, yet it let him look.

Such excoriation, such stretching of the vaginal walls, tunnel
into room; such remembrance of Jericho, prophecy of Berlin
when his mind was to have been on her comfort and healing.

Through the vulva was the way most tried to access her
yet they did not come close. Using

a half-dollar he formed the wire suture that closed
Anarcha's fistula on the thirtieth, it bears repeating, thirtieth
attempt.

For the rest of her life she slept in the Sims position:
on her left side, right knee brought to her chest; she so long,
four years, on his table came to find it comfortable, came to find
no other way to lose herself, relieve her mind,
ignore Sims' rising glory, his bragging in the journals
that he had seen the fistula *as no man had ever seen it before.*
Now they all can.

Anarcha who still does not know anesthesia except
for her willed loss of awareness went on peeing as she'd
always done, just not so frequently and in reduced
volume, hardly enough for a tea cup, but whenever
necessary, the doctor poked, prodded, practiced

then, successful, went gloved and shaven to help ladies
on whom white cloths were draped; divinity
on the table to indulge his tastefulness.

It should be noted
that Anarcha's fistula closed well,
sealed in infection, scarred
thickly

as if his hand remained.

1998

PATRICIA SMITH (b. 1955)

Born and raised on the impoverished West Side of Chicago, Smith is a nationally known performance poet who has won a number of poetry slam contests. A former reporter for the *Chicago Sun-Times*, she was also a columnist for the *Boston Globe* for a number of years. She has also taught at Georgia Tech University and at Cave Canem. A nonfiction book, *Africans in America* (1998), coauthored with Charles Johnson, accompanies a PBS television documentary on slavery. *Blood Dazzler* (2008) is her book-length poem sequence on Hurricane Katrina. A number of her poetry performances, including a compelling reading of "Skinhead," are on YouTube.

BLONDE WHITE WOMEN

They choke cities like snowstorms.

On the morning train, I flip through my *Ebony*,
marveling at the bargain basement prices
for reams of straightened hair
and bleaches for the skin. Next to me,
skinny pink fingers rest upon a briefcase,
shiver a bit under my scrutiny.
Leaving the tunnel, we hurtle into hurting sun.
An icy brush paints the buildings
with shine, fat spirals of snow
become blankets, and Boston stops breathing.

It is my habit to count them. So I search
the damp, chilled length of the train car
and look for their candle flames of hair,
the circles of blood at their cheeks,
that curt dismissing glare
reserved for the common, the wrinkled, the black.

I remember striving for that breathlessness,
toddling my five-year-old black butt around
with a dull gray mophead covering my
nappy hair, wishing myself golden.
Pressing down hard with my
carnation pink crayola, I filled faces
in coloring books, rubbed the waxy stick
across the back of my hand until the skin broke.

When my mop hair became an annoyance
to my mother, who always seemed to be mopping,
I hid beneath my father's white shirt,
the sleeves hanging down on either side of my head,
the coolest white light pigtails.
I practiced kissing, because to be blonde and white
meant to be kissed, and my fat lips slimmed
around words like "delightful" and "darling."
I hurt myself with my own beauty.

When I was white, my name was Donna.
My teeth were perfect; I was always out of breath.

In first grade, my blonde teacher
hugged me to her because I was the first
in my class to read, and I thought the rush
would kill me. I wanted her to swallow
me, to be my mother, to be the first fire
moving in my breast. But when she pried
me away, her cool blue eyes shining with
righteousness and too much touch,
I saw how much she wanted to wash.

She was not my mother,
the singing Alabama woman
who shook me to sleep
and fed me from her fingers.
I could not have been blacker
than I was at that moment.
My name is Patricia Ann.

Even crayons fail me now—
I can find no color darker,
more beautiful, than I am.
This train car grows tense with me.
I pulse, steady my eyes,
shake the snow from my short black hair,
and suddenly I am surrounded by snarling madonnas

demanding that I explain
my treachery.

1992

SKINHEAD

They call me skinhead, and I got my own beauty.
It is knife-scrawled across my back in sore, jagged letters,
it's in the way my eyes snap away from the obvious.
I sit in my dim matchbox,
on the edge of a bed tousled with my ragged smell,
slide razors across my hair,
count how many ways
I can bring blood closer to the surface of my skin.
These are the duties of the righteous,
the ways of the anointed.

The face that moves in my mirror is huge and pockmarked,
scraped pink and brilliant, apple-cheeked,
I am filled with my own spit.
Two years ago, a machine that slices leather
sucked in my hand and held it,
whacking off three fingers at the root.
I didn't feel nothing till I looked down
and saw one of them on the floor
next to my boot heel,
and I ain't worked since then.

I sit here and watch niggers take over my TV set,
walking like kings up and down the sidewalks in my head,
walking like their fat black mamas *named* them freedom.
My shoulders tell me that ain't right.

So I move out into the sun
where my beauty makes them lower their heads,
or into the night
with a lead pipe up my sleeve,
a razor tucked in my boot.
I was born to make things right.

It's easy now to move my big body into shadows,
to move from a place where there was nothing
into the stark circle of a streetlight,
the pipe raised up high over my head.
It's a kick to watch their eyes get big,
round and gleaming like cartoon jungle boys,
right in that second when they know

the pipe's gonna come down, and I got this thing
I like to say, listen to this, I like to say
"Hey, nigger, Abe Lincoln's been dead a long time."

I get hard listening to their skin burst.
I was born to make things right.

Then this newspaper guy comes around,
seems I was a little sloppy kicking some fag's ass
and he opened his hole and screamed about it.
This reporter finds me curled up in my bed,
those TV flashes licking my face clean.
Same ol' shit.
Ain't got no job, the coloreds and spics got 'em all.
Why ain't I working? Look at my hand, asshole.
No, I ain't part of no organized group,
I'm just a white boy who loves his race,
fighting for a pure country.
Sometimes it's just me. Sometimes three. Sometimes 30.
AIDS will take care of the faggots,
then it's gon be white on black in the streets.
Then there'll be three million.
I tell him that.

So he writes it up
and I come off looking like some kind of freak,
like I'm Hitler himself. I ain't that lucky,
but I got my own beauty.
It is in my steel-toed boots,
in the hard corners of my shaved head.

I look in the mirror and hold up my mangled hand,
only the baby finger left, sticking straight up,
I know its the wrong goddamned finger,
but fuck you all anyway.
I'm riding the top rung of the perfect race,
my face scraped pink and brilliant.
I'm your baby, America, your boy,
drunk on my own spit, I am goddamned fuckin' beautiful.

And I was born

and raised

right here.

1992

from BLOOD DAZZLER°

from TANKAS

Never has there been
a wind like this. Its throaty
howl has memorized
my name. And it calls, and it
calls, and lamb to ax, I come.

Go, they said. Go. Go.
Get out before the rain comes,
before you can't run,
before the mud smells your skin
and begins its swirl, its hug.

2008

MAN ON THE TV SAY

Go. He say it simple, gray eyes straight on and watered,
he say it in that machine throat they got.
On the wall behind him, there's a moving picture
of the sky dripping something worse than rain.
Go, he say. Pick up y'all black asses and run.
Leave your house with its splinters and pocked roof,
leave the pork chops drifting in grease and onion,
leave the whining dog, your one good watch,
that purple church hat, the mirrors.
Go. Uh-huh. Like our bodies got wheels and gas,
like at the end of that running there's an open door
with dry and song inside. He act like we supposed
to wrap ourselves in picture frames, shadow boxes,
and bathroom rugs, then walk the freeway, racing
the water. *Get on out.* Can't he see that our bodies
are just our bodies, tied to what we know?
Go. So we'll go. Cause the man say it strong now,
mad like God pointing the way outta Paradise.
Even he got to know our favorite ritual is root,
and that none of us done ever known a horizon,
especially one that cools our dumb running,
whispering urge and constant: *This way. Over here.*

2008

° **volume title:** *Blood Dazzler* is a book-length poem sequence about Hurricane Katrina.

COMPANY'S COMING

Hell, I rode the back of the last one.
It was all they said it was, but I rode her good.
The key to making it through
is to strap yourself hard against a thing,
keep your mouth shut tight
lest all that wrong weather gets in.
She gon' slap the black offa you now,
don't get me wrong, but that big fuss
don't last but a hot minute.
Just lay yourself flat while ol' girl
points her chaos toward your upturned ass,
just hold onto maybe while she blows away
what you thought would hold you down.
Ain't no feeling like the one when it's all over
and you still here. So go on, peek through the blinds.
See a mad-ass woman with us in her eye?
She picks her teeth with prayers. Get ready to ride.

2008

VOODOO II: MONEY

If magick brings it, it will be tainted, damp, ill-hued,
the wrong patriot will grimace from its center,
denominations will mean nothing. Money that passes
through hands blackened with the powder of ill wish,
hands spiced with incantation oils,
won't ever spend well. It will appear green and viable
only for a second, a second just wide enough
to turn you into a certified fool—then, as you hold
it in front of you like a shield against weather,
you will know. It's too thin to hold tomorrow back.

2008

VOODOO V: ENEMY BE GONE

The storm left a wound seeping,
a boulevard yawning, some
memories fractured, a
kiss exploded, she left
no stone resting, a bone
army floating, rats sated,
she left the horizon sliced

and ornery, she left in a hurry,
in a huff, in all her glory,
she took with her a kingdom
of sax and dream books,
a hundred scattered chants,
some earth burned in her
name, and she took flight,
all pissed and raucous, like
a world-hipped woman
makin' room.

2008

from WHAT TO TWEAK

Stifle the stinking, shut down the cameras,
wave Dubya° down from the sky.
Subtract the babies, unarm the flailers,
Hose that wailing bitch down!
Draw up a blueprint, consider detention,
throw them some cash from a bag.
Tell them it's God, ply them with preachers,
padlock the rest of the map.
Hand them a voucher, fly in some Colonel,
twist the volume knob hard.
Turn down the TV, distract them with vision,
pull out your hammer and nail.
Sponge off their shoulders, suckle their children,
prop them upright for the lens.
Tolerate ranting, dazzle with card tricks,
pin flags on absent lapels.
Try not to breathe them, fan them with cardboard,
say that their houses will rise.
Play them some music, swear you hear engines,
drape their stooped bodies with beads.
Salute their resilience, tempt them with future.
surrender your shoes to the mud.
Promise them trailers, pass out complaint forms,
draft a law wearing their names.
Say help is coming, say help is coming,
then say that help's running late.
Shrink from their clutches, lie to their faces,
explain how the levies grew thin.
Mop up the vomit, cringe at their crudeness,

---

78. *Dubya:* George W. Bush (b. 1946) forty-third president of the United States, 2001–2009.

audition their daughters for rape.
Stomp on their sleeping, outrun the gangsters,
pass out American flags.

2008

BACK HOME

Everything crawls—the green-black walls
move slow like prayer. The floor rocks
with all that's left living—leggy
scuttering, vermin, lumpy rain.
Everything floats dizzy samba,
weaving obstacles and channels,
and sometimes rats ride. This is home.
This is home as funk, churning moss
dripping from its arms, arms open
wide to take in my damp body.
Everything crawls. The drooped ceiling
crawls toward the floor, the light hard-crawls
through soft splintered slats. And I crawl
through upturned rooms, humming gospel,
closing tired eyes against my home's
languid rhythms of rot, begging
my new history to hold still.

2008

MOTOWN CROWN°

The Temps, all swerve and pivot, conjured schemes
that had us skipping school, made us forget
how mamas schooled us hard against the threat
of five-part harmony and sharkskin seams.
We spent our schooldays balanced on the beams
of moon we wished upon, the needled jetblack
45s that spun and hadn't yet
become the dizzy spinning of our dreams.
Sugar Pie, Honey Bun, oh you
loved our nappy hair and rusty knees.

---

poem title: Motown, the record company, was founded by Berry Gordy, Jr. (b. 1929) in Detroit, Michigan, in 1959. Its crossover success helped integrate popular music. Relocated to Los Angeles in 1972, it remained an independent company until 1988. The individual Motown artists celebrated in the sonnet sequence include Marvin Gaye (1939–1984); Michael Jackson (1958–2009); Smokey Robinson (b. 1940); Diana Ross (b. 1944); Levi Stubbs (1936–2008); Mary Wells (1943–1992); and Stevie Wonder (b. 1950). The groups mentioned include The Deceptions, The Marvelettes, The Temptations, and The Supremes.

Marvin Gaye slowed down while we gave chase
and then he was our smokin' fine taboo.
We hungered for the anguished screech of *Please*
inside our chests—relentless, booming bass.

Inside our chests, relentless booming bass
softened to the turn of Smokey's key.
His languid, liquid, luscious, aching plea
for bodies we didn't have yet made a case
for lying to ourselves. He could erase
our bowlegs, raging pimples, we could see
his croon inside our clothes, his pedigree
of milky flawless skin. Oh, we'd replace
our daddies with his fine and lanky frame,
I did you wrong, my heart went out to play
he serenaded, filling up the space
that separated Smoke from certain flame.
We couldn't see the drug of him—OK,
silk where his throat should be. He growled such grace.

Silk where his throat should be, and growling grace,
Little Stevie made us wonder why
we even *needed* sight. His rhythm eye
could see us click our hips and swerve in place
whenever *he* cut loose. Ooh, we'd unlace
our Converse All-Stars. Yeah, we wondered why
we couldn't get down *without* our shoes, we'd try
and dance and keep up with his funky pace
of hiss and howl and hum, and then he'd slow
to twist our hearts until he heard them crack,
ignoring what was leaking from the seams.
The rockin' blind boy couldn't help but show
us light. We bellowed every soulful track
from open window, 'neath the door—pipe dreams.

From open windows, 'neath the doors, pipe dreams
taught us bone, bouffant and nicotine
and served up Lady D, the boisterous queen
of overdone, her body built from beams
of awkward light. Her bug-eyed brash extremes

dizzied normal girls. The evergreen
machine, so clean and mean, dabbed kerosene
behind our ears and said *Now burn.* Our screams
meant only that our hips would now be thin,
that we'd hear symphonies, wouldn't hurry love,
as Diana said, *Make sure it gleams*
no matter what it is. Her different spin,
a voice like sugar air, no inkling of
a soul beneath the vinyl. The Supremes.

That soul beneath the vinyl, the Supremes
knew nothing of it. They were breathy sighs
and fluid hips, soul music's booby prize.
But Mary Wells, so drained of self-esteem,
was a pudgy, barstool-ridin' buck-toothed dream
who none of us would dare to idolize
out loud. She had our mamas' grunt and thighs
and we preferred to just avoid THAT theme—
as well as war and God and gov'ment cheese
and bullets in the street and ghetto blight.
While Mary's "My Guy" blared, we didn't think race,
'cause there was all that romance, and the keys
that Motown held. Unlocked, we'd soon ignite.
We stockpiled extra sequins, just in case.

We stockpiled extra sequins, just in case
the Marvelettes decided that our grit
was way beyond Diana's, that we fit
inside their swirl, a much more naughty place.
Those girls came from the brick, we had to brace
ourselves against their heat, much too legit
to dress up as some other thing. We split
our blue jeans trying to match their pace.
And soon our breasts commenced to pop, we spoke
in deeper tones, and Berry Gordy looked
and licked his lips. Our only saving grace?
The luscious, liquid languid tone of Smoke,
the soundtrack while our A-cup bras unhooked.
Our sudden Negro hips required more space.

Our sudden Negro hips required more space,
but we pretended not to feel that spill
that changed the way we walked. And yes, we still
couldn't help but feel so strangely out of place
while Motown filled our eager hearts with lace
and Valentines. Romance was all uphill,
no push, no prod, no shiny magic pill
could lift us to that light. No breathing space
in all that time. We grew like vines to sun,
and then we burned. As mamas shook their heads
and mourned our Delta names, we didn't deem
to care. Religion—there was only one.
We took transistor preachers to our beds
and Smokey sang a lyric dripping cream.

While Smokey sang a lyric dripping cream,
Levi tried to woo us with his growl:
Can't help myself. Admitted with a scowl,
his bit of weakness was a soulful scheme—
and we kept screaming, front row, under gleam
of lights, beside the speakers' blasting vowels,
we rocked and screamed. Levi, on the prowl,
glowed black, a savior in the stagelight's beam.
But then the stagelight dimmed, and there we were
in bodies primed—for what we didn't know.
We sang off-key while skipping home alone.
Deceptions that you sing to tend to blur
and disappear in dance, why is that so?
Ask any colored girl and she will moan.

Ask any colored girl and she will moan
an answer with a downbeat and a sleek
five-part croon. She's dazzled, and she'll shriek
what she's been taught: She won't long be alone,
or crazed with wanting more. One day she'll own
that quiet heart that Motown taught to speak,
she'll know that being the same makes her unique.
She'll rest her butt on music's paper throne
until the bassline booms, until some old
Temptation leers and says *I'll take you home*
and heal you in the way the music vowed.

She's trapped within his clutch, his perfumed hold,
dancing to his conjured, crafted poem,
remembering how. Love had lied so loud.
Remembering how love had lied so loud,
we tangled in the rhythms that we chose.
Seduced by thump and sequins, heaven knows
we tried to live our looming lives unbowed,
but bending led to break. We were so proud
to mirror every lyric. Radios
spit beg and mend, and precious stereos
told us what we were and weren't allowed.
Our daddies sweat in factories while we
found other daddies under limelight's glow.
And then we begged those daddies to create
us. Like Stevie, help us blindly see
the rhythms, but instead, the crippling blow.
We whimpered while the downbeat dangled bait.

We whimpered while the downbeat dangled bait,
we leapt and swallowed all the music said
while Smokey laughed and Marvin idly read
our minds and slapped us hard and slapped us straight,
and even then, we listened for the great
announcement of the drum, for tune to spread,
a Marvelette to pick up on the thread.
But as we know by now, it's much too late
to reconsider love, or claw our way
through all the glow they tossed to slow our roll.
What we know now we should have always known.
When Smokey winked at us and then said *They*
don't love you like I do, he snagged our soul.
We wound up doing the slow drag, all alone.

They made us do the slow drag, all alone.
They made us kiss our mirrors, deal with heat,
our bodies sudden bumps. They danced deceit
and we did too, addicted to the drone
of revelation, all the notes they'd thrown
our way: *Oh, love will change your life. The sweet*
sweet fairy tale we spin will certainly beat
the real thing any day. Oh, yes we own

you now. We sang you pliable and clueless,
waiting, waiting, oh the dream you'll hug
one day, the boy who craves you right out loud
in front of everyone. But we told you,
we know we did, we preached it with a shrug—
less than perfect love was not allowed.

Less than perfect love was not allowed.
Temptations begged as if their every sway
depended on you coming home to stay.
Diana whispered air, aloof and proud
to be the perfect girl beneath a shroud
of glitter and a fright she held at bay.
And Michael Jackson, flailing in the fray
of daddy love, succumbed to every crowd.
What would we have done if not for them,
wooing us with roses carved of sound
and hiding muck we're born to navigate?
Little did we know that they'd condemn
us to live so tethered to the ground.
While every song they sang told us to wait.

Every song they sang told us to wait
and wait we did, our gangly heartbeats stunned
and holding place. Already so outgunned
we little girls obeyed. And now it's late,
and CDs spinning only help deflate
us. The songs all say, *Just look what you've done,*
you've wished through your whole life. And one by one
your stupid sisters boogie to their fate.
So now, at fifty plus, I turn around
and see the glitter drifting in my wake
and mingling with the dirt. My dingy dreams
are shoved high on the shelf. They're wrapped and bound
so I can't see and contemplate the ache.
The Temps, all swirl and pivot, conjured schemes.

The Temps, all swirl and pivot, conjured schemes
inside our chests, relentless booming bass

then silk where throats should be. Much growling grace
from open window, 'neath the door, pipe dreams—
that soul beneath the vinyl. The Supremes
used to stockpile extra sequins just in case
Diana's Negro hips required more space,
while Smokey penned a lyric dripping cream.
Ask any colored girl, and she will moan,
remembering how love had lied so loud.
I whimpered while the downbeat dangled bait
and taught myself to slow drag, all alone.
Less than perfect love was not allowed
and every song they sang told me to wait.

2009

MARILYN CHIN (b. 1955)

Born in Hong Kong and raised in Portland, Oregon, where her father was a restaurant owner, Marilyn (Mei Ling) Chin was educated at the University of Massachusetts and the University of Iowa's Writers' Workshop. She now teaches at San Diego State University. In addition to her own poems, she has done translations, edited *Writing from the World* (1985), and was featured on the 1995 television series *The Language of Life,* broadcast on educational television.

HOW I GOT THAT NAME

AN ESSAY ON ASSIMILATION

I am Marilyn Mei Ling Chin.
Oh, how I love the resoluteness
of that first person singular
followed by that stalwart indicative
of "be," without the uncertain i-n-g
of "becoming." Of course,
the name had been changed
somewhere between Angel Island° and the sea,
when my father the paperson
in the late 1950s
obsessed with a bombshell blonde
transliterated "Mei Ling" to "Marilyn."
And nobody dared question
his initial impulse—for we all know
lust drove men to greatness,
not goodness, not decency.
And there I was, a wayward pink baby,
named after some tragic white woman
swollen with gin and Nembutal.
My mother couldn't pronounce the "r."
She dubbed me "Numba one female offshoot"
for brevity: henceforth, she will live and die
in sublime ignorance, flanked
by loving children and the "kitchen deity."
While my father dithers,
a tomcat in Hong Kong trash—
a gambler, a petty thug,

---

8. *Angel Island:* detention site for Chinese immigrants in San Francisco Bay; see the introduction to the selection of Angel Island poetry.

who bought a chain of chopsuey joints
in Piss River, Oregon,
with bootlegged Gucci cash.°
Nobody dared question his integrity given
his nice, devout daughters
and his bright, industrious sons
as if filial piety were the standard
by which all earthly men were measured.

Oh, how trustworthy our daughters,
how thrifty our sons!
How we've managed to fool the experts
in education, statistics and demography—
We're not very creative but not adverse to rote-leaning.
Indeed, they can *use* us.
But the "Model Minority" is a tease.
We know you are watching now,
so we refuse to give you any!
Oh, bamboo shoots, bamboo shoots!
The further west we go, we'll hit east;
the deeper down we dig, we'll find China.
History has turned its stomach
on a black polluted beach—
where life doesn't hinge
on that red, red wheelbarrow,
but whether or not our new lover
in the final episode of "Santa Barbara"°
will lean over a scented candle
and call us a "bitch."
Oh God, where have we gone wrong?
We have no inner resources!

Then, one redolent spring morning
the Great Patriarch Chin
peered down from his kiosk in heaven
and saw that his descendants were ugly.
One had a squarish head and a nose without a bridge.
Another's profile—long and knobbed as a gourd.
A third, the sad, brutish one
may never, never marry.
And I, his least favorite—

30. *Gucci cash:* income from selling stolen or illegal imitation Gucci products.
53. *"Santa Barbara":* television soap opera set in the California coastal city.

"not quite boiled, not quite cooked,"
a plump pomfret simmering in my juices—
too listless to fight for my people's destiny.
"To kill without resistance is not slaughter"
says the proverb. So, I wait for imminent death.
The fact that this death is also metaphorical
is testament to my lethargy.

So here lies Marilyn Mei Ling Chin,
married once, twice to so-and-so, a Lee and a Wong,
granddaughter of Jack "the patriarch"
and the brooding Suilin Fong,
daughter of the virtuous Yuet Kuen Wong
and G. G. Chin the infamous,
sister of a dozen, cousin of a million,
survived by everybody and forgotten by all.
She was neither black nor white,
neither cherished nor vanquished,
just another squatter in her own bamboo grove
minding her poetry—
when one day heaven was unmerciful,
and a chasm opened where she stood.
Like the jowls of a mighty white whale,
or the jaws of a metaphysical Godzilla,
it swallowed her whole.
She did not flinch nor writhe,
nor fret about the afterlife,
but stayed! Solid as wood, happily
a little gnawed, tattered, mesmerized
by all that was lavished upon her
and all that was taken away!

1994

ALTAR

I tell her she has outlived her usefulness.
I point to the corner where dust gathers,
where light has never touched. But there she sits,
a thousand years, hands folded, in a tattered armchair,
with yesterday's news, "the Golden Mountain Edition."
The morning sun slants down the broken eaves,
shading half of her sallow face.

On the upper northwest corner (I'd consulted a geomancer),°
a deathtrap shines on the dying bougainvillea.
The carcass of a goatmoth hangs upsidedown,
hollowed out. The only evidence
of her seasonal life is a dash
of shimmery powder, a last cry.

She, who was attracted to that bare bulb,
who danced around that immigrant dream,
will find her end here, this corner,
this solemn altar.

1994

8. *geomancer:* one who practices divination, prophesying from the pattern made when a handful of earth is cast down or dots are drawn at random and connected with lines.

JANICE N. HARRINGTON (b. 1956)

Janice N. Harrington was born in Vernon, Alabama, and grew up there and in Lincoln, Nebraska. She is a poet, a children's book author, and a professional storyteller. A former librarian, she now teaches creative writing at the University of Illinois at Urbana–Champaign. The two poems here are reprinted from her book *Even the Hollow My Body Made Is Gone* (2007).

FALLING

With lengths of string and canted chairs, my father
struggles to raise the wide wings and bright belly,
every attempt unraveling, breaking, or crashing.
On crooked knee he tries again, but it never flies.
In the ancient story, another father watches
as his beloved plunges into the sea, leaving
only these signs: wax and twine and the quills of gulls.
But what father ever binds the cords tight enough?
Shy from that scalding sea! Shy from that searing
light! Aspire less and take the midmost course,
the one your father chose. Lift yourself on wings
he made for you, and when you fall into the devouring
sea whisper *Daddy, Daddy, oh,* but loud enough
for him to hear, loud enough to soften wax or sever

a gull's extended wing. In a backyard, in Vernon,
a colored man attempts to teach his daughter *flight*
and *boundlessness,* their shadows stretching
wingtip to wingtip, while between them
an airplane teeters on a cotton string but never
flies. And black Icarus plummets into a Tuskegee
airfield, a black bird from a clear sky,
a crow's field holler when you are the only one
to hear it. Dark Icarus riven against
red sand, black Icarus swinging, swinging
from a yella pine. The black feather that falls
upon your shoulder weighs more than grief.

No, the plane never flew. But we forgive
our fathers their broken flights: sometimes.
Aileron, airfoil, wing root, wingtip, we lift
ourselves through perilous moments unaware,

beneath pinions of mercy. How are wings
made? Wax, twine, and the quills of gulls?
And in the ancient story, a fisherman,
a plowman, and a tenant farmer from Sulligent
look up in amazement, seeing father and daughter

walking across the clouds. It is evening now,
and the heart has done its barrel-rolls
and loop-the-loops, and whatever we've written
on this pale page turns to vapor and rains
down into the sea. There is only this last act: rising,
full throttle into a breathless fall.

2007

IF SHE HAD LIVED

If she had lived, the goat-faced girl,

she would have seen her reflection in the waters
of this fishpond and held its white-fleeced lilies
beneath her whiskered chin. If she had lived,

she would have walked in moonlight, pulling eel
from lampblack waters, while owls told their old spook
story, *Who'll cook for you? Who'll cook for you?*

If she had lived, she would have stooped
beneath the day's hem, back bent and arched,
chopping cotton as the minutes fell like hoe blades,
their sweated strokes sounding *thuh, thuh, thuh.*

Living, she would have proved that a colored woman
lay once with the Goat God, that a colored woman
held Faunus° between her thighs and loved him.
Their fierce rut amidst yellow-eyed asters and red sand:

their kindled groins beside the nests of fire ants.
She lay beneath him and they loved, and they loved,
her flesh drinking the clabbered sperm.
This happened to a colored woman in Alabama,

and she gave birth to a goat-faced girl.
They say she had the breasts of a grown woman.

---

14. *Faunus:* Roman god of fertility.

They say she was covered in hair. They say,
she had a goat's face: this child deformed.

The mother said the baby was born
with the face of fear, that ripe with this child,
she had seen a goat unexpectedly
and it frightened her, a goat and this warning:

that a woman must be careful, vision gives
birth to itself. The baby died, perhaps
it was born too old, perhaps a goat heart
is not strong enough. The baby died

and the mother buried her beside the garden,
or was it the fishpond? No, the baby is here,
in the Negro cemetery, her little fingers curled
inward, grasping. Later, the mother will cradle

her arms against her chest, her breasts spilling
milk. She will walk into the darkness remembering
her child, the goat-faced girl. The hooves of tears
mark her cheek, but she will not wipe them.

She stands in the dark, a colored woman, crooning,
crooning, crooning, and a wind comes: gentle.
A wind blows across her skin, across her lips, across
the ends of her fingers, making music—the sound of pipes.

In Alabama, a colored woman bore a deformed baby.
No, a colored woman bore the child
of a goat. No, a colored woman is grieving.
Her goat-faced girl, her baby is dead—that is the song, sing it.

Say, a colored woman is grieving her baby girl, sing it.
But this all happened long ago, the child is dead.
The woman is dead. They are gone, girl, woman, goat,
only the song remains. Only ruminant memory

taking our lives in its tough mouth.

2007

SESSHU FOSTER (b. 1957)

Sesshu Foster grew up in City Terrace, California, and received an M.F.A. from the University of Iowa. He taught English for a number of years at a Boyle Heights, Los Angeles, junior high school and now teaches at Francisco Bravo Medical Magnet. His books include *City Terrace Field Manual* (1996) and *World Ball Notebook* (2008), from which these prose poems are taken. In addition to teaching and writing his own poetry, he has coedited a collection of multicultural urban poetry, *Invocation L.A.* (1989).

WE'RE CAFFEINATED BY RAIN INSIDE CONCRETE UNDERPASSES

We're caffeinated by rain inside concrete underpasses,
rolling along treetops, Chinese elms, palm trees,
California peppers. We pushed a lawn mower for white
people, we got down on our hands and knees in their
San Marino driveways. We told our youth to grab hard a
piece of paper swirling like tickets in a bonfire, fire-
crackers at Chinese New Year, toilet paper in a bowl.
We coiled long green hoses. We oiled mean little
engines that buzzed like an evil desire that could spit a
steel slice or sharp stone to take your eye out. We
gripped rusty clippers, clipped leafy hedges, ground
sharper edges. We hauled their sacks of leftover leisure
that rotted at the curbside. We slapped our hands with
gloves, slammed white doors of Econoline vans, showed
up at sunrise in the damp perfume of the downtown
flower market. With all the Japanese gardeners gone,
we're Mexican now. The ones given five minutes a
week or fifteen minutes a month. They wrote us a
check, we wiped our hands on our pants or they did not
shake them. Fertilizer under our fingernails grown large,
yellow and cracked as moons. Instead of us, they saw
azaleas, piracanthus, oleanders, juniper shrubs, marigolds.
They didn't want to see us, they like nature in rows and
flowering things, not another kind of face. Notions
rattled in us like spare bolts in a coffee can. Our days off
rode us hard, like a desert storm on mountains far away.
Try to make our children see more than this man with
green stains, cracked skin, red eyes. More than the back
bent over stacked tools and coiled hoses. Coffee breath.

On dry boulevards fading into smog, kids just like ours
smash our windows and loot our tools. Our kids today
want to grow up to get lucky. Okay, we tell them, have
it your way, and we light our children like candles.

1996

YOU'LL BE FUCKED UP

You'll be fucked up. They'll take your things away
when you're not looking, they'll take your shit and
discard part in the dumpster, they'll take you to San
Diego and put you on a plane, they'll make up some
itinerary of churches and parades, they'll show you
Hollywood, you'll get driven up and down Sunset
Boulevard, around Melrose clothes boutiques, novelty
stores, Thai and Italian restaurants, California cuisine,
maybe a glimpse of hundreds of miles of smooth sand
dunes along the Baja coastline, inaccessible even by
4-wheel drive, and bit by bit they'll take out your teeth
and eyes, your sexual parts and your hair, your original
shoes and sunglasses will be put away, they'll take you
to Santa Barbara and drive you by some house in the
hills, have you listen to canned conversation down to
Montecito Country Club, somebody will be out playing
golf and they'll leave you in the car, by then you'll
know how to wait, your shit good and gone, everything
removed from lockers and computer files, you can check
the glove compartment but you won't even be wearing
your own shoes or eyeglasses, ideals or nightmares,
you'll be fucked and nothing will be yours, that's when
they will begin to say yes, they will say yes, yes, they
will say yes and no, no and yes, they will take you
to where you can see the waves starting far out at sea,
coming in across the big patches of light on the ocean
and moving across the far distant point, they will do
the talking and you won't care at all.

1996

LOOK AND LOOK AGAIN, WILL HE GLANCE UP ALL OF A SUDDEN

Look and look again, will he glance up all of a sudden,
his eyes lit from below in a satanic grin, his hanging
face, his mestizo hair black and dusty? The pallid paint
job is a put off, it's a cover for his indigenous passion,
his transsexual nature beneath fingernail scratches of

white finish. He wears a triangle of roses, madera
blushing carnation luster. Look and look again, are the
long lines of his muscles from the famine of history/
our desperate glories, the spiritual confrontation of that
lanky belly with the material world, or is the cascade
of his ribs a genetic sign of his hereditary disposition to
higher things, the tension of breath ascending, leaping
off the hard couch of bones? His tree a platform for the
helicopter ride of consciousness? That fragile excruciated
chest exploding inside with chamber music of quena,
bombo, charango & guitarrón? Norteño shivers along
that accordion torso? Did the grease slide out of this
Semitic meat and enter splinters of Roman wood,
mummifying his serene mind? This architecture is based
on fact like a crime novel, spliced with metaphors for
the human condition, neat as question marks. But if
he was just to sigh, grit his teeth with the exasperation
of an actor who washed out for the part of Samson in
a '50's Hollywood loincloth epic, and raise his fat
brown eyes to these chaparral hills under a mean sky,
he'd know these stones weren't gonna roll for him, not
here, not simply for the trembling Buddhist gravity of
his baby eyelashes.

1996

I'M ALWAYS GRATEFUL NO ONE HEARS THIS TERRIBLE RACKET

I'm always grateful no one hears this terrible racket:
the factories inside. I pull into King Taco, Brooklyn
& Soto, the doors of my face rapidly opening and
closing, electric eye busted, insects crawling in and out
of my ears. Nobody at the bus stop notices the clatter:
that makes me feel safe. But a cop cruiser crosses the
Willie Herron mural kitty-corner at the farmacia. It's
obscured, defaced, graffitied. The freeway thrashes, a
snake fastened to my leg. Epileptic with grief, it gums
my boots. My vehicle breathing hot, arms around my
neck. I feel like I'm with friends, the inverted cones
that descend from space. Eating tacos of butterflies.
Something's not quite right. That's easy to say, but
how to fix it? McDonald's is busy, getting big phone
calls, lots of drama. The sky airlifts teenagers into spheres
of heaven. Will they get shot there, too? Something
is sweet, I'm following it closely. There's a line, heating

up the street. I'm following something like honey. I
think it drips from brown eyes.

1996

THE JAPANESE MAN WOULD NOT APPEAR RIDING A HORSE

The Japanese man would not appear riding a horse
above the telephone pole like the marlboro man the
japanese man strode above the endive kale and parsley
weeding the glendale truck garden his life was not
picturesque like a hiroshige° block print or a flight of
golden cranes across a kimono it was not a samurai flick
though his cotton clothing absorbed his sweat like the
pages of a book absorb the ink of meaning and desire
itself formed in his mind something long and cool as his
woman a piece of iced celery when he heard a shout in
english stood upright and saw the labor contractor
standing on the flatbed of the white man's truck waving
him over this morning what did it mean? after seeing the
billboard in town NO JAPS WANTED THIS IS A WHITE
NEIGHBORHOOD/ the old issei sat in the cluttered
living room in the boyle heights bungalow with his
cigarette in the tin ashtray cradled in the linen napkin
his wife always placed on the arm of the couch for him
and the marlboro commercial projected from the tv
into stale smoke as the old man lifted the cigarette in
his freckled knobby fingers and took a long drag.

1996

LIFE MAGAZINE, DECEMBER, 1941

Life Magazine, December, 1941: "How to Tell Japs from
the Chinese" "Angry Citizens Victimize Allies With
Emotional Outburst At Enemy"

War hysteria? The Jap and the Chinese are discernible
not merely from the instructive, easily interpreted
diagrams/photographs on this page—our helpful captions
denote distinctive bone structures and facial features—the
Jap and the Chinese also have distinguishing social
psychologies which will serve you well. When you slap
the Jap, his skin will blanche, but if you kick the yellow
Chinaman, he may cuss you in a heathen tongue. If you
burn down Chinatown/ hang Chinese in trees, their

5. *hiroshige:* Ando Hiroshige (1797–1858), Japanese painter celebrated for his woodblock prints of landscapes.

tongues will curl and get black. But the Jap tends no
separate villages, each individual fiend must be beaten and
stomped. Drive out to the shack of the field hand with
laundry fluttering by the irrigation ditch/ it's hard to tell
what imported stoop labor inhabits this margin. You have
to shoot in the air and scream anything you want/ each
word imbued with hatred. At *LIFE* we are here to direct
your hatred to its proper object/ If the man inside the
shack is Kenji Uchioka, he may shoot at you with his
rifle/ watch out for that guy. If you locate him on the
city streets in a crowd, *LIFE* hastens to note, we in no
way condone mob violence/ patriotism has its ways and
means! You may ferret out the Japanese children from
interloping Asiatics by clever tactics/ harassment and fear,
look for urine puddled beneath classroom desks; be
forewarned/ keep your eyes open for that Uchioka guy.
Bust him down with the FBI in front of his family,
especially his little girl/ if you want to take him quietly.
Leavenworth, for the duration.

1996

I TRY TO PEE BUT I CAN'T

I try to pee but I can't. Nothing comes out. Except
for a thin black line. In the immense white lavatory
of the night, porcelain urinals shine like the whites
of eyes. Watts° burns. In a chocolate box of childhoods.
Rays of sunlight swirl with dust particles, then are
folded away. A procession moves up Whittier, low-
riders feeling a lovesick wet spot for the deaths of
JFK/Robert Kennedy. I listen to it through the wall.
It's always summer as far inside as we've come, back
up against this wall. You're a war child. You tell me,
which war is it? When Watts burns, maybe they will
cut us a break. I would like to see a break. I know,
you want me to come out with you. I would like to
see you, too. But I can't right now. Saturday, Sunday . . .
Two Marias head over to Evergreen Cemetery.
Monday . . . There is still too much light.

1996

4. *Watts:* twenty-square-mile Los Angeles ghetto of 100,000 people; in 1965 substantial sections burned during the single largest racial disturbance in American history to that date.

GAME 83

The city inside of us like bits of glass that would work their way out of the skin in years to come, a spot of blood on his forehead then a tiny sliver of glass. She told me a bump appeared years after she broke her ankle—it was a steel pin, once inserted, had come loose, rolling under the skin—they surgically removed it. She's back to running—playing soccer on the ankle she showed me. Manazar Gamboa in a film about Chavez Ravine at a reading Karla Diaz hosted at Bergamot Station, and years later, I heard people recall Manazar. Talk about Chavez Ravine, prison junk and liver failure. Kids follow storm drains underground, underneath avenues, back alleys and back yards. Emerge in weird industrial oases of concrete embankments, ivy, willows, creosote bush. Rainy winters boys fall in the storm flood and are swept down concrete channels to their deaths. Shining streets. In the turning of the year, fresh cold air of winter rains, look out from the city inside us.

2008

LI-YOUNG LEE (b. 1957)

Li-Young Lee was born to Chinese parents in Jakarta, Indonesia. His maternal grandfather was Yuan Shikai, China's first Republican president, who sought to make himself emperor. Lee's father had been a personal physician to Mao Zedong before relocating his family to Indonesia. His father spent nineteen months in an Indonesian prison camp in Macau. In 1959 the Lee family fled Indonesia to escape anti-Chinese sentiment and after a five-year journey through Hong Kong and Japan, they settled in the United States. Li-Young Lee attended the University of Pittsburgh, the University of Arizona, and the State University of New York at Brockport. This narrative gives material weight to Lee's status as a poet of the East Asian diaspora. He has taught at a numbers of universities and now lives in Chicago.

"Persimmons," often taken as Lee's signature poem, registers the strain of growing up in multiple worlds through linguistic conflict. "Little Father" embodies a new phase of his career, in which personal reflection becomes at once more haunting and more lyrical.

PERSIMMONS

In sixth grade Mrs. Walker
slapped the back of my head
and made me stand in the corner
for not knowing the difference
between *persimmon* and *precision.*
How to choose

persimmons. This is precision.
Ripe ones are soft and brown-spotted.
Sniff the bottoms. The sweet one
will be fragrant. How to eat:
put the knife away, lay down newspaper.
Peel the skin tenderly, not to tear the meat.
Chew the skin, suck it,
and swallow. Now, eat
the meat of the fruit,
so sweet,
all of it, to the heart.

Donna undresses, her stomach is white.
In the yard, dewy and shivering
with crickets, we lie naked,
face-up, face-down.
I teach her Chinese.

Crickets: *chiu chiu*. Dew: I've forgotten.
Naked: I've forgotten.
Ni, wo: you and me.
I part her legs,
remember to tell her
she is beautiful as the moon.

Other words
that got me into trouble were
fight and *fright, wren* and *yarn.*
Fight was what I did when I was frightened,
fright was what I felt when I was fighting.

Wrens are small, plain birds,
yarn is what one knits with.
Wrens are soft as yarn.
My mother made birds out of yarn.
I loved to watch her tie the stuff;
a bird, a rabbit, a wee man.

Mrs. Walker brought a persimmon to class
and cut it up
so everyone could taste
a *Chinese apple.* Knowing
it wasn't ripe or sweet, I didn't eat
but watched the other faces.

My mother said every persimmon has a sun
inside, something golden, glowing,
warm as my face.

Once, in the cellar, I found two wrapped in newspaper,
forgotten and not yet ripe.
I took them and set both on my bedroom windowsill,
where each morning a cardinal
sang, *The sun, the sun.*

Finally understanding
he was going blind,
my father sat up all one night
waiting for a song, a ghost.
I gave him the persimmons,
swelled, heavy as sadness,
and sweet as love.

This year, in the muddy lighting
of my parents' cellar, I rummage, looking
for something I lost.
My father sits on the tired, wooden stairs,
black cane between his knees,
hand over hand, gripping the handle.

He's so happy that I've come home.
I ask how his eyes are, a stupid question.
All gone, he answers.

Under some blankets, I find a box.
Inside the box I find three scrolls.
I sit beside him and untie
three paintings by my father:
Hibiscus leaf and a white flower.
Two cats preening.
Two persimmons, so full they want to drop from the cloth.

He raises both hands to touch the cloth,
asks, *Which is this?*

This is persimmons, Father.

Oh, the feel of the wolftail on the silk,
the strength, the tense
precision in the wrist.
I painted them hundreds of times
eyes closed. These I painted blind.
Some things never leave a person:
scent of the hair of one you love,
the texture of persimmons,
in your palm, the ripe weight.

1986

LITTLE FATHER

I buried my father
in the sky.
Since then, the birds
clean and comb him every morning
and pull the blanket up to his chin
every night.

I buried my father underground.
Since then, my ladders
only climb down,
and all the earth has become a house
whose rooms are the hours, whose doors
stand open at evening, receiving
guest after guest.
Sometimes I see past them
to the tables spread for a wedding feast.

I buried my father in my heart.
Now he grows in me, my strange son,
my little root who won't drink milk,
little pale foot sunk in unheard-of night,
little clock spring newly wet
in the fire, little grape, parent to the future
wine, a son the fruit of his own son,
little father I ransom with my life.

2001

MARTÍN ESPADA (b. 1957)

Born in Brooklyn, New York, of a Puerto Rican father and a Jewish mother—his father was a photographer who illustrated his first book—Espada now teaches at the University of Massachusetts, but his earlier experience is much wider. He was a night clerk in a transient hotel, a journalist in Nicaragua, a welfare rights paralegal, and later a tenant lawyer in Boston. In addition to writing his own poetry, he has edited collections of political poetry and of works by contemporary Latino poets. His political poetry is notable for making its points with great wit and bravado. In its capacity to use humor to raise consciousness, it recalls McGrath, but Espada's language is more direct.

BULLY

In the school auditorium,
the Theodore Roosevelt° statue
is nostalgic
for the Spanish-American war,
each fist lonely for a saber
or the reins of anguish-eyed horses,
or a podium to clatter with speeches
glorying in the malaria of conquest.

But now the Roosevelt school
is pronounced Hernández.
Puerto Rico has invaded Roosevelt
with its army of Spanish-singing children
in the hallways,
brown children devouring
the stockpiles of the cafeteria,
children painting Taíno ancestors
who leap naked across murals.

Roosevelt is surrounded
by all the faces
he ever shoved in eugenic spite
and cursed as mongrels, skin of one race,
hair and cheekbones of another.

---

2. *Roosevelt:* (1858–1919), twenty-sixth president of the United States (1901–1909). Roosevelt became famous when he organized a volunteer cavalry division known as the Rough Riders that served in Cuba at the outbreak of the Spanish-American War (1898). As president, his policy was aggressive and interventionist toward Latin America, as when he intervened in a Panamanian civil war in 1903.

Once Marines tramped
from the newsreel of his imagination;
now children plot to spray graffiti
in parrot-brilliant colors
across the Victorian mustache
and monocle.

1990

REVOLUTIONARY SPANISH LESSON

Whenever my name
is mispronounced,
I want to buy a toy pistol,
put on dark sunglasses,
push my beret to an angle,
comb my beard to a point,
hijack a busload
of Republican tourists
from Wisconsin,
force them to chant
anti-American slogans
in Spanish,
and wait
for the bilingual SWAT team
to helicopter overhead,
begging me
to be reasonable

1990

NIGGERLIPS

Niggerlips was the high school name
for me.
So called by Douglas
the car mechanic, with green tattoos
on each forearm,
and the choir of round pink faces
that grinned deliciously
from the back row of classrooms,
droned over by teachers
checking attendance too slowly.

Douglas would brag
about cruising his car
near sidewalks of black children
to point an unloaded gun,

to scare niggers
like crows off a tree,
he'd say.

My great-grandfather Luis
was un negrito too,
a shoemaker in the coffee hills
of Puerto Rico, 1900.
The family called him a secret
and kept no photograph.
My father remembers
the childhood white powder
that failed to bleach
his stubborn copper skin,
and the family says
he is still a fly in milk.

So Niggerlips has the mouth
of his great-grandfather,
the song he must have sung
as he pounded the leather and nails,
the heat that courses through copper,
the stubbornness of a fly in milk,
and all you have, Douglas,
is that unloaded gun.

1990

THE NEW BATHROOM POLICY AT ENGLISH HIGH SCHOOL

The boys chatter Spanish
in the bathroom
while the principal
listens from his stall

The only word he recognizes
is his own name
and this constipates him

So he decides
to ban Spanish
in the bathrooms

Now he can relax

1990

FEDERICO'S GHOST

The story is
that whole families of fruitpickers
still crept between the furrows
of the field at dusk,
when for reasons of whiskey or whatever
the cropduster plane sprayed anyway,
floating a pesticide drizzle
over the pickers
who thrashed like dark birds
in a glistening white net,
except for Federico,
a skinny boy who stood apart
in his own green row,
and, knowing the pilot
would not understand in Spanish
that he was the son of a whore,
instead jerked his arm
and thrust an obscene finger.

The pilot understood.
He circled the plane and sprayed again,
watching a fine gauze of poison
drift over the brown bodies
that cowered and scurried on the ground,
and aiming for Federico,
leaving the skin beneath his shirt
wet and blistered,
but still pumping his finger at the sky.

After Federico died,
rumors at the labor camp
told of tomatoes picked and smashed at night,
growers muttering of vandal children
or communists in camp,
first threatening to call Immigration,
then promising every Sunday off
if only the smashing of tomatoes would stop.

Still tomatoes were picked and squashed
in the dark,
and the old women in camp
said it was Federico,
laboring after sundown

to cool the burns on his arms,
flinging tomatoes
at the cropduster
that hummed like a mosquito
lost in his ear,
and kept his soul awake.

1990

THE SAINT VINCENT DE PAUL FOOD PANTRY STOMP

Waiting for the carton of food
given with Christian suspicion
even to agency-certified charity cases
like me,
thin and brittle
as uncooked linguini,
anticipating the factory-damaged cans
of tomato soup, beets, three-bean salad
in a welfare cornucopia,
I spotted a squashed dollar bill
on the floor, and with
a Saint Vincent de Paul food pantry stomp
pinned it under my sneaker,
tied my laces meticulously,
and stuffed the bill in my sock
like a smuggler of diamonds,
all beneath the plaster statue wingspan
of Saint Vinnie,
who was unaware
of the dance
named in his honor
by a maraca player
in the salsa band
of the unemployed.

1990

FIDEL IN OHIO°

The bus driver tore my ticket
and gestured at the tabloid
spread across the steering wheel.

---

poem title: Fidel Castro (b. 1926) Cuban revolutionary and political leader, president of Cuba since 1959, a survivor despite U.S. attempts to overthrow his government. The poem playfully takes Castro as a symbol of widespread U.S. ignorance about Latin America.

The headline:
FIDEL CASTRO DEAD
REPLACED BY IDENTICAL DOUBLE
Below, two photographs of Fidel,
one with cigar, one without.

"The resemblance is amazing,"
the driver said,
and I agreed.

1993

IMAGINE THE ANGELS OF BREAD

This is the year that squatters evict landlords,
gazing like admirals from the rail
of the roofdeck
or levitating hands in praise
of steam in the shower;
this is the year
that shawled refugees deport judges'
who stare at the floor
and their swollen feet
as files are stamped
with their destination;
this the year that police revolvers,
stove-hot, blister the fingers
of raging cops,
and nightsticks splinter
in their palms;
this is the year
that darkskinned men
lynched a century ago
return to sip coffee quietly
with the apologizing descendants
of their executioners.

This is the year that those
who swim the border's undertow
and shiver in boxcars
are greeted with trumpets and drums
at the first railroad crossing
on the other side;
this is the year that the hands
pulling tomatoes from the vine
uproot the deed to the earth that sprouts the vine,

the hands canning tomatoes
are named in the will
that owns the bedlam of the cannery;
this is the year that the eyes
stinging from the poison that purifies toilets
awaken at last to the sight
of a rooster-loud hillside,
pilgrimage of immigrant birth;
this is the year that cockroaches
become extinct, that no doctor
finds a roach embedded
in the ear of an infant;
this is the year that the food stamps
of adolescent mothers
are auctioned like gold doubloons,
and no coin is given to buy machetes
for the next bouquet of severed heads
in coffee plantation country.

If the abolition of slave-manacles
began as a vision of hands without manacles,
then this is the year;
if the shutdown of extermination camps
began as imagination of a land
without barbed wire or the crematorium,
then this is the year;
if every rebellion begins with the idea
that conquerors on horseback
are not many-legged gods, that they too drown
if plunged in the river,
then this is the year.

So may every humiliated mouth,
teeth like desecrated headstones,
fill with the angels of bread.

1996

BLUES FOR THE SOLDIERS WHO TOLD YOU

I'm like a country who can't remember the last war.
—DOUG ANDERSON

They told you that the enemy and the liberated throng
swaddle themselves in the same robes and rags,
wear the same masks with eyes that follow you,

pray in the same bewildering tongue, until your rifle
trembles to rake the faces at every checkpoint.
They told you about the corpse of a boy or girl
rolled at your feet, hair gray with the powder
of rubble and bombardment, flies a whirlpool blackening both eyes,
said you'll learn the words for apology too late to join
the ceremony, as flies become the chorus of your nightmares.
They told you about the double amputee from your town,
legs lopped off by the blast, his basketball friend
bumping home in a flag-draped coffin
the cameras will not film anymore,
about veterans who drench themselves in liquor
like monks pouring gasoline on their heads.

They told you in poems and stories
you did not read, or stopped reading
as your cheeks scorched with inexplicable fever,
and because they spoke with a clarity that burned your face,
because they saw with the vision of a telescope
revolving around the earth, they spent years wandering
through jails and bars, exiled to roads after midnight
where gas stations snap their lights off one by one,
seers unseen at the coffee shop waiting for bacon and eggs,
calling at 3 AM to say *I can't stop writing and you have to hear this.*
You will not hear this, even after the war is over
and the troops drown in a monsoon of desert flowers
tossed by the crowd, blooming in their mouths
to stop their tongues with the sweetness of it.

2006

THE TROUBLE BALL

for my father, Frank Espada

In 1941, my father saw his first big league ballgame at Ebbets Field
in Brooklyn: the Dodgers and the Cardinals. My father took his father's hand.
When the umpires lumbered on the field, the band in the stands
with a bass drum and trombone struck up a chorus of *Three Blind Mice.*
The peanut vendor shook a cowbell and hollered. The home team
raced across the diamond, and thirty thousand people shouted
all at once, as if an army of liberation rolled down Bedford Avenue.
My father shouted, too. He wanted to see The Trouble Ball.

On my father's island, there were hurricanes and tuberculosis, dissidents in jail
and baseball. The loudspeakers boomed: *Satchel Paige pitching for the Brujos*
of Guayama. From the Negro Leagues he brought the gifts of Baltasar the King;

from a bench on the plaza he told the secrets of a thousand pitches: The Trouble Ball,
The Triple Curve, The Bat Dodger, The Midnight Creeper, The Slow Gin Fizz,
The Thoughtful Stuff. Pancho Coímbre hit rainmakers for the Leones of Ponce;
Satchel sat the outfielders in the grass to play poker, windmilled three pitches
to the plate, and Pancho spun around three times. He couldn't hit The Trouble Ball.

At Ebbets Field, the first pitch echoed in the mitt of Mickey Owen,
the catcher for the Dodgers who never let the ball escape his glove.
A boy off the boat, my father shelled peanuts, waiting for Satchel Paige
to steer his gold Cadillac from the bullpen to the mound, just as he would
navigate the streets of Guayama. Yet Satchel never tipped his cap that day.
¿Dónde están los negros? asked the boy. *Where are the Negro players?*
No los dejan, his father softly said. *They don't let them play here.*
Mickey Owen would never have to dive for The Trouble Ball.

It was then that the only brown boy at Ebbets Field felt himself
levitate above the grandstand and the diamond, another banner
at the ballgame. From up high he could see that everyone was white,
and their whiteness was impossible, like snow in Puerto Rico,
and just as silent, so he could not hear the cowbell, or the trombone,
or the Dodger fans howling with glee at the bases-loaded double.
He understood why his father whispered in Spanish: everybody
in the stands might overhear the secret of The Trouble Ball.

At Ebbets Field in 1941, the Dodgers met the Yankees in the World Series.
Mickey Owen dropped the third strike with two outs in the ninth inning
of Game Four, flailing like a lobster in the grip of a laughing fisherman,
and the Yankees stamped their spikes across the plate to win. Brooklyn,
the borough of churches, prayed for his fumbling soul. This was the reason
statues of the Virgin leaked tears and the fathers of Brooklyn drank,
not the banishment of Satchel Paige to doubleheaders in Bismarck,
North Dakota. There were no rosaries or boilermakers for The Trouble Ball.

My father would return to baseball on 108th Street. He pitched for the Crusaders,
kicking high like Satchel, riding the team bus painted with four-leaf clovers, seasick
all the way to Hackensack or the Brooklyn Parade Grounds. One day he jammed
his wrist sliding into second, threw three more innings anyway, and never pitched again.
He would return to Ebbets Field to court my mother. The same year they were married
a waiter refused to serve them, a mixed couple sitting all night in the corner,
till my father hoisted him by his lapels and the waiter's feet dangled in the air,
a puppet and his furious puppeteer. My father was familiar with The Trouble Ball.

I was born in Brooklyn in 1957, when the Dodgers packed their duffle bags
and left the city. A wrecking ball swung an uppercut into the face

of Ebbets Field. I heard the stories: how my mother, lost in the circles
and diamonds of her scorecard, never saw Jackie Robinson accelerate
down the line to steal home. I wore my father's glove until the day
I laid it down to lap the water from the fountain in the park. By the time
I raised my head, it was gone like Ebbets Field. I walked slowly home.
I had to tell my father I would never learn to catch The Trouble Ball.

There was a sign below the scoreboard at Ebbets Field: *Abe Stark, Brooklyn's*
Leading Clothier. Hit Sign, Win Suit. Some people see that sign in dreams.
They speak of ballparks as cathedrals, frame the pennants from the game
where it began, Dodger blue and Cardinal red, and gaze upon the wall.
My father, who remembers everything, remembers nothing of that dazzling day
but this: *¿Dónde están los negros? No los dejan.* His hair is white, and still
the words are there, like the ghostly imprint of stitches on the forehead
from a pitch that got away. It is forever 1941. It was The Trouble Ball.

2011

HARD-HANDED MEN OF ATHENS

Theseus: What are they that do play it?
Philostrate: Hard-handed men, that work in Athens here,
Which never labour'd in their minds till now.
—A Midsummer Night's Dream,° Act V, Scene I

We are the hard-handed men of Athens, the rude Mechanicals:
the tailor, the weaver, the tinker, the bellows-mender.
Tonight we are actors in the forest, off the grid, surrounded
in the dark by fairies and spirits, snakes and coyotes.
Carnivorous vegans live in these woods. They leave the drum circle
to nibble at the sliced ham I smuggle in the folds of my costume.

I am three hundred pounds. The director of the company
saw me and said: "You are the Wall." Two weeks ago I fell
off a wall, stepping into the darkness like a cartoon character
walking on air, waving *bye-bye.* I belly-flopped in a puddle of mud.
An elderly bystander, as if on cue, spoke her only line: "Are you OK?"
I am not OK. I have a fractured elbow. I wear a sling under my Wall costume,
the Styrofoam bricks and plastic vines, the wooden beam across my shoulders.
I cannot remember my lines. I hide the script in my sling with the ham.

Epigraph: The plot of Shakespeare's comedy *A Midsummer Night's Dream* centers around the marriage of Theseus (Duke of Athens) and Hippolyta (Queen of the Amazons). The cast includes four Athenian lovers and six amateur actors who are manipulated by fairies who live in the forest where much of the play is set. Lysander is one of the young Athenians. Cobweb and Mustardseed are among the fairies.

The play begins. No one can find Lysander.° He is in the bathroom
with dysentery. Theseus improvises dialogue in iambic pentameter.
His voice echoes and scares the coyotes in the hills. They howl
back at him. A snake writes his name in the dirt by my feet.
I tell no one. I don't want the fairies to panic. Cobweb and Mustardseed
might run into the Tiki torches, and then their fairy wings would explode,
and the nearest hospital is forty miles away. The Tiki torches
are the only source of light off the grid. It's Shakespeare in the Dark.
The woman playing Peter Quince is mean to small children.
When Bottom turns into a donkey and the Mechanicals flee,
I stand behind her and let her bounce off my chest. She falls down.
I want her to fall down. I ask: "Are you OK?" She is not OK. Fairy Queen
Titania's bed sways in the trees, threatening to topple and kill us all.

At the wedding of Theseus, Duke of Athens, we play Pyramus and Thisbe.
The aristocrats laugh at us, real actors on loan from the highbrow
Shakespearean company in the valley, and we snarl back at them.
I am the Wall. I am inspired. I lift Pyramus and Thisbe into the air
and slam them together for their kiss. The beam across my shoulders
cracks. The crack alarms the carnivorous vegans on picnic blankets
watching the show. Some think the crack is my leg breaking. Some think
the crack is a gunshot. Suddenly it's Ford's Theatre and I'm Lincoln.
Or maybe I'm John Wilkes Booth. The jagged beam presses into my neck,
against the artery in my neck, like the fangs of a vampire hungry for ham.
One stumble and *A Midsummer Night's Dream* ends in a bloodbath.

I bellow my last line: "Thus Wall away doth go." I do a soft-shoe offstage.
Five people pull the Wall costume over my head. Somebody asks: "Are you OK?"
I am not OK. Then I see my son onstage. He is twelve. He is Moonshine.
He cradles a half-blind Chihuahua and says, "This dog, my dog."
He lifts his lantern high, and his lantern is the moon. Even the sneering
Hippolyta, Queen of the Amazons, must admit: "Well shone, Moon."
This moon shines like an uncirculated Kennedy half-dollar from the days
when Kennedy° was a martyred saint. The coyotes do not howl.
The crickets fall silent. Even the fairies cease their gossip and giggling.
We are the hard-handed men of Athens. This dog is our dog.

2013

---

15. *Lysander:*
° *Kennedy:* John F. Kennedy (1917–1963), thirty-fifth president of the United States.

THE RIGHT FOOT OF DON JUAN DE OÑATE Y SALAZAR°

On the road to Taos, in the town of Alcalde, the bronze statue
of Juan de Oñate, the conquistador, kept vigil from his horse.
Late one night a chainsaw sliced off his right foot, stuttering
through the ball of his ankle, as Oñate's spirit scratched
and howled like a dog trapped within the bronze body.

Four centuries ago, after his cannon fire burst to burn hundreds
of bodies and blacken the adobe walls of the Acoma Pueblo,
Oñate wheeled on his startled horse and spoke the decree:
all Acoma males above the age of twenty-five would be punished
by amputation of the right foot. Spanish knives sawed through ankles;
Spanish hands tossed feet into piles like fish at the marketplace.
There was prayer and wailing in a language Oñate did not speak.

Now, at the airport in El Paso, across the river from Juárez,
another bronze statue of Oñate rises on a horse frozen in fury.
The city fathers smash champagne bottles across the horse's legs
to christen the statue, and Oñate's spirit remembers the chainsaw
carving through the ball of his ankle. The Acoma Pueblo still stands.
Thousands of brown feet walk across the border, the desert
of Chihuahua, the shallow places of the Río Grande, the bridges
from Juárez to El Paso. Oñate keeps watch, high on horseback
above the Río Grande, the law of the conquistador rolled
in his hand, helpless as a man with an amputated foot,
spirit scratching and howling like a dog within the bronze body.

2013

---

poem title: Don Oñate y Salazar (1550–1626) was a Spanish conquistador and explorer. He founded the colonial province of Santa Fé de Nuevo México and became its first governor.

In 1595 King Philip II ordered him to colonize the northern frontier of New Spain. His supposed objective was to spread Roman Catholicism and establish new missions. He began the expedition in 1598, fording the Rio Grande, or Río del Norte, at the present-day El Paso in late April. That month he claimed all of New Mexico beyond the river for Spain. In October 1598 a skirmish erupted when Oñate's occupying Spanish military demanded supplies from the Acoma tribe—supplies the Acoma needed if they were to survive the winter. The Acoma resisted and twelve Spaniards were killed, including Don Juan Oñate's nephew. A war began and in January 1599, Oñate retaliated for his nephew's death. His soldiers killed 800 villagers, including men, women, and children. They enslaved the remaining 500, and by Don Juan's decree, they amputated the right foot of every Acoma man over the age of twenty-five. Women were forced into slavery.

In 1998 an American Indian commando group stealthily approached a bronze statue of the first conquistador, Don Juan de Oñate, at the Oñate Monument and Visitors Center a few miles north of Española, New Mexico. With an electric saw, the group slowly severed his right foot—boot, stirrup, star-shaped spur, and all. Estevan Arrellano, the Center's director, supervised the attachment of a new foot to the twelve-foot-tall statue. He remarked: "Give me a break—it was 400 years ago. It's OK to hold a grudge, but for 400 years?" The group that removed the foot also issued a statement: "We took the liberty of removing Oñate's right foot on behalf of our brothers and sisters of Acoma Pueblo. We see no glory in celebrating Oñate's fourth centennial, and we do not want our faces rubbed in it."

ATSURO RILEY (b. 1960)

Atsuro Riley grew up in South Carolina and now lives in California. In *Romey's Order,* his percussive wordplay enables him to create a Faulknerean picture of rural southern life and culture that draws on rhetorical resources from Gerald Manley Hopkins to Basil Bunting. His poem "Chord" has "Daddy rut-graving gravel driving off," "Mama mash-sucking sour loquats in the shed," and "Sylvia supper-calling her fish-camp fish with a bell." The poems that follow are all from *Romey's Order* (2010).

PICTURE

This is the house (and jungle-strangled yard) I come from and carry.

The air out here is supper-singed (and bruise-tingeing) and close. From where I'm hid (a perfect Y-crotch perch of medicine-smelling sweet-gum), I can belly-worry this (welted) branch and watch for swells (and coming squalls) along our elbow-curve of river, or I can hunker-turn and brace my trunk and limbs—and face my home.

Our roof is crimp-ribbed (and buckling) tin, and tar.

Our (in-warped) wooden porch-door is kick-scarred and splintering. The hinges of it rust-cry and -rasp in time with every Tailspin-wind, and jamb-slap (and after-slap), and shudder.

Our steps are slabs of cinder-crush and -temper, tamped and cooled.

See that funnel-blur of color in the red-gold glass?—Mama, mainly: boiling jelly. She's the apron-yellow (rickracked) plaid in there, and stove-coil coral; the quick silver blade-flash, plus the (magma-brimming) ladle-splash; that's her behind the bramble-berry purple, sieved and stored.

Out here, crickets are cricking their legs. Turtlets are cringing in their bunker-shells and burrows. Once-bedded nightcrawling worms are nerving up through beanvine-roots (and moonvines), —and dew-shining now, and cursive:

Mama will pressure-cook and scald and pan-scorch and frizzle.
Daddy will river-drift down to the (falling-down) dock.
I myself will monkey-shinny so high no bark-burns (or tree-rats, or tides)
or lava-spit can reach me.
I will hunt for after-scraps (and -sparks) and eat them all.

ROSES

The house with the nick- and snigger-name *Snort and Grunt.*
Shunned trailer-house, (pocked) scorn-brunt. Side-indented,
thorn-bined, boondocked in a hollow.

In a green-holler clamber-mire of itch-moss and bramble.
Tremblescent ditch-jellies, globberous spawn-floss. Drupes of
(dapple-clinkling) bottle-glass in trees.

Strangs them old oaks of his with NEHI *and liquor-pints. Magnesia!*
Yard-splayed magnolia-blooms, carved of tractor-tire. Milk-
painted (fangle-plaited) barbwire-scapes and -vines.

And -fronds. A palm-shape gold with birds at the end of the yard.
Elaborated branches, branching. What is fixing to be a rose-bush
caning and twining. Is leaves.

SKILLET

Was mine-drawn,
Was pig-iron;
—Is a cast-heft
Fact.

•

Chokedamp's in it,
Born blackdamp.
Blood-iron
Ore-stope, lode-lamps,
Turnturbulating crubble-corf and -barrows.
Trace-tastes of (blast-furnace) harrow-smelt and pour.
Holds the heat hard. *Rememories flavors: no warshing.*
Carks and plaques itself in layers, like a pearl.

BELL

The heard-tell *how her baby'd burned* downrivering and rippling.
Rill and wave of chicken/prayer/purlow murmuring back.
Brackwater cove-woods by her marsh-yard oak-creaking and -crying.
Mourn-cranes and eave-crow and crape-blinded windows keening black.
Raining; wrack.
The grieve-mother *Malindy Jean* porch-planking brunt and planging.
Breasting river (crossing-over) songs with cast-iron inside 'em.
The live heft-fact scorch-skillet willow-strung low and hanging.
Her heaving shovel-hafts and oars to make it ring.

2010

CLAUDIA RANKINE (b. 1963)

Claudia Rankine was born in Kingston, Jamaica, and raised in Jamaica and New York City. She was educated at Williams College and Columbia University. She has taught at Case Western Reserve University, Barnard College, University of Georgia, and in the writing program at the University of Houston. She now teaches at Pomona College. She is a poet, editor, playwright, and multimedia artist. Politically astute and invariably ironic about contemporary American life, she tracks its effects on language, institutions, and cultural understanding. She is also regularly concerned with the way the media creates and limits the character of individual consciousness. As a black woman, she frequently asks us to think about the status of race in America. The poems that follow are all from *Don't Let Me Be Lonely* (2004).

from DON'T LET ME BE LONELY: AN AMERICAN LYRIC

Or one begins asking oneself that same question differently. Am I dead? Though this question at no time explicitly translates into Should I be dead, eventually the suicide hotline is called. You are, as usual, watching television, the eight-o'clock movie, when a number flashes on the screen: 1-800-SUICIDE. You dial the number. Do you feel like killing yourself? the man on the other end of the receiver asks. You tell him, I feel like I am already dead. When he makes no response you add, I am in death's position. He finally says, Don't believe what you are thinking and feeling. Then he asks, Where do you live?

Fifteen minutes later the doorbell rings. You explain to the ambulance attendant that you had a momentary lapse of happily. The noun, happiness, is a static state of some Platonic ideal° you know better than to pursue. Your modifying process had happily or unhappily experienced a momentary pause. This kind of thing happens, perhaps is still happening. He shrugs and in turn explains that you need to come quietly or he will have to restrain you. If he is forced to restrain you, he will have to report that he is forced to restrain you. It is this simple: Resistance will only make matters more difficult. Any resistance will only make matters worse. By law, I will have to restrain you. His tone suggests that you should try to understand the difficulty in which he finds himself. This is further disorienting. I am fine! Can't you see that! You climb into the ambulance unassisted.

I forget things too. It makes me sad. Or it makes me the saddest. The sadness is not really about George W.° or our American optimism; the sadness lives in the recognition that a life can not matter. Or, as there are billions of lives, my sadness is alive alongside the recognition that billions of lives never mattered. I write this without breaking my heart, without bursting into anything. Perhaps this is the real source of my sadness. Or, perhaps, Emily Dickinson, my love, hope was never a thing with

---

Platonic ideal: related to the theory of forms described by classical Greek Philosopher Plato (c. 428–27 B.C.–c. 348–347 B.C.).

George W.: George Walker Bush (b. 1946), an American politician and businessman who was the forty-third president of the United States of America (2001–2009).

feathers. I don't know, I just find when the news comes on I switch the channel. This new tendency might be indicative of a deepening personality flaw: IMH°, The Inability to Maintain Hope, which translates into no innate trust in the supreme laws that govern us. Cornel West° says this is what is wrong with black people today—too nihilistic. Too scarred by hope to hope, too experienced to experience, too close to dead is what I think.

Timothy McVeigh° died at 7:14 a.m. and a news reporter asks relatives of his 168 victims if they have forgiven him. Perhaps because McVeigh is visually the American boy next door, this is yet another attempt by the media to immunize him from his actions. Still it is unclear to me why the reporter asks this now, but I nonetheless continue watching to hear what is said. Many say, No, no, I have not forgiven him. A few say, Yes.

What does it mean to forgive and how does forgiveness show itself? "Forgiveness forgives only the unforgivable," Jacques Derrida° claims. Timothy McVeigh never asked to be forgiven. He managed to suggest that both condemnation and forgiveness were irrelevant by quoting William Earnest Henley's° poem "Invictus": "It matters not how strait the gate, How charged with punishments the scroll, I am the master of my fate: I am the captain of my soul." The need for forgiveness does not seem to enter into McVeigh's final statement to the media. Even as his judicial execution by lethal injection is televised over closed-circuit television for the victims' families, he makes no sign that forgiveness is necessary to him.

So what is forgiveness and how does it show itself?

Forgiveness, I finally decide, is not the death of amnesia, nor is it a form of madness, as Derrida claims. For the one who forgives, it is simply a death, a dying down in the heart, the position of the already dead. It is in the end the living through, the understanding that this has happened, is happening, happens. Period. It is a feeling of nothingness that cannot be communicated to another, an absence, a bottomless vacancy held by the living, beyond all that is hated or loved.

Mr. Tools, for a while the only person in the world walking around with an artificial heart, said the weirdest thing was being without a heartbeat. His was a private and perhaps lonely singularity. No one else could say, I know how you feel. The only living being without a heartbeat, he had a whirr instead. It was not the same whirr of a siren, but rather the fast repetitive whirr of a machine whose insistent motion might eventually seem like silence.

IMH: ordinarily, internet slang for "in my head."

West: an academic philosopher and activist (b. 1953).

McVeigh: (1968–2001), American terrorist who detonated a truck bomb in front of the Alfred P. Murrah Federal Building in Oklahoma City on April 19, 1995. Commonly referred to as the Oklahoma City bombing, the attack killed 168 people and injured over 600. It was the deadliest act of terrorism within the United States prior to the September 11, 2001, attacks, and remains the most serious act of domestic terrorism in United States history.

Derrida: (1930–2004), French philosopher, father of deconstruction, born in Algeria.

Henley: (1849–1903), English poet, critic, and editor, best remembered for his 1875 poem "Invictus."

Mr. Tools had the ultimate tool in his body. He felt its heaviness. The weight on his heart was his heart. All his apparatus—artificial heart, energy coil, battery, and controller—weighed more than four pounds. The whirr if you are not Mr. Tools is detectable only with a stethoscope. For Mr. Tools, that whirr was his sign that he was alive.

Three days after the attack on the World Trade Center it rains. It rains through the night with a determination that peters off by morning. That same afternoon I go downtown to the site. The rain, I thought, would clear the air of smoke. It is still smoking because the debris is still burning. A rank smell is in the air. The rescue workers are there moving pieces of wreckage by hand. In the overcast, dim light they shadow the dead, are themselves deadened.

Their movements are so slow my eyes can rest in them. Something swallows the noise of the trucks. I see but do not hear them. The language of description competes with the dead in the air. My eyes burn and tear. Stacked up along the highway are the wooden stretchers that were never needed. Ink runs on the posters of the missing taped to the sides of buildings. The photographed faces are faded. In some places the rain cleared away the ash and the powdered concrete, in other places it matted the ash and concrete to window ledges, to car exteriors, to any and all available surfaces.

The policemen, their backs to the workers, stare at the public, the news people, everyone and anyone; each stands with his weight on one leg speaking under his breath to another. My sense is that whatever they are saying does not connect with the part of their brain that is there to police our curious grief.

I don't usually talk to strangers, but it is four o'clock and I can't get a cab. I need a cab because I have packages, but it's four o'clock and all the cabs are off duty. They are making a shift change. At the bus stop I say, It's hard to get a cab now. The woman standing next to me glances over without turning her head. She faces the street where cab after cab drives by with its light off. She says, as if to anyone, It's hard to live now. I don't respond. Hers is an Operation Iraqi Freedom answer. The war is on and the Department of Homeland Security has decided we have an elevated national-threat level, a code-orange alert. I could say something, but my packages are getting heavier by the minute and besides, what is there to say since rhetorically it's not about our oil under their sand but about freeing Iraqis from Iraqis and Osama is Saddam and Saddam is "that man who tried to kill my father" and the weapons of mass destruction are, well, invisible and Afghanistan is Iraq and Iraq is Syria and we see ourselves only through our own eyes and the British, but not the French, and Germany won't and Turkey won't join us but the coalition is inside Baghdad where the future is the threat the Americans feel they can escape though there is no escaping the Americans because war, this war, is about peace: "The war in Iraq is really about peace. Trying to make the world more peaceful. This victory in Iraq, when it happens, will make the world more peaceful."

2004

D. A. POWELL (b. 1963)

Born in Albany, Georgia, D. A. Powell later lived in California and was educated at the University of San Francisco before completing a degree at the Iowa Writers' Workshop. Often both witty and frank about gay sexuality, Powell layers images from popular culture with reflections on AIDS and contemporary social practices. His complex, inventive collage effects and long-line untitled poems have given his work both a distinctive texture and a unique appearance. Powell has taught at Columbia University, the University of Iowa, Sonoma State University, San Francisco State University, and served as the Briggs-Copeland Lecturer in Poetry at Harvard. He currently teaches at the University of San Francisco and edits the online magazine *Electronic Poetry Review.*

[THE COCKTAIL HOUR FINALLY ARRIVES: WHETHER ENDING A DAY AT THE OFFICE]

the cocktail hour finally arrives: whether ending a day at the office
or opening the orifice at 6am [legal again to pour in californica]:   the time is always right

we need a little glamour and glamour arrives: plenty of chipped ice
a green jurassic palm tree planted.   a yellow spastic monkey swinging

a pink classic flamingo impaled upon the exuberant red of cherries
dash of bitters.   vermouth sweet.   enough rye whiskey to kill

this longing: I take my drinks stiff and stuffed with plastic.   like my lovers
my billfold full of rubbers.   **OPENS** my mouth: its tiny neon lounge

2004

[DOGS AND BOYS CAN TREAT YOU LIKE TRASH. AND DOGS DO LOVE TRASH]

dogs and boys can treat you like trash.   and dogs do love trash
to nuzzle their muzzles.   they slather with tongues that smell like their nuts

but the boys are fickle when they lick you.   they stick you with twigs
and roll you over like roaches.   then off with another: those sluts

with their asses so tight you couldn't get them to budge for a turd
so unlike the dogs: who will turn in a circle showing & showing their butts

a dog on a leash: a friend in the world.   he'll crawl into bed on all fours
and curl up at your toes.   he'll give you his nose.   he'll slobber on cuts

a dog is not fragile; he's fixed.   but a boy: cannot give you his love
he closes his eyes to your kisses.   he hisses.   a boy is a putz°

with a sponge for a brain.   and a mop for a heart: he'll soak up your love
if you let him and leave you as dry as a cork.   he'll punch out your guts

when a boy goes away: to another boy's arms.   what else can you do
but lie down with the dogs.   with the hounds with the curs.   with the mutts

2004

---

putz: Yiddish slang for a stupid person.

[CAME A VOICE IN MY GULLET: RISE UP AND FEAST. THUNDEROUS]

a song of Simon Peter, concerning his dream

came a voice in my gullet: rise up and feast.   thunderous
a vestment dropping from the violet cope above
not a vestment: a vessel.   amphora the shape of lips

vessel of skin moiled and swollen: a fretting leprosy
and why would I wish a taste?   inside, all manner of beasts
creatures covered in scall charbon and quarter evil

the sea-things one discovers in the net and tosses back
& the coney the camel the tortoise the hare the swine
oysters as well as snails.   those without fins or scales

though I hungered as a sick lass with her empty box
I could not be filled.   not with the tainted reasty lot
in my bowels a raven ruffled its dismal neck and cawed

now I was devout and nothing common or dirty
inside me: not a wild meat not a fruit or spice exotic
for I was a stone: washed in the stream.   I was cut clean

still the air split with want.   the urgent voice seized
because these *are* the pleasures of the world.   *eat*
of the glands I tasted many.   hearts.   lights.   pluck

what had been circumcised fit me.   the uncircumcised too
for nothing was given for my body which was not sacred
the seed the root the tongue and pure blood that cleanses

2004

HEID E. ERDRICH (b. 1963)

Heid Erdrich is an Ojibwe from the Turtle Mountain Band in North Dakota. She was born in Breckenridge, Minnesota, and raised in nearby Wahpeton, North Dakota, where her Ojibwe mother and German American father taught at the Bureau of Indian Affairs boarding school. Erdrich was educated at Dartmouth and Johns Hopkins. She taught for over a decade at the University of St. Thomas and is now an independent scholar and a frequent visiting writer at educational and cultural institutions across the country. In Minnesota, Erdrich regularly works with galleries to present exhibits focused on Native American visual art, and she directs Wiigwaas Press, an Ojibwe language publisher.

TRUE MYTH

Tell a child she is composed of parts
(her Ojibway quarters, her German half-heart)
she'll find the existence of harpies° easy
to swallow. Storybook children never come close
to her mix, but manticores° make great uncles,
Sphinx° a cousin she'll allow, centaurs better to love
than boys—the horse part, at least, she can ride.
With a bestiary for a family album she's proud.
Her heap of blankets, her garbage grin, prove
she's descended of bears, her totem, it's true.
And that German witch with the candy roof,°
that was her ancestor too. If swans° can rain
white rape from heaven, then what is a girl to do?
Believe her Indian eyes, her sly French smile,
her breast with its veins skim milk blue—
She is the myth that is true.

1997

---

3. *harpies:* harpies as ugly winged bird-women, for example in Aeschylus's *The Eumenides*, are a late development in Greek mythology.

5. *manticores:* Persian legendary creatures similar to the Egyptian sphinx. It has the body of a red lion, a human head with three rows of sharp teeth (like a shark), and a trumpet-like voice. Other aspects of the creature vary from story to story. It may be horned, winged, or both. The tail is that of either a dragon or a scorpion, and it may shoot poisonous spines to either paralyze or kill its victims. It devours its prey whole and leaves no clothes, bones, or possessions behind.

6. *Sphinx:* a mythical creature with the body of a lion and a human head. In Greek tradition, it has the haunches of a lion, the wings of a great bird, and the face of a woman. She is mythologized as treacherous and merciless. Those who cannot answer her riddle are killed and eaten.

11. *candy roof:* in the Grimm Brothers fairy tale, Hansel and Gretel eat the roof top of the candy house they come upon when lost in the woods.

12. *swans:* in Greek myth, the god Zeus takes the form of a swan and rapes Leda, wife of the king Tyndareus of Sparta and mother of Helen of Troy.

THE THEFT OUTRIGHT

after Frost

We were the land's before we were.

Or the land was ours before you were a land.
Or this land was our land, it was not your land.

We were the land before we were people,
loamy roamers rising, so the stories go,
or formed of clay, spit into with breath reeking soul—

What's America, but the legend of Rock 'n' Roll?

Red rocks, blood clots bearing boys, blood sands
swimming being from women's hands, we originate,
originally, spontaneous as hemorrhage.

Un-possessing of what we still are possessed by,
possessed by what we now no more possess.

We were the land before we were people,
dreamy sunbeams where sun don't shine, so the stories go,
or pulled up a hole, clawing past ants and roots—

Dineh in documentaries scoff DNA evidence off.
They landed late, but canyons spoke them home.
Nomadic Turkish horse tribes they don't know.

What's America, but the legend of Stop 'n' Go?

Could be cousins, left on the land bridge,
contrary to popular belief, that was a two-way toll.
In any case we'd claim them, give them some place to stay.

2008

SOME ELSIE°

And there she sits, Elsie, in American Lit.,
at the Community College or Harvard or the U.
The sleek New York TA reads how her family

---

poem title: a response to William Carlos Williams' poem "To Elsie."

"married with a dash of Indian Blood"
and thus escaped the fate of the "pure products"
Wm. Carlos Wms. saw go crazy.

Does she sit, terrified or transfixed?
Waiting for someone to turn, look at her and think,
There she is, that Elsie.
So what if she was hemmed all around with murder?
Or if a few of her relatives had screws loose?
She'd deny bathing in filth from Friday to Sunday.
What a girl does on the weekend,
come on now, that's her own affair.

She endures the comments about her body,
"the great ungainly hips and flopping breasts"
What if her ample chest had been her pride?
What if, at first, she flushed at the sound of
"voluptuous water" and took it as a compliment?

What if, at first she thought, *Ah, at last*
a poem about someone I know.
Imagining that she'd strain after deer, too,
if stuck in the suburbs passing pills.
But now, even knowing her hips,
somehow become, the TA says, *a text,*
doesn't help the sting when she thinks
there's some truth she'd like to express,
broken brain or not.

2008

NATASHA TRETHEWEY (b. 1966)

There are three overarching subjects in Natasha Trethewey's work—history, the arts, and the social construction of her own family's identity and experience. Trethewey was born in Gulfport, Mississippi, on Confederate Memorial Day, exactly 100 years after it was first celebrated. Her parents—a black mother and a white father—had been married illegally a year before the U.S. Supreme Court struck down antimiscegenation laws in *Loving* v. *Virginia*. The history behind the reception of racially or ethnically mixed couples is integrated in much of her autobiographical work with analysis of her own and her parents' lives. But it is her general concern with history and current events that is the focus of the poems here. "Native Guard" is a poem sequence constructed out of the history of an all-black Union Army regiment composed mostly of former slaves. The three poems that follow—"Providence," "Liturgy," and "Believer"—are taken from *Beyond Katrina* (2010), her book-length meditation on the impact of the 2005 storm. Trethewey was educated at the University of Georgia, Hollins University, and the University of Massachusetts. She teaches at Emory University.

NATIVE GUARD

If this war is to be forgotten, I ask in the name of all things
sacred what shall men remember?
—Frederick Douglass°

NOVEMBER 1862

Truth be told, I do not want to forget
anything of my former life: the landscape's
song of bondage—dirge in the river's throat
where it churns into the Gulf, wind in trees
choked with vines. I thought to carry with me
want of freedom though I had been freed,
remembrance not constant recollection.
Yes: I was born a slave, at harvest time,
in the Parish of Ascension; I've reached
thirty-three with history of one younger
inscribed upon my back. I now use ink
to keep record, a closed book, not the lure
of memory—flawed, changeful—that dulls the lash
for the master, sharpens it for the slave.

---

epigraph: from Douglas's, "Address at the Grave of the Unknown Dead," Arlington, Virginia, May 30, 1871.

DECEMBER 1862

For the slave, having a master sharpens
the bend into work, the way the sergeant
moves us now to perfect battalion drill,
dress parade. Still, we're called supply units—
not infantry—and so we dig trenches,
haul burdens for the army no less heavy
than before. I heard the colonel call it
nigger work. Half rations make our work
familiar still. We take those things we need
from the Confederates' abandoned homes:
salt, sugar, even this journal, near full
with someone else's words, overlapped now,
crosshatched beneath mine. On every page,
his story intersecting with my own.

JANUARY 1863

O how history intersects—my own
berth upon a ship called the *Northern Star*
and I'm delivered into a new life,
Fort Massachusetts: a great irony—
both path and destination of freedom
I'd not dared to travel. Here, now, I walk
ankle-deep in sand, fly-bitten, nearly
smothered by heat, and yet I can look out
upon the Gulf and see the surf breaking,
tossing the ships, the great gunboats bobbing
on the water.° And are we not the same,
slaves in the hands of the master, destiny?
—night sky red with the promise of fortune,
dawn pink as new flesh: healing, unfettered.

JANUARY 1863

Today, dawn red as warning. Unfettered
supplies, stacked on the beach at our landing,
washed away in the storm that rose too fast,
caught us unprepared. Later, as we worked,

36–39. *I can look . . . on the water:* adapted from *Thank God My Regiment an Africa One: The Civil War Diary of Colonel Nathan W. Daniels.*

I joined in the low singing someone raised
to pace us, and felt a bond in labor
I had not known. It was then a dark man
removed his shirt, revealed the scars, crosshatched
like the lines in this journal, on his back.
It was he who remarked at how the ropes
cracked like whips on the sand, made us take note
of the wild dance of a tent loosed by wind.
We watched and learned. Like any shrewd master,
we know now to tie down what we will keep.

FEBRUARY 1863

We know it is our duty now to keep
white men as prisoners—rebel soldiers,
would-be masters. We're all bondsmen here, each
to the other. Freedom has gotten them
captivity. For us, a conscription
we have chosen—jailors to those who still
would have us slaves. They are cautious, dreading
the sight of us. Some neither read nor write,
are laid too low and have few words to send
but those I give them. Still, they are wary
of a negro writing, taking down letters.
X binds them to the page—a mute symbol
like the cross on a grave. I suspect they fear
I'll listen, put something else down in ink.

MARCH 1863

I listen, put down in ink what I know
they labor to say between silences
too big for words: worry for beloveds—
My Dearest, how are you getting along—
what has become of their small plots of land—
did you harvest enough food to put by?
They long for the comfort of former lives—
I see you as you were, waving goodbye.
Some send photographs—a likeness in case
the body can't return. Others dictate
harsh facts of this war: *The hot air carries*
the stench of limbs, rotten in the bone pit.
Flies swarm—a black cloud. We hunger, grow weak.
When men die, we eat their share of hardtack.

APRIL 1863°

When men die, we eat their share of hardtack
trying not to recall their hollow sockets,
the worm-stitch of their cheeks. Today we buried
the last of our dead from Pascagoula,
and those who died retreating to our ship—
white sailors in blue firing upon us
as if we were the enemy. I'd thought
the fighting over, then watched a man fall
beside me, knees-first as in prayer, then
another, his arms outstretched as if borne
upon the cross. Smoke that rose from each gun
seemed a soul departing. The Colonel said:
an unfortunate incident; said:
their names shall deck the page of history.

JUNE 1863°

Some names shall deck the page of history
as it is written on stone. Some will not.
Yesterday, word came of colored troops, dead
on the battlefield at Port Hudson; how
General Banks was heard to say *I have*
no dead there, and left them, unclaimed. Last night,
I dreamt their eyes still open—dim, clouded
as the eyes of fish washed ashore, yet fixed—
staring back at me. Still, more come today
eager to enlist. Their bodies—haggard
faces, gaunt limbs—bring news of the mainland.
Starved, they suffer like our prisoners. Dying,
they plead for what we do not have to give.
Death makes equals of us all: a fair master.

---

poem title: on April 9, 1863, 180 black men and their officers went onto the mainland to meet Confederate troops near Pascagoula, Mississippi. After the skirmish, as the black troops were retreating (having been outnumbered by the Confederates), white Union troops on board the gunboat *Jackson* fired directly at them and not at oncoming Confederates. Several black soldiers were killed or wounded.

poem title: during the battle of Port Hudson in May 1863, General Nathaniel P. Banks requested a truce to locate the wounded Union soldiers and bury the dead. His troops left the Native Guard dead and wounded where they lay. When Colonel Shelby, a Confederate officer, asked permission to bury the putrifying bodies in front of his lines, Banks refused, saying he had no dead there.

AUGUST 1864

Dumas was a fair master to us all.
He taught me to read and write: I was a man-
servant, if not a man. At my work,
I studied natural things—all manner
of plants, birds I draw now in my book: wren,
willet, egret, loon. Tending the gardens,
I thought only to study live things, thought
never to know so much about the dead.
Now I tend Ship Island graves, mounds like dunes
that shift and disappear. I record names,
send home simple notes, not much more than how
and when—an official duty. I'm told
it's best to spare most detail, but I know
there are things which must be accounted for.

1865°

These are things which must be accounted for:
slaughter under the white flag of surrender—
black massacre at Fort Pillow; our new name,
the Corps d'Afrique—words that take the *native*
from our claim; mossbacks and freedmen—exiles
in their own homeland; the diseased, the maimed,
every lost limb, and what remains: phantom
ache, memory haunting an empty sleeve;
the hog-eaten at Gettysburg, unmarked
in their graves; all the dead letters, unanswered;
untold stories of those that time will render
mute. Beneath battlefields, green again,
the dead molder—a scaffolding of bone
we tread upon, forgetting. Truth be told.

2006

PROVIDENCE

What's left is footage: the hours before
        Camille, 1969—hurricane
                parties, palm trees leaning

poem title: Confederate troops attacked Fort Pillow, a Union garrison fifty miles north of Memphis in April 1864. One news correspondent reported that, after gaining control of the fort, the Confederates disregarded attempts by the black troops to surrender and "an indiscriminate slaughter followed" in which Colonel Nathan Bedford purportedly ordered the black troops "shot down like dogs."

in the wind,
fronds blown back,

a woman's hair. Then after:
the vacant lots,
boats washed ashore, a swamp

where graves had been. I recall

how we huddled all night in our small house,
moving between rooms,
emptying pots filled with rain.

The next day, our house—
on its cinder blocks—seemed to float

in the flooded yard: no foundation

beneath us, nothing I could see
tying us   to the land.
In the water, our reflection
trembled,

disappeared
when I bent to touch it.

2006

BELIEVER

for Tamara Jones

The house is in need of repair, but is—
for now, she says—still hers. After the storm,
she laid hands on what she could reclaim:
the iron table and chairs etched with rust,
the dresser laced with mold. Four years gone,
she's still rebuilding the shed out back
and sorting through boxes in the kitchen—
a lifetime of bills and receipts, deeds
and warranties, notices spread on the table,
a barrage of red ink: PAST DUE. Now,
the house is a museum of everything

she can't let go: a pile of photographs—
fused and peeling—water stains blurring
the handwritten names of people she can't recall;
a drawer crowded with funeral programs
and church fans, rubber bands and paper sleeves
for pennies, nickels, and dimes. What stops me

is the stack of tithing envelopes. Reading my face,
she must know I can't see why—even now—
she tithes, why she keeps giving to the church.
First seek the kingdom of God, she tells me,
and the rest will follow— says it twice

as if to make a talisman of her words.

2010

LITURGY

To the security guard staring at the Gulf
thinking of bodies washed away from the coast,
  plugging her ears
against the bells and sirens—sound of alarm—
  the gaming floor
on the coast;

To Billy Scarpetta, waiting tables on the coast,
  staring at the Gulf
thinking of water rising, thinking of New Orleans,
  thinking of cleansing
the coast;

To the woman dreaming of returning to the coast,
  thinking of water rising,
her daughter's grave, my mother's grave—underwater—
  on the coast;

To Miss Mary, somewhere;

To the displaced, living in trailers along the coast,
  beside the highway,
in vacant lots and open fields; to everyone who stayed
  on the coast,
who came back—or cannot—to the coast;

To those who died on the coast.

This is a memory of the coast: to each his own
recollections, her reclamations, their
restorations, the return of the coast.

This is a time capsule for the coast: words of the people
—don't forget us—

the sound of wind, waves, the silence of graves,
the muffled voice of history, bulldozed and buried
under sand poured on the eroding coast,
the concrete slabs of rebuilding the coast.

This is a love letter to the Gulf Coast, a praise song, a dirge,
invocation and benediction, a requiem for the Gulf Coast.

This cannot rebuild the coast; it is an indictment,
    a complaint,
my *logos*— argument and discourse—with the coast.

This is my *nostos*— my pilgrimage to the coast, my memory,
    my reckoning—

native daughter: I am the Gulf Coast.

2010

SHERMAN ALEXIE (b. 1966)

Sherman Alexie's visibility and reputation increased so rapidly in the 1990s that at times he seemed more a natural phenomenon, like a summer thunderstorm, than a mere writer. But an astonishingly inventive writer he is. The son of a Spokane father and a part-Coeur d'Alene mother, Alexie grew up on the Spokane Indian Reservation in Wellpinit, Washington. He was educated first at Gonzaga University in Spokane and then at Washington State University in Pullman; he now lives in Seattle. His first book of poems and prose poems, *The Business of Fancydancing,* was selected as a Notable Book of the Year by the *New York Times Book Review* in 1992. His next poetry collection, *First Indian on the Moon,* appeared the following year, along with a volume of his short fiction, *The Lone Ranger and Tonto Fistfight in Heaven.* Alexie reworked the short story collection into a film script, which was released as a major motion picture, *Smoke Signals*, in 1998. That same year he was on public television in a panel discussion about race with U.S. president Bill Clinton. And he has continued to be a prolific writer of poetry and fiction, while simultaneously exploring other media. A musical collaboration with Jim Boyd, *Reservation Blues: The Soundtrack*, is based on a 1996 Alexie novel.

Proficient at adapting traditional stanzaic forms, Alexie writes poetry notable for its fusion of cultural criticism and a highly focused irreverence. He has an exuberant, inventive imagination that generates continual surprises and gives him the courage to try almost anything in his writing. Not all his experiments succeed, but no writer as productive as Alexie could succeed all the time. Meanwhile, he has followed Adrian Louis's example in writing poetry of astonishing frankness about both the Native American world and the surrounding dominant culture.

INDIAN BOY LOVE SONG (#2)

I never spoke
the language
of the old women

visiting my mother
in winters so cold
they could freeze
the tongue whole.

I never held my head
to their thin chests
believing in the heart.

Indian women, forgive me.
I grew up distant
and always afraid.

1992

from THE NATIVE AMERICAN BROADCASTING SYSTEM

9.

I am the essence of powwow,° I am
toilets without paper, I am fry bread
in sawdust, I am bull dung
on rodeo grounds at the All-Indian
Rodeo and Horse Show, I am

the essence of powwow, I am
video games with braids, I am spit
from toothless mouths, I am turquoise
and bootleg whiskey, both selling
for twenty bucks a swallow, I am

the essence of powwow, I am
fancydancers in flannel, I am host drum
amplified, I am *Fuck you*
don't come back and *Leave me*

the last hard drink. I am
the essence of powwow, I am the dream
you lace your shoes with, I am
the lust between your toes, I am
the memory you feel across the bottom
of your feet whenever you walk too close.

1993

EVOLUTION

Buffalo Bill opens a pawn shop on the reservation
right across the border from the liquor store
and he stays open 24 hours a day, 7 days a week

---

1. *powwow:* the term comes from the Algonquin word *pawauogs,* meaning shamanistic curing ceremonies, but the modern term has its roots in the dances, social events, and ceremonies of the plains and prairie tribes. Contemporary powwows are often not tribally exclusive; even when sponsored by a single tribal community, they are, in effect, nonexclusive, pan-Indian celebrations of Native American culture and history. Dancing of many historical varieties is their central feature. But the very largest powwows are no longer community celebrations but rather performances for white audiences who pay an admission fee.

and the Indians come running in with jewelry
television sets, a VCR, a full-length beaded buckskin outfit
it took Inez Muse 12 years to finish. Buffalo Bill

takes everything the Indians have to offer, keeps it
all catalogued and filed in a storage room. The Indians
pawn their hands, saving the thumbs for last, they pawn

their skeletons, falling endlessly from the skin
and when the last Indian has pawned everything
but his heart, Buffalo Bill takes that for twenty bucks

closes up the pawn shop, paints a new sign over the old
calls his venture THE MUSEUM OF NATIVE AMERICAN
  CULTURES
charges the Indians five bucks a head to enter.

1992

SCALP DANCE BY SPOKANE INDIANS

Before having Spokane Falls, Paul Kane dropped down to the nearby village of Kettle Falls to paint his now-famous "Scalp Dance by Spokane Indians" in oils on canvas. Its central figure, a woman who had lost her husband to the Blackfeet, whirled around a fire swashing and kicking in revenge a Blackfoot scalp on a stick. Behind her, eight painted women danced and chanted, as did the rest of the tribe to the beat of drums.

—FROM THE SPOKANE INDIANS: CHILDREN OF THE SUN
BY ROBERT H. RUBY AND JOHN A. BROWN

Always trying to steal a little bit of soul, you know? Whether it be poetry or oils on canvas. They call themselves artists but they are really archaeologists.

Really, that's all any kind of art is.

And who am I, you ask? I'm the woman in the painting. I'm the one dancing with the Blackfoot scalp on a stick. But I must tell you the truth. I never had a husband. The artist, Paul Kane, painted me from memory. He saw me at Fort Spokane, even touched his hand to my face as if I were some caged and tame animal in a zoo.

"I need to memorize that curve," he said.

In fact, I have never shared tipi and blanket with any man. When Paul Kane touched me I struck him down and only the hurried negotiations of a passing missionary saved me from Kane's anger. But far from that, I am also a healer, a woman who reserves her touch for larger things.

Paul Kane was nothing except an artist.

But you must remember Kane was also an observant man. He watched many Spokanes put themselves to death. He thought it was because of gambling losses. But no, it was because of all the loss that the Spokane Indians were forced to endure.

Like the loss of soul I felt when I found myself in that painting years later. Ever since Paul Kane had touched me that day, I had felt something missing: a tooth, a fingernail, a layer of skin.

You must also understand that we treated Paul Kane well even as he conspired to steal. Some sat still for his portraits and didn't smile because Kane insisted they remain stoic. That was his greatest mistake. Our smiles were everything; our laughter created portraits in the air, more colorful and exact than any in Kane's work.

I have seen all his paintings and Kane never let us smile. When you see me now in that painting, dancing with the scalp, you must realize that I didn't have a husband, that I never danced without a smile, that I never sat still for Kane.

That is the truth. All of it.

1993

HOW TO WRITE THE GREAT AMERICAN INDIAN NOVEL

All of the Indians must have tragic features: tragic noses, eyes, and arms.
Their hands and fingers must be tragic when they reach for tragic food.

The hero must be a half-breed, half white and half Indian, preferably
from a horse culture. He should often weep alone. That is mandatory.

If the hero is an Indian woman, she is beautiful. She must be slender
and in love with a white man. But if she loves an Indian man

then he must be a half-breed, preferably from a horse culture.
If the Indian woman loves a white man, then he has to be so white

that we can see the blue veins running through his skin like rivers.
When the Indian woman steps out of her dress, the white man gasps

at the endless beauty of her brown skin. She should be compared to nature:
brown hills, mountains, fertile valleys, dewy grass, wind, and clear water.

If she is compared to murky water, however, then she must have a secret.
Indians always have secrets, which are carefully and slowly revealed.

Yet Indian secrets can be disclosed suddenly, like a storm.
Indian men, of course, are storms. They should destroy the lives

of any white women who choose to love them. All white women love
Indian men. That is always the case. White women feign disgust

at the savage in blue jeans and T-shirt, but secretly lust after him.
White women dream about half-breed Indian men from horse cultures.

Indian men are horses, smelling wild and gamey. When the Indian man
unbuttons his pants, the white woman should think of topsoil.

There must be one murder, one suicide, one attempted rape.
Alcohol should be consumed. Cars must be driven at high speeds.

Indians must see visions. White people can have the same visions
if they are in love with Indians. If a white person loves an Indian

then the white person is Indian by proximity. White people must carry
an Indian deep inside themselves. Those interior Indians are half- breed

and obviously from horse cultures. If the interior Indian is male
then he must be a warrior, especially if he is inside a white man.

If the interior Indian is female, then she must be a healer, especially if she is inside
a white woman. Sometimes there are complications.

An Indian man can be hidden inside a white woman. An Indian woman
can be hidden inside a white man. In these rare instances,

everybody is a half-breed struggling to learn more about his or her horse culture.
There must be redemption, of course, and sins must be forgiven.

For this, we need children. A white child and an Indian child, gender
not important, should express deep affection in a childlike way.

In the Great American Indian novel, when it is finally written,
all of the white people will be Indians and all of the Indians will be ghosts.

1996

TOURISTS

1. JAMES DEAN°

walks everywhere now. He's afraid of fast cars
and has walked this far, arriving
suddenly on the reservation, in search
of the Indian woman of his dreams.

---

section head: *James Dean:* (1931–1955), American actor whose films include *Rebel Without a Cause* (1955) and *Giant* (1956), and who died in a car crash just after the latter film finished shooting. Idolized by a generation that came of age in the 1950s, David Thomson has described him as an actor "whose resignation and fatalism showed up the restricted personality of the world he lived in."

He wants an Indian woman who could pass
for Natalie Wood.° He wants an Indian woman
who looks like the Natalie Wood
who was kidnapped by Indians
in John Ford's° classic movie, "The Searchers."
James Dean wants to rescue somebody beautiful.
He still wears that red jacket,
you know the one. It's the color of a powwow fire.
James Dean has never seen
a powwow, but he joins right in, dancing
like a crazy man, like a profane clown.
James Dean cannot contain himself.
He dances in the wrong direction. He tears
at his hair. He sings in wild syllables
and does not care. The Indian dancers stop
and stare like James Dean was lightning
or thunder, like he was bad weather.
But he keeps dancing, bumps into a man
and knocks loose an eagle feather.
The feather falls, drums stop.
This is the kind of silence
that frightens white men. James Dean
looks down at the feather
and knows that something has gone wrong.
He looks into the faces of the Indians.
He wants them to finish the song.

2. JANIS JOPLIN°

sits by the jukebox in the Powwow Tavern,
talking with a few drunk Indians
about redemption. She promises each of them
she can punch in the numbers
for the song that will save their lives.
All she needs is a few quarters, a beer,
and their own true stories. The Indians

---

6. *Natalie Wood:* (1938–1981), Hollywood actress who began her film career as a child, and later played roles in such films as *Rebel Without a Cause, Splendor in the Grass* (1961), and *West Side Story* (1961).

9. *John Ford:* (1895–1973), one of the most famous American film directors of the 1940s, 1950s, and early 1960s; his films include a number of westerns starring John Wayne, *The Searchers* (1956) being the most memorable.

section head: *Janis Joplin:* (1943–1970), one of the most influential and charismatic performers during the heyday of American rock music; a rebel with a throaty, thunderous delivery, she became a legend after her death from a drug overdose.

are as traditional as drunk Indians can be
and don't believe in autobiography,
so they lie to Janis Joplin about their lives.
One Indian is an astronaut, another killed JFK,
while the third played first base
for the New York Yankees. Janis Joplin knows
the Indians are lying. She's a smart woman
but she listens anyway, plays them each a song,
and sings along off key.

3. MARILYN MONROE°

drives herself to the reservation. Tired and cold,
she asks the Indian women for help.
Marilyn cannot explain what she needs
but the Indian women notice the needle tracks
on her arms and lead her to the sweat lodge°
where every woman, young and old, disrobes
and leaves her clothes behind
when she enters the dark of the lodge.
Marilyn's prayers may or may not be answered here
but they are kept sacred by Indian women.
Cold water is splashed on hot rocks
and steam fills the lodge. There is no place like this.
At first, Marilyn is self-conscious, aware
of her body and face, the tremendous heat, her thirst,
and the brown bodies circled around her.
But the Indian women do not stare. It is dark
inside the lodge. The hot rocks glow red
and the songs begin. Marilyn has never heard
these songs before, but she soon sings along.
Marilyn is not Indian, Marilyn will never be Indian
but the Indian women sing about her courage.
The Indian women sing for her health.
The Indian women sing for Marilyn.
Finally, she is no more naked than anyone else.

1996

---

section head: *Marilyn Monroe:* (1926–1962), American movie actress whose films include *River of No Return* (1954), *Bus Stop* (1956), and *Some Like It Hot* (1959); she became both a sex symbol and, after her suicide, a symbol of the terrible psychological price Hollywood stardom can exact from women.

51. *sweat lodge:* built of branches shaped as a dome, with a cover of blankets or skins, ceremonial sweat lodges with their concentrated heat connect participants to the past, the earth, and the spirit world; the United States government tried to outlaw sweat lodge rituals in the nineteenth century.

RICHARD SIKEN (b. 1967)

Richard Siken was educated at the University of Arizona and currently lives in Tucson, Arizona, where he is a full-time social worker caring for developmentally disabled adults. He is also a coeditor at Spork Press, which published the quarterly literary magazine *Spork* from 2001 to 2010 and continues to issue it occasionally, along with chapbooks and novels. To make these dual lives possible, Siken has regularly worked twenty-hour shifts on the weekend to free up time to edit for the press and write his poetry during the week. Siken's book of poetry, *Crush,* from which both of the poems here are reprinted, arguably takes frankness about gay sexuality further than anyone has before. Siken says the 1991 death of his companion influenced the writing of the book: "[it] is a little more about elegy and a little more desperate" as a consequence. Some of his speakers are consumed with sexual obsessions. Others vacillate between resentment and forgiveness. Reckless, youthful sex has a place in some of the poems. On the other hand, he has said, "If you think that life is brutal and short, then the book is uplifting. I don't know if it's grim. I think it's true."

VISIBLE WORLD

Sunlight pouring across your skin, your shadow
flat on the wall.
The dawn was breaking the bones of your heart like twigs.
You had not expected this,
the bedroom gone white, the astronomical light
pummeling you in a stream of fists.
You raised your hand to your face as if
to hide it, the pink fingers gone gold as the light
streamed straight to the bone,
as if you were the small room closed in glass
with every speck of dust illuminated.
The light is no mystery,
the mystery is that there is something to keep the light
from passing through.

2004

A PRIMER FOR THE SMALL WEIRD LOVES

1

The blond boy in the red trunks is holding your head underwater
because he is trying to kill you,
and you deserve it, you do, and you know this,
and you are ready to die in this swimming pool

because you wanted to touch his hands and lips and this means
your life is over anyway.
You're in the eighth grade. You know these things.
You know how to ride a dirt bike, and you know how to do
long division,
and you know that a boy who likes boys is a dead boy, unless
he keeps his mouth shut, which is what you
didn't do,
because you are weak and hollow and it doesn't matter anymore.

2

A dark-haired man in a rented bungalow is licking the whiskey
from the back of your wrist.
He feels nothing,
keeps a knife in his pocket,
peels an apple right in front of you
while you tramp around a mustard-colored room
in your underwear
drinking Dutch beer from a green bottle.
After everything that was going to happen has happened
you ask only for the cab fare home
and realize you should have asked for more
because he couldn't care less, either way.

3

The man on top of you is teaching you how to hate, sees you
as a piece of real estate,
just another fallow field lying underneath him
like a sacrifice.
He's turning your back into a table so he doesn't have to
eat off the floor, so he can get comfortable,
pressing against you until he fits, until he's made a place for himself
inside you.
The clock ticks from five to six. Kissing degenerates into biting.
So you get a kidney punch, a little blood in your urine.
It isn't over yet, it's just begun.

4

Says to himself
The boy's no good. The boy is just no good.
but he takes you in his arms and pushes your flesh around
to see if you could ever be ugly to him.

You, the now familiar whipping boy, but you're beautiful,
he can feel the dogs licking his heart.
Who gets the whip and who gets the hoops of flame?
He hits you and he hits you and he hits you.
Desire driving his hands right into your body.
Hush, my sweet. These tornadoes are for you.
You wanted to think of yourself as someone who did these kinds of things.
You wanted to be in love
and he happened to get in the way.

5

The green-eyed boy in the powder-blue t-shirt standing
next to you in the supermarket recoils as if hit,
repeatedly, by a lot of men, as if he has a history of it.

This is not your problem.
You have your own body to deal with.
The lamp by the bed is broken.
You are feeling things he's no longer in touch with.
And everyone is speaking softly,
so as not to wake one another.
The wind knocks the heads of the flowers together.
Steam rises from every cup at every table at once.
Things happen all the time, things happen every minute
that have nothing to do with us.

6

So you say you want a deathbed scene, the knowledge that comes
before knowledge,
and you want it dirty.
And no one can ever figure out what you want,
and you won't tell them,
and you realize the one person in the world who loves you
isn't the one you thought it would be,
and you don't trust him to love you in a way
you would enjoy.
And the boy who loves you the wrong way is filthy.
And the boy who loves you the wrong way keeps weakening.
You thought if you handed over your body
he'd do something interesting.

7

The stranger says there are no more couches and he will have to
sleep in your bed. You try to warn him, you tell him
you will want to get inside him, and ruin him,
but he doesn't listen.
You do this, you do. You take the things you love
and tear them apart
or you pin them down with your body and pretend they're yours.
So, you kiss him, and he doesn't move, he doesn't
pull away, and you keep on kissing him. And he hasn't moved,
he's frozen, and you've kissed him, and he'll never
forgive you, and maybe now he'll leave you alone.

2004

Graphic Interpretations

S

Lion-girl of the Rue Payenne
Is that your mate with the mauve mouth who wants in?

Face powder settles on the brows of the walls
While hair from the tap flows into fingerbowls

Your first breast is the envy of all paradoxes
Invisible dainty spiders eat holes in your stockings

ERENADE TO LEONOR

As you step from one room's hemisphere to another
Your second breast wrangles with a young bat's brother

It's all you can do to prove you're not his sister
Before he goes you'll give him a devious picture

If he looks through the evening's window upside down
Glue a smile on his back, on his knee a frown

When he gazes at the moon's mirror wrongside up
Will you make his tongue spin like a star or a top?

Oh your tricks are as real as a clock striking four
Your perfume bottles fill with the breath of this paramour

Your talons dyed with blue, the blue tears of night
Scratch at his eyes with unexpected daylight

As the cat with the violet lips leaps in
To visit the lion-girl of the Rue Payenne

Charles Henri Ford

Rival Pleasure discovery 28

too gorgeous to hide

STIFF SWITCHBLADE torture tested Organ

nerve Loaded with Off-Season Take off

Unheard of Speed-up all

through the meat

Hey, Dad

don't let one little

pimple SPOIL A BEAUTIFUL EX-BUSBOY

INFECTING memories to bring home thump, thump

every single piece OF Tough customer

should GET LOST here

Charles Henri Ford

WE REAL COOL
BY GWENDOLYN BROOKS
The Pool Players
Seven at the Golden Shovel

WE REAL COOL. WE
LEFT SCHOOL. WE

LURK LATE. WE
STRIKE STRAIGHT. WE

SING SIN. WE
THIN GIN. WE

JAZZ JUNE. WE
DIE SOON.

Designed by Cledie Taylor
"We Real Cool" from Selected Poems by Gwendolyn Brooks

BROADSIDE No. 6, December 1966
BROADSIDE PRESS, 12651 OLD MILL PLACE, DETROIT, MICHIGAN 48238

KRAL MAJALES

And the Communists have nothing to offer but fat cheeks and eyeglasses and lying policemen
and the Capitalists proffer Napalm and money in green suitcases to the Naked,
and the Communists create heavy industry but the heart is also heavy
and the beautiful engineers are all dead, the secret technicians conspire for their own glamor
in the Future, in the Future, but now drink vodka and lament the Security Forces,
and the Capitalists drink gin and whiskey on airplanes but let Indian brown millions starve
and when Communist and Capitalist assholes tangle the Just man is arrested or robbed or had his head cut off,
but not like Kabir, and the cigarette cough of the Just man above the clouds
in the bright sunshine is a salute to the health of the blue sky.
For I was arrested thrice in Prague, once for singing drunk on Narodni street,
once knocked down on the midnight pavement by a mustached agent who screamed out *BOUZERANT*,
once for losing my notebooks of unusual sex politics dream opinions,
and I was sent from Havana by plane by detectives in green uniform,
and I was sent from Prague by plane by detectives in Czechoslovakian business suits,
Cardplayers out of Cezanne, the two strange dolls that entered Joseph K's room at morn
also entered mine, and ate at my table, and examined my scribbles,
and followed me night and morn from the houses of lovers to the cafés of Centrum—
And I am the King of May, which is the power of sexual youth,
and I am the King of May, which is industry in eloquence and action in amour,
and I am the King of May, which is long hair of Adam and the Beard of my own body
and I am the King of May, which is Kral Majales in the Czechoslovakian tongue,
and I am the King of May, which is old Human poesy, and 100,000 people chose my name,
and I am the King of May, and in a few minutes I will land at London Airport,
and I am the King of May, naturally, for I am of Slavic parentage and a Buddhist Jew
who worships the Sacred Heart of Christ the blue body of Krishna the straight back of Ram
The Beads of Chango the Nigerian singing Shiva Shiva in a manner which I have invented,
and the King of May is a middleeuropean honor, mine in the XX century
despite space ships and the Time Machine, because I heard the voice of Blake in a vision,
and repeat that voice. And I am the King of May that sleeps with teenagers laughing.
And I am the King of May, that I may be expelled from my Kingdom with Honor, as of old,
To shew the difference between Caesar's Kingdom and the Kingdom of the May of Man—
and I am the King of May, tho paranoid, for the Kingdom of May is too beautiful to last for more than a month—
and I am the King of May because I touched my finger to my forehead saluting
a luminous heavy girl with trembling hands who said "one moment Mr. Ginsberg"
before a fat young Plainclothesman stepped between our bodies—I was going to England—
and I am the King of May, returning to see Bunhill Fields and walk on Hampstead Heath,
and I am the King of May, in a giant jetplane touching Albion's airfield trembling in fear
as the plane roars to a landing on the grey concrete, shakes & expells air,
and rolls slowly to a stop under the clouds with part of blue heaven still visible.
And *tho* I am the King of May, the Marxists have beat me upon the street, kept me up all night in Police Station, followed me thru Springtime Prague, detained me in secret and deported me from our kingdom by airplane.
Thus I have written this poem on a jet seat in mid Heaven.

May 7, 1965 Allen Ginsberg

Robert LaVigne

oyez

MOLOCH

What sphinx of cement and aluminum bashed open their skulls and ate up their brains and imagination?

Moloch! Solitude! Filth! Ugliness! Ashcans and unobtainable dollars! Children screaming under the stairways! Boys sobbing in armies! Old men weeping in the parks!

Moloch! Moloch! Nightmare of Moloch! Moloch the loveless! Mental Moloch! Moloch the heavy judger of men!

Moloch the incomprehensible prison! Moloch the crossbone soulless jailhouse and Congress of sorrows! Moloch whose buildings are judgement! Moloch the vast stone of war! Moloch the stunned governments!

Moloch whose mind is pure machinery! Moloch whose blood is running money! Moloch whose fingers are ten armies! Moloch whose breast is a cannibal dynamo! Moloch whose ear is a smoking tomb!

Moloch whose eyes are a thousand blind windows! Moloch whose skyscrapers stand in the long streets like endless Jehovahs! Moloch whose factories dream and croak in the fog! Moloch whose smokestacks and antennae crown the cities!

Moloch whose love is endless oil and stone! Moloch whose soul is electricity and banks! Moloch whose poverty is the specter of genius! Moloch whose fate is a cloud of sexless hydrogen! Moloch whose name is the Mind!

Moloch in whom I sit lonely! Moloch in whom I dream angels! Crazy in Moloch! Cocksucker in Moloch! Lacklove and manless in Moloch!

Moloch who entered my soul early! Moloch in whom I am a consciousness without a body! Moloch who frightened me out of my natural ecstasy! Moloch whom I abandon! Wake up in Moloch! Light streaming out of the sky!

Moloch! Moloch! Robot apartments! invisible suburbs! skeleton treasuries! blind capitals! demonic industries! spectral nations! invincible madhouses! granite cocks! monstrous bombs!

They broke their backs lifting Moloch to Heaven! Pavements, trees, radios, tons! lifting the city to Heaven which exists and is everywhere about us!

Visions! omens! hallucinations! miracles! ecstasies! gone down the American river!

Dreams! adorations! illuminations! religions! the whole boatload of sensitive bullshit!

Breakthroughs! over the river! flips and crucifixions! gone down the flood! Highs! Epiphanies! Despairs! Ten years' animal screams and suicides! Minds! New loves! Mad generation! down on the rocks of Time!

Real holy laughter in the river! They saw it all! the wild eyes! the holy yells! They bade farewell! They jumped off the roof! to solitude! waving! carrying flowers! Down to the river! into the street!

1956

Six hundred broadsides were hand-printed at the Penmaen Press in Lincoln, Massachusetts during January 1978. Three hundred were printed on French Rives paper, numbered 1-300 and signed by Allen Ginsberg and Lynd Ward. The text is Part II of *HOWL*, copyright 1956, 1959 by Allen Ginsberg. Reprinted by permission of City Lights Books. The original wood engraving is copyright 1978 by Lynd Ward.

Allen Ginsberg

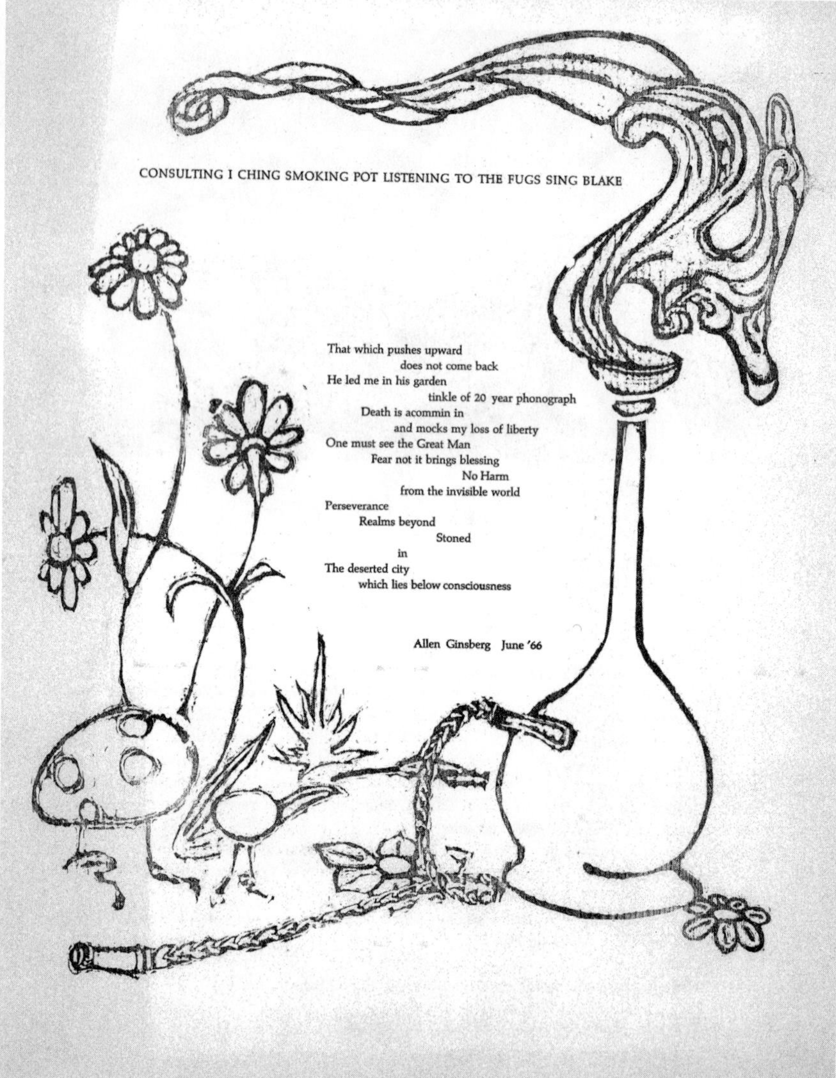

CONSULTING I CHING SMOKING POT LISTENING TO THE FUGS SING BLAKE

That which pushes upward
does not come back
He led me in his garden
tinkle of 20 year phonograph
Death is acommin in
and mocks my loss of liberty
One must see the Great Man
Fear not it brings blessing
No Harm
from the invisible world
Perseverance
Realms beyond
Stoned
in
The deserted city
which lies below consciousness

Allen Ginsberg June '66

Printed by Kriya Press of Sri Ram Ashrama, Pleasant Valley, New York 1967
Limited edition of one hundred copies of which this is number 62

WILLIAM EVERSON

A Canticle to the Waterbirds

CLACK YOUR BEAKS you cormorants and kittiwakes,
North on those rock-croppings finger-jutted into the rough Pacific surge;
You migratory terns and pipers, who leave but the temporal clawtrack written on sandbars there of your presence;
Grebes and pelicans; you comber-picking scoters and you shorelong gulls;
All you keepers of the coastline north of here to the Mendocino beaches;
All you beyond upon the cliff-face thwarting the surf at Hecate Head;
Hovering the under-surge where the cold Columbia grapples at the bar;
North yet to the Sound, whose islands float like a sown flurry of chips upon the sea:
Break wide your harsh and salt-encrusted beaks unmade for song
And say a praise up to the Lord.

And you freshwater egrets east in the flooded marshlands skirting the sea-level rivers, white one-legged watchers of shallows;
Broad-headed kingfishers minnow-hunting from willow stems on meandering valley sloughs;
You too, you herons, blue and supple-throated, stately, taking the air majestical in the sunflooded San Joaquin,
Grading down on your belted wings from the upper lights of sunset,
Mating over the willow clumps or where the flatwater rice fields shimmer;
You killdeer, high-criers, far in the moon-suffusion sky;
Bitterns, sand-waders, all shore-walkers, all roost-keepers,
Populates of the 'dobe cliffs of the Sacramento:
Open your water-dartling beaks,
And make a praise up to the Lord....

William Everson

This excerpt was printed in Goudy types on T. H. Saunders handmade paper in an edition of sixty by Felicia Rice and Gary Young on the occasion of the poet receiving the 1991 Artist of the Year Award from the Santa Cruz County Arts Commission. The woodcut is by Daniel O. Stolpe.

THE FORM FALLS IN ON ITSELF,
ITS IDENTITY VANISHING. THERE
ON THE BARE GROUND THE PIECES
CRAWL TOWARDS ONE ANOTHER.

SOMBER IN THE MORNING
SICK OF LOVE AND DEATH
THE WORLD IS WHAT
I TOUCH AND SEE

LOOK AT MY SMOOTH FACE
COVER MY FAILINGS
I SMILE I ADD
TO THE PICTURE OF HEALTH

HAVE YOU HEARD
THEY FOUND A TURD
ON THE PRESIDENT'S PLATE
AFTER THE BIRD OF PEACE
FLEW OVER. DAVID IGNATOW

David Ignatow
1971

WHEN THE WAR IS OVER

by W. S. Merwin

When the war is over
We will be proud of course the air will be
Good for breathing at last
The water will have been improved the salmon
And the silence of heaven will migrate more perfectly
The dead will think the living are worth it we will know
Who we are
And we will all enlist again

O Mother Gaia

sky cloud gate milk snow

wind-void-word

I bow in roadside gravel

Gary Snyder

A DIFFERENCE

How is a *room* unlike a *moor*?
They're not the same, you may be sure.
A *room* has walls, a *moor* does not.
Inquire of any honest Scot
And he will say, I have no doubt,
That one's indoors and one is out.
A *room*, then, fits inside a dwelling;
A *moor* is its reverse in spelling,
And has such wild outdoorish weather,
Such rocks, such miles and miles of heather
All full of flocks of drumming grouse,
You wouldn't have one in the house.

A DIFFERENCE

Credits

Ai. "The Root Eater," "Twenty-Year Marriage," Copyright © 1973 by Ai, from THE COLLECTED POEMS OF AI. Used by permission of W. W. Norton & Company, Inc. "The German Army, Russia, 1943". Copyright © 1979 by Ai, Copyright © 1985 by Ai, from THE COLLECTED POEMS OF AI. Used by permission of W. W. Norton & Company, Inc. "The Testimony of J. Robert Oppenheimer," Copyright © 1985 by Ai, from THE COLLECTED POEMS OF AI. Used by permission of W. W. Norton & Company, Inc.

Sherman Alexie. "Evolution," "Indian Boy Love Song (#2)," Reprinted from THE BUSINESS OF FANCYDANCING © 1992 by Sherman Alexie, by permission of Hanging Loose Press. "No. 9 (from The Native American Broadcasting System)," "Scalp Dance," by Spokane Indians Reprinted from FIRST INDIAN ON THE MOON © 1993 by Sherman Alexie, by permission of Hanging Loose Press. "How to Write the Great American Indian Novel," "Tourists," Reprinted from THE SUMMER OF BLACK WIDOWS © 2000 by Sherman Alexie, by permission of Hanging Loose Press.

A. R. Ammons. "Corsons Inlet". Copyright © 1963 by A. R. Ammons, from COLLECTED POEMS 1951–1971 by A. R. Ammons. Used by permission of W. W. Norton & Company, Inc. "Coon Song," and "Gravelly Run," Copyright © 1960 by A. R. Ammons, from COLLECTED POEMS 1951–1971 by A. R. Ammons. Used by permission of W. W. Norton & Company, Inc.

John Ashberry. "The Dream Only of America" from The Tennis Court Oath © 1962 by John Ashbery. Reprinted by permission of Wesleyan University Press, www.wesleyan.edu/wespress. "Farm Implements and Rutabagas in a Landscape" from THE DOUBLE DREAM OF SPRING by John Ashbery. Reprinted by permission of Georges Borchardt, Inc., for the author. All rights reserved. "Mixed Feelings", copyright © 1975 by John Ashbery from SELF-PORTRAIT IN A CONVEX MIRROR by John Ashbery. Used by permission of Viking Penguin, a division of Penguin Group (USA) LLC. "Daffy Duck in Hollywood," "Street Musicians," "Syringa," from HOUSEBOAT DAYS by John Ashbery. Copyright © 1975, 1977, 2008 by John Ashbery. Reprinted by permission of Georges Borchardt, Inc., on behalf of the author. All rights reserved. "Paradoxes and Oxymorons" from SHADOW TRAIN by John Ashbery. Copyright © 1980, 1981, 2008, by John Ashbery. Reprinted by permission of Georges Borchardt, Inc., for the author. All rights reserved. "Dull Muave," and "The Problem of Anxiety" from CAN YOU HEAR, BIRD by John Ashbery. Copyright © 1995 by John Ashbery. Reprinted by permission of Georges Borchardt, Inc., on behalf of the author. All rights reserved. "A Kind of Chill" from A WORLDLY COUNTRY: NEW POEMS by JOHN ASHBERY. Copyright © 2007 by John Ashbery. Reprinted by permission of HarperCollins Publishers. "Spooks Run Wild" from PLANISPHERE by JOHN ASHBERY. Copyright © 2009 BY JOHN ASHBERY. Reprinted by permission of HarperCollins Publishers. "Marine Shadow," and "Words to That Effect," from QUICK QUESTION by JOHN ASHBERY. Copyright © 2012 by John Ashbery. Reprinted by permission of HarperCollins Publishers.

Amiri Baraka. "Black Art," "SOS," and "when We'll Worship Jesus," Reprinted by permission of SLL/Sterling Lord Literistic, Inc. Copyright by Amiri Baraka.

Charles Bernstein. Used by permission of Charles Bernstein, from "Foreign Body Sensation" from The Sophist (los Angeles: Sun & Moon Press, 1987). Used by permission of Charles Bernstein, from "The Kiwi Bird in the Kiwi Tree" from Rough Trades (Los Angeles: Sun & Moon Press, 1991). Used by permission of Charles Bernstein, from "Riddle of the Fat Faced Man" from Rough Trades (Los Angeles: Sun & Moon Press, 1991). Used by permission of Charles Bernstein, from "The Boy Soprano" from With Strings (Chicago: University of Chicago Press, 2001).

John Berryman. Reprinted by permissions of Farrar, Straus and Giroux, LLC: Dream Songs #1, 4, 5, 14, 22, 29, 40, 45, 46, 55, 76, 382, and 384 from THE DREAM SONGS by John Berryman. Copyright © 1969 by John Berryman. Copyright renewed by Kate Donahue Berryman.

Elizabeth Bishop. Reprinted by permissions of Farrar, Straus and Giroux, LLC: "The Armadillo," "At the Fishouses," "Crusoe in England," "Filling Station," "the Fish," "In the Waiting Room," "The Man-Moth," "One Art," "Pink Dog," "Questions of Travel" from THE COMPLETE POEMS 1927–1979 by Elizabeth Bishop. Copyright © 1979, 1983 by Alice Helen Methfessel.

Paul Blackburn. "At the Crossroad," and "At the Well," From Collected Poems of Paul Blackburn. Copyright © 1985 by Joan Blackburn. Reprinted by permission of Persea Books Inc., New York. All rights reserved.

Robert Bly. "Counting Small-Boned Bodies." Reprinted by permission of the "Free Poetry Institute for the Study of Nonvoilence." Robert Bly, "Hearing Gary Snyder Read." Reprinted under Broadside's 1971 mark, "May Be Reproduced Without Permission."

William Bronk. "At Tikal," "I Thought It Was Harry," "Left Alone," "The Mayan Glyphs Unread," "Where It Ends," Reprinted by permission of the Trustees of Columbia University in the City of New York.

Gwendolyn Brooks. "A Song in the Front Yard," "Gay Chaps at the Bar," "Malcolm X," "Of De Witt Williams on His Way to Lincoln Cemetery," "The Ballad of Rudolph Reed," "The Blackstone Rangers," "The Boy Died in My Alley," "To The Diaspora," "To Those of My Sisters Who Kept Their Naturals," "We Real Cool," "Young Afrikans," Reprinted by consent of Brooks Permissions. "We Real Cool," Reprinted by consent of Brooks Permissions.

Ana Castillo. "Seduced by Natassja Kinski," and "Hummingbird Heart," From I ASK THE IMPOSSIBLE. Copyright © 2000 by Ana Castillo. Published in English by Anchor Books. Reprinted by permission of Ana Castillo.

Lorna Dee Cervantes. "Refugee Ship" is reprinted with permission from the publisher of "The Americas Review" by Lorna Dee Cervantes (© 1990 Arte Público Press- University of Houston). "Poema Para los Californios Muertos" from Emplumada, by Lorma Dee Cervamtes. © 1982. Reprinted by permission of the University of Pittsburgh Press. "Starfish" from Emplumada, by Lorma Dee Cervamtes. © 1982. Reprinted by permission of the University of Pittsburgh Press.

Marilyn Chin. "Altar," and "How I Got That Name," from THE PHOENIX GONE, THE TERRACE EMPTY. Reprinted by permission of Milkweed Editions.

Lucille Clifton. "at the cemetery, walnut grove plantation, south carolina, 1989," "i am accused of tending to the past," "next," "poem to my uterus," "reply," and "to my last period," from The Collected Poems of Lucille Clifton. Copyright © 1991 by Lucille Clifton. Reprinted with the permission of The Permissions Company, Inc. on behalf of BOA Editions, Ltd., www.boaeditions.org. Lucille Clifton, "brothers" from The Book of Light. Copyright © 1993 by Lucille Clifton. Reprinted with the permission of The Permissions Company, Inc. on behalf of Copper Canyon Press, www.coppercanyonpress.org.

Sandra Cisneros. "Little Clown, My Heart," Reprinted by permission of Bergholz Agency.

Gregory Corso. "Bomb," and "Marriage," By Gregory Corso, from THE HAPPY BIRTHDAY OF DEATH, copyright © 1960 by New Directions Publishing Corp. Reprinted by permission of New Directions Publishing Corp.

Jayne Cortez. "Do You Think," and "I Am New York City," Reprinted from "ON THE IMPERIAL HIGHWAY: NEW AND SELECTED POEMS" © 2009 by Jane Cortez, by Permission of Hanging Loose Press.

Robert Creeley. "After Lorca," "Age," "America," "The Flower," "I Know a Man," from The Collected Poems of Robert Creeley: 1945–1975 © 2006 by the Regents of the University of California. Published by the University of California Press. Reprinted by permission of the University of California Press. "For Love" from The Collected Poems of Robert Creeley 1945–1975. Copyright © 1962 by Robert Creeley. Reprinted by permission of The Permissions Company, Inc., on behalf of the Estate of Robert Creeley.

Joy Davidman. "For the Nazis," Reprinted with permission of the Literary Estate of Joy Davidman.

James Dickey. "Falling," and "The Sheep Child," from *The Whole Motion: Collected Poems 1945–1992* © 1992 by James Dickey. Reprinted by permission of Wesleyan University Press, www.wesleyan.edu/wespress.

Mark Doty. "Homo Will Not Inherit" from ATLANTIS by MARK DOTY. Copyright © 1995 by Mark Doty. Reprinted by permission of HarperCollins Publishers. "The Embrace" from SWEET MACHINE by MARK DOTY. Copyright © 1998 by Mark Doty. Reprinted by permission of HarperCollins Publishers.

Rita Dove. "Parsley," and "Receiving the Stigmata," from Museum, Carnegie Mellon University Press, Pittsburgh, PA. © 1983 by Rita Dove. Reprinted by permission of the author.

Henry Dumas. "Son of Msippi," "Kef 24," "Kef 16," "Fish," "Knees of a Natural Man," "Low Down Dog Blues," "Black Star Line," "Peas," and "Yams," Reprinted by permission of Henry Dumas Estate, Eugene B. Redmond, Executor.

Robert Duncan. "Often I Am Permitted to Return to a Meadow," By Robert Duncan, from THE OPENING OF THE FIELD, copyright © 1960 by Robert Duncan. Reprinted by permission of New Directions Publishing Corp. "My Mother Would Be a Falconress," "The Torso (Passages 18)," "Up Rising (Passages 25)," By Robert Duncan, from BENDING THE BOW, copyright © 1968 by Robert Duncan. Reprinted by permission of New Directions Publishing Corp.

Anita Endrezze. "Birdwatching at Fan Lake," "Return of the Wolves," and "La Morena and Her Beehive Hairdo," From Throwing Fire at the Sun, Water at the Moon by Anita Endrezze. © 2000 Anita Endrezzee. Reprinted by permission of the University of Arizona Press.

Louise Erdrich. "Indian Boarding School: The Runaways," from JACKLIGHT (later in ORIGINAL FIRE: SELECTED AND NEW POEMS). Reprinted by permission of The Wylie Agency. "Dear John Wayne," from THAT'S WHAT SHE SAID: A COLLECTION OF CONTEMPORARY FICTION AND POETRY BY NATIVE AMERICAN WOMEN (later in ORIGINAL FIRE SELECTED AND NEW POEMS). Reprinted by permission of The Wylie Agency. "The Fence" from ORIGINAL FIRE by LOUISE ERDRICH. Copyright © 1989 by Louise Erdrich. Reprinted by permission of HarperCollins Publishers.

William Everson. "A Canticle to the Waterbirds," and "The Making of the Cross." From The Veritable Years: Poems 1949–1966 by William Everson. Reprinted by permission of Black Sparrow Books, an imprint of David R. Godine, Publisher, Inc. Copyright © 1998 by Jude Everson and the William Everson Literary Estate. Reprinted by permission of William Everson and Daniel O. Stope.

Carolyn Forché. "The Colonel," from THE COUNTRY BETWEEN US. Reprinted by permission of Harper Collins Publishers. "The Museum of Stones," from *The New Yorker*, 3/26/2007. Reprinted by permission of Carolyn Forché. "The Lightkeeper," from *The New Yorker*, 5/3/2010. Reprinted by permission of Carolyn Forché. "Morning on the Island," from *The Nation*, 4/19/2010. Reprinted by permission of Carolyn Forché.

Charles Henri Ford. "Plaint," "Flag of Ecstasy," "Pastoral for Pavlik." Reprinted by permission of the Literary Estate of Henri Ford. "Serenade to Leonor," © 2013 Artists Rights Society (ARS), New York / ADAGP, Paris. "28," Reprinted by permission of the Literary Estate of Henri Ford.

Sesshu Foster. "We're caffinated by rain inside concrete underpasses," "You'll be fucked up," "The Japanese man would not appear riding a horse," "Look and look again, will he glance up all of a sudden," "I try to pee but I can't," and "I'm always grateful no one hears this terrible racket," Copyright © 1996 by Sesshu Foster. Reprinted by permission of Kaya Press. *Life Magazine*, December, 1941 Copyright © 1996 by Sesshu Foster. Reprinted by permission of Kaya Press.

Kathleen Fraser. "In Commemoration of the Visit of Foreign Commercial Representatives to Japan, 1947" from il cuore: the heart, Selected Poems, 1970–1995 © 1997 by Kathleen Fraser. Reprinted by permission of Wesleyan University Press, www.wesleyan.edu/wespress.

Lawson Fusao Inada. Excerpts from "Listening Images" from Legends from Camp. Copyright © 1993 by Lawson Fusao Inada. Reprinted with the permission of The Permissions Company, Inc., on behalf of Coffee House Press, www.coffeehousepress.org.

Allen Ginsberg. "Howl," "Love Poem on Theme by Whitman", "A Supermarket in California," from COLLECTED POEMS 1947–1980 by Allen Ginsberg. Copyright © 1984 by Allen Ginsberg. Reprinted by permission of HarperCollins Publishers. Allen Ginsberg "Ran- Wet Asphalt Heat, Garbage Curbed Cans Overflowing," "Who To Be Kind To." "Sphincter" from COSMOPOLITAN GREETINGS POEMS 1986–1992 by ALLEN GINSBERG. Copyright © 1994 by Allen Ginsberg. Reprinted by permission of HarperCollins Publishers. "Moloch," BY PERMISSION OF RAOBIN WARD SAVAGE & NANDA WEEDON WARD.

Louise Glück. "The Drowned Children" from THE FIRST FOUR BOOKS OF POEMS by LOUISE GLÜCK. Copyright © 1968, 1971, 1972, 1973, 1974, 1975, 1976, 1977, 1978, 1979, 1980, 1985, 1995 by Louise Glück. Reprinted by permission of HarperCollins Publishers. "The Wild Iris," "Vespers ("You thought we didn't know")," and "Vespers ("More than you love me, very possibly"), from THE WILD IRIS by LOUISE GLÜCK. Copyright © 1992 by Louise Glück. Reprinted by permission of HarperCollins Publishers. "Penelope's Song," "Quiet Evening," "Parable of the King," "Parable of the

Hostages," "Circe's Power," "Circe's Grief," "Reunion," and "Telemachus' Burden," Copyright © 1996 by Louise Glück. Reprinted by permission of HarperCollins Publishers. Reprinted by permissions of Farrar, Straus and Giroux, LLC: "Before the Storm," and "A Village Life," from A VILLAGE LIFE by Louise Glück. Copyright © 2009 by Louise Glück.

Albert Goldbarth. "Coinages: A Fairy Tale," "Swan," from The Kitchen Sink: New and Selected Poems 1972–2007. Copyright © 2007 by Albert Goldbarth. All reprinted with the permission of The Permissiosn Company, Inc., on behalf of Graywolf Press, www.graywolfpres.org. Albert Goldbarth, "1400" from To Be Read in 500 Poems. Copyright © 2009 by Albert Goldbarth. All reprinted with the permission of The Permissiosn Company, Inc., on behalf of Graywolf Press, www.graywolfpres.org.

Jorie Graham. "From the New World," and "History," from REGION OF UNLIKENESS by JORIE GRAHAM. Copyright © 1991 by Jorie Graham. Reprinted by permission of HarperCollins Publishers.

Judy Grahn. "Carol," "I Have Come to Claim Marilyn Monroe's Body," "Plainsong," "The Woman Whose Head is On Fire," from *Love Belongs to Those Who do the Feeling* by Judy Grahn. Copyright © 2008 by Judy Grahn. Reprinted by permission of Red Hen Press.

Barbara Guest. "Couch Space," "Twilight Polka Dots," "Words," from *The Collected Poems of Barbara Guest* © 2008 by the Estate of Barbara Guest. Reprinted by permission of Wesleyan University Press, www.wesleyan.edu/wespress.

Jessica Hagedorn. "Ming the Merciless," Copyright © 2002 by Jessica Hagedorn. All rights reserved.

Michael Harper. "Song: I Want a Witness," "Blue Ruth: America," "Brother John," "American History," "We Assume: On the Death of Our Son, Reuben Masai Harper," "Reuben, Reuben," "Deathwatch," and "Dear John, Dear Coltrane," Reprinted by permission of Michael S. Harper and University of Illinois Press.

Janice N. Harrington. "Falling," and "If She Had Lived," from Even the Hollow My Body Made is Gone. Copyright © 2007 byJ Janine N. Harrington. Reprinted with the permission of The Permissions Company, Inc., on behalf of BOA Editions, Ltd., www.boaeditions.org.

Mary Cornelia Hartshorne. "Fallen Leaves," "Hills of Doon," and "Wind in Mexico."

Robert Hass. "Rusia en 1931," and "A Story About the Body," from HUMAN WISHES by ROBERT HASS. Copyright © 1989 by Robert Hass. Reprinted by permission of HarperCollins Publishers. "Forty Something," and "Sonnet," from SUN UNDER WOOD: NEW POEMS by ROBERT HASS. Copyright © 1996 by Robert Hass. Reprinted by permission of HarperCollins Publishers.

Robert Hayden. Copyright © 1962, 1966 by Robert Hayden, "Aunt Jemima of the Ocean Waves," "Middle Passage," and "Runagate Runagate", from COLLECTED POEMS OF ROBERT HAYDEN by Robert Hayden, edited by Frederick Glaysher. Used by permission of Liveright Publication Corporation. Copyright © 1966 by Robert Hayden, "A Letter from Phyllis Wheatley," "Night, Death, Mississippi,"from COLLECTED POEMS OF ROBERT HAYDEN by Robert Hayden, edited by Frederick Glaysher. Used by permission of Liveright Publishing Corporation. Copyright © 1970 by Robert Hayden, "The Dogwood Trees," "Elegies for Paradise Valley", from COLLECTED POEMS OF ROBERT HAYDEN by Robert Hayden, edited by Frederick Glaysher. Used by permission of Liveright Publishing Corporation. Copyright © 1978 by Robert Hayden, "O Daedalus, Fly Away Home," "Those Winter Sundays", from COLLECTED POEMS OF ROBERT HAYDEN by Robert Hayden, edited by Frederick Glaysher. Used by permission of Liveright Publishing Corporation.

Anthony Hecht. "The Book of Yolek," "A Hill," "More Light! More Light!,"from COLLECTED EARLIER POEMS by Anthony Hecht, copyright © 1990 by Anthony E. Hecht. Used by permission of Alfred A. Knopf, a division of Random House, Inc. Any third party use of this material, outside of this publication, is prohibited. Interested parties must apply directly to Random House, Inc. for permission.

Lyn Hejinian. "A pause, a rose, something on paper," from *My Life*. Reprinted by permission of Lyn Hejinian. "Nos. III, XIX, XXIV, XXX, XXXII, XXXVII," from The Distance. Reprinted by permission of Lyn Hejinian.

William Heyen. "Riddle," Reprinted by permission of William Heyen. From Crazy Horse in Stillness: "Forces," "White & Gold," "One World," "Bone & Velvet," "Mother," "The Count," "Surveyors," "Rot," "V," "Resolve," "Treaty," "Snowbirds," "The Slowing," "The Paper It's Written On," "The Tooth," "Wakan Tanka," "Disequilibrium," and "Eclipse," Reprinted by permission of William Heyen.

Garrett Kaoru Hongo. From THE RIVER OF HEAVEN by Garrett Hongo, copyright © 1988 by Garrett Hongo. Used by permission of Alfred A. Knopf, a division of Random House, Inc. Any third party use of this material, outside of this publication, is prohibited. Interested parties must apply directly to Random House, Inc. for permission. From CORAL ROAD: POEMS by Garrett Hongo, copyright © 2011 by Garretrt Hongo. Used by permission of Alfred A. Knopf, a division of Random House, Inc. Any third party use of this material, outside of this publication, is prohibited. Interested parties must apply directly to Random House, Inc. for permission.

Susan Howe. "The Falls Fight," and "Hope Atherton's Wanderings," from Singularities © 1990 by Susan Howe. Reprinted by permission of Wesleyan University Press, www.wesleyan.edu/wespress.

Andrew Hudgins. "At Chancellorsville: The Battle of the Wilderness," "He Imagines His Wife Dead," and "The Summer of the Drought," Reprinted by permission of Andrew Hudgins and Houghton Mifflin Harcourt.

David Ignatow. "The Form Falls in On Itself," © 1971.

Thomas James. "Dissecting a Pig," and "Mummy of a Lady Named Jemutesonekh" from LETTERS TO A STRANGER by Thomas James. Copyright © 1973 by Thomas James. Reprinted by permission of Houghton Mifflin Harcourt Publishing Company. All rights reserved.

Japanese American Concentration Camp Haiku. "Shiho Okamoto (Being arrested)," "Sadayo Taniguchi (Handcuffed and taken away)," "Kyotaro Komuro (Lingering summer heat)," "Taro Katay, (Shouldering)," "Komuro (Passed guard tower)," "Okamoto (In the shade of summer sun)," "Shonan Suzuki (Withered grass on ground)," "Hakuro Wada (Young grass red and shriveled)," "Hyakuissei Okamoto (Dandelion has bloomed)," "Shizuku Uyemaruko (On certain days)," "Wada (Released seagull)," "Ryokuin Matsui (Sprinkling water outside)," "Komuro (Want to be with children)," "Wada (Even the croaking of frogs)," "Hangetsu Tsunekawa (Sentry at main gate)," "Shokoshi Saga (Thin shadow of tule reed)," "Tokuji Hirai (Looking at summer moon)," "Suzuki (Moon shadows on internment camp)," "Hirai (Early moon has set)," "Suiko Matsushita (Rain shower from mountain)," "Kyokusui (Thorns of the iron fence)," "Neiji Ozawa (Desert rain falling)," "Senbinshi Takaoka (Frosty morning)," "Oshio (Stepping through snow)," "Jyosha Yamada (Black clouds instantly shroud)," "Takaoka (Winter wind)," "Hekisamei Matsuda (Doll without a head)," "Sei Sagara (Suddenly awakened)," "Hyakuissei Okamoto (Jeep patrolling slowly)," "Shizuku Uyemaruko (Grieving within)," "Okamoto (In the sage brush)," "Matsushita (Oh shells——)," Haikus from MAY SKY, translated by Violet Kazue de Cristoforo.

Randall Jarrell. Reprinted by permissions of Farrar, Straus and Giroux, LLC: "The Death of the Ball Turret Gunner," "A Front," "Losses," "Second Air Force," "Protocols" from THE COMPLETE POEMS by Randall Jarrell. Copyright © 1969, renewed 1997 by Mary von S. Jarrell.

Donald Justice. "Absences," "Early Poems," "An Old Fashioned Devil," "Presences," "The Wall," from COLLECTED POEMS OF DONALD JUSTICE by Donald Justice, copyright © 2004 by Donald Justice. Used by permission of Alfred A. Knopf, a division of Random House, Inc. Any third party use of this material, outside of this publication, is prohibited. Interested parties must apply directly to Random House, Inc. for permission.

Bob Kaufman. "The Biggest Fisherman," "Crootey Songo," "No More Jazz at Alcatraz," from Cranial Guitar: Selected Poems. Copyright © 1996 by Eileen Kafman. Reprinted with the permission of The Permissions Company, Inc., on behalf of Coffee House Press, www.coffeehousepress.org. "From Jail Poems, Nos. 1–3," By Robert Kaufman, from SOLITUDES CROWDED WITH LONELINESS, copyright (C01965 by Bob Kaufman. Reprinted by permission of New Directions Publishing Corp.

Weldon Kees. "June 1940," and "Travels in North America." Reprinted from The Collected Poems of Weldon Kees edited by Donald Justice by permission of the University of Nebraska Press. Copyright 1962, 1975, by the University of Nebraska Press. © renewed 2003 by the University of Nebraska Press.

Jack Kerouac. "The Perfect Love of Mind Essence," Reprinted by permission of John Sampas.

Galway Kinnell. "The Bear," and "The Porcupine" from THREE BOOKS by Galway Kinnell. Copyright © 1993 by Galway Kinnell. Reprinted by permission of Houghton Mifflin Harcourt Publishing Company. All rights reserved. "The Vow" from WHEN ONE HAS LIVED A LONG TIME ALONE by Galway Kinnell, copyright © 1990 by Galway Kinnell. Used by permission of Alfred A. Knopf, a division of Random House, Inc. Any third party use of this material, outside of this publication, is prohibited. Interested parties must apply directly to Random House, Inc. for permission.

Etheridge Knight. "Eastern guard tower," "To write a blues song," and "Making jazz swing in" from The Essential Etheridge Knight, by Etheridge Knight, © 1986. Reprinted by permission of the University of Pittsburgh Press. "For Black Poets Who Think of Suicide," "For Malcolm, a Year Later," "Hard Rock Returns to Prison From The Hospital For The Criminal Insane," "The Idea of Ancestry," "A Poem for Myself," "Television Speaks," from *The Essential Etheridge Knight*, by Etheridge Knight, © 1986. Reprinted by permission of the University of Pittsburgh Press.

Yusef Komunyakaa. "Communiqué," "The Dog Act," "Fog Galleon," "The Nazi Doll," "Prisoners," "Tu Do Street," and "Work," from Pleasure Dome: New and Collected Poems © 2001 by Yusef Komunyakaa. Reprinted by permission of Wesleyan University Press, www.wesleyan.edu/wespress.

Aaron Kramer. "Denmark Vesey," From Aaron Kramer, WICKED TIMES: SELECTED POEMS, ed. Cary Nelson and Donald Gilzinger, Jr. (Urbana: U of Illinois Press, 2004). Reprinted with permission.

Maxine Kumin. "Oblivion," "Pantoum, With Swan," "Saga," "Voices from Kansas," "With William Meredith in Bulgaria," Reprinted by permission of Maxine Kumin.

Li-Young Lee. "Persimmons" from Rose. Copyright © 1986 by Li-Young Lee. All reprinted with the permission of The Permissions Company, Inc., on behalf of BOA Editions, Ltd., www.boaeditions.org. Li-Young Lee, "Little Father" from Book of My Nights. Copyright © 2001 by Li-Young Lee. All reprinted with the permission of The Permissions Company, Inc., on behalf of BOA Editions, Ltd., www.boaeditions.org.

Denise Levertov. "The Ache of Marriage," By Denise Levertov, from POEMS 1960–1967, copyright © 1964 by Denise Levertov. Reprinted by permission of New Directions Publishing Corp. "Life at War," "Olga Poems," and "What Were They Like?," By Denise Levertov, from POEMS 1960–1967, copyright © 1966 by Denise Levertov. Reprinted by permission of New Directions Publishing Corp.

Phillip Levine. "For Fran", "The Horse", "Animals Are Passing From Our Lives", copyright © 1991 by Philip Levine, "Belle Isle, 1949", "They Feed They Lion", copyright © 1968, 1969, 1970, 1971, 1972 by Philip Levine, "Francisco, I'll Bring You Red Carnations" from NEW SELECTED POEMS by Philip Levine, copyright © 1984, 1991 by Philip Levine. Used by permission of Alfred A. Knopf, a division of Random House, Inc. Any third party use of this material, outside of this publication, is prohibited. Interested parties must apply directly to Random House, Inc. for permission. "Fear and Fame" from WHAT WORK IS by Philip Levine, copyright © 1991 by Philip Levine. Used by permission of Alfred A. Knopf, a division of Random House, Inc. Any third party use of this material, outside of this publication, is prohibited. Interested parties must apply directly to Random House, Inc. for permission. "On the Meeting of Garcia Lorca and Hart Crane" copyright © 1994 by Philip Levine, from THE SIMPLE TRUTH by Philip Levine. Used by permission of Alfred A. Knopf, a division of Random House, Inc. Any third party use of this material, outside of this publication, is prohibited. Interested parties must apply directly to Random House, Inc. for permission.

Audre Lorde. Copyright © 1968 by Audre Lorde. "Coal", from THE COLLECTED POEMS OF AUDRE LORDE by Audre Lorde. Used by permission of W. W. Norton & Company, Inc. Copyright © 1986 by Audre Lorde. "Call," "Outlines," and "Sisters in Arms", from THE COLLECTED POEMS OF AUDRE LORDE by Audre Lorde. Used by permission of W. W. Norton & Company, Inc.

Adrian C. Louis. "Coyote Night," and "Dust World" from Among the Dog Eaters. Copyright © 1992 by Adrian C. Louis. All reprinted with the permission of The Permissions Company, Inc., on behalf of West End Press, Albuquerque, New Mexico, www.westend.org. Adrian C. Louis, "Wakinyan," and "Without Words," from Fire Water World. Copyright © 1989 by Adrian C. Louis. All reprinted with the permission of The Permissions Company, Inc., on behalf of West End Press, Albuquerque, New Mexico, www.westendpress.org. "A Colossal American Copulation," From Ceremonies of the Damned by Adrian C. Louis. Copyright © 1997 by Adrian C. Louis. Reprinted with permission of the University of the Nevada Press. "Petroglyphs of Serena From Ceremonies of the Damned," by Adrian C. Louis. Copyright © 1997 by Adrian C. Louis. Reprinted with permission of the University of the Nevada Press.

Robert Lowell. Reprinted by permissions of Farrar, Straus and Giroux, LLC: "Inauguration Day: January 1953," "A Mad Negro Soldier Confined at Munich," "Commander Lowell," "To Speak of Woe That Is in Marriage," "Man and Wife," "Memories of West Street and Lepke," "Skunk Hour," "For the Union Dead," "The Mouth of the Hudson," "July in Washington," "The March I," "The March II," "Central Park," and "Epilogue" from COLLECTED POEMS by Robert Lowell. Copyright © 2003 by Harriet Lowell and Sheridan Lowell.

Thomas McGrath. "After the Beat Generation," "Against the False Magicians," "A Little Song About Charity," "Ars Poetica: Or: Who Lives in the Ivory Tower?," "Crash Report," "Deep South," "First Book of Genesis According to the Diplomats," "Ode for the American Dead in Asia," from THE MOVIE AT THE END OF THE WORLD: COLLECTED POEMS by Thomas McGrath. Copyright © 1972 by Thomas McGrath. This material is used by permission of Ohio University Press, www.ohioswallow.com. Thomas McGrath, "Poem at the Winter Solstice" from Echoes Inside the Labyrinth (Thunder's Mouth Press, 1983). Copyright © 1983 by Thomas McGrath. Reprinted with the permission of The Permissions Company, Inc., on behalf of the Estate of Thomas McGrath and Middlepoint Press, Inc.

James Merrill. "The Broken Home," "Lost in Translation," "An Urban Convalescence," "Willowware Cup" from COLLECTED POEMS by James Merrill, edited by J.D. McClatchy and Stephen Yenser, copyright © 2001 by the Literary Estate of James Merrill at Washington University. Used by permission of Alfred A. Knopf, a division of Random House, Inc. Any third party use of this material, outside of this publication, is prohibited. Interested parties must apply directly to Random House, Inc. for permission.

W. S. Merwin. "The Drunk in the Furnace" from Migration: New and Selected Poems. Copyright © 1960 by W. S. Merwin. All reprinted with the permission of The Permissions Company, Inc., on behalf of Copper Canyon Press, www.coppercanyonpress.org. "It is March," "Caesar," "The Room," "December Among the Vanished," "For the Anniversary of My Death," "When the War is Over," "The Asians Dying," "For a Coming Extinction," "Looking for Mushrooms at Sunrise," "The Gardens of Zuni," and "Beginning" by W. S. Merwin, currently collected in THE SECOND FOUR BOOKS OF POEMS by W. S. Merwin. Copyright © 1960, 1961, 1962, 1963, 1964, 1965, 1966, 1967, 1968, 1969, 1970, 1971, 1972, 1973, 1993 by W. S. Merwin, used by permission of The Wylie Agency LLC. "The Horse," "Sun and Rain," and "Berryman" by W. S. Merwin, currently collected in MIGRATION by W. S. Merwin. Copyright © 2005 by W. S. Merwin, used by permission of The Wylie Agency LLC. "Daylight," and "The Name of the Air," from THE PUPIL: POEMS by W. S. Merwin, copyright © 2001 by W. S. Merwin. Used by permission of Alfred A. Knopf, a division of Random House, Inc. Any third party use of this material, outside of this publication, is prohibited. Interested parties must apply directly to Random House, Inc. for permission. W. S. Merwin, "Far Along the Story," and "Worn Words," from The Shadow of Sirius. Copyright © 1960 by W. S. Merwin. All reprinted with the permission of The Permissions Company, Inc., on behalf of Copper Canyon Press, www.coppercanyonpress.org.

N. Scott Momaday. "A Benign Self-Portrait," "The Burning," "Buteo Regalis," "Carriers of the Dream Wheel," "Crows in a Winter Composition," "December 29, 1980," "Plainview: 3," "Purple," "Rings of Bone," "The Shield That Came Back," and "The Stalker," Reprinted by permission of N. Scott Momaday. From AGAIN IN THE MORNING: The Snow Mare, by N. Scott Momaday. Copyright © 2011 University of New Mexico Press. Reprinted by permission of University of New Mexico Press. From IN THE BEAR'S HOUSE: To an Aged Bear, by N. Scott Momaday. Copyright © 1999 University of New Mexico Press. Reprinted by permission of University of New Mexico Press.

Thylias Moss. "There Will Be Animals." From *Pyramid of Bone*. Pp. 12–13. © 1989 by the Rector and Visitors of the University of Virginia. Reprinted by permission of the University of Virginia Press. "The Lynching," and "Interpretation of a Poem by Frost," From *Rainbow Remnants* by Thylias Moss. Copyright © 1991 by Thylias Moss. Reprinted by permission of Persea Books Inc., New York. All rights reserved. "Ambition," and "Crystals," From *Last Chance for the Tarzan Holler* by Thylias Moss. Copyright © 1988 by Thylias Moss. Reprinted by permission of Persea Books Inc., New York. All rights reserved.

Harryette Mullen. from *Trimmings* Harryette Mullen, ["Atkimbo bimbos, all a jangle"], ["Punched in like slopwork"], ["Animal pelts"], ["Opens up a little leg"], ["A fish caught"], ["Her ribbon"], ["Aren't you glad you use petroleum"], ["Kills bugs dead"], ["A daughter turned against the grain"], ["Off the pig, ya dig?"], ["Ad infinitum perpetual infants goo"], and ["Flies in buttermilk"] from Recyclopedia. Copyright © 2006 by Harryette Mullen. Reprinted with the permission of The Permissions Company, Inc., on behalf of Graywolf Press, www.graywolfpress.org. from *S*PeRM**K*T* Harryette Mullen, ["Atkimbo bimbos, all a jangle"], ["Punched in like slopwork"], ["Animal pelts"], ["Opens up a little leg"], ["A fish caught"], ["Her ribbon"], ["Aren't you glad you use petroleum"], ["Kills bugs dead"], ["A daughter turned against the grain"], ["Off the pig, ya dig?"], ["Ad infinitum perpetual infants goo"], and ["Flies in buttermilk"] from Recyclopedia. Copyright © 2006 by Harryette Mullen. Reprinted with the permission of The Permissions Company, Inc., on behalf of Graywolf Press, www.graywolfpress.org.

Sharon Olds. "The Pope's Penis" from THE GOLD CELL by Sharon Olds, copyright © 1987 by Sharon Olds. Used by permission of Alfred A. Knopf, a division of Random House, Inc. Any third party use of this material, outside of this publication, is prohibited. Interested parties must apply directly to Random House, Inc. for permission. "Ideographs," "Photograph of the Girl," "Things That Are Worse Than Death," from THE DEAD AND THE LIVING by Sharon Olds, copyright © 1987 by Sharon Olds. Used by permission of Alfred A. Knopf, a division of Random House, Inc. Any third party use of this material, outside of this publication, is prohibited. Interested parties must apply directly to Random House, Inc. for permission. "The Waiting" from THE FATHER by Sharon Olds, copyright © 1992 by Sharon Olds. Used by permission of Alfred A. Knopf, a division of Random House, Inc. Any third party use of this material. "Her Father's Cadaver" from THE WELLSPRING by Sharon Olds, copyright © 1996 by Sharon Olds. Used by permission of Alfred A. Knopf, a division of Random House, Inc. Any third party use of this material, outside of this publication, is prohibited. Interested parties must apply directly to Random House, Inc. for permission. "Known to be Left," and "Left-Wife Goose," from STAG'S LEAP by Sharon Olds, copyright © 2012 by Sharon Olds. Used by permission of Alfred A. Knopf, a division of Random House, Inc. Any third party use of this material, outside of this publication, is prohibited. Interested parties must apply directly to Random House, Inc. for permission.

Michael Palmer. "All Those Words," "Autobiography," "Fifth Prose," "I Have Answers to All of Your Questions," "Song of the Round Man," By Michael Palmer, from THE LION BRIDGE, copyright © 1984 by Michael Palmer. Reprinted by permission of New Directions Publishing Corp.

Robert Pinsky. Reprinted by permissions of Farrar, Straus and Giroux, LLC: "Dying," "Shirt," "The Unseen," from THE FIGURED WHEEL: NEW AND COLLECTED POEMS 1966–1996 by Robert Pinsky. Reprinted by permissions of Farrar, Straus and Giroux, LLC: "Vieni, Creator Spiritus" from GULF MUSIC by Robert Pinsky. Copyright © 2007 by Robert Pinsky.

Sylvia Plath. "The Colossus" from THE COLOSSUS AND OTHER POEMS by Sylvia Plath, copyright © 1957, 1958, 1959, 1960, 1961, 1962 by Sylvia Plath. Used by permission of Alfred A. Knopf, a division of Random House, Inc. Any third party use of this material, outside of this publication, is prohibited. Interested parties must apply directly to Random House, Inc. for permission. "The Bee Meeting" from ARIEL: POEMS by SYLVIA PLATH. Copyright © 1961 by Ted Hughes. Reprinted by permission of HarperCollins Publishers. "The Arrival of the Bee Box" from ARIEL: POEMS by SYLVIA PLATH. Copyright © 1962 by Ted Hughes. Reprinted by permission of HarperCollins Publishers. "Stings" from ARIEL: POEMS by SYLVIA PLATH. Copyright © 1963by Ted Hughes. Reprinted by permission of HarperCollins Publishers. "The Swarm" from ARIEL: POEMS by SYLVIA PLATH. Copyright © 1964 by Ted Hughes. Reprinted by permission of HarperCollins Publishers. "Wintering" from ARIEL: POEMS by SYLVIA PLATH. Copyright © 1965 by Ted Hughes. Reprinted by permission of HarperCollins Publishers. All lines from "DADDY" FROM ARIEL by SYLVIA PLATH. Copyright © 1963 by Ted Hughes. Reprinted by permission of HarperCollins Publishers. "Ariel" from ARIEL: POEMS by SYLVIA PLATH. Copyright © 1966 by Ted Hughes. Reprinted by permission of HarperCollins Publishers. All lines from "LADY LAZARUS" FROM ARIEL by SYLVIA PLATH. Copyright © 1963 by Ted Hughes. Reprinted by permission of HarperCollins Publishers.

Frank O'Hara. Frank O'Hara: From LUNCH POEMS: from "Alma," section 3 only (two prose paragraphs), pp. 4–5, "Cornkind,"pp. 42–43, "Music," pp. 1–2, "Poem (Lana Turner Has Collapsed)," pp. 78, "The Day Lady Died," "A Step Away From Them." "On Seeing Larry Rivers' Washington Crossing the Delaware at the Museum of Modern Art" "Poem (The Eager note on my door...)" from Meditations in an Emergency, copyright © 1957 by Frank O'Hara. Used by permission of Grove/Atlantic, Inc. Any third party use of this material, outside of this publication, is prohibited. "A True Account of Talking to the Sun at Fire Island," "Why I Am Not a Painter," from THE COLLECTED POEMS OF FRANK O'HARA by Frank O'Hara, edited by Donald Allen, copyright © 1971 by Maureen Granville-Smith, Administratix of the Estate of Frank O'Hara, copyright renewed 1999 by Maureen O'Hara Granville-Smith and Donald Allen. Used by permission of Alfred A. Knopf, a division of Random House, Inc. Any third party use of this material, outside of this publication, is prohibited. Interested parties must apply directly to Random House, Inc. for permission.

Mary Oliver. "Black Snake This Time," "At Great Pond," "Morning Walk," from WEST WIND: Poems and Prose by Mary Oliver. Cpyright © 1997 by Mary Oliver. Reprinted by permission of Houghton Mifflin Harcourt Publishing Company. All rights reserved.

Charles Olson, "Cole's Island," "Maximus, to himself," "Variations Done for Gerald Van De Wiele." from Selected Poems by Charles Olson, edited by Robert Creeley © 1994 by the Estate of Charles Olson and the University of Connecticut. Published by the University of California Press. Reprinted by permission of University of California Press.

Tillie Lerner Olsen." I Want You Women Up North To Know," published in *The Partisan* (March 1934).

D. A. Powell. ("came a voice in my gullet,") ["the cocktail hour finally arrives,"] ["dogs and boys can treat you like trash,"] from Cocktails. Copyright © 2004 by D. A. Powell. Used with the permission of The Permissions Company, Inc., on behalf of Graywolf Press, Minneapolis, Minnesota, www.graywolfpress.org.

Dudley Randall. "A Different Image," and "Ballad of Birmingham," was reprinted by permission of the Dudley Randall Estate, from *Roses and Revolutions: The Selected Writings of Dudley Randall* (Wayne State University Press, 2009).

Claudia Rankine. Excerpts from Don't Let Me Be Lonely: An American Lyric. Copyright © 2004 by Claudia Rankine. Reprinted with the permission of The Permissions Company, Inc., on behalf of Graywolf Press, www.graywolfpress.org.

Ishmael Reed." I am a Cowboy in the Boat of Ra," and "Oakland Blues," Excerpted from the book, *NEW AND COLLECTED POEMS 1964–2007*. Copyright © 2007 by Ishmael Reed. Permission granted by Lowenstein Associates, Inc.

Adrienne Rich. "Aunt Jennifer's Tigers", "Shooting Script", from THE FACT OF A DOORFRAME: Poems Selected and New, 1950–1984 by Adrienne Rich. Copyright © 1984 by Adrienne Rich. Copyright © 1975, 1978 by W. W. Norton & Company, Inc. Copyright © 1981 by Adrienne Rich. Used by permission of W. W. Norton & Company, Inc. "Trying to Talk with a Man", "Diving into the Wreck", "Twenty-one Love Poems", "Power", "Part XIII *Dedications)" from "An Atlas of the Difficult World", from LATER POEMS: SELECTED AND NEW, 1971–2012 by Adrienne Rich. Copyright © 2013 by The Adrienne Rich Literary Trust. Copyright © 2001, 2007, 2004, 2001, 1999, 1995, 1991, 1989, 1986, 1981 by Adrienne Rich. Copyright © 1978, 1973 by W. W. Norton & Company, Inc. Used by permission of W. W. Norton & Company, Inc. "Behind the Motel," and "Hotel," from TELEPHONE RINGING IN THE LABYRINTH: POEMS 2004–2006 by Adrienne Rich. Copyright © 2007 by Adrienne Rich. Used by permission of W. W. North & Company, Inc.

Atsuro Riley. "Bell," "Picture," "Roses," "Skillet," from Romey's Order. The University of Chicago Press, Ltd., London. © 2010 by the University of Chicago. All rights reserved. Published in 2010. Printed in the United States of America. Reprinted by permission of University of Chicago Press.

Alberto Ríos. "Madre Sofía," Reprinted by permission of Alberto Ríos. Alberto Ríos, "What Happened to Me" from The Smallest Muscle in the Human Body. Copyright © 2002 by Alberto Ríos. Reprinted with the permission of The Permissions Company, Inc. on behalf of Copper Canyon Press, www. coppercanyonpress.org.

Carolyn M. Rodgers. "how i got ovah," "and when the revolution came," and "mama's God," FROM HOW I GOT OVAH: NEW AND SELECTED POEMS by Carolyn M. Rodgers, copyright © 1968, 1969, 1970, 1971, 1972, 1973, 1975 by Carolyn M. Rodgers. Copyright renewed © 2003 by Carolyn M. Rodgers. Used by permission of Doubleday, a division of Random House, Inc. Any third party use of this material, outside of this publication, is prohibited. Interesting parties must apply directly to Random House, Inc. for permission.

Wendy Rose. "Truganinny" from The Halfbreed Chronicles. Copyright © 1985 by Wendy Rose. Reprinted with the permission of The Permissions Company, Inc., on behalf of West End Press, www.westendpress.org.

Jimmy Santiago Baca. "Mi Tío Baca El Poeta De Socorro," and "The Painters," Reprinted by permission of Jimmy Santiago Baca.

Anne Sexton. "Her Kind" from TO BEDLAM AND PART WAY BACK by Anne Sexton. Copyright © 1960 by Anne Sexton, renewed 1988 by Linda G. Sexton. Reprinted by permission of Houghton Mifflin Harcourt Publishing Company. All rights reserved. "The Truth the Dead Know" from ALL MY PRETTY ONES by Anne Sexton. Copyright © 1962 by Anne Sexton, renewed 1990 by Linda G. Sexton. Reprinted by permission of Houghton Mifflin Harcourt Publishing Company. All rights reserved. "And One for My Dame" from LIVE OR DIE by Anne Sexton. Copyright © 1966 by Anne Sexton, renewed 1994 by Linda G. Sexton. Reprinted by permission of Houghton Mifflin Harcourt Publishing Company. All rights reserved. "Jesus Asleep" from THE BOOK OF FOLLY. Copyright © 1972 by Anne Sexton, renewed 2000 by Linda G. Sexton. Reprinted by permission of Houghton Mifflin Harcourt Publishing Company. All rights reserved. "Jesus Raises Up the Harlot" from THE BOOK OF FOLLY. Copyright © 1972 by Anne Sexton, renewed 2000 by Linda G. Sexton. Reprinted by permission of Houghton Mifflin Harcourt Publishing Company.

All rights reserved. "The Room of My Life" from THE AWFUL ROWING TOWARD GOD by Anne Sexton. Copyright © 1975 by Loring Conant, Jr., Executor of the Estate of Anne Sexton. Reprinted by permission of Houghton Mifflin Harcourt Publishing Company. All rights reserved.

Richard Siken. "A Primer for the Small Weird Loves," and "Visible World," from *Crush*, Copyright © 2005 by Yale University. Published by Yale University Press. All rights reserved. Republished by permission of Yale University Press.

Patricia Smith. "Blond White Women," and "Skinheads," Reprinted from Big Towns, Big Talk with permission from Zoland Books, an imprint of Steerforth Press. Patricia Smith, from "Tankas": "Company's Coming," "Go, they said. Go. Go. ," "Man on the TV Say," "Money," "Never has there been," "Voodoo II," "Voodoo V," Copyright © 2008 by Patricia Smith. Reprinted with the permission of The Permissions Company, Inc., on behalf of Coffee House Press, www.coffeehousepress.org. "Back Home," and "Stifle the stinking, shut down the cameras," from Blood Dazzler. Copyright © 2008 by Patricia Smith. Reprinted with the permission of The Permissions Company, Inc., on behalf of Coffee House Press, www.coffeehousepress.org. "Motown Crown," Reprinted by permission of Patricia Smith.

Welton Smith. "Malcolm."

William Stafford. "At the Bomb Testing Site," "At the Un-National Monument Along the Canadian Border," "The Indian Cave Jerry Ramsey Found," "Traveling Through the Dark" from *The Way It Is: New and Selected Poems*. Copyright © 1960, 1962, 1974, 1975, 1998 by William Stafford and the Estate of William Stafford. Reprinted with the permission of The Permissions Company, Inc., on behalf of Graywolf Press, Minneapolis, Minnesota, www.graywolfpress.org.

Timothy Steele. "April 27, 1937," and "Daybreak, Benedict Canyon," (Columbis, OH: Swallow/Ohio U Press). Reprinted by permission of Swallow/Ohio U Press.

Ron Stillman. "Ketjak," from The Age of Huts (compleat), pp. 3–5, 39–40. © 2007 by the Regents of the University of California. Reprinted by permission of Ron Silliman and University of California Press. Ron Silliman, "Sunset Debris," from The Age of Huts (compleat), pp. 11–12. © 2007 by the Regents of the University of California. Reprinted by permission of Ron Silliman and University of California Press. Ron Silliman, "The Chinese Notebook," from The Age of Huts (compleat), pp. 43–66. © 2007 by the Regents of the University of California. Reprinted by permission of Ron Silliman and University of California Press. *Toner*. Reprinted by permission of Ron Silliman.

Ruth Stone. "American Milk," "Drought in the Lower Fields," "From the Arboretum," "I Have Three Daughters," "In an Iridescent Time," "Pokeberries," and "Some Things You'll Need to Know Before You Join the Union," Reprinted by permission of Bianca Stone for The Estate of Ruth Stone.

Mark Strand. "The Prediction," and "Where Are the Waters of Childhood," from SELECTED POEMS by Mark Strand, copyright © 1979, 1980 by Mark Strand. Used by permission of Alfred A. Knopf, a division of Random House, Inc. Any third party use of this material, outside of this publication, is prohibited. Interested parties must apply directly to Random House, Inc. for permission.

Gary Synder. "Axe Handles," and "Riprap," Copyright © 2009 by Gary Snyder from Riprap and Cold Mountain Poems. Reprinted by permission of Counterpoint. "Beneath My Hand and Eye the Distant Hills. Your Body," Reprinted by permission of Gary Snyder. "I Went Into the Maverick Bar," and "Straight-Creek——Great Burn," By Gary Snyder from TURTLE ISLAND, copyright © 1974 by Gary Snyder. Reprinted by permission of New Directions Publishing Corp. "O Mother Gaia," Copyright © 2009 by Gary Snyder from Axe Handles. Reprinted by permission of Counterpoint.

Mona Van Duyn. From A TIME OF BEES by Mons Van Duyn. Copyright © 1964 by the Mona Van Duyn. Copyright renewed 1981 by Mona Van Duyn for "Toward a Definition of Marriage". Used by permission of the publisher.

Paul Violi. "Index," Reprinted by permission of the Estate of Paul Violi. "A Moveable Snack," and "Tanka," Reprinted from "THE CURIOUS BUILDER" © by Paul Violi, by permission of Hanging Loose Press.

Derek Walcott. Reprinted by permissions of Farrar, Straus and Giroux, LLC: "A Far Cry from Africa," "The Fortunate Traveller," "Laventille," from COLLECTED POEMS 1948–1984 by Derek Walcott. Copyright © 1986 by Derek Walcott. Reprinted by permissions of Farrar, Straus and Giroux, LLC: "Book One, Chapter 1" from OMEROS by Derek Walcott. Copyright © 1990 by Derek Walcott.

Margaret Walker. "For My People" from THIS IS MY COUNTRY: NEW AND COLLECTED POEMS by Margaret Walker. Copyright © 1989 by Margaret Walker Alexander. Published by the University of Georgia Press, Athens, Georgia 30620, www.ugapress.org. All rights reserved. Reprinted by permission of University of Georgia Press.

Richard Wilbur. "The Pardon" from CEREMONY AND OTHER POEMS by Richard Wilbur. Copyright © 1950 and renewed 1978 by Richard Wilbur. Reprinted by permission of Houghton Mifflin Harcourt Publishing Company. All rights reserved. "A Baroque Wall-Foundation in the Villa Sciarra," and "Love Call Us to the Things of This World" from THINGS OF THIS WORLD by Richard Wilbur. Copyright © 1956 and renewed 1984 by Richard Wilbur. Reprinted by permission of Houghton Mifflin Harcourt Publishing Company. All rights reserved. "Advice to a Prophet" from ADVICE TO A PROPHET AND OTHER POEMS by Richard Wilbur. Copyright © 1961, renewed 1989 by Richard Wilbur. Used by permission of Houghton Mifflin Harcourt Publishing Company. All rights reserved. "Children of Darkness" from THE MIND-READER by Richard Wilbur. Copyright © 1971, and renewed 1999 by Richard Wilbur. Reprinted by permission of Houghton Mifflin Harcourt Publishing Company. All rights reserved. "A Difference" from OPPOSITES, MORE OPPOSITES, AND A FEW DIFFERENCES: Poems and Drawings by Richard Wilbur. Copyright © 2000 by Richard Wilbur. Reprinted by permission of Houghton Mifflin Harcourt Publishing Company. All rights reserved.

C. D. Wright. "Obedience of the Corpse" from Just Whistle.: A Valentine. Copyright © 2005 by C. D. Wright. All reprinted with the permission of The Permissions Company, Inc. on behalf of Copper Canyon Press, www.coppercanyonpress.org. C, D, Wright, "And Nothing," "Because Conditions are ideal for Crowing," "The Body, Alive, Not Dead but Dormant," "The Corpse was in the Bed," "On the Morn of," "A Partition Separates It From Other Bodies," and "Song of the Gourd," from Steal Away: Selected and New Poems. Copyright © 2005 by C. D. Wright. All reprinted with the permission of The Permissions Company, Inc. on behalf of Copper Canyon Press, www.coppercanyonpress.org. C. D. Wright, "Dear Dying Town," "Only the Crossing Counts," "What Would Oppen Say," from Cooling Time: An American Poetry Vigil. Copyright © 2005 by C. D. Wright. All reprinted with the permission of The Permissions Company, Inc. on behalf of Copper Canyon Press, www.coppercanyonpress.org.

Charles Wright. "Clear Night," "Spider Crystal Ascension," from Country Music: Selected Early Poems © 1982 by Charles Wright. Reprinted by permission of Wesleyan University Press, www.wesleyan.edu/wespress. Reprinted by permissions of Farrar, Straus and Giroux, LLC: "Homage to Paul Cezanne" from THE WORLD OF THE TEN THOUSAND THINGS: POEMS 1980–1990 by Charles Wright. Copyright © 1990 by Charles Wright.

James Wright. "Autumn Begins in Martins Ferry," "Beginning," "A Blessing," "A Centenary Ode: Inscribed to Little Crow, Leader of the Sioux Rebellion in Minnesota, 1862," "Lying in a Hammock at William Duffy's Farm in Pine Island, Minnesota," "Saint Judas" from Collected Poems © 1971 by James Wright. Reprinted by permission of Wesleyan University Press, www.wesleyan.edu/wespress.

Ray A. Young Bear. "In Viewpoint: Poem for 14 Catfish and The Town of Tama, Iowa," and "It is the Fish-faced Boy Who Struggles," Reprinted by permission of Ray Young Bear.

Index of Poem Titles

Index of Poets

About the Editor

Cary Nelson is Jubilee Professor of Liberal Arts and Sciences and Professor of English and Criticism and Interpretive Theory at the University of Illinois at Urbana–Champaign. He has also served on the Executive Council of the Modern Language Association, and from 2006 to 2012 he served as national president of the American Association of University Professors (AAUP), in which capacity he made television appearances on Fox News and C-SPAN, as well as radio broadcasts on Voice of America, National Public Radio, and many other stations. He is the author of *The Incarnate Word: Literature as Verbal Space* (1973), *Our Last First Poets: Vision and History in Contemporary American Poetry* (1981), *Repression and Recovery: Modern American Poetry and the Politics of Cultural Memory, 1910–1945* (1989), *Shouts from the Wall; Posters and Photographs Brought Home from the Spanish Civil War by American Volunteers* (1996), *Manifesto of a Tenured Radical* (1997), *No University Is an Island: Saving Academic Freedom* (2010), *When Death Rhymed: Poem Cards and Poetry Panics of the Great Wars* (forthcoming), and the coauthor of *Academic Keywords: A Devil's Dictionary for Higher Education* (1999), *Office Hours: Activism and Change in the Academy* (2004), and *Principles to Guide Academy-Industry Relationships* (2014). His edited or coedited books include *Theory in the Classroom* (1986), *W. S. Merwin: Essays on the Poetry* (1987), *Regions of Memory: Uncollected Prose by W. S. Merwin* (1987), *Marxism and the Interpretation of Culture* (1988), *Edwin Rolfe: A Biographical Essay* (1990), *Cultural Studies* (1992), Edwin Rolfe's *Collected Poems* (1993), *Higher Education Under Fire: Politics, Economics, and the Crisis of the Humanities* (1994), *Madrid 1937: Letters of the Abraham Lincoln Brigade from the Spanish Civil War* (1996), *Disciplinarity and Dissent in Cultural Studies* (1996), *Will Teach for Food: Academic Labor in Crisis* (1997), *The Aura of the Cause: A Photo Album for North American Volunteers in the Spanish Civil War* (1997), *Anthology of Modern American Poetry* (2000), *The Wound and the Dream: Sixty Years of American Poems about the Spanish Civil War* (2002), Aaron Kramer's *Wicked Times: Selected Poems* (2004), and *The Oxford Handbook of Modern and Contemporary American Poetry* (2012). He is the author of over 200 essays, along with guest contributions to the *New York Times*, the *Wall Street Journal*, and other publications. His personal website is www.cary-nelson.org.